London

timeout.com/london

Published by Time Out Guides Ltd, a wholly owned subsidiary of Time Out Group Ltd.
Time Out and the Time Out logo are trademarks of Time Out Group Ltd.

© Time Out Group Ltd 2008
Previous editions 1989, 1990, 1992, 1994, 1995, 1997, 1998, 1999, 2000, 2001, 2002, 2003, 2004, 2005, 2006, 2007.

10 9 8 7 6 5 4 3 2 1

This edition first published in Great Britain in 2008 by Ebury Publishing
A Random House Group Company
20 Vauxhall Bridge Road, London SW1V 2SA

Random House Australia Pty Limited 20 Alfred Street, Milsons Point, Sydney, New South Wales 2061, Australia
Random House New Zealand Limited 18 Poland Road, Glenfield, Auckland 10, New Zealand
Random House South Africa (Pty) Limited Isle of Houghton, Corner Boundary
Road & Carse O'Gowrie, Houghton 2198, South Africa

Random House UK Limited Reg. No. 954009

For further distribution details, see www.timeout.com

ISBN: 978-1-846700-49-1

A CIP catalogue record for this book is available from the British Library

Printed and bound by Firmengruppe APPL, aprinta druck, Wemding, Germany

The Random House Group Limited supports The Forest Stewardship Council (FSC), the leading international forest
certification organisation. All our titles that are printed on Greenpeace approved FSC certified paper carry the FSC
logo. Our paper procurement policy can be found at http://www.rbooks.co.uk/environment

Time Out Guides Limited
Universal House
251 Tottenham Court Road
London W1T 7AB
Tel + 44 (0)20 7813 3000
Fax + 44 (0)20 7813 6001
Email guides@timeout.com
www.timeout.com

Editorial

Editor Simon Coppock
Deputy Editor Charlie Godfrey-Faussett
Copy Editors Francis Gooding, Lisa Ritchie, John Watson
Listings Editors Shane Armstrong, Carol Baker, Alex Brown, Gemma Pritchard
Proofreader Tamsin Shelton
Indexer Anna Norman

Managing Director Peter Fiennes
Financial Director Gareth Garner
Editorial Director Ruth Jarvis
Deputy Series Editor Dominic Earle
Editorial Manager Holly Pick
Assistant Management Accountant Ija Krasnikova

Design

Art Director Scott Moore
Art Editor Pinelope Kourmouzoglou
Senior Designer Henry Elphick
Graphic Designer Gemma Doyle
Junior Graphic Designer Kei Ishimaru
Digital Imaging Simon Foster
Advertising Designer Jodi Sher

Picture Desk

Picture Editor Jael Marschner
Deputy Picture Editor Katie Morris
Picture Researcher Helen McFarland
Picture Desk Assistant Troy Bailey

Advertising

Sales Director Mark Phillips
Advertising Sales Manager Alison Wallen
Sales Executives Ben Holt, Alex Matthews, Jason Trotman
Advertising Assistant Kate Staddon
Copy Controller Declan Symington

Marketing

Group Marketing Director John Luck
Marketing Manager Yvonne Poon
Sales and Marketing Director North America Lisa Levinson

Production

Group Production Director Mark Lamond
Production Manager Brendan McKeown
Production Controller Caroline Bradford
Production Coordinator Susan Whittaker

Time Out Group

Chairman Tony Elliott
Financial Director Richard Waterlow
Group General Manager/Director Nichola Coulthard
Time Out Magazine Ltd MD Richard Waterlow
Time Out Communications Ltd MD David Pepper
Time Out International MD Cathy Runciman
Group Art Director John Oakey
Group IT Director Simon Chappell

Contributors

Introduction Simon Coppock. **History** Charlie Godfrey-Faussett (*City seer, I'll wager, Soho, so long* Peter Watts; *Time Out: 40 years of London* Paul Fairclough). **London Today** Simon Coppock (*Transports of delight?* Peter Watts). **Architecture** Charlie Godfrey-Faussett. **Surveillance Society v the New Decadents** Simone Baird (*Smokin'* Edmund Gordon). **Where to Stay** Peterjon Cresswell, John Watson; additional reviews by Simon Coppock, Charlie Godfrey-Faussett, Lesley McCave, Anna Norman, Daniel Smith (*Getting all the Kit* Lisa Ritchie, Ruth Jarvis; *Selling the Savoy* Charlie Godfrey-Faussett; *Cheap 'n' charming* Simon Coppock). **Sights Introduction** Simon Coppock. **The South Bank & Bankside** Charlie Godfrey-Faussett. **The City** Joe Bindloss. **Holborn & Clerkenwell** Cyrus Shahrad. **Bloomsbury & Fitzrovia** Francis Gooding (*Wellcome Collection* Simon Coppock). **Covent Garden & the Strand** Francis Gooding (*All aboard!* Charlie Godfrey-Faussett). **Soho & Leicester Square** Peterjon Cresswell. **Oxford Street & Marylebone** Cyrus Shahrad. **Paddington & Notting Hill** Edoardo Albert. **Piccadilly & Mayfair** Francis Gooding. **Westminster & St James's** Francis Gooding (*Ceremonial city* Simon Coppock). **Chelsea** Cyrus Shahrad. **Knightsbridge & South Kensington** Francis Gooding (*Sikorski Museum* Peter Watts). **North London** Patrick Mulkern. **East London** Simon Coppock, Francis Gooding (*The two Brick Lanes, Sun, sound and sea* Simon Coppock). **South-east London** Ronnie Haydon (*Dome is where the art is* Peterjon Cresswell). **South-west London** Tracey Graham (*Northcote Road* Rhodri Marsden). **West London** Edoardo Albert. **Restaurants & Cafés** Contributors to *Time Out Eating & Drinking* (*Sure can pick 'em* Guy Dimond; *What a source* Ronnie Haydon; *Cultured cafés, Best of British* Simon Coppock). **Pubs & Bars** contributors to *Time Out Bars, Pubs & Clubs* (*Sure can pick 'em* Tom Lamont; *Ale and hearty, Who's wine-ing now?* Charlie Godfrey-Faussett). **Shops & Services** Lisa Ritchie (*Words & music* Francis Gooding, Simon Coppock). **Festivals & Events** Cathy Limb (*Carnival of controversy* Edmund Gordon). **Children** Ronnie Haydon (*Teen sensation* John Lewis). **Comedy** Tracey Graham (*Making Hay?* Malcolm Hay). **Dance** Tim Benzie. **Film** Francis Gooding. **Galleries** Martin Coomber. **Gay & Lesbian** Tim Benzie. **Music** John Lewis. **Nightlife** Simone Baird. **Sport & Fitness** Tom Davies. **Theatre** Caroline McGinn. **Trips Out of Town** contributors to *Time Out Weekend Breaks* (*Boomtown Brighton* Simon Coppock). **Getting Around** Gemma Pritchard. **Resources A-Z** Gemma Pritchard. **References & further reading** Simon Coppock (*Reading corners* Francis Gooding).

Maps john@jsgraphics.co.uk.

Photography pages 3, 7, 41, 43, 47, 54, 60, 61, 69, 71, 77, 91 (top), 95, 97, 103, 107, 111, 129, 133, 134, 140, 146, 159, 161, 162, 169, 219, 233, 237, 239, 247, 248, 250, 253, 259, 285, 286, 287, 289, 295 Britta Jaschinski; pages 11, 149 Christina Theisen; pages 12, 18 Mary Evans Picture Library; page 15 World History Archive/TopFoto; page 19 http://mcnaught.orpheusweb.co.uk/HarryB; page 22 Insight-Visual UK/Rex Features; page 23 Museum of London, UK/The Bridgeman Art Library; pages 28, 89 Andreas Schmidt; page 30 BAA; pages 31, 125, 324 Tim Motion; page 35 Leon Chew; pages 5, 37, 91 (bottom left and right), 100, 101, 113, 117, 121, 122, 132, 136, 143, 151, 153, 156, 173, 176, 180, 181, 185, 187 190, 191, 263, 273, 279, 281, 283, 300, 301, 303, 312 Jon Perugia; pages 39, 73, 157, 305 (right), 309 Rob Greig; page 50 Troy Bailey; pages 53, 126, 130, 154, 192, 195, 269, 319, 355 Heloise Bergman; pages 57, 149, 305 (left) Olivia Rutherford; page 80 Hadley Kincade; pages 83, 171, 172 Tove Breitstein; pages 105, 118, 164, 260, 276 Andrew Blackenbury; page 119 Paul Mattson; pages 166, 236 Gemma Day; pages 193, 203, 214, 217, 223, 226, 227, 229, 254, 256 Ming Tang Evans; page 206 Jitka Hynkova; pages 200, 234 Alys Tomlinson; pages 208, 224 Oliver Knight; page 212 Tricia de Courcy Ling; page 220 Paula Glassman; page 230 Ross Fortune; page 264 Richard Lea-Hair; page 267 Simon Khamara; page 270 Hanne Lund; page 274 Jacob Perimutter; page 282 Dee Conway; pages 290, 291 Helene Binet; page 298 Jonas Rodin; page 316 Rogan McDonald; page 327 Steve Bardens/Rex Features; pages 310, 315, 333 Michelle Grant; page 336 RSC Henry IV part 2; pages 341, 352, 353 Amanda C. Edwards.

The following images were provided by the featured establishments/artists: pages 51, 66, 147, 183, 266, 271, 306, 329, 339, 348.
The Editor would like to thank all contributors to previous editions of *Time Out London*, whose work forms the basis for parts of this book.

Contents

Introduction

Friday night. We're running a little late on our way to a hotel bar off Trafalgar Square. The square is full, with people sat on each step up to the National Gallery, more standing on the empty plinth. There's a film playing on the big screen – some elegantly constructed 1940s propaganda for the indomitable variety of British life during the war, with a soaring classical soundtrack. Saturday morning, somewhat the worse for cocktails, we re-enter the square to a different buzz – drums and dancers are here now, celebrating a religious festival. Sunday morning. We're at our local tube station, hoping to nip into town for a couple of hours. Our main route is out of action. As is our back-up choice. Even our third, worst-case scenario tube is closed. Of course we can still get the bus. Just as everyone else has.

That's London for you. Fun? Yes. Full of surprises? Always. Frustrating? Oh yes. The painful truth for residents – and every word of this guide was written by resident experts – is that it is you visitors who are likely to get the best out of our city. While we're busy throwing impotent curses at the tube derailment that's made us late for work, you can blithely head up to the surface for an impromptu stroll around this glorious, curmudgeonly old city. While we struggle home crushed closer to

our colleagues than we'd normally get to our partners, you can be idling over another pint of Pride. While we're at the keyboard earning our extortionate rent, you can be enjoying an afternoon of world-class culture, totally gratis, at the British Museum. Or Tate Modern. Or the Natural History Museum.

Even for visitors, there are problems. There are nearly as many grumpy waitresses and rude barmen as there are effusive shopgirls and charming cabbies. Hotels are expensive. Bars and food are too. But we've put this book together to take you to the best places and the biggest bargains – as well as to the sort of places where quality is so high you don't mind forking out. Until you get your credit card bill, that is.

What's happening in the city now? There are new museums (hello, Wellcome Collection) and grand reopenings (take a bow London's Transport Museum). There are brilliant new restaurants (Wild Honey) and handsome old cafés (don't ever leave us Pellicci). There are the twisted nightclubs and the tranquil Royal Parks. And, above all, there are street events, crazy fiestas and music festivals breaking out all over town, almost every weekend.

London, at the moment, is a fantastic city to be in. Welcome and be glad. You couldn't have chosen a better time to visit.

ABOUT TIME OUT CITY GUIDES

This is the 16th edition of *Time Out London*, one of an expanding series of more than 50 guides produced by the people behind the successful listings magazines in London, New York, Chicago, Sydney and many more cities around the world. Our guides are all written and updated by resident experts who have striven to provide you with all the most up-to-date information you'll need to explore London, whether you're a local or a first-time visitor.

THE LOWDOWN ON THE LISTINGS

Above all, we've tried to make this book as useful as possible. Addresses, telephone numbers, websites, transport information, opening times, admission prices and credit card details have all been included in the listings, as have details of other selected services and facilities. However, owners and managers can change their arrangements at any time. Before you go out of your way, we

strongly advise you to call and check opening times and other particulars. While every effort has been made to ensure the accuracy of the information contained in this guide, the publishers cannot accept responsibility for any errors it may contain.

PRICES AND PAYMENT

Our listings detail which of the four major credit cards – American Express (AmEx), Diners Club (DC), MasterCard (MC) and Visa (V) – are accepted by individual venues. Many businesses will also accept other cards, such as Maestro and Carte Blanche, as well as travellers' cheques issued by a major financial institution.

The prices we've supplied should be treated as guidelines, not gospel. Fluctuating exchange rates and inflation can cause charges, particularly in shops and restaurants, to change rapidly. If prices vary wildly from those we've quoted, ask whether there's a good reason, then

please email to let us know. We aim to give the best and most up-to-date advice, and we always want to know if you've been badly treated or overcharged.

THE LIE OF THE LAND
Thanks to the chaotic street plan – or, rather, the lack of one – London is one of the most complicated of all major world cities to find your way around. It's a major part of the city's charm, since getting lost can open up all sorts of pleasant surprises, but it isn't much fun when you've a particular objective in mind. To make life a bit easier, we've included an area designation for every venue in this guide. Our area divisions are based on local usage and are clearly marked on the colour-coded map that appears on pp392-393. Most entries also have a grid reference that points to our fully indexed colour street maps at the back of the book (pp394-407).

The precise locations of hotels (**❶**), bars (**❶**) and restaurants (**❶**) have all been pinpointed on these maps; the section also includes a transport map and a street index.

Advertisers

TELEPHONE NUMBERS
The area code for London is 020; landlines follow this with eight digits in two groups of four. The 020 code is not used internally within London and is not given in our listings. From abroad, dial your country's exit code (in the US, it's 01), followed by 44 (the international code for the UK), then 20 for London (thereby dropping the first zero of the area code) and the eight-digit number. Mobile phone numbers have a five-digit code, usually starting 07, then a six-digit number. Freephone numbers start 0800, national-rate numbers 0870 and local-rate numbers 0845. For more on telephones and codes, *see pp373-374*.

ESSENTIAL INFORMATION
For all the practical information you might need for visiting the city, including customs and immigration information, disabled access, emergency telephone numbers, the lowdown on the local transport network and a list of useful websites, turn to the Directory at the back of this guide. It starts on p356.

LET US KNOW WHAT YOU THINK
We hope you enjoy *Time Out London*, and we'd like to know what you think of it. We welcome tips for places that you consider we should include in future editions, and take notice of your criticism of our choices. You can email us at guides@timeout.com.

There is an online version of this guide, along with guides to more than 50 other international cities, at **www.timeout.com**.

SOMERSET HOUSE

This beautiful neoclassical building stands on the banks of the Thames by Waterloo Bridge.

Visit The Courtauld Gallery's world-famous Impressionist and Post-Impressionist masterpieces, and the newly-opened Embankment Gallery's art, design, fashion and photography exhibitions.

Relax in the spectacular Edmond J. Safra Fountain Court, and don't miss the open air films and concerts in the summer or London's most beautiful ice rink in the winter.

Open daily Admission to Somerset House is free. Entry fees apply to galleries and events.

Tel: 020 7845 4600
Strand, London WC2

www.somersethouse.org.uk

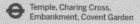 Temple, Charing Cross, Embankment, Covent Garden

THE COURTAULD Gallery

ROUTEMASTER

RM 1218

In Context

Features

Boudicca at the Roman walls of London.

History

Razed, plagued or bombed, London's always booming.

Going on 20 centuries in existence, London has seen it all. Fire, disease, riots and bombing countered by wealth, creativity and overweening self-confidence. Sometimes it is only the city's versatility and adaptability that seem constant: it has always been a port, fort, market, seat of government and multinational meeting place. According to novelist Ford Madox Ford in *The Soul of London*: 'England is a small country. The world is infinitesimal. But London is illimitable.'

While the capital's size and rapid expansion have long fascinated visitors, the city's origins are much less grand. Celtic tribes lived in scattered communities along the banks of the Thames before the Romans arrived in Britain, but no evidence suggests there was a settlement on the site of the future metropolis before the invasion of the Emperor Claudius in AD 43. During the Roman conquest of the country, they forded the Thames at its shallowest point (near today's London Bridge) and, later, built a timber bridge here. A settlement developed on the north side of this crossing.

Over the next two centuries, the Romans built roads, towns and forts in the area, and trade flourished. Progress was brought to a halt in AD 61 when Boudicca, the widow of an East Anglian chieftain, rebelled against the imperial forces who had seized her land, flogged her and raped her daughters. She led the Iceni in a savage revolt, destroying the Roman colony at Colchester before marching on London. The Roman inhabitants were massacred and their settlement razed. The following year Boudicca was defeated at the Battle of Watling Street and legend has it that she's buried beneath what's now platform 10 at King's Cross Station.

After order was restored, the town was rebuilt and, around AD 200, a two-mile-long, 18-foot-high wall constructed around it. Chunks of the wall survive today, and early names of the original gates – Ludgate, Newgate, Bishops-gate and Aldgate – are preserved on the map of the modern city. The street known as London Wall traces part of its original course.

By the fourth century, racked by barbarian invasions and internal strife, the Roman Empire was in decline. In 410, the last troops were withdrawn and London became a ghost town.

CHRISTIANITY ARRIVES IN LONDON

During the fifth and sixth centuries, history gives way to legend. The Saxons crossed the North Sea and settled in eastern and southern England. Apparently avoiding the ruins of

London, they built outside the city walls. Pope Gregory sent Augustine to convert the English to Christianity in 596. Ethelbert, Saxon King of Kent, proved a willing convert, and consequently Augustine was appointed the first Archbishop of Canterbury. Since then, the Kentish city has remained the centre of the English Christian Church. London's first Bishop, though, was Mellitus: one of Saint Augustine's missionaries, he converted the East Saxon King Sebert and, in 604, founded a wooden cathedral dedicated to St Paul inside the old city walls. On Sebert's death, his fickle followers reverted to paganism, but later generations of Christians rebuilt what is now St Paul's Cathedral.

London continued to expand. The Venerable Bede, writing in 731, described 'Lundenwic' as 'the mart of many nations resorting to it by land and sea'. This probably refers to a settlement west of the Roman city in the vicinity of today's Aldwych (Old English for 'old town'). During the ninth century, the city faced a new danger from across the North Sea: the Vikings. The city was sacked in 841 and 851, when the Danish raiders returned with 350 ships. It was not until 886 that King Alfred of Wessex – aka Alfred the Great – regained the city, re-establishing London as a major trading centre with a merchant navy and new wharfs at Billingsgate and Queenhithe.

'London now had two hubs: Westminster, the centre of government, and the City.'

Throughout the tenth century the city was prospering. Churches were built, parishes established and markets set up. However, the 11th century brought more harassment from the Vikings, and the English were even forced to accept a Danish king, Cnut (Canute, 1016-35), during whose reign London replaced Winchester as the capital of England.

In 1042, the throne reverted to an Englishman, Edward the Confessor, by many accounts a genuinely saintly man, who devoted himself to building England's grandest church two miles west of the City on an island in the river marshes at Thorney (meaning 'the isle of brambles'). He replaced the timber church of St Peter's with a huge abbey, 'the West Minster' (Westminster Abbey; consecrated in December 1065), and moved his court to the new Palace of Westminster. Just a week after the consecration, Edward died. But London now had two hubs: Westminster, the centre of the royal court, government and law, and the City of London, the commercial centre.

WILLIAM EARNS HIS NICKNAME

On Edward's death, there was a succession dispute. William, Duke of Normandy, claimed that the Confessor, his cousin, had promised him the English crown, but the English chose Edward's brother-in-law Harold. Piqued, William gathered an army and invaded; on 14 October 1066 he defeated Harold at the Battle of Hastings and marched on London. City elders then had to offer William the throne, and he was crowned in Westminster Abbey on Christmas Day 1066.

Recognising the need to win over the prosperous City merchants by negotiation rather than force, William granted the burgesses and the Bishop of London a charter – still kept at Guildhall – that acknowledged their rights and independence in return for taxes. But, 'against the fickleness of the vast and fierce population', he also ordered strongholds to be built at the city wall, including the White Tower (the tallest building in the Tower of London) and the now-lost Baynard's Castle at Blackfriars. The earliest surviving written account of contemporary London was penned 40 years later by a monk, William Fitz Stephen, who conjured up the walled city and pastures and woodland outside the perimeter.

PARLIAMENT AND RIGHTS

The Model Parliament, which agreed the principles of government, was held in Westminster Hall in 1295, presided over by Edward I and attended by barons, clergy and representatives of knights and burgesses. The first step towards establishing personal rights and political liberty – not to mention curbing the power of the king – had already been taken in 1215 with the signing of the Magna Carta by King John. In the 14th century, subsequent assemblies gave rise to the House of Lords (which met at the Palace of Westminster) and the House of Commons (which met in the Chapter House at Westminster Abbey). The king and his court had frequently travelled the kingdom during the 12th and 13th centuries, but now the Palace of Westminster was the seat of law and government, and noblemen and bishops began to build themselves palatial houses along the Strand from the City to Westminster, with gardens that stretched down to the river.

Relations between the monarch and the City were never easy. Londoners guarded their privileges with self-righteous intransigence, and resisted attempts by successive kings to squeeze money out of them to finance wars and building projects. Subsequent kings were forced to turn to Jewish and Lombard moneylenders, but the City merchants were as intolerant of foreigners as of the royals. Rioting, persecution and the occasional lynching and pogrom were commonplace in medieval London.

The privileges granted to the City merchants under Norman kings, allowing independence and self-regulation, were extended by the monarchs who followed, in return for finance. In 1191, during the reign of Richard I, the City of London was formally recognised as a commune – a self-governing community – and in 1197 it won control of the Thames, which included lucrative fishing rights that the City retained until 1857. In 1215, King John confirmed the city's right 'to elect every year a mayor', a position of great authority with power over the Sheriff and the Bishop of London. A month later the mayor joined the rebel barons in signing the Magna Carta.

Over the next two centuries, the power and influence of the trade and craft guilds (later known as the City Livery Companies) increased as trade with Europe grew, and the wharfs by London Bridge were crowded with imported cloth, furs, wine, spices and precious metals. Port dues and taxes were paid to Customs officials, including part-time poet Geoffrey Chaucer, whose *Canterbury Tales* were the first published work of English literature.

The City's markets, already established, drew produce from miles around: livestock at Smithfield, fish at Billingsgate and poultry at Leadenhall. The street markets, or 'cheaps', around Westcheap (now Cheapside) and Eastcheap were crammed with a variety of goods. As commerce increased, foreign traders and craftsmen settled around the port; the population within the city wall grew from about 18,000 in 1100 to well over 50,000 in the 1340s.

THE PEASANTS ARE REVOLTING

Not surprisingly, lack of hygiene became a serious problem. Water was provided in cisterns at Cheapside and elsewhere, but the supply, which came more or less direct from the Thames, was limited and polluted. The street called Houndsditch was so named because Londoners threw their dead animals into the furrow that formed the City's eastern boundary, while in the streets around Smithfield (the Shambles) butchers dumped the entrails of slaughtered beasts in the gutters.

These appalling conditions provided the breeding ground for the greatest catastrophe of the Middle Ages: the Black Death of 1348 and 1349, which killed about 30 per cent of England's population. The plague came to London from Europe, carried by rats on ships, and was to recur in London several times during the next three centuries, becoming a perennial hazard of London life.

The outbreaks of disease left the labour market short-handed, causing unrest among the overworked peasants. The imposition of a poll tax of a shilling a head proved the final straw, leading to the Peasants' Revolt of 1381. Thousands marched on London, led by Jack Straw from Essex and Wat Tyler from Kent. In the rioting and looting that followed, the Savoy Palace on the Strand was destroyed, the Archbishop of Canterbury murdered and hundreds of prisoners set free. When the 14-year-old Richard II rode out to Smithfield to face the rioters, Wat Tyler was fatally stabbed by Lord Mayor William Walworth. The other ringleaders were subsequently rounded up and hanged. But no more poll taxes were imposed.

ROSES, WIVES AND BLOODY MARY

Under the Tudor monarchs (1485-1603) and spurred by the discovery of America and the ocean routes to Africa and the Orient, London became one of Europe's largest cities. The first Tudor monarch, Henry VII, is usually noted for ending the Wars of the Roses, raging in England for many years between the Houses of York and Lancaster. He defeated Richard III at the Battle of Bosworth and married Elizabeth of York. But in London he's also noted for Henry VII's Chapel, the addition he made to the eastern end of Westminster Abbey and a triumph of Renaissance architecture.

Henry VII was succeeded in 1509 by Henry VIII. Henry's first marriage to Catherine of Aragon failed to produce an heir, so in 1527 the King determined the union should be annulled. When the Pope refused to co-operate, Henry defied the Catholic Church, demanding to be recognised as Supreme Head of the Church in England and ordering the execution of anyone who opposed the plan (including his chancellor Sir Thomas More). Thus it was that England began the transition to Protestantism. The subsequent dissolution of the monasteries transformed the face of the medieval city with confiscations and redevelopment of property.

On a more positive note, Henry found time to develop a professional navy, founding the Royal Dockyards at Woolwich in 1512 and at Deptford the following year. He also established palaces at Hampton Court and Whitehall, and built a residence at St James's Palace. Much of the land he annexed for hunting became the Royal Parks, including Greenwich, Hyde, Regent's and Richmond parks.

After Henry, there was a brief Catholic revival under Queen Mary (1553-8), though her marriage to Philip II of Spain met with much opposition in London. She had 300 Protestants burned at the stake at Smithfield, earning her the nickname 'Bloody Mary'.

RENAISSANCE REBIRTH

Elizabeth I's reign (1558-1603) saw a flowering of English commerce and arts. The founding of the Royal Exchange by Sir Thomas Gresham in 1566 allowed London to emerge as Europe's leading commercial centre. The merchant venturers and the first joint-stock companies (Russia Company and Levant Company) established new trading enterprises, while adventuring seafarers Francis Drake, Walter Raleigh and Richard Hawkins sailed to the New World and beyond. In 1580, Elizabeth knighted Drake on his safe return from a three-year circumnavigation; eight years later, he and Charles Howard defeated the Spanish Armada.

As trade grew, so did London. It was home to some 200,000 people in 1600, many living in dirty, overcrowded conditions; plague and fire were day-to-day hazards. The most complete picture of Tudor London is given in John Stow's *Survey of London* (1598), a fascinating first-hand account by a diligent Londoner whose monument stands in the City church of St Andrew Undershaft.

These were the glory days of English drama, popular with all social classes but treated with disdain by the Corporation of London, which banned theatres from the City in 1575. The Rose (1587) and the Globe (1599, now recreated; *see p80*), were erected at Bankside, providing

City seer William Blake

William Blake's London is a wide and wonderful thing. Poet, artist and all-round visionary, Blake's footprint can be detected in all parts of town, from Lambeth to Peckham, Soho to Newgate, Battersea to Bunhill Fields. Born in 1757 near Golden Square, one of Soho's forgotten spaces, Blake trained as an engraver at Great Queen Street, spending days diligently copying the medieval statues in Westminster Abbey. While working on Great Queen Street in 1780, Blake got caught up in the mob that made up the Gordon Riots – a three-day orgy of anti-Catholic and anti-state destruction – and watched them batter down the gates of the vicious and hated Newgate prison, on the site of which the Old Bailey now stands.

Blake married at St Mary's, Battersea, after which his poetry was first published and he began to socialise with London's radicals and reformers – including Tom Paine, artist Henry Fuseli and publisher Joseph Johnson. He also illustrated *Original Stories from Real Life*, a book by the pioneering proto-feminist Mary Wollstonecraft. Like many of his stripe, Blake was a firm supporter of the French Revolution in its early days, but became disillusioned as the Terror descended.

By now, Blake was living in Hercules Road, Lambeth, and seeing visions in Peckham Rye (a tree full of angels) and South Molton Street (the devil). This inspired the increasingly mystical content of his work: *Songs of Innocence and Experience*, *The Book of Thel*, *The Marriage of Heaven and Hell* and then *Jerusalem* were all illustrated books of poetry, written in Biblical style and full of religious imagery. *Jerusalem* in particular is crammed with London references. Always poor, Blake also continued to take on engraving work, famously illustrating Dante's *Inferno* and Milton's *Paradise Lost*.

Blake died in 1827 while still working on *Inferno*. He was buried at Bunhill Fields (*see p94*), a graveyard on the edge of the City that catered for noncomformists or dissenters – Protestants who worshipped outside the established Church. The exact location of Blake's grave was thought lost – although he is commemorated by a stone set on a mass grave – but was recently rediscovered by two Blake obsessives, Luis and Carol Garrido. The Friends of William Blake are currently campaigning to mark the exact location with an appropriate marker.

LONDON Wetland CENTRE
WWT

DISCOVER THE WILDER SIDE OF LONDON

Explore the London Wetland Centre and discover the beautiful wildlife that lives in this 100 acre wetland haven. Visit the Bird Airport observatory, discover rare and endangered birds in World Wetlands or just relax in the Water's Edge café. Let your children run wild in the Explore adventure area and Discovery Centre.

Open 7 days a week from 9.30am to 5pm
T: 020 8409 4400   Visit wwt.org.uk/london

WWT London Wetland Centre, Queen Elizabeth's Walk, Barnes, SW13 9WT
Alight at Barnes Station or take the no. 283 Duck Bus from Hammersmith Tube

homes for the works of popular playwrights Christopher Marlowe and William Shakespeare. Deemed officially 'a naughty place' by royal proclamation, 16th-century Bankside was a kind of Shoreditch of its time: a mix of art, entertainment and prostitution, within easy reach of the City. This was where you came for bear-baiting, cock-fighting and raucous taverns, or to visit one of many 'stewes' (brothels).

The Tudor dynasty ended with Elizabeth's death in 1603. Her successor, the Stuart King James I, narrowly escaped assassination on 5 November 1605, when Guy Fawkes and his gunpowder were discovered underneath the Palace of Westminster. The Gunpowder Plot was hatched in protest at the failure to improve conditions for the persecuted Catholics, but only resulted in an intensification of anti-papist sentiment. The non-event is commemorated as Bonfire Night even now; the burning of Guy in effigy celebrated with cheery fireworks.

Aside from the Gunpowder Plot, James I deserves to be remembered for hiring Inigo Jones to design court masques (musical dramas) and the first – beautiful and influential – examples of classical Renaissance style in London. The Queen's House (1616; *see p177*), the Banqueting House (1619; *see p137*) and St Paul's, Covent Garden (1631; *see p115*), can still be visited.

ROYALISTS AND ROUNDHEADS

Charles I succeeded his father in 1625, but gradually fell out of favour with the City of London and an increasingly independent-minded and antagonistic Parliament – taxation was again the main source of disquiet. The last straw came in 1642 when Charles intruded on the Houses of Parliament in an attempt to arrest five MPs. The country slid into civil war (1642-9) between the supporters of Parliament (the Roundheads, led by Puritan Oliver Cromwell) and of the King (the Royalists).

Both sides knew that control of the country's major city and port was vital for victory. London's sympathies were firmly with the Parliamentarians and, in 1642, 24,000 citizens assembled at Turnham Green, west of the City, to face Charles's army. Fatally for his future fortunes, the King lost his nerve and withdrew. He was never seriously to threaten the capital again; eventually, the Royalists were defeated elsewhere in the country. Charles was tried for treason and, though he denied the legitimacy of the court, he was declared guilty. Taken to the Banqueting House in Whitehall on 30 January 1649, where he declared himself a 'martyr of the people', and was beheaded. To this day, a commemorative wreath is laid at the site of the execution on the last Sunday in January each year.

For the next 11 years the country was ruled as a Commonwealth by Cromwell. His son Richard's subsequent rule was as brief as Oliver's had been stern and, due to the Puritan closing of theatres, banning of Christmas (a Catholic superstition) and strictures on the wickedness of any sort of fun, the restoration of the exiled Charles II in 1660 was greeted with relief and great rejoicing. The Stuart King had Cromwell exhumed from Westminster Abbey and his body hung in chains at Tyburn. His carcass was then thrown into a pit and his severed head displayed on a pole outside the abbey until 1685.

PLAGUE, FIRE AND REVOLUTION

In 1665 came the most serious outbreak of bubonic plague since the Black Death. By the time the winter cold had put paid to the epidemic, nearly 100,000 Londoners had died. On 2 September 1666, a second disaster struck. The fire that spread from a carelessly tended oven in Farriner's baking shop on Pudding Lane was to rage for three days and consume four-fifths of the City, including 89 churches, 44 livery company halls and some 13,000 houses.

The Great Fire at least allowed planners the chance to rebuild London as a rational, modern city. Many blueprints were considered, but, in the end, Londoners were so impatient to get on with business that the City was reconstructed largely on its medieval street plan, albeit in brick and stone rather than wood. The towering figure of the period was the prolific Sir Christopher Wren, who oversaw work on 51 of the 54 rebuilt churches. Among them was his masterpiece, the new St Paul's (*see p93*), completed in 1710 and, in effect, the world's first Protestant cathedral.

In the wake of the Great Fire, many well-to-do former City dwellers moved to new residential developments west of the old quarters, an area subsequently known as the West End. In the City, the Royal Exchange was rebuilt, but merchants increasingly used the new coffeehouses to exchange news. With the expansion of the joint-stock companies and the chance to invest capital, the City emerged as a centre not of manufacturing, but of finance.

Anti-Catholic feeling still ran high. The accession in 1685 of Catholic James II aroused such fears of a return to papistry that a Dutch Protestant, William of Orange, was invited to take the throne with his wife, Mary Stuart (James's daughter). James fled to France in 1688 in what became known – by its beneficiaries – as the 'Glorious Revolution'. The Bank of England was founded during William III's reign, in 1694, initially to finance the King's wars with France.

A street scene during the **plague**. *See p17.*

CREATION OF THE PRIME MINISTER

After the death of Queen Anne (who, though the daughter of James II, had sided with her sister Mary and brother-in-law William during the Glorious Revolution), the throne passed to George, great-grandson of James I, who was born and raised in Hanover, Germany. Thus, a German-speaking king – who never learned English – became the first of four long-reigning Georges in the Hanoverian line.

During George I's reign (1714-27), and for several years afterwards, Sir Robert Walpole's Whig party monopolised Parliament. Their opponents, the Tories, supported the Stuarts and had opposed the exclusion of the Catholic James II. On the King's behalf, Walpole chaired a group of ministers (the forerunner of today's Cabinet), becoming, in effect, Britain's first prime minister. Walpole was presented with 10 Downing Street (constructed by Sir George Downing) as a residence; it remains the official home of all serving prime ministers.

During the 18th century, London grew with astonishing speed, in terms of both population and construction. New squares and many streets of terraced houses spread across Soho, Bloomsbury, Mayfair and Marylebone, as wealthy landowners and speculative developers – encouraged to overlook the risk by the size of

the potential rewards – cashed in on the new demand for leasehold properties. South London too became more accessible with the opening of the first new bridges for centuries: Westminster Bridge (1750) and Blackfriars Bridge (1769) joined London Bridge, then the only crossing.

GIN RUINS POOR, RICH MOCK MAD

In the older districts, however, people were still living in terrible squalor and poverty, far worse than the infamous conditions of Victorian times. Some of the most notorious slums were located around Fleet Street and St Giles's (north of Covent Garden), only a short distance from streets of fashionable residences maintained by large numbers of servants. To make matters worse, gin ('mother's ruin') was readily available at very low prices, and many poor Londoners drank excessive amounts in an attempt to escape the horrors of daily life. The well-off seemed complacent, amusing themselves at the popular Ranelagh and Vauxhall pleasure gardens or with organised trips to the Bedlam asylum to mock the patients. Similarly, public executions at Tyburn – near today's Marble Arch – were popular events in the social calendar.

The outrageous imbalance in the distribution of wealth encouraged crime, and there were daring daytime robberies in the West End. Reformers were few, though there were exceptions. Henry Fielding, author of the picaresque novel *Tom Jones*, was also an enlightened magistrate at Bow Street Court *(see p115)*. In 1751, he and his blind half-brother John set up a volunteer force of 'thief-takers' to back up the often ineffective efforts of parish constables and watchmen who were the only law-keepers in the city. This crime-busting group of early cops, known as the Bow Street Runners, were the forerunners of today's Metropolitan Police (established in 1829).

Riots were commmon, frequently in reaction to middlemen charging extortionate prices or to merchants adulterating food. But the worst riots in the city's violent history were the anti-Catholic Gordon Riots of June 1780. Named after ringleader Lord George Gordon, they left 300 people dead – Romantic poet and mystic William Blake *(see p15* **City seer)** was among those swept along.

Meanwhile, five major new hospitals were founded by private philanthropists. St Thomas's and St Bartholomew's were long-established monastic institutions for the care of the sick, but Westminster (1720), Guy's (1725), St George's (1734), London (1740) and the Middlesex (1745) went on to become world-famous teaching hospitals. Thomas Coram's Foundling Hospital *(see p109)* was another remarkable achievement of the time.

INDUSTRY AND CAPITAL-ISM

It wasn't just the indigenous population of London that was on the rise. Country people, whose common land had been replaced by sheep enclosures, were faced with starvation wages or unemployment, and drifted into the towns in large numbers. Just outside the old city walls, the East End drew in many poor immigrant labourers to build the docks towards the end of the 18th century. London's total population had grown to almost a million by 1801, the largest of any city in Europe. By 1837, when Queen Victoria came to the throne, five more bridges and the capital's first passenger railway (running from Greenwich to London Bridge) gave hints that unprecedented expansion might be around the corner.

As well as being the administrative and financial capital of the British Empire, which by the end of Victoria's reign spanned a fifth of the globe, London was also its chief port and the world's largest manufacturing centre, with breweries, distilleries, tanneries, shipyards, engineering works and many other grim and grimy industries lining the south bank of the Thames. On the one hand, London had splendid buildings, fine shops, theatres and museums; on the other, it was a city of poverty, pollution, disease and prostitution. Residential areas were becoming polarised into districts with fine terraces maintained by squads of servants, or overcrowded, insanitary, disease-ridden slums.

The growth of the metropolis in the century before Victoria came to the throne had been

I'll **wager** Harry Bensley

The most famous wager to have been struck in a London gentlemen's club is surely that of Phileas Fogg, who one day at the Reform Club on Pall Mall pledged that he could circumnavigate the globe in 80 days. Author Jules Verne was drawing on the tradition that the exclusive environment of these private clubs encouraged bored, wealthy, uninhibited and reckless young men to strike up these extraordinary bets. White's (on St James's Street) was particularly famous for such wagers. One story is that two members bet a considerable sum on which of two raindrops would reach the bottom of a window pane first. Another tale concerns a member who collapsed, leading to two of his friends promptly having a bet on whether he was dead or not, then arguing that any attempt to revive him would damage the integrity of the wager. Another member bet £1,000 that a man could live for 12 hours under water, while in 1751 Lord Chesterfield bet his brother that he would never wager more than a guinea.

Given London's speculative culture, we should not be too surprised at the tale of Harry Bensley, a businessman who was losing heavily at cards one night in 1907 at the National Sporting Club on Regent Street and found himself making an extraordinary bet to cover his losses. Bensley would attempt to walk around the world without being identified, wearing a deep-sea diver's helmet and pushing a pram to make things more interesting. To which end he set off from Trafalgar Square on New Year's Day, with only £1, a set of postcards and a change

of underpants to sustain him. The facts throughout are disputed, but it is certain that by 1914 Bensley had enlisted in the British Army. He was invalided out of the trenches in 1915. Many of his business interests were in Russia and he lost his fortune after the Revolution in 1917, spending the rest of his life working in a menial jobs before dying in a Brighton bedsit in 1956. The whole fantastic story is recounted by Ken McNaught, Bensley's great-grandson, at mcnaught. orpheusweb.co.uk/HarryB.

Osatsuma

MODERN JAPANESE DINING

56 Wardour Street, London, W1 020 7437 8338
www.osatsuma.com
⊖ PICCADILLY CIRCUS LEICESTER SQUARE
Open M-T 12-11 W-T 12-11.30 F-S 12-12 Sun 12-10.30

spectacular, but during her reign (1837-1901), thousands more acres were covered with roads, houses and railway lines. If you visit a street within five miles of central London, its houses will be mostly Victorian. By the end of the 19th century, the city's population had swelled to more than six million – an incredible growth of five million in 100 years.

Despite social problems – memorably depicted in the writings of Charles Dickens – major steps were being taken to improve conditions for the majority of Londoners by the turn of the century. The Metropolitan Board of Works installed an efficient sewerage system, street lighting and better roads. The worst slums were replaced by low-cost building schemes funded by philanthropists such as the American George Peabody, who established the Peabody Donation Fund, which continues to this day to provide subsidised housing to the working classes. The London County Council (created in 1888) also helped to house the poor.

The Victorian expansion would not have been possible without an efficient public transport network with which to speed workers into and out of the city from the new suburbs. The horse-drawn bus appeared on London's streets in 1829, but it was the opening of the first passenger railway seven years later that heralded the commuters of the future. The first underground line, which ran between Paddington and Farringdon Road, opened in 1863 and proved an instant success, attracting more than 30,000 travellers on the first day. Soon after, the world's first electric track in a deep tunnel – the 'tube' – opened in 1890 between the City and Stockwell, later becoming part of the Northern Line.

THE CRYSTAL PALACE

If any one event crystallised the Victorian period of industry, science, discovery and invention it was the Great Exhibition of 1851. Prince Albert, the Queen's Consort, helped organise this triumphant event, for which the Crystal Palace, a giant building of iron and glass was erected in Hyde Park. It looked like a giant greenhouse, which is hardly surprising as it was designed not by a professional architect but by the Duke of Devonshire's gardener, Joseph Paxton. Condemned by art critic John Ruskin as the model of dehumanisation in design, the Palace came to be presented as the prototype of modern architecture. During the five months it was open, the Exhibition drew six million visitors. The profits were used by the Prince Consort to establish a permanent centre for the study of the applied arts and sciences: the enterprise survives today in the South Kensington museums of natural history,

science, and decorative and applied arts, and in three colleges (of art, music and science; *see p149*). After the Exhibition, the Palace was moved to Sydenham (*see p173*) and used as an exhibition centre until it burned down in 1936.

Meanwhile the Royal Geographical Society was sending navigators to chart unknown waters, botanists to bring back new species and geologists to study the earth. And many of their specimens ended up at the Royal Botanic Gardens at Kew (*see p183*).

ZEPPELINS ATTACK FROM THE SKIES

London entered the 20th century as the capital of the largest empire in history. Its wealth and power were there for all to see, set in stone in grandstanding monuments like Tower Bridge and the Midland Grand Hotel at St Pancras Station, both of which married the retro stylings of High Gothic with modern iron and steel technology. During the brief reign of Edward VII (1901-10), London regained some of the gaiety and glamour it had lacked in the dour later years of Victoria's reign. A touch of Parisian chic came to London with the opening of the Ritz Hotel in Piccadilly; Regent Street's Café Royal hit the heights of its popularity as a meeting place for artists and writers; the gentlemen's clubs entered a new era of lunacy (*see p19* **I'll wager**); and 'luxury catering for the little man' was provided at the new Lyons Corner Houses (the Coventry Street branch, which opened in 1907, could accommodate an incredible 4,500 people).

'The mighty city knew what it meant to be helpless.'

Road transport too was revolutionised. By 1911, horse-drawn buses were abandoned, replaced by the motor cars that put-putted around the city's streets, and the motor bus, introduced in 1904.

Disruption came in the form of devastating air raids during World War I. The first bomb over the city was dropped from a Zeppelin near the Guildhall in September 1915, and was followed by gruelling nightly raids on the capital; bomb attacks from German Gotha GV bombers began in July 1917. In all, around 650 people lost their lives as a result of Zeppelin raids, but the greater impact was psychological – the mighty city had experienced helplessness.

ROARING BETWEEN THE WARS

Political change happened quickly once the war had ended. David Lloyd George's government averted revolution in 1918-19 by promising (but not delivering) 'homes for heroes' – for the embittered returning soldiers. But the Liberal

Soho, so long George Melly

The death of George Melly in the summer of 2007 saw many of the old anecdotes dusted off for one last airing: such as the time he appeared on stage in full drag pretending to be 'Georgina'; the fact that he joined the Royal Navy because he liked the uniforms; and the numerous tales of alcoholic and sexual excess, many of them focused in and around Soho at its most decadent. But these affectionate obituaries also supplied us with the answer to one of London's seemingly insoluble questions: 'What did George Melly actually *do*?'

The answer is 'A lot. Of everything.' Melly was born in Liverpool in 1926 into an open-minded family, an attitude he took with him to public school at Stowe, where he earned a reputation as a voracious seducer of younger

boys and emerged a convinced homosexual. He joined the Navy, where he first showed a talent for entertaining his colleagues with bawdy song and developed a fascination for Surrealist art. After leaving the Navy, he began work at a Soho gallery and discovered women there after being seduced by the gallery owner's wife (while her husband 'sat there in his socks, watching'). Melly also began to sing in nightclubs in the traditional jazz scene, playing with trumpeter Mick Mulligan. By now Melly was a well-known face on the bohemian scene that centred around Soho haunts such as the Colony Room and Ronnie Scott's, and as such was getting drawn into numerous avenues – as well as singing, he was writing storylines for cartoon strips, which led to him becoming pop critic at the *Observer*. With the trad scene slowing down, writing became his bread and butter: Melly reviewed telly and also films for the *Observer*, scripted the films *Smashing Time* and *Take a Girl Like You* and wrote his first book, *Revolt Into Style*, an analysis of pop culture, in 1970.

Melly was established as a personality and his return to performance saw him drawing crowds for his ability to spin a good story as much as his skill at holding a note. He became a regular BBC broadcaster, continued to write and drink and womanise (his second marriage was 'open'), but rarely lost a friend because of these habits, such was his good humour, wit and grace. Melly later released three volumes of hilarious and candid autobiography (*Scouse Mouse, Rum, Bum and Concertina* and *Owning Up*), all of which served to cement his reputation as 'Good Time George'. Melly, by now a London icon, died in July 2007.

Party's days in power were numbered, and in 1924 the Labour Party, led by Ramsay MacDonald, formed its first government.

After the trauma of World War I, a 'live for today' attitude prevailed in the Roaring Twenties among the young upper classes, who flitted from parties in Mayfair to dances at the Ritz. But this meant little to the mass of Londoners, who were suffering greatly in the post-war slump. Civil disturbances, brought on by the high cost of living and rising unemployment, resulted in the nationwide General Strike of 1926, when the working

classes downed tools en masse in support of the striking miners. Prime Minister Baldwin encouraged volunteers to take over the public services and the streets teemed with army-escorted food convoys, aristocrats running soup kitchens and students driving buses. After nine days of chaos, the strike was called off by the Trades Union Congress (TUC).

The economic situation only worsened in the early 1930s following the New York Stock Exchange crash of 1929; by 1931 more than three million Britons were jobless. During these years, the London County Council (LCC) began to have a greater impact on the city, clearing slums and building new houses, creating parks and taking control of education, transport, hospitals, libraries and the fire service.

London's population increased dramatically between the wars too, peaking at nearly 8.7 million in 1939. To accommodate the influx, the suburbs expanded quickly, particularly to the north-west with the extension of the Metropolitan Line to an area that became known as 'Metroland'. Identical, gabled, double-fronted houses sprang up in their hundreds of thousands, from Golders Green to Surbiton.

At least Londoners were able to entertain themselves in their matching homes: film and radio had arrived. When London's first radio broadcast was beamed from the roof of Marconi House in the Strand in 1922, families were soon gathering around enormous Bakelite wireless sets to hear the BBC (the British Broadcasting Company; from 1927 the British Broadcasting Corporation). TV broadcasts started on 26 August 1936, when the first telecast went out live from Alexandra Palace, though only very few could afford televisions until the 1950s.

THE BLITZ

Abroad, events had taken on a frightening impetus. Neville Chamberlain's policy of appeasement towards Hitler's increasingly aggressive Germany collapsed when the Germans invaded Poland, and on 3 September 1939 Britain declared war. The government implemented precautionary measures against air raids – including the evacuation of 600,000 children and pregnant mothers – but the expected bombing raids did not happen during the autumn and winter of 1939-40, a period that became known as the Phoney War. That came to an abrupt end in September 1940, when hundreds of German bombers dumped high explosives on east London and the docks, destroying entire streets. Those killed and injured in that opening salvo numbered more than 2,000. The Blitz had begun. The raids on London continued for 57 consecutive nights, then intermittently for a further six months. Londoners reacted with tremendous stoicism, famously asserting 'business as usual'. After a final massive raid on 10 May 1941, Germany had left a third of the City and the East End in ruins.

From 1942 onwards, the tide of the war began to turn, but Londoners had a new terror to face: the V1, or 'doodlebug'. Dozens of these deadly, explosive-packed, pilotless planes descended on the city in 1944, causing widespread destruction. Later in the year, the more powerful V2 rocket was launched. The last fell on 27 March 1945 in Orpington, Kent, around six weeks before Victory in Europe (VE Day) was declared on 8 May 1945.

YOU'VE NEVER HAD IT SO GOOD

World War II left Britain almost as shattered as Germany. Soon after VE Day, a general election was held and Churchill was heavily defeated by the Labour Party under Clement Attlee. The new government established the National Health Service in 1948, and began a massive nationalisation programme that included public transport, electricity, gas, postal and telephone services. For most people, however, life remained regimented and austere. In war-ravaged London, the most immediate problem

The **Great Fire** of London. *See p17.*

40 Time Out years
of London

When *Time Out* first landed in hip hangouts and boutiques in late 1968, it would have seemed far-fetched to suggest that this folded A2 sheet, dropped off by rickety delivery-boy's bicycle, would go on to chronicle the social, cultural and political life of the capital for another 40 years. Since then, the magazine has evolved and grown – just like the city – but its love of detailing London's richness remains undimmed.

Up before the beak

Time Out was unique in listing London's alternative scene, but it wasn't the only magazine to spring from the counter-culture. When in 1971, our friends at *Oz* found themselves in the Old Bailey dock, we devoted our cover to their cause. The hippie pranksters had given over an issue of their magazine to schoolboys and the result outraged the establishment with its cover of 'naked chicks' under the phrase 'the schoolkids issue'. Charged with producing 'obscene, lewd, indecent and sexually perverted articles', the editors duly took the rap. Only widespread protests saw their harsh sentences overturned.

Hooligans

In this age of Japanese World Cup finals and the Miami Dolphins at Wembley, it's hard to picture a simpler time when dads and their boys stood on the terraces eating pies and shouting 'the ref's blind!'. But there was a darker side to early 1970s football that *Time Out* rather relished. This was personified by lank-haired soccer hooligans, each one a miniature general marshalling his Saturday afternoon battalions in 'tear-ups' across London.

Brixton burns

In the early 1980s, serious disorder wasn't just confined to football stadiums. Before the Falklands War, Margaret Thatcher was a deeply unpopular prime minister. Unemployment had doubled under her, inflation stood at 18% and when in 1981 frustration boiled over in cities across the country, it was Brixton that made the headlines. In fact the riot was concentrated around just a few roads, but it spoke of a wider crisis between black Londoners and the police. You may think that headline 'We control the streets of London and that's all there is to it' was the boast of a street-corner wide boy. In fact, it was the assertion of the Metropolitan Police as their cars burnt.

Snow blind

Just as the 20th century began a full 14 years late, so *Time Out* snagged the tardy arrival of the 1970s. It wasn't pretty either. As longhairs all over the capital began to switch their import preferences from Morocco to Columbia in a blizzard of snow and hideous matching white suits, the scene chronicled by *Time Out* began to fracture and dilute. Before long it would be impossible to sit in befugged silence through *Dark Side of the Moon* without hearing the life story of your nearest neighbour. Twice.

The sex issue

Time Out has covered sex in just about every conceivable way, from erotic movies to suburban swingers and outdoor adventures. So in January 1987 we weren't about to join the nay-sayers who told us that the emergence of AIDS meant the party was over. The government did its bit in informing and educating, but their ads, full of tombstones and thunderclap skies, made us want to remind our readers that sex wasn't a battlefield – it was supposed to be fun.

Music rules

It's fitting that football hooliganism peaked with the end of punk and faded with the loved-up late 1980s. It was impossible to witness football fans waving inflatable parrots on terraces where fighting had been rife without wondering just what they'd been necking with their Lucozade the night before. Acid house transformed London's nightlife and *Time Out* chronicled it all ten years on, just as ten years earlier we'd anatomised the angry energy of punk, our cover design capturing the rawness of the fanzines that surrounded the scene.

Ken Livingstone had already made our cover when London got its first elected mayor, but he was to write our editorial five years on in very different circumstances. When, on 7 July 2005, London's transport network was hit by four suicide bombs, the *Time Out* staffers who made it to the office across the paralysed city realised that the magazine couldn't ignore the terrible events still unfolding around them. Production for the following week was already well advanced, but there was no hesitation in scrapping the existing cover. In its place, our designers created a quiet classic that spoke volumes about the magazine's relationship with the city it has covered for four decades. Stark and reflecting the defiant unity Londoners showed in those weeks, it read simply 'Our City'.

faced by local authorities was a critical shortage of housing. Prefabricated bungalows provided a temporary solution for some, but the huge new high-rise housing estates that the planners devised were often badly built and proved to be unpopular with their residents.

There were bright spots. London hosted the Olympics in 1948; three years later came the Festival of Britain, resulting in the first, full redevelopment the riverside site into the South Bank Centre. As the 1950s progressed, life and prosperity gradually returned, leading Prime Minister Harold Macmillan in 1957 famously to proclaim that 'most of our people have never had it so good'. However, many Londoners were leaving. The population dropped by half a million in the late 1950s, causing a labour shortage that prompted huge recruitment drives in Britain's former colonies. London Transport and the National Health Service were both particularly active in encouraging West Indians to emigrate to Britain. Unfortunately, as the Notting Hill race riots of 1958 illustrated, the welcome these new immigrants received was rarely friendly. There were several areas of tolerance, among them Soho, which, during the 1950s, became famed for its mix of races and the café and club life they brought with them – the heyday of bon viveurs like George Melly (*see p22* **Soho, so long**).

THE SWINGING SIXTIES

By the mid 1960s, London had started to swing. The innovative fashions of Mary Quant and others broke Paris's stranglehold on couture: boutiques blossomed along the King's Road, while Biba set the pace in Kensington. Carnaby Street became a byword for hipness as the city basked in its new-found reputation as the music and fashion capital of the world – made official, it seemed, when *Time* magazine devoted its front cover to 'swinging London' in April 1966. The year of student unrest in Europe, 1968, saw the first issue of *Time Out* hit the streets in August; it was a fold-up sheet, sold for 5d. (For London's recent past, as seen by the mag, *see p24* **Time Out: 40 years of London**.) The decade ended with the Beatles naming their final album *Abbey Road* after their studios in NW8, and the Rolling Stones playing a free gig in Hyde Park that drew around 500,000 people.

Then the bubble burst. Many Londoners remember the 1970s as a decade of economic strife and the decade in which the IRA began its bombing campaign on mainland Britain.

The 1980s were the decade of Thatcherism. The Conservatives won the general election in 1979 under Britain's first woman prime minister, Margaret Thatcher, instituting a monetarist economic policy that depended

on cuts to public services that widened the divide between rich and poor. Riots in Brixton (1981) and Tottenham (1985) were linked to unemployment and heavy-handed policing, especially keenly felt in London's black communities. The Greater London Council (GLC), led by Ken Livingstone, mounted opposition to the government with a series of populist measures. It was abolished in 1986.

The replacement of Thatcher by John Major in October 1990 signalled a short-lived upsurge of hope among Londoners. A riot in Trafalgar Square had helped to see off both Maggie and her inequitable Poll Tax. Yet the early 1990s were scarred by continuing recession and more IRA terrorist attacks.

THINGS CAN ONLY GET BETTER?

In May 1997, the British people ousted the tired Tories and gave Tony Blair's Labour Party the first of three general election victories. The initial enthusiasm didn't last. The government hoped the Millennium Dome would be a 21st-century rival to the 1851 Great Exhibition. It wasn't. Badly mismanaged, the Dome ate some £1 billion on the way to becoming a national joke.

Nobody was laughing when the government's plans to invade Iraq in 2003 generated the largest public demonstration in London's history: over one million participated – to no avail. The new millennium saw Ken Livingstone, former leader of the GLC, become London's first directly elected mayor and head of the new Greater London Assembly (GLA). He was re-elected in 2004 for a second term, a thumbs up for his first term's policies, which included a congestion charge that sought to ease traffic gridlock by forcing drivers to pay £8 to enter the city centre.

The summer of 2005 was topsy-turvy. First came the city's elation at winning the bid to host the 2012 Olympics. Then a day later jubilation turned to shock, when bombs on tube trains and a bus killed 52 people and injured 700. These were followed two weeks later by similar, unsuccessful, attacks. In the immediate aftermath the number of people travelling on tubes and buses was fewer and more people took to cycling to work, but very quickly the first 'Not Afraid' T-shirts began to appear and London emerged with a revitalised sense of itself and bloody-minded determination to keep on with its ordinary life.

The run-up to the 2012 Olympics remains high on the agenda, with the Olympic torch arriving in town this year, as well as Eurostar trains from the continent gliding into their brand new terminus at St Pancras (*see p109*). A city in transition, then? True enough – things are just as they've always been.

Key events

AD 43	The Romans invade; a bridge is built on the Thames; Londinium is founded.
61	Boudicca burns Londinium; the city is rebuilt and made the provincial capital.
122	Emperor Hadrian visits Londinium.
200	A city wall is built; Londinium becomes capital of Britannia Superior.
410	Roman troops evacuate Britain.
c600	Saxon London is built to the west.
604	St Paul's is built by King Ethelbert.
841	The Norse raid for the first time.
c871	The Danes occupy London.
886	King Alfred of Wessex takes London.
1013	The Danes take London back.
1042	Edward the Confessor builds a palace and 'West Minster' upstream.
1066	William I is crowned in Westminster Abbey; London is granted a charter.
1067	The Tower of London begun.
1123	St Bartholomew's Hospital founded.
1197	Henry Fitzalwin is the first mayor.
1213	St Thomas's Hospital is founded.
1215	The mayor signs the Magna Carta.
1240	First Parliament sits at Westminster.
1290	Jews are expelled from London.
1348-9	The Black Death.
1381	The Peasants' Revolt.
1388	Tyburn becomes place of execution.
1397	Richard Whittington is Lord Mayor.
1476	William Caxton sets up the first ever printing press at Westminster.
1512-3	Royal Dockyards at Woolwich and Deptford founded by Henry VIII.
1534	Henry VIII cuts off Catholic Church.
1555	Martyrs burned at Smithfield.
1566	Gresham opens the Royal Exchange.
1572	First known map of London printed.
1599	The Globe Theatre opens.
1605	Guy Fawkes fails to blow up James I.
1642	The start of the Civil War.
1649	Charles I is executed; Cromwell establishes Commonwealth.
1664-5	The Great Plague.
1666	The Great Fire.
1675	Building starts on the new St Paul's.
1686	The first May Fair takes place.
1694	The Bank of England is established.
1710	St Paul's is completed.
1750	Westminster Bridge is built.
1766	The city wall is demolished.
1769	Blackfriars Bridge opens.
1773	The Stock Exchange is founded.
1780	The Gordon Riots take place.
1784	The first balloon flight over London.
1803	The first horse-drawn railway opens.
1812	PM Spencer Perceval assassinated.
1820	Regent's Canal opens.
1824	The National Gallery is founded.
1827	Regent's Park Zoo opens.
1829	London's first horse-drawn bus runs; the Metropolitan Police Act is passed.
1833	The London Fire Brigade is set up.
1835	Madame Tussaud's opens.
1836	The first passenger railway opens; Charles Dickens publishes his first novel *The Pickwick Papers*.
1843	Trafalgar Square is laid out.
1848-9	Cholera epidemic sweeps London.
1851	The Great Exhibition takes place.
1853	Harrods opens its doors.
1858	The Great Stink: pollution in the Thames reaches hideous levels.
1863	The Metropolitan Line, the world's first underground railway, opens.
1866	London's last major cholera outbreak; the Sanitation Act is passed.
1868	The last public execution is held at Newgate prison.
1884	Greenwich Mean Time established.
1888	Jack the Ripper prowls the East End; London County Council is created.
1890	The Housing Act enables the LCC to clear the slums; the first electric underground railway opens.
1897	Motorised buses introduced.
1915-8	Zeppelins bomb London.
1940-1	The Blitz devastates much of the city.
1948	London hosts the Olympic Games.
1951	The Festival of Britain takes place.
1952	The last London 'pea-souper' smog.
1953	Queen Elizabeth II is crowned.
1966	England win World Cup at Wembley.
1975	Work begins on the Thames Barrier.
1981	Riots in Brixton.
1982	The last of London's docks close.
1986	The GLC is abolished.
1990	Poll Tax protesters riot.
1992	Canary Wharf opens; an IRA bomb hits the Baltic Exchange in the City.
1997	Labour wins the national election.
2000	Ken Livingstone is elected mayor; Tate Modern and the London Eye open.
2003	London's biggest public demonstration ever against the war on Iraq.
2005	London wins bid to host the 2012 Olympics. Suicide bombers kill 52.
2007	Gordon Brown takes over from Tony Blair as prime minister.

London Today

The ancient city keeps on changing – these days, in a hurry.

It isn't often that an election becomes a spectacle, but the 1 May 2008 contest for London's mayor – since 2000 directly elected by Greater London's 7.5 million registered voters – could be just that. It's looking like a straight, bruising fight between two larger-than-life characters, personalities so strong they need no surnames: it's Boris versus Ken.

Boris Johnson, the blond, tousle-haired Tory MP for Henley and former editor of *The Spectator*, apparently playing politics for laughs. Ken Livingstone, the scratchy-voiced incumbent looking to secure his third term. The former seems to personify an avuncular London of tradition, where old Routemaster buses run again and we sup warm beer in the warm glow of Empire; the latter, a more serious-minded London, a global, progressive and open city.

Behind these loose first impressions, the details are intriguing. Livingstone is a career politician of 30 years standing, the man whose 'Loony Left' Greater London Council was such a torment to Margaret Thatcher that she had it disbanded – such a leftie, in fact, that Tony Blair wouldn't have him as Labour Party candidate in that inaugural 2000 election. Livingstone introduced what is effectively a green tax (the Congestion Charge, levied on any car that enters a steadily growing area of central London), raising revenue for sorely needed public transport improvements while at the same time bullying drivers into ditching the motor. Livingstone is also the man who got rid of those loved Routemaster buses, replacing them in part with the loathed 18-metre-long bendy buses, the man who won the Olympics for London and who signed a deal with the socialist Hugo Chávez for cheap Venezuelan oil.

Johnson, by contrast, is new generation Tory, a Notting Hill Conservative in the same way that Blair was Islington Labour. The product of an expensive education (Eton, Oxford), Johnson combines an affable demeanour and apparently relaxed attitude to modern life. He cycles. He jogs. He hosts the occasional TV quiz show. He is cuddly in a way that was until recently unimaginable in the patrician Conservative Party. Indeed the aimable idiot persona has so far enabled him to get away with comments that would have sunk anyone else – referring to 'piccaninnies' in one of his columns, for example. His politics are flexible, but broadly free market, free speech, small state, low tax. His concerns? The whole electorate were invited to vote for their preferred Tory candidate: Johnson won an invigorating 80 per cent of the votes cast, but – despite attracting good media coverage – only 20,000 votes were cast.

Turnout should be much much better in May, with tart initial exchanges between the front-runners. Livingstone calls Johnson a 'charming rogue', warning against the election becoming 'Celebrity Big Mayor', a reference to a low-rent reality TV show. Boris hit back with a simple assertion of serious intent, and hit Ken with wasting taxpayers' money. Livingstone retorts: 'Boris Johnson does not put forward any serious major constructive proposals for London policy simply because he does not have any'. Then mentions in passing the three big things he did about crime, housing and transport before lunch that day (or in the preceding fortnight, at any rate). And for good measure, trumpets his success in securing the deal for Crossrail (*see p30* **Transports of delight?**), praising the development opportunities it will create and explaining how it 'passes through London's boroughs of greatest deprivation'. That's both poor and rich voters on board, then.

It isn't all about the leading candidates. The bit-part players tell us almost as much about the current state of London. Brian Paddick, the gay former police chief who presided over a controversial relaxation of anti-cannabis laws in south London in 2001, is currently an eye-catching candidate for the Liberal Democrat nomination. His ticket? Crime, transport and green issues. The Greens themselves will put up a candidate; so too will the far-right BNP.

Of course, this is politics. Who knows whether one or both of the main candidates will be forced to withdraw by scandal or personal tragedy, decide to have a sex change, or merely reverse their position on an essential issue? But the key themes are pretty much clear: transport, housing, crime. Green policies will merit lip service, mainly in relation to transport. 'Black holes' will be identified in funding, only to be denied outright, explained as merely marginal and/or the accuser's numbers brought into question. Two further topics will also be aired: immigration and London's status as a global city – with implacable reference to our coming role as 2012 Olympic city, and accompanying envious or condescending glances at New York and Paris. Boris has already claimed he will measure his success not against that slip of a Ken Livingstone, but against the mayor of mighty New York, Michael Bloomberg.

Such comparisons with New York may suggest envy, but Paris is nowadays a safe subject. When our gossipy French hotel receptionist blithely told us about moving to London because he hated his countrymen,

we could mischievously point out that London is now France's seventh largest city. He almost wailed – but it's true. Maybe 200,000 French people are resident in London. They're young too, averaging just 29 years old. Forget East European plumbers and the South-east Asian hordes fleeing poverty: it's the old enemy France we need to keep our jobs safe from.

Happily, London is showing signs of accepting its hybridity – god knows the city's had long enough to so, with immigration a constant throughout its history. One interesting development was the opening within a month of each other in late 2007 of three sexy new arts centres, each dedicated to cultural diversity, each by up-and-coming architect David Adjaye. The Stephen Lawrence Centre in Deptford, Shoreditch's Rivington Place and the Bernie Grant Centre in Tottenham are all sleek, stylish and open modern buildings – a considerable feat in Deptford, where two windows were shot at, possibly by far-right extremists provoked by the mere mention of murdered black teenager Lawrence's name. These buildings won't attract cameraphone-wielding visitors like the iconic Gherkin does. But the Gherkin is really just an especially fine example of the City showing off, flexing its big-money biceps like it has done since Gresham set up the Royal Exchange in Elizabethan times. Whereas in Adjaye, we may be seeing something new.

'By the time you read this, amphibian-loving Mayor Ken may be history.'

There are also, however, several instances of the emperor's new clothes. For one, the rebranding by the British Film Institute of the sensibly descriptive National Film Theatre as something known as a BFI Southbank. For another, the branding consultants getting their teeth into the 2012 Olympics. They came up with a logo, designed to appeal to The Kids but routinely derided as vapid and already out of date. Meanwhile, the capital's training facilities remain shabby, with Crystal Palace closed down by an asbestos scare. And the costs? For the Olympic Stadium it is no longer £280 million, but £496 million. Some bright spark neglected to include inflation and VAT.

Boris Johnson accepted his candidacy for London mayor with a rabble-rousing threat: 'King Newt's days are numbered.' By the time you read this, the amphibian-loving Mayor Ken may indeed be history. Whose city will it be then? Perhaps it belongs to anyone with a story to tell about the place. Which is as much as to admit: Whose city is it? Yours, if you want it.

Transports of delight?

London's transport infrastructure has long been a source of pride and frustration for the city's residents. We have the oldest and most comprehensive underground railway in the world, but we also have the least reliable; there's a huge network of buses, but they never seem to get anywhere, despite the introduction of the Congestion Charge, which aimed to reduce the number of cars in the centre of town. Don't even get us started on the prices.

However, relief could be on hand in the form of a new wave of transport solutions. First to be completed is the new Eurostar terminal at St Pancras. **St Pancras International** will allow trains to reach Paris 15 minutes earlier than before, while also relieving congestion at Waterloo, one of London's busiest commuter stations. At the same time St Pancras will replace the old Thameslink station at nearby King's Cross, allowing larger trains to be used on the vital commuter service – the only north–south cross-London line. The changes have already encouraged redevelopment throughout the King's Cross–St Pancras area. It's hardly surprising that Transport for London is planning a similar transformation on tired and overcrowded Victoria station.

The tube is now in a constant state of redevelopment, some good (long overdue improvements to access), some annoying (entire lines closed at weekends), but one long-standing project is the rebuilding of the

Heathrow Terminal 4 tube station on the Piccadilly Line. This is to help deal with the increase of passengers expected when the massive new **Terminal 5** (*pictured*) opens in summer 2008. Designed by Richard Rogers, the terminal will enable the airport to handle 90 million passengers a year – its current capacity is supposedly 45 million, but passenger numbers are aleady 68 million.

Going some way towards compensating for this added damage to the climate, TfL is trialling new green buses, marked with a green sycamore leaf motif – the first of 70 hydrogen fuel cell buses to be introduced by 2010. There's also a largely successful campaign to encourage cycling, with more cycle paths throughout the city.

Other eco-friendly projects had included proposed tram lines – but most of these were shelved when the **Crossrail** deal was announced in 2007. Talked about since the 1980s, this massively ambitious £16 billion project now has a funding plan, although final assent is yet to be granted by Parliament. Crossrail will run 73.6 miles of track under London, easing commuter pressure between the West End and Canary Wharf, and linking Heathrow in the west to major new housing tracts in the east. As property developers lick their lips, other Londoners disconsolately eye the prospect of a decade of deep-level drilling and disruption between now and the putative opening date of 2017.

Architecture

Renaissance, Georgian, Victorian and modern – largely.

Like never before, London's architecture is on the up. Quite literally. Ken Livingstone likes tall buildings and most borough councils have concurred, giving their approval in the past five years to more skyscraper proposals than in the previous two decades put together. Even a fleeting glance around suggests that these towering projects (*see p32* **The only way is up…**) will significantly alter the character of a city that has long been broadly brick-built and low-rise. It has become a truism to say that London exists in a constant state of creative flux, but some fluxes are more extreme than others. Though it may yet be some time before the place resembles Chicago, which first reached for the sky after being razed by fire in 1871, modern London also sprang into being after a terrible conflagration, the Great Fire of 1666.

The fire destroyed five-sixths of the City of London, burning some 13,200 houses and 89 churches. History does not relate exactly how many people perished. Recorded fatalities

(among worthies of note) were few. The devastation is commemorated by Sir Christopher Wren's 202-foot Monument (*see p97*); many of the finest buildings in the City still stand as testament to the talents of this man, the architect of the great remodelling, and his successors.

London was a densely populated place built largely of wood, where fire control was very primitive. It was only after the three-day inferno that the authorities insisted on a few basic building regulations. Brick and stone became the construction materials of choice, and key streets were widened to act as firebreaks. In spite of grand proposals from architects (including Wren) who hoped to reconfigure it along classical lines, London reshaped itself around its old street pattern, with buildings that had survived the Fire standing as monuments to earlier ages. Chief of these was the Norman **Tower of London** (*see p101*), begun soon after William's 1066 conquest and extended over the next 300 years; the Navy cheated the advancing flames of the Great Fire by blowing up the surrounding houses before the inferno could get to it. Then there is **Westminster Abbey** (*see p138*), begun in 1245 when the site lay far outside London's walls and completed in 1745 by church architect Nicholas Hawksmoor's west

towers. Though the abbey is the most French of England's Gothic churches, deriving its spirit from across the channel, the chapel added by Henry VII, completed in 1512, is pure Tudor. Centuries later, Washington Irving gushed: 'Stone seems, by the winning labour of the chisel, to have been robbed of its weight and density, suspended aloft, as if by magic.'

The only way is up…

London has never really done tall buildings. None of your Eiffel Towers or Empire States here after all. Sure, since 1078 there's been the **Tower of London**, but it's only 90 feet high. And **Tower Bridge** (1894), that's only 141 feet. Even **Big Ben** (1858) is really quite small, though more than twice as high as Tower Bridge, at 322 feet. In fact, until the 1960s, or 1955 if you count the 370-foot chimneys of **Battersea Power Station**, **St Paul's Cathedral** (completed in 1710) remained the city's tallest building, all 367 feet of it. The construction of the Post Office Tower (completed in 1964; now called the **BT Tower**, *see p110*) set a new height record (582 feet), though until quite recently it did not officially exist, being left off Ordnance Survey maps for security reasons. Post-war reconstruction of the Blitzed city was gathering pace and high-rise architecture seemed to hold out the promise of affordable housing for cash-strapped boroughs. London saw a flurry of new buildings rising higher than anything known in the city before, notably the **Millbank Tower** (1961; 387 feet) next to Tate Britain on the Thames; **Centre Point** (1966; 385 feet) the high-rise at the junction of Oxford Street and Tottenham Court Road, later topped by the **Euston Tower**

(1970; 408 feet). In the City of London, the bewildering **Barbican Centre** (1973-76; 404 feet; *see p94*) continued the trend for residential skyscrapers into the 1970s, while in west London Ernö Goldfinger's 393-foot **Trellick Tower** (1972; *see p130*) rapidly became an infamous citadel of crime and drugs. Two years later, **Guy's Hospital Tower** (469 feet) proved that the National Health Service could do tall too. Then tower blocks went out of fashion. Only at the end of the decade did the equally uninspiring NatWest Tower (1980; now called **Tower 42;** *see p100*) set a new record at 600 feet, which it held for ten years until the opening of Cesar Pelli's monolithic **One Canada Square** (1991; *see p167*) on Canary Wharf, currently the tallest building in the city at 771 feet.

It wasn't until 2002 that Pelli's tower was joined by anything of comparable height, namely **25 Canada Square** (655 feet). The following year saw the completion of the much-more-interesting **30 St Mary Axe** or Gherkin (590 feet; *see p100*). Since 2000, the **London Eye** (*see p76*) has been wowing Londoners and visitors alike with the view from 443 feet. Over the coming years it will also provide a panoramic perspective on the new skyscrapers' race to the top.

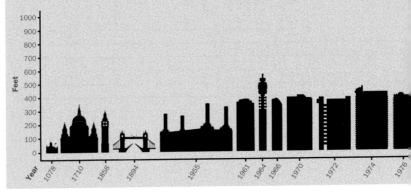

The European Renaissance came late to Britain, making its London debut with Inigo Jones's 1622 **Banqueting House** (*see p137*). The sumptuously decorated ceiling added in 1635 by Rubens celebrated the Stuart monarchy's Divine Right to rule, though 14 years later King Charles I provided an even greater spectacle as he was led from the room and beheaded on a stage outside. Tourists also have Jones to thank for **St Paul's Covent Garden** (*see p115*) and the immaculate **Queen's House** (*see p177*) at Greenwich, but these are not his only legacies. He also mastered the art of piazzas (notably at Covent Garden), porticos and pilasters, changing British architecture forever. His work influenced the careers of

In the City, first up, is 201 Bishopsgate and the **Broadgate Tower**, designed by Skidmore, Owings & Merrill (SOM), near Liverpool Street station, a 35-storey tower (538 feet) due for completion this year, with a new shopping plaza at its base. Docklands will also be sponsoring some competitors in the race to be London's tallest, with a new set of new towers higher than Canada Square on the **Riverside** development, slated to be ready by 2009. Not to be outdone, in the same year the City hopes to see the **Bishopsgate Tower** by KPF (Kohn Pedersen Fox), inspired by the John Hancock Centre in Chicago. At 60 storeys, with its lower floors already dubbed 'Marilyn Monroe's skirt', this 945-foot structure is likely, for a time, to become London's tallest building. The first in the city to be solely designed using parametric 'smart' or 'generative' modelling, its eco-friendly spiral design will not be for the fainthearted. Nearby, in 2010, at **110 Bishopsgate**, the Heron Tower by the same architects will stand 794 feet tall. At **122 Leadenhall**, the Richard Rogers partnership is responsible for the 737-foot 'Cheese Grater', a wedge-shaped 48-storey skyscraper.

More controversially, on the South Bank at 1 Blackfriars, the 574-foot **Jumeirah Tower** (aka the Beetham Tower), at the southern end of Blackfriars Bridge, is awaiting the final go-ahead from the government and hopes to be complete by 2012. Also on the south bank, further downstream near London Bridge, the most hotly debated of them all is projected. The current favourite to become London's tallest building in time for the Olympics is the **Shard** (1,016 feet). Designed by Renzo Piano, this striking glass spike is due to house the offices of Transport for London and a Shangri-La hotel.

Meanwhile, as Londoners express increasing concern about the effect of this type of project on the London skyline and their local environment (one of them includes only six extra parking places, for example), the Mayor has drawn up 26 'protected vistas', designed to enshrine various views, especially of St Paul's and Westminster, from strategic points around the city. They include the panoramic views from Alexandra Palace, Parliament Hill, Kenwood, Primrose Hill, Greenwich and Blackheath. And talking of views, one thing's pretty certain: at this rate, come the Olympics, there will be a significant number of brand new vantage points from which a lucky few will be able to gaze down on the rest of us.

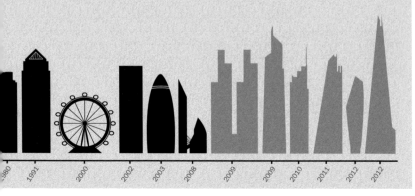

succeeding generations of architects and introduced a habit of venerating the past that it would take 300 years to kick.

Nothing cheers a builder like a natural disaster, and one can only guess at the relish with which Christopher Wren and co began rebuilding after the Fire. They brandished classicism like a new broom: the pointed arches of English Gothic were rounded off, Corinthian columns made an appearance and church spires became as multi-layered as a wedding cake.

Wren blazed the trail with daring plans for **St Paul's Cathedral** (*see p93*), spending an enormous – for the time – £500 on the oak model of his proposal. But the scheme, incorporating a Catholic dome rather than a Protestant steeple, was too Roman for the establishment and the design was rejected. Wren quickly produced a redesign and gained planning permission by incorporating a spire, only to set about a series of mischievous U-turns to give us the building – domed and heavily suggestive of an ancient temple – that has survived to this day.

'Nothing cheers a builder like a natural disaster.'

Wren's architectural baton was picked up by Nicholas Hawksmoor and James Gibbs, who benefited from a 1711 decree that 50 extra churches should be built. Gibbs became busy in and around Trafalgar Square, building the steepled Roman temple of **St Martin-in-the-Fields** (*see p137*), as well as the baroque **St Mary-le-Strand** and the tower of **St Clement Danes** (for both, *see p116*).

Gibbs's work was well received, but the more prolific and experimental Hawksmoor had a rougher ride. **St George's** (*see p109*) in Bloomsbury cost three times its £10,000 budget and took 15 years to build. It too aims to evoke the spirit of the ancients. Rather than a spire, there is a stepped pyramid topped by a statue of George I in a toga.

One of a large family of Scottish architects, Robert Adam found himself at the forefront of a movement that came to see Italian baroque as a corruption of the real thing. Architectural exuberance was eventually dropped in favour of a simpler interpretation of the ancient forms. The best surviving work of Adam and his brothers James, John and William can be found in London's great suburban houses **Osterley Park**, **Syon House** (*see p191*) and **Kenwood House** (*see p158*), but the project for which they are most famous no longer stands. In 1768, they embarked on the cripplingly expensive **Adelphi** housing estate off the Strand. Most of the complex was pulled down in the 1930s

and replaced by an office block. Only a small part of the original development survives in what is now the **Royal Society of Arts** (8 John Adam Street, Covent Garden, WC2).

Just as the first residents were moving into the Adelphi, a young unknown called John Soane was embarking on a domestic commission in Ireland. It was never completed, but Soane went on to build the **Bank of England** (*see p95*) and **Dulwich Picture Gallery** (*see p173*). The Bank was demolished between the wars, leaving only the perimeter walls and depriving London of Soane's masterpiece, though his gracious Stock Office has been reconstructed in the museum. A more authentic glimpse of what those bankers might have enjoyed can be gleaned from a visit to Soane's house, now the quirky **Sir John Soane's Museum** (*see p103*), an extraordinary and exquisite architectural experiment.

A near-contemporary of Soane's, John Nash was arguably a less talented architect, but his contributions have proved comparable to those of Wren. Among his buildings are the inner courtyard of **Buckingham Palace** (*see p142*), the **Theatre Royal Haymarket** (Haymarket, SW1) and **Regent Street** (Soho/Mayfair, W1). The latter began as a proposal to link the West End to the planned park further north, as well as a device to separate the toffs of Mayfair from Soho riff-raff or, in Nash's words, a 'complete separation between the Streets occupied by the Nobility and Gentry, and the narrow Streets and meaner houses occupied by mechanics and the trading part of the community'.

By the 1830s, the classical form of building had been established in England for some 200 years, but this didn't prevent a handful of upstarts from pressing for change. In 1834, the **Houses of Parliament** (*see p138*) burned down, leading to the construction of Sir Charles Barry's Gothic masterpiece. This was the beginning of the Gothic Revival, a move to replace what was considered foreign and pagan with something that was native and Christian.

Barry sought out Augustus Welby Northmore Pugin. Working alongside Barry (and not always in agreement – of Barry's symmetrical layout he famously remarked, 'All Grecian, sir. Tudor details on a classic body.'), Pugin created a Victorian fantasy that would today be condemned as the Disneyfication of history.

Architects would often decide that buildings weren't Gothic enough; as with the 15th-century **Great Hall** (*see p97*) at the **Guildhall**, which gained its corner turrets and central spire only in 1862. The argument between classicists and goths erupted in 1857, when the government hired Sir George Gilbert Scott, a leading light of the Gothic movement, to design a new HQ for the Foreign Office. Scott's design incensed anti-

In Context

goth Lord Palmerston, then prime minister, whose diktats prevailed. But Scott exacted his revenge by building an office in which everyone hated working, and by going on to construct Gothic edifices all over town, among them the **Albert Memorial** (*see p149*) and **St Pancras Chambers** (*see p109*), the station frontage housing the Midland Grand Hotel.

St Pancras was completed in 1873, after the Midland Railway commissioned Scott to build a London terminus that would dwarf that of its rivals next door at King's Cross. Using the project as an opportunity to show his mastery of the Gothic form, Scott built an asymmetrical castle that obliterated views of the train shed behind, itself an engineering marvel completed earlier by William Barlow. Other charming and imposing neo-Gothic buildings around the city include the **Royal Courts of Justice** (*see p116*), the **Natural History Museum** (*see p151*), and **Tower Bridge** (*see p101*). Under the influence of the Arts and Crafts movement, medievalism easily morphed into mock-Tudor, such as the wonderful black-and-white **Liberty Store** (*see p238*). World War I and the coming of modernism led to a spirit of renewal and a starker aesthetic. **Freemason's Hall** (*see p115*) and the BBC's **Broadcasting House** (*see p125*) are good examples of the pared-down style of the 1920s and '30s. The latter is currently being extended and modernised.

Perhaps the finest example of between the wars modernism can be found at **London Zoo** (*see p127*). Built by Russian émigré Bertold Lubetkin and the Tecton group, the spiral ramps of the Penguin Pool (no longer used by penguins) were a showcase for the possibilities of concrete. The material was also put to good use on the Underground, enabling the quick, cheap building of cavernous spaces with sleek lines and curves.

There was nothing quick or cheap about the art deco **Daily Express** (*see p88*) building (Fleet Street, the City, EC4). A black glass and chrome structure built in 1931, it is an early example of 'curtain wall' construction where the façade is literally hung on an internal frame. The building has been refurbished, but the original deco detailing – crazy flooring, snake handrails and funky lighting – remains intact. Public access is not guaranteed, but it's worth sticking your head around the door of what the *Architects' Journal* has called a 'defining monument of 1930s London'.

The aerial bombing of World War II left large areas of London ruined, providing another opportunity for builders to cash in. Lamentably, the city was little improved by the rebuild; in many cases, it was worse off. The destruction left the capital with a dire housing shortage, so architects were given a chance to demonstrate the grim efficiency with which they could house large numbers of families in tower blocks.

Houses of Parliament.

There were post-war successes, however, including the **Royal Festival Hall** (*see p77*) on the South Bank. The sole survivor of the 1951 Festival of Britain, the RFH was built to celebrate the war's end and the centenary of the Great Exhibition. The neighbouring **Hayward Gallery** is an exemplar of the 1960s vogue for Brutalist architecture. The 1970s and '80s offered up a pair of alternatives to Brutalism: post-modernism and high-tech. The former is represented by Cesar Pelli's **One Canada Square** (*see p167*) at Canary Wharf in Docklands, an oversized obelisk that has become the archetypal expression of 1980s architecture and holds an ambiguous place in the city's affections. Richard Rogers' **Lloyd's of London** building (*see p98*) is London's best-known example of high-tech, in which commercial and industrial aesthetics cleverly combine to produce what is arguably one of the most significant British buildings since the war. Mocked on completion in 1986, the building still manages to outclass newer projects.

'Tellingly, all three of these landmarks are in the east.'

Equally ground-breaking was Future Systems' **NatWest Media Centre** at Lord's Cricket Ground (St John's Wood Road, St John's Wood, NW8). Built from aluminium in a boatyard and perched high above the pitch, it's one of London's most daring constructions to date, especially given the traditional setting. And Will Alsop's multicoloured **Peckham Library** (171 Peckham Hill Street, Peckham, SE15) redefined community architecture, winning the Stirling Prize in 2000.

Thanks to the Heritage Lottery Fund, much new architecture is to be found cunningly inserted into old buildings. Herzog & de Meuron's fabulous transformation of a power station on Bankside into **Tate Modern** (*see p81*) is perhaps the most famous example, while Lord Norman Foster's exercise in complexity at the **British Museum** (*see p107*), where the £100 million Great Court created the largest covered square in Europe, is one of the most impressive – every one of its 3,300 triangular glass panels is unique.

Any discussion of the city's architecture is, of course, impossible without mention of Foster. With his **City Hall** and already iconic **30 St Mary Axe** (formerly the Swiss Re Tower aka 'The Gherkin') in the City, his prolific practice set new standards in sports design with the new **Wembley Stadium** – the soaring arch has become another instantly recognisable symbol of the country's sporting life.

You'll have to hop on the DLR and head south to see the other great London building by Herzog & de Meuron, Deptford's **Laban** dance centre (Creekside, Deptford, SE8), which won them the Stirling Prize in 2003. The capital also has its first building by the acclaimed Daniel Libeskind, who has designed a small graduate centre for the **London Metropolitan University** (Holloway Road, Holloway, N7).

But superstar architects from overseas haven't snaffled up all the major commissions. On Whitechapel Road, E1, David Adjaye has designed his second new-build **Idea Store** (www.ideastore.co.uk), following on from his acclaimed building in Poplar (Chrisp Street, E14). With its sleek and crisp aesthetic, it's a world away from the traditional Victorian library in design as well as name and function. As if to confirm his status as a major player, he is also responsible for the new **Rivington Place** gallery (*see p165*), its design influenced by a Sowei mask from Sierra Leone.

Tellingly, all three of these new landmarks are in the east. As the capital's focus shifts firmly towards the Olympics-inspired regeneration of east London, they are surely just the forerunners of a huge period of change that will have a major impact on the capital's built environment. To see where things might be going, get off the tube at Goodge Street and visit **New London Architecture** (Building Centre, 26 Store Street, Bloomsbury, WC1, 7692 4000). Opened in 2005, this permanent exhibition aims to provide an overview of the key developments in London for the general visitor and design professional alike. The centre's impressive centrepiece is a 39-foot-long scale model of London, stretching from Battersea Power Station in the south up to King's Cross and out to Docklands and Stratford in the east.

It's a fascinating bird's-eye view of what the capital looks like now, and what it might soon become. Currently, there are more than 150 unbuilt schemes on the model, including spectacular 1,000-foot proposals for the City and London Bridge (*see p32* **The only way is up…**). As jaw-dropping as these are, they represent just a fraction of the £100 billion-worth of redevelopment projected for London over the next couple of decades. Especially interesting is the section of the model with the proposed Olympics 2012 facilities, which the bid team used as part of its campaign. The NLA model also provides a great way to get an understanding of how different parts of the capital link up, and how big things are. The model is accompanied by a regularly changing exhibition on a specific aspect of the capital's built environments.

Surveillance Society v the New Decadents

Dressing up for a dressing down:
Big Brother is watching the party.

Fall down the narrow staircase of Soho's Black Gardenia, a speakeasy-style jazz dive, and you'd be forgiven for thinking you'd fallen through a hole in time. Men in zoot suits lean against a tiny bar, nodding to impromptu jazz and blues outfits; the barmaid is dolled to red-lipped, 1940s tart perfection, with only her inky tattoos to suggest she's from the 21st century. There's no predicting what will happen down here, nor when you'll make it back out on to Dean Street – it's just that kind of bar. On parallel Wardour Street, at the Soho Revue Bar, Lady Luck is the most famous retro happening in town. Hosted by the decadent DJ El Nino and his stunning bride, Lady Kamikaze, this is where men in tailored trousers, white vests, tight waistcoats and trilbies whirl girls around with amazing aplomb. It's sleazy enough not to be quaint and the music is hip-jiggling fierce.

London is also experiencing a revival in dressing other. Alt-drag performers are sweeping over London's dancefloors. Less *Priscilla Queen of the Desert* than Leigh

Bowery – the man who made outrageously imaginative dressing-up an artform all his own back in the naughty 1980s – these troupers are experimental and savage, never pretty. They flock to the likes of Bar Music Hall in Shoreditch to pose and preen alongside fashionista club kids. Scottee – DJ, promoter, performer and every alt-drag boy's ambition – co-hosts Foreign here with drag queen du jour, Jodie Harsh. The boy in a couture piece of mustard yellow lycra guarding the door, with only his clipboard to keep the long, long queue of hopefuls at bay? That's Dean, and if you aren't dressed the part you ain't getting past. Once the final electro, edgy pop or mashed-up record has been played, it's all up to one of the bars on Kingsland Road for an afterparty (if we told you exactly which one, we'd be spoiling the fun). Then, of course, it's on to someone's shabby flat until sometime Monday.

Excess, oh yes. Yet in the battle against 'anti-social behaviour' (anything from littering and

smoking to public drunkenness, vandalism and threatening behaviour, punishable with an Anti-Social Behaviour Order or ASBO), Londoners are caught on camera on average 300 times every day. Methods of surveillance are becoming ever more Orwellian: speaking CCTV cameras that chastise litter louts are being tried out in Middlesbrough. Back in London, Westminster Council has introduced mobile cameras carried on cars, and the overall number of CCTV cameras in the borough will rise from 205 in July 2007 to a predicted 350 by the end of 2008.

The UK watchdog CameraWatch has repeatedly claimed that the majority of cameras are operated illegally, and according to the BBC, a 2007 Information Commissioners Office report highlighted the need for the public to be made more aware of the 'creeping encroachment' of surveillance apparatus on their civil liberties. Did we mention Orwell? There are 32 cameras within 200 yards of the house where the *1984* author lived until his death. Does it really

Smokin'!

It's not long since London's two million-odd smokers could light up in any pub, café, casino or restaurant they liked. Now they are pariahs, forced to huddle on street corners without so much as a wheeze of protest. It's hard to deny that with the ban has come a subtle yet distinct change in the city's character. The elegant **Macanudo Fumoir**, in Claridge's, for example, has lost much of its louche atmosphere, and now presents something of a misnomer. The familiar smoky aroma of the local pub has given way to the scent of stale beer – scant improvement. But perhaps the biggest victims are the proprietors of London's numerous hookah bars (at least a dozen on the Edgware Road alone), many of whom have seen custom tail off dramatically.

Some establishments have avoided the ban by hosting 'private' events, where staff aren't employed and drink isn't charged for. One such venue is **Bastion Host** (Unit 4, 210 Cambridge Heath Road, Bethnal Green, E2 9NQ, 8983 6960, www.bastionhostlondon. com), a small art gallery that holds regular exhibitions sponsored by Cobra Beer. These are by invitation only, but if you make the right friends you might get to enjoy free drinks in a refreshingly smoke-friendly atmosphere.

Another loophole has been found by Cuban-themed bar **Floridita** (100 Wardour Street,

Soho, W1F OTN, 7314 4000), which allows customers to 'sample' cigars in the adjoining tobacconist's shop. Drinks can't be taken from the bar to the shop, but there are jugs of water and newly installed coffee tables to make things more comfortable.

More permanent solutions have come in a number of ingenious forms. The **Bavarian Beerhouse** (190 City Road, Shoreditch, EC1V 2QH, 7608 0925) is offering customers a range of Bavarian snuff, and serving a variety of 'Snuff and Schnapps' specials. Similarly, **Pearl** (252 High Holborn, Holborn, WC1V 7EN, 7829 7000, www.pearl-restaurant.com) has created a surprisingly palatable nicotine-based cocktail, the Nicotini, consisting of tobacco-infused rum and demerera sugar, to space out those irritating cravings.

But most places have simply made do with spaces for outdoor seating and numerous heaters. Well-located pubs and bars that have expansive gardens or courtyards in which to smoke include Soho's **Endurance** (90 Berwick Street, W1F 0QB, 7437 2944), **Big Chill House** in King's Cross (*see p318*) and **93 Feet East** on Brick Lane (*see p313*), while plenty of cafés have provided outside tables under awnings. Trendy club **EGG** (*see p319*), also in King's Cross, even has a large heated garden with its own bar and DJ.

matter? After all, there isn't likely to be a police crackdown on alt-drag boys in smeared lipstick and customised frocks, nor on vintage-obsessed retro girls and sharp-suited lads. Certainly not all of London's promoters feel that measures against anti-social behaviour are a bad thing. 'Hackney police have noticeably increased their presence in the area,' says Scottee. 'We have a large percentage of younger clubbers, so I'm happy with the increase in surveillance. I think it ensures London clubbers have a safe time and get home in one piece.'

'Lethal Bizzle, one of the brightest DJs on the grime scene, puts it succinctly: "Police fuck shit up".'

Westminster Council – although clearly aware of public concern about the erosion of civil liberties – makes a similar case about CCTV. Matthew Norwell, acting assistant director for the crime and disorder reduction department, says, 'From my perspective, it's about appropriate solutions to appropriate problems. Five years ago, the West End had problems with low-level disorder and visible manifestations of the late night economy. The police and council needed an effective way of dealing with the problem and through policing, CCTV and licensing, it's better managed.' But doesn't that mean that going out just isn't as much fun as it was? 'What does that mean? Is it fun to be the victim of street crime or have your evening made unpleasant? Now, more people can go out and enjoy the West End safely.'

No one would argue against a safe journey home, but there are already some indications of where policing that relies on tight licensing and surveillance technology could be heading. The grime scene, which exploded in 2004, is based on a riotous, dancefloor-destroying mess of ravey synths, UK garage-like bass and quick-fire MCs, most of them black. Born out of London council estates, it's a popular and high-energy music that could be all over dancefloors in the capital. But it's not – you can count the number of regular nights on one hand.

Former club promoter Neil Boorman ran a grime night at Old Street's 333 club. Despite being trouble-free, 'from the word go, we felt that the police didn't want us in their backyard. The only way to have a hassle-free night and not lose all your money when the police cancelled it at the last minute would be to fax the line-up to the police for approval and to be prepared to take people off the bill.'

Lethal Bizzle, one of the brightest DJs on the grime and urban scene, puts it more succinctly: 'Police fuck shit up.' Bizzle shot to fame with his dynamite track, 'Pow', but the success was a double-edged sword. It was this single, his manager Nadian Khan believes, that caused the police to refuse to let him play anywhere. When a grime dancefloor goes off, it looks just like an indie moshpit – lots of kids jumping up and down. This, Khan argues, makes people think something bad is about to happen. 'When indie kids jump around,' says Bizzle, 'it's moshing. When black people do it, it's a riot.' Lethal should know: he got around the apparent police ban by playing at indie gigs. The likelihood of seeing a straight-up grime night, other than at a safe, 'arty' venue like the ICA, remains small.

Nor has grime been the only victim of the close attentions of the authorities. Before nu-rave swept through our high street shops in a fit of slogan T-shirts and fluoro colours, it was a small party scene in east London. In 2006, bands like the Klaxons and Sh*t Disco sought out empty rooftop apartments or boarded-up warehouses, threw parties and hoped the police wouldn't shut them down, using legislation passed in the 1990s to counter the original rave scene. The Klaxons have gone on to Mercury Award success, but others from the scene are still smarting from their time putting on parties.

'The police are all over Myspace, looking for illegal parties now. Who's going to take a risk like that?'

'Everyone got really excited by the illegal raves going on around Dalston,' says DJ and promoter Rory. 'They were messy and exciting and you never knew what was going to happen – sometimes bands would come and DJ badly, other times the soundsystem wouldn't work. But the police kept busting parties before they even started, saying that it was dangerous and all that crap. They started off just sending us away, but then at the end of 2006, they started confiscating all the equipment. If you borrow equipment and lose it? Easily forty-thou. The police are all over Myspace, looking for illegal parties now. Who's going to take a risk like that?'

According to George of the twisted cabaret duo Bourgeois & Maurice, the 'dress-up or piss-off' ethos at clubs like Foreign is a direct reaction to this: 'I think what's happening at the moment with DIY self-promotion and dress-up culture is a sort of punk movement in its own way and it is a reaction to feeling like a public voice has been taken away.'

Despite the difficulties promoters face from more stringent licensing, the loudest grumbling is about public health and environmental legislation, especially the July 2007 ban on smoking in public places and the Congestion Charge on cars in central London, levied since 2003 and enforced by cameras.

'We have to pay a congestion charge. Now we can't even smoke in public places. What law are we in for next?'

'People work hard in London,' says DJ El Nino, who believes such measures directly affect his club, and for the worse. 'They are entitled to a free social life. But we can't park in London because of all the restrictions. We have to pay a congestion charge. Now we can't even smoke in public places. What law are we in for next? It's affected nights out. Half the people are outside having a smoke – you can't take your drink outside with you, though. What social life do you have if you can't sit and have a drink and a smoke while listening to music?'

The Rakehell's Revels is perhaps the very definition of new-old decadence, a weekly rewind to the 1920s held in the Café Royal's opulent Grill Room. David Piper, the host of the Revels, is pragmatic about the smoking ban. 'I can't say it's changed attitudes very much… Habits maybe. Especially for my night – where smoking fits the image more, and to have to go outside on to Regent Street and share it with a noxious hotdog stand and general idiots ruins the flow somewhat. But I think it's impossible to fight or rebel against – rebelling against not being able to smoke in a club seems a bit petty – and most people don't have any sort of inclination to fight the world around them at all. Besides, the normal outlets for having a good time – getting very drunk, taking lots of drugs, etc – are still very much available. Party people, that is to say, those who tend to be able to have a good time whatever the circumstances, are still happy and having a good time.'

He may be on to something: Londoners are intent on getting it on and getting out of it, on putting effort and ingenuity into creating as many and as lurid opportunities for pleasure as possible. Smoking areas outside clubs have already become prime flirting zones – dubbed 'smirting'. Perhaps the best way to fight back is simply to join in the craziness, wink at the cameras when you see them and make sure you're wrapped up nice and warm if you're heading outside for a smoke.

Where to Stay

Where to Stay   42

Features

B&B Belgravia. *See p62.*

Where to Stay

Prices are increasing – but so are the quality and variety of London's hotels.

The bad news first: room prices rose nearly 20% to an average, according to Hotels.com, of £119 a night – cheap for New Yorkers and Muscovites, but the rest of us are struggling. What's going on? For one thing, demand remains high. The competition means facilities should keep improving, but there's no reason to expect prices to drop. Commentators have suggested a staggering 10% of the city's deluxe rooms are currently closed for refurbishment, keeping demand high and doubtless driving prices up even further once the swanky refits open. Of the current refurbishments, the Savoy is the most significant, closing for the whole of 2008 (*see also p63* **Selling the Savoy**); yang to the Savoy's yin, the Connaught (7499 7070, www.connaughthotellondon.com) reopens in December after £50 million of renovations.

Here's the good news. Hoteliers seem to have got the idea that not everyone has a superluxe business account to draw on. The *Financial Times* reports that more than two-thirds of this year's new rooms are expected to fall in

the 'budget' category, and the growth of stylish affordable options is already impressive. **B&B Belgravia** and the **Mayflower** group were the pioneers, but our current favourite is the **Hoxton Hotel**. **Yotel** are opening a new pod hotel (*see p66* **Cheap 'n' charming**), but they'll soon be facing competition: the nitenite chain (www.nitenite.com) of 'micro-boutiques' have acquired a site in Waterloo. Hostels too have been getting their act together: the new **Clink Hostel** is really impressive.

The talk this year is still – as it was always going to be – about Kit Kemp, whose **Haymarket Hotel** duly received its rave reviews (*see p60* **Getting all the Kit**). But boutique minimalism and flair have filtered down to corporate digs and even the better mid-range properties offer facilities like DVD players and robes, so the top end has to offer something special. Perhaps that's why luxury chains are creating boutiquey sub-brands: Hilton's **Trafalgar** has now been joined by Hyatt's **Andaz Liverpool Street**. And keep an eye on Shoreditch: by mid 2008 Conran's Boundary Project (www.theboundary.co.uk) should be up and running. We're excited.

The best | Hotels

For sheer luxury
Kit Kemp's boutique hotels (*see p60* **Getting all the Kit**) are wonderful, but we also adore the corner suites at **One Aldwych** (*see p49*).

For style on the cheap
The £125 weekend rate at **City Inn Westminster** (*see p62*) might get you a superb river view, while the 'Poblito' rooms are a snip at **Church Street Hotel** (*see p68*). But for the best budget style, *see p66* **Cheap 'n' charming**.

For period drama
Hazlitt's (*see p50*) and the **Rookery** (*see p45*) evoke the 18th century; the **Gore** (*see p67*) is a fitting tribute to the Victorians.

For afternoon tea
Dress up for the classic experience at the **Ritz** (*see p61*) and **Claridge's** (*see p59*), or sip from Zandra Rhodes crockery for Fashion Tea at the **Mandeville** (*see p42*).

INFORMATION AND BOOKING
Many of London's swankier hotels are found in Mayfair (W1). Bloomsbury (WC1) is good for mid-priced hotels and B&Bs. For cheap hotels, try Ebury Street near Victoria (SW1), Bloomsbury's Gower Street, Earl's Court (SW5), Bayswater, Paddington (W2) and South Kensington (SW7).

Always try to book ahead. If you can't, the obliging staff at **Visit London** (1 Lower Regent Street, Piccadilly Circus, 0870 156 6366, www.visitlondon.com) will look for a place within your selected area and price range for free. You can also check availability and reserve rooms on its website.

PRICES AND CLASSIFICATION
We don't list official star ratings, which tend to reflect facilities rather than quality; instead, we've classified hotels within each area heading

> ❶ Green numbers given in this chapter correspond to the location of each hotel as marked on the street maps. *See pp394-407.*

according to the price of a double room per night, beginning with the most expensive.

Because they rely on business custom, many high-end hotels quote prices exclusive of VAT. Don't be caught out. We include this 17.5 per cent tax in the listed rates; room rates change frequently though, so confirm them before you book. B&Bs excepted, breakfast isn't usually included. Hotels are constantly offering special deals, particularly (sometimes dramatically) at weekends for hotels that depend on business custom; check websites or ask when you book. Also check discount hotel websites – such as www.alpharooms.com or www.london-discount-hotel.com – for prices that can fall well below the rack rates we list.

FACILITIES AND ACCESSIBILITY

In this chapter, we list the main services offered by each hotel but concierges can often arrange far more, including theatre tickets and meal reservations. We have also tried to note which hotels offer rooms adapted for disabled customers, but it's always best to confirm the precise facilities. **Tourism For All** (0845 124 9971, www.tourismforall.org.uk) has details of wheelchair-accessible places. We've also stated which hotels offer parking facilities, but again enquire in advance rather than just pitch up in your car: spaces are sometimes limited.

The South Bank & Bankside

Moderate

Southwark Rose

47 Southwark Bridge Road, South Bank, SE1 9HH (7015 1480/www.southwarkrosehotel.co.uk). London Bridge tube/rail. **Rates** £170 double. **Rooms** 84. **Credit** AmEx, MC, V. **Map** p404 P8 ❶

It's a little more arty these days, the Rose, with work by Paris-based Japanese photographer Mayumi embellishing a lobby that also features a three-rose logo and notices for weekend deals for £159. Convenient for Tate Modern, Borough Market and Shakespeare's Globe, a ten-minute walk from London Bridge station, the hotel and its rooms are every bit purpose-built and budget-conscious, all sleek, dark wood, crisp white linen and mosaic-tiled bathrooms. Good-value suites are equipped with kitchenettes and an extra sofabed, and guests can use the gym at Novotel next door.

Bar. Disabled-adapted rooms. Internet (wireless, £10/day). Parking (£16/day). Restaurant. Smoking rooms. TV (pay movies).

Cheap

Premier Inn London County Hall

County Hall, Belvedere Road, South Bank, SE1 7PB (0870 238 3300/www.premiertravelinn.com).

Straight out of a Dickens novel – the fabulous **Rookery**. *See p45.*

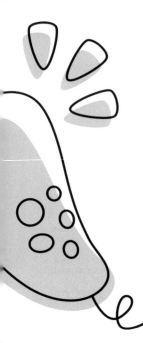

Waterloo tube/rail. **Rates** £99-£139 double. **Rooms** 316. **Credit** AmEx, DC, MC, V. **Map** p401 M9 ➋

Recently rebranded the Premier Inn, with accompanying purple walls, bedspreads and headboards, it retains the USP of rooms for £99 slap bang next to the London Eye, which a number of them even look out on. Unsurprisingly, it is institutional in feel: the Premier Inn comprises five floors of long corridors above a lobby so busy that queue-control barriers are in place. The neat rooms are surprisingly spacious, though, with teabags and coffee sachets beside a kettle plonked on an open wardrobe.

Bar. Disabled-adapted rooms. Internet (wireless, £10/day). Restaurant. Smoking rooms. TV.
Other locations throughout the city.

The City

Deluxe

Andaz Liverpool Street

40 Liverpool Street, EC2M 7QN (7961 1234/ www.london.liverpoolstreet.andaz.com). Liverpool Street tube/rail. **Rates** £120-£385 double. **Rooms** 267. **Credit** AmEx, DC, MC, V. **Map** p405 R6 ➌

It's all change at the former Great Eastern Hotel. A faded railway hotel until its £70m overhaul by Conran in 2000, it became a Hyatt in 2006, and was duly converted in 2007 into the first property of the group's new Andaz portfolio. Andaz means 'personal style' in Hindi, and the name reflects the new vibe: out with gimmicky menus, closet-sized minibars and even the lobby reception desk, and in with down-to-earth service, eco-friendliness and uncomplicated luxury. Despite the changes, bedrooms still wear the regulation style-mag uniform: Eames chairs, chocolate shagpile rugs and white Frette linens, and management is keen to maintain the hotel's East End character (City boys like to hire the hotel's very own Freemasons temple, which also stages comedy nights). Although the area has its fair share of decent eating and drinking options, you won't have to set foot outside: Catch (formerly Fishmarket), Japanese Miyako (Myabi) and the soon-to-be-renamed Aurora (serving modern European cuisine) are just some of the in-house options. Of the rooms, the open-plan suites are the best.

Bars (3). Restaurants (5). Business centre. Concierge. Disabled-adapted rooms. Gym. Internet (broadband/ wireless, free). Room service. Smoking rooms. TV (free movies).

Expensive

Threadneedles

5 Threadneedle Street, EC2R 8AY (7657 8080/ www.theetoncollection.com). Bank tube/DLR. **Rates** £193-£370 double. **Rooms** 69. **Credit** AmEx, MC, V. **Map** p405 Q6 ➍

Occupying a Victorian banking hall, the former HQ of the Midland Bank, its lobby and bar area centre-pieced by a magnificent atrium, Threadneedles

successfully integrates modern design with monumental space. Because of the obvious constraints of developing a listed building, rooms aren't uniform shapes and many of them still have original 19th-century windows. The decor is soothingly neutral, with Korres natural toiletries in the serene limestone bathrooms. Little stress-busting comforts reflect its business-friendly location: fleecy throws, a scented candle lit at turndown, a 'movie treats' menu of pop-corn, ice-cream and Coke. In-house Bonds in the same block offers arguably the best cocktails in London, and one of the finest wine lists.

Bar. Concierge. Disabled-adapted rooms. Internet (wireless, £20/day). Restaurant. Room service. TV (pay movies).

Holborn & Clerkenwell

Expensive

Rookery

12 Peter's Lane, Cowcross Street, Clerkenwell, EC1M 6DS (7336 0931/www.rookeryhotel.com). Farringdon tube/rail. **Rates** £149-£240 double. **Rooms** 33. **Credit** AmEx, DC, MC, V. **Map** p402 O5 ➎

Hidden away down a tiny alley linking Cowcross Street with St John's Lane, the Rookery is a kind of Dickensian Tardis. You'd never guess from the outside that this unassuming row of 18th-century buildings conceals a wonderfully comfortable hotel. Like its sibling Hazlitt's (*see p50*), it's decorated in period style, with Gothic oak beds, plaster busts and clawfoot bathtubs, without neglecting modern comforts: Egyptian cotton sheets and plush towels draped over heated towel racks; broadband internet and LCD TVs. All the rooms, surprisingly generous in size, are individually furnished. Topping it all is the Rook's Nest, a huge split-level suite with views of St Paul's. Judging from the guest book, no one ever wants to leave. *Photos p43.*

Bar. Concierge. Internet (free dataport/wireless). Room service. TV.

Moderate

Malmaison

Charterhouse Square, Clerkenwell, EC1M 6AH (7012 3700/www.malmaison.com). Barbican tube/ Farringdon tube/rail. **Rates** £125-£250 double. **Rooms** 97. **Credit** AmEx, DC, MC, V. **Map** p402 O5 ➏

Certain touches remind you that this is one of a growing chain, but this four-year-old hotel has charm. Location is key: it's set in a lovely, leafy, cobblestone square, next to Smithfield Market with its lively restaurants, bars and pubs. The reception is stylishly kitted out with a lilac and cream che-quered floor, exotic plants and a petite champagne bar, while purples, dove-grey and black wood dominate the rooms and two suites. Rooms are equipped to the standard you'd expect, with nice extra touches including free broadband access and

creative lighting; for something more luxurious, the hotel's new suite – the Square – has a four-poster bed, Bose sound system and original artworks. With the City and Inns of Court nearby, the clientele is largely businessmen and lawyers during the week, but lower weekend prices attract non-business types for the weekend. The gym, a subterranean brasserie and a suite of meeting rooms with a rooftop bar complete the picture.
Bar. Disabled-adapted rooms. Gym. Internet (broadband, free). Restaurant. Room service. TV.

Zetter
86-88 Clerkenwell Road, Clerkenwell, EC1M 5RJ (7324 4444/www.thezetter.com). Farringdon tube/ rail. **Rates** £155-£399 double. **Rooms** 59. **Credit** AmEx, MC, V. **Map** p402 O4 ❼
Billing itself as a restaurant with rooms, the Zetter is in fact more than that: it's a fun, laid-back, modern hotel with some interesting design notes. There's a refreshing lack of attitude – the polyglot staff clearly enjoy their job. The rooms, stacked up on five galleried storeys overlooking the intimate bar area, are sleek and functional, but cosied up with choice home comforts like hot-water bottles and old Penguin paperbacks, while the walk-in Raindance showers are stocked with Elemis products. Those on the St John's Square side are quieter. Top-floor suites have great rooftop views, and the prices beat the West End hands down. The restaurant does modern Mediterranean food well, its wide picture windows making for amusing people-watching breakfasts.
Bar. Concierge. Disabled-adapted rooms. Internet (dataport/wireless, free). Restaurant. Room service. Smoking rooms. TV (pay movies/music/DVD).

Bloomsbury & Fitzrovia

Deluxe

Sanderson
50 Berners Street, Fitzrovia, W1T 3NG (7300 1400/ www.morganshotelgroup.com). Oxford Circus tube. **Rates** £320-£500 double. **Rooms** 150. **Credit** AmEx, DC, MC, V. **Map** p406 V1 ❽
Although now seven years old and surrounded by bland 1960s façades, the Sanderson remains one of the city's most stylish hotels. A Schrager/Starck creation, the hotel's sleek design verges on the surreal, starting at the lobby, with its sheer flowing curtains and Dali red-lips sofa. The campery continues as you take the purple lift up to the generously sized guest rooms with their silver-leaf sleigh beds, piled high with cushions, and super-modern glassed-in bathroom areas with powerful steam showers and beautiful stand-alone baths. When it's time to mingle, you can slip downstairs to join the celebs at the Long Bar and recently opened Suka restaurant, offering Zak Pelaccio's contemporary Malaysian cuisine. A business centre is planned for 2008.
Bars (2). Business services. Concierge. Disabled-adapted rooms. Gym. Internet (dataport/wireless, £15/day). Restaurant. Room service. Spa. TV (DVD).

Expensive

Charlotte Street Hotel
15-17 Charlotte Street, Fitzrovia, W1T 1RJ (7806 2000/www.firmdale.com). Goodge Street or Tottenham Court Road tube. **Rates** £250-£310 double. **Rooms** 52. **Credit** AmEx, DC, MC, V. **Map** p399 K5 ❾
This gorgeous hotel is a fine exponent of Kit Kemp's trademark style (*see p60* **Getting all the Kit**), fusing trad English furnishings with avant-garde art. The huge beds are ridiculously comfortable.
Bar. Concierge. Gym. Internet (broadband/wireless, from 30p/min to £20/day). Restaurant. Room service. Smoking rooms. TV (DVD).

myhotel bloomsbury
11-13 Bayley Street, WC1B 3HD (7667 6000/www. myhotels.co.uk). Goodge Street or Tottenham Court Road tube. **Rates** £163-£276 double. **Rooms** 78. **Credit** AmEx, DC, MC, V. **Map** p399 K5 ❿
It was back in 1999 that this sleek Conran-designed hotel first combined Asian fusion decor and feng shui – now the chain is to open a third outpost (*see p348*). Subtle improvements continue to be made – the bathrooms have been refreshed over the last year – but the essentials remain: an aquarium (with an odd number of fish) and floral arrangements in the calming lobby, strategically placed crystals and scented candles, a wonderfully chill library in the cellared basement. Rooms are minimalist, but exoticised (think buddha heads and south-east Asian furnishings) and fully accessorised (plasma screens, Wi-Fi). The top-floor myspace is a fabulous self-contained apartment and studio – retrofuturist to a tee, and with access to a private rooftop terrace with great views. If you overdo things at the buzzy street-level bar, Jinja (Shinto for 'shrine') offers treatments. The website offers weekend rates, sometimes as low as £125; myhotel chelsea (*see p63*) is less urban.
Bar. Concierge. Gym. Internet (dataport/wireless, free). Restaurant. Room service. Smoking rooms. TV (pay movies/DVD).

Moderate

Academy Hotel
21 Gower Street, Bloomsbury, WC1E 6HG (7631 4115/www.theetoncollection.com). Goodge Street tube. **Rates** £205 double. **Rooms** 49. **Credit** AmEx, DC, MC, V. **Map** p399 K5 ⓫
Comprising five Georgian townhouses, the Academy has a restrained country-house style – decor in most rooms is soft, summery florals and checks, although eight suites have more sophisticated colour schemes. Guests are cocooned from busy Bloomsbury and those in the split-level doubles get plenty of breathing space at decent rates. The library and conservatory open on to fragrant walled gardens where drinks and breakfast are served in summer.
Bar. Internet (dataport/wireless, £6/hr). Room service. TV.

Harlingford Hotel

61-63 Cartwright Gardens, Bloomsbury, WC1H 9EL (7387 1551/www.harlingfordhotel.com). Russell Square tube/Euston tube/rail. **Rates** £99 double. **Rooms** 43. **Credit** AmEx, MC, V. **Map** p399 L4

Enter the Harlingford, its stately gold lettering marking the right corner of a sweeping Georgian crescent that is lined with hotels, and you'll hear the sound of a gentle water fountain from a garden behind the receptionist's desk. There's no question, the Harlingford is a stylish trailblazer in this bed-and-breakfast enclave. The tasteful guests' lounge, scattered with trendy light fittings and modern prints, almost makes you forget it is a budget hotel. The staff are eager to please, and the adjacent garden and tennis court located in a pretty square are available to guests.
TV.

Jenkins Hotel

45 Cartwright Gardens, Bloomsbury, WC1H 9EH (7387 2067/www.jenkinshotel.demon.co.uk). Russell Square tube/Euston tube/rail. **Rates** £89 double. **Rooms** 14. **Credit** MC, V. **Map** p399 K3

'Nothing's changed here – not even the owners!' was the reply of the ruddy-faced proprietor when we asked, his hand gesturing towards the restlessly changing hotel trade that lines the same sweeping crescent as the Harlingford (*see above*). The Jenkins is traditional – once inside, you could be in a Sussex village guesthouse – and attracts much repeat custom. It's been a hotel since the 1920s, so it's fitting that an episode of Agatha Christie's *Poirot* was filmed in room nine. But don't expect a period look – just tidy, freshly painted en suite rooms with pretty bedspreads, crisp, patterned curtains and a small fridge. Guests have access to a tennis court.
TV.

Morgan

24 Bloomsbury Street, Bloomsbury, WC1B 3QJ (7636 3735/www.morganhotel.co.uk). Tottenham Court Road tube. **Rates** £100 double. **Rooms** 21. **Credit** MC, V. **Map** p399 K5

Round the corner from the British Museum, this cheap and cheerful hotel has been run by the three Shoreditch-bred Ward siblings since the 1970s. While the place has no aspirations to boutique status, the 17 air-conditioned rooms and four suites have extras beyond basic B&B standard: modern headboards with handy inbuilt reading lamps, smart brocade drapes, bathrooms with granite sinks and – as in the top hotels – a phone by the loo. The cosy, panelled breakfast room, with its framed London memorabilia, is the perfect setting for a full English. The hotel's annexe of spacious flats, equipped with stainless-steel kitchenettes, is one of London's best deals.
Internet (wireless, free). TV.

Cheap

Arosfa

83 Gower Street, Bloomsbury, WC1E 6HJ (7636 2115/www.arosfalondon.com). Goodge Street tube. **Rates** £75 double. **Rooms** 16. **Credit** MC, V. **Map** p399 K4

Arosfa means 'place to stay' in Welsh, but we reckon that description sells this townhouse B&B short. Yes, the accommodation is fairly spartan, but it is also spotless, and all the rooms have en suite shower/WC (albeit tiny). Arosfa also has a great location – in the heart of Bloomsbury, just opposite a huge Waterstone's – and a pleasing walled garden. Wireless internet is available on a shared terminal in the lounge, which is done out like a Victorian grandparent's drawing room.
Internet (wireless, free; shared terminal, free). TV.

Sanderson.

Ashlee House

261-265 Gray's Inn Road, Bloomsbury, WC1X 8QT (7833 9400/www.ashleehouse.co.uk). King's Cross tube/rail. **Rates** £23-£27 double; £9-£22 dorm bed. **Beds** 172. **Credit** MC, V. **Map** p399 L3 ⑯

The more established of a pair of classy hostels run by an ambitious, efficient Irish family, Ashlee House is a short walk from its sister operation, the Clink Hostel. Features standard to the Clink will soon be added here: coded card keys, trendy bed steps and so on. Not that the Ashlee lacks panache, far from it. The funky lobby is decorated with sheepskin-covered sofas and has wallpaper digitally printed with London scenes. The rooms are more basic: each one contains between two and 16 beds, and a sink. Breakfast is served in a large communal kitchen; a £5 deposit gets you a crockery and cutlery set for self-catering, set beside a comfortable communal area filled with Chesterfields. There's a TV room with nightly film screenings and an Xbox, internet, luggage storage and laundry.
Internet (shared terminals, £1/hr). TV (lounge).

Clink Hostel

78 King's Cross Road, Finsbury, WC1X 9QG (7183 9400/www.clinkhostel.com). King's Cross tube/rail. **Rates** £24-£30 double; £15 dorm bed. **Beds** 300. **Credit** MC, V. **Map** p399 M3 ⑰

With the newer of its two main buildings due to open by early 2008, the impressive, imposing Clink is well ahead of the field as far as London hostels are concerned – for style, comfort, facilities and, above all, setting. A 300-year-old courthouse where Dickens once scribbled and the Clash stood before the beak, the Clink was taken over by the management of Ashlee House and converted into a contemporary lodging for up to 500 backpackers, 300 in the older wing opened in summer 2007. The lobby, a listed building (even the 'Quiet, Please' notice) gives on to two beautiful, wood-panelled courtroom-cum-communal areas. The dormitory floors are done out in a handy colour code that is repeated on funky bed steps (designed in-house). The beds, based on the increasingly popular Japanese pods, are sectioned off for privacy, with a reading light and little safety box above each. Natural light and a view of the King's Cross skyline, broken by St Pancras's spire, are a feature wherever you sleep. *Photos pp50-51.*
Bar. Internet (shared terminals, £1/hr). TV (lounge).

Generator

37 Tavistock Place, Bloomsbury, WC1H 9SE (7388 7666/www.generatorhostels.com). Russell Square tube. **Rates** (per person) £35-£56 double; £12.50-£50 dorm bed. **Beds** 837. **Credit** MC, V. **Map** p399 L4 ⑱

'I Survived the Generator' beermugs, 'Boy Meets Girl' G-strings and Polaroids of people mooning on the noticeboard greet you – backpackers come here for a purpose. This is where Club 18-30 meets youth hostel, a large building set back from the main road, done out in Hacienda-style industrial: steel surfaces, exposed pipes and neon signs. Drinking contests, happy house or karaoke nights, and hangover breakfasts are par for the course, making guests oblivious to the sometimes surly staff and otherwise sombre surroundings. There's also a movie lounge, travel agent, shop, internet room and kitchen.
Bar. Internet (shared terminals).

Covent Garden & the Strand

Deluxe

Covent Garden Hotel

10 Monmouth Street, Covent Garden, WC2H 9LF (7806 1000/www.firmdale.com). Covent Garden or Leicester Square tube. **Rates** £283-£376 double. **Rooms** 58. **Credit** AmEx, MC, V. **Map** p407 X2 ⑳

A perennial favourite in Kemp's gilt-edged portfolio of hotels (*see p60* **Getting all the Kit**), the Covent Garden is snug and stylish.
Bar. Business centre. Concierge. Gym. Internet (dataport/wireless, £20/day). Parking (£36/day). Restaurant. Room service. Smoking rooms. TV (DVD).

One Aldwych

1 Aldwych, the Strand, WC2B 4RH (7300 1000/ www.onealdwych.com). Covent Garden/Temple tube/Charing Cross tube/rail. **Rates** £258-£505 double. **Rooms** 105. **Credit** AmEx, DC, MC, V. **Map** p407 Z3 ㉑

Enter through the breathtaking Lobby Bar (*see p226*) and you know you're in for a treat. Despite weighty history – the 1907 building was designed by the architects behind the Ritz – One Aldwych is thoroughly modern. Upstairs, everything, from Frette linen through bathroom mini-TVs to the environmentally friendly loo-flushing system and chemical-free REN toiletries, has been chosen with care. Flowers and fruit are replenished daily and a card with the next day's weather forecast appears at turndown. The location is perfect for Theatreland, but you'll be looking for excuses to avoid setting foot outside: the hotel's cosy little screening room has good-value brunch- or dinner-and-movie packages; Axis restaurant serves upmarket modern European fare (you can peer down on diners from the balcony bar); and Indigo covers breakfast and lighter meals. There are treatments, a gym and a steam room, and a swimming pool where classical music accompanies your laps. If you can, book one of the three round corner suites that are stacked in the corner tower – they're very romantic. *Photo p53.*
Bars (2). Business services. Coffeeshop. Concierge. Disabled-adapted rooms. Gym. Internet (dataport, £15.50/day; wireless, free). Parking (£35/day). Pool (1, indoor). Restaurants (2). Room service. Smoking rooms. Spa. TV (pay movies/DVD).

St Martins Lane Hotel

45 St Martin's Lane, Covent Garden, WC2N 4HX (7300 5500/www.stmartinslane.com). Leicester Square tube/Charing Cross tube/rail. **Rates** £375-£558 double. **Rooms** 204. **Credit** AmEx, DC, MC, V. **Map** p407 X4 ㉒

Clink Hostel. *See p49.*

When it opened as a Schrager property nearly a decade ago, the St Martins was the toast of the town. The flamboyant lobby was constantly buzzing, and guests giggled at Philippe Starck's playful decor. Although Starck objects – such as the gold tooth stools in the lobby – have become positively mainstream and the space lacks the impact of its heyday, it's still an exclusive place to stay. The all-white bedrooms have comfortable minimalism down to a T, with floor-to-ceiling windows, gadgetry secreted in sculptural cabinets and sleek limestone bathrooms with toiletries from the Agua spa at sister property Sanderson (*see p46*). Asia de Cuba fusion restaurant is as good-looking as ever, and the Light Bar remains dramatic. To work off the excess, there's the trendy, industrial-look Gymbox next door, to which guests have free access. Avoid rooms on the smoking floors unless you're a dedicated puffer.
Bar. Business services. Concierge. Disabled-adapted rooms. Gym. Internet (dataport/high-speed). Parking. Restaurant. Room service. TV (pay movies/DVD).

Soho & Leicester Square

Expensive

Hazlitt's

6 Frith Street, Soho, W1D 3JA (7434 1771/www. hazlittshotel.com). Tottenham Court Road tube. **Rates** £240-£252 double. **Rooms** 23. **Credit** AmEx, DC, MC, V. **Map** p406 W2 ㉓
Three Georgian townhouses comprise this charming place, named after William Hazlitt, the spirited 18th-century essayist, critic and philosopher who lodged (and died in abject poverty) here. Now it provides your best chance to enjoy an upmarket version of the Soho accommodation of his period. In the superior double front rooms, it's easy to imagine the child prodigy Mozart strolling home with his dad after a recital: they also lodged on Frith Street on the

composer's introduction to England in 1765. Quieter standard doubles are at the back of the house. All the rooms are individual, named after various great writers, with fireplaces, superb carved wooden four-posters and half-testers, free-standing bathtubs and handsome cast-iron Shanks toilet cisterns. It gets creakier and more crooked the higher you go, culminating in enchanting garret single rooms (also very comfortable) with rooftop views. Air-conditioning, web TV hidden in antique cupboards and triple-glazed windows come as standard. There's no house restaurant or bar, but then you have all of Soho to enjoy just outside the front door.
Business services. Concierge. Internet (dataport/ wireless, free). Room service. Smoking rooms. TV (DVD).

Soho Hotel

4 Richmond Mews (off Dean Street), Soho, W1D 3DH (7559 3000/www.firmdale.com). Tottenham Court Road tube. **Rates** £335-£366 double. **Rooms** 91. **Credit** AmEx, DC, MC, V. **Map** p406 W2 ㉔
Kemp's 2004 shot at urban hip is still her most edgy creation. It's all very cool, but also wonderfully quiet and comfortable. *See p60* **Getting all the Kit**.
Bar. Business services. Concierge. Disabled-adapted rooms. Gym. Internet (dataport/wireless, £20/day). Room service. Smoking rooms. TV (DVD).

Cheap

Piccadilly Backpackers

12 Sherwood Street, Soho, W1F 7BR (7434 9009/ www.piccadillybackpackers.com). Piccadilly Circus tube. **Rates** £55-£62 double; £12-£22 dorm bed. **Beds** 700. **Credit** AmEx, MC, V. **Map** p406 V4 ㉕
It's like Piccadilly Circus, the little doorway currently festooned with scaffolding behind Glasshouse Street. International hostellers swarm into London's (the world's?) most central venue, attracted by the rates

Where to Stay

and location. The accommodation is basic, although graphic art students have painted the rooms on the third floor in an attempt to perk things up a little. Ten rooms feature 'pods' – six beds arranged three up, three down, in pigeonhole fashion. In the common room you can surf 100 channels on the widescreen TV or get online in the 24-hour internet café. There's a travel shop and a backpackers' bar nearby at 4 Golden Square (7287 9241).
Internet (shared terminals/wireless, £1.50/hr). TV (lounge).

Oxford Street & Marylebone

Expensive

Cumberland

Great Cumberland Place, off Oxford Street, W1H 7DL (0870 333 9280/www.guoman.com). Marble Arch tube. **Rates** £140-£370 single; £164-£376 double; £340-£458 suite. **Rooms** 900 (1,019 incl annexe). **Credit** AmEx, DC, MC, V. **Map** p395 F6
Perfectly located by Marble Arch tube (turn the right way and you're there in seconds), the Cumberland is a bit of a monster. There are 900 rooms, plus another 119 in an annexe just down the road, and a huge, echoing lobby with dramatic, large-scale modern art, wall panels that change colour through the day and a somewhat severe waterfall sculpture. The rooms are minimalist, with acid-etched headboards, neatly modern bathrooms and plasma TVs – nicely designed, but rather small. The hotel's excellent modern British dining room is the exclusive Rhodes W1 (*see p206*) opened in spring 2007, but there are also a pricey brasserie with attached cocktail bar, and a boisterous late-night DJ bar Carbon, with its trash-industrial decor. On a weekend, breakfast can feel a little like the feeding of the 5,000.
Bars (2). Concierge. Gym. Internet (dataport/high-speed). Restaurants (2). Room service. TV.

Mandeville

Mandeville Place, Marylebone, W1U 2BE (7935 5599/www.mandeville.co.uk). Bond Street tube. **Rates** £150-£275 double. **Rooms** 142. **Credit** AmEx, DC, MC, V. **Map** p398 G6
Seeking to transform an unremarkable traditional hotel into something more appropriate to the area, the Mandeville's owners gave interior designer Stephen Ryan the opportunity to make a style statement. The hotel's dreary Boswells pub duly became the DeVille restaurant, with neo-Victorian wallpaper and life-size mannequins, while the DeVigne bar (where the wasabi martini is a thing of joy) sports an eye-popping combination of mink suede sofas, primary-coloured leather stools and Dutch Master paintings given a Day-Glo lippy makeover. Those expecting further theatrics in the bedrooms will be disappointed, however. The rooms are perfectly nice, with faux leather headboards, Versace-esque classical-print curtains and Italian marble bathrooms, but don't feel big enough or glam enough to match the prices. Still, the pink suite is pleasingly eccentric, with movie-star mirrors in the upstairs bathroom and a terrific rooftop terrace under a retractable awning.
Bar. Concierge. Disabled-adapted rooms. Internet (dataport, £5/hr; wireless). Room service (24hr). Restaurant. TV (satellite).

Moderate

Montagu Place

2 Montagu Place, Marylebone, W1H 2ER (7467 2777/www.montagu-place.co.uk). Baker Street tube. **Rates** £129-£229 double. **Rooms** 16. **Credit** AmEx, DC, MC, V. **Map** p395 F5
The Montagu is a stylish, small hotel in a pair of Grade II-listed Georgian townhouses. Catering primarily for the midweek business traveller, its 16 rooms are divided into Comfy, Fancy and Swanky categories, the difference being size – Swanky are the largest, with enormous bathrooms, while Comfy are the smallest and, being at the back, have no street views. All rooms have deluxe pocket-sprung beds (queens in the smaller rooms, kings in the two larger categories), as well as cafetières with freshly ground coffee and flatscreen TVs (DVD players are available from reception). The look is boutique-hotel sharp, except the uneasy overlap of bar and reception – though that means you can get a drink at any time and retire to the graciously modern lounge. An affordably classy affair. *Photos p54.*
Bar. TV (widescreen/DVD).

Sherlock Holmes Hotel

108 Baker Street, Marylebone, W1U 6LJ (7486 6161/www.sherlockholmeshotel.com). Baker Street tube. **Rates** (incl breakfast at weekends) £116-£470 double. **Rooms** 119. **Credit** AmEx, DC, MC, V. **Map** p398 G5
How do you transform a dreary, chintz-filled Hilton into a hip boutique hotel? It's elementary: hype up the Baker Street address, banish the bland decor and

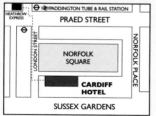

create a sleek lobby bar. That's what the Park Plaza chain did when it snapped up the Sherlock Holmes a few years ago. Guests can mingle with local office workers in the casually chic bar, which extends to a lounge in the style of a glossed-up gentlemen's club and an organic restaurant. The rooms, meanwhile, resemble hip bachelor pads: beige and brown colour scheme, leather headboards, pinstripe scatter cushions and spiffy bathrooms. Split-level 'loft' suites take advantage of the first floor's double-height ceilings. There's a decent gym with sauna, steam rooms and beauty treatments, and the inevitable memorabilia ranges from expressionist paintings of Holmes and Watson to magnifying glasses.
Bar. Business centre. Concierge. Disabled-adapted rooms. Gym. Internet (broadband/dataport/wireless). Restaurant. Room service. TV (pay movies).

Sumner
54 Upper Berkeley Street, Marylebone, W1H 7QR (7723 2244/www.thesumner.com). Marble Arch tube. **Rates** (incl breakfast) £135-£170 double. **Rooms** 20. **Credit** AmEx, DC, MC, V. **Map** p395 F6 ③⓪
The team behind the highly regarded Five Sumner Place relocated in 2006 to this fine old Georgian townhouse just off the Edgware Road and around the corner from Marble Arch, Oxford Street and Hyde Park. Top interior designers have gone to work on the ground-floor public spaces, which are cool and Nordic in shades of slate and grey. Depending on your predilections the results are either hip and minimal or reminiscent of a Harley Street waiting room. The 20 bedrooms are different in feel, still contemporary but with warmer tones,

and the deluxe options feature custom-designed Ligne Roset furniture and huge walk-in showers. Room sizes vary but are generally spacious, and those at the front are bathed in natural daylight from large (triple-glazed) windows.
Disabled access. Internet (wireless). TV (widescreen).

22 York Street
22 York Street, Marylebone, W1U 6PX (7224 2990/ www.22yorkstreet.co.uk). Baker Street tube. **Rates** £100-£120 double. **Rooms** 12. **Credit** AmEx, MC, V. **Map** p398 G5 ③①
There's no sign on the door; people usually discover this immaculately kept B&B by word of mouth. Unpretentious and comfortable, it's perfect for those who loathe hotels and hate designer interiors. The rooms in these two graceful neighbouring Georgian townhouses aren't *Wallpaper* material, but they are subtly tasteful, with wooden floors, antique pieces and French quilts. Breakfast is an occasion, served at a huge, curving wooden table in the traditional kitchen. There's a cosy sitting room in the basement with free internet access and a lounge with coffee room upstairs. It's three minutes' walk to Regent's Park and the shops and restaurants of Marylebone.
Internet (wireless). TV.

Cheap

Weardowney Guesthouse
9 Ashbridge Street, Marylebone, NW8 8DH (7725 9694/www.weardowney.com). Marylebone tube/rail. **Rates** £75-£96 double. **Rooms** 7. **Credit** AmEx, DC, MC, V. **Map** p395 E4 ③②

The stunning Lobby Bar at **One Aldwych**. *See p49.*

Amy Wear and Gail Downey are fashion models turned knitwear designers. Having moved out of the house they shared for ten years, they opened it as a quiet corner establishment for paying guests. Above their own boutique, there are just seven rooms, with either a double bed or twin; only three are en suite, the others sharing a bathroom between two rooms. Rooms are adorned with hand-knitted throws and curtains, as well as prints, art and photos from the pair's creative associates. General improvements have been made to the running of the place – a housekeeper now takes care of laundry and breakfast. Lodgers, who can use the downstairs kitchen and pretty roof terrace, tend to be models, designers and others from the fashion industry. *Photo p57. Internet (wireless, free). TV.*

Montagu Place.
See p51.

Paddington & Notting Hill

Deluxe

Hempel

31-35 Craven Hill Gardens, Paddington, W2 3EA (7298 9000/www.the-hempel.co.uk). Lancaster Gate or Queensway tube/Paddington tube/rail. **Rates** £347-£370 double. **Rooms** 47. **Credit** AmEx, DC, MC, V. **Map** p394 C6 ⊛

Suave in low-lit creams and soft beiges, the Hempel remains a bastion of the minimalism espoused by original designer Anouska Hempel, despite being sold in 2005 and given something of a shake-up. The new owners have attempted to cultivate an air of extreme exclusivity, courting celebrities and their lackeys with two new bars and wildly luxurious fittings (like Pour rugs at £10,000 a pop, Zents bathroom products, even canned minibar oxygen). They've kept such features as the bed suspended from the ceiling by iron bars (in the 'Lioness's Den'), but completely refitted all rooms, primarily with sleek modern Italian furnishings. The effect may be a little constrained – rooms can seem a bit formal – but the quality of the package wins through. Plans for the coming year include a spa – we can't wait. *Bar. Business services. Concierge. Disabled-adapted rooms. Gym. Internet (dataport/high-speed/wireless). Restaurant. Room service. TV (pay movies/music/DVD).*

Expensive

Guesthouse West

163-165 Westbourne Grove, Notting Hill, W11 2RS (7792 9800/www.guesthousewest.com). Notting Hill Gate tube. **Rates** (incl continental breakfast) £182-£217 double. **Rooms** 20. **Credit** AmEx, MC, V. **Map** p394 B6 ⊛

Set in an impressive three-floor, cream-coloured building, Guesthouse West is a stylish, affordable antidote to exorbitant hotels. It keeps prices down by cutting out room service and offering instead a handy list of local businesses. The look is Notting Hillbilly hip: the retro lobby bar, licensed to serve until 10pm, has a

changing art display and the front terrace is perfect for posing. Minimalist bedrooms have enough extras to keep hip young things happy: wireless internet, flatscreen TVs, Molton Brown toiletries. *Bar. Internet (high-speed/wireless). Restaurant. TV (pay movies/music/DVD).*

Miller's Residence

111A Westbourne Grove, Bayswater, W2 4UW (7243 1024/www.millersuk.com). Bayswater or Notting Hill Gate tube. **Rates** (incl continental breakfast) £176-£270 double. **Rooms** 8. **Credit** AmEx, MC, V. **Map** p394 B6 ⑤

This gloriously atmospheric pad, hidden behind an unmarked door in an unprepossessing side street, is a cross between a baronial family pile and a Portobello arcade. It's owned by antiques expert Martin Miller (who set up Miller's Antiques price guides back in the 1960s), and furnished with his finds, with chandeliers, antique vases and cabinets of curios at every turn. Rooms, some featuring four-poster beds, may be named after 19th-century poets, but they come with 21st-century perks such as air-conditioning and CD and DVD players (there's a large DVD library in reception). The drawing room, where a generous breakfast buffet is laid out in the morning, is an Aladdin's cave of artefacts; it's even more atmospheric in the evenings, when it's highly conducive to relaxing by the elaborately carved fireplace with a whisky from the free bar. In keeping with the authenticity and age of the place, there's no lift. There's also no restaurant, but you've got plenty of choice right on the doorstep. *Internet (wireless). TV.*

New Linden

59 Leinster Square, Bayswater, W2 4PS (7221 4321/www.newlinden.co.uk). Bayswater tube. **Rates** £120-£160 double. **Rooms** 51. **Credit** AmEx, MC, V. **Map** p394 B6 ㊱

Part of the excellent group comprising the Mayflower Hotel and Twenty Nevern Square (for both, *see p70*), the New Linden had nearly completed renovations (with just the public rooms in desperate need of an update) as we went to press, but it's already looking to be as much of an affordable showpiece as its sisters. Bedrooms have white or cream walls, wooden floors and streamlined modern or antique Eastern furnishings. Marble bathrooms (in varied playful designs, some with deluge shower heads), flatscreen TVs and CD players come as standard. Some of the suites have balconies and one split-level family room retains elaborate period pillars and cornicing. The location – just down from the trendy shops on Westbourne Grove, between Notting Hill and Kensington Gardens – is a big plus. *Concierge. Internet (wireless). TV.*

Portobello Hotel

22 Stanley Gardens, Notting Hill, W11 2NG (7727 2777/www.portobello-hotel.co.uk). Holland Park or Notting Hill Gate tube. **Rates** (incl breakfast) £190-£310 double. **Rooms** 23. **Credit** AmEx, MC, V. **Map** p394 A6 ㊲

Now equipped with a lift to help guests scale the four floors after taking advantage of the 24hr bar, this decadent Notting Hill mansion has been hosting stars from Kate Moss to Van Morrison for nearly 40 years. All rooms are stylishly equipped with a large fan, tall house plants and round-the-clock room service. Most overlook a pretty rose garden. The spectacular beds range from a Balinese four-poster to a ship's bunk and a couple of seductive oriental affairs that resemble Berber tents. In many rooms the Victorian bathtubs take centre stage, including one with a Victorian 'bathing machine'. Alice Cooper used his tub to house his boa constrictor, which he fed with white mice from the local pet shop. Other themed pads include the beguiling Moroccan Room, strewn with carpets and cushions, and the serene Japanese Water Garden Room with an elaborate spa bath, buddhas and its own private grotto. *Bar. Internet (wireless). Room service (24hr). TV (free in-house movies).*

Cheap

Garden Court Hotel

30-31 Kensington Gardens Square, Bayswater, W2 4BG (7229 2553/www.gardencourthotel.co.uk). Bayswater or Queensway tube. **Rates** (incl breakfast) £75-£115 double. **Rooms** 32. **Credit** MC, V. **Map** p394 B6 ㊳

Run by the same family since the 1950s, in a grand place built in the 1850s, this budget hotel has been brought bang up to date with the installation of a lift and an airy lounge with wooden floors and brown leather sofas facing the fireplace. It also has a bit of character: a giant antique Beefeater statue stands guard in the lobby, and the cheery bedrooms have modish modern wallpaper. As the name suggests, the hotel has a small walled garden; guests have access to the private square too. *Internet (shared terminal, £1/30mins). TV.*

Pavilion

34-36 Sussex Gardens, Paddington, W2 1UL (7262 0905/www.pavilionhoteluk.com). Edgware Road tube/Marylebone or Paddington tube/rail. **Rates** £85-£100 double. **Rooms** 29. **Credit** AmEx, MC, V. **Map** p395 E5 ㊴

In a row of dowdy hotels between Paddington and Hyde Park, the Pavilion is a shining star. Or more like a disco ball. This B&B is as kitsch as its famous guests Duran Duran, Jarvis Cocker and numerable contestants from *Pop Idol*. The rooms are a riot: the Highland Fling is a tartan theme park, with plaid bedspreads and stag antlers; Better Red Than Dead is an extravaganza of crimson, vermilion and burgundy. A favoured shag pad is Honky Tonk Afro with its mirror ball, fuzzy dice and heart-shaped mirrored headboards. OK, so the location's not exactly rocking and the bathrooms are small, but there's more personality in this humble budget hotel than in many of the capital's big-name boutiques. *Internet (wireless, £10/day). Parking (£10/day). Room service (24hr). TV.*

Stylotel

160-162 Sussex Gardens, Paddington, W2 1UD (7723 1026/www.stylotel.com). **Rates** *£80 double.* **Rooms** 39. **Credit** AmEx, MC, V. **Map** p395 E6 ⑩

Love it or loathe it, the Stylotel turns the notion of a budget London property on its head. This recent overhaul of a traditional townhouse hotel appears to take some design cues from efficient European youth hostels – fastidiously clean laminate flooring, royal blue colour scheme – but what sets it apart is the attention to detail. Funky materials and features such as galvanised steel floors, frosted glass and the cubic, blue faux leather sofas of the retro-futurist lounge and reception are echoed in the rooms. There, apart from the capsule-like bathroom units, most things are designed by the owner's son: stippled aluminium panelling, padded headboards in that same blue faux leather, metal boxes with glass sides and tops that serve double duty as bedside table and lamp, and welded metal bedframes that lift the thick mattresses high enough to scoot luggage beneath. Add flatscreen TVs, wireless internet, an enthusiastic manager and a colourful breakfast room (a hot breakfast is included), and you've got a hip bargain for today's kids (though an octogenarian couple were on a repeat stay when we visited). *Concierge. Internet (wireless, £2/hr). Smoking rooms. TV.*

Vancouver Studios

30 Prince's Square, Bayswater, W2 4NJ (7243 1270/www.vancouverstudios.co.uk). Bayswater or Queensway tube. **Rates** *£99-£110 double.* **Rooms** 48. **Credit** AmEx, DC, MC, V. **Map** p394 B6 ㉛

Having just spent £1m on expansion (they now offer a six-person luxury duplex for £350 a night), the Vancouver is still ahead of the game in this lodging-dense location. Staying here feels more like renting a small flat than putting up in a hotel. The fresh, unfussy studios are equipped with kitchenettes, flatscreen TVs and DVD players. The sitting room, which guests share with two resident cats, is cosy and funky, with Mexican upholstery, cacti and an old-fashioned gramophone. It opens on to a lush, walled garden with a gurgling fountain. There are also handy on-site facilities such as a laundry room, and free wireless internet for laptop-carrying guests. If you get lost in the interlinked Prince's and Leinster Squares, look out for twin red phone boxes on the Bayswater Road side of this quiet locality. *Internet (dataport/shared terminal/wireless). TV (DVD).*

Piccadilly Circus & Mayfair

Deluxe

Brown's

Albemarle Street, Mayfair, W1S 4BP (7493 6020/ www.roccofortecollection.com). Green Park tube. **Rates** *£529-£722 double.* **Rooms** 117. **Credit** AmEx, DC, MC, V. **Map** p406 U5 ㊷

Brown's was opened in 1837 by Lord Byron's butler, James Brown, and became the quintessential Mayfair hotel. The first British telephone call was made from here in 1876, five years after Napoleon III and Empress Eugenie took refuge in one of the

For models it's just like home: **Weardowney Guesthouse**. *See p53*.

suites after fleeing the Third Republic. Franklin Roosevelt, Haile Selassie and Rudyard Kipling have all been guests. Kipling wrote the *Jungle Book* here and now has a suite named in his honour. In 2003 the Rocco Forte Collection acquired the place and gave it a £24m top-to-toe refurbishment. The public spaces resonate history – non-residents can visit the English Tea Room by the lobby, with its original wood panelling, fireplaces and Jacobean plaster ceilings for afternoon tea (3-6pm, £35). The Donovan Bar, named after 1960s snapper Terence Donovan, is sheer class, and the Grill offers traditional British cuisine with a modern twist. All 117 bedrooms, super-large and extremely comfortable, have been reconfigured, kept in character with original artwork, book collections and, in the suites, fireplaces. *Bar. Business centre. Concierge. Disabled-adapted rooms. Gym. Internet (high-speed/wireless). Restaurant. Room service (24hr). Spa. TV (music/pay movies).*

Claridge's

55 Brook Street, Mayfair, W1K 4HR (7629 8860/ www.claridges.co.uk). Bond Street tube. **Rates** £668-£778 double. **Rooms** 203. **Credit** AmEx, DC, MC, V. **Map** p398 H6 ⑬

Claridge's is synonymous with history and class, its decorative character linked to its 1898 reopening and signature art deco redesign. Photographs of Churchill and the arrival of sundry royals grace the grand entrance. While remaining traditional, its bars and restaurant are actively fashionable – Gordon Ramsay offers contemporary French cuisine in his restaurant and A-listers gather in the Claridge's bar. The Fumoir has, they say, the country's largest selection of Macanudo cigars – although, since the smoking ban of 2007, you'll have to smoke them elsewhere. The rooms divide equally between deco original and Victorian, with period touches such as deco toilet flushes in the swanky marble bathrooms. Bedside panels control the mod-con facilities at the touch of a button. A private butler serves the penthouse suites (yours for £5,000 a night), with several bedrooms, bathrooms and a private terrace. *Bars (2). Business services. Concierge. Gym. Internet (dataport/high-speed/wireless). Restaurants (3). Room service (24hr). Smoking rooms. TV (DVD/pay movies).*

Dorchester

53 Park Lane, Mayfair, W1K 1QA (7629 8888/ www.thedorchester.com). Hyde Park Corner tube. **Rates** £505-£681 double. **Credit** AmEx, DC, MC, V. **Map** p400 G7 ⑭

A glitzy Park Lane fixture since 1931, the Dorchester is enjoying its first major upgrade since a complete refurbishment in 2002. The Alain Ducasse team of Nicola Canuti and Bruno Riou launched a restaurant here in November 2007, a month after the reopening of Alexandra Champalimaud's redesigned trio of rooftop suites, all marble and glass-beaded wallpaper. The view over Hyde Park from the expansive terrace is the same one Elizabeth Taylor would have seen when she agreed to star in *Cleopatra* – she took

the call here. Of the 49 other suites, General Eisenhower planned the D-Day landings in one and Prince Philip held his stag-do in another. This opulence is reflected in the grandest lobby in town, complete with Liberace's piano. The hotel continually upgrades older rooms to the same high standard as the rest, with floral decor, antiques and lavish marble bathrooms; some have park views. The Dorchester employs 90 full-time chefs – both China Tang and the Grill Room (*see p208*) live up to their reputations. At the other end of the price scale, the revamped spa is affordable for non-residents. *Bar. Concierge. Disabled-adapted rooms. Gym. Internet (dataport/high-speed/web TV). Parking. Restaurants (3). Room service (24hr). Smoking rooms. Spa. TV (pay movies/music/DVD).*

Haymarket Hotel

1 Suffolk Place, off Piccadilly Circus, SW1Y 4BP (7470 4000/www.firmdale.com). Piccadilly Circus tube. **Rates** £288-£364 double. **Rooms** 50. **Credit** AmEx, DC, MC, V. **Map** p406 W5 ㊻

This is the latest opening from Kit Kemp's Firmdale Group, located in a monumental Regency building (*see p60* **Getting all the Kit**). Rooms are generously sized (as are their bathrooms), individually decorated and discreetly stuffed with facilities; there are only 50 of them, so there is plenty of personal attention from the switched-on staff. *Photos p60. Bar. Concierge. Disabled-adapted rooms. Gym. Internet (wireless, £20/day). Pool (1, indoor). Restaurant. Room service. Smoking rooms. Spa. TV (DVD/pay movies).*

Metropolitan

19 Old Park Lane, Mayfair, W1K 1LB (7447 1000/ www.metropolitan.como.bz). Hyde Park Corner tube. **Rates** £428-£793 double. **Rooms** 150. **Credit** AmEx, DC, MC, V. **Map** p400 H8 ㊼

Christina Ong's chic, contemporary Metropolitan is celebrating its tenth anniversary with a set of no-holds-barred package stays – 24-carat gold offerings in Seduce Me at the Met; a London helicopter tour for Excess at the Met – completely in keeping with the upscale character of her landmark venue. The sassier, younger sister of the more staid Halkin (*see p65*), the Met forms part of a celeb-friendly group of hotels and resorts called COMO, long established in Bali, Bangkok and the Turks & Caicos Islands. Look no further than the destination dining spot Nobu or the paparazzi-plagued Met Bar to appreciate its credentials. Ong's background in retail and interior design stand out in the relaxed lobby bar area and throughout the spacious rooms, soundproofed from the regular hum of Mayfair traffic and their creamy furnishings now brought out by plum carpets. All 60 TV channels and a DVD library come free of charge, as do the in-house Shambhala smellies in the marble bathrooms. The gym has recently been refitted with superior equipment, with personal trainers and massages also available. With its park-view rooms, the hotel that set a new standard for modern urban retreats is still a cut above the rest.

Getting all the Kit

Before it even opened in spring 2007, the Haymarket had been designated the best hotel in London – even the world – by travel magazines. But then the husband and wife team behind it, Tim and Kit Kemp, have a serious track record. Along with Anouska Hempel (**Blakes**, *see p65*), they pretty much invented the boutique hotel for London back in the mid 1980s. The Kemps' Firmdale group now comprises seven hotels: the **Haymarket** (*see p59; pictured*), **Charlotte Street** (*see p46*), **Covent Garden** (*see p49*), **Number Sixteen** (*see p67*), the **Soho Hotel** (*see p50*), the **Knightsbridge** (10 Beaufort Gardens, SW3 1PT, 7584 6300) and the **Pelham** (15 Cromwell Place, South Kensington, SW7 2LA, 7589 8288). Kit Kemp, the design half of the couple (Tim handles the numbers), pioneered the 'modern English' decorative style that is now one of the capital's dominant design notes. This style matches traditional touches – pinstriped wallpaper, pristine white quilts, floral upholstery – with bold, contemporary elements. Every Firmdale room is unique, but most have two trademark elements: upholstered mannequins and shiny granite and oak bathrooms.

What has kept the Kemps' hotels ahead of the growing boutique competition? One appealing factor is the combination of lively public spaces with exclusive private ones. Most of their hotels have busy and buzzy restaurants and bars: the classy Oscar at Charlotte Street; Brasserie Max, with its retro zinc bar and 1920s Paris feel, at the Covent Garden; loungey Refuel at the Soho. Three of the hotels have excellent screening rooms, and the Haymarket has upped the ante with its pool bar. Yet each property also has a drawing room and library (with a well-stocked honesty bar), where residents can retire for a quiet drink or read – an especially popular feature with paparazzi-hounded celebs.

There's a winning restlessness about Kemp. Like an enthusiastic little girl with a doll's house collection, she constantly updates rooms and moves items from one hotel to another – a boon for regular guests. Nor is her signature style a repeated design formula: each hotel reflects its location. Charlotte Street (once a dental warehouse) pays homage to the Bloomsbury set with hand-made furniture by members of the group of Victorian intellectuals, as well as paintings

by the likes of Duncan Grant and Vanessa Bell. Number Sixteen is an appealingly fresh take on the B&Bs that proliferate in its South Kensington locale, complete with with bird- and butterfly-themed modern art in the drawing room and a pretty, sprawling garden in which you can take breakfast. The Soho resembles a converted loft, offsetting classically Kemp bold stripes and traditional florals with shocking pinks and groovy acid greens – you wouldn't suspect the place had been a multi-storey carpark were you not clued in by a mural.

And now we have the Haymarket, probably the most luxurious of the lot. The block-size building was designed by John Nash, the architect of Regency London. It is an aesthetic pleasure simply to inhabit the spaces he created, one that Kemp's decor, with sinuous sculptures, fuchsia paint and shiny sofas, somewhat against the odds, manages to enhance. Then there's the couldn't-be-more-central location and accompanying street views, and that basement swimming pool and bar which – yes – is open to non-residents. Looks like Kit Kemp's done it again.

Bar. Business centre. Concierge. Gym. Internet (dataport/high-speed/wireless). No-smoking floors. Parking. Restaurant. Room service (24hr). Smoking rooms. Spa. TV (pay movies/DVD).

Ritz

150 Piccadilly, W1J 9BR (7493 8181/www.theritz london.com). Green Park tube. **Rates** £529-£646 double. **Rooms** 136. **Credit** AmEx, DC, MC, V. **Map** p400 J8 ⑲

Founded by hotelier extraordinaire César Ritz, the hotel celebrated its centenary in 2006 and remains the epitome of luxury. Recently embellished by the addition of the adjoining 18th-century Grade-II listed William Kent House and its five lavish reception rooms, the Ritz echoes this grandeur in its public areas, rooms and suites. The real show-stopper is the ridiculously ornate, vaulted Long Gallery, an orgy of chandeliers, rococo mirrors and marble columns – jackets are compulsory for gentlemen, naturally, although this rule is lifted for breakfast. The high-ceilinged, Louis XVI-style bedrooms have been painstakingly renovated to their former glory in a range of restrained pastel colours. Less restrained are the swanky 24-carat gold leaf features and the magnificently heavy curtains. Amid this old-world luxury, mod cons include wireless internet, large TVs and a gym. Tours are even available, as is a fine afternoon tea served in the Palm Court.
Bar. Business centre. Concierge. Gym. Internet (dataport/high-speed/wireless, £20/day). Restaurant. Room service. Smoking floor. TV (DVD/VCR).

Expensive

No.5 Maddox Street

5 Maddox Street, Mayfair, W1S 2QD (7647 0200/www.living-rooms.co.uk). Oxford Circus tube. **Rates** £300-£435 double suite; £558 2-bed suite; £752 3-bed suite. **Rooms** 12. **Credit** AmEx, DC, MC, V. **Map** p406 U2 ⑲

The PR material has it: an inner-city sanctuary. This bolthole just off Regent Street is perfect for visiting film directors looking to be accommodated in a chic apartment at a reasonable long-term rate. Here they can shut the discreet brown front door, climb the stairs and flop into a home from home with all contemporary cons. Upgrades are on the way for the TV sets and toiletries, both now past their sell-by date of the late 1990s when the East-meets-West decor style was all the rage: bamboo floors and dark wood furniture mixed with sable throws and the obligatory crisp white sheets. Equally, the spacious kitchen cupboards and fridge are full of authentic vintage sweets and organic treats to satisfy most cravings and entertain guests. Many bring their partners and offspring. There's no bar, but there's the Patara, a decent Thai restaurant, on the ground floor. Room service will shop for you too – everything's right on the doorstep.
Business centre. Concierge. Internet (dataport/ high-speed/wireless, £15/day, £60/wk). Private kitchen. Room service. TV (DVD/music).

Westminster & St James's

Deluxe

City Inn Westminster

30 John Islip Street, Westminster, SW1P 4DD
(7630 1000/www.cityinn.com). Pimlico tube. **Rates**
£116-£351 double. **Rooms** 420. **Credit** AmEx, DC,
MC, V. **Map** p401 K10 ⑩

There's nothing particularly flashy about this new-build hotel, but if you were a sturdy spitter you could surely hit Tate Britain (*see p141*) from the upper floors. The owners have wisely made art a theme, collaborating with the Chelsea College of Art to ensure there's changing art through the lobbies and meeting rooms. The rooms too are well thought, with all the added extras (CD/DVD library, with players in the rooms, plus free broadband and flatscreen TVs) and service is charmingly efficient. On-site facilities include the impressive Millbank Lounge (*see p230*), with its vaunted 75 whiskies, and the less-convincing City Café, outside which you can sit on a Ron Arad chair on the covered Art Street. All rooms have floor-to-ceiling windows, so river-facing suites on the 12th and 13th floors have superb night views – when the businessmen go home for the weekend you might grab one for as little as £125.
Bars (2). Business centre. Concierge. Disabled-adapted rooms. Gym. Parking (£30/day). Restaurant. Room service (24hr). Smoking rooms. TV (CD/DVD/pay movies).

Trafalgar

2 Spring Gardens, off Trafalgar Square, SW1A 2TS (7870 2900/www.thetrafalgar.com). Charing Cross tube/rail. **Rates** £293-£351 doubles. **Rooms** 129. **Credit** AmEx, DC, MC, V. **Map** p407 X5 ㊿

The Trafalgar is a Hilton – but you'd hardly notice. It is the chain's first 'concept' hotel. Although it's housed in one of the imposing edifices on the famous square (the former Cunard HQ, in fact, where the ill-fated *Titanic* was conceived), the mood is young and dynamic. The rooms (all of which are a good size) have a masculine feel, with minimalist walnut furniture and white or chocolate walls. The bathtubs are made for sharing with the tap in the middle, and full-size, bespoke, aromatherapy-based toiletries are a nice touch. Just to the right of the open reception on the ground floor is the Rockwell Bar, which serves a brilliant selection of bourbon and mixes cocktails for every taste. DJs play every night, with things getting pretty fierce of a weekend – although thick walls should ensure no sound escapes to the bedrooms. Breakfast downstairs is accompanied each morning by a different musician, ranging from Latin American bossa guitarist to a harpist. Yet even with all these attractions, it is the none-more-central location that's the biggest draw – the few corner suites look directly into the square (prices reflect location) and, during summer or Christmas opening times, those without a room view can enjoy themselves from the small rooftop champagne bar.

Bars (2). Concierge. Disabled-adapted rooms. Gym. Internet (dataport, £15/day). Restaurant. Room service (24hr). Smoking floor. TV (CD/DVD/pay movies/games).

Moderate

B&B Belgravia

64-66 Ebury Street, Belgravia, SW1W 9QD (7823 4928/www.bb-belgravia.com). Victoria tube/rail. **Rates** (incl breakfast) £107 double. **Rooms** 17. **Credit** AmEx, MC, V. **Map** p400 H10 ㉒

Opened in 2004, this is one of the most attractive B&Bs we've seen. The black and white lounge (leather sofa, arty felt cushions, modern fireplace) could be straight out of *Elle Decoration*. But it's not precious: you'll find a laptop equipped with free internet connection and above it games and stuffed toys to keep the kids entertained, plus a collection of DVDs to watch on the flatscreen TV. There's also a high-tech espresso machine, and guests can take their drinks out to tables in the large back garden. The bedrooms are chic, with dove grey walls and contemporary panelled headboards, and come with flatscreen TVs. They've had fun with the sleek bathrooms – one has the basin on the windowsill, another has a large window on to the street (with a sliding frosted glass panel for the modest).
Disabled-adapted rooms. Internet (high-speed). TV.

Windermere Hotel

142-144 Warwick Way, Pimlico, SW1V 4JE (7834 5163/www.windermere-hotel.co.uk). Victoria tube/rail. **Rates** (incl breakfast) £114-£139 double. **Rooms** 20. **Credit** AmEx, MC, V. **Map** p400 H11 ㊸

Minutes from Victoria Station, Warwick Way is lined with small hotels and B&Bs. The Windermere edges ahead of the competition with better than expected facilities (including flatscreen TVs with satellite, free internet, power showers and its own restaurant), smart rooms light on the chintz and a hospitable atmosphere coupled with terrific levels of service (a dozen staff for just 20 rooms). Pick of the colourful but not overpowering rooms is no.31, a top-floor double that gets flooded with light from big windows and offers quintessential London rooftop views. The breakfasts are also excellent (included in room rates) and guests get a discount at the neighbouring municipal car park.
Bar. Business services. Internet (dataport). Restaurant. Room service (until 11pm). TV.

Cheap

Morgan House

120 Ebury Street, Belgravia, SW1W 9QQ (7730 2384/www.morganhouse.co.uk). Pimlico tube/Victoria tube/rail. **Rates** (incl breakfast) £72-£92 double. **Rooms** 11. **Credit** MC, V. **Map** p400 G10 ㊼

The Morgan is an archetypal small English B&B. The passages are narrow and the rooms small. The recently spruced-up decor is more serviceable than striking, with pastel walls, traditional iron or wooden beds and print curtains, although framed prints, fireplaces in most rooms and the odd chandelier lend a gracious air. The top-floor rooms are airy and contemporary, including a family room that sleeps four (in a double plus bunk beds). There's a pleasant patio garden, where guests can chill on a warm evening with a bottle of wine. *TV.*

Chelsea

Expensive

Cadogan
*75 Sloane Street, SW1X 9SG (7235 7141/www.
steinhotels.com/cadogan). Sloane Square tube.* **Rates**
£347-£464 double. **Rooms** 65. **Credit** AmEx, DC,
MC, V. **Map** p397 F10 ⑮
Time has rather caught up with this terribly British hotel. Beautiful wood panels and mosaic flooring at both entrances, plus an old-fashioned cage lift, remind you of naughtier times: Edward VII visited his mistress Lillie Langtry here and Oscar Wilde was arrested in room 118. The signature suites are great fun for history buffs (the Oscar Wilde is dressed in crushed velvet and feather prints; the Lillie Langtry is a period cream and pink confection),

but the other bedrooms are a bit of a mixed bag – some are rather dowdy, others (like a verdant junior suite with central arch) genuinely romantic. The residents' bar feels like a traditional hotel lounge bar, and the handsome Langtry restaurant serves trad British food with an occasional twist (beef tea served as a tiny tower of sliced beef and vegetables, the consommé poured over it at the table). Truly magical, though, are the private Cadogan Place gardens opposite – only guests and residents of the grand square are permitted access to this enchanting combination of formal lawns and twisty wooded paths.
*Bar. Business centre. Concierge. Gym. Internet
(wireless, £10/day). Restaurant. Room service.
TV (DVD).*

myhotel chelsea
*35 Ixworth Place, SW3 3QX (7225 7500/www.
myhotels.com). South Kensington tube.* **Rates**
£276-£417 double. **Rooms** 45. **Credit** AmEx,
DC, MC, V. **Map** p397 E11 ⑯
The Chelsea myhotel feels a world away from its sleekly modern Bloomsbury sister (*see p46*), feeling softer, more feminine – precious certainly, perhaps in both senses. Pink walls, a floral sofa and a plate of scones in the lobby offer a posh English foil to feng shui touches such as the aquarium and candles, elements that doubtless appeal to a slightly older clientele and SW3's legion shoppers. The feminine

Selling the Savoy

Sometimes the monogrammed slippers and branded toiletries aren't enough to take home as a memento of your stay. Although several hotels have discreetly begun to act as showrooms for their furniture designers and bedmakers, becoming sort of living catalogues of home furnishing, last year, just before Christmas, the Savoy went one better and offered punters the chance to snap up much of the historic contents of the place.

Built in 1889, the hotel is London's original grande dame. Monet painted the river from his room; Noël Coward played in the Thames Foyer; Vivien Leigh met Laurence Olivier in the Savoy Grill. Here, a bartender introduced Londoners to the martini at the American Bar. So what bits of this extraordinary history are on offer? Everything from bedsteads, curtains and bed linen to butler's trays, trompe l'oeil and marquetry screens… even a three-tier planter from the central reservation of the only spot in Britain where cars drive on the right, all going for a song at Bonham's auction house. Some items had no reserve, meaning you could have snapped up some Savoy for just £20.

Had a particularly romantic dance in the Lancaster Ballroom? Why, you could have taken home the parquet flooring – yours for about half a grand, in 100 separate sections. Enjoyed memorable tunes at a Sunday morning jazz brunch in the River Restaurant? That white Grotrian-Steinweg grand piano could have tinkled away chez vous for just a few thousand. Anyone looking to bask in the reflected glory of some of the hotel's legendary celebrity guests was in for a treat. Among the 3,000 items in the auction were the Georgian mahogany serpentine chest of drawers from actor Richard Harris's suite – perfect as a hell-raising drinks cabinet – and a pre-war gilt-mounted cylinder bureau from the riverside Monet Suite, guaranteed to create an impression. History does not relate whether Winston Churchill's ashtray, John Wayne's shaving mirror, Charlie Chaplin's umbrella stand or Marilyn Monroe's trouser press also went under the hammer. But the patina of a century's celebrity hospitality has been spread to caring new owners in far-flung private corners of the known world.

mood continues in the rooms with dusky pink wallpaper, white wicker headboards and velvet cushions, although it manages at the same time to feel fresh and modern rather than chintzy (every room has a 21in TV and DVD player). The modernised country farmhouse feel of the bar-restaurant might work better for breakfast than a late-night cocktail, but the conservatory-style library in a central courtyard is a fine place to sink into one of the ample stylish comfy chairs and listen to the water feature or your own choice of CD. The myhotel Jinja room offers treatments if the elegant free weights have proved a temptation too far.
Bar. Business centre. Concierge. Gym. Internet (dataport/wireless). Restaurant. Room service. Spa. TV (DVD).

Knightsbridge & South Kensington

Deluxe

Baglioni
60 Hyde Park Gate, Kensington, SW7 5BB (7368 5700/www.baglionihotellondon.com). High Street Kensington or Gloucester Road tube. **Rates** £452-£482 double. **Rooms** 68. **Credit** AmEx, DC, MC, V. **Map** p394 C9 ⑤⑦
Upscale Italian with one of the most desirable locations in London, the Baglioni and its exciting designer style cannot fail to impress. Yet, although occupying a Victorian mansion opposite Kensington Palace and with a butler service on each floor, the Baglioni has none of the snooty formality of some of its deluxe English counterparts. The ground-floor Italian restaurant and bar are part baroque, part Donatella Versace: spidery black chandeliers, burnished gold ceilings, gigantic vases and a truly magnificent mirror from Venice. The chic bedrooms are more subdued: black floorboards, taupe and gold-leaf walls, dark wood furniture enlivened by jewel-coloured cushions and soft throws. Instead of the usual marble, the swanky black-panelled bathrooms have hammered iron sinks imported from Morocco. Health spa treatments range from a four-step anti-ageing itinerary to Botox.
Bar. Business centre. Concierge. Disabled-adapted rooms. Gym. Internet (dataport/high-speed/web TV/wireless). Parking (£38/day). Restaurant. Room service (24hr). Spa. TV (DVD/movies/music).

Blakes
33 Roland Gardens, South Kensington, SW7 3PF (7370 6701/www.blakeshotels.com). South Kensington tube. **Rates** £382-£441 double. **Credit** AmEx, DC, MC, V. **Map** p397 D11 ⑤⑧
As original as when Anouska Hempel opened it in 1983 – oranges and birdsong fill the dark, oriental lobby – Blakes and its maximalist decor have stood the test of time, a living casebook for interior design students. Each room is in a different style, with influences from Italy, India, Turkey and China. Exotic antiques picked up on the designer's travels – intricately carved beds, Chinese birdcages, ancient trunks – are complemented with sweeping drapery and piles of plump cushions. Downstairs is the eclectic, Eastern-influenced restaurant, complemented by a gym and wireless internet for a celebrity clientele enticed by the discreet, residential location.
Bar. Business services. Concierge. Internet (dataport/wireless, £12/day). Restaurant. Room service (24hr). TV (pay movies/DVD).

Halkin
Halkin Street, Belgravia, SW1X 7DJ (7333 1000/www.halkin.como.bz). Hyde Park Corner tube. **Rates** £446 double. **Rooms** 41. **Credit** AmEx, DC, MC, V. **Map** p400 G9 ⑤⑨
The first hotel of Singaporean fashion magnate Christina Ong (whose COMO group also includes the Metropolitan, *see p59*) was ahead of the East-meets-West design trend when it opened in 1991. Repeat custom accounts for more than half of its trade. Its subtle design – a marriage of European luxury and oriental serenity – looks more current than hotels half its age. The 41 rooms, located off curving black corridors, combine stylish classical sofas with black lacquer tables and South-east Asian artefacts. Each floor is loosely themed by element, influencing the colour of the carpets and the marble bathrooms. Egyptian cotton sheets are common throughout. A high-tech touch-screen bedside console controls everything from the 'do not disturb' sign to the air-con. Gracious and discreet behind a Georgian-style façade, the Halkin is equally renowned for its Michelin-starred restaurant, Nahm (*see p213*).
Bar. Concierge. Disabled-adapted rooms. Internet (high-speed/wireless). Parking (£45/day). Restaurant. Room service (24hr). TV (pay movies/DVD).

Lanesborough
1 Lanesborough Place, Hyde Park Corner, SW1X 7TA (7259 5599/www.lanesborough.com). Hyde Park Corner tube. **Rates** £535-£652 double. **Rooms** 95. **Credit** AmEx, DC, MC, V. **Map** p400 G9 ⑥⓪
The Lanesborough is justifiably considered one of London's more historic luxury hotels even though its impressive redevelopment was only completed in 1991. Occupying an 1820s Greek Revival building by National Gallery designer William Wilkins right on Hyde Park Corner, it contains 95 luxurious guest rooms, traditionally decorated with antique furniture and lavish marble bathrooms featuring customised toiletries. Electronic keypads control everything from the air-conditioning to the 24hr room service at the touch of a button. Other well-considered touches include the complimentary high-speed internet access, free movies and personalised business cards. The Library Bar (which serves outstanding cocktails) and Conservatory (for afternoon tea) maintain the high standards.
Bar. Business centre. Concierge. Disabled-adapted rooms. Gym. Internet (dataport/wireless). Parking (£40/day). Restaurant. Room service (24hr). Spa. TV (DVD/movies).

Milestone Hotel & Apartments

1 Kensington Court, Kensington, W8 5DL
(7917 1000/www.milestonehotel.com). High Street
Kensington tube. **Rates** £294-£364 double. **Rooms**
57. **Credit** AmEx, DC, MC, V. **Map** p394 C9 ⑥

Wealthy American visitors make annual pilgrimages here, their arrival greeted by the comforting, gravel tones of their regular concierge, as English as roast beef, and the glass of sherry in the room. Yet amid old-school luxury thrives inventive modernity. Rooms overlooking Kensington Gardens feature the inspired decor of South African owner Beatrice Tillman: the Safari suite contains tent-like draperies and leopard-print upholstery; the spectacular Tudor Suite has an elaborate inglenook fireplace, minstrels' gallery and a pouffe concealing a pop-up TV. Butlers are on 24hr call. Full-sized Penhaligon's toiletries are offered throughout. A recent addition (ten rooms are refurbished each year) is the infinity pool, complementing the range of treatments. House restaurant Cheneston's serves modern British cuisine with a wine list overseen by the UK's number two sommelier.

Bar. Business services. Concierge. Disabled-adapted rooms. Gym. Internet (dataport/wireless). Pool (1, indoor). Restaurant. Room service (24hr). Smoking floors. TV (DVD/pay movies).

Expensive

Bentley Kempinksi

Harrington Gardens, South Kensington, SW7 4JX
(7244 5555/www.thebentley-hotel.com). Gloucester
Road tube. **Rates** £458 double. **Rooms** 64. **Credit**
AmEx, DC, MC, V. **Map** p396 C10 ⑥

Although it isn't large, the Bentley's style is on a grand scale: Louis XV-style furniture, gilt mirrors, gleaming marble – 600 tons of it, all imported – and a sweeping circular staircase perfect for making an entrance. Chandeliers abound in this opulent boutique hotel, in the bedrooms as well as the lobby. The former also feature plush carpets, satin bedspreads and dark marble bathrooms with gold fittings and jacuzzi tubs. Glitzy restaurant 1880 is named after the date of the original building set on this quiet

Cheap 'n' charming

Yes, London hotels are expensive. Yes, the rising room rates are likely to continue rising. But there are signs of hope. While it's hard to recommend staying at an **easyHotel** (*see p71*) unless price really is your only consideration, the scheduled opening of a second **Yotel** (www.yotel.com; *pictured*) in Heathrow airport in December 2007 is cause for minor celebration. If it's like its sister establishment just off the main concourse in Gatwick airport, it does the job with cheeky efficiency. First off, you can book your room for as long as you need – from a minimum of four hours (double from £55), for those of you who need a bed but aren't intending to spend your time in it sleeping, longer if you're filling

an awkward gap between flights or between last train and an early check-in. The design is fun: each bed is contained in a sort of pod, with a wraparound headboard that has a side-panel for all the electronics – air-con, lighting and controls for a not entirely convenient TV-cum-internet screen opposite the bed. There's a reasonably roomy bathroom (with two-head shower) separated from the bed area by a glass partition, while Muji goods and microwaved food are delivered to your door from the Galley (a manned reception area). Even the lack of external windows is easily forgotten with windows on to the main corridor a steady ambient glow.

Of course the Yotels aren't much use when you're in town, so we're delighted to see a growing number of affordably stylish options in London itself. **B&B Belgravia** (*see p62*) and the Mayflower Group (**New Linden**, *see p55*; **Mayflower**, *see p70*; **Twenty Nevern Square**, *see p70*) offer suave digs for not much over £100 a night, while weekend rates at the **Hoxton** (*see p68*) and **Stylotel** (*see p57*) are often well below that. Things are even bright among the city's hostels, with the arrival of the superb **Clink** (*see p49*).

Kensington street; the Malachite Bar is a dimly lit, decadent hideaway in deep red, green and leopard-print. The real showpiece is the classical spa, with gold-laced mosaics and a full-size Turkish hammam. *Bar. Business centre. Concierge. Disabled-adapted rooms. Gym. Internet (dataport/high-speed, £5.99/hr). Restaurants (2). Room service (24hr). Smoking rooms. Spa. TV (pay movies/music/DVD).*

Gore

189 Queen's Gate, South Kensington, SW7 5EX (7584 6601/www.gorehotel.com). South Kensington tube. **Rates** £199-£351 double. **Rooms** 50. **Credit** AmEx, DC, MC, V. **Map** p397 D9 ⊕

Recently refurbished and now under new management, the Gore retains a special atmosphere. It's a fin-de-siècle period piece founded by descendants of Captain Cook in a couple of grand Victorian townhouses. The lobby and staircase are close hung with old paintings, and the bedrooms have fantastic 19th-century carved oak beds, sumptuous drapes and shelves of old books. The suites are spectacular: the Tudor Room has a huge stone-faced fireplace and a minstrels' gallery, while tragedy queens should plump for the Venus room and Judy Garland's old bed (and replica ruby slippers). Bistrot 190 gets good reviews, and provides a casually elegant setting for great breakfasts, while the warm, wood-pannelled 190 bar has a salubrious charm. It's recently been enhanced by the arrival of Cinderella's Carriage, a red velvet bedecked snug bookable on guarantee of a minimum £100 spend. Hyde Park, the Royal Albert Hall and the museums are all just a short walk away. *Bar. Concierge. Internet (dataport/wireless). Restaurant. Room service (7am-midnight daily). Smoking floor. TV.*

Number Sixteen

16 Sumner Place, South Kensington, SW7 3EG (7589 5232/www.firmdale.com). South Kensington tube. **Rates** £217-£311 double. **Rooms** 42. **Credit** AmEx, MC, V. **Map** p395 D10 ⊕

There's no slacking in style at Kit Kemp's most affordable hotel. Bedrooms are generously sized, bright and very light. *See p60* **Getting all the Kit**. *Bar. Business centre. Concierge. Internet (dataport/ wireless, £20/day). Parking (£37/day). Room service (24hr). TV (DVD).*

Moderate

Aster House

3 Sumner Place, South Kensington, SW7 3EE (7581 5888/www.asterhouse.com). South Kensington tube. **Rates** £146-£185 double. **Rooms** 13. **Credit** MC, V. **Map** p397 D10 ⊕

Set in a listed building in a quiet, residential area, this award-winning B&B attempts to live up to its upmarket address. The slightly kitsch lobby leads to a lush garden, with a duckpond, and a palm-filled conservatory where guests take breakfast over the morning's papers. The bedrooms are comfortable, with traditional floral upholstery, air-conditioning

and smart marble bathrooms (ask for one with a power shower). Staff can lend guests mobile phones for their stay, and the rooms all have wireless internet connectivity. The museums and big-name shops are all close at hand. A good, affordable option. *Internet (dataport/wireless). TV.*

Cheap

Meininger

Baden-Powell House, 65-67 Queen's Gate, South Kensington, SW7 5JS (7590 6910/www.meininger-hostels.com). Gloucester Road or South Kensington tube. **Rates** £49 double; £13-£25 dorm bed. **Rooms** 46. **Credit** MC, V. **Map** p397 D10 ⊕

This classy German hostel chain's first London operation is set in the large conference centre for the Scouts' Association, which still owns this modern, six-storey building opposite the Natural History Museum, opened by the Queen in 1961. With its purple colour scheme and artwork an appreciative nod to the movement, which hires out the events rooms, the lodging quarters have had a complete makeover: the breakfast room has an expansive view of London traffic and its equally large second-floor terrace is equipped with benches and a table-tennis table. The three main floors offer airy dormitory, twin and single accommodation, all bedrooms en suite with TV, wireless access and air-conditioning, as well as bedside tables and lamps. The more basic dorms are on the top floor. Families and big groups are welcome – children are safely catered for. Self-catering or bar, but there is 24hr tea and coffee provision for both communal and single or twin rooms. *Internet (shared terminal, £2/hr). TV.*

Vicarage Hotel

10 Vicarage Gate, Kensington, W8 4AG (7229 4030/www.londonvicaragehotel.com). High Street Kensington or Notting Hill Gate tube. **Rates** (incl breakfast) £88-£114 double. **Rooms** 17. **Credit** AmEx, MC, V. **Map** p394 B8 ⊕

The glowing reviews from guidebooks mounted in the hallway testify to the understandable popularity of this off-Ken High Street hotel. A Victorian townhouse on a quiet dogleg of Vicarage Gate, across from Kensington Gardens, the Vicarage has a glitzy lobby, with red and gold wallpaper, ornate mirrors and a chandelier, and rooms in traditional B&B pastel, furnished with faux antiques and floral fabrics. Nine of them have bathrooms. *TV.*

North London

Moderate

Colonnade

2 Warrington Crescent, Little Venice, W9 1ER (7286 1052/www.theetoncollection.com/colonnade). Warwick Avenue tube. **Rates** £147-£212 double. **Rooms** 43. **Credit** AmEx, MC, V.

If you're looking for somewhere to stay while your new home is being renovated, you could slip between the sheets in the same room that Freud did in 1938 while awaiting the move into what would be his final address (*see p158*). These days, the former Esplanade Hotel goes by a new name, and a mezzanine has been added to the high-ceilinged Freud Suite, but this handsome double-fronted Victorian mansion just north of optimistically named Little Venice retains its old-school charm. The lobby is suffused with rich autumn colours – russet carpet, brown leather chairs, forest-green drapes – and the pricier rooms are opulent but not overly fussy, with plush carpets, stuffed armchairs, gilt-framed mirrors, thick duvets and bright, decent-sized bathrooms. Unfortunately, those colour and texture combinations make some of the lower-ceilinged standard doubles feel a bit oppressive; toned-down furnishings in the single rooms work better. Breakfast (£10-£15) is served in the glass-topped tapas bar and cocktail lounge sunk in the front garden.
Bar. Internet (wireless, £15/day). Parking (£20/day). Restaurant. Room service (24hr). TV.

Cheap

Hampstead Village Guesthouse
2 Kemplay Road, Hampstead, NW3 1SY (7435 8679/www.hampsteadguesthouse.com). Hampstead tube/Hampstead Heath rail. **Rates** (incl breakfast) £75-£90 double. **Rooms** 9. **Credit** AmEx, MC, V.
Popular with visiting academics and their families, this comfy bed and breakfast occupies a Victorian pile in picturesque Hampstead. This is the place to stay if you hate hotels – the nine guest rooms in Annemarie van der Meer's sprawling home contain an eclectic collection of furniture, paintings and books... it's like staying in the spare room of an intellectual relative (one who'll lend you a mobile or a laptop, mind). Space is used to maximum effect, with quirky devices – children love the wardrobe that conceals a fold-out bed. There's a fridge in each room and most of the rooms are en suite (although some bathrooms are tiny); one even has a steel tub in the middle of the floor. There's also a modern studio in a converted garage, sleeping five. Breakfast is served in the kitchen or secluded garden.
Internet (wireless). TV.

East London

Moderate

Hoxton Hotel
81 Great Eastern Street, Shoreditch, EC2A 3HU (7550 1000/www.hoxtonhotels.com). Old Street tube/rail. **Rates** (incl breakfast) £169 double. **Rooms** 205. **Credit** AmEx, MC, V. **Map** p403 Q4 ⑥⑨
The Hoxton Hotel proves that budget needn't be boring. Opened in September 2006, it is a perfect fit for its hip Shoreditch location. The large glass front wall maintains a link between the activity out on the

street and the busy double-height foyer with its areas of lounge seating grouped around two fires – a kind of postmodern country lodge. A large and well-designed bar and restaurant – visible to passers-by and open to the public – lends a genuine air of excitement to the place. The rooms aren't big, but they are well thought out – the flatscreen TV turns to a cheekily tiny chaise longue or the Frette linen bed, free internet, a free Pret Lite breakfast, fresh milk in the fridge. Grab a room at the back on the fifth or sixth floor and you'll be blessed with great urban views at night; otherwise all rooms are identical. It's doubtful you'll get a better deal in London – especially if you manage to book one of the few £1 rooms released every three months.
Bars. Business centre. Disabled-adapted rooms. Internet (dataport/wireless, free). Restaurant. Room service (24hr). TV (pay movies).

South-east London

Moderate

Church Street Hotel
29-33 Camberwell Church Street, Camberwell, SE5 8TR (7703 5984/www.churchstreethotel.com). Denmark Hill rail/36, 436 bus. **Rates** (incl breakfast) £120-£180 double. **Rooms** 31. **Credit** AmEx, MC, V.
Craftsman José Raido and his Galician family are behind this attractive and original new hotel, opened in summer 2007. It's near the busy bus junction of Camberwell Green, right on the frontier of London's Latin American quarter. Avoiding the temptation to give their premises a hokey Spanish name, José and his team have gone big on the detail within. All the funky bathroom tiles in the bright, high-ceilinged bedrooms, for example, came from Guadalajara, perfectly matched with imported cinema posters and other Mexicana. The Somerset bed frames were forged by José himself. Bathroom products are from the Greek Korres range – organic, like the pastries and cereals offered for breakfast in an icon-filled dining room that also serves as 24hr honesty bar. Even those paying £70-£90 for the shared-bathroom 'Poblito' rooms are entitled to breakfast and an eyeful of bright design. Tea and coffee are complimentary, while the small jars of hot pepper dip in each room come courtesy of José's father. A downstairs restaurant is due soon. *Photos p71.*
Bar. Business centre. Internet (wireless). Parking (£5/day). Restaurant. Room service (24hr). TV.

South-west London

Moderate

Windmill on the Common
Windmill Drive, Clapham Common Southside, Clapham, SW4 9DE (8673 4578/www.windmill clapham.co.uk). Clapham Common or Clapham South tube. **Rates** (incl breakfast) £125-£140. **Rooms** 29. **Credit** AmEx, MC, V.

Perched on the edge of Clapham Common, the Windmill is a pleasant neighbourhood pub in a building dating from 1729 – although the hotel wing behind the car park has a plaque dated 1883. No matter – this is a comfortable, reasonably priced hotel and a lovely short stroll from Clapham Common or Clapham South tube stops. The tidy bedrooms are being redecorated, ten at a time, and ten are designated 'premium', coming with stocked fridge and fluffy towels. A full English breakfast is provided for all guests and a three-night non-premium weekend rate of £270 per room is not a bad deal at all. *Bar. Disabled-adapted room. Internet (dataport). Parking. Restaurant. Room service (until 10.30pm). TV.*

Cheap

Riverside Hotel
23 Petersham Road, Richmond-upon-Thames, Surrey TW10 6UH (8940 1339/www.riverside richmond.co.uk). Richmond tube/rail. **Rates** £90-£95 double. **Rooms** 12. **Credit** AmEx, DC, MC, V.
There are changes afoot at the Riverside – but not anything to spoil the tranquil view by the Thames Footpath, a short walk but a world away from the traffic-choked high street at Richmond's centre. The family that has run the Riverside for the past two decades – it has been a hotel since the 1930s – is converting eight rooms into flats, leaving a dozen still rented out to guests at reasonable (and negotiable) rates. All, comfortable and high-ceilinged, are done out in traditional style, and the hotel is within easy reach of Richmond Park and Kew Gardens. *Internet (dataport/wireless, £6/day). TV.*

West London

Expensive

High Road House
162 Chiswick High Road, Chiswick, W4 1PR (8742 1717/www.highroadhouse.co.uk). Turnham Green tube. **Rates** £140-£160. **Rooms** 14. **Credit** AmEx, DC, MC, V.
This addition to Nick Jones's Soho House group opened on Chiswick High Road in 2006, generously sparing west London's media crowd the slog into W1. Unsurprisingly, it's always packed, not least the terrace brasserie downstairs. Above it is a members' bar and restaurant featuring a modern British menu composed by Steve Beadle, and above that, two floors of guest rooms, 14 in all. Ilse Crawford's design cocoons guests in a white world of unadorned walls, digital technology and treats from teas to retro sweeties. All have ten-inch cabbage-head showers and white-tiled bathrooms with retro fittings, Cowshed products and some thoughtful 'in case you forgot' products. Food (in-room and out) is excellent, with service to match. *Bars (2). Concierge. Disabled-adapted rooms. Internet (wireless). Restaurants (2). Room service (7am-1am daily). TV (pay movies/DVD).*

Rockwell
181 Cromwell Road, Earl's Court, SW5 0SF (7244 2000/www.therockwellhotel.com). Earl's Court tube. **Rates** £160-£180 double. **Rooms** 40. **Credit** AmEx, MC, V. **Map** p396 B10 ⑥⑨
Housed in a restored Victorian terrace, Rockwell isn't your average London four-star. For a start, it's

The **Rockwell** – elegant within, Victorian up front.

independently owned, meaning no identikit furniture but rather rooms of different sizes and shapes that are all thoughtfully kitted out, with funky wallpaper and Egyptian cotton bed linen. Thanks to triple glazing, you'd never know busy Cromwell Road is just outside. The hotel has quickly built up a reputation among design-savvy travellers, and has already been used as a backdrop for several major fashion shoots. The small reception area is the epitome of understated elegance, with well-stocked bookshelves, a modern fireplace and cool jazz on the stereo, while the One-Eight-One restaurant, bar and outside walled garden are worthy destinations in their own right. On the downside, corridors are a bit dingy, and bathrooms in the smaller rooms are on the poky side – but at least they come with White Company toiletries and fluffy robes. And, frankly, at these prices, we're not complaining.
Bar. Internet (broadband). Restaurant. TV (pay movies/DVD).

Moderate

Base2Stay

25 Courtfield Gardens, Earl's Court, SW5 0PG (0845 262 8000/www.base2stay.com). Earl's Court tube. **Rates** £99-£189. **Rooms** 67. **Credit** AmEx, MC, V. **Map** p396 B10 ❼

Opened in spring 2006, Base2Stay looks good, with its modernist limestone and taupe tones. It claims to offer 'a synthesis of boutique hotel and serviced apartment' and the prices are certainly agreeable, so where have the corners been cut? The answer is simple: frills. The 'kitchenette' that supposedly dispenses with the need for a hotel bar or dining area is a microwave, sink, mini-fridge and kettle squeezed into a cupboard in the bedroom – but given there's nowhere but the bed for more than one person to sit, you'll probably want to take advantage of the small discounts offered at nearby restaurants (20% at Strada, 10% at Wagamama). Not that the rooms are disagreeable, with cream walls, taupe and chocolate accents, and sepia print photos; the first-floor rooms have ridiculously high ceilings and the bunk bed rooms are great for kids. As long as you don't mind the lack of perks, you get an affordable room less than five minutes from the tube station.
Disabled-adapted rooms. Internet (wireless). TV (flatscreen/pay movies).

Hotel 55

55 Hanger Lane, Ealing, W5 3HL (8991 4450/ www.hotel55-london.com). North Ealing tube. **Rates** (incl breakfast) £130 double. **Rooms** 25. **Credit** AmEx, MC, V.

Turn the corner from North Ealing tube, past the pleasant Greystoke pub and up to Hanger Lane and a surprise awaits at this junction of bucolic west London and traffic-choked North Circular. Where there was once the prosaic Glencairn Hotel, a popular stop for lonely truck drivers, is now the contemporary, design-led Hotel 55. True, it ticks the boxes of many of London's other contemporary, design-led

hotels – Molton Brown bath products, sheets of Egyptian cotton, 24hr lounge bar – but considering the price and location, this is no bad thing at all. Individuality is provided by the modern canvases of Indian artist Sudhir Deshpande, the natural woods integral to the design of Babettli Azzone, and a lovely landscaped garden.
Bar. Disabled-adapted rooms. Internet (wireless). TV.

Mayflower Hotel

26-28 Trebovir Road, Earl's Court, SW5 9NJ (7370 0991/www.mayflower-group.co.uk). Earl's Court tube. **Rates** (incl continental breakfast) £92-£115 double. **Rooms** 46. **Credit** AmEx, MC, V. **Map** p396 B11 ⑪

At the forefront of the budget-hotel style revolution, the Mayflower Hotel has given Earl's Court – once a far from glamorous B&B wasteland – a kick up the backside. Following a spectacular makeover a few years back, the Mayflower proves cheap really can be chic. The minimalist lobby is dominated by a gorgeous teak chair that came all the way from Jaipur; there's a fashionably battered leather sofa and even a couple of caged love birds in the café-cum-lounge. The wooden-floored rooms are furnished in an Eastern style with hand-carved beds and sumptuous fabrics or sleek modern headboards and units, with architectural fragments or contemporary paintings to match. In some rooms, ceiling fans add a tropical feel, which extends to the palm trees in the garden. At such low rates, marble bathrooms, CD players, room safes and wireless internet are hitherto unheard-of luxuries.
Bar (juice bar). Business centre. Internet (wireless). Parking (£20/day, booking essential). TV.

Twenty Nevern Square

20 Nevern Square, Earl's Court, SW5 9PD (7565 9555/www.twentynevernsquare.co.uk). Earl's Court tube. **Rates** (incl breakfast) £90-£150 double. **Rooms** 20. **Credit** AmEx, DC, MC, V. **Map** p396 A11 ⑫

The words 'stylish' and 'Earl's Court' don't usually appear in the same sentence, but it's the less-than-posh location of this immaculate boutique hotel that keeps the place's rates reasonable. Tucked away in a secluded (private) garden square, it feels far away from its less-than-lovely locale. The modern-colonial style was created by its well-travelled owner, who personally sourced many of the exotic furnishings (as well as those in even cheaper sister hotel the Mayflower; *see above*). Rooms are clad in a mixture of Eastern and European antique furniture, and sumptuous silk curtains and bedspreads; in the sleek marble bathrooms, toiletries are tidied away in decorative caskets. The beds are the real stars, though, from elaborately carved four-posters to Egyptian sleigh styles, all with luxurious mattresses. The Far East feel extends into the lounge and the airy conservatory bar-cum-breakfast room, with its pale walls and dark wicker furniture.
Bar. Internet (dataport/wireless). Parking (£20/day). Room service (24hr). Smoking rooms. TV (DVD).

Cheap

easyHotel

14 Lexham Gardens, Earl's Court, W8 5JE (www. easyhotel.com). Earl's Court tube. **Rates** from £25 double. **Rooms** 34. **Credit** MC, V. **Map** p396 B10 ⑦

First came easyJet, then easyCar and easyCruise… Since August 2005, entrepreneur Stelios Haji-Ioannou has applied his no-frills approach to this compact hotel for compact wallets, adding two further easyHotels in 2007, with plans for Luton and Heathrow locations in 2008 (the latter in competition with the new Yotel, *see p66* **Cheap 'n' charming**). The 34 rooms come in three sizes – small, really small and tiny – the last of which is the precise width of the bed. Forget cats, there's not even room to swing a shoulder bag (and hardly anywhere to put one down). The rooms come with a bed, a pre-fab bathroom unit (toilet, sink and showerhead almost on top of the sink) and that's it. There's no wardrobe, no hairdryer, no lift and no breakfast, and you only get a window if you pay extra for it. Just one person mans reception 24 hours a day, and there are no services, food, entertainment or public areas. The rooms, which are bookable online only, start at an admittedly low £25 – but the prices vary according to demand, so book early or expect to pay an average rate of around £40-£50. To make a genuine saving, avoid such fripperies as TV (£5) and housekeeping (£10). Check-in and check-out are at a less than generous 3pm and 10am respectively.
TV (£5 supplement).

Other locations 36-40 Belgrave Road, Victoria, SW1V 1RG; 44-48 West Cromwell Road, Kensington, SW5 9QL.

Apartment rental

The companies we have listed below specialise in holiday lets, although some of them have minimum stay requirements (making this an affordable option only if you're planning a relatively protracted visit to the city). Typical daily rates on a reasonably central property are around £70-£90 for a studio or one-bed, up to £100 for a two-bed, although, as with any aspect of staying in London, the sky's the limit if you want to pay it. Respected all-rounders with properties around the city include **Astons Apartments** (7590 6000, www. astons-apartments.com), **Holiday Serviced Apartments** (0845 060 4477, www.holiday apartments.co.uk) and **Palace Court Holiday Apartments** (7727 3467, www.palacecourt. co.uk). **Accommodation Outlet** (7287 4244, www.outlet4holidays.com) is a recommended lesbian and gay agency that has some excellent properties in Soho, in particular.

Camping & caravanning

If the thought of putting yourself at the mercy of English weather in some far-flung suburban

Church Street Hotel. *See p68.*

field doesn't put you off, the transport links into central London might do the job instead. Still, you can't argue with the prices.

Crystal Palace Caravan Club *Crystal Palace Parade, SE19 1UF (8778 7155). Crystal Palace rail/ 3 bus.* **Open** *Mar-Oct* 8.30am-6pm Mon-Thur, Sat, Sun; 8.30am-8pm Fri. *Nov-Feb* 9am-6pm Mon-Thur, Sat, Sun; 9am-8pm Fri. **Rates** *Caravan* £5-£8. *Tent* £5-£15. **Credit** MC, V.

Lee Valley Campsite *Sewardstone Road, Chingford, E4 7RA (8529 5689/www.leevalley park.org.uk). Walthamstow Central tube/rail then 215 bus.* **Open** *Apr-Oct* 8am-9pm daily. **Rates** £6.45; £2.90 under-16s; free under-2s. *Electricity* £3/day. **Credit** MC, V.

Lee Valley Leisure Centre Camping & Caravan Park *Meridian Way, Pickett's Lock, Edmonton, N9 0AS (8803 6900/www. leevalleypark.org.uk). Edmonton Green rail/W8 bus.* **Open** 8am-10pm daily. **Rates** £6.45; £2.90 reductions; free under-5s. **Credit** MC, V.

Staying with the locals

Several agencies can arrange for individuals and families to stay in Londoners' homes. Prices for a stay are around £20-£85 for a single and £45-£105 for a double, including breakfast, and depending on the location and degree of comfort. Agencies include **At Home in London** (8748 1943, www.athomeinlondon.co.uk), **Bulldog Club** (0870 803 4414, www.bulldogclub.com), **Host & Guest Service** (7385 9922, www. host-guest.co.uk), **London Bed & Breakfast Agency** (7586 2768, www.londonbb.com) and **London Homestead Services** (7286 5115, www.lhslondon.com). There may be a minimum stay. Alternatively, you can browse around noticeboard-style 'online community' websites such as **Gumtree** (www.gumtree.com).

University residences

During the university vacations much of London's dedicated student accommodation is opened up to visitors, providing them with a source of basic but cheap digs.

International Students House *229 Great Portland Street, Marylebone, W1W 5PN (7631 8300/www.ish.org.uk). Great Portland Street tube.* **Rates** (per person) £12-£21 dormitory; £34 single; £26.50 (per person) twin. **Available** all year. **Map** p398 H4 ❼⓸

King's College Conference & Vacation Bureau *Strand Bridge House, 138-142 Strand, Covent Garden, WC2R 1HH (7848 1700/www.kcl. ac.uk/kcvb). Temple tube.* **Rates** £19.50-£39 single; £42-£58 twin. **Available** end of June-mid Sept. **Map** p407 Z3 ❼⓹

LSE *Bankside House, 24 Sumner Street, South Bank, SE1 9JA (7107 5773/www.lsevacations.co.uk). London Bridge tube.* **Rates** £42 single; £64 twin/ double. **Available** July-Sept. **Map** p404 O8 ❼⓺

The London School of Economics has vacation rentals across town, but Bankside House (tucked just behind Tate Modern) is the best located.

Walter Sickert Hall *29 Graham Street, Islington, N1 8LA (7040 8822/www.city.ac.uk/ems). Angel tube.* **Rates** £32-£40 single; £60 twin. **Available** June-Sept (executive rooms available all year). **Map** p402 O3 ❼⓻

Youth hostels

If you're not a member of the International Youth Hostel Federation (IYHF), you'll pay an extra £3 a night, but you can avoid paying this fee by joining the IYHF for £13 (£6.50 for under-18s) at any hostel, or through www.yha. org.uk. The selected hostels include breakfast in the price. All under-18s receive a 25 per cent discount. Youth hostel beds are arranged either in twin rooms or dormitories.

Earl's Court *38 Bolton Gardens, SW5 0AQ (7373 7083/www.yha.org.uk). Earl's Court tube.* **Open** *Reception* 24hrs daily. *Access* 24hrs daily. **Rates** £13.95-£31.95. **Map** p396 B11 ❼⓼

Holland Park *Holland Walk, W8 7QU (7937 0748/www.yha.org.uk). High Street Kensington tube.* **Open** *Reception* 24hrs daily. *Access* 24hrs daily. **Rates** £14.95-£70. **Map** p394 A8 ❼⓽

Oxford Street *14 Noel Street, W1F 8GJ (7734 1618/www.yha.org.uk). Oxford Circus tube.* **Open** *Reception* 7am-11pm daily. *Access* 24hrs daily. **Rates** £16.50-£60.95. **Map** p406 V2 ❽⓿

St Pancras *79-81 Euston Road, NW1 2QE (0870 770 6044/www.yha.org.uk). King's Cross tube/rail.* **Open** *Reception* 24hrs daily. *Access* 24hrs daily. **Rates** £13.95-£31.95. **Map** p399 L3 ❽⓵

St Paul's *36 Carter Lane, EC4V 5AB (7236 4965/ www.yha.org.uk). St Paul's tube/Blackfriars tube/rail.* **Open** *Reception* 24hrs daily. *Access* 24hrs daily. **Rates** £14.95-£60. **Map** p404 O6 ❽⓶

Thameside *20 Salter Road, SE16 5PR (0870 770 6010/www.yha.org.uk). Rotherhithe tube.* **Open** *Reception* 7am-11pm daily. *Access* 24hrs daily. **Rates** £15.95-£31.95.

YMCAs

You may need to book months ahead; this Christian organisation is mainly concerned with housing young homeless people. Some hostels open to all are given below (all are unisex), but you can get a full list from the **National Council for YMCAs** (8520 5599, www.ymca.org.uk).

Barbican YMCA *2 Fann Street, EC2Y 8BR (7628 0697/www.ymca.org.uk). Barbican tube/ rail.* **Map** p402 P5 ❽⓷

Kingston & Wimbledon YMCA *200 The Broadway, SW19 1RY (8542 9055/www.ymca. org.uk). South Wimbledon tube/Wimbledon tube/rail.*

London City YMCA *8 Errol Street, EC1Y 8SE (7628 8832/www.ymca.org.uk). Barbican or Old Street tube/rail.* **Map** p402 P4 ❽⓸

Sightseeing

Lord's Cricket Ground. *See p157.*

please
KEEP OFF
THE GRASS

Introduction

How to approach the Big Smoke.

London is a wonderful place to visit, but its size can make it overwhelming. With an understanding of its geography and transport, it's a little easier to navigate.

GETTING AROUND

The tube is the most straightforward way to get around, and you are rarely far from a station in central London. Services are frequent and, outside rush hours, you'll usually get a seat. But mix your tube journeys with bus rides to get a handle on London's topography – you can get free bus maps from many large tube stations and from the **Britain & London Visitor Centre** on Lower Regent Street (*see p374*).

Although the wonderful old hop-on/hop-off Routemaster buses have been withdrawn from general service, two Heritage Routes are run specifically for visitors: *see p139* **Big red bus**. It's also a good idea to add river services to your transport portfolio (*see p360*). For more on all methods of transport, *see pp356-362*.

AN OVERVIEW

The **South Bank** (*pp76-79*) is, obviously, the south bank of the Thames but, less obviously, it's also the centre of the nation's arts scene. **Bankside** (*pp79-81*), east of the South Bank and across from the City, rose to prominence in recent years with the launching of Tate Modern. In the historic **City** (*pp88-101*) reminders of London's ramshackle, though occasionally great, past jostle with today's citadels of high finance. The areas north and east of here, the old warehouse hinterlands of **Shoreditch** and **Hoxton** (for both, *see pp165-166*), are known for their galleries and nightlife. Heading back west, **Clerkenwell** (*p104*) used to do the dirty work for the medieval city, but now has some of London's best restaurants and bars, while **Holborn** (*pp102-104*) is the legal quarter; it is also where the City meets the 'West End', which is what would be referred to in America as 'Downtown'. The heart of the West End is **Soho** (*pp119-121*), which – for all that it never quite lives up to its infamy – is fun nevertheless. North are literary **Bloomsbury** (*pp106-109*), home to the British Museum; **Fitzrovia** (*pp110-111*), which services its many advertising and media agencies with decent places to eat and drink; and coming area **King's Cross** (*pp109-110*), with the British Library and the brand new Eurostar terminal St Pancras International. East of Soho is genuine visitor-magnet **Covent Garden** (*pp112-118*), with its attractive market and Piazza and the fantastic Transport Museum.

South of Soho are **Chinatown** (*pp121-122*) and horribly crowded Leicester Square (*p123*), the latter a place to buy half-price theatre tickets (*p333*) and catch blockbuster movies. South again is the official centre of London, Trafalgar Square (*pp135-137*), and the officious centre of Britain, **Westminster** (*pp137-142*). Bordering the precincts of power is pretty St James's Park, overlooked by Buckingham Palace (*p142*), and then to the north aristocratic **St James's** (*pp142-144*), divided by Piccadilly from the similarly aristocratic and exclusive area of **Mayfair** (*pp131-134*).

Piccadilly runs west from Piccadilly Circus (*p131*) to Hyde Park Corner and then into **Knightsbridge** (*pp148-149*), home of designer shopping (and Harrods). The similarly privileged areas of **Chelsea** (*pp145-147*) and **South Kensington** (*pp149-153*), location of London's three great Victorian museums, lie south and south-west of Knightsbridge.

All of the areas in bold above are delineated on our colour-coded area map, *see pp392-393*.

PRACTICALITIES

To avoid queues and overcrowding, try to avoid visiting major attractions at the weekend – and using any form of public transport during rush hour (roughly 8-9.30am and 4.30-7pm Mon-Fri). Many attractions are free to enter (all the big museums, for example), so if you're on a budget you can tick off large numbers of places on your must-see list just for the price of getting there. The **London Pass** (www.londonpass. com) gives pre-paid access to more than 50 sights and attractions; unless you're prepared to visit several sights a day for four or five days, you're unlikely to get your money's worth – although it does mean you can jump ticket queues at places like the ultra-popular Tower of London.

We've given last entry times where they precede an attraction's official closing time by more than an hour. Some smaller venues may close early when they're quiet, and many places close all day on certain public holidays (notably Christmas and Easter) – always phone ahead if you're having to go out of your way.

Sightseeing tours

By boat
City Cruises *7740 0400/www.citycruises.com.*
City Cruises' Rail River Rover (£11; £5.50 reductions) combines hop-on, hop-off travel on any of its regular cruises (pick-up points: Westminster, Waterloo, Tower and Greenwich piers) with unlimited travel on the Docklands Light Railway.
London RIB Voyages *7928 2350/www.london ribvoyages.com.* **Tickets** £26.50-£39.
Part speedboat ride, part sightseeing tour, the RIB powers up to 12 passengers from the London Eye to either Canary Wharf (£26.50) or the Thames Barrier (£39) and back in 80mins. Book in advance.

By bus
Big Bus Company *48 Buckingham Palace Road, Westminster, SW1W 0RN (7233 9533/www.bigbus tours.com).* **Open-top bus tours** *3 routes* 30mins-3hrs. Tickets include river cruise & walking tours. **Departures** every 20-30mins. *Summer* 8.30am-6pm daily. *Winter* 8.30am-4.30pm daily. **Pick-up** 20+ stops incl Haymarket, Green Park (near the Ritz), Marble Arch (Speakers' Corner). **Fares** £22; £10 reductions; free under-5s. **Credit** AmEx, DC, MC, V.
Original London Sightseeing Tour *Jews Row, Wandsworth, SW18 1TB (8877 1722/www.the originaltour.com).* **Departures** *Summer* 9am-7pm daily.*Winter* 9am-5.30pm daily. **Pick-up** 90 stops incl Grosvenor Gardens, Marble Arch (Speakers' Corner), Embankment tube, Baker Street tube & Trafalgar Square. Free cruise. **Fares** £19; £12 5-15s; £72 family; free under-5s. **Credit** AmEx, MC, V.

By duck
London Duck Tours *55 York Road, Waterloo, SE1 7NJ (7928 3132/www.londonducktours.co.uk).* **Tours** *Feb-Dec* phone for details. **Pick-up** Chicheley Street (behind the London Eye). **Fares** £18; £12-£14 reductions; £55 family. **Credit** MC, V.
City of Westminster tours in an amphibious vehicle. The road and river trip, lasting 75 minutes, starts at the London Eye and enters the Thames at Vauxhall.

By bicycle
For more on bicycle hire and tours, *see p362.*

By helicopter
Cabair *Elstree Aerodrome, Borehamwood, Herts WD6 3AW (8953 4411/www.cabairhelicopters.com).* **Fares** £149/person. **Credit** AmEx, DC, MC, V.
Helicopter tours (lasting 30 mins) that follow the Thames. Flights are on Sunday and select Saturdays, although a four-person weekday tour and lunch package can be arranged for £1,500.

By taxi
Black Taxi Tours of London *7 Durweston Mews, Marylebone, W1U 6DF (7935 9363/www.blacktaxi tours.co.uk).* **Cost** £90-£100. **No credit cards**.
A tailored two-hour tour for up to five people.

On foot
Original London Walks (7624 3978, www.walks. com) offer an astonishing 140 walks; other good choices are **And Did Those Feet** (8806 4325, www. chr.org.uk), **Performing London** (01234 404774, www.performinglondon.co.uk) and **Silver Cane Tours** (7720 715295, www.silvercanetours.com).

The best Sightseeing

Borough Market
Skip the breakfast buffet and eat your way instead round London's best food market (*see p255*), then stroll back to central London past the attractions of the South Bank.

Brick Lane
Get the buzz in Dray Walk, then take your pick of Banglatown or the Shoreditch bars (*see p162* **Street scene**).

British Museum
The riches of the collection are stunning, but it's the drama of the glass-covered Great Court that makes the heart leap, especially on a sunny day. *See p107.*

London's Transport Museum
One of London's most enjoyable museums is reborn (*see p117* **All aboard!**). Not satisfied? Take the heritage route on an old-fashioned double-decker bus (*see p139* **Big red bus**).

St Paul's Cathedral
There can be few more dramatic sights than the first view of St Paul's as you approach up Ludgate Hill. And London offers few better panoramas than from outside the dome of Wren's masterpiece. *See p93.*

Wellcome Collection
London is full of bizarre museums, but this newcomer has leapt to the top of the list: glass eyes, a torture chair, memento mori and interactive modern art. Compelling – if a touch frightening. *See p111* **Odd curiosity stop**.

Underground
The world's oldest subterranean railway is a place of endless fascination: see a deco classic like Arnos Grove station or admire the cathedral-like modern grandeur of Canary Wharf. It's also a dab hand at getting people around.

The South Bank & Bankside

The big wheel, views, movies and art – the riverside here is a wonder.

It may have taken more than half a century, but the south bank of the river from Westminster to Tower Bridge can justly claim to be one of the capital's great success stories. After the Festival of Britain established the Royal Festival Hall and later the Southbank Centre here in 1951, the riverside struggled to prove itself a sufficiently attractive alternative to the West End for arts and entertainment. In the 1970s, the Brutalist architecture of the Hayward Gallery and grey concrete blocks of the National Theatre made a defiantly modernist statement – and a visit here somehow all the more daunting. It was perhaps the inclusion of this section of riverbank on the Queen's Silver Jubilee Walkway in 1977 that marked the beginning of the change in the area's fortunes. The following two decades would see the inspired development of Oxo Tower Wharf and the reconstruction of the Globe Theatre. Since the turn of the new millennium, the South Bank and Bankside have hardly looked back: with the London Eye revolving, Tate Modern thriving, the Golden Jubilee and Millennium footbridges busy, visitor numbers have finally achieved critical mass. Today this leafy length of riverside thrums with crowds enjoying the views across the water to Somerset House, St Paul's and the Tower of London, and its string of popular attractions. The Royal Festival Hall and Southbank Centre are fully open again after two years of refurbishment, the concert hall's interior and river frontage both dramatically enhanced, and even the new spaces created for BFI Southbank beneath Waterloo Bridge have a certain kind of glamour.

The South Bank

Lambeth Bridge to Hungerford Bridge

Map p401

Embankment or Westminster tube/Waterloo tube/rail.
Narrowly the westernmost crossing to the South Bank, Lambeth Bridge in fact lands east of the river, opposite the Tudor gatehouse of **Lambeth Palace**; since the 12th century, this has been the official residence of the Archbishops of Canterbury. The palace is not normally open to the public, except on holidays, but the church next door, St Mary at Lambeth, serves as the **Museum of Garden History** (*see p77*).

Just south of Westminster Bridge is the charming **Florence Nightingale Museum** (*see p77*), part of St Thomas's Hospital; north of the bridge is the start of London's major riverside tourist zone. The **British Airways London Eye** (*see below*) packs in the crowds, while in the grand County Hall (once the residence of London's city government) are the **London Aquarium** and **Dalí Universe** (for both, *see p77*).

British Airways London Eye

Riverside Building, next to County Hall, Westminster Bridge Road, SE1 7PB (0870 500 0600/www.ba-londoneye.com). Westminster tube/Waterloo tube/rail.
Open *Oct-May* 10am-8pm daily. *June-Sept* 10am-9pm daily. **Admission** £14.50; £7.25-£11 reductions (only applicable Mon-Fri Sept-June); free under-5s.
Credit AmEx, MC, V. **Map** p401 M8.
Hard to believe that this giant wheel was originally intended to turn beside the Thames for only five years: it has proved so popular that no one wants it to come down, and it's now scheduled to keep spinning for another 20 years. The 443ft frame, whose 32 glass capsules each hold 25 people, commands superb views over the heart of London and beyond. A 'flight' takes half an hour, allowing plenty of time to ogle the Queen's back garden and follow the silver snake of the Thames. Some people book in advance (although they take a gamble with the weather), but it's also possible to turn up and queue for a ticket on the day. Night flights offer a more twinkly experience. There can be long queues in summer, and security is tight.

One of the two **Golden Jubilee Bridges**.

Dalí Universe

County Hall Gallery, County Hall, Riverside Building, Queen's Walk, SE1 7PB (7620 2720/www.dali universe.com). Westminster tube/Waterloo tube/rail. **Open** 9.30am-7pm Mon-Thur, Sat; 9.30am-8pm Fri. **Admission** £12; £10 reductions; £30 family. **Credit** AmEx, DC, MC, V. **Map** p401 M9.

Trademark attractions such as the Mae West Lips sofa and the *Spellbound* painting enhance the main exhibition here, curated by long-term Dalí friend Benjamin Levi. There are sculptures, watercolours (including his flamboyant tarot cards), rare etchings and lithographs, all exploring his favourite themes: Dreams and Fantasy, Femininity and Sensuality, and Religion and Mythology. Be sure to check out too the interesting series of Bible scenes by the Catholic-turned-atheist-turned-Catholic again. The gallery also shows works by new artists.

Florence Nightingale Museum

St Thomas's Hospital, 2 Lambeth Palace Road, SE1 7EW (7620 0374/www.florence-nightingale.co.uk). Westminster tube/Waterloo tube/rail. **Open** 10am-5pm Mon-Fri; 10am-4.30pm Sat, Sun. **Admission** £5.80; £4.80 reductions; £16 family; free under-5s. **Credit** AmEx, MC, V. **Map** p401 M9.

The nursing skills and campaigning zeal that made Florence Nightingale's Crimean War work the stuff of legend are honoured here with a chronological tour through her remarkable life. On returning from the battlefields of Scutari she opened the Nightingale Nursing School here in St Thomas's Hospital. Displays of period mementoes – clothing, furniture, books, letters and portraits – include her stuffed pet owl, Athena. Free children's activities take place every other weekend.

London Aquarium

County Hall, Riverside Building, Westminster Bridge Road, SE1 7PB (7967 8000/tours 7967 8007/www. londonaquarium.co.uk). Westminster tube/Waterloo tube/rail. **Open** 10am-6pm daily. **Admission** £13.25; £9.75-£11.50 reductions; £34 family; free under-3s. **Credit** MC, V. **Map** p401 M8.

The aquarium, one of Europe's largest, displays its inhabitants according to geographical origin, so there are tanks of bright fish from the coral reefs and the Indian Ocean, temperate freshwater fish from the rivers of Europe and North America, and crustaceans and rockpool plants from shorelines. Tanks are devoted to jellyfish, sharks, piranhas and octopuses, there's a touch pool with giant rays in it, and a side tank contains rather impressive robotic fish.

Museum of Garden History

Lambeth Palace Road, SE1 7LB (7401 8865/ www.museumgardenhistory.org). Lambeth North tube/Waterloo tube/rail. **Open** 10.30am-5pm Tue-Sun. **Admission** free. *Suggested donation £3; £2.50 reductions.* **Credit** AmEx, MC, V. **Map** p401 L10.

John Tradescant, intrepid plant hunter and gardener to Charles I, is buried here at the world's first museum of horticulture. In the graveyard a replica of a 17th-century knot garden has been created in his honour. Topiary and box hedging, old roses, herbaceous perennials and bulbs give all-year interest, and most plants are labelled with their country of origin and year of introduction to these islands. A magnificent stone sarcophagus in the graveyard garden contains the remains of William Bligh, captain of the mutinous HMS *Bounty*. Inside are displays of ancient tools, exhibitions about horticulture through the ages, a collection of antique gnomes, a shop and, in the north transept, a wholesome café.

Hungerford Bridge to Blackfriars Bridge

Maps p401 & p404

Embankment or Temple tube/Blackfriars or Waterloo tube/rail.

When riverside warehouses were cleared to make way for the **Southbank Centre** in the 1950s, the big concrete boxes that form the Royal Festival Hall, Purcell Room and Queen Elizabeth Hall were hailed at the time as a daring statement of modern architecture. Together with the National Theatre and the Hayward Gallery, they comprise one of the largest and most popular arts centres in the world. The centrepiece, Sir Leslie Martin's **Royal Festival Hall** (1951), has been given

Sightseeing

a £75 million overhaul: the improvement of its river frontage includes several retail outlets and restaurants but the internal alterations are most striking: the main auditorium has had its acoustics enhanced and seating refurbished; the upper floors now include a members' area and an improved Poetry Library with meeting rooms, where readings are given against the superb backdrop of the Eye and Big Ben.

The **Hayward Gallery** (*see below*) next door is a landmark of Brutalist architecture. Its new pavilion was designed in collaboration with light artist Dan Graham. The gallery's trademark neon-lit tower, designed in 1970 by Phillip Vaughan and Roger Dainton, is a kinetic light sculpture of yellow, red, green and blue tubes controlled by the direction and speed of the wind.

Tucked under Waterloo Bridge is **BFI Southbank** (*see p288*), the UK's premier arthouse cinema, run by the British Film Institute. New developments along one side have delivered new ticket desks, a stylish bar-café-restaurant, a gallery, studio cinema and the Mediatheque (*see p289* **The Film of History**). Out front is a small second-hand book market. **Waterloo Bridge** itself dates from 1942 and was designed by Sir Giles Gilbert Scott to replace an earlier structure. It was largely built by women and famously provides some of the finest views of the City, especially at dusk.

East of the bridge is Denys Lasdun's terraced **Royal National Theatre** (*see p333*), which has popular free outdoor performances in summer (*see p266*) and free chamber music within during winter. A little further along, the deco tower of the **Oxo Tower Wharf** was designed to circumvent advertising regulations for the stock cube company that used to own the building. Earmarked for demolition in the 1970s, it was saved by the Coin Street Community Builders, whose exhibition centre on the ground floor tells the full story. It now provides affordable housing, interesting designer shops and galleries, two restaurants on the second floor (our current favourite is **Bincho**; *see p196*) and a rooftop restaurant, bar and bistro with more wonderful views.

Hayward Gallery

Belvedere Road, SE1 8XX (information 7921 0813/ box office 0870 169 1000/www.hayward.org.uk). Embankment tube/Waterloo tube/rail. **Open** 10am-6pm Mon-Thur, Sun; 10am-10pm Fri, Sat. **Admission** £8; £5-£7 reductions; £4 under-16s; free under-12s. **Credit** AmEx, MC, V. **Map** p401 M8. In the Hayward's foyer extension and its mirrored, elliptical glass Waterloo Sunset Pavilion, casual visitors can watch cartoons on touch screens as they sip their Starbucks. Art-lovers dismayed by the latter nonetheless enjoy the pavilion and the excellent exhibition programme.

Around Waterloo

Map p404

Waterloo tube/rail.

At the southern end of Waterloo Bridge stands the £20million **BFI IMAX** cinema (*see p288*), plonked in the middle of the roundabout in the 1990s, making imaginative use of a desolate space that had become notorious for its grim 'cardboard city', where the homeless gathered to sleep. Further south, on the corner of Waterloo Road and the street called the Cut is the restored Victorian façade of the **Old Vic Theatre** (*see p335*). Known in Victorian times as the 'Bucket of Blood' for its penchant for melodrama, it is now in the hands of Hollywood actor Kevin Spacey. Further down the Cut is the new home of the **Young Vic** (*see p340*), a hotbed of theatrical talent, recently renovated and rebuilt. There are some good eateries down here, notably the **Anchor & Hope** gastropub and **Baltic** (for both, *see p196*). North of the Cut, off Cornwall Road, are several atmospheric terraces of mid 19th-century artisans' houses (*see p84* **Walk**).

Bankside

Map p404

Borough or Southwark tube/London Bridge tube/rail.

The area known as Bankside, south of the river between Blackfriars Bridge and London Bridge, was in Shakespeare's day the epicentre of bawdy Southwark, since it was beyond the jurisdiction of the City fathers. As well as playhouses such as the Globe and the Rose stirring up all sorts of trouble, there were the famous 'stewes' (brothels), seedy inns and other dens of iniquity. Presiding over all this depravity, the Bishops of Winchester as landlords made a tidy income from the fines they levied on 'Winchester Geese' – prostitutes.

It is no longer 'Geese' that flock to Bankside but culture vultures, drawn in massive numbers to the soaring spaces of **Tate Modern** (*see p81*), the former power station turned gallery. Spanning the river in front of the Tate, the **Millennium Bridge** was the first new Thames crossing in London since Tower Bridge opened in 1894. The bridge opened on 10 June 2000 and promptly closed again two days later because of an excessive swaying motion (the 'wobble'). After £5 million worth of modifications (engineers installed dampers under the deck) it reopened on 27 February 2002. It remains an extremely elegant structure, a 'ribbon of steel' in the words of its conceptualists, architect Sir Norman Foster and sculptor Anthony Caro. Cross it and you'll find yourself at the foot of the stairs leading up to St Paul's (*see p93*).

Tate Modern.

Continuing east, the river walk passes dinky little **Shakespeare's Globe** (*see below*) and, beyond Southwark Bridge, the **Anchor Bankside** pub (34 Park Street, 7407 1577); built in 1775 on the site of an even older inn, the Anchor has been a brothel, a chapel and a ship's chandlers. Dr Johnson is thought to have written parts of his dictionary here.

All that's left of the grand Palace of Winchester, home of successive bishops, is the rose window of the Great Hall on Dickensian-looking Clink Street, a short walk from the river, next to the site of the former Clink prison, now the **Clink Prison Museum** (*see below*). Round the corner is the entrance to **Vinopolis, City of Wine** (*see p81*), while at its eastern end Clink Street pulls up short at a dock containing a terrific replica of Drake's ship, the **Golden Hinde** (*see below*).

Bankside Gallery

48 Hopton Street, SE1 9JH (7928 7521/www. banksidegallery.com). Southwark tube/Blackfriars tube/rail. **Open** 11am-6pm daily. **Admission** free; donations appreciated. **Credit** DC, MC, V. **Map** p404 O7.
This little gallery is the home of the Royal Watercolour Society and the Royal Society of Painter-Printmakers. Annual shows include the watercolourists in March and October, the painter-printmakers in May, and wood engravers generally every other August. The shop has books and art materials, alongside prints and watercolours.

Clink Prison Museum

1 Clink Street, SE1 9DG (7403 0900/www.clink. co.uk). London Bridge tube/rail. **Open** 10am-6pm Mon-Fri; 10am-9pm Sat, Sun. **Admission** £5; £3.50 reductions; £12 family. **Credit** MC, V. **Map** p404 P8.
This small and pretty grisly exhibition looks behind the bars of the hellish prison that was owned by the Bishops of Winchester between the 12th and the 18th centuries. Thieves, prostitutes and debtors all served their sentences within its walls during an era

when boiling people in oil was thoroughly legal. On display for the 'hands-on' experience are devices of torture and the fetters whose clanking gave the prison its name.

Golden Hinde

St Mary Overie Dock, Cathedral Street, SE1 9DE (0870 011 8700/www.goldenhinde.org). Monument tube/London Bridge tube/rail. **Open** 10am-6pm daily. **Admission** £6; £4.50 reductions; £10 family. **Credit** MC, V. **Map** p404 P8.
Weekends see this reconstruction of Sir Francis Drake's little 16th-century flagship swarming with children dressed up as pirates for birthday dos. The meticulously recreated ship is fascinating to explore. Thoroughly seaworthy, this replica has even reprised Drake's circumnavigatory voyage. 'Living History Experiences' (some overnight), in which participants dress in period clothes, eat Tudor fare and learn the skills of the Elizabethan seafarer, are a huge hit with the young, as are the pirate parties (phone for prices and book well in advance).

Rose Theatre

56 Park Street, SE1 9AR (7593 0026/www.rose theatre.org.uk). London Bridge tube/rail. **Open** *May-Sept* by appointment only. **Credit** AmEx, MC, V. **Map** p404 P8.
Built by Philip Henslowe and operational from 1587 until 1606, the Rose was the first playhouse to be erected at Bankside. Funds are currently being sought for new excavation work in search of as yet uncovered portions of the old theatre, which could restore its original ground plan. In the meantime, it is only accessible as part of the guided tour of Shakespeare's Globe (*see below*).

Shakespeare's Globe

21 New Globe Walk, SE1 9DT (7902 1400/box office 7401 9919/www.shakespeares-globe.org). Mansion House or Southwark tube/London Bridge tube/rail. **Open** *Exhibition & tours* 10am-5pm daily. *Tours* every 15 mins. **Admission** £9; £6.50-£7.50 reductions; £20 family. **Credit** AmEx, MC, V. **Map** p404 O7.

The original Globe Theatre, where many of William Shakespeare's plays were first staged and which he co-owned, burned down in 1613 during a performance of *Henry VIII*. Nearly 400 years later, it was rebuilt not far from its original site under the auspices of actor Sam Wanamaker (who, sadly, didn't live to see it up and running), using construction methods and materials as close to the originals as possible. You can tour the theatre outside the May to September performance season; when the theatre's historically authentic (and frequently very good) performances are staged, the tour is around the Rose Theatre site instead (*see p80*). In the UnderGlobe beneath the theatre is a fine exhibition on the history of the reconstruction, Bankside and its Elizabethan theatres, and the London of Shakespeare; it's open year-round. A tour and exhibition visit lasts around 90 minutes.

Tate Modern

Bankside, SE1 9TG (7401 5120/7887 8888/www. tate.org.uk). Blackfriars tube/rail. **Open** 10am-6pm Mon-Thur, Sun; 10am-10pm Fri, Sat. *Tours* 11am, noon, 2pm, 3pm daily. **Admission** free. *Temporary exhibitions* prices vary. **Map** p404 O7.

A powerhouse of modern art, Tate Modern is awe inspiring even before you step inside thanks to its industrial architecture. It was built as Bankside Power Station and designed by Sir Giles Gilbert Scott, architect of Battersea Power Station (*see p179*) and the designer of the famous British red telephone box. Bankside was shut down in 1981 and opened as an art museum in 2000. The original cavernous turbine hall is used to jaw-dropping effect as the home of large-scale, temporary installations (the latest, a huge crack in the floor by Doris Salcedo, will be removed in April 2008). The permanent collection draws from the Tate organisation's deep reservoir of modern art (international works from 1900 and on) and features heavy-hitters such as Matisse, Rothko, Giacometti and Pollock. In 2006, the galleries were completely rehung, with the artworks grouped according to movement (Surrealism, Minimalism, Post-war abstraction) rather than theme.

If you don't know where to start, take one of the guided tours (ask at the information desk). There are also various tour packages, some combined with Shakespeare's Globe (*see p80*) and others including lunch or dinner (the Level 2 café is recommended; *see p275*). The Tate-to-Tate boat service – decor courtesy of Damien Hirst, bar on board – links with Tate Britain (*see p141*) and runs every 20 minutes, stopping along the way at the Eye (*see p76*). Tickets are available from ticket desks at the Tates, on board, online or by phone (7887 8888, £4.30 adult).

Vinopolis, City of Wine

1 Bank End, SE1 9BU (0870 241 4040/www. vinopolis.co.uk). London Bridge tube/rail. **Open** *Jan-Nov* noon-9pm Mon, Fri, Sat; noon-6pm Tue-Thur, Sun. *Dec* noon-6pm daily. Last entry 2hrs before closing. **Admission** £17.50-£32.50; free under-16s. **Credit** MC, V. **Map** p404 P8.

This glossy attraction is more of an introduction to wine-tasting than a resource for cognoscenti, but you do need to have some interest to get a kick out it. Participants are furnished with a wine glass and an audio guide. Exhibits are set out by country, with five opportunities to taste wine or champagne from different regions. Gin crashes the party courtesy of a Bombay Sapphire cocktail, and a whisky-tasting area and a microbrewery (the Brew Wharf) were recently added. Highlights include a virtual voyage through Chianti on a Vespa and a virtual flight to the wine-producing regions of Australia. The complex also has a tourist information centre.

Borough

Map p405

Borough or Southwark tube/London Bridge tube/rail.

At Clink Street the riverside route cuts inland, skirting the edge of the district of Borough. The landmark here is the Anglican **Southwark Cathedral** (*see p83*), formerly St Saviour's and before that the monastic church of St Mary Overie. Shakespeare's brother Edmund was buried in the graveyard here and there's a monument to the playwright inside. Just south of the cathedral is **Borough Market**, a busy food market dating back to the 13th century. It's wholesale only for most of the week but on Thursdays, Fridays and Saturdays it hosts London's best food market (*see p255*). There are several excellent eating options under and around its brick arches including **Tapas Brindisa** (*see p196*), **fish!** (7407 3803, www. fishdiner.co.uk) and **Roast** (*see p195*). There are also a handful of fine pubs including the popular **Market Porter** (9 Stoney Street, 7407 2495) and the **Globe** (8 Bedale Street, 7407 0043), which features heavily in the Bridget Jones films – her bachelorette pad is above the pub, a location likely to be removed by the impending expansion of the railway viaduct. Not far away, at 77 Borough High Street, is the **George** (7407 2056), London's last surviving galleried coaching inn, boasting Dickens as a former regular.

The area around Borough High Street was lively, especially until 1750, because nearby London Bridge was the only dry crossing point on the river below Kingston Bridge, which lies far to the west of the city. There are a couple of small, quirky museums in the area, including the **Bramah Museum of Tea & Coffee** (*see p83*) and the **London Fire Brigade Museum** (94A Southwark Bridge Road, 7587 2894, www. london-fire.gov.uk), which traces the history of firefighting in the capital from the Great Fire in 1666 to the present day in an old-fashioned way. Entry to the museum is only possible by guided tour, booked in advance (10.30am, 2pm Mon-Fri; £3, £2 reductions).

Sightseeing

Around London Bridge Station tourist attractions clamour for attention. One of the grisliest, with its displays of body parts and surgical implements, is the **Old Operating Theatre, Museum & Herb Garret**, although it's the considerably less scary **London Dungeon** (for both, *see below*) that draws the biggest queues at weekends. Competing with the blood-curdling shrieks emanating from its entrance are the dulcet tones of Vera Lynn, broadcast in an attempt to lure visitors into **Winston Churchill's Britain at War Experience** (*see below*).

Old Operating Theatre, Museum & Herb Garret.

Bramah Museum of Tea & Coffee

40 Southwark Street, SE1 1UN (7403 5650/www. bramahmuseum.co.uk). London Bridge tube/rail. **Open** 10am-6pm daily. **Admission** £4; £3.50 reductions; £10 family. **Credit** AmEx, DC, MC, V. **Map** p404 P8.

As a nation we get through 100,000 tons of teabags a year, a fact that would appal the founder of this delightful museum, former tea-taster Edward Bramah. His collection displays pots, caddies and ancient coffee makers. They work as visual aids to the role they have played in the history of different nations. The exhibition doesn't take long to work round, but it's tempting to linger in the café where a pianist usually tinkles away in the early afternoon. Pre-book for afternoon cream teas (£7).

London Dungeon

28-34 Tooley Street, SE1 2SZ (7403 7221/www. thedungeons.com). London Bridge tube/rail. **Open** *Sept-June* 10.30am-5.30pm daily. *July, Aug* 9.30am-7.30pm daily. **Admission** £19.95; £13.95-£14.95 reductions. **Credit** AmEx, MC, V. **Map** p405 Q8.

A jokey celebration of torture, death and disease under the Victorian railway arches of London Bridge. Visitors are led through a dry-ice fog past gravestones and hideously rotting corpses to experience nasty symptoms from the Great Plague exhibition: an actor-led medley of corpses, boils, projectile vomiting, worm-filled skulls and scuttling rats. Other OTT revisions of horrible London history include the Great Fire and the Judgement Day Barge, where visitors play the prisoners (death sentence guaranteed).

Old Operating Theatre, Museum & Herb Garret

9A St Thomas's Street, SE1 9RY (7188 2679/ www.thegarret.org.uk). London Bridge tube/rail. **Open** 10.30am-5pm Mon-Wed, Fri-Sun; 10.30am-7pm Thur. **Admission** £5.25; £3-£4.25 reductions; £12.95 family; free under-6s. **No credit cards**. **Map** p405 Q8.

The tower that houses this salutary revelation of antique surgical practice used to be part of the chapel of St Thomas's Hospital. When the hospital was moved to Lambeth in the 1860s most of the buildings were torn down to make way for London Bridge Station and it was not until 1956 that this atmospheric old garret was discovered in the loft of the church. Visitors enter via a vertiginous wooden spiral staircase to view the medicinal herbs on display. Further in is the centrepiece of the museum: a pre-anaesthetic Victorian operating theatre dating from 1822, with tiered viewing seats for students. Just as disturbing are the displays of operating equipment that look like torture implements. Other cases hold strangulated hernias, leech jars and amputation knives.

Southwark Cathedral

London Bridge, SE1 9DA (7367 6700/tours 7367 6734/www.dswark.org/cathedral). London Bridge tube/rail. **Open** 8am-6pm daily (closing times vary on religious holidays). *Services* 8am, 8.15am, 12.30pm, 12.45pm, 5.30pm Mon-Fri; 9am, 9.15am, 4pm Sat; 8.45am, 9am, 11am, 3pm, 6.30pm Sun. *Choral Evensong* 5.30pm Tue (boys & men), Fri (men only); 5.30pm Mon, Thur (girls). **Admission** (incl audio tour) £2.50. **Credit** AmEx, MC, V. **Map** p404 P8.

The oldest bits of this building, one of the few places south of the river that Dickens had a good word for, date back more than 800 years. The retro-choir was where the trials of several Protestant martyrs took place during the reign of Mary Tudor. After the Reformation, the church fell into disrepair, and used as a bakery and part as a pigsty; in 1905 it became a cathedral. An interactive museum called the Long View of London, a refectory and a lovely garden are some of the millennial improvements. There are memorials to Shakespeare, John Harvard (benefactor of the US university) and Sam Wanamaker (the force behind Shakespeare's Globe), as well as stained-glass windows with images of Chaucer, who set his pilgrims off to Canterbury from Borough High Street.

Sightseeing

Walk Under the arches

Start London Eye (Westminster or Waterloo tube). **Finish** Tower Bridge (London Bridge tube). **Time** 1hr 15 mins.

The riverside walk from the London Eye to Tower Bridge via Tate Modern is a big hit with visitors – crowds of 'em. This alternative route links those three iconic sights in about the same distance, but drops the crowds and explores the less familiar and more lived-in hinterland of the South Bank. Begin at the **London Eye** by turning your back on the thing and walking away – at the top of Chicheley Street there's a great photo-op for a shot of your loved one with the spokes of the big wheel radiating from their head.

Cross York Road and head down Leake Street, with a good view of the futuristic former Eurostar terminal, looking for a new job now that Paris trains arrive at St Pancras. The design made Nicholas Grimshaw's name in 1993. Leake Street enters an old white-tiled brick tunnel, aka bridge number 1/A1, supporting the entire width of Waterloo, the largest train station in the UK. And the tunnel proves a time warp as it emerges on bustling **Lower Marsh**, a street market since Victorian times and still about as 'local' as central London gets. As well as stalls selling fruit and veg, clothes and 'fancy goods', an intriguing array of independent shops and cafés are here: second-hand scooters and first-rate

coffee at Scooterworks; vintage threads at What the Butler Saw and Radio Days; and rare classical music at Gramex.

Stroll down Lower Marsh and you'll arrive at Waterloo Road, where the grand **Old Vic** theatre (*see p335*), founded in 1818 and the first home (from 1963-76) of the National Theatre under Larry Olivier, stands at the top of the Cut. Next door is the National Theatre Studio, the 'experimental engine house' of the National Theatre, a role that was first played by the **Young Vic** (*see p340*), further along the Cut on the left. Founded here in 1970, this vibrant theatre space has just been given a new lease of life. Palestra, the office block at the end of the Cut, was designed by Will Alsop and finished in 2006.

Just before the Young Vic, a left turn down tiny Windmill Walk leads under a railway arch into a small remnant of 19th-century London. Brad Street has a charming chimneyscape. Follow Windmill Walk to find the **King's Arms** (*see p221*). The pub fronts on to Roupell Street, an almost unaltered terrace of Victorian artisans' cottages. It's worth nipping a short way down Theed Street to catch the view down Whittlesey Street towards the spire of St John's Church. At the end of Roupell Street, cross into Meymott Street and turn left down Colombo Street. The old **Rose & Crown Pub** (no.47, 7928 4285) has a beer

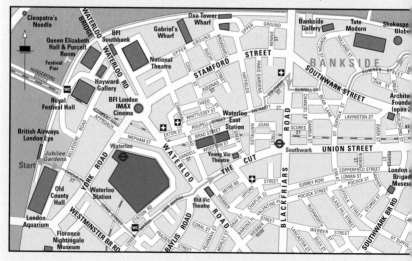

Sightseeing

garden on Paris Garden, once famous for bear baiting. At the end of Colombo Street, cross the busy Blackfriars Road into Burrell Street, passing through Railway Arch no.406, the number picked out in fairy lights. Just along Southwark Street on the right is **Kirkaldy's Testing & Experimenting Works** with the motto 'Facts not Opinions' above the front door. In 1874 David Kirkaldy installed his 'big testing machine' here (it can still be seen on the first Sunday of each month) to measure load-bearing in construction materials. Just opposite, Sumner Street leads left to the back of **Tate Modern** (see p81) passing the new Blue Fin building (85 Southwark Street) designed by Allies & Morrison whose offices are opposite, above the stylish café **Table** (see p195).

Fork left into Park Street to pass behind Shakespeare's Globe (see p337) and under Southwark Bridge Road to the **original site** of the Globe Theatre, excavated in 1989. Bricks in a courtyard mark out the foundations. Stick with the Park Street as it turns sharp right – a plaque records that here 'the Austrian Butcher' General Haynau, brutal suppressor of the Hungarian revolutionaries of 1848, was recognised and attacked by two draymen (brewery carters) – to curve round left into **Borough Market** (see p81) for a fine view of the market and Southwark Cathedral. After making your way through the market, a short detour down Southwark Street leads to the **Hop Exchange**, a great wrought-iron-galleried space where the produce of the Kentish hop fields (hence the county's fine white horse insignia on the balustrades) was once sold to supply London's breweries. Across the way on Borough High Street can be found the **George Inn** (see p81), a galleried coaching inn of the type that inspired the design of theatres like the Globe. Almost as ancient is **King's Head Yard**, a couple of doors up towards London Bridge on the right. Walk down here to find your way through King's College London and the old arcaded quads of Guy's Hospital to emerge on St Thomas Street near the **Old Operating Theatre & Herb Garret** (see p83). Turn right and then head left through the grim tunnel of Stainer Street to Tooley Street, where there's a faintly surreal glimpse of HMS *Belfast* down Battle Bridge Lane on the left, before you reach **More London Riverside**. This generic downtown development has been very successful, including as it does City Hall and a trickle-down 'desire line' path that affords views of Tower Bridge, but it's also the kind of soulless cityscape into which much of London is being transformed. In summer console yourself with entertaining outdoor theatre in the Scoop – before following the riverbank to **Tower Bridge**.

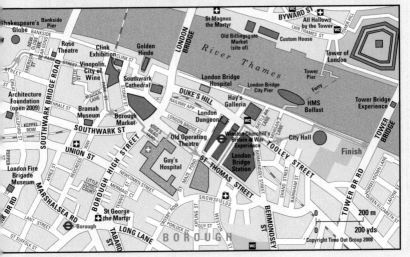

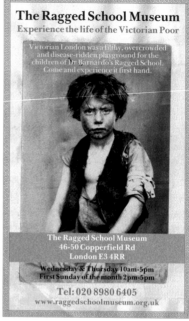

Winston Churchill's Britain at War Experience

64-66 Tooley Street, SE1 2TF (7403 3171/www. britainatwar.co.uk). London Bridge tube/rail. **Open** *Apr-Sept* 10am-6pm daily. *Oct-Mar* 10am-5pm daily. **Admission** £9.95; £4.85-£5.75 reductions; £25 family; free under-5s. **Credit** AmEx, MC, V. **Map** p405 Q8.

This old-fashioned exhibition recalls the privations endured by the British during World War II. Visitors descend from street level in an ancient lift to a reconstructed tube station shelter that doubles as a movie theatre showing documentaries from the period. The experience continues with displays about London during the Blitz, including real bombs, rare documents, photos and reconstructed shopfronts. The displays on rationing, food production and Land Girls are fascinating, and the set-piece walk-through bombsite (you enter just after a bomb has dropped on the street) is quite disturbing.

London Bridge to Tower Bridge

Map p405

Bermondsey tube/London Bridge tube/rail.

Across Tooley Street from the pleasures of the London Dungeon and Britain at War Experience stands **Hay's Galleria**, once an enclosed dock, now dominated by a peculiar kinetic sculpture called *The Navigators*. Here the twinkling **Christmas Shop** (7378 1998, www.thechristmasshop.co. uk) stays doggedly festive, and half-hearted craft stalls await custom. Exiting on the riverside, you can walk east past the great grey hulk of **HMS Belfast** (*see below*) to Tower Bridge.

Beyond the battleship you pass the pristine environs of **City Hall**, the home of the current London government. Designed by Sir Norman Foster, the eco-friendly rotund glass structure leans squiffily away from the river (to prevent it casting shade on the walkers below – how thoughtful). The building has an exhibition blowing the Mayor's trumpet on the ground floor, a café on the lower ground floor and a pleasant 'amphitheatre' called the Scoop, used for lunch breaks, sunbathing and a range of outdoor events in summer.

Near Tower Bridge, a noticeboard announces when the bridge is next due to open (which it does about 900 times a year for tall ships to pass through). The bridge is one of the lowest crossings over the Thames – hence twin lifting sections (bascules) were designed by architect Horace Jones and engineer John Wolfe Barry. Their original steam-driven hydraulic machinery can still be seen at the **Tower Bridge Exhibition** (*see p101*).

Further east, the former warehouses of Butler's Wharf are now mainly about upmarket riverside dining. Shad Thames is the main thoroughfare behind the wharves, where in days long gone dockworkers unloaded tea, coffee and spices into huge warehouses; those warehouses are now divided into pricey apartments and offices, and house the **Design Museum** (*see below*).

Up past the Design Museum across Jamaica Road and down Tanner Street is historic **Bermondsey Street**, site of the **London Fashion & Textile Museum** (83 Bermondsey Street, 7407 8664, www.ftmlondon.org), founded by Zandra Rhodes and recently reopened as part of the Newham College of Further Education. Further south, around Bermondsey Square (where Bermondsey Street meets Tower Bridge Road), it's all Starbucks and delis, new cobbles and hanging baskets, although eel and pie shop **M Manze** (*see p195*) has been here since 1902. The Friday **antiques market** (4am-2pm) is great for browsing, but will probably have been picked clean of bargains by the dealers before you've had time for breakfast.

Design Museum

Shad Thames, SE1 2YD (7403 6933/www.design museum.org). Tower Hill tube/London Bridge tube/ rail. **Open** 10am-5.45pm daily. **Admission** £7; £4 reductions; free under-12s. **Credit** AmEx, MC, V. **Map** p405 S9.

Exhibitions in this white 1930s-style building (a former warehouse) focus on modern and contemporary design. The Tank is a diminutive outdoor gallery of constantly changing installations by leading contemporary designers, while the smart Blueprint Café has a balcony overlooking the Thames. A major touring exhibition on the architect Richard Rogers will open here in April 2008, fresh from celebrating the 30th anniversary of one of his landmark projects, the Pompidou Centre in Paris.

HMS Belfast

Morgan's Lane, Tooley Street, SE1 2JH (7940 6300/ www.iwm.org.uk). London Bridge tube/rail. **Open** *Mar-Oct* 10am-6pm daily. *Nov-Feb* 10am-5pm daily. **Admission** £9.95; £5.30-£6.15 reductions; free under-16s (must be accompanied by an adult). **Credit** MC, V. **Map** p405 R8.

This 11,500-ton battlecruiser, the last surviving big gun World War II ship in Europe, is a floating branch of the Imperial War Museum. It makes an unlikely playground for children, who tear easily around its cramped complex of nine decks, boiler, engine rooms and gun turrets. The *Belfast* was built in 1938, provided cover for convoys to Russia and was instrumental in the Normandy Landings. She also supported UN forces in Korea before being decommissioned in 1965. Now the ship's guns are trained, over a distance of 12.5 miles – in fun, not in anger – on the London Gateway services of the M1.

Sightseeing

The City

Big bucks and billionaires, not bowlers and brollies.

The beating financial heart of the capital – and of the country – the City of London sees a million visitors every day, but most are bankers, brokers, lawyers and traders. Any international bank worth the name has an office somewhere inside the Square Mile, the precinct of land contained by the old Roman walls of London. During the Victorian era, the bankers of the City presided over the largest economy on earth. The streets of the City are still flush with cash, though there aren't quite as many oyster bars as there were during the hedonistic years of the 1980s. Apart from the two big crowd-pullers – St Paul's and the Tower of London – the City might not immediately appear to have much to offer casual visitors, but dive into the throng of office workers and you'll find that the streets are paved with historical treasures. Dotted here and there among the office blocks are Roman ruins, medieval monuments, churches constructed by Wren and Hawksmoor and settings from Dickens, Shakespeare and even Dan Brown.

From the start London has been divided in two, with Westminster the centre of politics and the City the capital of commerce. Many of the City's administrative affairs are still run on a feudal basis, under the auspices of the arcane borough council once known as the Corporation of London. Now rebranded the City of London, it is the richest local authority in Britain. The sheer wealth of this part of London is hard for ordinary mortals to conceive – the City was able to bounce back after losing half its population to the Black Death and half its buildings first to the Great Fire and much later to Nazi bombing during the Blitz. To really understand the City you need to visit on a weekday when the great economic machine is running at full tilt; at weekends, almost everything closes and the

streets fall eerily quiet. During the annual Open House in September (see p270), you can often get inside some of the City's iconic buildings, including 30 St Mary Axe, the Lloyd's building, Mansion House and the Bank of England.

City of London Information Centre

St Paul's Churchyard, EC4M 8BX (7332 1456/ *www.cityoflondon.gov.uk*). St Paul's tube. **Open** 9.30am-5.30pm Mon-Fri. **No credit cards.** Map p404 O6.
Run by the City of London, the striking, brand-new office on the Thames side of St Paul's has information and brochures on sights, events, walks and talks in the Square Mile.

Fleet Street

Map p404

Temple tube/Blackfriars tube/rail.
Without Fleet Street, the daily newspaper might never have been invented. Marking the route of the vanished River Fleet, which still gurgles somewhere below street level, Fleet Street was a major artery for the delivery of goods into the City, including the first printing press, which was installed behind **St Bride's Church** (see p90) in 1500 by William Caxton's assistant, Wynkyn de Worde, who also set up a bookstall in the churchyard of St Paul's. In 1702, London's first daily newspaper, the *Daily Courant*, rolled off the presses and, in 1712, Fleet Street saw the first of many libel cases when the *Courant* leaked the details of a private parliamentary debate. By the end of World War II, half a dozen newspaper offices were churning out scoops and scandals between the Strand and Farringdon Road. Most of the newspapers moved away after Rupert Murdoch won his war with the print unions in the 1980s; the last of the news agencies, Reuters, finally followed suit in 2005. Today the only periodical published on Fleet Street is a comic – the much-loved *Beano*. You can see some interesting relics from the media days, though, including the Portland-stone **Reuters building** (no.85), the Egyptian-influenced **Daily Telegraph building** (no.135) and the sleek, black **Daily Express building** (nos.121-128), designed by Owen Williams in the 1930s and arguably the only art deco building of note in London (stand across the road for a glimpse into the magnificent chrome-lined lobby).

Tucked away on an alley behind St Bride's Church is the **St Bride Foundation Institute** (7353 3331, www.stbridefoundation.org) with a library (noon-5.30pm Tue, Thur; noon-9pm Wed) dedicated to printing and typography. Back on Fleet Street is **St Dunstan-in-the-West** (7405 1929, www.stdunstaninthewest.org; free tours 11am-3pm Tue), where the poet John Donne was rector in the 17th century. The church was rebuilt in the 1830s, but the eye-catching clock with chimes beaten by clockwork giants dates to 1671. It is now designated the Diocese of London's Church for Europe.

Next door, no.186 is the house where Sweeney Todd, the 'demon barber of Fleet Street', allegedly murdered his customers before selling their bodies to a local pie shop. The legend itself is in fact a porky pie – Todd was invented by the editors of a Victorian penny

dreadful in 1846 and propelled to fame by a stage play and Stephen Sondheim musical.

Opposite St Dunstan is **Prince Henry's Room** (no.17, 7936 4004). Housed in one of the few buildings still standing from before the Great Fire, the museum was closed for refurbishment as we went to press – but its display on the life and times of London's great diarist and chronicler of the fire, Samuel Pepys (1633-1703), should reopen in late 2008.

Fleet Street has always been known for its alehouses. Half the newspaper editorials in London were once composed over liquid lunches at pubs like the Old Bell Tavern (no.95, 7583 0216) and the Punch Tavern (no.99, 7353 6658), where the satirical magazine *Punch* was launched in 1841; both pubs are closed at weekends. On the other side of the road, **Ye Olde Cheshire Cheese** (no.145, 7353 6170)

Sightseeing

An aerial view of the **City of London**.

was a favourite watering hole of Dickens, Yeats and Dr Samuel Johnson, who lived around the corner at 17 Gough Square (*see below*). At no.66, the **Tipperary** (7583 6470) is the oldest Irish pub outside Ireland – it opened in the 1700s and sold the first pint of Guinness on the British mainland shortly after.

Dr Johnson's House

17 Gough Square, off Fleet Street, EC4A 3DE (7353 3745/www.drjohnsonshouse.org). Chancery Lane or Temple tube/Blackfriars tube/rail. **Open** *May-Sept* 11am-5.30pm Mon-Sat. *Oct-Apr* 11am-5pm Mon-Sat. *Tours* by arrangement, groups of 10 or more only. **Admission** £4.50; £1.50-£3.50 reductions; £10 family; free under-5s. *Tours* free. **No credit cards.** **Map** p404 N6.

Famed as the author of one of the first – and surely the most significant – dictionary of the English language, Dr Samuel Johnson (1709-84) also wrote poems, a novel and one of the earliest travelogues, an acerbic account of a tour of the Western Isles with James Boswell. You can tour the stately Georgian townhouse off Fleet Street where Johnson came up with his inspired definitions – 'to make dictionaries is dull work,' was his definition of the word 'dull'.

St Bride's Church

Fleet Street, EC4Y 8AU (7427 0133/www.stbrides. com). Temple tube/Blackfriars tube/rail. **Open** 8am-6pm Mon-Fri; 11am-3pm Sat; 10am-1pm, 5-7.30pm Sun. Times vary Mon-Sat, so phone ahead to check. **Admission** free. **Map** p404 N6.

Hidden away down an alley south of Fleet Street, St Bride's is still popularly known as the journalists' church. In the north aisle is a shrine dedicated to journos killed in action. Down in the crypt a very fine museum displays a number of fragments of the churches that have existed on this site since the sixth century. According to local legend, the Wren-designed spire was the inspiration behind the traditional tiered wedding cake.

The Temple

Map p404 N5

Temple tube/Blackfriars tube/rail.

At its western end, Fleet Street becomes the Strand at **Temple Bar**, the City's ancient western boundary and once the site of Wren's great gateway, now relocated beside St Paul's (*see p93*). This area has long been linked to the law and here on the edge of Holborn (*see p102*) stand the splendid neo-Gothic **Royal Courts of Justice** (7947 6000, www.hmcourts-service.gov.uk). Two of the highest civil courts in the land sit here, the High Court and Appeals Court – justice at its most bewigged and ermine-robed – and visitors are welcome to observe the process of law in any of the 88 courtrooms. Across the road are the interconnected courtyards of the **Middle**

Temple (7427 4800, www.middletemple.org.uk) and **Inner Temple** (7797 8183, www.inner temple.org.uk), two of the Inns of Court that provided training and lodging for London's medieval lawyers. Access is usually reserved for lawyers and barristers, but tours of the Inner Temple can be arranged for £10 per person (minimum five people, call 7797 8241 to book).

The site was formerly the headquarters of the Knights Templar, an order of warrior monks founded in the 12th century to protect pilgrims travelling to the Holy Land. The Templars built the original **Temple Church** (*see below*) in 1185, but they fell foul of Catholic orthodoxy during the Crusades and the order was disbanded for heresy. Dan Brown used the Temple Church as a setting for his bestselling conspiracy novel *The Da Vinci Code* (2003). Robin Griffith-Jones, the master of Temple Church, has produced a robust response to his claims at www.beliefnet.com/templechurch.

Temple Church

King's Bench Walk, EC4Y 7BB (7353 8559/ www.templechurch.com). Temple tube. **Open** 2-4pm Wed; 11am-12.30pm, 1-4pm Thur, Fri; 11am-12.30pm Sat; 12.30-3.30pm Sun. *Services* 8.30am, 11.15am Sun; 1.15pm Thur. *Organ recital* Wed (phone for details). Opening times vary, especially at weekends; phone or check website for details. **Admission** free. **Map** p404 N6.

Inspired by Jerusalem's Church of the Holy Sepulchre, the Temple Church was the private chapel of the mystical Knights Templar. The rounded apse contains the worn gravestones of several Crusader knights, but the church was refurbished by Wren and the Victorians, and few original features survived the bombing of the Blitz. These days most visitors are avid *Da Vinci Code* fans.

St Paul's & around

Map p404 O6

St Paul's tube.

After Big Ben, the towering dome of **St Paul's Cathedral** (*see p93*) is probably the definitive symbol of London, an architectural two fingers up to the Great Fire and later, in a famous photograph, to the German bombers that tried to destroy the city. The first cathedral to St Paul was built on the Ludgate Hill site in 604, but it fell to Viking marauders and its Norman replacement – a magnificent Gothic structure with a 490-foot spire – burned to the ground in the Great Fire. The new St Paul's was commissioned from Sir Christopher Wren in 1673 as the centrepiece of London's resurgence from the ashes. Modern buildings now encroach on St Paul's from all sides but the open-air gallery at the top of the dome still provides the finest viewpoint in the City.

St Paul's Cathedral. *See p93.*

Immediately north of the cathedral is the redeveloped **Paternoster Square**, a modern plaza incorporating striking carved stone heads by the sculptor Emily Young and a sundial that only very rarely tells the time. The name harks back to the days when priests from St Paul's walked the streets chanting the Lord's Prayer (the opening line being *Pater noster*, 'Our Father'). Also of interest here is Wren's statue-covered **Temple Bar**, which previously stood at the intersection of Fleet Street and the Strand, marking the boundary between the City of London and neighbouring Westminster. During the Middle Ages, the monarch was only allowed to pass through the Temple Bar into the City with the approval of the Lord Mayor of London. The archway was dismantled as part of a Victorian road-widening programme in 1878 and became a garden ornament for a country estate in Hertfordshire, before being installed in its current location in 2004 after a public campaign.

Glamour Grandeur
Sleaze Disease

Discover a great city in the making

FREE ENTRY

150 London Wall, EC2Y 5HN
⊖ St Paul's, Barbican
www.museumoflondon.org.uk

MUSEUM OF LONDON

SPICES SLAVERY
SKYSCRAPERS

MUSEUM IN DOCKLANDS

How the world came to the East End

KIDS GO FREE

⊖ Canary Wharf   ⊖ West India Quay

West India Quay, London E14 4AL

www.museumindocklands.org.uk

Registered charity number: 1060415

South of St Paul's, a cascade of steps runs down to the **Millennium Bridge**, which spans the river to **Tate Modern** (see p81). The stairs take you close to the 17th-century **College of Arms** (see below), the official seat of heraldry in Great Britain. East of the cathedral is narrow Bow Lane, lined with bijou shops, bistros and champagne bars. The lane is bookended by **St Mary-le-Bow** (7248 5139, www.stmaryle bow.co.uk, 7am-6pm Tue-Thur, 7am-4pm Fri), whose peals once defined anyone born within earshot as a true Cockney, and **St Mary Aldermary** (7248 4906, www.stmaryalder mary.co.uk, 11am-3pm Mon, Wed, Thur), with its pin-straight spire, designed by Wren's office.

There are more Wren creations south of St Paul's (St James Garlickhythe, St Nicholas Cole Abbey, St Mary Somerset, St Benet and St Andrew-by-the-Wardrobe) and one to the west (St Martin-within-Ludgate). For a mapped route around them, see p98 **Walk**. North-west of the cathedral is the **Old Bailey** (see below).

Old Bailey (Central Criminal Court)

Corner of Newgate Street & Old Bailey, EC4M 7EH (7248 3277). St Paul's tube. **Open** *Public gallery* 10am-1pm, 2-4.30pm Mon-Fri. **Admission** free. No under-14s; 14-16s only if accompanied by adults. **Map** p404 O6.

A gilded statue of blind (meaning impartial) justice stands atop London's most famous criminal court. Although the current building was only completed in 1907, the site has hosted some of the most controversial trials in British history, including that of Oscar Wilde. More recently, the Kray brothers and IRA bombers have been put in the dock here. The public is welcome to attend trials but bags, cameras, dictaphones, mobile phones and food are prohibited (and no storage facilities are provided).

College of Arms

130 Queen Victoria Street, EC4V 4BT (7248 2762/www.college-of-arms.gov.uk). St Paul's tube/ Blackfriars tube/rail. **Open** 10am-4pm Mon-Fri. *Tours* by arrangement. **Admission** free. **No credit cards. Map** p404 O7.

Originally created to identify competing knights at medieval jousting tournaments, coats of arms soon became an integral part of family identity for the landed gentry of Britain. Visitors interested in track- ing down their family history can arrange tours.

St Paul's Cathedral

Ludgate Hill, EC4M 8AD (7236 4128/www.st pauls.co.uk). St Paul's tube. **Open** 8.30am-4pm Mon-Sat. *Galleries, crypt & ambulatory* 9.30am- 4pm Mon-Sat. Special events may cause closure; check before visiting. *Tours of cathedral & crypt* 11am, 11.30am, 1.30pm, 2pm Mon-Sat. **Admission** *Cathedral, crypt & gallery* £9.50; £3.50-£8.50 reductions; £22.50 family; free under-6s. *Tours* £3; £1-£2.50 reductions. **Credit** (shop) AmEx, MC, V. **Map** p404 O6.

The passing of three centuries has done nothing to diminish the magnificence of London's most famous cathedral. In the last decade, restoration has stripped most of the Victorian grime from the walls and the extravagant main façade looks as brilliant today as it must have when first unveiled in 1708. If you look south from St Paul's, you can see the source of the soot that once blackened the gleaming Portland stone – the coal-fired power station that now hous- es Tate Modern (see p81). Ironically, the construc- tion of St Paul's was originally funded by a tax on coal coming into the Port of London.

Sir Christopher Wren had to fight to get his plans for this epic cathedral past the authorities – many politicians thought it too large and expensive. His first two designs were rejected and he was forced to keep the construction of his third design a secret in order to create the massive dome for which St Paul's is now famous. In fact, there are three domes – the inner and outer domes are separated by a hidden brick dome that supports the entire structure (believed to weigh 64,000 tons).

Most visitors walk around in awe at the vast open spaces and grandiose memorials to national heroes such as Nelson, Wellington, Lawrence of Arabia and General Gordon of Khartoum. You can also look down on it all from the Whispering Gallery inside the dome, reached by 259 steps from the main hall (the acoustics here are so good that a whisper can be bounced clearly to the other side of the dome). Steps continue to the outdoor Golden Gallery (530 steps), which offers giddying views over London – come here to orient yourself before setting off in search of other monuments in the City.

Before leaving St Paul's, head down to the maze- like crypt, which contains a shop and café and memorials to such dignitaries as Alexander Fleming, William Blake and Florence Nightingale, plus the small, plain tombstone of Christopher Wren himself, inscribed with the epitaph, 'Reader, if you seek a monument, look around you'. As well as tours of the main cathedral and self-guided audio tours (£3.50, £3 reductions), you can join special tours of the Triforium – visiting the library and Wren's 'Great Model' – at 11.30am and 2pm on Monday and Tuesday and at 2pm on Friday (pre-book on 7246 8357, £14.50 including admission). *Photos p91.*

North to Smithfield

Maps p402 O5 & p404 O5

Barbican or St Paul's tube.
North of St Paul's on Foster Lane is **St Vedast-alias-Foster** (7606 3998, www. vedast.net, 8am-6pm Mon-Fri), another finely proportioned Wren church, restored after World War II using spare trim from other churches in the area. Nearby, off Aldersgate Street, peaceful, fern-filled **Postman's Park** contains the Watts Memorial to Heroic Sacrifice: a wall of Victorian ceramic plaques, each of

which commemorates an heroic but fatal act of bravery, such as the sad story of Sarah Smith, a pantomime artiste at the Prince's Theatre, who received 'terrible injuries when attempting in her inflammable dress to extinguish the flames which had engulfed her companion (1863)'.

Further west on Little Britain (named after the Duke of Brittany, not the TV show) is St Bartholomew-the-Great (see below) founded along with St Bartholomew's Hospital in the 12th century. Popularly known as St Bart's, the hospital treated air-raid casualties throughout World War II – shrapnel damage from German bombs is still clearly visible on the outside walls. Scottish nationalists now come here to lay flowers at the monument to William Wallace, who was executed in front of the church on the orders of Edward I in 1305. Just beyond St Bart's is bustling Smithfield Market (see p104).

St Bartholomew-the-Great

West Smithfield, EC1A 9DS (7606 5171/www.greatstbarts.com). Barbican tube/Farringdon tube/rail. **Open** 8.30am-5pm Mon-Fri (until 4pm Nov-Feb); 10.30am-4pm Sat; 2.30-6.30pm Sun. *Services* 9am, 11am, 6.30pm Sun; 12.30pm Tue; 8.30am Thur. **Admission** £4; £3 reductions; £10 family. **Map** p402 O5.

This wonderfully atmospheric medieval church was built over the remains of the 12th-century priory hospital of St Bartholomew, founded by Prior Rahere, a former courtier of Henry I. The church was chopped about during Henry VIII's reign and the interior is now firmly Elizabethan. You may recognise the main hall from the movies *Shakespeare in Love* and *Four Weddings and a Funeral*. Benjamin Franklin trained here as a printer in 1724 before launching his political career in America.

Museum of St Bartholomew's Hospital

West Smithfield, EC1A 7BE (7601 8152). Barbican or Farringdon tube/rail. **Open** 10am-4pm Tue-Fri. **Admission** free; donations welcome. **Map** p402 O5.

Be glad you are living in the 21st century. Many of the displays in this small museum inside St Bart's Hospital relate to the days before anaesthetics, when surgery and carpentry were kindred occupations. Every Friday at 2pm visitors can take a guided tour of the museum (£5, book ahead on 7837 0546) that takes in the Hogarth paintings in the Great Hall, the little church of St Bartholomew-the-Less, neighbouring St Bartholomew-the-Great and Smithfield.

North of London Wall

Map p402 P5

Barbican tube/Moorgate tube/rail.

From St Bart's, the road known as London Wall runs east to Bishopsgate, following the approximate route of the old Roman walls. Tower blocks have sprung up here like daisies, but the odd lump of weathered stonework can still be seen poking up between the office blocks, marking the path of the old City wall. You can patrol the remaining stretches of the wall, with panels (some barely legible) pointing out the highlights along a route of almost two miles. The walk starts near the **Museum of London** (see p95) and continues to the Tower of London.

The area north of London Wall was reduced to rubble by German bombs in World War II. In 1958, the City of London and London County Council clubbed together to buy the land for the construction of 'a genuine residential neighbourhood, with schools, shops, open spaces and amenities'. What Londoners got was the **Barbican**, a vast concrete estate of 2,000 flats that feels a bit like a university campus after the students have all gone home. Casual visitors may get the eerie feeling they have been miniaturised and transported into a giant architect's model, but design enthusiasts will recognise the Barbican as a prime example of 1970s brutalism, softened a little by time and rectangular ponds of friendly resident ducks.

The main attraction here is the Barbican arts complex, with its library, cinema, theatre and concert hall – each reviewed in the appropriate chapters – plus an art gallery (see below) and the **Barbican Conservatory** (noon-5pm Sun), a giant greenhouse full of exotic ferns and palms. Unfortunately, pedestrian access was not high on the architects' list of priorities – the Barbican is a maze of blank passages and dead-end walkways, not much improved by a recent injection of millions of pounds into renewal and refurbishment. Marooned amid the concrete towers is the only pre-war building in the vicinity: the heavily restored 16th-century church of **St Giles Cripplegate** (7638 1997, www.stgilescripplegate.com, 11am-4pm Mon-Fri), where Oliver Cromwell was married and John Milton buried.

North-east of the Barbican on City Road are **John Wesley's House** (see p95) and **Bunhill Fields**, the nonconformist cemetery where William Blake (see p15 **City seer**), the preacher John Bunyan and novelist Daniel Defoe are buried.

Barbican Art Gallery

Barbican Centre, Silk Street, EC2Y 8DS (7638 8891/7382 7006/www.barbican.org.uk). Barbican tube/Moorgate tube/rail. **Open** 11am-8pm Mon, Wed, Fri-Sun; 11am-6pm Tue, Thur. **Admission** £8; £4-£6 reductions; under-12s free. **Credit** (shop) AmEx, MC, V. **Map** p402 P5.

The art gallery at the Barbican Centre isn't quite as 'out there' as it would like you to think, but the exhibitions on design, architecture and pop culture are usually pretty diverting, as are their often attention-grabbing titles.

Museum of London

150 London Wall, EC2Y 5HN (0870 444 3851/ www.museumoflondon.org.uk). Barbican or St Paul's tube. **Open** 10am-5.50pm Mon-Sat; noon-5.50pm Sun. **Admission** free; suggested donation £2. **Credit** (shop) AmEx, MC, V. **Map** p402 P5.

Opened in 1976, this expansive museum, which is set in the middle of a decidedly unpromising roundabout on London Wall, these days shares the job of recreating London's history with the Museum in Docklands (*see p168*). The chronological displays begin with 'London Before London': flint axes from 300,000 BC found in Glasshouse Street, Piccadilly; bones from an aurochs and hippopotami; and the Bronze Age Dagenham idol, a fertility image carved from a single piece of Scots pine. 'Roman London' includes an impressive reconstructed dining room complete with mosaic floor. Windows overlook a sizeable fragment of the City wall, whose Roman foundations have clearly been built upon many times over the centuries. Sound effects and audio-visual displays illustrate the medieval city, with clothes, shoes and armour on display. From Elizabethan and Jacobean London, heyday of the Globe Theatre, comes the Cheapside Hoard, an astonishing cache of jewellery unearthed in 1912. The downstairs galleries (Victorian London, 'World City' and Lord Mayor's coach) are closed for remodelling until autumn 2009. The website has details of temporary exhibitions and activities for children.

John Wesley's House & Museum of Methodism

Wesley's Chapel, 49 City Road, EC1Y 1AU (7253 2262/www.wesleyschapel.org.uk). Moorgate or Old Street tube/rail. **Open** 10am-4pm Mon-Sat; after the service until 1.45pm Sun. *Tours* arrangements on arrival; groups of 10 or more phone ahead. **Admission** free; donations welcome. **Map** p403 Q4.

The founder of Methodism, John Wesley (1703-91), was a man of legendary self-discipline. You can see the minister's nightcap, preaching gown and personal experimental electric-shock machine on a tour of his austere home on City Road. The adjacent chapel has a small museum on the history of Methodism and fine memorials of dour, sideburn-sporting preachers. Downstairs (to the right) are some of the finest public toilets in London, built in 1899 with original fittings by Sir Thomas Crapper.

Bank & around

Map p405 Q6

Mansion House tube/Bank tube/DLR.
Few places in London have quite the same sense of pomp and circumstance as Bank. Above Bank Station, seven streets come together to mark the symbolic heart of the Square Mile, ringed by some of the most important buildings in the City. Constructed from steely Portland stone, the Bank of England, the Royal Exchange and Mansion

Bank of England.

House form a stirring monument to the importance of money: most decisions concerning the British economy are still made within this small precinct.

Easily the most dramatic building here is the **Bank of England**, founded in 1694 to fund William III's war against the French. It's a veritable fortress, with no accessible windows and just one public entrance, leading to the **Bank of England Museum** (*see p96*). The outer walls were constructed in 1788 by Sir John Soane, whose personal museum can still be seen in Holborn (*see p103*). Although millions have been stolen from its depots elsewhere in London, the bank itself has never been robbed. Today it is responsible for printing the nation's banknotes and setting the base rates for borrowing and lending.

On the south side of the square is the Lord Mayor of London's official residence, **Mansion House** (7626 2500, group visits by written application two months in advance to the Diary Office, Mansion House, Walbrook, EC4N 8BH), an imposing neoclassical building constructed by George Dance in 1753. It's the only private residence in the UK to have its own court and prison cells for unruly guests. Just behind Mansion House is the superbly elegant church of **St Stephen Walbrook** (7626 9000, www.ststephenwalbrook.net, 11am-4pm Mon-Fri), built by Wren in 1672, with its gleaming coffered ceiling and incongruous altar – dubbed 'the camembert' – sculpted by Sir Henry Moore.

To the east of Mansion House is the **Royal Exchange**, the Parthenon-like former home of the London Stock Exchange, which was founded way back in 1565 to facilitate the newly invented trade in stocks and shares with Antwerp. In 1972, the exchange shifted to offices on Threadneedle Street, thence to Paternoster Square, and today the Royal Exchange houses a posh champagne bar and the staggeringly expensive emporiums of Tiffany's, de Beers and Chanel. Flanking the Royal Exchange are statues of James Henry Greathead, who invented the machine that cut the tunnels for the London Underground, and Paul Reuter, who founded the Reuters news agency here in 1851.

The period grandeur is undermined somewhat by the monstrosity on the west side of the square, **No.1 Poultry**; the name fits – it's a total turkey, especially as it replaced the beautiful 1870s Mappin & Webb building. A short walk down Queen Victoria Street will lead you to the eroded foundations of the **Temple of Mithras**, constructed by Roman soldiers in AD 240-250. Beliefs from the cult of Mithras were incorporated into Christianity when Rome abandoned paganism in the fourth century.

Further south, on Cannon Street, you can observe the **London Stone**, thought to mark the centre point of London or a Roman temple or a druidic altar, depending who you talk to – some even have the effrontery to claim it's just a lump of rock. Nearby on College Hill is the late Wren church of **St Michael Paternoster Royal** (7248 5202, 9am-5pm Mon-Fri), the final resting place of London's first Lord Mayor, Richard 'Dick' Whittington. Later transformed into a rags-to-riches pantomime hero, the real Dick Whittington was a wealthy merchant who was elected Lord Mayor four times between 1397 and 1420. The role of Dick Whittington's cat is less clear – many now believe that the cat was actually a ship, but an excavation to find Whittington's tomb in 1949 did uncover the body of a mummified medieval moggy.

South-east of Bank on Lombard Street is Hawksmoor's striking **St Mary Woolnoth**, squeezed in between the 17th-century banking houses with their gilded signboards. The gilded grasshopper at 68 Lombard Street is the heraldic emblem of Sir Thomas Gresham, who founded the Royal Exchange. Further east on Lombard Street is Wren's **St Edmund the King** (7626 5031, www.spiritualitycentre.org, 10am-6pm Mon-Fri), which now houses a centre

for modern spirituality. Other significant churches in the area include Wren's handsome red-brick **St Mary Abchurch**, off Abchurch Lane, and **St Clement**, on Clement's Lane, immortalised in the nursery rhyme 'Oranges and Lemons'. Over on Cornhill are two more Wren churches; **St Peter-upon-Cornhill** was mentioned by Dickens in *Our Mutual Friend*, while **St Michael Cornhill** contains a bizarre statue of a pelican feeding its young with pieces of its own body – a medieval symbol for the Eucharist – sculpted by someone who had plainly never seen a pelican.

North-west of the Bank of England is the **Guildhall**, City of London headquarters. You can tour the Great Hall (*see p97*), Art Gallery and Library (for both, *see p97*), plus the **Clockmakers' Museum** (*see below*), and the church of **St Lawrence Jewry**, another restored Wren construction with an impressive gilt roof.

Bank of England Museum

Entrance on Bartholomew Lane, EC2R 8AH (7601 5545/www.bankofengland.co.uk/museum). Bank tube/DLR. **Open** 10am-5pm Mon-Fri. *Tours* by arrangement. **Admission** free. *Tours* free. **Map** p405 Q6.

Housed inside the former Stock Offices of the Bank of England, this engaging museum explores the history of the national bank. As well as ancient coins and original artwork for British banknotes, the museum offers a rare chance to manhandle a real 13kg gold bar (closely monitored, more's the pity, by CCTV). Child-friendly temporary exhibitions take place in the museum lobby.

Clockmakers' Museum

Guildhall Library, Aldermanbury, EC2V 7HH (Guildhall Library 7332 1868/www.clockmakers.org). Mansion House or St Paul's tube/Bank tube/DLR/Moorgate tube/rail. **Open** 9.30am-4.45pm Mon-Sat. **Admission** free. **Map** p404 P6.

The proud history of the Worshipful Company of Clockmakers of London is showcased here. Hundreds of ticking, chiming clocks and watches are displayed in cases and cabinets on the walls, from the egg-sized pocket watches of Elizabethan gentlemen to the giant marine chronometers that guided the ships of the British Empire. They don't all keep the same time – that would be asking a little much – but the collection offers a fascinating window through time, from the first primitive iron carriage clocks to the creation of the modern-day wristwatch. Among other venerable timepieces are Marine Chronometer H5, built by John Harrison (1693-1776) to solve the problem of longitude; the exquisitely enamelled gold watch created by Conyers Dunlop for Charlotte, wife of George III; and the plain but hard-wearing Smith's Imperial wristwatch worn by Sir Edmund Hillary on the first – Rolex-sponsored – ascent of Everest in 1953.

Clockmakers' Museum.

Great Hall

Gresham Street, EC2P 2EJ (7606 3030/tours ext 1463/www.corpoflondon.gov.uk). St Paul's tube/Bank tube/DLR. **Open** *May-Sept* 10am-5pm daily. *Oct-Apr* 10am-5pm Mon-Sat. *Tours* by arrangement; groups of 10 or more only. **Admission** free. **Map** p404 P6.

The City of London and its progenitors have been holding grand ceremonial dinners here for more than 800 years. Memorials to national heroes line the walls, shields of the 100 livery companies grace the ceiling, and every Lord Mayor since 1189 gets a namecheck on the windows. Many famous trials have taken place here over the centuries, including the treason trial of Lady Jane Grey, 'the nine days queen', in 1553.

Guildhall Art Gallery

Guildhall Yard, off Gresham Street, EC2P 2EJ (7332 3700/www.guildhall-art-gallery.org.uk). Mansion House or St Paul's tube/Bank tube/DLR/ Moorgate tube/rail. **Open** 10am-5pm Mon-Sat; noon-4pm Sun. **Admission** £2.50; £1 reductions; free under-16s. Free to all after 3.30pm daily, all day Fri. **Credit** (over £5) MC, V. **Map** p404 P6.

The City of London's gallery contains numerous portraits of stuffy politicians and a few surprises, including works by Constable and Reynolds, some charming paintings by the Pre-Raphaelites and an absorbing display of topographical works showing London down the ages. The centrepiece of the permanent exhibition is the *Siege of Gibraltar* by John Copley – thought to be the largest painting in Britain – which spans two floors of the purpose-built gallery. Alongside hang other smaller works by Copley, portraits of Nelson and other national heroes. The majority of the Pre-Raphaelite works are in the galleries on the lower floors. A sub-basement contains the scant remains of London's Roman amphitheatre, constructed around AD 70 for gladiatorial combat.

Guildhall Library

Aldermanbury, EC2V 7HH (7332 1868/www.city oflondon.gov.uk). St Paul's tube/Bank tube/DLR. **Open** 9.30am-5pm Mon-Sat. **Admission** free. **Map** p404 P6.

A one-stop shop for books, manuscripts and prints relating to the history of London. Original historic works can be requested for browsing (bring ID) and the bookshop has an excellent stock of London books and old maps of the capital. The library has a regularly changing exhibition of work from the collection.

Monument & around

From Bank, King William Street runs south-east towards London Bridge, passing the small square containing the **Monument** (7626 2717, www.themonument.info), designed by Sir Christopher Wren and his (usually overlooked) associate Robert Hooke as a memorial to the Great Fire of London. The 202 feet from the ground to the tip of the golden flame is the distance east to Farriner's bakery in Pudding Lane, where the fire began on the 2 September 1666. During refurbishment the spiral staircase that climbs inside the column up to the viewing gallery is closed to visitors; it should reopen in December 2008.

South of the Monument on Lower Thames Street is the moody-looking church of **St Magnus the Martyr** (*see p98*), and nearby are several relics from the days when this part of the City was a busy port, including the old Customs House and Billingsgate Market, London's main fish market until 1982. North of the Monument along Gracechurch Street is the atmospheric **Leadenhall Market**, constructed in 1881 by Horace Jones (who also built the market at Smithfield; see p104). The vaulted roof was restored to its original Victorian finery in 1991 and city workers come here in droves to lunch at the pubs, cafés and restaurants, including the Lamb Tavern (see p222). Fantasy fans may recognise the market as Diagon Alley from *Harry Potter & the Philosopher's Stone*.

Behind the market is Sir Richard Rogers' high-tech **Lloyd's of London** building, constructed in 1986, with all its ducts, vents, stairwells and lift shafts on the outside, like an oil rig dumped in the heart of the City – we still think it's brilliant. The original Lloyd's Register of Shipping, decorated with evocative bas-reliefs of sea monsters and nautical scenes, is on Fenchurch Street. Just south on Eastcheap (derived from the Old English 'ceap' meaning 'barter') is Wren's **St Margaret Pattens**, with an original 17th-century interior.

St Magnus the Martyr

Lower Thames Street, EC3R 6DN (7626 4481/ www.stmagnusmartyr.org.uk). Monument tube.
Open 10am-4pm Tue-Fri; 10am-1pm Sun. *Mass* 11am Sun; 12.30pm Tue, Thur; 1.15pm Fri.
Admission free; donations appreciated.
No credit cards. Map p405 Q7.
Downhill from the Monument, this looming Wren church marked the entrance to the original London Bridge, which was lined with shops, churches and fortifications. The bridge was cleared of buildings in 1758, then sold brick and mortar in 1971 to an Arizona millionaire who, so the story goes, believed he was buying Tower Bridge. A cute scale model of the old bridge is displayed inside the church (the Museum in Docklands, see p168, has an even better one), along with a statue of axe-wielding St Magnus, the 12th-century Earl of Orkney. The church is mentioned at one of the climaxes of TS Eliot's *The Wasteland*: 'Where the walls of Magnus Martyr hold Inexplicable splendour of Ionian white and gold.'

Walk The hidden Wrens

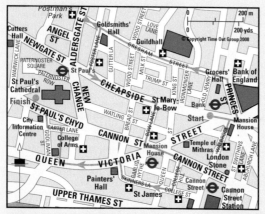

Start your exploration at Bank. South down Walbrook, just behind Mansion House, is one of Wren's most elegant constructions, **St Stephen Walbrook** (see p96). It has an inspired domed ceiling borrowed from Wren's original design for St Paul's. Returning to Bank, stroll north along Prince's Street, beside the Bank of England's blind wall. Look right along Lothbury to find **St Margaret Lothbury** (7606 8330, www.stml. org.uk, 7am-6pm Mon-Fri).

Start Bank tube. **Finish** St Paul's Cathedral. **Time** 1hr 30mins.

After the Great Fire of London in 1666, Sir Christopher Wren won a royal commission to rebuild the capital's religious monuments, creating 53 iconic churches, including his magnum opus, St Paul's Cathedral. More than 20 of the architect's other churches survive intact. They are generally quiet places, where the architect's genius can still be appreciated in peace – although many offer superb lunchtime organ recitals and other musical performances.

The grand screen dividing the choir from the nave was designed by Wren himself, while other works here by his favourite woodcarver, Grinling Gibbons, were recovered from various churches damaged in World War II.

A short walk west along Gresham Street brings you to **St Lawrence Jewry** (7600 9478, 8am-1pm Mon-Fri), which backs on to the Guildhall, headquarters of the City of London. In this the City's official church, you can hear the renowned Klais organ and see the grand gilt ceiling during the lunchtime organ recitals (1-1.45pm Tue).

Tower of London

Map p405 R7/8
Tower Hill tube/Tower Gateway DLR.

Marking the eastern edge of the City, the
Tower of London (*see p101*) was the palace
of the medieval kings and queens of England.
Home to the Crown Jewels and the Royal
Armoury, it's one of Britain's best-loved tourist
attractions and, accordingly, is mobbed by
visitors seven days a week. Inside, you can see
famous treasures of state, reconstructed royal
chambers, the spot where two of Henry VIII's
wives were beheaded and the Bloody Tower,
where Sir Walter Raleigh was imprisoned and
the princes Edward V and Richard brutally
murdered, allegedly on the orders of Richard III.

At the south-east corner of the Tower is
Tower Bridge (*see p101*), built in 1894. It
is still London's most distinctive bridge. Used
as a navigation aid by German bombers, it
escaped the firestorm of the Blitz. East across
Bridge Approach is **St Katharine's Docks**,
the first London docks to be formally closed
when the River Thames silted up in the 1960s.
The restaurants around the marina offer more
dignified dining than those around the Tower.

Immediately north of the Tower, **Trinity
Square Gardens** are a humbling memorial
to the tens of thousands of merchant seamen
killed in the two World Wars. Just beyond is
one of the City's finest Edwardian buildings,
the former Port of London HQ at 10 Trinity
Square, with a towering neoclassical façade
and gigantic statues symbolising Commerce,
Navigation, Export, Produce and Father
Thames. Next door is **Trinity House**,
the headquarters of the General Lighthouse
Authority, founded by Henry VIII for the
upkeep of shipping beacons along the river.

Continuing west, glance north along Wood
Street to see the isolated tower of **St Alban**,
built by Wren in 1685 but ruined in World War
II and now an eccentric private home. At the
end of the street is **St Anne & St Agnes**
(7606 4986, 10.30am-5pm Mon-Fri, Sun),
laid out in the form of a Greek cross. Recitals
take place here on weekday lunchtimes.

Turn south down Foster Lane, passing
another imposing Wren church, **St Vedast-
alias-Foster** (*see p93*). From the end of
Foster Lane, the cathedral is almost close
enough to touch, but there are more fine
churches to see before you get to explore
Wren's crowning glory. Turn left into
Cheapside. A brief walk east will take
you to the corner of pedestrianised Bow
Lane and the attractively proportioned **St
Mary-le-Bow** (*see p93*), constructed by
Wren between 1671 and 1680.

Grab a swift espresso along Bow Lane
then continue south to **St Mary Aldermary**
(*see p93*), the only Gothic church by Wren
to survive World War II. Inside, you can
see a fabulous moulded plaster ceiling
and an original wooden sword rest (London
parishioners carried arms right up until the
19th century). Roman coins are sold here
to fund the renovation of the church.

Head east along Cannon Street and turn
south along College Hill to reach **St Michael
Paternoster Royal** (*see p96*), one of the last
Wren churches to be built in the City. Dick
Whittington, the first Lord Mayor of London,
is depicted with his (possibly mythical) cat
on the stained-glass windows.

Now turn west along Skinners Lane
to Garlick Hill (named after a medieval garlic
market) and **St James Garlickhythe** (7236
1719, www.stjamesgarlickhythe.org.uk,
10.30am-4pm Mon-Fri), the official church
of London's vintners and joiners, built by
Wren in 1682. The church was hit by bombs
in World War I and World War II and partly
ruined by a falling crane in 1991, but the
interior has been convincingly restored.

OK, now you've earned St Paul's. Follow
Trinity Lane to Queen Victoria Street and turn
left, passing another stately Wren church:
St Nicholas Cole Abbey, the first church
rebuilt after the Great Fire. Finally, turn north
along pedestrianised Peter's Hill, with St
Paul's rising before you like a beacon.

St Paul's (*see p93*) is arguably London's
finest building. It's easy to spend several
hours exploring the memorials to British
national heroes and climbing to the top of
the iconic dome for the view over the City,
with the spires of Wren's churches poking up
between the office blocks. Pay your respects
at Wren's humble tomb in the crypt, before
making one more detour to Paternoster
Square to see another of his works, the
Temple Bar archway that once marked the
boundary between the City and Westminster
at the western end of Fleet Street.

Sightseeing

The surrounding streets and alleys have evocative names: Crutched Friars, Savage Gardens and Pepys Street. The famous diarist lived in nearby Seething Lane and observed the Great Fire of London from **All Hallows by the Tower** (*see below*). Pepys is buried in the church of St Olave on Hart Street, nicknamed 'St Ghastly Grim' by Dickens for the leering skulls at the entrance.

North of the Tower are **St Botolph's-without-Aldgate** (*see below*) and the tiny stone church of **St Katharine Cree** (7283 5733, 10.30am-4pm Mon-Thur, 10.30am-1pm Fri) on Leadenhall Street, one of only eight churches to survive the Great Fire. Inside is a memorial to Sir Nicholas Throckmorton, Queen Elizabeth I's ambassador to France, who was imprisoned for treason on numerous occasions, despite – or perhaps because of – his friendship with the temperamental queen. Just north of St Katharine is Mitre Square, site of the fourth Jack the Ripper murder. Nearby on Bevis Marks, the superbly preserved **Bevis Marks Synagogue** (7626 1274, 11am-1pm Mon-Fri, 10.30am-12.30pm Sun) was founded in 1701 by Sephardic Jews fleeing the Spanish Inquisition. Services are still held in Portuguese as well as Hebrew. Next door is the classy Bevis Marks Restaurant (7283 2220, www.bevismarkstherestaurant.com).

Bevis Marks connects with **St Mary Axe**, named after a vanished church that is said to have contained an axe used by Attila the Hun to behead English virgins. Here you'll find Lord Norman Foster's **30 St Mary Axe**, arguably London's finest modern building. It's known as 'the Gherkin' (even 'the Erotic Gherkin') for reasons that are obvious once you see it. Nearby are two more medieval churches that survived the Great Fire – St Helen's Bishopsgate (*see p101*) and St Andrew Undershaft.

To the west of St Mary Axe is the ugly and rather dated **Tower 42** (25 Old Broad Street). It was the tallest building in Britain until the construction of 1 Canada Square (*see p167*) in Docklands in 1990. Behind, on Bishopsgate, is Gibson Hall, the ostentatious former offices of the National Provincial Bank of England.

One block north, St Mary Axe intersects with **Houndsditch**, where Londoners threw dead dogs and other rubbish in medieval times. The ditch ran outside the London Wall (*see p94*), dividing the City from the East End (*see p161*).

All Hallows by the Tower

Byward Street, EC3R 5BJ (7481 2928/www.all hallowsbythetower.org.uk). Tower Hill tube/Tower Gateway DLR. **Open** 9am-5.30pm Mon-Fri; 10am-5pm Sat, Sun. *Tours* phone for details, donation requested. *Services* 11am Sun; 12.30pm Mon, Wed, Fri; 8.30am Tue, Thur. **Admission** free; donations appreciated. **Map** p405 R7.

Often described as London's oldest church, All Hallows is built on the foundations of a seventh-century Saxon church. Much of what survives today was reconstructed after World War II but several Saxon details can be seen in the main hall, where the Knights Templar were tried by Edward II in 1314. The undercroft contains a museum with Roman and Saxon relics and a Crusader altar. William Penn, the founder of Pennsylvania, was baptised here in 1644. A former vicar of All Hallows, the Rev 'Tubby' Clayton, founded the friendship society born of the experience of trench warfare in World War I, Toc H.

St Botolph's-without-Aldgate

Aldgate High Street, EC3N 1AB (7283 1670/ www.stbotolphs.org.uk). Aldgate tube. **Open** 10am-3pm Mon-Thur; 10am-12.30pm Sun. *Eucharist* 10.30am Sun; 1.05pm Mon (during school term), Thur. **Admission** free; donations appreciated. **Map** p405 R6.

The oldest of three churches of St Botolph in the City, this handsome monument was built at the gates of Roman London as a homage to the patron saint of travellers. The building was reconstructed by George Dance in 1744 and a beautiful ornamental ceiling was added in the 19th century by John Francis Bentley, who also created Westminster Cathedral.

St Ethelburga Centre for Reconciliation & Peace

78 Bishopsgate, EC2N 4AG (7496 1610/ www.stethelburgas.org). Bank tube/DLR/Liverpool Street tube/rail. **Open** 11am-3pm Wed, Fri. **Admission** free; donations appreciated. **Map** p405 R6.

Built around 1390, the tiny church of St Ethelburga was reduced to rubble by an IRA bomb in 1993 and rebuilt as a centre for peace and reconciliation. Behind the chapel is a Bedouin tent where events are held to promote dialogue between the faiths (phone or check the website for details), an increasingly heated issue in modern Britain. Meditation classes are held here on Tuesdays and Thursdays.

Tower of London.

St Helen's Bishopsgate

*Great St Helen's, off Bishopsgate, EC3A 6AT
(7283 2231/www.st-helens.org.uk). Bank tube/DLR/
Liverpool Street tube/rail.* **Open** 9.30am-12.30pm Mon-
Fri. *Services* 10.30am, 6pm Sun. *Lunchtime meetings*
1-2pm Tue, Thur. **Admission** free. **Map** p405 R6.
Founded in 1210, St Helen's is actually two churches
knocked into one, which explains its unusual shape.
The church survived the Great Fire and the Blitz, but
was partly wrecked by IRA bombs in 1992 and 1993.
The hugely impressive 16th- and 17th-century
memorials inside include the grave of Thomas
Gresham, founder of the Royal Exchange (*see p96*).

Tower Bridge Exhibition

*Tower Bridge, SE1 2UP (7403 3761/www.tower
bridge.org.uk). Tower Hill tube/Tower Gateway
DLR.* **Open** *Apr-Sept* 10am-6.30pm daily. *Oct-
Mar* 9.30am-6pm daily. **Admission** £6; £3-£4.50
reductions; £14 family; free under-5s. **Credit**
AmEx, MC, V. **Map** p405 R8.
Opened in 1894, this is the 'London bridge' that
wasn't sold to America. Originally powered by
steam, the drawbridge is now opened by electric
rams when big ships need to venture this far
upstream (you can check when the bridge is next
due to be raised on the website). An entertaining
exhibition on the history of the bridge is displayed
in the old steamrooms and the west walkway, which
provides a crow's-nest view along the Thames.

Tower of London

*Tower Hill, EC3N 4AB (0870 950 4466/www.hrp.org.
uk). Tower Hill tube//Tower Gateway DLR/Fenchurch
Street rail.* **Open** *Mar-Oct* 10am-6pm Mon, Sun; 9am-
6pm Tue-Sat. *Nov-Feb* 10am-5pm Mon, Sun; 9am-5pm
Tue-Sat. **Admission** £16; £9.50-£13 reductions;
£45 family; free under-5s. **Credit** AmEx, MC, V.
Map p405 R8.
If you haven't been to the Tower of London before,
go now. Despite the exhausting crowds and long
climbs up inaccessible stairways, this is easily one
of Britain's finest historical attractions. Who would
not be fascinated by a close-up look at the crown of
Queen Victoria or the armour (and prodigious
codpiece) of King Henry VIII? The buildings of the
Tower span 900 years of history and the bastions
and battlements house a series of interactive
displays on the lives of British monarchs – and the
often excruciatingly painful deaths of traitors.

The highlight, though, has to be the Crown Jewels,
if only because they occupy such a hallowed position
in the British psyche. Numerous films have been
made about attempts to steal the jewels, but only one
person ever came close. The villainous Colonel Blood
tried it in 1671 – and, when he was captured,
somehow managed to negotiate a complete pardon.
Travelators glide past such treasures of state as the
Monarch's Sceptre, mounted with the Cullinan I
diamond, and the Imperial State Crown, worn by the
Queen each year for the opening of Parliament.

The other big draw is the Royal Armoury in the
White Tower, with four floors of swords, armour,
poleaxes, halberds, morning stars (spiky maces) and
other gruesome tools for separating human beings
from their body parts. Executions of prisoners of
noble birth were carried out on the green in front of
the Tower – the site is marked by a glass pillow,
sculpted by poet and artist Brian Catling in 2006.
In fact, prisoners were still being held and executed
here as recently as 1941. The historical displays
in the surrounding towers are refreshed every year –
the current focus is on the lives of royalty and famous
prisoners at the tower, including such English icons
as Sir Walter Raleigh and Guy Fawkes.

Tickets are sold in the kiosk just to the west of the
palace and visitors enter through the Middle Tower,
but there's also a free audio-visual display in the
Welcome Centre outside the walls. There's plenty
here to fill a whole day, but you can skip to the
highlights using the audio tour, or by joining one of
the highly recommended and entertaining free tours
led by the Yeoman Warders (Beefeaters), who also
care for the Tower's ravens.

Holborn & Clerkenwell

Butchers, clubbers and lawyers mix it up on the edge of the City.

Sometimes it can feel as though the entire spectrum of London life is colliding in full colour between Holborn and Clerkenwell: from the barristers whose offices pepper the picturesque Inns of Court to the left-leaning yuppies wearing tracks between their loft conversions and the latest fancy gastropub; from butchers hauling meat around Smithfield Market at the crack of dawn to the bug-eyed clubbers weaving unsteadily between them. The area has been at times devoutly religious (a site of monastic orders and nunneries in the Middle Ages) and fiercely revolutionary (a hotbed of Lollard, Chartist and Communist dissent down the centuries); it has been both periodically ravaged by fire and at the mercy of a watery geography. The former Fleet River, boarded over in 1733 and now running as a sewer beneath Farringdon Road, once threatened to overwhelm the neighbourhood with effluent and illness. Its future seems finally to have been secured, however, thanks to ongoing property development and the affiliated provision of local amenities, which combine with its unusual history to make it one of the most interesting corners of the capital.

Holborn

Map p399
Holborn tube.
Most will find little to love in the immediate surroundings of Holborn tube station, a hectic crossroads dominated by chain stores and faceless office blocks. Never mind: a sharp left on Remnant Street and ragged nerves are recharged in the unexpectedly lovely **Lincoln's Inn Fields**. London's largest square comes complete with gnarled oaks casting dappled

shade over a crumbling bandstand and tennis courts overlooked by the upmarket restaurant the **Terrace** (7430 1234), where Caribbean-influenced cuisine is served in an eco-friendly building that's part barn, part modern art installation. On the south side of the park, the neoclassical façade of the Royal College of Surgeons houses the **Hunterian Museum** (*see p103*), a collection of medical marvels; facing it from the north side is the **Sir John Soane's Museum** (*see p103*), a magic box of architectural oddities that's as gloriously eccentric as the architect who lived here and collected them: one of the most unusual attractions in the city. To the east of the square lies **Lincoln's Inn** (7405 1393, www.lincolns inn.org.uk), one of the capital's four Inns of Court, its grounds teeming with barristers but open to pottering members of the public hoping to ogle its odd mix of Gothic, Tudor and Palladian architecture while imbibing its Oxbridge air of studious integrity. On nearby Portsmouth Street lies the **Old Curiosity Shop** – now an upmarket shoe store – its creaking 16th-century timbers certainly known to Dickens, once a resident of Bloomsbury, although whether or not they inspired his novel remains open to debate.

Another of London's few timber buildings to survive the Great Fire can be found looming over Chancery Lane tube station. This is the wooden frontispiece of **Staple Inn** (7632 2127), yet another warren of beavering barristers, although its partial occupation by a large Vodafone retailer lowers the tone. Opposite, Gray's Inn Road runs north to **Gray's Inn** (7458 7800, www.graysinn.org.uk), where sculpted gardens dating back to 1606 are open to the public between 10am and 2.30pm Monday to Friday. Also in the area is the dramatic **Pearl Assurance Building** (252 High Holborn), now a hotel and restaurant frequented by lawyers, and the **London Silver Vaults** (7242 3844, www.thesilvervaults.com), opened in 1876 as a series of strong rooms for the upper classes to secure their valuables and now a hive of dealers buying, selling and repairing silverware. Equally liable to turn brown eyes green with envy are the glittering window displays of **Hatton Market**, London's jewellery and diamond centre since medieval times; today it's a leafy lane populated by bright-eyed couples browsing for bands of gold: a short walk – but a million miles aesthetically speaking – from the Cockney fruit stalls and knock-off sock merchants of nearby **Leather Lane** street market (10am-2.30pm Mon-Fri).

Further on is enigmatic **Ely Place**, its postcode notably absent from the street sign as a result of it falling technically under the jurisdiction of Cambridgeshire. The street has a rich literary history: the church garden of ancient **St Etheldreda** (*see below*) produced strawberries so delicious that they made the pages of Shakespeare's *Richard III* (a celebratory Strawberrie Fayre is still held on the street each June); Ely Place was also the home of *David Copperfield*'s Mr and Mrs Waterbrook. The 16th-century boozer **Ye Old Mitre** (*see p225*) was reputedly a favourite of Dr Johnson and remains one of the most atmospheric of the city's pubs.

Hunterian Museum

Royal College of Surgeons, 35-43 Lincoln's Inn Fields, WC2A 3PE (7869 6560/www.rcseng.ac.uk/museums). Holborn tube. **Open** 10am-5pm Tue-Sat. **Admission** free. **Map** p399 M6.

John Hunter (1728-93) was a pioneering surgeon and anatomist, appointed physician to King George III. Through his life he amassed a huge collection of many thousands of medical specimens. After he died, the collection was enhanced and expanded by others; today it can be viewed in this recently refurbished museum housed at the Royal College of Surgeons. The sparkling glass cabinets of the new space offset the goriness of some of the exhibits – these include the brain of 19th-century mathematician Charles Babbage and Winston Churchill's dentures. A gallery displays important 18th-century painting and sculpture by Stubbs, Chantrey, Rysbrack and Shipley, among others. *Photos p105.*

St Etheldreda

14 Ely Place, EC1N 6RY (7405 1061/www.st etheldreda.com). Chancery Lane tube/Farringdon tube/rail. **Open** 8.30am-7pm daily. **Admission** free; donations appreciated. **Map** p402 N5.

St Etheldreda, dedicated to the saintly seventh-century Queen of Northumbria, is Britain's oldest Catholic church and London's only surviving example of 13th-century Gothic architecture. Saved from the Great Fire of London by a sudden change in the wind, this is the last remaining building of the Bishop of Ely's palace. The crypt is dark and atmospheric, untouched by the noise of nearby traffic. The church's stained-glass windows (which, deceptively, are actually from the 1960s) are stunning.

Sir John Soane's Museum

13 Lincoln's Inn Fields, WC2A 3BP (7405 2107/www.soane.org). Holborn tube. **Open** 10am-5pm Tue-Sat; 10am-5pm, 6-9pm 1st Tue of mth. *Tours* 11am Sat. **Admission** free; donations appreciated. *Tours £5; free reductions.* **Map** p399 M5.

A leading architect of his day – he was responsible for the building that houses the Bank of England – Sir John Soane (1753-1837) obsessively collected art, furniture and architectural ornamentation, partly for enjoyment and partly for research. In the early 19th century, he turned his house into a museum to which 'amateurs and students' should have access. Much of the museum's appeal derives from the domestic setting. Rooms are modestly sized but modified by Soane with ingenious devices to channel and direct natural daylight and to expand available space, including walls that open out like cabinets to display some of his many paintings (works by Canaletto and Turner, as well as two series by Hogarth). The Breakfast Room has a beautiful and much-imitated domed ceiling inset with convex mirrors, but the real wow is the Monument Court, a multi-storey affair stuffed with an array of sculpted

Sightseeing

The Inns of Court.

stone detailing removed from ancient and medieval buildings. At the lowest level of the court is a sarcophagus of alabaster so fine that it's almost translucent. It was carved for the pharaoh Seti I (1291-78 BC) and discovered in his tomb in Egypt's Valley of the Kings, before being removed by 19th-century treasure hunters. Soane bought it after the British Museum declined the opportunity.

Clerkenwell & Farringdon

Map p402

Farringdon tube/rail.

Few places encapsulate London's capacity for reinvention quite like Clerkenwell, an erstwhile religious centre taking its name from the parish clerks that regularly performed Biblical mystery plays on its streets. The nuns of St Mary's, meanwhile, occupied what is now **St James Church** (Clerkenwell Close, 7251 1190, www.jc-church.org), home to a memorial to Protestants burned at the stake by Mary Tudor, although the most lasting holy legacy is that of the 11th-century knights of the Order of St John. The remains of their priory can today be seen in the extant **St John's Gate**, which dates from 1504 and is home to the **Museum & Library of the Order of St John** (*see below*).

By the 17th century, Clerkenwell was turning into a fashionable locale in its own right, but during the Industrial Revolution it was buried beneath warehouses and factories. Numerous printing houses were set up on its streets, a heritage that ultimately combined with Clerkenwell's reputation as a safe haven for liberals (both 16th-century Lollards and 19th-century Chartists saw it as a spiritual home of sorts). In 1903 Lenin is believed to have met Stalin for a drink in what is now the **Crown Tavern** (43 Clerkenwell Green, 7253 4973), one year after moving publication of *Iskra* to neighbouring 37A, now the **Marx Memorial Library** (7253 1485, www.marx-memorial-library.org). The left-leaning *Guardian* newspaper also moved here in 1964, originally to an office on Gray's Inn Road, then to 119 Farringdon Road (in 2008 it is due to relocate again, along with the *Observer*, north-west to purpose-built offices in King's Cross).

Industrial dereliction and decay were, however, the theme locally until property development in the 1980s and '90s turned the neighbourhood into one of London's most desirable residential areas, teeming with gleefully stereotypical *Guardian* readers frequenting artfully distressed gastropubs like the pioneering **Eagle** (159 Farringdon Road), or the brilliant artisan food shops, fashion boutiques, restaurants and bohemian bars strung along **Exmouth Market**.

Museum & Library of the Order of St John

St John's Gate, St John's Lane, EC1M 4DA (7324 4005/www.sja.org.uk/museum). Farringdon tube/rail. **Open** 10am-5pm Mon-Fri; 10am-4pm Sat. *Tours* 11am, 2.30pm Tue, Fri, Sat. **Admission** free. *Tours* free. Suggested donation £5; £4 reductions. **Credit** MC, V. **Map** p402 O4.

Today the Order of St John is best known in London for its provision of ambulance services, but its roots lie in Christian medical practices during the Crusades of the 11th, 12th and 13th centuries. This museum charts the history of the medieval Order of Hospitaller Knights through a fascinating collection of objects and artworks from Jerusalem, Malta, the Ottoman Empire and elsewhere. In the mid 18th century, long after the dissolution of the Order, the gatehouse served as a tavern from which the *Gentleman's Magazine*, the world's first general-interest rag, was published by Edward Cave; it also happened to provide Dr Johnson with his first job. A separate collection relates specifically to the evolution of the modern ambulance service.

Smithfield

Map p402

Farringdon tube/rail.

In a city increasingly dependent on tasteless supermarket produce, **Smithfield Market** provides a colourful link to an age in which meat was a matter of national pride. Yet its fortunes remain in a constant state of flux: today the old general market is a sometime squat used as little more than wall space for fly posters, while only the meat market remains operating out of what was once the largest food market in the capital. Designed by Horace Jones, it opened for business in 1868 but was shattered by bombs in World War II. Early risers will find traders setting up their stalls at first light inside the metal structure – its ornate arched ceiling and bizarre colour scheme (white, purple, blue and green) meeting with a row of traditional red phone boxes in the photogenic Central Avenue. The **Cock Tavern** (7248 2918) is licensed from 6am to serve beer and breakfast to famished meat handlers.

Nowadays Smithfield is most notable for its abundance of swanky eateries, including **Smiths of Smithfield** (*see p199*), **Club Gascon** (*see p199*) and **St John** (*see p197*). Also nearby is **Fabric** (*see p317*), the chaotic and cavernous superclub, still drawing queues of Bambi-eyed bass addicts that stretch all the way around the market on popular nights. More academic and peaceful by some distance is **Charterhouse**, a Carthusian monastery founded in 1370, now Anglican almshouses retaining the original 14th-century chapel and a 17th-century library.

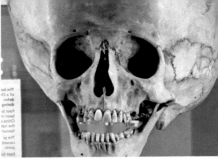

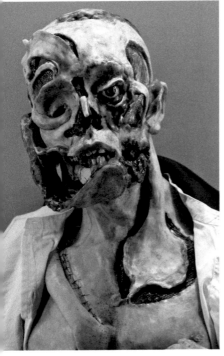

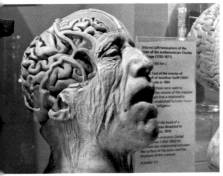

Hunterian Museum. *See p103.*

Bloomsbury & Fitzrovia

Bohemians and squares.

Bloomsbury's elegant Georgian terraces and gracious squares are home to two of London's major cultural landmarks. The historical treasures housed behind the stern neoclassical façade of the **British Museum** are undoubtedly the main attraction, but just to the north is one of the world's greatest repositories of knowledge, the **British Library**. The learned atmosphere of the area is reinforced by the cluster of university buildings, with their attendant bookshops and cafés. To the north, the once-insalubrious King's Cross area is undergoing huge redevelopment as a result of the new **St Pancras International** station, while the alleys of Fitzrovia, to the west of Tottenham Court Road, retain subtle traces of the area's former bohemianism.

Bloomsbury

Map p399

Holborn, Euston Square, Russell Square
or Tottenham Court Road tube.
Often associated with the group of academics, writers and artists who once colonised its townhouses, Bloomsbury's floral name has more prosaic origins: it's taken from 'Blemondisberi', the manor (or 'bury') of William Blemond, who acquired the area in the early 13th century. It remained rural until the 1660s, when the fourth Earl of Southampton built Bloomsbury Square around his house. The Southamptons intermarried with the Russells, the Dukes of Bedford, and together they developed the area as one of London's first planned suburbs. Over the next couple of hundred years, they built a series of grand squares: charming **Bedford Square** (1775-80) is London's only complete Georgian square,

while huge **Russell Square**, for years a run-down haunt of drunks and junkies, has been restored as an attractive public park with a popular café with outdoor terrace.

The area's charm is the sum of its parts, best experienced as an idle afternoon's meander, browsing Great Russell Street's **bookshops** and relaxing in historic pubs. The blue plaques here are a 'who's who' of English literature: William Butler Yeats lived at 5 Upper Woburn Place, Edgar Allan Poe at 83 Southampton Row and TS Eliot at 28 Bedford Place; 6 Store Street was the birthplace of Anthony Trollope. The house of Charles Dickens at 48 Doughty Street is now the **Charles Dickens Museum** (*see p109*). As for the famous Bloomsbury Group (denounced by DH Lawrence as 'this horror of little swarming selves'), its headquarters was at 50 Gordon Square, where EM Forster, Lytton Strachey, John Maynard Keynes, Clive and Vanessa Bell, and Duncan Grant would discuss literature, art, politics and, above all, each other. Virginia and Leonard Woolf lived at 52 Tavistock Square, and Wyndham Lewis's Rebel Art Centre occupied 38 Great Ormond Street. On Bloomsbury's western border, Malet Street, Gordon Street and Gower Street are dominated by the University of London. The most notable building is Gower Street's **University College**, founded in 1826. Inside is the 'Autoicon' of utilitarian philosopher and founder of the university Jeremy Bentham – his preserved cadaver, fully clothed, sitting in a glass-fronted cabinet. The university's main library is housed in university City-like **Senate House**, over on Malet Street. It is one of London's most imposing examples of monumental art deco. Monolithic and brooding, it was the model for Orwell's Ministry of Truth in his dystopic novel *1984*.

South of the university sprawls the **British Museum** (*see p107*), with its vast collection of archaeological and artistic treasures. Running off Great Russell Street, which is where you'll find the museum's main entrance, are three attractive parallel streets (Coptic, Museum and Bury), among them the **Cartoon Museum** (*see p107*), while Bloomsbury Way has Hawksmoor's newly restored **St George's Bloomsbury** (*see p109*). Nearby **Sicilian Avenue** is an Italianate, pedestrian precinct of colonnaded shops that links with Southampton Row.

North-east of here is **Lamb's Conduit Street**, a convivial neighbourhood with interesting shops, one of London's finest old pubs (the **Lamb**; *see p225*) and, at the top of the street, **Coram's Fields** (*see p278*), a delightful children's park built on the grounds of the former Thomas Coram's Foundling Hospital. The legacy of the great Coram family is now commemorated in the beautiful **Foundling Museum** (*see p109*).

British Museum

Great Russell Street, WC1B 3DG (7323 8000/ recorded information 7323 8783/www.thebritish museum.ac.uk). Russell Square or Tottenham Court Road tube. **Open** *Galleries* 10am-5.30pm Mon-Wed, Sat, Sun; 10am-8.30pm Thur, Fri. *Great Court* 9am-6pm Mon-Wed, Sun; 9am-11pm Thur-Sat. *Highlights tours* (90mins) 10.30am, 1pm, 3pm daily. *Eye opener tours* (50mins) phone for details. **Admission** free; donations appreciated. *Temporary exhibitions* prices vary. *Highlights tours* £8; £5 reductions. *Eye opener tours* free. **Credit** (shop) DC, MC, V. **Map** p399 K/L5.

Officially London's most popular tourist attraction, the British Museum is a neoclassical marvel built in 1847 by Robert Smirke, one of the pioneers of the Greek Revival style. As impressive is Lord Norman Foster's glass-roofed Great Court, opened in 2000 and now claimed to be 'the largest covered public square in Europe'. This £100m landmark surrounds the domed Reading Room (used by the British Library until its move to King's Cross; *see p110*, where Marx, Lenin, Dickens, Darwin, Hardy and Yeats once worked. Star exhibits of the museum include ancient Egyptian artefacts – the Rosetta Stone on the ground floor, mummies upstairs – and Greek antiquities including the marble freizes from the Parthenon known as the Elgin Marbles. The Celts gallery has the Lindow Man, killed in 300BC and preserved in peat. The Wellcome Gallery of Ethnography holds an Easter Island statue and regalia from Captain Cook's travels.

The King's Library, which opened in 2004, is the finest neoclassical space in London, and home to a permanent exhibition, 'Enlightenment: Discovering the World in the 18th Century', a 5,000-piece collection devoted to the formative period of the museum. The remit covers physics, archaeology and the natural world: the objects displayed range from 18th-century Indonesian puppets to a beautiful orrery.

You won't be able to see everything in one day, so buy a souvenir guide and pick out the showstoppers, or plan several visits. Highlights tours focus on specific aspects of the collection; Eye opener tours offer introductions to world cultures.

Cartoon Museum

35 Little Russell Street, WC1N 2HH (7580 8155/ www.cartoonmuseum.org). Tottenham Court Road tube. **Open** 10.30am-5.30pm Tue-Sat; noon-5.30pm Sun. **Admission** £4; free-£3 reductions. **Credit** (shop) DC, MC, V. **Map** p407 Y1.

On the ground floor of this transformed former dairy the best in British cartoon art is displayed in chronological order, starting with the early 18th century, when high-society types back from the Grand Tour introduced the Italian practice of *caricatura* to polite company. From Hogarth it moves through

The **British Museum**, a civilised place in which to explore mighty civilisations.

Camden Lock – a London original.

Explore one of London's most creative shopping districts and meet some real personalities. Nestled within the bustling streets of Camden Town is the original gem beside the canal. A haven for London's style purveyors with an eye for eclectic design and a passion for ethical trading; its a boho mix of global inspiration.

Every day an army of independent shops and market traders in and around the award-winning Camden Lock Market Hall are open, with a stream of new talent and quirky shopping ideas. Relax on the cafe terraces and into the evening soak up the vibrant Camden scene at Dingwalls, Jongleurs and the Lockside Lounge.

CAMDEN LOCK Open everyday and until 7pm on Thursdays
www.camdenlockmarket.com

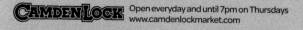

A FAMILY COLLECTION | A NATIONAL MUSEUM | AN INTERNATIONAL TREASURE HOUSE

Just minutes from the bustle of Oxford St, explore one of the world's greatest collections of art, shown in the intimate and opulent setting of the collectors' former London home.

- Old Master Paintings, Armour, Furniture, Ceramics, Sculpture
- Free Entry, Free Exhibitions, Family Activities, Public Events
- Free tours, trails & armour handling
- Beautiful glazed courtyard restaurant

Hertford House, Manchester Sq, London W1U
020 7563 9550 www.wallacecollection.org

Britain's cartooning 'golden age' (1770-1830) to examples of wartime cartoons, ending up with modern satirists such as Gerald Scarfe, the wonderfully loopy Ralph Steadman and the *Guardian's* Steve Bell. Upstairs is a celebration of UK comic art, with original 1921 *Rupert the Bear* artwork by Mary Tourtel, Frank Hampson's *Dan Dare*, Leo Baxendale's *Bash Street Kids* and a painted *Asterix* cover by that well-known Brit Albert Uderzo. There is a shop, but it isn't half as good as Gosh!, the comic store just round the corner at 39 Great Russell Street (7636 1011, www.goshlondon.com).

Charles Dickens Museum

48 Doughty Street, WC1N 2LX (7405 2127/www. dickensmuseum.com). Chancery Lane or Russell Square tube. **Open** 10am-5pm Mon-Sat; 11am-5pm Sun. *Tours* by arrangement. **Admission** £6; £3-£5 reductions; £14 family. **Credit** (shop) AmEx, DC, MC, V. **Map** p399 M4.

London is scattered with plaques marking the many addresses where the peripatetic Charles Dickens lived but never quite settled. This is the only one of his many London homes that is still standing. Dickens lived here for three years between 1837 and 1840, during which time he wrote *Nicholas Nickleby* and *Oliver Twist*. Ring the doorbell to gain access to four floors of Dickensiana, from posters advertising his public speaking to personal letters, manuscripts and his writing desk, exhibited in rooms decorated as they would have been when he lived here. Plans were afoot to close the museum for renovations in 2008 – check the website for news.

Foundling Museum

40 Brunswick Square, WC1N 1AZ (7841 3600/ www.foundlingmuseum.org.uk). Russell Square tube. **Open** 10am-6pm Tue-Sat; noon-6pm Sun. **Admission** £5; £4 reductions; free under-16s. **Credit** MC, V. **Map** p399 L4.

This museum recalls the social history of the Foundling Hospital, set up in 1739 by a compassionate shipwright and sailor, Captain Thomas Coram. Returning to England from America in 1720, he was appalled by the number of abandoned children on the streets. Securing royal patronage, he persuaded the artist William Hogarth and the composer GF Handel to become governors; Hogarth decreed the building should become the first public art gallery, and artists including Gainsborough, Reynolds and Wilson donated work. The museum uses pictures, manuscripts and objects to recount the social changes of the period. There are also temporary exhibitions and a monthly programme of classical and early music concerts.

Petrie Museum of Egyptian Archaeology

University College London, Malet Place, WC1E 6BT (7679 2884/www.petrie.ucl.ac.uk). Euston Square, Goodge Street or Warren Street tube. **Open** 1-5pm Tue-Fri; 10am-1pm Sat. **Admission** free; donations appreciated. **Map** p399 K4.

The museum, set up in 1892 by eccentric traveller and diarist Amelia Edwards (*A Thousand Miles Up the Nile*), is named after Flinders Petrie, one of the most exhaustive excavators of ancient Egyptian treasures. Where the British Museum's Egyptology collection is strong on the big stuff, the Petrie focuses on the minutiae of ancient life. Its aged wooden cabinets are full of pottery shards, grooming accessories, jewellery and primitive tools. Highlights include artefacts from the heretic pharaoh Akhenaten's short-lived capital Tell el Amarna. Among the oddities are a 4,000-year-old skeleton of a man who was buried in an earthenware pot. That some corners of this small museum are so gloomy staff offer torches only adds to the fun.

St George's Bloomsbury

Bloomsbury Way (7405 3044/www.stgeorges bloomsbury.org.uk). Holborn or Tottenham Court Road tube. **Open** 1-2pm Tue-Fri; 11.30am-5pm Sat; 2-5.30pm Sun. **Admission** free. **Map** p399 L5.

Consecrated in 1730, St George's is a grand and typically disturbing work by Nicholas Hawksmoor, with an offset, stepped spire inspired by the Mausoleum at Halicarnassus. It reopened in October 2006 following major renovations: highlights include the mahogany reredos, and 10ft-high sculptures of lions and unicorns clawing at the base of the steeple. As well as guided tours, there are regular concerts – check the website for details.

Wellcome Collection

183 Euston Road, NW1 2BE (7611 2222/www. wellcomecollection.org). Euston Square tube/Euston tube/rail. **Open** 10am-6pm Tue, Wed, Fri, Sat; 10am-10pm Thur; 11am-6pm Sun. *Library* 10am-6pm Mon, Wed, Fri; 10am-8pm Tue, Thur; 10am-4pm Sat. **Admission** free. **Map** p399 K4.

See p111 **Odd curiosity stop.**

King's Cross & St Pancras

Map p399

King's Cross tube/rail.

In 1835, a monument to the recently deceased King George IV was built at the junction of Pentonville Road, Gray's Inn Road and Euston Road. George had been an unpopular king, and the monument didn't last long. But Georgie had the last laugh: the area formerly known as Battle Bridge was from then on known as King's Cross. As we go to press, the old name seems more apt – much of the area looks like a war zone, with boarded-up and semi-demolished buildings, dust, rubble and chaos. The reason? A £500m makeover of the area is underway, with King's Cross being readied for a new role as a major European transport hub. The glorious centrepiece will be a renovated and restored **St Pancras Station**, welcoming the high-speed Eurostar train from Brussels and Paris to its gorgeous Victorian glass-and-iron train shed (which for many years had the largest clear-span in the world). Sir George Gilbert Scott's magnificent Gothic hotel building, which fronts the station, will also reopen – although not until 2009. Developers envisage St Pancras International as somewhere to linger. It will have the longest champagne bar in Europe, shops, a gastropub, major displays of public art and even – we are promised – a farmers' market. For current details, see www.stpancras.com.

Once all the building work is done, the gaping badlands to the north of St Pancras and King's Cross stations will have been transformed into a mixed-use nucleus called King's Cross Central. Until then, there are still a few places to explore: the **London Canal Museum** (*see below*), secreted north of King's Cross Station right by the new Kings Place recital rooms (*see p304*); kids' favourite **Camley Street Natural Park** (12 Camley Street, 7833 2311), an unexpected little wild garden between the stations beside the canal; and a little further north the delightful churchyard of **St Pancras Old Church** (*see below*).

British Library
96 Euston Road, NW1 2DB (7412 7332/www.bl.uk).
Euston Square tube/Euston or King's Cross tube/rail. **Open** 9.30am-6pm Mon, Wed-Fri; 9.30am-8pm Tue; 9.30am-5pm Sat; 11am-5pm Sun. **Admission** free; donations appreciated. **Map** p399 K/L3.
'One of the ugliest buildings in the world,' opined a Parliamentary committee on the opening of the new British Library in 1997. But don't judge a book by its cover: the interior is a model of cool, spacious functionality, and the reading rooms are a joy to use (although only open to card holders). This is one of the greatest libraries in the world, with holdings of over 150 million items. It receives a copy of every new publication produced in the UK and Ireland, from the daily papers to the most obscure academic treatises. In the John Ritblat Gallery, the library's main treasures are displayed: the Magna Carta, the Lindisfarne Gospels and original manuscripts from Chaucer, as well as Beatles lyrics. The focal point of the building is the King's Library, a six-storey glass-walled tower housing George III's collection. The temporary exhibitions are often superb, and the restaurant and café aren't bad either.

London Canal Museum
12-13 New Wharf Road, off Wharfdale Road, N1 9RT (7713 0836/www.canalmuseum.org.uk).
King's Cross tube/rail. **Open** 10am-4.30pm Tue-Sun. **Admission** £3; £2 reductions; £1.50 children; free under-8s. **Map** p399 M2.
The museum is housed in a former 19th-century ice warehouse, used by Carlo Gatti for his ice-cream, and includes an exhibit on the history of the ice trade. This is perhaps the most interesting part of the exhibition; the collection looking at the history

of the waterways and those who worked on them is rather sparse by comparison. The canalside walk from here to Camden Town is most enjoyable.

St Pancras Old Church & St Pancras Gardens
St Pancras Road, NW1 1UL (7387 4193).
Mornington Crescent tube/King's Cross tube/rail. **Open** *Gardens* 7am-dusk daily. *Services* 9am Mon-Fri; 7pm Tue; 9.30am Sun. **Admission** free. **Map** p399 K2.
The Old Church, whose site may date back to the fourth century, has been ruined and rebuilt many times. The current structure is handsome, but it's the restored churchyard that delights. Among those buried here are writer William Godwin and his wife, Mary Wollstonecraft; over this grave, their daughter Mary Godwin (author of *Frankenstein*) declared her love for poet Percy Bysshe Shelley. The grave of Sir John Soane is one of only two Grade I-listed tombs (the other is Karl Marx's, in Highgate Cemetery; *see p159*); its dome influenced Gilbert Scott's design for the classic red British phone box.

Fitzrovia

Maps p398 & p399
Tottenham Court Road or Goodge Street tube.
Squeezed in between Tottenham Court Road, Oxford Street, Great Portland Street and Euston Road, Fitzrovia may not be as famous as Bloomsbury but its history is just as rich. The origins of the name are hazy: some believe it comes from Fitzroy Square, which was named after Henry Fitzroy, son of Charles II; others insist it is due to the famous **Fitzroy Tavern** (16 Charlotte Street, 7580 3714), ground zero for London bohemia of the 1930s and '40s, a favourite with such regulars as Dylan Thomas and George Orwell. Fitzrovia had its share of artists too: James McNeill Whistler lived at 8 Fitzroy Square, a number later taken over by British Impressionist Walter Sickert, while Roger Fry's Omega Workshops had its studio at no.33.

Fitzrovia's raffish image is almost entirely a thing of the past. It's better known now as a high-powered media centre. ITN started broadcasting from 48 Wells Street, and Channel 4's first office was at 60 Charlotte Street from 1982. The district's icon is the **BT Tower**, completed in 1964 as the Post Office Tower. Its revolving restaurant and observation deck were open to the public and featured in almost any film that wanted to prove how prodigiously London was swinging (*Bedazzled* is just one example). Until, that is, the IRA exploded a bomb in the toilets; the restaurant now revolves for the benefit of corporate functions. **Charlotte Street** and neighbouring byways remain a good destination for dining and drinking.

Odd curiosity stop
Wellcome Collection

A newcomer in a city with an embarrassment of riches when it comes to museums, the **Wellcome Collection** (*see p109*) stakes its claim pretty impressively. Founder Sir Henry Wellcome, a pioneering 19th-century pharmacist and entrepreneur, amassed a vast and idiosyncratic collection of artefacts, implements and curios relating to the medical trade. These fascinating and often-grisly items – ranging from delicate ivory carvings of pregnant women to used guillotine blades, from a viciously bladed torture chair to Napoleon's toothbrush – form the core of the collection, but the museum offers much more.

The curators have been diligently adding serious works of modern art to Sir Henry's offbeat booty, most of which are on display in a smaller room to one side of the main chamber of curiosities. One of the most arresting is John Isaacs' *I can't help the way I feel*, a six-foot polystyrene, resin and steel statue of a man who appears to be burying himself in the fleshy folds of his own stomach. Horrid – but as a means of confronting the viewer with an image of obesity, hard to beat. More subtle, but no less interesting, is Marc Quinn's sculpture *Silvia Petretti – Sustiva, Tenofivir, 3TC (HIV)*. Graeco-Roman in style, the statue is of a woman with HIV... and the material used is mixed from the drugs she must take each day to stay alive.

Throughout, a broad-ranging and intelligent dialogue between art and science gives the collection a depth that is lacking from many science museums. Recent exhibitions have also been excellent, exploring connections between videos of open-heart surgery, Andy Warhol prints and ancient Chinese medical handbooks, for example. And if you feel the need for a spoonful of sugar to help all that medicine go down, there's a superb Peyton & Byrne café at hand on the ground floor, serving full meals, fabulous cakes and a good selection of teas.

All Saints

7 Margaret Street, W1W 8JG (7636 1788/www.
allsaintsmargaretstreet.org.uk). Oxford Circus tube.
Open 7am-7pm daily. *Services* 7.30am, 8am, 1.10pm, 6pm, 6.30pm Mon-Fri; 7.30am, 8am, 6pm, 6.30pm Sat; 8am, 10.20am, 11am, 5.15pm, 6pm Sun. **Admission** free. **Map** p406 U1.
A quiet respite from the tumult of nearby Oxford Street, this 1850s church was designed by William Butterfield, one of the great Gothic Revivalists. The church is squeezed into a tiny site, but its soaring architecture and a lofty spire – the second-highest in London – disguise the fact. Behind the polychromatic brick façade, the shadowy but lavish interior is one of the capital's most impressive, with luxurious marble, flamboyant tile work, and glittering stones built into its pillars.

Pollock's Toy Museum

1 Scala Street (entrance on Whitfield Street),
W1T 2HL (7636 3452/www.pollockstoymuseum.
com). Goodge Street tube. **Open** 10am-5pm Mon-Sat.
Admission £3; £1.50-£2 reductions; free under-3s.
Credit (shop) MC, V. **Map** p398 J5.
Housed in a wonderfully creaky Georgian townhouse, Pollock's is named after Benjamin Pollock, the last of the Victorian toy theatre printers. By turns beguiling and creepy, the museum is a nostalgia-fest of old board games, tin trains, porcelain dolls and Robertson's gollies. It's fascinating for adults but less so for children, for whom the displays may seem a bit static – describing a pile of painted woodblocks stuffed in a cardboard box as a 'Build a skyscraper' kit may only make them feel lucky to be going home to a PlayStation.

Covent Garden & the Strand

Forget the mime. Go for the Impressionism.

The melee of tourist groups can make a visit to Covent Garden a struggle, but it has plenty to offer even the more independent-minded visitor. There's good shopping for a start (mostly north of the market proper), London's Transport Museum is enormous fun, and Inigo Jones's austere St Paul's Church easily upstages the living statues and jugglers that crowd its rear portico. If you prefer high art to street art, the Royal Opera House is here, and the superb Courtauld collection at Somerset House is only a short walk away. To the south, the once-elegant Strand links Trafalgar Square with the Aldwych and Fleet Street, its heavy traffic marking the divide between Covent Garden and the Thameside Embankment.

Covent Garden

Map p407
Covent Garden or Leicester Square tube.
Back in the 13th century, this area of pastureland, as its corrupted name suggests, was the property of the Abbey (or 'convent') of Westminster. Having been wrested from the churchmen in the 1540s during Henry VIII's dissolution of England's monasteries, the land came into the hands of John Russell, first Earl of Bedford, in 1552; his family still owns tracts of land hereabouts. During the century that followed, his descendants extensively developed the area. The fourth Earl of Bedford employed the sought-after architect Inigo Jones, who created the Italianate open square that remains the centrepiece of today's Covent Garden. St Paul's Church

formed its western boundary and the remaining three sides consisted of tall terraced houses. Fashionable London flocked to the area and paid handsomely for the privilege of residency.

The first recorded market in Covent Garden appeared on the south side of the square in 1640, selling fruit and vegetables. It attracted coffeehouses and theatres, as well as gambling dens and brothels. During the next three centuries, the market grew until it had become London's pre-eminent fruit and vegetable wholesaler, employing over 1,000 porters. A flower market was added (where the Transport Museum now stands) and the market building itself was redesigned by the architect Charles Fowler. By 1918, it had been upgraded with new buildings and market halls.

In the second half of the 20th century, it was obvious that the congested streets of central London were unsuitable for market traffic and the decision was taken to move the traders out (for a last look at the market shortly before it closed, watch Alfred Hitchcock's 1972 thriller *Frenzy*). In 1974, with the market gone, the threat of property development loomed for the empty stalls and offices. It was only through mass squats and demonstrations that the area was saved. Today there exists a thriving residential community alongside a mix of established shops and small enterprises, with a sprinkling of cultural venues to continue the theatrical heritage. Chain stores have moved in, but it's still a nice place to stroll – wonderfully so if you catch it early on a fine morning.

Covent Garden Piazza

Inigo Jones's Piazza remains an attractive space and Charles Fowler's market hall gets lovelier with age. Visitors flock here for a combination of gentrified shopping, outdoor restaurant and café seating, street artists and classical renditions in the lower courtyard. The majority of the street entertainment takes place under the portico of **St Paul's** (*see p115*). It was here that Samuel Pepys observed what is thought to be Britain's first Punch & Judy show ('an Italian puppet play', as he described it), on 9 May 1662.

St Paul's launched an Avenue of the Stars in 2005, immortalising British and Commonwealth entertainers. Those honoured so far include Olivier, Chaplin and Alec Guinness.

Tourists favour the **old covered market** (7836 9136, www.coventgardenmarket.co.uk), which combines a collection of small, sometimes quirky shops, many of them with a twee, touristy appeal, with upmarket chain stores such as Hobbs, Whistles and Crabtree & Evelyn; more serious-minded shopping can be found in the boutiques to the north of Covent Garden tube station. The **Apple Market**, in the North Hall, has arts and crafts stalls every Tuesday to Sunday, and antiques on Monday. Across the road, the tackier **Jubilee Market** deals mostly in novelty T-shirts and other tat.

The Piazza and market is best viewed from the Amphitheatre Café Bar's terrace loggia at the **Royal Opera House** (*see below*).

London's Transport Museum

The Piazza, WC2E 7BB (7379 6344/www.ltmuseum. co.uk). Covent Garden tube. **Open** 10am-6pm Mon-Thur, Sat; 11am-9pm Fri. **Admission** £8; £6.50 reductions; free under-16s. **Map** p407 Z3.

After its eagerly awaited reopening in late 2007, you can again visit one of the city's most joyful museums. Here preserved buses, trams and trains trace the city's transport history from the horse age to the present day (*see p117* **All aboard!**). *Photo p117.*

Royal Opera House

Bow Street, WC2E 9DD (7304 4000/www.royal operahouse.org). Covent Garden tube. **Open** 10am-3pm Mon-Sat. **Admission** free. *Stage tours* £9; £7-£8 reductions. **Credit** AmEx, DC, MC, V. **Map** p407 Y3.

The Royal Opera House (founded in 1732 by John Rich on the profits of his production of John Gay's *Beggar's Opera*) has witnessed no fewer than three fires in its lifetime. The current building is the third on the site, the second having been sublet in 1855 to John Anderson, who had already seen two theatres burnt down and made this his third – on the final day of his lease. But that's the least of the dramas associated with this stage. Between 1735 and 1759 Handel premièred, among many other works, *Samson*, *Judas Maccabaeus* and *Solomon* here. Frenzied opera-lovers twice rioted against ticket price rises, for 61 nights in 1809, while the 1763 fracas came within an iron pillar of bringing down the galleries. It's possible to explore the massive eight-floor building as part of an organised tour, including the main auditorium, nosing into the costume workshops and sometimes even a rehearsal. Certain parts of the building are also open to the general public, including the glass-roofed Floral Hall, the Crush Bar (so named because in Victorian times the only thing served during intermissions was orange and lemon crush) and the Amphitheatre Café Bar, with its terrace overlooking the Piazza. Productions scheduled for 2008 include Puccini's *Tosca* and Verdi's *Don Carlo*.

St Paul's Churchyard Garden. See p115.

Sightseeing

St Paul's Covent Garden

Bedford Street, WC2E 9ED (7836 5221/
www.actorschurch.org). Covent Garden or Leicester
Square tube. **Open** 9am-4.30pm Mon-Fri; 9am-
12.30pm Sun. *Services* 1.10pm Wed; 11am Sun.
Choral Evensong 4pm 2nd Sun of mth. **Admission**
free; donations appreciated. **Map** p407 Y3.

Known as the Actors' Church for its association with
Covent Garden's theatres, this magnificently spare
building was designed by Inigo Jones in 1631. Actors
commemorate on its walls range from those lost in
obscurity – AR Philpott, 'Pantopuck the Puppetman'
– to those destined for immortality – among them
Vivien Leigh (her plaque inscribed with words from
Shakespeare's *Antony & Cleopatra*: 'Now boast thee,
death, in thy possession lies a lass unparallel'd') and,
yes, Boris Karloff. George Bernard Shaw set the first
scene of *Pygmalion* under the church's rear portico,
and the first known plague victim, Margaret Ponteous,
is buried in the pleasant churchyard. *Photos p113.*

Elsewhere in Covent Garden

The area offers a mixed bag of entertainment,
eateries and shops. On the area's western
border, from opposite ends of St Martin's Lane
– and the social spectrum – the well-known lapdancing establishment **Stringfellows** (16-19
Upper St Martin's Lane, 7240 5534) faces down
the **Coliseum** (*see p305*), home of the English
National Opera. **Brydges Place**, running off
St Martin's Lane just south of the opera house,
is the narrowest alley in London; only one
person can walk down it at a time.

Closer to the Piazza, most of the older,
more unusual shops have been superseded
by a homogeneous mass of cafés. High-profile
fashion designers have all but domesticated
main shopping street **Long Acre**, although
excellent travel bookshop **Stanfords** (*see
p242*) still holds out for the independents.
More interesting shopping experiences lie
in the streets north of Long Acre, notably the
attractive trio of **Neal Street**, **Monmouth
Street** and **Earlham Street**. Earlham is
home to the **Donmar Warehouse** (*see p340*),
a former banana-ripening depot that is now
an intimate theatre; Sam Mendes was artistic
director here before taking off for Hollywood
and fame with *American Beauty*. On Shorts
Gardens next door is pungent and wonderful
Neal's Yard Dairy (no.17, 7240 5700),
purveyor of exceptional UK cheeses, while
down a little passageway one door along is
Neal's Yard itself, known for its co-operative
cafés, herbalists and head shops.

Where Monmouth and Earlham Streets meet
Shorts Gardens is **Seven Dials**, named after
the number of sundials incorporated into the
central monument (the seventh being formed by
the pillar itself). The original pillar, an infamous

criminal rendezvous, was torn down in 1773
by a mob who believed that there was treasure
buried at its base. There wasn't.

South of Long Acre and east of the Piazza,
historical depravity is called to account at the
former **Bow Street Magistrates Court**.
Once it was home to the Bow Street Runners,
precursor to the Metropolitan Police, and site of
Oscar Wilde's conviction in 1895 for 'indecent
acts'. Suffragette Emily Pankhurst and East
End mobsters the Kray Twins were also tried
here. However, on 14 July 2006 the judge's
gavel fell for the last time; the building has
been sold and is set to become a boutique hotel.
To the south, Wellington and Catherine Streets
mix theatres – including, notably, the grand
Theatre Royal, where you can join one of the
entertaining tours – with an excess of eateries.

Freemasons' Hall (7831 9811; call for
details of the guided tours) – the impressive
white building at the point where Long Acre
becomes Great Queen Street – is worth a peek
for its solemn, symbolic architecture.

The Strand & Embankment

Map p407

Embankment tube or Charing Cross tube/rail.
Until as recently as the 1860s, the bustling street
known as the Strand ran beside the Thames –
in fact, it was originally the river's bridlepath.
In the 14th century, it was lined with grand
residences whose gardens ran down to the
water. It wasn't until the 1870s that the
Thames was pushed back with the creation of
the Embankment and its adjacent gardens. By
the time George Newnes's famed *Strand*
magazine was introducing its readership to
Sherlock Holmes (1891), the street after which
the magazine was named boasted the Savoy
and its theatre, the Cecil Hotel (long since
demolished), Simpson's, King's College and
Somerset House (*see p116*), leading Disraeli to
describe it as 'perhaps the finest street in Europe'.

Nobody would make such a claim today –
there are too many overbearing office blocks
and underwhelming restaurants – but there's
still plenty of interest. In 1292, the body of
Eleanor of Castile, consort to King Edward I,
completed its funerary procession from Lincoln
to the small hamlet of Charing, at the western
end of what is now the Strand, and the occasion
was then marked by the last of 12 elaborate
crosses. A replica of the Eleanor Cross was
erected in 1865 on the forecourt of **Charing
Cross Station**, where it remains today,
looking like the spire of a sunken cathedral.
Across the road is Maggie Hambling's eccentric
sarcophagal memorial to a more recent queen:
A Conversation with Oscar Wilde.

Sightseeing

The Embankment itself can be approached down **Villiers Street**, where Rudyard Kipling, author of *The Jungle Book*, lived at no.43. Pass through the tube station to where **boat tours** with on-board entertainment embark. Just east stands **Cleopatra's Needle**, an obelisk presented to the British nation by the viceroy of Egypt, Mohammed Ali, in 1820 (it was to be another 59 years before it was finally set in place beside the Thames). It was originally erected in around 1500 BC by the pharaoh Tuthmosis III at a site near modern-day Cairo, before being moved to Alexandria, Cleopatra's capital, in 10 BC; by this time, however, the great queen was already 20 years dead. The plinth contains a full set of British Empire coins, Bibles in various languages, a railway guide and copies of newspapers from 1879, the year it was erected.

Back on the Strand, the majestic **Savoy Hotel** opened in 1889, financed by the profits made from Gilbert and Sullivan's light operas at the neighbouring Savoy Theatre (which pre-dates the hotel by eight years). Interestingly, Savoy Court, which connects the hotel's magnificent deco entrance with the Strand, is the only street in the whole of the British Isles where the traffic drives on the right.

Benjamin Franklin House

36 Craven Street, WC2N 5NF (7925 1405/ www.benjaminfranklinhouse.org). Charing Cross tube/rail. **Open** pre-book tours by phone or online. **Box office** 10.30am-5pm Wed-Sun. **Admission** £7; £5 reductions; free under-16s. **Credit** AmEx, MC, V. **Map** p407 Y5.

Restoration of the house where Franklin – scientist, diplomat, philosopher, inventor and Founding Father of the United States – lived between 1757 and 1775 was completed in 2006. It is now open to the public as a centre for academic research on Franklin. The house is not a museum in the conventional sense, but it can be explored on well-run, pre-booked tours lasting a short but intense 45 minutes (at noon, 1pm, 2pm, 3.15pm, and 4.15pm on Wednesday to Sunday). These are led by an actress in character as Franklin's landlady Margaret Stevenson, using projections and sound to conjure up the world and times in which Franklin lived. *Photos p118.*

The Aldwych

Map p405

Temple tube.

At the eastern end of the Strand is the Aldwych, a grand crescent that dates back only to 1905, although the name 'ald wic' (old settlement) has its origins in the 14th century. To the south is the splendidly regal **Somerset House** (*see below*); even if you aren't all that interested

in the galleries, it's worth visiting the fountain courtyard, especially in December and January when it's the venue for a hugely popular open-air icerink. Beyond Somerset House you pass **King's College**, its 1960s buildings sitting uneasily with Robert Smirke's 1829 originals. In front of the college is **St Mary-le-Strand** (7836 3126, open 11am-4pm daily), James Gibbs's first public building, built 1714-17. The church was originally intended to have a statue of Queen Anne on a column beside it, but she died before it could be built and the plan was scrapped. On Strand Lane, reached via Surrey Street, is the so-called **'Roman' bath** where Dickens took many a cold plunge. Back near King's College, on the Strand and on Surrey Street, are entrances to one of London's ghost tube stations: the 1907 Aldwych station (although the signs say 'Strand', the station's earlier name). It has been closed since 1994 and functions chiefly as a frequent film set (*see p286* **The city is the star**).

On a traffic island just east of the Aldwych is **St Clement Danes** (7242 8282). It's believed that a church was first built here by the Danish in the ninth century, but the current building is mainly Sir Christopher Wren's handiwork. It is the main church of the RAF. Just beyond the church are the **Royal Courts of Justice** (*see below*) and the original site of Temple Bar, which marked the boundary between Westminster and the City of London; Temple Bar is now next to St Paul's Cathedral.

Turning back towards the Strand, on the north of the Aldwych, is a trio of imperial buildings: Australia House, Bush House (home to the BBC's World Service) and India House, offices of the Indian High Commission.

Royal Courts of Justice

Strand, WC2A 2LL (7947 6000/www.court service.gov.uk). Temple tube. **Open** 9am-5pm Mon-Fri. **Admission** free. **Map** p399 M6.

The magnificent Royal Courts preside over the most serious civil cases in British law. Members of the public are allowed to attend these trials (with exceptions made for sensitive cases), so if you want to see the justice system in action, step inside. There are few trials in August and September. Note that cameras and children under 14 are not permitted.

Somerset House

Strand, WC2R 1LA (7845 4600/www.somerset house.org.uk). Temple or Embankment tube/ Charing Cross tube/rail. **Open** 10am-6pm (last entry 5.15pm) daily. **Admission** Courtyard & terrace free. *1 museum* £5; £4 reductions. *2 museums* £8; £7 reductions. *3 museums* £12; £11 reductions. Free students & under-18s daily; Courtauld Gallery free 10am-2pm Mon. *Tours* phone for details. **Credit** *Shop* MC, V. **Map** p401 M7.

All aboard!

After undergoing two years of the most thorough refurbishment since its move to Covent Garden in 1980, **London's Transport Museum** (*see p113*) is up and running once again. As well as remodelling the interior of the magnificent old flower market building, with its great arched windows and soaring iron columns, to provide even more display space, the museum has emerged with a much more confident focus on social history and design. Appropriately, it's now also much easier to get around.

How does the museum go about illustrating the 200-year history of public transport in the capital? After an introductory art installation, 'World Cities', putting the city's transport in a global context by comparison with Delhi, New York, Paris, Tokyo and Shanghai, the collections are in broadly chronological order, beginning with the Victorian gallery. Taking pride of place is a replica of the horse-drawn carriage that provided Shillibeer's first bus service in 1829. And that's just the first of the extraordinary array of vehicles – trams, buses, trains and tubes – that can be seen here, in retirement from their vital role ferrying people across the expanding metropolis. A major new display recreates a suburban living room – where visitors are welcome to lounge – of the type made popular by the speculative development of the Metropolitan Line.

Another gallery is dedicated to the museum's truly impressive collection of poster art, much better represented post-refurb. Under the inspirational leadership of Frank Pick, in the early 20th century London Transport developed one of the most coherent and accessible brand identities in the world. As well as Harry Beck's now iconic tube map, the underground's distinctive roundel and Edward Johnston's bespoke typeface, Pick commissioned a wide variety of artists to produce original advertisements and noticeboards for the transport system that have now become classics of their kind.

One of the main aims of the new museum is to put people and their stories at the heart of the presentation of its artefacts, while also raising questions about the future of public transport in the capital. But the famous tube-driving simulator is still here. So too is a purpose-built, computerised, all-singing, all-dancing exhibit called Connections, incorporating some 55,000 model buildings in its depiction of the individual journeys made in countless numbers throughout the city every day. Another display features transport ideas that are 'coming soon'. Unlike the many tube trains affected by ongoing investment in their ageing infrastructure, it looks like London's Transport Museum, at least, has arrived in style.

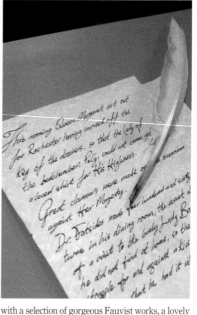

Benjamin Franklin House. *See p116.*

The original Somerset House was a Tudor palace commissioned by the Duke of Somerset in 1547. It was extended and refurbished several times over two centuries, but began to suffer from poor maintenance and in 1775 was demolished to make way for an entirely new building. The architect Sir William Chambers spent the last 20 years of his life working on the vast neoclassical mansion that now overlooks the Thames at Waterloo Bridge. It was built to accommodate learned societies such as the Royal Academy, but various governmental offices also took up residence, including the Inland Revenue. The taxmen are still here, but the rest of the building is open to the public, and houses three formidable art and museum collections (*see below*), the beautiful fountain court, a little café and a fairly classy restaurant.

Courtauld Institute of Art Gallery
7848 2526/www.courtauld.ac.uk/gallery.
The Courtauld has one of Britain's greatest collections of paintings, and it contains several works of world importance. Although there are some outstanding works from earlier periods (be sure you don't miss the wonderful *Adam & Eve* by Lucas Cranach), the collection's strongest suit is holdings of Impressionist and post-Impressionist paintings. There are some popular masterpieces: Manet's astonishing *A Bar at the Folies-Bergère* is undoubtedly the centrepiece, alongside plenty of superb Monets and Cézannes, important Gauguins (including *Nevermore*), and some excellent Van Goghs and Seurats. On the top floor, we get to the 20th century

with a selection of gorgeous Fauvist works, a lovely room of Kandinskys and plenty more besides. An essential stop if you have any interest in art. The little café, hidden away downstairs, is a joy and the forthcoming 75th anniversary show 'The Courtauld Cézannes' (26 June-21 Sept 2008) should be terrific.

Gilbert Collection
7420 9400/www.gilbert-collection.org.uk.
In 1949, British-born Sir Arthur Gilbert uprooted to California, where he subsequently made millions in real estate. He developed a predilection for all that glisters, collecting silver, gold and all sorts of gemmed, gilded and shiny objects. In 1996, Britain became the beneficiary of this opulence when he donated his entire collection, saying 'I felt it should return to the country of my birth' – he even continued buying new pieces after the museum had been opened. The dazzling arsenal of objects is now proudly displayed at Somerset House. Two floors are shamelessly bedecked with candelabras, mosaics, vases, urns, plates, mosaics and snuff boxes. The museum holds themed exhibitions throughout the year.

Hermitage Rooms
7845 4630/www.hermitagerooms.co.uk.
The Hermitage Rooms host rotating exhibitions of items belonging to the Winter Palace in St Petersburg; the rooms even recreate in miniature the decor of their Russian twin. New shows arrive twice a year and can include everything from paintings and drawings to decorative art and fine jewellery.

Soho & Leicester Square

Who would want to sanitise Soho – or linger in Leicester Square?

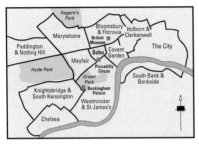

London's hip square mile is the stuff of legend, etched on vinyl and captured on celluloid, an open-most-hours party zone, louche, libertine but losing this lustre with each half-baked campaign seemingly needed to revitalise it. The latest, I Love Soho, is responsible for the love-heart merchandise peddled in a few bars – but little else. Westminster Council, never the most enlightened of bodies, has put in motion a scheme to regenerate the most atmospheric of Soho sidewalks, Berwick Street (*see p122* **Street scene**). Why would Soho need saving, you may ask yourself, as you pick your way

through its namesake square, which throngs with loiterers and malingers, while party-minded individuals of all sexual persuasions spill out of bars on the radial streets. Trade, say the powers that be. Not the rough variety, the walk-ups and indiscreet postcards offering easy pleasure, nor streets noisy with post-midnight revelry, but the shops and stalls to drive daytime tourism: a Portobello perhaps, a Covent Garden or a Camden.

Fenced in by the trading thoroughfares of the Charing Cross Road, Oxford and Regent Streets, and Shaftsbury Avenue, Soho is being doomed to draw in moneyed shoppers rather than the musos, boozers, gays and perverts who have been crossing its threshold since the late 1800s.

For bar owners and restaurateurs, business is better than ever. A media hub, dotted with post-production offices, Soho seems to be forever doing lunch or going for post-work drinks. The Soho of literary legend and music fame is long gone, and many of its venues have either moved (the Marquee) or moved on (the Coach & Horses of Bernard and Balon lore). In the interregnum, the pink pound ascended, turning spinal Old Compton Street and its tributaries into a late-night hangout long before the rest of town caught on to the idea.

In between today's gay bars and party troughs stands attractive evidence of Soho's mongrel heritage: French churches, Italian cafés and delicatessens, the Swiss Centre and Chinatown. Two pubs, the French House and De Hems, accommodated the Resistance in exile, French and Dutch. Blue plaques – Mozart, Marx, John Logie Baird – barely scratch the surface of Soho's rich history. Forever unconventional, continental by definition, Soho is still London at its most game – surely something to be celebrated rather than campaigned against?

Soho Square

Map p406
Tottenham Court Road tube.
Soho Square forms the neighbourhood's northern gateway. This tree-lined quadrangle was laid out in 1681 and initially called King's

Soho Square.

Square – a weather-beaten statue of Charles II stands just north of centre. Locked at night, by day its grassy spaces are filled with canoodling couples while snacking workers occupy its benches, one of which bears a plaque dedicated to tragic singer Kirsty MacColl, whose song 'Soho Square' celebrated the place. Night and day, traffic cruises around it, waiting for one of the area's few parking bays to become free. The centrepiece is a little mock Tudor hut used to store gardeners' equipment. The denominations of the two churches on the square testify to the area's long-standing European credentials: as well as the French Protestant church, you'll find St Patrick's, one of the first Catholic churches built in England after the Reformation. Film and media companies have head offices here, as well as the English Football Association – that's Soho Square in the background when another soccer scandal story is being covered by on-the-spot TV news.

Two classic Soho streets run south from the square. **Greek Street**, named after the church that once stood here, is lined with an eclectic range of restaurants and drinkeries, starting with the **Gay Hussar** (no.2, 7437 0973), London's only Hungarian restaurant and popular with Labour politicians in the 1970s – in 2003, the restaurant's 50th anniversary year, it hosted Michael Foot's 90th birthday party. The nearby **Pillars of Hercules** pub (no.7, 7437 1179), former haunt of writers Martin Amis and Ian McEwan, supports an arch leading to Manette Street and the Charing Cross Road. There you'll find a side entrance to **Foyles** (*see p241*), London's best-known bookshop, with a first-floor café. Opposite, the **Crobar** (17 Manette Street, 7439 0831) is a rock-themed late-night haunt. Back on Frith Street, **Garlic & Shots** (no.14, 7734 9505) is another past-midnight favourite, as is the more fashionable **Thirst** (no.53, 7437 1977). More upmarket French-influenced choices include **L'Escargot Marco Pierre White** (no.48, 7437 2679) and the corner **Café Bohème** (13 Old Compton Street, 7734 0623), serving croissaints for breakfast, plats du jour during the day and original cocktails way into the night. On the next corner down stands the **Coach & Horses** (no.29, 7437 5920), legendary louche hang-out, somewhat tamer since the retirement of famously rude landlord Norman Balon. Nearby pâtisserie **Maison Bertaux** (no.28; *see p202*) and champagne bar **Kettners** (29 Romilly Street, 7734 6112) add a touch of class.

Parallel to Greek Street is **Frith Street**, once home to Mozart (1764-65, no.20), painter John Constable (1810-11, no.49) and humanist essayist William Hazlitt, who died in 1830 at

no.6, now a discreet and charming hotel (*see p50*) named in his memory. Opposite the hotel is garlanded new restaurant Arbutus (*see p203*) and, a little further down, the legendary **Ronnie Scott's** (*see p314*), Britain's best-known jazz club. Across from Ronnie's is the similarly mythologised **Bar Italia** (no.22, 7437 4520), an authentically Italian café and restaurant; a large portrait of Rocky Marciano dominates the narrow, chrome bar, 24-hour opening dominates the thinking of many of its patrons. Back up towards Soho Square, the **Dog & Duck** (18 Bateman Street; *see p227*), an Orwell favourite, is an authentic pub with decent ales.

Old Compton Street & around

Map p406

Leicester Square or Tottenham Court Road tube.
Old Compton Street, linking the Charing Cross Road to Wardour Street via Greek, Frith and Dean Streets, is gay central. Tight T-shirts congregate around **Balans** (no.60; *see p299*), **Compton's** (nos.51-53; *see p302*) and the **Admiral Duncan** (no.54; *see p301*). Another gay-friendly spot, the **Boulevard Bar & Dining Room** (no.59, 7287 0770), was formerly the 2 i's Coffee Bar, birthplace of rock 'n' roll in London, where stars and svengalis mingled in the late 1950s and early 1960s.

Visit the street in the morning for a sense of the immigrant Soho of old, with cheeses and cooked meats from **Camisa** (no.61, 7437 7610) and roasting beans from the **Algerian Coffee Stores** (no.52, 7437 2480) scenting the air, and **Pâtisserie Valerie** (no.44, 7437 3466, www. patisserie-valerie.co.uk) doing a brisk trade in buttery croissants. Around the corner, the **French House** (49 Dean Street; *see p226*) was de Gaulle's London base for the French Resistance in World War II and later became a favourite of painters Francis Bacon and Lucian Freud. It's small, cliquey and still serves Breton cider and beer in half-pint glasses – crowds of smokers gather outside. Dean Street is also the address of the members-only **Groucho Club** (no.45), a media haunt lower on kudos since a corporate takeover in 2006. A few doors along, **Sunset Strip** (no.30) is the sole remaining legitimate strip club in Soho. It's hard to believe Karl Marx, who lived both at no.28 and no.44 from 1850 to 1856, would have approved. Further north is the **Soho Theatre** (no.21; *see p340*), with a programme of new plays and comedy. Possibly the best Indian restaurant in town, the **Red Fort** (no.77; *see p203*) is a big draw, as is its downstairs cocktail bar, Akbar.

Leicester Square.

Parallel to Dean Street, **Wardour Street** today provides offices for an assortment of film and TV production companies but is best known for its rock history. What's now upscale tapas joint **Meza** (no.100, 7314 4002, www. mezabar.co.uk) was for nearly three decades the Marquee club, where Led Zeppelin played their first London gig and Hendrix appeared four times. The latter's favourite Soho haunt was the nearby **Ship** pub (no.116, 7437 8446), still with a sprinkling of music-themed knick-knacks, although the Marquee moved home ten years ago. Punk band the Jam played a secret gig at the venue a year after releasing their top-ten hit 'A-Bomb in Wardour Street'. Nearby St Anne's Court is home of Trident Studios, where Lou Reed's *Transformer* and David Bowie's *Hunky Dory* and *Ziggy Stardust* were recorded. (The Ziggy album cover was, however, shot in Mayfair; *see p131*.) Adjoining Brewer Street was where a young Bowie, as David Jones, played a gig in 1964 at the Jack of Clubs (no.10, now **Madam Jo Jo's**; *see p318*). One street west again, **Berwick Street** feels like the real Soho deal (*see p122* **Street scene**).

Tiny **Walkers Court**, linking Berwick and Brewer Streets, has a squeeze of strip joints and sex shops, while through on **Rupert Street** are a number of clip joints and gay bars.

West Soho

Map p406
Piccadilly Circus tube.
Soho gets quieter west of Berwick Street. Here Brewer Street has a few interesting shops, including the **Vintage Magazine Store** (nos.39-43, 7439 8525) for everything

from retro robots to pre-war issues of *Vogue*. On Great Windmill Street is the **Windmill Theatre** (nos.17-19), which gained fame in the 1930s and 1940s for its 'revuedeville' shows with erotic 'tableaux' – naked girls who remained stationary in order to stay within the law. The story of the theatre was retold in the 2005 film *Mrs Henderson Presents*. The place is now a lapdancing joint.

North of Brewer Street is **Golden Square**. Developed in the 1670s, it became the political and ambassadorial district of the late 17th and early 18th centuries, and remains home to some of the area's grandest residential buildings – many of which are now filled by media companies. North of the square is **Carnaby Street**: four decades ago it was the epitome of swinging London, but became a rather seamy commercialised backwater. Along with **Newburgh Street** and **Kingly Court** nearby, it has recently undergone a revival. Interesting independents now sit alongside tourist traps doing no more than trade happily off the history of the area. There are also a growing number of good bars hereabouts, not least **Two Floors** (3 Kingly Street; *see p228*).

Chinatown & Leicester Square

Maps p406 & p407
Leicester Square tube.
Shaftesbury Avenue is the very heart of Theatreland. The Victorians built seven grand theatres here; six of them still stand. By far the most impressive is the gorgeous **Palace Theatre** on Cambridge Circus. It opened in

1891 as the Royal English Opera House, but grand opera flopped here and the theatre reopened as a music hall two years later. The theatre has been home mostly to musicals, which have included *The Sound of Music* in 1961, *Jesus Christ Superstar* in 1972 and *Les Misérables*, which ran here from 1985 to 2004, racking up 7,602 performances. Opposite the theatre, what's now the Med Kitchen occupies premises that were once home to Marks & Co, the booksellers immortalised in Helene Hanff's *84 Charing Cross Road*. Second-hand bookshops still line the road to the south.

Behind, south of Shaftesbury Avenue and west of Charing Cross Road, is **Chinatown**. The Chinese are relative latecomers to Soho. London's original Chinatown was around Limehouse in east London, but hysteria about Chinese opium dens and criminality led to 'slum clearances' in 1934 (interestingly, the surrounding slums were deemed to be in considerably less urgent need of clearance). It wasn't until the 1950s that the Chinese put down roots here, attracted by the cheap rents along Gerrard and Lisle Streets. The ersatz oriental gates, stone lions and pagoda-topped phone boxes around **Gerrard Street** suggest a Chinese theme park, but this remains a close-knit residential and working enclave, a genuine focal point for the Chinese community in London. The area is crammed with restaurants, Asian grocery stores and a host of small shops selling iced-grass jelly, speciality teas and cheap air tickets to Beijing. Adjoining Gerrard Street is Macclesfield Street, best known for housing Benelux-themed pub **De Hems** (no.11, 7437 2494), where the Dutch Resistance would meet in the early 1940s.

Street scene Soho central

Old Soho is suffering wave after wave of new initiatives and branding exercises, but **Berwick Street** at least is making a sturdy last stand. While the rest of London's sassiest square mile succumbs to chains and clean-up campaigns, this amiable thoroughfare offers authenticity by the pound. Built in the early 1700s, with its market already in place later that century, by the early 20th century Berwick Street was thriving thanks to the Jewish community's arcade of drapers, dressmakers, jewellers and tailors around the fruit stalls. Signs engraved on façades above shopfronts – 'The Silk House

1929' and 'V Falber & Sons' – recall an era that ended with World War II. The fruit and veg stalls, along with sweets, nuts and even a fishmonger, remain (9am-6pm Mon-Sat).

A more recent mercantile phenomenon is also on the wane. When Oasis shot this street scene to feature on the cover of *(What's the Story) Morning Glory?*, Berwick Street was best known for its music shops. Now that vinyl and CD have given way to eBay and downloads, some of these niche venues have gone or are selling stock off fast. A successful operation such as **Sister Ray** (nos.34-35, 7734 3297) sees fit to run: 'Last

Soho & Leicester Square

South of Chinatown is **Leicester Square**, reasonably pleasant by day, but by night a hellish sinkhole of semi-undressed inebriates out on a big night 'up west'. How different it once was. In the 17th century, the square was one of London's most exclusive addresses, and in the 18th century it was home to the royal court of Prince George (later George II). Satirical painter William Hogarth had a studio here (1733-64), as did 18th-century artist Sir Joshua Reynolds; both are commemorated by busts in the small gardens that lie at the heart of the square, although it's the statue of a tottering Charlie Chaplin that gets all the attention. There's no particular reason for Chaplin to be here, other than that Leicester Square is considered the home of British film thanks to its numerous cinemas, notably the monolithic **Odeon Leicester Square** (*see p287*). This cinema once boasted the UK's largest screen – and possibly has the UK's highest ticket prices. The Odeon and neighbouring Empire are regularly used for movie premières. Unless numbed by alcohol, most Londoners avoid the cheap fast fooderies, expensive cinemas and tacky pavement artists and buskers – so should you. The **Cork & Bottle** (44-46 Cranbourn Street; *see p227*) on the other hand is a popular basement wine bar with a directory of vintages, tasty cheeses and cold cuts. The south side of the square is where you'll find the **tkts booth** (*see p333*), retailer of cut-price, same-day theatre tickets. North in Leicester Place is the **Prince Charles Cinema** (*see p288*), which screens an eclectic mix of cult classics at knockdown prices. Next door to the Prince Charles, the French Catholic church of **Notre Dame de France** contains murals by Jean Cocteau.

year we sold 15 tons of vinyl – thank you!' across its shop window. Meanwhile, **Renewal Records** (no.30) is offering 50 per cent discounts and opposite **Mr CD** (no.80) has a £1 CD sale. Music journalists once sold off piles of promotional copies around here to supplement their income – now record companies send out MP3s instead.

As if to buck the trend, independent underground label Berwick Street Records was set up in 2005 in homage to the vinyl valley. **Vinyl Junkies** (no.94, 7439 2775) still does a steady trade – just look at the carrier bags at people's feet around the landmark **Endurance** (no.90, 7437 2944). A jukebox pub and gastrobar combined (with tables outside out the back), here you can stick on the Specials, the Libertines and Daft Punk to accompany your beer-battered cod. The Endurance harks back to a time when members of the punk elite would congregate in the long-gone King of Corsica pub on the same site. Next door is the vegetarian diner **Beatroot** (no.92, 7437 8591), where steaming portions of low-priced meat-free delights are served in three box sizes.

If you ask for coffee in the Endurance, you'll be directed across the road to **flat white** (no.17, 7734 0370, www.flat-white.co.uk). On the same block are a couple of upscale eateries, the continental **Bar du Marché** (no.19, 7734 4606) and **Mediterranean** (no.18, 7437 0560), though raising the bar higher, over the road, is Alan Yau's design-led teahouse and pioneering all-day dim sum

eaterie **Yauatcha** (15-17 Broadwick Street, 7494 8888). The building by Richard Rogers and interior by Christian Liagre could hardly contrast more strongly with the illuminated-gas-fire style and genuine retro feel of the **Blue Posts** pub (no.22, 7437 5008) on the other side of the street. Unceasingly popular (try getting in on a Thursday evening), this corner boozer is set in a gabled house with 'Watney's Ales' still stencilled on the windows – and feels no compunction to bring out the best crockery for guests. Seats of scuffed lime, charity-shop illustrations of London and birdlife on the walls, and tables of tacky MDF surround an island bar where egalitarian chatter in the finest Soho tradition still reigns. Builders, post-production editors, restaurateurs and market traders, all gabble and glug as one. Overseeing proceedings is a portrait of Jessie Matthews, star of stage and radio (1907-81), Berwick Street born and bred. Fittingly, she's the only personality (Marx, Mozart, pah!) to have a plaque here.

Outside, other retro touches – shop signs bearing the long-since superseded 0171 phone code, street names in *Abbey Road*-style block lettering – catch your eye before it is inevitably drawn to the remnants of the sex industry. Doorways sport hand-lettered signs inviting punters to walk up the scruffy stairways within. Berwick Street winds up with Harmony, Spankarama and Eros Movieland before running into narrow **Walker's Court**, Soho's last remaining red-light quarter, traversed in the blink of an eye.

Sightseeing

92

Oxford Street & Marylebone

Frocks, docs and crocs.

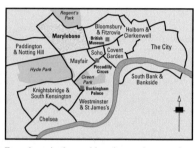

Few places in the world conjure up images of shopping at its most chaotic quite like Oxford Street, its one-and-a-half-mile length continuing to rule supreme in the retail stakes despite increasing competition from out-of-town shopping centres and the fact that many locals won't set foot there unless absolutely necessary. Tourists – of which there are many – head north of Oxford Street mainly to ogle the waxworks of Madame Tussauds, although neighbouring Marylebone also boasts leafy squares, luxurious eating options and streets lined with smaller, more enticing boutiques. Nearby Regent's Park, meanwhile, offers respite for those who'd rather soak up the sun than splash out the cash.

Oxford Street

Map p398

Bond Street, Marble Arch, Oxford Circus or Tottenham Court Road tube.
The relentless trade here accounts for ten per cent of all spending in the capital, but few Londoners hold Oxford Street in high esteem. The road has existed in some form or other since the 12th century, gaining notoriety as the route by which carriages would convey condemned men from Newgate Prison to the gallows at Tyburn (*see p125*), stopping only for a last pint at the **Angel** pub (61 St Giles High Street, 7240 2876). In 1772, it saw the grand opening of James Wyatt's Pantheon; modelled on the Roman equivalent, it featured society balls, exhibitions, opera and theatre

until its closure in 1814. It was demolished in 1937 and a Marks & Spencer now occupies the site (173 Oxford Street). In the 19th century, the street became primarily a shopping district, and it remains so to this day, its western and more salubrious stretch punctuated with large department stores: **John Lewis** (nos.278-306, 7629 7711), **Debenhams** (nos.334-348, 08445 616161) and **Selfridges** (no.400, 0800 123 400). The latter, opened in 1909, is especially grand, with much of the building completed in the art deco heyday of the 1920s. Elsewhere, major architectural interest is limited to Oxford Circus's four identical convex corners, constructed between 1913 and 1928, although the overwhelming crush of the crowds and the rush of traffic can hamper any curiosity – a problem that may yet be resolved by controversial plans to pedestrianise Oxford Street, banning cars by 2009 and installing a tram system by 2013.

At the western end of Oxford Street is **Marble Arch**, originally erected by John Nash in 1827 as an entrance to the rebuilt Buckingham Palace but moved to its current location in 1851 when a fuming Queen Victoria found it too narrow for her state coach to pass through. These days the arch stands forlorn on a hectic traffic island, although tourists still admire its Carrara marble construction and sculptures celebrating Nelson and Wellington's victories over France.

North of Oxford Circus

Map p398

Great Portland Street, Oxford Circus or Regent's Park tube.
Immediately north of Oxford Circus runs Langham Place, notable for the Bath stone façade of John Nash's **All Souls Church**. Its bold combination of a Gothic spire and classical rotunda wasn't always popular: in 1824, one year after it was officially opened, the church was condemned in a House of Commons speech as a 'deplorable and horrible object', and a contemporary newspaper cartoon showed Nash impaled on its spire.

Opposite the church you'll find the BBC head-quarters in **Broadcasting House**, an oddly asymmetrical art deco building that is shipshape in more ways than one. Prominent among the building's carvings is a statue of Shakespeare's Prospero and Ariel, his spirit of the air – or, in this case, the airwaves. (*Ariel* is also the name of the BBC's internal magazine.) The statue caused controversy when it was unveiled due to the flattering size of the manhood of the airy sprite; artist Eric Gill was summoned back to make it more modest. Major renovation work, due for completion in 2011, will see Broadcasting House become home to BBC News, national radio and the World Service.

Over the road is the **Langham Hotel**, opened in 1865 as the UK's first grand hotel and a landmark accommodation option ever since, its history peppered with notable guests from Mark Twain and Napoleon III to Noël Coward and Oscar Wilde (who was commissioned to write *The Picture of Dorian Gray* during a dinner here). The BBC owned the building between 1965 and 1986, during which time episodes of legendary radio comedy *The Goon Show* were broadcast from the ballroom.

North of here, Langham Place turns into **Portland Place**, designed by Robert and James Adam as the glory of 18th-century London. The aristocrats moved out long ago and its Georgian terraced houses are now mostly occupied by embassies and swanky offices. At no.66 is the **Royal Institute of Architects** (RIBA), with a bookshop, first-floor café and one of the finest architectural libraries in the world. Running parallel to Portland Place is **Harley Street**, famous for housing the offices of high-cost dentists and doctors, and **Wimpole Street**, erstwhile home to the poet Elizabeth Barrett Browning (no.50) and Sir Arthur Conan Doyle (2 Upper Wimpole Street). More recently, a young Paul McCartney woke up at no.57, the house of then-girlfriend Jane Asher's parents, and dashed to the piano to transcribe the tune that had been playing in his dream. Originally entitled 'Scrambled Eggs' ('Scrambled eggs/Oh baby how I love your legs'), the song was later given new words and renamed 'Yesterday'.

Marylebone

Map p398

Baker Street, Bond Street, Marble Arch, Oxford Circus or Regent's Park tube.
North of Oxford Street, the increasingly fashionable district known as 'Marylebone Village' has become a magnet for moneyed Londoners, but it wasn't always so idyllic. The area once laboured under the morbid attraction

of Tyburn gallows, with crowds of thousands gathering to watch countless executions over a period of roughly 600 years (the last execution took place here in 1783). The neighbourhood's modern name is a contraction of its parish church, St Mary by the Bourne – the 'bourne' in question is Tyburn stream, which is now entirely covered over but filters into the Thames near Pimlico. **St Marylebone Church** stands in its fourth incarnation

Oxford Street.

of the **Conran Shop** (no.55, 7723 2223) and independent book emporium **Daunt Books** (no.83, 7224 2295), this last a cross between a library and a tiered Edwardian conservatory. Quainter still is winding Marylebone Lane, home to shoe designer **Tracey Neuls** (no.29, 7935 0039) and womenswear boutique **KJ's Laundry** (no.74, 7486 7855), as well as an atmospheric corner pub, the **Golden Eagle** (no.59, 7935 3228), which hosts regular old-style piano singalongs (Tue, Thur, Fri).

Marylebone is a popular foodie destination, with upmarket eateries like the **Providores & Tapa Room** (109 Marylebone High Street, 7935 6175) snuggling up to delicatessens like **La Fromagerie** (2-4 Moxon Street, 7935 0341) and the century-old lunchroom **Paul Rothe & Son** (35 Marylebone Lane, 7935 6783). Marylebone Farmers' Market takes place in the Cramer Street car park every Sunday (10am-2pm).

Further south, 19th-century **St James's Roman Catholic Church** (22 George Street) boasts a soaring neo-Gothic interior dramatically lit by stained-glass windows – Vivien Leigh (née Hartley) married barrister Herbert Leigh Hunt here in 1932 – and the **Wallace Collection**'s arsenal of art and artefacts is a short walk away on Manchester Square. The square was also home to the former offices of EMI Records, the railings of which the Fab Four peered over for the cover photos of their Red Album and Blue Album. The auditorium of nearby **Wigmore Hall** (36 Wigmore Street) remains a jewel in London's classical music crown.

Madame Tussauds

Marylebone Road, NW1 5LR (0870 400 3000/www. madame-tussauds.com). Baker Street tube. **Open** 9.30am-6pm (last entry 5pm) daily. **Admission** *9.30am-5.30pm* £25; £10-£22.50 reductions; £78 family (internet booking only, only available 24hrs in advance). *5.30-6pm* £16; £11-£14 reductions; £50 family. **Credit** MC, V. **Map** p398 G4.
Tussauds compensates for its inherently static attractions with a flurry of attendant activity. As you enter the first room, you're dazzled by fake paparazzi flashbulbs. Starry-eyed kids can take part in a 'Divas' routine with Britney, Beyoncé and Kylie, and Robbie Williams has a hidden sensor activated by kisses to produce a 'twinkle' in his eye. Figures are constantly being added to keep up with new stars, movies and TV shows – the latest include Leonardo DiCaprio, Bollywood heart-throb Shah Rukh Khan and *Pirates of the Caribbean* stars Orlando Bloom and Keira Knightley. Other rooms contain public figures past and present, from Henry and his six wives to Blair and Bush, by way of the Beatles c1964. Below stairs, the Chamber of Horrors surrounds you with hanged corpses and eviscerated victims of torture. For an extra £2 over-12s can be terrorised by serial killers in the Chamber Live. At

Marylebone High Street.

at the northern end of the High Street, its charming garden hosting designer clothing and artisan food stalls at the **Cabbages & Frocks Markets** each Saturday between 11am and 5pm (www.cabbagesandfrocks.co.uk).

Many visitors to Marylebone head directly for the waxworks of **Madame Tussauds**, although there's also a small and often over-looked museum at the neighbouring **Royal Academy of Music** (7873 7373). The area's beating heart, however, is **Marylebone High Street**, teeming with interesting shops that include women's clothing store Sixty 6 (no.66, 7224 6066), classy home furnishings courtesy the kitsch Spirit of London Ride, climb aboard a moving black taxi pod for a whirlwind trundle through 400 years of the city's history. The Planetarium has been replaced by the Wonderful World of Stars, a 360-degree animated take on celebrity – as viewed by aliens – from the makers of *Wallace & Gromit*.

Wallace Collection

Hertford House, Manchester Square, W1U 3BN (7935 0687/www.wallacecollection.org). Bond Street tube. **Open** 10am-5pm daily. **Admission** free. **Credit** (shop) AmEx, MC, V. **Map** p398 G5.

This handsome late 18th-century house contains a collection of furniture, paintings, armour and objets d'art. It all belonged to Sir Richard Wallace, who, as the illegitimate offspring of the fourth Marquess of Hertford, inherited the treasures his father amassed in the last 30 years of his life. Room after grand room contains Louis XIV and XV furnishings and Sèvres porcelain, and the galleries are hung with lush paintings by Titian, Velázquez, Boucher, Fragonard, Gainsborough and Reynolds; Franz Hals's *Laughing Cavalier* (neither laughing, nor a Cavalier) is one of the best known. There are also regular temporary exhibitions. The lovely Wallace restaurant, in the glass-roofed courtyard, is a new Oliver Peyton outfit. On the front lawn stands a Wallace fountain of the type that Sir Richard commissioned as farewell gifts to Paris, the city of his youth and his first love.

Regent's Park

Map p398

Baker Street or Regent's Park tube.

Regent's Park (open 5am-dusk daily) is one of London's most popular open spaces. Originally a hunting ground of Henry VIII, it remained a royals-only retreat long after it was formally designed by John Nash in 1811, only opening to the public for the first time in 1845. Repairs of wartime damage to the grounds stagnated until well into the 1970s, but the park is now a spectacular place to while away a lunch hour or spend an entire day. The animal noises and odours of **London Zoo** carry a surprising distance, while at the lovely **Open Air Theatre** performances of *A Midsummer Night's Dream* are an integral part of London summers. Rowing boat hire, spectacular rose gardens, ice-cream stands and the **Garden Café** (7935 5729, www.thegardencafe.co.uk) complete the picture.

West of Regent's Park looms the golden dome of the **London Central Mosque** (www.iccuk.org) and the northern end of **Baker Street**, which is, unsurprisingly, pretty heavy on nods to the world's favourite freelance detective. Not least among them is the **Sherlock Holmes Museum** (7935 8866, www.sherlock-holmes.co.uk) at no.239. Here the Holmes stories are earnestly re-enacted: there's a bobby guarding the front door and Victorian maids man the tills at the (rather tacky) shop. Serious fans will probably find more of interest among the books and photos of the Sherlock Holmes Collection at **Marylebone Library** (7641 1206, by appointment only) or, eschewing Baker Street altogether, heading to the Murder One bookshop (76-78 Charing Cross Road, 7539 8820, www.murderone.co.uk), which has probably the largest collection of Sherlock Holmes-related books for sale anywhere. They could also make a pilgrimage to Conan Doyle's former home on Upper Wimpole Street or the Langham Hotel (for both, *see p125*), which features in several of his stories.

From crime fiction to music fact, another true story of Baker Street involves the Beatles having painted no.94 with a mind-boggling psychedelic mural before opening it in December 1967 as the Apple Boutique, a clothing store run on such whimsical hippie principles that it quickly began losing huge amounts of money and was forced to close within six months. Fab Four pilgrims head to the **London Beatles Store** (no.231, 7935 4464, www.beatlesstorelondon.co.uk), where the ground-floor shop offers a predictable array of Beatles-branded accessories alongside genuine collectibles and vintage records. The gallery above (admission £1) has original album artwork, photographs and a few of Paul's rather dodgy sketches. Next door, Presley store **Elvisly Yours** (7486 2005) caters to those more into blue suede shoes than yellow submarines.

London Zoo

Regent's Park, NW1 4RY (7722 3333/www.zsl.org/london-zoo). Baker Street or Camden Town tube then 274, C2 bus. **Open** *Late Oct-mid Mar* 10am-4pm daily. *Mid Mar-late Oct* 10am-5.30pm daily. **Admission** £14.50; £10.75-£12.70 reductions; £45 family; free under-3s. **Credit** AmEx, MC, V. **Map** p398 G2.

Opened in 1828, this was the world's first scientific zoo, and today umbrella charity ZSL stresses its commitment to worldwide conservation. The zoo's habitats keep pace with the times – the elephants have been given room to roam at sister-site Whipsnade Wild Animal Park in Bedfordshire, and the penguins have been moved from Lubetkin's famous modernist pool to a more suitable space. The new 16,000sq ft walk-through squirrel monkey enclosure allows you to get close to the animals in an open environment based on a Bolivian rainforest, while the African Bird Safari, another new walk-through habitat, has replaced three small, outdated bird enclosures. In 2007, the Gorilla Kingdom opened, a forest walk among the big apes and the creatures that share their world. It's advisable to follow one of the recommended routes around the zoo to avoid missing anything; check the daily programme to get a good view at feeding times.

Sightseeing

Paddington & Notting Hill

The Middle Eastern West End and a noted hill of celebrity boutiques.

Unless you're a devotee of Victorian railway engineering there's no very compelling reason to visit Paddington, and Bayswater offers little to visitors other than to those intrigued by London's expat enclaves – this is the focal point of London's Middle Eastern community. Notting Hill, however, remains a major tick on many itineraries, not least because of the indefatigable Portobello Market.

Edgware Road & Paddington

Maps p395
Edgware Road, Lancaster Gate,
Marble Arch or Paddington tube/rail.
Edgware Road rules a definite north–south line marking where the central West End stops and central west London begins. Its straightness and length give a clue to its origins (it was a Roman road) but it is best known these days as the heart of the city's Middle East end. If you want to pick up your copy of *Al Hayat*, cash a cheque at the Bank of Kuwait or catch Egyptian football, this is the place to come. It is home to the **Maroush** (*see p208*) mini-empire of restaurants.

North of the Marylebone Road flyover, the landscape gets bleaker, but there are some highlights: **Church Street** has a local food and general market that is rapidly gentrifying at its eastern end, thanks to the fascinating **Alfie's Antiques Market** (*see p259*).

The fact that the name Paddington has been immortalised by a certain small, ursine Peruvian émigré is appropriate, given that the area has long served as a home to refugees and

immigrants. It was a country village until the 19th century. Then came the Grand Junction Canal in 1801, linking London to the Midlands, and in 1838 the railway. The current **Paddington Station** was built in 1851 to the specifications of the great engineer Isambard Kingdom Brunel. The triple roof of iron and glass is a fine example of Victorian engineering.

In the 1950s, there was poverty and over-crowding, but the area's proximity to central London meant property developers eventually recognised its potential. The slick **Paddington Central** development east of the station is a case in point, with its million square feet of office space, canalside apartments and restaurants – on Sheldon Square, the Chinese Pearl Liang (no.8, 7289 7000) and Japanese Yakitoria (no.25, 3214 3000, www.yakitoria.co.uk) are both notable. Also east of the station is St Mary's Hospital, where Alexander Fleming discovered penicillin.

Alexander Fleming Laboratory Museum

St Mary's Hospital, Praed Street, W2 1NY (7886 6528/www.st-marys.nhs.uk/about/fleming_museum.htm). Paddington tube/rail. **Open** 10am-1pm Mon-Thur. *By appointment* 2-5pm Mon-Thur; 10am-5pm Fri. **Admission** £2; £1 reductions; free under-5s. **No credit cards. Map** p395 D5.
Only 80 years ago pneumonia was often fatal and tuberculosis 'the captain of the armies of death'. In 1928, Fleming noticed that the Staphylococcus bacteria on a discarded culture plate were being killed and humanity was handed a powerful weapon against bacterial enemies – a weapon that is losing its potency as 'superbugs' adapt to antibiotics. This is the room where the ground-breaking discovery of penicillin happened and it preserves many artefacts.

Bayswater

Map p394
Bayswater or Queensway tube.
West of Paddington is Bayswater, an area of grand Victorian housing, much of which has been converted into flats and hotels. At the junction with Leinster Terrace, 100 Bayswater Road is where playwright Sir James Barrie lived

Notting Hill: have bag, will shop. *See p130.*

from 1902 to 1909; here he wrote *Peter Pan*. Further up the side street, 23-24 Leinster Gardens warrants close scrutiny; the façades of these adjacent houses are no more than elaborate set decoration – a painted wall built to hide an opening to the Underground line below.

Queensway, the vertical spine of the area, was known as Black Lion Lane until it was renamed in honour of Queen Victoria. Like Edgware Road, it is full of Middle Eastern cafés and restaurants. There's a slightly different eastern flavour on Moscow Road, just off Queensway, in the form of the Greek Orthodox **Cathedral of St Sophia** (7229 7260, www.st sophia.org.uk, open 11am-2pm Mon, Wed-Fri) where Byzantine icons and golden mosaics glow in the candlelight. Near the top of the street, grand old **Whiteleys** (Queensway, 7229 8844, www.whiteleys.com) has turned from department store into franchise heaven and unofficial dating ground for half the Middle East. William Whiteley, the store's founder, called himself 'The Universal Provider' – a bold claim from someone who was shot dead in 1907 by a man claiming to be his bastard son.

Heading north over the junction with Bishops Bridge Road is the **Porchester Centre** (7792 2919), one of the few surviving examples of the Victorian Turkish baths that were once common in Britain. A left at the top of Queensway takes you into **Westbourne Grove**, which starts humble but gets posher the further west you go. Once you cross Chepstow Road you're really into Notting Hill. The shopping is stellar, but you'll have to clear purchases with your bank

manager. Here you will find **Bill Amberg**'s gorgeous leather accessories (21-22 Chepstow Corner, 7727 3560), and luxury scents and candles at **Maison Diptyque** (195 Westbourne Grove, 7727 8673), while across the street is jet-set holiday boutique **Heidi Klein** (no.174, 7243 5665, www.heidiklein.co.uk). There are similar riches on **Ledbury Road**, including covetable fashion and home accessories at **Aimé** (no.32, 7221 7070,www.aimelondon.com). Along with the boutiques is the tip-top deli **Tavola** (no.155, 7229 0571), owned by restaurateur Alastair Little, and Tom Conran's celeb-frequented **Tom's** (no.226, 7221 8818). Ledbury Road also has a branch of cool deli-café **Ottolenghi** (no.63, 7727 1121; *see also p214*). Predictably, the one museum in the area is a homage to consumerism.

Museum of Brands, Packaging & Advertising

Colville Mews, Lonsdale Road, W11 2AR (7908 0880/www.museumofbrands.com). Notting Hill Gate tube. **Open** 10am-6pm Tue-Sat; 11am-5pm Sun. **Admission** £5.80; £2-£3.50 reductions; free under-7s. **Credit** MC, V. **Map** p394 A6.

Robert Opie began collecting the things that most of us throw away when he was 16. Over the years the collection has grown to include everything from milk bottles to vacuum cleaners and cereal packets. The emphasis is on British consumerism through the last century, though there are items as old as an ancient Egyptian doll. The greatest interest is for British nostalgists who relish the cascading time-travel experience of watching brands such as HP Sauce transmogrify over the years. *Photo p130.*

Museum of Brands. *See p129.*

Notting Hill

Map p394

Notting Hill Gate, Ladbroke Grove or Westbourne Park tube.

The triangle made by the tube stations of Notting Hill Gate, Ladbroke Grove and Westbourne Park contains some lovely squares, houses and gardens, along with a host of fashionable restaurants, bars and shops, many exploiting the lingering street cred of the fast disappearing black and working-class residents.

Notting Hill Gate is not itself an attractive high street, but the leafy avenues south are; so is Pembridge Road, to the north, leading to the boutique-filled streets of Westbourne Grove and Ledbury Road, and more notably to **Portobello Road** and its famed market (*see p239*). The name honours the capture of Puerto Bello from the Spaniards in 1739. Beginning at Pembridge Road, the **Sun in Splendour** (no.7, 7313 9331) is Notting Hill's oldest pub. Over the road is a charming terrace of two-storey cottages: no.22 has a plaque commemorating the residency of George Orwell in 1927-28 – he began his first book (*Down and Out in Paris and London*) here. A little further north, 19 Denbigh Terrace has been home to both Peter Cook and Richard Branson. The **Electric** Cinema (*see p287*), built in 1910, has a gorgeous façade of cream faience tiles and an equally beautifully maintained interior. Next door, the Electric Brasserie (no.191, 7908 9696, www.the-electric.co.uk) is buzzily fashionable.

Blenheim Crescent boasts three notable independent booksellers in **Blenheim Books** (no.11, 7792 0777, www.blenheimbooks.co.uk), **Books for Cooks** (no.4; *see p242*) and the **Travel Bookshop** (nos.13-15, 7229 5260, www.thetravelbookshop.com), the store on which Hugh Grant's bookshop was based in the movie *Notting Hill* – a film that did more to undermine the area's bohemian credibility than a fleet of Starbucks. The location of Grant's apartment in the film (actually then the home of the film's screenwriter Richard Curtis) is a block north at 280 Westbourne Park Road.

Under the Westway, the elevated section of the M40 motorway that links London with the West Country, is small but busy **Portobello Green Market**. Here you'll find the best vintage fashion stalls. Look out for the excellent second-hand boot and shoe stall and brilliant vintage handbag stall (usually outside the Falafel King café), along with wonderful vintage clothing stall Sage Femme, which can normally be found outside the Antique Clothing Shop. North of the Westway, Portobello's vitality fizzles out. It sparks back to life at Golborne Road, the heartland of London's North African community and the address of the excellent, no-frills **Moroccan Tagine** café (no.95, 8968 8055). Here too are the rival Portuguese café-delis **Lisboa Pâtisserie** (no.57, 8968 5242) and **Café Oporto** (no.62A, 8968 8839). **Trellick Tower**, the concrete building at the north-eastern end of Golborne Road, is one of London's most divisive bits of architecture. Love it or hate it, it's a significant piece of modernism by Ernö Goldfinger. At its western end, Golborne Road connects with Ladbroke Grove, which can be followed north to the famously spooky **Kensal Green Cemetery**.

Kensal Green Cemetery

Harrow Road, Kensal Green, W10 4RA (8969 0152/www.kensalgreen.co.uk). Kensal Green tube. **Open** *Apr-Sept* 9am-6pm Mon-Sat; 10am-6pm Sun. *Oct-Mar* 9am-5pm Mon-Sat; 10am-5pm Sun. *Tours* 2pm Sun; (incl catacombs) 2pm 1st & 3rd Sun of mth. **Admission** free. *Tours* £5 (£4 reductions) donation. **No credit cards**.

Behind the neoclassical gate is a green oasis of the dead. The resting place of both the Duke of Sussex, sixth son of King George III, and his sister, HRH Princess Sophia, was the place to be buried in the 19th century. Wilkie Collins, Anthony Trollope and William Makepeace Thackeray all lie here, but it is the mausoleums of lesser folk that make the most eye-catching graves.

Piccadilly Circus & Mayfair

Bright lights and the high life.

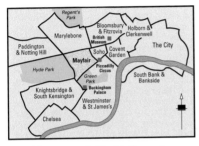

Not without reason is Mayfair the most expensive property on the Monopoly board: here you'll find some of London's most glamorous and venerable shops and squares. From the old-world decorum of the arcades to the shock of the new in the area's cluster of commercial art galleries, you'll need to bring more than play money if you plan on shopping. Slightly less ritzy – though home to the hotel of decidedly larger-than-Monopoly dimensions and reputation – Piccadilly stretches out along Mayfair's southern edge, from the roaring traffic at Hyde Park Corner to the flashing billboards and swirling crowds of Piccadilly Circus.

Piccadilly Circus & Regent Street

Map p406
Oxford Circus or Piccadilly Circus tube.
Bustling, hectic **Piccadilly Circus** is an uneasy mix of the tawdry and the grandiose. It certainly has little to do with the original vision of its architect John Nash. His 1820s design for the intersection of two of the West End's most elegant streets, Regent Street and Piccadilly, was a harmonious circle of curved frontages. But 60 years later Shaftesbury Avenue muscled in, creating the present lopsided and slightly pandemonious traffic junction. Alfred Gilbert's memorial fountain in honour of child-labour abolitionist Earl Shaftesbury was erected in 1893. Properly known as the Shaftesbury Memorial, the statue that tops it was intended

to show the Angel of Christian Charity, but to critics and public alike it looked like **Eros**, and their judgement has stuck. The illuminated advertising panels first appeared late in the 19th century and have been present ever since.

Connecting Piccadilly Circus to Oxford Circus to the north and Pall Mall to the south, **Regent Street** is a broad, curving boulevard. It was designed by Nash in the early 1800s, with the aims of improving access to Regent's Park and bumping up property values in Haymarket and Pall Mall. The grandeur of the sweeping road is impressive – even if much of Nash's architecture was destroyed in the early 20th century. Halfway up, on the left side, **Heddon Street** is where the iconic photo was taken that graces the cover of David Bowie's *Ziggy Stardust* album – the building that he is posed in front of is now the Moroccan-flavoured Mô Tea Room, next door to famed North African eaterie **Momo** (*see p211*); the bright K West sign visible on the cover was long since stolen by a Bowie fan, never to be seen again. Further north on Regent Street are mammoth children's emporium **Hamleys** (nos.188-196, 0870 333 2455, www.hamleys. com) and landmark **Liberty** store (*see p238*).

Mayfair

Map p400
Bond Street or Green Park tube.
The image of gaiety suggested by its name – deriving from a long-departed fair that used to take place here each May – is belied by the staid atmosphere of modern-day Mayfair. It's easy to feel like you don't belong in some of the deadly quiet residential streets that, over the centuries, attracted many of London's biggest wigs. Even on busy shopping streets you may feel out of place without the reassuring heft of a platinum card – if you do have one of those, though, there's no better place in the capital to burn it up.

The Grosvenor and Berkeley families bought the rolling green fields that would become Mayfair in the mid 17th century. In the 1700s, they developed the pastures into a posh new neighbourhood. In particular they built a series of squares surrounded by elegant houses. The

Piccadilly Circus.

most famous of these, **Grosvenor Square** (that's 'Grove-ner'), built 1725-31, is now dominated by the supremely inelegant US Embassy. A product of the Cold War era, it takes up one whole side of the square and its only decorative touches are a fierce-looking eagle and a mass of post-9/11 protective barricades. Out front, a big statue of President Dwight Eisenhower has pride of place (Franklin D Roosevelt stands in the park nearby).

When in London, Eisenhower stayed at the exclusive hotel **Claridge's** (*see p59*), a block east on Brook Street. **Brook Street** has impressive music credentials: GF Handel lived and died (1759) at no.25, and Jimi Hendrix roomed briefly next door at no.23. These adjacent buildings have been combined into a museum dedicated to Handel's memory (*see p133*). This part of Mayfair, however, is all about shopping. **South Molton Street**, which connects Brook Street with Oxford Street to the north, is no longer the hip enclave it once was, but it still boasts the fabulous boutique-emporium **Browns** (*see p245*), while **New Bond Street** is an A-Z of every top-end, mainstream fashion house you can name.

Beyond New Bond Street, **Hanover Square** is another of the area's big squares, now a busy traffic chicane. Just south is **St George's Church**, built in the 1720s and once everybody's favourite place to get married. Among the luminaries who uttered their vows at the altar were George Eliot and Teddy Roosevelt (not

to each other, of course). Handel, who married nobody, attended services here. South of St George's, salubrious **Conduit Street** is where fashion shocker **Vivienne Westwood** (no.44) faces the more staid **Rigby & Peller** (no.22A), corsetière to the Queen. At no.9 is London's most audacious restaurant, **Sketch** (*see p211*).

Running south off Conduit Street is the most famous Mayfair shopping street of all, **Savile Row**, home of bespoke British tailoring. At no.15 is the estimable **Henry Poole & Co**, which over the years has cut suits for clients including Napoleon Bonaparte, Charles Dickens, Winston Churchill and Charles de Gaulle. No.3 was the home of Apple Records, the Beatles' recording studio. The group famously played their last gig at this address on 30 January 1969, up on the roof – the set lasted 45 minutes until it was halted by the police following complaints from a local bank manager about 'a breach of the peace'.

Two streets west, **Cork Street** is the West End's gallery row, where you can almost always see interesting work on display – though usually small, some shows can rival anything the public museums offer on a similar scale. A couple of streets over again is Albemarle Street, where you'll find the scientific Royal Institution (no.21), home to the **Faraday Museum** (7409 2992, www.rigb.org). After a lengthy refurbishment, the Institution and museum will be reopening in spring 2008.

Shepherd Market

The third of Mayfair's famed squares is **Berkeley Square**, which is just west of Albemarle Street. No.44 is one of the square's original houses, built in the 1740s, and once called by noted architectural historian Nikolaus Pevsner 'the finest terrace house of London'. **Curzon Street**, which runs off the south-west corner of Berkeley Square, was home to MI5, Britain's secret service, from 1945 until the 1990s; it's also the northern boundary of **Shepherd Market**, which is named after a food market set up here by architect Edward Shepherd in the early 18th century, and the true heart of the neighbourhood. From 1686, this was where the raucous May Fair was held, until it was shut down for good in the late 18th century after city leaders complained of 'drunkenness, fornication, gaming and lewdness'. You'll still manage the drunkenness easily enough in what is now a pleasant, upscale area with a couple of good pubs (**Ye Grapes** at 16 Shepherd Market and the **Shepherd's Tavern** at 50 Hertford Street) and some of London's most agreeable pavement dining. Perhaps more surprising, there are still prostitutes working from neighbouring tatty apartment blocks.

Flat 12, 9 Curzon Place, which is just north-west of Shepherd Market, is notable for rock exits. In 1974, after attending Mick Jagger's 32nd birthday party in Chelsea, Mama Cass Elliot of the Mamas and Papas, returned to Curzon Place. She went to bed and never woke up – heart failure due to obesity was the verdict. In 1978, the Who's drummer Keith Moon checked out on the same premises, cause of death: an overdose.

Handel House Museum

25 Brook Street (entrance in Lancashire Court), W1K 4HB (7495 1685/www.handelhouse.org). Bond Street tube. **Open** 10am-6pm Tue, Wed, Fri, Sat; 10am-8pm Thur; noon-6pm Sun. **Admission** £5; £2-£4.50 reductions; free under-5s. **Credit** MC, V. **Map** p398 H6.

George Frideric Handel moved to Britain from his native Germany aged 25 and settled in this Mayfair house 12 years later, remaining here until his death in 1759. The house has been beautifully restored with original and recreated furnishings, paintings and a welter of the composer's scores (in the same room as photos of Jimi Hendrix, who lived next door). The pro-gramme of events is surprisingly dynamic for such a small museum, and includes recitals every Thursday.

Piccadilly & Green Park

Map p400

Green Park, Hyde Park Corner or Piccadilly Circus tube.

Piccadilly's name is derived from a type of suit collar (the 'picadil') in vogue during the 18th century; the first of the area's main buildings was built by tailor Robert Baker and, indicating the source of his wealth, nicknamed 'Piccadilly Hall'. A stroll through the handful of Regency shopping arcades confirms that the rag trade is still flourishing in the area, and you are mere minutes away from Savile Row (*see left*) and Jermyn Street. The newly renovated **Burlington Arcade**, its entrance next door to the Royal Academy, is the oldest and most famous of these. Resplendent in top hats and livery, its security staff (known as 'beadles') are on hand to ensure that there is no singing, whistling or hurrying in the arcade: such uncouth behaviour is prohibited by archaic bylaws that remain on the books (although laws forbidding unaccompanied women or ladies with pushchairs to enter the arcade have been repealed). High-end retail continues to be represented on Piccadilly itself by **Fortnum & Mason** (*see p238*), London's most prestigious food store, founded in 1707 by a former footman to Queen Anne and splendidly refurbished to celebrate its third century. A couple of doors away at no.187, **Hatchard's** (*see p241*) the Bookseller dates back to 1801. The simple-looking church at no.197 is **St James's** (*see*

p134). This was the personal favourite of its architect Sir Christopher Wren. The interior contains superb limewood carving by his colleague Grinling Gibbons, including the font in which William Blake (*see p15* **City seer**) was baptised in 1757. There's often a market out front, and a coffeeshop with outdoor seating is tucked into a corner by the garden. The church doubles as a music venue.

On the north side of Piccadilly, the former Burlington House (1665) is now home to the **Royal Academy of Arts** (*see p134*), which hosts several lavish, crowd-pleasing exhibitions each year and has a pleasant courtyard café.

West down Piccadilly, smartly uniformed doormen mark the **Wolseley** (*see p211*), a former car showroom reopened in 2004 as an instant classic of a restaurant, and the **Ritz** (*see p61*). The green expanse just beyond the Ritz is **Green Park**. Once a plague pit, where the city's epidemic victims were buried, it may not match the grandeur of St James's or Regent's parks, but it has its own charm. This is most evident in spring, when the slopes are covered in daffodils. Further along Piccadilly, work your way past the queue outside the Hard Rock Café to the Duke of Wellington's old home, **Apsley House** (*see p134*), opposite **Wellington Arch** (*see p134*), both at Hyde Park Corner.

West is Hyde Park (*see p152*) and the posh enclave of Belgravia (*see p148*), while to the south lies Buckingham Palace (*see p142*).

Savile Row.

Wellington Arch.

Apsley House

149 Piccadilly, W1J 7NT (7499 5676/www.english-heritage.org.uk). Hyde Park Corner tube. **Open** *Nov-Mar* 10am-4pm Tue-Sun. *Apr-Oct* 10am-5pm Tue-Sun. *Tours* by arrangement. **Admission** £5.30; £4 reductions. *Tours* phone in advance. *Joint ticket with Wellington Arch* £6.90; £5.20 reductions; £17.30 family. **Credit** MC, V. **Map** p400 G8.

Called No.1 London because it was the first London building encountered on the road from the village of Kensington after crossing the Knights' Bridge, Apsley House was built by Robert Adam in the 1770s. The Duke of Wellington had it as his London residence for 35 years. Although his descendants still live here, several rooms are open to the public providing a superb feel for the man and his era. Admire the extravagant porcelain dinnerware and plates or ask for a demonstration of the crafty mirrors in the scarlet and gilt picture gallery, where a fine Velázquez and a Correggio hang near Goya's portrait of the Iron Duke after he defeated the French in 1812 (a last-minute edit, as X-rays revealed that Wellington's head had been brushed over that of Joseph Bonaparte, Napoleon's brother).

Royal Academy of Arts

Burlington House, Piccadilly, W1J 0BD (7300 8000/www.royalacademy.org.uk). Green Park or Piccadilly Circus tube. **Open** 10am-6pm Mon-Thur, Sat, Sun; 10am-10pm Fri. **Admission** varies. **Credit** AmEx, DC, MC, V. **Map** p406 U4.

Britain's first art school was founded in 1768 and moved to the extravagantly Palladian Burlington House a century later. It is now best known for the galleries, which stage a roster of populist temporary exhibitions. Those in the John Madejski Fine Rooms are drawn from the RA's holdings – ranging from Constable to Hockney – and are free. The Academy's biggest event is the Summer Exhibition, which for more than two centuries has drawn from works entered by the public.

St James's Piccadilly

197 Piccadilly, W1J 9LL (7734 4511/www.st-james-piccadilly.org). Piccadilly Circus tube. **Open** 8am-6.30pm daily. *Evening events* times vary. **Admission** free. **Map** p406 V4.

Consecrated in 1684, St James's is the only church Sir Christopher Wren built on an entirely new site. A calming building, with few architectural airs or graces, it was bombed to within an inch of its life in World War II but painstakingly reconstructed. Grinling Gibbons's delicate limewood garlanding around the sanctuary survived and is one of the few real frills. This is a busy church as, along with its inclusive ministry, it runs a counselling service, stages regular classical concerts, provides a home for the William Blake Society and hosts markets in the churchyard: antiques on Tuesday, arts and crafts from Wednesday to Saturday. There's also a handy café tucked into a corner by the quiet garden.

Wellington Arch

Hyde Park Corner, W1J 7JZ (7930 2726/www.english-heritage.org.uk). Hyde Park Corner tube. **Open** *Apr-Oct* 10am-5pm Wed-Sun. *Nov-Mar* 10am-4pm Wed-Sun. **Admission** £3.20; £1.60-£2.40 reductions; free under-5s. *Joint ticket with Apsley House* £6.90; £5.20 reductions; £17.30 family. **Credit** MC, V. **Map** p400 G8.

Built in the late 1820s to mark Britain's triumph over Napoleonic France, Decimus Burton's Wellington Arch was shifted from its original location to accommodate traffic at Hyde Park Corner in 1882. It was initially topped by an out-of-proportion equestrian statue of Wellington, but since 1912 Captain Adrian Jones's 38-ton bronze *Peace Descending on the Quadriga of War* has finished it with a flourish. It was restored in 1999 by English Heritage, and has three floors of displays, covering the history of the arch and the Blue Plaques scheme. From the balcony, you can see the Houses of Parliament and Buckingham Palace, though trees obstruct much of the view in summer.

Westminster & St James's

The city's centre – a place of power, pomp and coincidence.

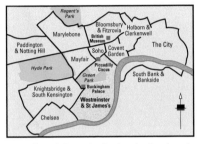

Westminster's imposing landmarks date largely from the 19th century, but the foundations of power on which they rest stretch back almost a thousand years. In the 11th century, Edward the Confessor moved the royal palace west from the City to marshland then known as Thorney Island, and the area remains London's – arguably England's – heart. The British government has its seat in the **Houses of Parliament**; the monarch's most famous residence, **Buckingham Palace**, overlooks Green Park and the Mall; and **Westminster Abbey**, where a church has stood since the eighth century, has been the place of coronation for royalty since William the Conqueror was crowned on Christmas Day in 1066. There are plenty of other unmissable sights too: **Trafalgar Square**, the **National Gallery** and **Tate Britain** should all be visited, as should lovely **St James's Park**.

Trafalgar Square

Map p407

Leicester Square tube or Charing Cross tube/rail.
Despite having spent several decades hemmed in on all sides by traffic, Trafalgar Square has always been a natural gathering point. Since its north side was returned to pedestrians in 2003, that civic function has been even more apparent. Protest marches start and finish here, and it is a venue for concerts and festivals, as well as for impromptu demonstrations and celebrations. The piazza was conceived by the monument-obsessed Prince Regent, later

George IV. He commissioned John Nash (who also designed Piccadilly Circus; *see p131*) to create a grand square that paid homage to Britain's naval power. The square was not completed until 1840, after the deaths of both the King and Nash. The focal point is **Nelson's Column**, a tribute to the heroic Vice Admiral Horatio Nelson, who died during the Battle of Trafalgar in 1805. This Corinthian column, designed by William Railton, is topped by a statue of Nelson. The granite fountains were added in 1845 (then redesigned by Lutyens in 1939) and the bronze lions – the work of Sir Edwin Landseer – in 1867. Statues of George IV and a couple of Victorian military heroes anchor three of the square's corners. On the south side of the square a **statue of Charles I**, dating from the 1630s, faces down Whitehall. Immediately behind the statue, which was the first equestrian bronze in England, a plaque marks the original site of an Eleanor Cross (*see p136* **Stuck in the middle**). Neoclassical buildings overlook the square: James Gibbs's **St Martin-in-the-Fields** (*see p137*) and one of the world's great art museums, the **National Gallery** (*see below*). The smaller **National Portrait Gallery** (*see p137*) is as impressive.

National Gallery

Trafalgar Square, WC2N 5DN (7747 2885/www.nationalgallery.org.uk). Leicester Square tube/Charing Cross tube/rail. **Open** (incl Sainsbury Wing) 10am-6pm Mon, Tue, Thur-Sun; 10am-9pm Wed. *Tours* 11.30am, 2.30pm Mon, Tue, Thur, Fri, Sun; 11.30am, 2.30pm, 6pm, 6.30pm Wed; 11.30am, 12.30pm, 2.30pm, 3.30pm Sat. **Admission** free. *Special exhibitions* prices vary. **Credit** (shop) MC, V. **Map** p407 X5.
Founded in 1824, the National Gallery has a collection that grew from just 38 paintings into one of the greatest in the world, comprising more than 2,000 Western European pieces. There are masterpieces from virtually every school of art, from religious works of the 13th century to van Gogh. The modern Sainsbury Wing (1991) concentrates on the Renaissance, with unmissable gems including Piero della Francesca's *Baptism of Christ* and the beautiful Wilton Diptych. The wings of the main building overflow with paintings by the Great Masters, with

Stuck in the middle

It would be nice to think that the centre of London – the exact, official centre of this noble city – was somewhere suitably grand. Perhaps it's **Nelson's Column** (*see p135*)? Certainly memorable. How about Apsley House, with its unbeatable address: no.1, London? Sorry, no.

Let's try the **Tower of London** (*see p101*), then. Back when giants still ruled these isles, King Bran (known to us from a Welsh epic, *The Mabinogion*) was mortally wounded in battle against the Irish. He gave the order that he should be decapitated and his head buried under the city, where it would continue to protect his land against invasion. It is said William the Conqueror's White Tower was erected on the very spot, surely giving it a persuasive claim as the mythological centre of the city? Nope.

Less ancient but still venerable – and with the added bonus of actually existing – is another contender: the **London Stone**. This rounded lump of limestone, set into the wall at 111 Cannon Street (opposite Cannon Street Station) and recorded as the Lonenstane at least as far back as the 11th century, is thought by some to be a

Roman milestone, silently marking the spot from which measurements in the occupied province were taken 2,000 years ago. Or another Roman contender might be **Cornhill**, highest hill in the Square Mile, site of the main Roman basilica.

No, and no again. For the truth, fast-forward 1,000 years. Ask a Londoner, and they might well tell you about the monument in front of Charing Cross Station. In 1290, after the death of his wife Eleanor, the uxurious Edward I ordered that crosses be erected to mark the 12 points at which her funeral train halted on its journey from Lincoln to Westminster Abbey. In 1863, long after the original cross had been turned into paving for Whitehall, the current replica cross was erected outside the station. And the centre of London? It's the site of that final cross.

The trouble is, the site of the last cross wasn't in fact in front of Charing Cross Station. The official central point of the city is a touch south of Trafalgar Square, just behind the equestrian statue of Charles I standing on a woozily skewed roundabout, where the original Eleanor Cross once stood. Only a plaque (*pictured*) now marks the place.

such highlights as Holbein's *Ambassadors* and Velázquez's *Rokeby Venus*, as well as important works by Turner and Constable. The real crowd-pullers, however, are more modern: Monet's huge *Water-Lilies* is just one of dozens of Impressionist masterworks, while Van Gogh's *Chair* and Seurat's *Bathers at Asnières* are also stars. You can't see everything in one visit, but there are guided tours of

the major works and excellent free audio guides. Eating options are terrific too: the National Dining Rooms (*see p211*) and, facing St Martin-in-the-Fields (*see p137*) from the East Wing, the National Café, whose late opening seems unknown to most visitors. A major exhibition in 2008 (until 19 May) will celebrate the work of Pompeo Batoni, the great portrait painter of 18th-century Grand Tourists.

National Portrait Gallery

*2 St Martin's Place, WC2H 0HE (7306 0055/www.
npg.org.uk). Leicester Square tube/Charing Cross
tube/rail.* **Open** 10am-6pm Mon-Wed, Sat, Sun; 10am-
9pm Thur, Fri. **Admission** free. *Special exhibitions*
prices vary. **Credit** AmEx, MC, V. **Map** p407 X4.
From Tudor royalty to present-day celebs (and from
Tudor celebs to present-day royalty), the sitters for
portraits in the NPG are of interest for contributions
not only to history but also to culture, sport, science
and government. Exhibits are organised chronolog-
ically from top to bottom: start on the second floor
and work your way down. The gallery's subject
matter, manageable size and attractive design make
it wonderfully personable, and the top-floor restaurant has great views. The prestigious BP Portrait
Award exhibition is an annual highlight.

St Martin-in-the-Fields

*Trafalgar Square, WC2N 4JJ (7766 1100/Brass
Rubbing Centre 7766 1122/box office 7839 8362/
www.stmartin-in-the-fields.org). Leicester Square tube/
Charing Cross tube/rail.* **Open** Church 8am-6pm daily.
Services 8am, 5.30pm Mon-Fri; 8am, 1.15pm, 5.30pm,
6pm Wed; 9am Sat; 8am, 10am, 2.15pm (in Chinese),
5pm, 6.30pm Sun. *Brass Rubbing Centre* 10am-6pm
Mon-Sat; noon-6pm Sun. *Evening concerts* 7.30pm
Thur-Sat & alternate Tue. *Free concerts* 1pm Mon, Tue,
Fri. **Admission** free. *Brass rubbing* £3-£15. *Evening
concerts* prices vary. **Credit** MC, V. **Map** p407 X4.
A church has stood here since the 13th century, 'in
the fields' between Westminster and the City; this
one was built in 1726 by James Gibbs, who designed
it in a curious combination of neoclassical and
baroque styles. This is the parish church for
Buckingham Palace (note the royal box to the left of
the gallery), but is better known for its classical
music concerts (*see p307*). It has undergone a £36m
refurbishment, the final phases of which are due for
completion in April 2008; the interior, with superb
plaster- and stonework, is fully restored, the glass
has been replaced, and various extraneous Victorian
additions have been removed to return the building
to its original condition. The crypt, its excellent café
and the London Brass Rubbing Centre should all
have been expanded and modernised, and there will
be two brand-new glass pavilion entrances.

Whitehall to Parliament Square

Map p401

Westminster tube or Charing Cross tube/rail.
Lined with government buildings, the long,
gentle curve of **Whitehall** is named after Henry
VIII's magnificent palace, which burned to the
ground in 1698. At the top of the street, the
Banqueting House (*see below*), London's first
entirely Italianate building, survived the blaze;
it faces **Horse Guards**, which has acquired
a new museum (*see p143* **Ceremonial city**).
The street is also still home to the Ministry

of Defence, the Foreign Office and the Treasury.
Further down Whitehall is Sir Edwin Lutyens's
dignified memorial to the dead of both world
wars, the **Cenotaph**, which is near **Downing
Street** (closed to the public), the home address
of both the prime minister (no.10) and chancellor
(no.11). King Charles Street runs parallel, flanked
by the Foreign Office, ending with the **Cabinet
War Rooms** (*see p138*), the operations centre
used by Churchill during World War II air
raids, along with the **Churchill Museum**.
  A few hundred feet from the Cenotaph stands
the much newer **memorial to the women
of World War II**, featuring 17 sets of work
clothes hanging on pegs. Designed by the
sculptor John Mills, it was inspired by the
advice given in 1945 to the seven million
or so women who had contributed to the war
effort: 'Hang up your uniforms and overalls
and go home – the job is done.'
  At the end of Whitehall, **Parliament
Square** was laid out in 1868, surrounded by
architecture on an appropriately grand scale.
It's overlooked by the fantastical, neo-Gothic
Middlesex Guildhall (1906-13) on the west
side, while to the south are **Westminster
Abbey** (*see p138*) and the somewhat smaller
St Margaret's Church (*see p138*), where
Samuel Pepys and Churchill were each married.
The square itself is dotted with statues of British
politicians, such as Disraeli and Churchill. The
single previous outsider – Abraham Lincoln,
sitting sombrely to one side – has now been
joined by a new statue of Nelson Mandela.
  If it is true, as some say, that few buildings
in London really dazzle, the extravagant
Houses of Parliament (*see p138*) are an
exception. Formally still known as the Palace
of Westminster, the only surviving part of the
medieval royal palace is Westminster Hall (and
the **Jewel Tower**, just south of Westminster
Abbey; *see p138*). One note: the legendary **Big
Ben** is actually the name of the bell, not the
clock tower that houses it. Opposite Big Ben
is **Portcullis House**, an office block for MPs
completed in 2000 by architect Michael Hopkins
– he also designed the high-tech Westminster
tube station that the building sits upon. At the
end of Westminster Bridge stands a statue of
the warrior queen Boudicca and her daughters,
gesticulating toward Parliament.

Banqueting House

*Whitehall, SW1A 2ER (0870 751 5178/www.hrp.
org.uk). Westminster tube/Charing Cross tube/rail.*
Open 10am-5pm Mon-Sat. **Admission** £4.50;
£3-£3.50 reductions; free under-5s. **Credit** MC, V.
Map p401 L8.
Designed by the great neoclassicist Inigo Jones to
replace the previous wood and canvas structure,
this was the first true Renaissance building in

London. The austere simplicity of the exterior belies the sumptuous ceiling in the beautifully proportioned first-floor hall, painted by Rubens. Charles I commissioned the Flemish artist to glorify his father James I, 'the wisest fool in Christendom', and the ceiling imagery extols the virtues of wise rule. A bust over the entrance commemorates the fact that after several years of unwise rule Charles lost the Civil War, and was beheaded in front of Banqueting House in 1649. The event is marked annually on 31 January with a small ceremony. Call to check the hall is open before you visit: it sometimes closes for corporate functions. Lunchtime concerts are held here on the first Monday of every month except August.

Cabinet War Rooms & Churchill Museum

Clive Steps, King Charles Street, SW1A 2AQ (7930 6961/www.iwm.org.uk). St James's Park or Westminster tube. **Open** 9.30am-6pm daily. **Admission** £11; £8.50 reductions; free under-15s. **Credit** MC, V. **Map** p401 K9.

This small underground set of rooms was Churchill's bunker during World War II. Almost nothing has been changed since it was closed on 16 August 1945: every book, chart and pin in the map room remains in place, as does the BBC microphone he used when making his famous addresses. The furnishings are spartan, vividly evoking the wartime atmosphere, which is enhanced by the audio guide's sound effects – wailing sirens, wartime speeches. Occupying an underground space adjoining the War Rooms is the Churchill Museum, an in-depth look at the great man's life and times. In 2008, the museum will stage a temporary exhibition exploring wartime thrift and recycling, and a memorial show to coincide with the 90th anniversary of the end of World War I.

Houses of Parliament

Parliament Square, SW1A 0AA (Commons information 7219 4272/Lords information 7219 3107/tours information 0870 906 3773/www. parliament.uk). Westminster tube. **Open** (when in session) *House of Commons Visitors' Gallery* 2.30-10.30pm Mon, Tue; 11.30am-7.30pm Wed; 10.30am-6.30pm Thur; 9.30am-3pm Fri. *House of Lords Visitors' Gallery* from 2.30pm Mon, Tue; from 3pm Wed; from 11am Thur; occasional Fri. *Tours* summer recess only; phone for details. **Admission** *Visitors' Gallery* free. *Tours* £7; £5 reductions; free under-5s. **Credit** MC, V. **Map** p401 L9.

The ornate architecture here is the ultimate expression of Victorian self-confidence, even if its style was a throwback to the Middle Ages. Completed in 1860, it was the creation of architect Charles Barry, who won an architectural competition to replace the original Houses of Parliament, destroyed by fire in 1834. Barry was assisted on the interiors by Augustus Pugin. Although the first Parliament was held here in 1275, Westminster did not become its permanent home until the young Henry VIII decided to move to Whitehall in 1532. Parliament was originally housed in the choir stalls of St Stephen's

Chapel, where members sat facing each other from opposite sides, a tradition that continues today. Of the original palace, only the Jewel Tower (*see below*) and the almost mythically ancient Westminster Hall, one of the finest medieval buildings in Europe, remain.

In all there are 1,000 rooms, 100 staircases, 11 courtyards, eight bars and six restaurants (plus a visitors' cafeteria). None of them is open to the public, but you can watch the Commons or Lords in session from the galleries. In truth there's not much to see: most debates are sparsely attended and unenthusiastically conducted. Visitors queue at St Stephen's Entrance (it's well signposted) and, in high season, may have to wait a couple of hours. The best spectacle is Prime Minister's Question Time at noon on Wednesday, but you need to book advance tickets through your embassy or MP, who can also arrange tours. Parliament goes into recess in summer, at which times tours of the main ceremonial rooms, including Westminster Hall and the two houses, are available to the general public.

Jewel Tower

Abingdon Street, SW1P 3JY (7222 2219/www. english-heritage.org.uk). Westminster tube. **Open** *Apr-Oct* 10am-5pm daily. *Nov-Mar* 10am-4pm daily. **Admission** £2.90; £1.50-£2.20 reductions; free under-5s. **Credit** MC, V. **Map** p401 L9.

Emphatically not the home of the Crown Jewels (for which you need the Tower of London; *see p101*), this old stone tower was built in 1365 to house Edward III's treasure. Along with Westminster Hall, it is one of only two surviving parts of the medieval Palace of Westminster. From 1621 to 1864 the tower stored Parliamentary records, but now has only a small exhibition on Parliament's past.

St Margaret's Church

Parliament Square, SW1P 3JX (7654 4840/www. westminster-abbey.org/stmargarets). St James's Park or Westminster tube. **Open** 9.30am-3.45pm Mon-Fri; 9.30am-1.45pm Sat; 2-5pm Sun (times may change at short notice due to services). *Services* 11am Sun; phone to check for other days. **Admission** free. **Map** p401 L9.

Some of the most impressive pre-Reformation stained glass in London can be found here: the east window (1509) commemorates the marriage of Henry VIII and Catherine of Aragon, while later windows celebrate Britain's first printer, William Caxton, buried here in 1491; explorer Sir Walter Raleigh, executed in Old Palace Yard; and writer John Milton (1608-74), who married his second wife, Katherine Woodcock, in St Margaret's. Founded in the 12th century, the church was rebuilt from 1486 to 1523. Since 1614, this has been the official church of the House of Commons (the bells are rung when a new Speaker is chosen).

Westminster Abbey

20 Dean's Yard, SW1P 3PA (7222 5152/tours 7654 4900/www.westminster-abbey.org). St James's Park or Westminster tube. **Open** *Chapter House, Nave & Royal Chapels* 9.30am-3.45pm Mon, Tue, Thur, Fri; 9.30am-7pm Wed; 9.30am-1.45pm Sat. *Abbey Museum*

Big red bus

For over 50 years the conductor-operated Routemaster bus served London both as a uniquely practical means of travel and an international symbol of the capital. At the start of 2006, the red double-deckers headed a list of the nation's most popular icons, along with Stonehenge and the FA Cup. Enduringly popular for their open-backed design, which allowed passengers to hop on or off whenever they liked, the model was finally withdrawn from service in December 2005, despite prior assurance from Mayor Ken Livingstone that this would not happen (to wit: 'only a ghastly dehumanised moron would want to get rid of the Routemaster'). The decision probably remains the single most unpopular thing the Mayor has done while in office.

Slightly happier news for Routemaster-lovers arrived when Transport for London announced that the bus would live on along two 'heritage' routes. Beautifully refurbished Routemasters now run through the central London sections of routes 9 and 15. The vehicles used first went into service between 1960 and 1964. They have been lovingly repainted in their original colour scheme, complete with a cream-coloured horizontal stripe, and fitted with new engines that meet European emission standards.

Elsewhere the Routemasters have been replaced by reviled, double-length 'bendy buses', the bane of cyclists and a uniquely ill-fitting vehicle for London's busy, cramped and twisting network of roads.

The heritage Routemasters, meanwhile, run daily every 15 minutes from 9.30am to 6.30pm, supplementing normal bus services. Route 9 runs from the Aldwych via the Strand, Trafalgar Square and Piccadilly Circus to the Royal Albert Hall; Route 15 runs from Trafalgar Square to Tower Hill and allows passengers to get a glimpse of the Strand, Fleet Street and St Paul's Cathedral.

Routemaster fares match the rest of the bus network (*see p360*), and Travelcards are accepted. You must buy tickets or cards before you board, rendering redundant that other much missed feature of the Routemaster: the conductor. Ding ding!

10.30am-4pm Mon-Sat. *Cloisters* 8am-6pm Mon-Sat. *Garden* Apr-Sept 10am-6pm Tue-Thur. Oct-Mar 10am-4pm Tue-Thur. *Services* 7.30am, 8am, 12.30pm, 5pm Mon-Fri; 8am, 9am, 3pm Sat; 8am, 10am, 11.15am, 3pm, 5.45pm, 6.30pm Sun. **Admission** £10; £7 reductions; £24 family; free under-11s with paying adult. **Credit** MC, V. **Map** p401 K9.

Westminster Abbey has been synonymous with British royalty since the middle of the 11th century, when Edward the Confessor built a new church on the site just in time for his own funeral (it was consecrated only eight days before he died). Since then a who's who of the monarchy has been buried here and, with two exceptions (Edward V and

St James's Park. *See p142.*

Edward VIII), every English king since William the Conqueror (1066) has been crowned in the abbey. Of the original abbey, only the Pyx Chamber (which was the royal treasury) and the Norman undercroft remain. The Gothic nave and choir were rebuilt in the 13th century, and the Henry VII Chapel, with its spectacular fan vaulting, was added between 1503 and 1512. Nicholas Hawksmoor's west towers completed the building in 1745.

The interior is cluttered with monuments to statesmen, scientists, musicians and poets. Poets' Corner contains the graves of Dryden, Samuel Johnson, Browning and Tennyson – although it has plaques for many more, most are buried elsewhere. Centrepiece of the octagonal Chapter House is its faded 13th-century tiled floor, while the pretty garden of the Little Cloister offers respite from the crowds, especially during free lunchtime concerts.

Millbank

Map p401

Pimlico or Westminster tube.

Millbank runs along the river from Parliament to Vauxhall Bridge (and provides the most straightforward walking route to Tate Britain). Immediately south of the Houses of Parliament are the **Victoria Tower Gardens**, which contain a statue of suffragette leader Emmeline Pankhurst, a cast of Rodin's glum-looking *Burghers of Calais* and the Buxton Drinking Fountain commemorating the emancipation of slaves. On the other side of the road, Dean Stanley Street leads to **Smith Square**, home to **St John's, Smith Square**, an exuberant baroque fantasy built as a church in 1713-28 but now a venue for classical music (*see p307*). **Lord North Street**, running north from the square, is one of the best-preserved Georgian streets in London – as well as being one of the city's most prestigious addresses.

Further along the river, just north of Vauxhall Bridge, stands **Tate Britain** (*see below*), with its excellent collection of British art. It occupies the former site of the Millbank Penitentiary, one of Britain's fouler Victorian prisons, eventually demolished in 1890. (The ghost of a past inmate is supposed to haunt the cellars of the nearby **Morpeth Arms** at 55 Millbank.) Across the river, the curious cream and green-glass postmodernist block is the highly conspicuous HQ of the Secret Intelligence Service (SIS), which people more commonly refer to as MI6.

Tate Britain

Millbank, SW1P 4RG (7887 8000/www.tate.org.uk). Pimlico tube. **Open** 10am-5.50pm daily. *Tours* 11am, noon, 2pm, 3pm Mon-Fri; noon, 3pm Sat, Sun. **Admission** free. *Special exhibitions* prices vary. **Credit** (shop) MC, V. **Map** p401 K11.

Younger, sexier Tate Modern (*see p81*) gets all the wolf whistles, but the collection at Tate Britain is at least as strong – for historical art in London, it is second only to the National Gallery. With the opening of Tate Modern, plenty of space was freed up to accommodate fine British art from the 16th century to the present, pleasing pretty much everyone with work spanning five centuries. You'll find art by Hogarth, Gainsborough, the Blakes (William and Peter), Constable (who gets three rooms to himself), Reynolds, Bacon and Moore; Turner has the large Clore Gallery all to himself. Nor does Tate Britain skimp on more recent artists, notwithstanding its sibling rival's name: Howard Hodgkin, Lucian Freud and David Hockney are all represented, and the Art Now series of installations showcases up and coming British artists. The shop is well stocked with posters and art books, and the slightly old-fashioned restaurant has a cracking wine list. You can also have the best of both art worlds, thanks to the Tate-to-Tate boat service (*see p81*).

Exhibitions planned for 2008 include a Francis Bacon retrospective and a show exploring British art in the Islamic world. Most years, the controversy-courting and often-compelling annual Turner Prize exhibition for contemporary art is held at Tate Britain from October to January.

Victoria

Map p400

Pimlico tube or Victoria tube/rail.

Victoria Street, stretching from Parliament Square to Victoria Station, links political London with a rather more colourful and chaotic backpackers' London. Victoria Coach Station, one of the city's main arrival termini for visitors from the rest of Europe, is a short distance away in Buckingham Palace Road; Belgrave Road provides an almost unbroken line of cheap (and often grim) old B&Bs and hotels – as well as an easyHotel (*see p71*).

Not to be confused with Westminster Abbey (*see p138*) in Parliament Square, **Westminster Cathedral** (*see below*) is partly hidden by office blocks, and comes as a pleasant surprise. North of Victoria Street, back towards Parliament Square, is **Christchurch Gardens**, burial site of Thomas ('Colonel') Blood, the 17th-century rogue who nearly got away with stealing the Crown Jewels in 1671 (and did get away with a pardon for his crime). Nearby is **New Scotland Yard**, with its famous revolving sign and, just north of that, **55 Broadway**, home of London Underground.

Westminster Cathedral

42 Francis Street, SW1P 1QW (7798 9055/www.westminstercathedral.org.uk). Victoria tube/rail. **Open** 7am-7pm Mon-Fri, Sun; 8am-7pm Sat. *Services* 7am, 8am, 10.30am, 12.30pm, 1.05pm,

5.30pm Mon-Fri; 8am, 9am, 10.30am, 12.30pm, 6pm Sat; 8am, 9am, 10.30am, noon, 5.30pm, 7pm Sun. **Admission** free; donations appreciated. *Campanile* £5; £3 reductions. **No credit cards. Map** p400 J10. Westminster Cathedral is spectacular – and bizarre. Part wedding cake, part sweet stick, the neo-Byzantine confection is Britain's premier Catholic cathedral, built between 1895 and 1903 by John Francis Bentley, who was inspired by the Hagia Sophia in Istanbul. The land on which it is built had formerly been a bull-baiting ring and a pleasure garden before being bought by the Catholic Church in 1884. With such a festive exterior, you'd expect an equally ornate interior. Not so: the inside has yet to be finished. Even so, you get a taste of what the faithful will eventually achieve from the magnificent columns and mosaics (made from more than 100 kinds of marble). Eric Gill's sculptures of the Stations of the Cross (1914-18) are justly famous. Simple and objective, they were controversial at the time of installation, labelled Babylonian and crude by crit-ics. The nave of Westminster Cathedral is the broad-est in England, and dark wood floors and flickering candles add to the drama. The view from the 273ft bell tower is superb – it's even got a lift.

St James's Park

Map p400 & p401

St James's Park tube.
Originally a royal deer park for St James's Palace, the park's pastoral landscape owes its current shape to John Nash, who redesigned it in the early 19th century under the orders of George IV. The view of **Buckingham Palace** (*see below*) from the bridge over the lake is wonderful, especially at night when the palace is floodlit. The lake is now a sanctuary for wildfowl, among them pelicans (fed at 3pm daily, though also known to snack on passing pigeons) and Australian black swans.

On the south side of the park, Wellington Barracks, home of the Foot Guards, contains the **Guards' Museum** (*see p143*). Running along the north side is the grand processional route of the **Mall**, which connects Buckingham Palace with Trafalgar Square. Now tarmacked in pink to match the Queen's forecourt, the Mall was not designed with its current purpose in mind: Charles II had it laid out before the palace was even a royal residence. He wanted a new pitch for 'pallemaille', a game imported from France that involved hitting a ball with a mallet. Nearby Pall Mall, his favourite pitch, had become too crowded for the sport.

On the north side of the Mall is **Carlton House Terrace**, the last project completed by John Nash before his death in 1835. It was built on the site of Carlton House, which was George IV's home until he decided it wasn't fit for a king and enlarged Buckingham House

into a palace to replace it. Part of the terrace now houses the **Institute of Contemporary Arts** (ICA; *see p144*). The steps beside the ICA lead up to the **Duke of York column**, which commemorates Prince Frederick, Duke of York, commander-in-chief of the British Army during the wars with the French. He's the 'Grand old Duke of York' from the nursery rhyme.

Buckingham Palace & Royal Mews

The Mall, SW1A 1AA (7766 7300/Royal Mews 7766 7302/www.royalcollection.org.uk). Green Park or St James's Park tube/Victoria tube/rail. **Open** *State Rooms* mid July-Sept 9.45am-6pm (last entry 3.45pm) daily. *Queen's Gallery* 10am-4.30pm daily. *Royal Mews* Oct-July 11am-4pm daily. Aug, Sept 10am-5pm daily. **Admission** *Palace* £14; £8-£12.50 reductions; £36 family; free under-5s. *Queen's Gallery* £8; £4-£7 reductions; £20 family; free under-5s. *Royal Mews* £7; £4.50-£6 reductions; £18.50 family; free under-5s. **Credit** AmEx, MC, V. **Map** p400 H9.
The world's most famous palace, built in 1703, started life as a grand house for the Duke of Buckingham, but George III liked it so much he bought it, in 1761, for his young bride Charlotte. It became known as the Queen's House and 14 of their 15 children were born here. His son, George IV, hired John Nash to convert it into a palace, and con-struction on the 600-room building began in 1825. But the project was beset with problems from the start, and Nash – whose plans had always been disliked by Parliament and who ran grossly over budget – was dismissed in 1830. In 1837, when Victoria came to the throne, the building was still near uninhabitable, with faulty drains, windows that did not close, and a lack of both ventilation and sinks. The reliable but unimaginative Edward Blore was hired to finish the job, and his changes resulted in the current appearance of the palace. The east front – the part of the palace most familiar to visitors – was added at this time; previously, the Marble Arch had stood on the east side as the entrance to a long open courtyard, but Blore had it moved to the top of Park Lane, and blocked in the courtyard by constructing what is usually seen now as the 'front' of the palace. After seeing the building, critics dubbed its architect 'Blore the Bore'.

Visitors may judge the interiors for themselves. In August and September (and this year, for the first time, January, March and April too), while the Windsors are off on their holidays, the ostentatious State Apartments – used for banquets and investi-tures – are open to the public; in 2008, visitors also get to see the Ballroom set for a State Banquet. The Queen's Gallery, open for most of the year, contains highlights of Elizabeth's decorative and fine art col-lection: paintings by Rubens and Rembrandt, Sèvres porcelain, ornately inlaid cabinets and the Diamond Diadem (familiar from millions of postage stamps). Further along Buckingham Palace Road, the Royal Mews has royal carriages (the gilded State Coach among them), the official Rolls-Royces and, when they're not Trooping the Colour (*see p267*), horses.

Ceremonial city

'They're changing guard at Buckingham Palace/Christopher Robin went down with Alice./We saw a guard in a sentry-box./ "One of the sergeants looks after their socks,"/Says Alice.' When it comes to the **Changing of the Guard**, not much has changed since AA Milne wrote his poem. On alternate days from 10.45am, one of the five Foot Guards regiments lines up in scarlet coats and tall bearskin hats in the forecourt of Wellington Barracks; at exactly 11.27am the soldiers march, accompanied by their regimental band, to Buckingham Palace (see p142) to relieve the sentries there in a 45-minute ceremony. The protocol is impressively arcane: for example, if there are four guards at the front rather than two, it means that Her Majesty is in residence.

Not far away, at Horse Guards Parade in Whitehall, the Household Cavalry mount the guard daily at 11am (10am on Sunday). This is our preferred viewing, since the crowds aren't as thick as at the palace, and you aren't held far back from the action by

railings. After the old and new guard have stared each other out in the centre of the parade ground for quarter of an hour, if you nip through to the Whitehall side, you'll catch the departing old guard perform their hilarious dismount choreography – a synchronised, firm slap of approbation to the neck of each horse before the gloved troopers all swing off.

Not much has changed, but there is one major improvement. The new **Household Cavalry Museum** (see below) opened in 2007, allowing visitors to peer at the Guards' medals and cuirasses (even try one on during special kids' activity days) and watch video diaries of serving soldiers. Best of all, a glass screen is all that separates the museum from the stables, enabling you to see (and smell) those magnificent horses being rubbed down. No sign of sock-washing sergeants, though.

The Changing of the Guard schedule is subject to change: see www.changing-the-guard.com/sched.htm for updates. For **Beating Retreat** and **Trooping the Colour**, see p267; for **gun salutes**, see p264.

Guards' Museum

Wellington Barracks, Birdcage Walk, SW1E 6HQ (7414 3428/www.theguardsmuseum.com). St James's Park tube. **Open** 10am-4pm daily. **Admission** £3; £2 reductions; free under-16s. **Credit** (shop) AmEx, MC, V. **Map** p400 J9.
A small museum that presents the 350-year history of the Foot Guards, using splendid uniforms, medals, period paintings and intriguing memorabilia, such as their stuffed Victorian mascot Jacob the Goose, run over by a van in barracks, and a pair of desert

sandals from World War II that were commissioned by a founding forerunner of the SAS.

Household Cavalry Museum

Horse Guards, Whitehall, SW1A 2AX (7414 2392/ www.householdcavalry.co.uk). Embankment tube/ Charing Cross tube/rail. **Open** 10am-6pm (last entry 4.45pm) daily. **Admission** £6; £4 children & reductions; £18 family ticket. **Credit** AmEx, DC, MC, V. **Map** p401 K8.
See above **Ceremonial city**.

Institute of Contemporary Arts

The Mall, SW1Y 5AH (box office 7930 3647/www. ica.org.uk). Piccadilly Circus tube/Charing Cross tube/ rail. **Open** *Galleries* noon-7.30pm daily. **Membership** *Daily* £2, £1.50 reductions Mon-Fri; £3, £2 reductions Sat, Sun; free under-14s. *Annual* £35; £25 reductions. **Credit** AmEx, DC, MC, V. **Map** p401 K8.

Founded in 1948 by the group associated with poet and art critic Herbert Read, the ICA (which moved to the Mall in 1968) continues to happily challenge traditional notions of art from its incongruously establishment-looking home. The cinema (*see p286*) shows London's artiest films; the theatre stages performance art, quality avant-garde gigs, debates and club nights; and the exhibitions are frequent talking points. There's a bar and café for a post-show discussion, and a small, selectively stocked book and DVD shop with a good selection of arts periodicals.

St James's

Maps p400 & p406

Green Park or Piccadilly Circus tube.

One of central London's quietest and most exclusive areas, St James's is bordered by Piccadilly, Haymarket, the Mall and Green Park. The area was laid out in the 1660s and has long been associated with the aristocracy who wanted to be close to the royal palaces. This is a London that has remained unchanged for centuries: its squares and hushed streets are charming, resolutely rich and rather conceited.

The area is typified by **Pall Mall**, lined by stately, members-only, gentlemen's clubs (think drawing rooms and open fires rather than thongs and poles). These include the **Reform Club** (nos.104-105), site of Phileas Fogg's famous bet in Jules Verne's *Around the World in Eighty Days* (*see also p19* **I'll wager**).

North of Pall Mall, **St James's Square** was the most fashionable address in London for the 50 years after it was laid out in the 1670s: seven dukes and seven earls were residents by the 1720s. Among today's occupants is the **London Library**, founded by Thomas Carlyle in 1841 in disgust at the inefficiency of the British Library. It's the world's largest independent lending library, but open to members only. The material needs of clubland's gents are met by the anachronistic retailers and restaurants of **Jermyn Street**, perhaps old-fashioned shirt shop **Harvie & Hudson** (nos.96-97) or classic British dining room **Wiltons** (no.55, 7629 9955), which opened in 1742 as a stall selling oysters, shrimps and cockles. More of the same is round the corner on St James's Street.

Just off St James's Street is the Queen Mother's old residence, **Clarence House** (*see below*). Adjacent to Clarence House, **St James's Palace** was originally built for Henry VIII in the 1530s. It has remained the official residence

of the sovereign throughout the centuries, despite the fact that since 1837 the monarchs have all actually lived at Buckingham Palace (*see p142*). It has great historic significance to the monarchy: Mary Tudor surrendered Calais here, Elizabeth I lived here during the campaign against the Spanish Armada, and Charles I was confined here before his execution in 1649.

Today St James's Palace is used by the Princess Royal (the title given to the monarch's eldest daughter, who is Princess Anne) and various minor royals. Tradition still dictates that foreign ambassadors to the UK are received at 'the Court of St James's'. Although the palace is closed to the public, you can attend Sunday services at its historic **Chapel Royal** (1st Sun of mth, Oct-Easter Sunday; 8.30am, 11.15am).

Across Marlborough Road lies the **Queen's Chapel**, which was the first classical church to be built in England. Designed by Inigo Jones in the 1620s for Charles I's intended bride, the Infanta of Castile, the chapel now stands in the grounds of **Marlborough House** (built by Sir Christopher Wren). The chapel is only open to the public during Sunday services (Easter-July; 8.30am, 11.15am). A little further north, on St James's Place, the beautiful, 18th-century **Spencer House** (*see below*) is the ancestral townhouse of the late Princess Diana's family.

Clarence House

The Mall, SW1A 1AA (7766 7303/www.royal collection.org.uk). Green Park tube. **Open** *Aug-mid Oct* 10am-4.30pm daily. **Admission** £7; £4 under-17s; free under-5s. *Tours* pre-booked tickets only. **Credit** AmEx, MC, V. **Map** p400 J8.

Standing austerely beside St James's Palace, Clarence House was erected between 1825 and 1827, based on designs by John Nash. It was built for Prince William Henry, Duke of Clarence, who lived there as King William IV until 1837. The house has been much altered by its many royal inhabitants, the most recent of whom was the Queen Mother, who died in 2002. Prince Charles and his two sons have since moved in, but parts of the house are open to the public in summer: five receiving rooms and the small but significant British art collection accumulated by the Queen Mother. Tickets are hard to come by, usually selling out by the end of August.

Spencer House

27 St James's Place, SW1A 1NR (7499 8620/www. spencerhouse.co.uk). Green Park tube. **Open House** Feb-July, Sept-Dec 10.30am-5.45pm Sun. *Gardens* spring & summer; phone to check. **Admission** *Tours* £9; £7 reductions. Under-10s not allowed. **No credit cards. Map** p400 J8.

Designed by John Vardy and built for John Spencer, this house was completed in 1766. The Spencers moved out just over a century ago and the lavishly restored building is now used chiefly as offices and for corporate entertaining, hence the limited access.

Chelsea

Here mods and mojos have long since morphed into Manolos and Mojitos.

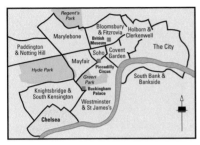

When the editor of *Vogue* declared London 'the most swinging city in the world' in 1965, she had probably been to Chelsea, a historic fishing village turned royal retreat, which by then had blossomed into a heaving centre of all things hip and happening. Nowhere was this more true than on the King's Road, a mecca for the youth following the opening of Mary Quant's boutique Bazaar in 1955. Over subsequent decades the pavements became a catwalk for mods and miniskirts, peaceniks and punks. The King's Road gave birth to the Rolling Stones and the Sex Pistols, while the Sound Techniques studio on Old Church Street recorded Pink Floyd, the Who and even Elton John. Chelsea has since grown grey and graceful, its wild abandon all but evaporated and its streets teeming with perma-tanned yuppies, pricey fashion houses and air-conditioned poodle parlours. At the same time, it is a richly historical place that can both surprise and charm – so long as you're prepared to dive into the villagey side streets.

Sloane Square & the King's Road

Map p396 & p397

Sloane Square tube then various buses.

Sloane Square remains central to the Chelsea experience, little more than a glorified roundabout roaring with traffic but popular nonetheless. Come summer, the terraces of the swanky brasseries teem with stereotypical Sloane Rangers sipping rosé, the air thick with cigar smoke and conversations about ski chalets; the new **Chelsea Brasserie** (Sloane Square Hotel, nos.7-12, 7881 5999, www.sloane

squarehotel.co.uk) is probably the best option. The bower-shaded benches in the middle of the square are a charming counterpoint to the looming façades of Tiffany & Co, Gieves & Hawkes and the enormous **Peter Jones** department store, the latter in a refurbished 1930s building with excellent views from its top-floor café. A certain edginess is lent to proceedings by the **Royal Court Theatre** (*see p335*), which shocked the nation with its 1956 première of John Osborne's *Look Back in Anger* and continues to run a programme of left-field productions.

Sloane Square is also home to an interesting fountain commemorating the passion of Charles II for his mistress, rags-to-riches folk heroine Nell Gwynne. It was Charles who gave the King's Road its name, this being the route that bore his carriage to Kew (the fact that it passed Nell's house was a bonus). At its eastern end is the very clean, very modern **Duke of York Square**, presided over by a statue of Hans Sloane, the physician and collector whose haul formed the basis for the British Museum – the kids who love the square for its cooling fountains and ice-cream parlour would be more interested to learn that Hans also invented milk chocolate. From early 2008 the square will also host the mercilessly modern art of the **Saatchi Gallery**. Having long since left its County Hall premises, Saatchi will open in 50,000 square feet of former military barracks, the Duke of York's Headquarters.

The once-adventurous shops along the King's Road are now an insipid mix of trendier-than-thou fashion houses and tawdry high street chains, enlivened by a few gems: **John Sandoe Books** (*see p242*) and **Antiquarius** (*see p259*) represent a glorious past, **Shop at Bluebird** (*see p247*) suggests future directions. Wander Cale Street for the likes of jewellery boutique **Felt** (7349 8829, www.felt-lond on.com) or **Traditional Toys** (7352 1718, www.traditionaltoy.com), or head for **Chelsea Farmers' Market**, on adjoining Sydney Street, to find a clutter of artfully distressed rustic sheds housing everything from Julianne Balai's design accessories (7376 5680, www.juliannebalai.com) to dog grooming from Pet Pavilion (7376 8800,www.petpavilion.co. uk). Sydney Street also leads to St Luke's

Sightseeing

Chelsea Physic Garden.

Church, where Charles Dickens married Catherine Hogarth in 1836.

Towards the western end of the King's Road is the **Bluebird** café and restaurant (*see p213*), housed in a dramatic art deco garage and worth a peek even if you can't afford to eat there. A little further up, the World's End store at no.430 occupies what was once Vivienne Westwood's notorious leather and fetish wear boutique SEX; a green-haired Johnny Rotten auditioned for the Sex Pistols here in 1975 by singing along to an Alice Cooper record on the shop's jukebox, making it a place of punk pilgrimage for many years to come.

Cheyne Walk & Chelsea Embankment

Map p397

Sloane Square tube then various buses.
Chelsea was still a humble fishing village in the 16th century when it first became associated with royalty – Sir Thomas More moved here in 1520, with Henry VIII acquiring the manor of Chelsea 12 years later. Intellects and literary luminaries flocked here too, from Samuel Pepys to George Eliot, Dante Gabriel Rossetti, Henry James and TS Eliot.

Then as now, Chelsea's popularity derived from its combination of proximity to the city and peacefulness, the latter lending a village feel that befits a place of retirement for the Chelsea Pensioners, former British soldiers living in the splendour of the **Royal Hospital Chelsea** (*see p147*). In summer they regularly don their red coats and tricorn hats when venturing beyond

the gates. The **National Army Museum** (*see p147*) is next door, although every May the area forgoes war stories in favour of potting tips for the annual Chelsea Flower Show (*see p266*).

Cheyne Walk is less peaceful than it once was due to embankment traffic, but still offers charming views of the Thames and plenty of spots for a sit-down. Over its western end loom the towers of the disused **Lots Road Power Station**, charged with providing electricity to the London Underground network from its construction in 1902 until it was shut down one century later. Nearby the single wrought-iron gate once marked an entrance to the Victorian society-hangout Cremorne Pleasure Gardens. The Pleasure Gardens are long-since built over, but Cremorne Road does have a riverside garden that offers views over the shiny offices, a glass-domed design centre and marina of **Chelsea Harbour** (www.chelsea-harbour.co.uk).

A short walk eastward along Cheyne Walk leads to 15th-century Crosby Hall, the scene of Gloucester's plotting in Shakespeare's *Richard III* and home of Sir Thomas More (it was here that he wrote *Utopia*). Next door, a gold-faced statue of Sir Thomas looks out over the river from the garden of **Chelsea Old Church** (*see p147*), where he once sang in the choir and may well be (partially) buried. Follow adjoining Old Church Road north and you'll find the **Chelsea Arts Club** (no.143), founded in 1871 at the suggestion of Whistler and home to charming gardens that are only open to its members.

Further east on Cheyne Walk, the park benches of **Chelsea Embankment Gardens** face Albert Bridge, which still has signs ordering troops to 'Break step when marching over this bridge'. In the small gardens you'll find a statue of the great historian Thomas Carlyle – the 'sage of Chelsea', whose home is preserved (**Carlyle's House**; *see p147*). For a green-fingered treat, carry on to the **Chelsea Physic Garden**. For those preferring blue to green, Chelsea FC's home ground, **Stamford Bridge**, is a short drive away on Fulham Road, which also has **Bibendum** (7581 5817,www.bibendum.co.uk), a restaurant housed in the former offices of the Michelin tyre company, a building that mixes art nouveau and art deco influences to great effect.

Carlyle's House

24 Cheyne Row, SW3 5HL (7352 7087/www.nat ionaltrust.org.uk). Sloane Square tube/11, 19, 22, 49, 211, 239, 319 bus. **Open** *Apr-Oct* 2-5pm Wed-Fri; 11am-5pm Sat, Sun. **Admission** £4.75; £2.40 reductions; £11.90 family. **Map** p397 E12.

Thomas Carlyle and his wife Jane, both towering intellects, moved to this four-storey, Queen Anne house in 1834. In 1896, 15 years after Carlyle's death, the house was preserved as a museum, offering an intriguing snapshot of Victorian life. The writer's quest for quiet (details of his valiant attempts to soundproof the attic) strikes a chord today – he was plagued by the sound of revelry from Cremorne Pleasure Gardens, and by the clucking of next door's poultry. It seems antisocial behaviour is nothing new.

Chelsea Old Church

Cheyne Walk, Old Church Street, SW3 5DQ (7795 1019/www.chelseaoldchurch.org.uk). Sloane Square tube/11, 19, 22, 49, 319 bus. **Open** 2-4pm Tue-Thur; 1.30-5pm Sun. *Services* 8am, 10am, 11am, 12.15pm Sun. *Evensong* 6pm. **Admission** free; donations appreciated.

Most of the ancient church, which dates back to the 13th century, was destroyed by a bomb in 1941. Legend has it that the Thomas More Chapel, which remains on the south side, has his headless body buried somewhere under the walls (his head, after being spiked on London Bridge, was 'rescued' and buried in a family vault in St Dunstan's Church, Canterbury). Guides are on hand on Sundays.

Chelsea Physic Garden

66 Royal Hospital Road (entrance on Swan Walk), SW3 4HS (7352 5646/www.chelseaphysicgarden. co.uk). Sloane Square tube/11, 19, 239 bus. **Open** *Apr-Oct* noon-dusk Wed; noon-5pm Thur, Fri; noon-6pm Sun. *Tours* times vary; phone to check. **Admission** £7; £4 reductions; free under-5s. *Tours* free. **Credit** (shop) AmEx, MC, V. **Map** p397 F12.

The 165,000sq ft grounds of this lovely botanic garden are filled with healing herbs and vegetables, rare trees and dye plants. The world's first rock garden was built here in 1772, using old stone from the Tower of London. The physic garden opened to the public in 1893, but nowadays hours are restricted. Free tours trace the history of the medicinal beds, where herbs are grown for their efficacy in treating illnesses.

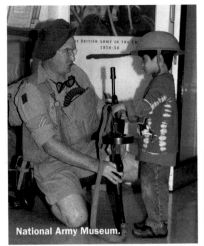

National Army Museum.

National Army Museum

Royal Hospital Road, SW3 4HT (7730 0717/ www.national-army-museum.ac.uk). Sloane Square tube/11, 137, 239 bus. **Open** 10am-5.30pm daily. **Admission** free. **Credit** (shop) AmEx, MC, V. **Map** p397 F12.

Some eccentric displays make this museum dedicated to the history of the British Army more entertaining than the modern exterior suggests. The collection kicks off with 'Redcoats', a gallery that starts at Agincourt in 1415 and ends with the American War of Independence. Upstairs, 'The Road to Waterloo' marches through the 20-year struggle against the French, featuring 70,000 model soldiers and bloodstained souvenirs of Waterloo. Also on display is the kit of Olympian medal winner Dame Kelly Holmes (an ex-army athlete), while Major Michael 'Bronco' Lane, conqueror of Everest, has donated his frostbitten fingertips.

Royal Hospital Chelsea

Royal Hospital Road, SW3 4SR (7881 5200/www. chelsea-pensioners.org.uk). Sloane Square tube/11, 19, 22, 137, 211, 239 bus. **Open** *Oct-Apr* 10am-noon, 2-4pm Mon-Sat. *May-Sept* 10am-noon, 2-4pm Mon-Sat; 2-4pm Sun. **Admission** free. **Map** p397 F12.

About 350 Chelsea Pensioners (retired soldiers) live here. Their quarters, the Royal Hospital, was founded in 1682 by Charles II and the building was designed by Sir Christopher Wren, with later adjustments by Robert Adam and Sir John Soane. Retired soldiers are eligible to apply for a final posting here if they are over 65 and in receipt of an Army or War Disability Pension for Army Service. The in-pensioners are organised into companies, along military lines, with a governor and other officers. They have their own club room, bowling green and gardens. The museum (open at the same times as the Hospital) has more about their life.

Knightsbridge & South Kensington

Houses of learning and temples to Mammon.

Knightsbridge is where the real cash gets splashed. Rows of designer shops, world-famous department stores and crowded, fashionable restaurants attract a global clientele for whom money is no object. For all that, the area is neither hip nor particularly stylish. South Kensington is a little less stuffy, and not just because of the acres of parkland that open up along its northern edge. The area boasts a world-beating complement of cultural landmarks, each within minutes of the other: three of London's finest museums; three internationally respected colleges; a renowned concert hall; and, nearby in Kensington Gardens, excellently curated contemporary art.

Knightsbridge

Map p397

Knightsbridge tube.
Knightsbridge in the 11th century was a village celebrated for its taverns, highwaymen and the legend that two knights once fought to the death on the bridge that spanned the Westbourne River (later dammed to form Hyde Park's Serpentine boating lake). Nowadays, the urban princesses would be far too busy unsheathing their credit cards to notice a duelling knight. Modern Knightsbridge is a shoppers' paradise, with voguish **Harvey Nichols** (*see p238*) holding court at the top of **Sloane Street**, which leads down to Sloane Square and Chelsea (*see p145*). Expensive brands – Gucci, Prada, Chanel, Christian Dior – dominate this otherwise unremarkable road.

East of Sloane Street is Belgravia, characterised by a cluster of embassies around **Belgrave Square**. Hidden behind the stucco-clad parades fronting the square are numerous tiny mews well worth exploring if only for the great pubs they conceal, notably the nostalgic **Nag's Head** (*see p231*), the shabbily grand **Grenadier** (18 Wilton Row, SW1X 7NR, 7235 3074) and the **Star Tavern** (6 Belgrave Mews West, SW1X 8HT, 7235 3019), which in the 1960s was where Great Train Robbers rubbed shoulders with movie stars such as Elizabeth Taylor. **St Paul's Knightsbridge** on Wilton Place is an appealing Victorian church, with scenes from the life of Jesus depicted on tiling on the nave, and a wonderful wood-beamed ceiling.

For tourists, Knightsbridge means one thing: **Harrods** (*see p238*). From its tan bricks and olive green awning to its green-coated doormen, it is an instantly recognisable retail legend – all the more so at night when it's lit up like a Vegas casino. Originally a family grocer's, it now employs about 5,000 people. Owner Mohammed Al Fayed continues to add to the richness of eccentricity here, notably with his Egyptian Hall and memorial to son Dodi and Princess Diana, but he'll have to go some to match past extravagances – such as the 1967 purchase by the Prince of Albania of a baby elephant for Ronald Reagan.

The western end of Knightsbridge is dominated by the imposing mass of the **Brompton Oratory** (*see below*), a church of suitably lavish proportions for an area long associated with extravagant displays of wealth. To really see how the rich live, wander behind the Oratory and north through the park to emerge on Ennismore Garden Mews, one of the loveliest streets in London; Michael Caine and Terence Stamp shared a flat here in the 1950s.

Brompton Oratory

Thurloe Place, Brompton Road, SW7 2RP (7808 0900/www.bromptonoratory.com). South Kensington tube. **Open** 6.30am-8pm daily. *Services* 7am, 10am, 12.30pm, 6pm Mon-Fri; 7am, 10am, 6pm Sat; 7am, 7am, 8am, 9am, 10am, 11am, 12.30pm, 4.30pm, 7pm Sun. **Admission** free; donations appreciated. **Map** p397 E10.

The second-biggest Catholic church in the country (after Westminster Cathedral) is formally known as the Church of the Immaculate Heart of Mary, but (being the home of the Congregation of the Oratory of St Philip of Neri) it is almost universally known as the 'Brompton Oratory'. Whatever you call it, the place is awesome. Completed in 1884, it feels older – partly because of the baroque Italianate style, but also because many of the marbles, mosaics and statuary pre-date the structure. Mazzuoli's late 17th-century apostle statues, for example, were once in Siena's cathedral. The vast main space culminates in a magnificent Italian altarpiece, and a number of ornate confessionals stand in the chapels flanking the nave. The 11am Solemn Mass sung in Latin on Sundays is enchanting, as are the Vespers, sung at 3.30pm (the website has details). In the Cold War, the KGB used the church as a dead-letter box.

South Kensington

Map p397
Gloucester Road or South Kensington tube.
This is the land of plenty, as far as cultural and academic institutions are concerned. With its heavyweight museums, three lofty colleges and a landmark concert hall, the area was once known as 'Albertopolis' in honour of the prince who oversaw the inception of all the above. Today £186,000 won't buy much, but this sum, the profits of the 1851 Great Exhibition, bought 3,789,000 square feet of land for the building of institutions to 'extend the influence of Science and Art upon Productive Industry'. Prince Albert did not survive to see the resulting trio of world-class museums: the **Natural History Museum**, the **Science Museum** and the **Victoria & Albert** (for all, *see p151*). Don't try to see all three on the same day; each will reward multiple return visits.

The three colleges in question are **Imperial College**, the **Royal College of Art** and the **Royal College of Music** (Prince Consort Road, 7589 3643; call for details of concerts and Wednesday openings of the musical instrument museum). The last of these forms a unity with the **Royal Albert Hall**, the great performance space inaugurated in 1871 and since used for boxing bouts, motor shows, marathons (524 circuits of the arena equals 26 miles), table tennis championships, the Eurovision Song Contest, Miss World, sumo wrestling, and rock concerts. Perhaps most significantly, the Hall's murky acoustics test conductors and musicians during the annual summer Proms concerts (*see p305*). Looking from here across Kensington Gore gives a great view of the **Albert Memorial**, a vast golden tribute to the royal benefactor.

South of the museums, around the lovely tube station with its small arcade, is the heart of South Kensington. Outside the station at the junction of Old Brompton Road and Onslow Square is a statue of Hungarian composer Béla Bartók, who used to stay at nearby Sydney Place whenever he performed in London. Just north of the station is Cromwell Place where, at no.7, Francis Bacon kept a studio in the 1940s before relocating a few hundred feet west to 7 Reece Mews, where he lived and worked from 1961 until his death in 1992.

Albert Memorial
Kensington Gardens (opposite Royal Albert Hall), SW7 (tours 7495 0916). South Kensington tube. **Tours** 2pm, 3pm 1st Sun of mth. **Admission** free. *Tours £4.50; £4 reductions.* **No credit cards.** **Map** p395 D8.
'I would rather not be made the prominent feature of such a monument,' was Prince Albert's reported response when the subject of commemoration came up. Quite what he would have made of this extraordinary memorial, unveiled 15 years after his death, is hard to imagine. It is, however, one of the great sculptural achievements of the Victorian period. Created by Sir George Gilbert Scott, it centres around a gilded Prince Albert holding a catalogue of the 1851 Great Exhibition. He's guarded on four

Albert Memorial.

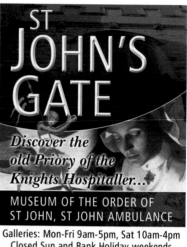
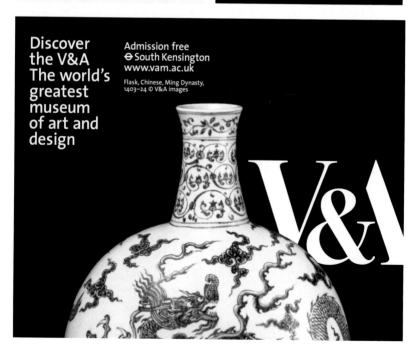

Science Museum.

outer corners by representations of the continents of Africa, America, Asia and Europe; pillars are crowned with bronze statues of the sciences; the arts are shown in a series of intricate mosaics; and the freize at the base of the monument depicts major artists, architects and musicians. The dramatic 180ft spire is inlaid with semi-precious stones.

Natural History Museum

Cromwell Road, SW7 5BD (information 7942 5725/switchboard 7942 5000/www.nhm.ac.uk). South Kensington tube. **Open** 10am-5.50pm daily. **Admission** free; charges apply for special exhibitions. *Tours* free. **Credit** (shop) MC, V. **Map** p397 D10.

This cathedral to the Victorian passion for knowledge, designed by Alfred Waterhouse, is every bit as impressive as the giant cast of a *Diplodocus* skeleton that greets you in the main hall; in fact, the building frequently overwhelms the exhibits. If you've come with children, you may not see much more than the Dinosaur gallery, with its star turn, the animatronic *Tyrannosaurus rex*. But there's much more – millions of plants, animals, fossils, rocks and minerals. Some of the galleries still have the sober and serious feel of the Victorian era; others, like Creepy Crawlies, are so beloved of children you can hardly get near the exhibits. Entry to the Earth Galleries (once the Geological Museum) is dramatic: you travel via an escalator, passing through a giant suspended globe and twinkling images of the star system. A gallery called Restless Surface has a mock-up of a Kobe supermarket, where the floor shakes to video coverage of the 1995 earthquake. Opening in late 2007 is a gallery called the Vault, which will give the inside track on a variety of precious metals, gems and crystals.

Many of the museum's 22 million specimens – including 'Archie', a 26ft-long Giant Squid caught in 2004 – are now housed in the new Darwin Centre buildings, where they take up nearly 17 miles of shelving; the Centre, home also to museum scientists and researchers, can be toured by arrangement.

Outside, the Wildlife Garden (Apr-Oct, £1.50) is the museum's living exhibition, with a range of British lowland habitats.

Science Museum

Exhibition Road, SW7 2DD (7942 4000/booking & information 0870 870 4868/www.sciencemuse um.org.uk). South Kensington tube. **Open** 10am-5.45pm daily. **Admission** free; charges apply for special exhibitions. **Credit** MC, V. **Map** p397 D9.

The Science Museum demonstrates with great aplomb how good science is interwoven with daily life, displaying engines, cars, aeroplanes, ships, medicine, computers and a variety of domestic exhibits. Landmark inventions such as Stephenson's *Rocket*, Arkwright's spinning machine, Whittle's turbojet and the Apollo 10 command module are celebrated in the Making the Modern World gallery. The ground floor houses an IMAX cinema, while the Who Am I? gallery in the Wellcome Wing explores discoveries in genetics, brain science and psychology. The newly expanded, hands-on Launchpad gallery has levers, pulleys, explosions and all sorts of absorbing experiments for kids (and their associated grown-ups) to get involved in. The temporary exhibitions for 2008 include shows on the development and use of plastics, and an exploration of the high-tech science used during the Cold War.

Sikorski Museum

20 Princes Gate, SW7 1PT (7589 9249/www. sikorskimuseum.co.uk). South Kensington tube. **Open** 2-4pm Mon-Fri; 10am-4pm 1st Sun of mth. **Admission** free. **Map** p397 D9. *See p152* **Odd curiosity stop**.

Victoria & Albert Museum

Cromwell Road, SW7 2RL (7942 2000/www.vam. ac.uk). South Kensington tube. **Open** 10am-5.45pm Mon-Thur, Sat, Sun; 10am-10pm Fri. *Tours* 10.30am,

11.30am, 12.30pm, 1.30pm, 2.30pm, 3.30pm daily. **Admission** free; charges apply for special exhibitions. **Credit** (shop) MC, V. **Map** p397 E10.

The 150-year-old V&A dazzles: its grand galleries contain around four million pieces of furniture, ceramics, sculpture, paintings, posters, jewellery and metalwork from across the world. Items are grouped by theme, origin or age. The museum boasts the finest collection of Italian Renaissance sculpture outside Italy, while home-grown treasures – the Great Bed of Ware, Canova's *The Three Graces*, Henry VIII's writing desk – are housed in the British Galleries, where you'll also find a range of interactive exhibits for children. Take time to admire the Fashion galleries, which run from 18th-century court dress right up to a summer 2005 chiffon number. The Architecture gallery has videos, models, plans and descriptions of various architectural styles, and the museum's famous Photography collection holds over 500,000 images. Opened in 2006, the Jameel Gallery shows Islamic art from the seventh century to the fall of the Ottoman Empire. Its centrepiece is the massive Ardabil carpet, the world's oldest and arguably most splendid floor covering. The V&A's abundance of temporary shows also draws crowds; visitors can look forward to China Design Now (15 Mar-13 July), a celebration of modern and contemporary artists' books in Blood on Paper (15 Apr-29 June) and Chanel-meets-surfing in Fashion and Sport (5 Aug-23 Nov).

Hyde Park & Kensington Gardens

Maps p394 & p395

Hyde Park Corner, Knightsbridge, Lancaster Gate or Queensway tube.

At 1.5 miles long and about a mile wide, **Hyde Park** (7298 2000, www.royalparks.gov.uk) is the largest of London's Royal Parks. The land was once part of a medieval manor, before being bequeathed to the monks of Westminster Abbey. In 1536, it was appropriated by Henry VIII for hunting deer. Despite opening to the public in the early 1600s, the parks were only frequented by the upper echelons of society. At the end of the 17th century, William III, averse to the dank air of Whitehall Palace, relocated to **Kensington Palace** (*see right*). A corner of Hyde Park was sectioned off to make grounds for the palace and, although today the two merge, Kensington Gardens was closed to the public until King George II opened it on Sundays to those wearing formal dress. Nowadays, if you're a child, the best element of Kensington Gardens is the **Diana, Princess of Wales Memorial Playground** (*see p278*). Adults may prefer the **Serpentine Gallery** (*see p153*). Across the road is the ring-shaped **Princess Diana Memorial**

Odd curiosity stop Sikorski Museum

South Kensington is famous for its big three museums – the Natural History Museum, the V&A and the Science Museum – but it's also home to one of London's many intriguing small museums, the **Sikorski Museum** (*see p151*). Founded by Polish nationals escaping the German invasion of 1939, it's named after Wladyslaw Sikorski, a military hero of World War I and the Polish-Soviet War, who became prime minister of the London-based Polish Government in Exile before dying in a plane crash in mysterious circumstances in 1943. When World War II ended, many Poles refused to return to a country that was now occupied by the Soviet Union, so the Government in Exile was maintained here at 20 Princes Gate until the collapse of communism in 1990.

In a fine building overlooking Hyde Park, the museum is defiantly traditionalist – the restoration of the Polish monarchy is a subject that can be broached here – and provides an insight into the fighting spirit of the exiled community. Honoured here especially is the memory of Lieutenant-

General Wladyslaw Anders, who led 'Anders Army', later the Polish Second Corps, some 25,000 soldiers released from Stalin's POW camps, through Iraq, to Palestine. One of his men, Menachem Begin, later became prime minister of Israel, and the Corps went on to play an important role in the bloody battle for Monte Cassino. A full-size model of Wojtke, the Polish army's mascot bear, takes pride of place at the foot of the stairs in the hall, along with a plaque commemorating the extraordinary contribution of Polish fighter pilots to victory in the Battle of Britain. Highlights of the collection are around 10,000 items of military memorabilia, some beautiful engravings of major events in Polish history and an Enigma cipher machine – a Polish mathematician helped to crack the Nazi's battlefield code. There are harrowing pictures from Polish concentration camps too.

In latter years, the museum has also housed the Polish Institute, a cultural centre that holds regular film screenings, lectures and music recitals for the dramatically increasing Polish diaspora.

Fountain, created by US architect Kathryn Gustafson. Almost as soon as it had been unveiled by the Queen, in July 2004, the fountain was in the headlines for the wrong reasons: people slipping on the granite while paddling.

Back across the road and further north, by the Long Water, is a bronze statue of **Peter Pan** by Sir George Frampton, erected in 1912: it was beside Hyde Park's Round Pond eight years earlier that playwright JM Barrie met Jack Lewellyn Davies, the boy who was the inspiration for Peter. Other sculptures include GF Watts's violently animated *Physical Energy* and Jacob Epstein's *Rima, Spirit of Nature*.

Hyde Park has long been a focal point for freedom of speech. It became a hotspot for mass demonstrations in the 19th century and remains so today – a march against war in Iraq in 2003 was (according to police) the largest in British history. The legalisation of public assembly in the park led to the establishment of **Speakers' Corner** in 1872 (close to Marble Arch tube), where ranters – sane and otherwise – have the floor. This isn't the place to come for balanced political debate, but Marx, Engels, Lenin, Orwell and the Pankhursts have all attended.

A rather more orderly entertainment takes place at 10.30am daily (9.30am on Sundays), when you can watch the Household Cavalry emerge from their barracks on South Carriage Drive. They ride across the park to Horse Guards Parade, prior to the **Changing of the Guard** (*see p143* **Ceremonial city**). The park perimeter is popular with skaters, as well as with bike- and horse-riders (for the riding school, *see p328*). If you're exploring on foot and the vast expanses defeat you, look out for the Liberty Drives (May-Oct). Driven by volunteers (there's no fare, but offer a donation if you can), these electric buggies pick up groups of sightseers and ferry them around the park. Cyclists should stick to the designated tracks; only under-tens are allowed to ride on the footpaths.

At the western side of the park is the **Serpentine**, London's oldest boating lake and home to ducks, coots, swans and tufty-headed grebes. You can rent rowing boats and pedalos from March to October.

Kensington Palace

Kensington Gardens, W8 4PX (0844 482 7777/ booking line 0870 751 5180/www.hrp.org.uk). Bayswater, High Street Kensington or Queensway tube. Open Mar-Oct 10am-5pm daily. Nov-Feb 10am-4pm daily. Admission £12; £6-£10 reductions; £33 family; free under-5s. Credit MC, V. Map p394 B8.

Sir Christopher Wren extended this Jacobean mansion to palatial proportions on the instructions of William III, who afterwards moved in with his wife Mary II. The asthmatic king considered that what was then a countryside location would be better for

Victoria & Albert Museum. *See p151.*

his health. The sections of the palace that the public are allowed to see give the impression of intimacy, although the King's Apartments, which you enter via Wren's lofty King's Staircase, are pretty grand. In the King's Gallery hang portraits of the first glamorous royals to live here. It appears from the Queen's Apartments, however, that William and Mary lived quite simply in these smaller rooms. The Royal Ceremonial Dress Collection is a display of the tailor's and dressmaker's art, with lavish ensembles worn for state occasions and a permanent collection of 14 dresses worn by Diana, Princess of Wales, the palace's most famous resident. Make time for tea in Queen Anne's Orangery (built 1704-5) and admire the horticultural perfection that is the Sunken Garden.

Serpentine Gallery

Kensington Gardens (nr Albert Memorial), W2 3XA (7402 6075/www.serpentinegallery.org). Lancaster Gate or South Kensington tube. Open 10am-6pm daily. Admission free; donations appreciated. Credit AmEx, MC, V. Map p395 D8.

The secluded location, sitting pretty to the west of the Long Water, makes this small and airy gallery for contemporary art an attractive destination. A rolling two-monthly programme of exhibitions featuring up-to-the-minute artists keeps the Serpentine in the arts news, as does the annual Serpentine Pavilion commission. Every spring an internationally renowned architect, who has never built in the UK before, is commissioned to design and build a new pavilion, which is open to visitors from June until September. There are also a lively programme of events and an excellent bookshop.

North London

Music, markets, mayhem and the purview of the middle-classes.

Camden Market.

A couple of centuries ago there was no north London. Beyond Marylebone, St Pancras and Clerkenwell stretched pastureland and private estates, with villages, hamlets and inns strung along Roman roads and country lanes. Then, in the 1790s, landowners initiated lucrative housing developments in Somers Town, Pentonville, Camden Town and Kentish Town; the Regency period saw the expansion of salubrious enclaves around St John's Wood, Regent's Park and Islington, the vanguard of a steady creep north towards the high villages of Hampstead, Highgate, Holloway and Hornsey. The construction of the Underground in Victorian times facilitated the inexorable surge of suburbia, so that by the 20th century the boundaries of the metropolis had been pushed as far north as Edgware, Finchley, Barnet and Enfield. Today the north London touchstone for visitors is Camden (the Lock, the markets, the vibe), but the more adventurous venture up to Hampstead and Highgate or along Islington's busily boisterous Upper Street. Saved from

developers long ago, the wild meadows and ancient woodland of Hampstead Heath provide a vital lung for Londoners, with Parliament Hill and, further out, Alexandra Palace, offering unrivalled views of London's landmarks.

Camden

Camden Town or Chalk Farm tube.

Camden has long been associated with the rougher side of life. Originally, it was just two taverns on the road to Hampstead, the Mother Black Cap and Mother Red Cap (now the World's End pub), a haunt of highwaymen and other rogues. Cheap lodging houses dominated the area around the time when the Regent's Canal was being dug in 1816, and it was rough in Victorian times too, according to Dickens, who grew up in Bayham Street. In the mid 1800s, Irish and Greek immigrants put down roots, many of them working on the new railways. The area remains largely working class, with a sizeable student community attracted by low rents since the 1960s – hence the indie music scene for which Camden is known. Of course, there are growing pockets of gentrification: the spacious houses in Albert Street, Gloucester Crescent and Camden Square, in particular, have long since been colonised by white-collar professionals and Alan Bennett.

There are also signs that Camden is enjoying a renaissance, with the revivals in 2006 of two major music and arts venues at the northern (the **Roundhouse**; *see p311*) and southern (**Koko**; *see p311*) ends of Camden High Street. Otherwise, traditional sights are few, but there's no lack of colour – every night Camden Town tube is garlanded with exotica, whether punks and goths in full regalia, vocal street preachers or the less photogenic junkies. Opposite the tube **Inverness Street** is a fruit market by day (8.30am-5pm daily) and a hub of activity by night, teeming with bars banging out anything from dirty electro and Latin house to rock 'n' roll. At the top end of the street, the **Good Mixer** (no.30, 7916 7929) is where Blur and Oasis drank before Britpop hyped itself to death.

Most visit for the various sites collectively known as **Camden Market** (*see right*), which stretches north from the tube along the alt-retail experience that is Camden High Street to the canal, its locks and beyond. No longer just a hangout for students and teens, this is one of London's big tourist attractions, particularly at weekends when crowds can be unbearable. Far better to explore on a weekday, if you can.

Cutting through the market is **Regent's Canal**, which opened in 1820 to provide a link between east and west London. The route was opened to the public as a scenic path in 1968, and the canal's industrial trappings have been transformed over the decades. Any stretch is worth a stroll (you can follow the canal all the way east to the Thames at Limehouse, but the most popular walk is west from Camden Lock around the top of Regent's Park, passing **London Zoo** (*see p127*). You can also stroll up into **Primrose Hill** (*see p166*), where you'll find decent eating and drinking venues. Narrowboat cruises and floating restaurants travel between picturesque **Little Venice** (Warwick Avenue tube) and Camden Lock in summer and on winter weekends, passing through a mercifully short, dank tunnel under St John's Wood. Try Jason's Trip (7286 3428, www.jasons.co.uk), Jenny Wren and My Fair Lady (7485 4433, www.walkersquay.com) or the London Waterbus Company (7482 2660, www.londonwaterbus.com).

Away from Camden High Street, west of the tube, the expanded **Jewish Museum** (Raymond Burton House, 129-131 Albert Street, NW1 7NB, 7284 1997, www.jewishmuseum.org.uk) is due to reopen in February 2009.

By night, Camden is still a great place to catch a gig. It has far more than its fair share of excellent small venues, including the legendary **Dublin Castle** (*see p313*), where the likes of Madness and Blur first cut their teeth (signed posters adorn the walls), as well as **Barfly**, **Green Note**, the **Jazz Café** and the **Underworld** (for all, *see pp312-314*). But the place is poorly furnished with eating and drinking options. You could try noodles on Jamestown Road at **Wagamama** (no.11, 7428 0800; *see also p200*) or **Hi Sushi Salsa** (no.28; *see p215*); on the Parkway, **Fresh & Wild** (no.49, 7428 7575) offers organic snacks, while **Jamon Jamon** (no.38, 7284 0606) does excellent tapas. Camden Lock's enormous pan-Asian bar-restaurant **Gilgamesh** (*see p232*) is worth a look if only to have your mind boggled by the riotously OTT decor.

Camden Market

Camden Canal Market *off Chalk Farm Road, south of junction with Castlehaven Road, NW1 9XJ (7485 8355/www.camdenlock.net).* **Open** 10am-6pm daily.
Camden Lock *Camden Lock Place, off Chalk Farm Road, NW1 8AF (7485 7963/www.camdenlock market.com).* **Open** 10am-6pm Mon-Wed, Fri-Sun; 10am-7pm Thur.
Camden Market *Camden High Street, junction with Buck Street, NW1 (7351 5353/www.camden markets.org).* **Open** 9.30am-5.30pm daily.
Electric Ballroom *184 Camden High Street, NW1 8QP (7485 9006/www.electric-ballroom.co.uk).* **Open** 10am-6pm Sat, Sun; record & film fairs occasional Sats throughout the year.
Stables *off Chalk Farm Road, opposite junction with Hartland Road, NW1 8AH (7485 5511/www.stablesmarket.com).* **Open** 10am-6pm daily (reduced stalls Mon-Fri).
All *Camden Town or Chalk Farm tube.*
Camden Market (formerly Buck Street Market), just next to the tube, flogs cheap sunglasses and cut-price interpretations of current fashions. The Electric Ballroom sells second-hand clothes and young designers' wares; it's neither cheap nor very exciting, but does have cut-price CDs. Both are fairly negligible, whereas Camden Lock has the advantage of being attractive thanks to a courtyard setting beside the canal. There are pleasant cafés, a couple of good bars and shops selling things you might actually want to buy. Crafty stalls sell mostly decorative items from funky lighting to ethnic art and antiques. North of the courtyard that contains Gilgamesh (*see p232*) is the Stables area, with food huts and railway arches housing vintage clothing and clubwear shops – by the time you read this some of these will have been moved on to make space for a multimillion-pound redevelopment of the area. Antiques and contemporary designer furniture are sold at the very north of the site at the part of the market known as the Horse Hospital (it once cared for horses injured while pulling barges).

The new Camden?

When Dickens recalled his childhood home in Camden, he described it as 'shabby, dingy, damp, and as mean a neighbourhood as one would desire not to see'. If anything the area had become even seamier by Edwardian times when Walter Sickert painted a famous picture of a murdered prostitute in a grubby bedsit. Now famous for its markets, Camden Town – the heaving High Street and busy canalside, the shops and bars – has long been a tat bazaar, a mecca for goths, indie kids, drunks and junkies. But changes may be afoot.

Approval has been granted for a £12 million private redevelopment of **Stables Market**, seeing the construction of a multistorey, glass complex of boutiques and bars that has displaced many existing stallholders. Already established on its own plot is the massive **Gilgamesh** (*see p232*), a 'restaurant lounge' approached by escalator, with outré decor and sliding glass roof; it's as far removed from the familiar Camden vibe as could be imagined, although a wall of glass does directly overlook the grim viaduct of a goods railway. Plans are in the offing to open another African-themed space called Zulu in the space beneath.

Yet many first-timers' introduction to Camden Town is still via the claustrophobic hole of the tube station. While there have been minor enhancements at platform level, plans to redevelop the corner site around the ticket hall have stalled. Local councillor Chris Naylor says: 'There's no doubt we have to get a new station, but the previous design was way too big and not sensitive to Camden's feel at all.' Camden Council has also set aside £24 million for a five-year 'boulevard project' – enhanced paving and lighting, new cycle lanes, hardy saplings, hanging baskets, security cameras – but apart from improvements to Inverness Street market and Chalk Farm Road, little has been done so far. Almost every lick of paint is controversial, with residents intensely worried that Camden might become a chain-clogged High Street. Indeed, even in showpiece Stables Market things are volatile: At Proud, an independent gallery-bar-gig space seen by some as representing the best of the new Camden, closed suddenly in 2007. Perhaps the goths and indie kids needn't move on just yet.

Around Camden

Primrose Hill, to the west of Camden, with its elegant terraces, is as pretty as the actors and pop stars who live here. Past the park and its namesake hill (with grand views over London), **Regent's Park Road** becomes a pleasant mix of smart shops, independent restaurants and cafés. The long-established **Primrose Pâtisserie** (no.136, 7722 7848) serves delicious slabs of cold apple crumble, and upmarket Greek eaterie **Lemonia** (no.89, 7586 7454) draws a devoted crowd from far and wide, but our current favourite blow-out here is **Odette's** (*see p215*). There are also quality gastropubs on Gloucester Avenue such as the **Engineer** (no.65, 7722 0950) and the **Lansdowne** (no.90, 7483 0409).

St John's Wood

St John's Wood or Swiss Cottage tube.
Rural calm prevailed in St John's Wood until well into the 19th century, when the only developments around the wooded hills and meadows were smart stucco villas. The pure air attracted artists, scientists and writers: George Eliot often held receptions at her house (The

Priory, North Bank). A blue plaque marks the house at 44 Grove End Road once owned by the popular Victorian classicist painter Sir Lawrence Alma-Tadema; the house is closed to the public. The inexpensive but pretty dwellings continued to suit rich men, who often used them to house their mistresses, until building work by the Great Central Railway in 1894 destroyed the lubricious rural idyll.

Sensitive redevelopment during the 1950s has left the area smart, desirable and fabulously expensive – just take a look at the chic boutiques along the High Street. **Lord's**, the world's most famous cricket ground, is the reason why most people visit. A short hop north is the recording facility of **Abbey Road Studios** (3 Abbey Road). The building has a fine musical tradition: Sir Edward Elgar opened the place in 1931, conductor Sir Malcolm Sargent lived next door and, of course, bands from the Beatles to Pink Floyd and Oasis have recorded here. The cover of the Fab Four's final album (1969) conferred iconic status on a zebra crossing outside and legions of devotees still line up to be photographed there. Since 1980, countless film scores have been recorded at Abbey Road, from the Star Wars prequels to the latest Harry Potter.

Up the Finchley Road from St John's Wood is Swiss Cottage, best visited for a look at the superb library designed by Sir Basil Spence and the modern **Hampstead Theatre** (*see p340*).

Lord's Tour & MCC Museum

St John's Wood Road, NW8 8QN (7616 8595/ www.lords.org). St John's Wood tube. **Tours** *Nov-Mar* noon, 2pm daily. *Apr-Oct* 10am, noon, 2pm daily. **Admission** £10; £7-£6 reductions; £27 family; free under-5s. **Credit** MC, V.
The wearers of the famous egg-and-bacon striped tie have come to love the NatWest Media Centre, the funky raised pod that dominates the self-proclaimed home of cricket. The centre joins the portrait-bedecked Long Room on the guided tour (you'll need to book), along with the expected collection of battered bats, photos and blazers. There's plenty of WG Grace ephemera, a stuffed sparrow with the ball that killed it and, of course, the urn that contains the Ashes, cricket's greatest prize.

Hampstead

Hampstead or Golders Green tube/ Gospel Oak or Hampstead Heath rail.
Exclusive Hampstead was a popular retreat in times of plague and remains a delightful place for a restorative wander. It has long been the favoured roosting place for literary and artistic bigwigs; Keats and Constable called it home in the 19th century, while the modern British sculptors Barbara Hepworth and Henry Moore lived the London village idyll here in the 1930s.

Hampstead tube station stands at the top of the steep High Street. The Georgian terraces of nearby **Church Row**, a beautiful street, lead to **St John-at-Hampstead** church (7794 5808), whose cemetery is less ostentatious than near-neighbour Highgate, but just as restfully bucolic. Among the notables buried here are Constable and comedian Peter Cook. Climb steep, narrow **Holly Walk** to Mount Vernon and check out a plaque to Robert Louis Stevenson on the corner house. Carry on to Holly Mount for Hampstead's antique **Holly Bush** pub (*see p232*), which was painter George Romney's stable block (his house still stands to the side on Holly Bush Hill). Another minute's climb brings you to **Fenton House** (*see p158*), and eventually up past the **Hampstead Scientific Society Observatory** (Lower Terrace, 8346 1056, www.hampsteadscience.ac.uk/astro), which is only open mid October to mid April on clear weekend evenings. A stroll along Judges Walk reveals a line of horse chestnuts and limes virtually unchanged since they were the subject of one of Constable's paintings in 1820.

At the summit of Hampstead is Whitestone Pond, where weary horses once refreshed themselves. Follow North End Way past Jack Straw's Castle (a weatherboarded former pub), wander down into the wooded West Heath (a dog walker's paradise, gay cruising territory after sundown) and you'll stumble upon the secluded **Hill Garden** and its Pergola (open

The statue of WG Grace at **Lord's**.

8.30am-dusk daily), a haven that locals like to keep a closely guarded secret. Make sure you've packed provisions, there are no facilities here.

East of Heath Street, a maze of attractive streets shelters **Burgh House** on New End Square (7431 0144), a Queen Anne house with a small local history museum and gallery space; 44 Well Walk, Constable's home for the last ten years of his life; and **2 Willow Road** (*see below*), architect Ernö Goldfinger's residence in the 1930s. Nearby, on Keats Grove, is **Keats House** (7435 2062), where Keats wrote many of his best poems; the house closes in 2008 for restoration.

Hampstead Heath provides some of the city's finest countryside. Its charming contours and woodlands conspire to make it feel far larger and more rural than it is (791 acres, with another 112 acres in the adjoining Kenwood estate). The views of London from the top of Parliament Hill are wonderful and on hot days the bathing ponds (men's, women's and mixed) are a godsend. As the source of the Fleet, one of the 'lost rivers' of London, the ponds are reasonably fresh, and are open all year round as long as algae levels are safe. There's also a brutally designed, unheated lido at Gospel Oak (7485 5757). The heath is popular for flying kites and sailing model boats, and there are concerts at two bandstands on Sunday afternoons in summer. At the north end of the park are **Kenwood House** (*see right*) and the atmospheric, 16th-century **Spaniards Inn** (8731 6571); highwayman Dick Turpin's father was once landlord here. The Grade II-listed building straddles Spaniards Way, causing a bottleneck that must be one of the most ancient examples of 'traffic calming' in the city.

Amongst the handsome residential streets in south-west Hampstead is the former home (and now museum) of Sigmund Freud (*see right*). Nearby, the innovative **Camden Arts Centre** (Arkwright Road, corner of Finchley Road, 7472 5500) has a reputation for distinctive shows by contemporary artists. The centre has landscaped gardens and a café that hosts film screenings and live performances on Wednesday evenings.

Fenton House

3 Hampstead Grove, NW3 6RT (7435 3471/ www.nationaltrust.org.uk). Hampstead tube. **Open** *Mar* 2-5pm Sat, Sun. *Apr-Oct* 2-5pm Wed-Fri; 11am-5pm Sat, Sun. **Tours** phone for details. **Admission** *House & gardens* £5.40; £2.70 under-18s; free under-5s. *Gardens* £1. *Joint ticket with 2 Willow Road* £7.20. **Credit** MC, V.

Devotees of early music will be impressed by the collection of harpsichords, clavichords, virginals and spinets in this late 17th-century house. The bequest was made on condition that qualified musicians be allowed to play them, so you might be lucky enough to hear them in action (or phone for details of lunch and evening concerts during the summer). The

porcelain collection won't appeal to everyone – the 'curious grotesque teapot' certainly lives up to its billing – but, for fans, there's work by Meissen and Rockingham. The maze-like sunken gardens are a delight, with the small orchard coming into its own for the Apple Day fête (usually early Oct).

Freud Museum

20 Maresfield Gardens, NW3 5SX (7435 2002/ www.freud.org.uk). Finchley Road tube. **Open** noon-5pm Wed-Sun. **Admission** £5; £3 reductions; free under-12s. **Credit** AmEx, MC, V.

After Anna Freud's death in 1982, the house she and her father Sigmund shared for the last year of his life became a museum. The analyst's couch sits in the study, round glasses and unsmoked cigars setting the scene, and the copious library is impressive. Upstairs is Anna's weaving room and a gallery. This is one of the few buildings in London to have two blue plaques: commemorating both father and daughter (she was a pioneer in child psychiatry).

Kenwood House/Iveagh Bequest

Hampstead Lane, NW3 7JR (8348 1286/www. english-heritage.org.uk). Hampstead tube/Golders Green tube then 210 bus. **Open** *Apr-Oct* 11am-5pm daily. *Nov-Mar* 11am-4pm daily. **Tours** (for groups by appointment only) £5. **Admission** free; donations appreciated. **Credit** MC, V.

Built in 1616, Kenwood House was remodelled (1764-79) by Robert Adam for William Murray, first Earl of Mansfield (it was Murray's decision as Chief Justice in a test case in 1772 that made it illegal to own slaves in England). Brewing magnate Edward Guinness bought the property in 1925, filling it with his art collection. Now English Heritage is in charge, trying to ensure that Guinness's wish 'that the atmosphere of a gentleman's private park should be preserved'. Art includes Vermeer's *The Guitar Player*, a panoramic view of Old London Bridge by Claude de Jongh (1630), Gainsborough's *Countess Howe*, and one of the world's most entrancing self-portraits (Rembrandt, c1663). Outside, Humphrey Repton's 1793 landscape remains mostly unchanged. An ivy tunnel leads from the flower garden, to a terrace with views over the lakes – one of Repton's famous 'surprises'. Part of the grounds is now listed as a Site of Special Scientific Interest for its rare invertebrates and species of bat. The charming Brew House Café is always busy.

2 Willow Road

2 Willow Road, NW3 1TH (7435 6166/www.nat ionaltrust.org.uk). Hampstead tube/Hampstead Heath rail. **Open** *Mar, Nov* 11am-5pm Sat. *Apr-Oct* noon-5pm Thur, Fri; 11am-5pm Sat. **Tours** noon, 1pm, 2pm Mon-Fri; 11am, noon, 1pm, 2pm Sat. **Admission** £5.10; £2.60 children; £12.80 family; free under-5s. *Joint ticket with Fenton House £7.30.* **No credit cards**

This atmospheric 1939 building is the National Trust's only example of international modernism. It's the centre residence in a terrace of three houses designed by Hungarian-born émigré architect Ernö Goldfinger (also responsible for Notting Hill's Trellick

Tower; *see p130*). The house was designed to be flexible, with movable partitions, folding doors, and a spiral staircase. The palette of colours grows lighter and brighter progressing upwards through the house. Home to the architect and his wife until their deaths, it contains art by Max Ernst and Henry Moore.

Highgate

Archway or Highgate tube.
The name comes from a tollgate that once stood on the site of the Gate House pub on the High Street. Legend has it that Dick Whittington, having walked away from the city as far as the foot of Highgate Hill, heard the Bow Bells peal out 'Turn again, Whittington, thrice Mayor of London'. The event is commemorated on the Whittington Stone, near the hospital. The area is today best known for the burial grounds of **Highgate Cemetery** (*see right*), last resting place of such important figures as Karl Marx. Adjoining is **Waterlow Park**, donated by low-cost housing pioneer Sir Sydney Waterlow in 1889. The park has terrific views, ponds, a mini-aviary, tennis courts and the 16th century **Lauderdale House** (8348 8716, www.lauderdalehouse.co.uk). Once home to Charles II's mistress, Nell Gwynn, it now has a nice garden café.

North of Highgate tube, shady **Highgate Woods** were mentioned (under another name) in the Domesday Book. Much of the ancient woodland remains as a conservation area with a nature trail, adventure playground and café hosting live jazz during the summer. A leafy walk leads from here along the line of a former railway through Crouch End, comfortable, middle-class and densely populated by the acting fraternity – David Tennant and Simon Pegg among the soap stars – to Finsbury Park.

Highgate Cemetery
Swains Lane, N6 6PJ (8340 1834/www.highgate-cemetery.org). Highgate tube. **Open** *East Cemetery Apr-Oct* 10am-4.30pm Mon-Fri; 11am-4.30pm Sat, Sun. *Nov-Mar* 10am-3.30pm Mon-Fri; 11am-3.30pm Sat, Sun. *West Cemetery* by tour only. **Tours** *Dec-Feb* 11am, noon, 1pm, 2pm, 3pm, 4pm Sat, Sun. *Mar-Nov* 2pm Mon-Fri. **Admission** £3. *Tours* £5. **No credit cards.**
With its dramatic tombs topped by towering angels, shrouded urns and broken columns, Highgate exudes a romantic atmosphere of ivy-covered neglect. The original 1839 West Cemetery – visitable by tour only: book ahead, arrive half an hour early, and no photography – is nonetheless breathtaking. Long paths wind through gloomy catacombs and the graves of notables such as poet Christina Rossetti, scientist Michael Faraday and lesbian writer Radclyffe Hall. Prize sites include the tombs lining Egyptian Avenue (pharaonic styling being all the rage in the 1830s) and the ring of neoclassical tombs known as the Lebanon Circle. The East Cemetery, added just 15 years later and not as atmospheric, allows you to wander freely as you seek the memorials to Karl Marx and George Eliot. The cemetery closes during burials, so call ahead.

Islington

Map p402
Angel tube/Highbury & Islington tube/rail.
Henry VIII owned houses for hunting in this once-idyllic village, by the 19th century it was already known for its shops, theatres and music

Hampstead Heath.

Sightseeing

halls. The new Regent's Canal meant the arrival of industrial slums from 1820, and the area declined into one of London's poorest boroughs. However, its Georgian squares and Victorian terraces have been gentrified in recent decades.

Surfacing from Angel tube, it's worth taking a wander north-eastwards to check out an arm of the Regent's Canal as it emerges from nearly 3,000 feet of tunnel under Islington. Outrageous 1960s playwright Joe Orton lived nearby at 25 Noel Road, where he was bludgeoned to death in 1967 by partner Kenneth Halliwell. Heading north from the tube along Upper Street, you pass old **Camden Passage** antiques market (*see p259*) on the right and the Business Design Centre on the left, before you reach the triangle of Islington Green and, eventually, **Highbury**. En route, there are countless boutiques, the **Screen on the Green** cinema (*see p288*), the **Almeida Theatre** (*see p339*) and the often-raucous **King's Head** theatre pub (*see p340*).

Taking this route you'll graze the south entrance of the N1 Centre shopping mall, near the Angel, which includes a music venue (the **Carling Academy Islington**; *see p309*), a Vue cineplex and lots of chain stores. This behemoth is symptomatic of changes that threaten to turn what was a unique locale into something much more familiar. Try **Alpino's** (*see p214*) for a slurp of old Islington.

Along Upper Street take a detour east to **Canonbury Square**, a Regency creation and once home to George Orwell (no.27) and Evelyn Waugh (no.17A). It now houses the **Estorick Collection of Modern Italian Art**.

Just beyond the end of Upper Street is **Highbury Fields**, to which 200,000 Londoners fled in 1666 to escape the Great Fire. Smart Highbury is best known as home to Arsenal football club, which moved in 2006 from the small but perfectly formed art deco Highbury Stadium to the new 60,000-capacity Emirates Stadium down the road, where there are occasional 90-minute guided tours ending at the **Arsenal Museum** (call 7704 4160 to book).

Estorick Collection of Modern Italian Art

39A Canonbury Square, N1 2AN (7704 9522/ www.estorickcollection.com). Highbury & Islington tube/rail/271 bus. **Open** 11am-6pm Wed-Sat; noon-5pm Sun. **Admission** £3.50; £2.50 reductions; free under-16s, students. **Credit** AmEx, MC, V.
Britain's only gallery devoted to modern Italian art. Eric Estorick was a US political scientist, writer and art collector whose collection includes some fine work by Italian Futurists such as Balla's *Hand of the Violinist* and Boccioni's *Modern Idol*, as well as pieces by Carra, Russolo and Severini. The museum has a library, a shop and café. A tenth anniversary celebratory exhibition will be taking place in 2008.

Dalston & Stoke Newington

Dalston Kingsland rail/30, 38, 56, 67, 149, 242, 243, 277 bus; Stoke Newington rail/73 bus.
Though scruffy and, at times, intimidating, Dalston is a vibrant place, with shops, Ridley Road's market stalls, cafés, all-night restaurants and clubs. It's also home to the **Dalston Jazz Bar** (4 Bradbury Street, 7254 9728), good for late drinks and live jazz; around the corner on Gillett Square is the **Vortex Jazz Club** (*see p315*), part of the Dalston Culture House.

Stoke Newington is sometimes seen as the place people move to when they can't afford Islington. We like it for Stoke Newington High Street: here you'll find Keralan vegetarian restaurant **Rasa** (no.55, 7249 0344), second-hand bookshops and one-off boutiques selling new and vintage clothes, and the colourful **Route 73 Kids** toy store (no.92, 7923 7873). The street's bookended by two green spaces: **Clissold Park** (7923 3660) is fine enough, with its small zoo, lake and tearoom, but **Abney Park Cemetery** (7275 7557, www.abney-park.org.uk) is a treasure. An old boneyard centred on a derelict Gothic revival chapel, it's also a nature reserve with rare butterflies, woodpeckers and bats.

Further north

The tidy suburban streets at north London's perimeter are enlivened by immigrant communities that have made them their home. Golders Green, Hendon and Finchley have large Jewish enclaves: there's been a Jewish cemetery on Hoop Lane since 1895, where cellist Jacqueline du Pré is buried. TS Eliot, Marc Bolan and Anna Pavlova all ended up at Golders Green Crematorium (8455 2374).

The neighbourhoods of Tottenham and Haringey have sizeable Greek Cypriot, Turkish Cypriot and Kurdish communities. The groups live side by side in Green Lanes, where food-related business success is evident in the thriving kebab shops, supermarkets and bakeries. But, the real draw up here is Alexandra Palace.

Alexandra Park & Palace

Alexandra Palace Way, N22 7AY (park 8444 7696/ information 8365 2121/boating 8889 9089/www. alexandrapalace.com). Wood Green tube/Alexandra Palace rail/W3, W7, 84A, 144, 144A bus. **Open** *Park* 24hrs daily. *People's Palace* phone for details.
'The People's Palace', when it opened in 1873, was supposed to provide affordable entertainment for all. It burned down just 16 days later. Rebuilt, it became the site of the first TV broadcasts by the BBC in 1936, but in 1980 was destroyed by fire once more. The born-yet-again palace has remained intact and yields panoramic views of London. It provides ice skating and boating, and hosts fairs, concerts and events.

East London

Fashion, food and fun – the East End is giving the West End a run for its money.

Long central to the mythology of old London – on the one side cheeky barrow boys and irrepressible Cockney sparrows, on the other gangsters, poverty and a ready supply of cheap labour – the east now looks more like the city's future. Ragged around the edges, as cursed with decades of underinvestment as it is blessed with the buzz of redevelopment and new money, as blowsy and old-fashioned as it is hip, east London is the embodiment of the whole city's changing cultural and social landscape.

Centuries of immigration, driven by the promise of available work and the proximity of the docks, have left this part of town quilted with a patchwork of cultures, languages, ethnic groups and religions. This is apparent even in the districts closest to the City – Whitechapel, adjacent Spitalfields and Brick Lane – which are now best known for being home to the city's Bangladeshi community, but increasingly also to arty bohemians and City money. Immediately north, Shoreditch and Hoxton could hardly be

more different in character: cheap rents and ready warehouse space brought in artists and designers during the 1980s, and where they went, fashion diligently followed. Though still shabby, the area is a vast playground for London's bright young things, with its bars, shops and galleries spilling over into surrounding districts.

Docklands, the area around London's last working dockyards at the time of their 1980s redevelopment, is dominated by the skyscrapers of Canary Wharf at the northern end of the Isle of Dogs, still a work in progress (*see p32* **The only way is up…**). Parts of Thames-side Wapping and Limehouse maintain a pleasingly dark Victorian atmosphere, augmented by some made-over pubs and small restaurants.

Northwards, Hackney is another borough in transformation. Its once-poor reputation is being renovated as rocketing prices around the City and Canary Wharf force the middle classes north and east. To the north, villagey Walthamstow benefits from having the ancient trees of Epping Forest on its doorstep.

Spitalfields, old and new.

Spitalfields

Maps p403 & p405

Aldgate East tube or Liverpool Street tube/rail.
Spitalfields, famous for its covered market, is best approached from Liverpool Street Station up Brushfield Street. You'll know you're on the right track when you spy the unforgettable spike spire of **Christ Church Spitalfields** (*see p163*) at the end of the street. Before the market is new shopping area Crispin Place, announced by a courtyard shaded by a sail-like curved awning. Slick shops here sell upmarket clothes, cosmetics, homeware and gourmet olive oil, and there's a decent cluster of eating places.

The redevelopment of **Spitalfields Market** (*see p239*) has hardly been very rapid. The uncharitable could alight on 1991 when, just like London's other old central markets, the original Spitalfields fruit and veg traders were banished to more traffic-accessible suburbs. Developers sought to demolish the handsome covered-market building, but vigorous campaigns were launched to preserve the market's character. When redevelopment began in earnest in 2002, the market was retained, but in truth buildings like the Norman Foster-

Sightseeing

Street scene The two Brick Lanes

Join the crowds flowing east from Spitalfields Market (*see p161*) along Hanbury Street during the weekend, and the direction you turn at the end will determine which Brick Lane you see. Turn right and you're in 'Banglatown', the name adopted by the ward back in 2002. Until you hit the bland modern offices beside the kitsch Banglatown arch, it's almost all Bangladeshi cafés, curry houses (*see p218*), grocery stores, money transfer services and sari shops. With the exception of the **Pride of Spitalfields** pub (3 Heneage Street, 7247 8933), serving a stalwart Sunday roast and fine real ales, there's little sign you're in the East End.

Jamme Masjid Mosque, between Fournier Street and Princelet Street, is a key symbol of Brick Lane's hybridity. It began life as a Huguenot chapel, became a synagogue and was finally converted, back in 1976, into a mosque – in other words, immigrant communities have been layering their experiences on this street at least since 1572, when the St Bartholomew's Day Massacre forced the non-conformist Huguenots out of France.

The newest layer is gentrification: turn left from Hanbury Street, and it's all about young urban bohemians. On a Sunday there's the lively local **market**, while pedestrianised Dray Walk, part of the **Old Truman Brewery** complex (nos.91-95), is crowded every day. It's full of hip independent businesses: **Story Deli** (*see p217*), the **Big Chill Bar** (*see p232*), **A Butcher of Distinction** (*see p248*), **Junky Styling** (*see p248*) and even the new, gig-friendly **Rough Trade** (*see p261*) are here, along with the **Rootmaster** (www.root-master.co.uk), a vegetarian café in an old red bus. Heading north on Brick Lane, you'll find the **Vibe Bar** (7377 2899, www.vibe-bar.co.uk) as well as **Luna & Curious** (*see p256*), a bookshop and the second-hand clothes at **Rokit** (nos.101 & 107, 7375 3864, 7247 3777). On the right, Grimsby Street is good for graffiti – full-colour throw-ups are not uncommon, whereas stencils prevail almost everywhere else. Further up in Cheshire Street is **Mimi** (*see p251*), **Beyond Retro** (*see p249*) and, archetypal new Brick Lane, modishly old-fashioned **Labour & Wait** (*see p260*), where a tin of twine costs £6.50.

designed office of corporate lawyers Allen & Overy could be anywhere in the City. Even shops that seem to have been here since Dickens's day are recent inventions: along Brushfield Street the charming grocery shop **A Gold** (*see p255*) was lovingly restored seven years ago; the owners of the **Market Coffee House** (nos.50-52, 7247 4110) put reclaimed wood panelling and creaky furniture into an empty shell; and the deli **Verde & Co** (no.40, 7247 1924) was opened by its owner, author Jeanette Winterson, inspired by the local food shops she found in – whisper it – France. Enter the covered market from Crispin Place and you'll see the new glass-walled **Kinetica** (7392 9674, www.kinetica-museum .org), a gallery that focuses on new media and kinetic art – ranging from Burning Man-style robots to early 20th-century sideshow automata. The Friday fashion market and main Sunday market thrive, despite the disruption and uncertainty of continuing development.

If you are in the area on Sunday, you'll get another perspective on Spitalfields by heading a few streets south to the famously salt-of-the-earth **Petticoat Lane Market**, which centres on Middlesex Street. At the foot of Goulston Street, **Tubby Isaacs** seafood stall has been selling whelks, cockles and crabs since 1919.

A block north of Spitalfields Market is **Dennis Severs**' House (*see below*), an atmospherically restaged Huguenot dwelling, while across from the market, on the east side of Commercial Street, in the shadow of Christ Church, the **Ten Bells** (84 Commercial Street, 7366 1721) is where one of Jack the Ripper's prostitute victims drank her last gin (it's pleasant enough, but head to the Commercial Tavern at no.142 if you want a drink – just as lively but usually less crowded). The streets between here and Brick Lane to the east are dourly impressive, lined with tall, shuttered Huguenot houses; **19 Princelet Street** is sometimes open to the public. This unrestored 18th-century house was home first to French silk merchants and later Polish Jews who built a synagogue in the garden. For details of open days, see www.19princeletstreet.org.uk.

Christ Church Spitalfields

Commercial Street, E1 6QE (7247 7202/www.christ churchspitalfields.org). Liverpool Street tube/rail. **Open** 11am-4pm Tue; 1-4pm Sun. **Admission** free. **Map** p401 S5.

Built in 1729 by architect Nicholas Hawksmoor, the marvellous Christ Church Spitalfields has in recent years been cleaned and restored to its original state (tasteless alterations had followed a 19th-century lightning-strike). Most tourists get no further than cowering before the overbearing spire, but the revived interior is impressive, its pristine whiteness in marked contrast to its architect's dark reputation.

The formidable 1735 Richard Bridge organ is almost as old as the church. The resident Gabrieli Consort & Players give regular performances, and the church is open for services and worship.

Dennis Severs' House

18 Folgate Street, E1 6BX (7247 4013/www.dennis severshouse.co.uk). Liverpool Street tube/rail. **Open** noon-4pm 1st & 3rd Sun of mth; noon-2pm Mon following 1st & 3rd Sun of mth; times vary Mon evenings. **Admission** £8 Sun; £5 noon-2pm Mon; £12 Mon evenings. **Credit** V. **Map** p403 V5.

The ten rooms of this original Huguenot house have been decked out to recreate snapshots of life in Spitalfields between 1724 and 1914. A tour through this compelling 'still-life drama', as American creator Dennis Severs dubbed it, takes you through the cellar, kitchen, dining room, smoking room and upstairs to the bedrooms. With hearth and candles burning, smells lingering and objects scattered apparently haphazardly, it's designed to feel as though the inhabitants had deserted the rooms only moments before you entered.

Brick Lane

Maps p403 & p405
Aldgate East tube.

Irony of ironies: tatty old **Brick Lane** is world-famous for its curries (there's now a Brick Lane restaurant in Manhattan and a namesake street in Dhaka), but the rise in reputation has been mirrored by a decline in quality (*see p218*). It does, however, sell brilliant Bengali sweets (drop in on Madhubon Sweet Centre at no.42 to prove the case) and all manner of rare groceries. For details of what's happening all along Brick Lane, *see p162* **Street scene**.

Whitechapel

Map p405
Aldgate East or Whitechapel tube.

Not one of the prettier parts of London, the district that takes its name from the white stones used to build a now-demolished church centres on busy but anonymous Whitechapel Road. One of the bright spots is **Whitechapel Art Gallery** (*see p165*), still worth travelling for, despite extensive ongoing work as it expands next door into the former library. The neighbouring alley (which also currently provides access to the gallery) has a wall of anarchists' portraits and the **Freedom Press Bookshop** (7247 9249), on the first floor just round the corner, should you need to bone up on some radical ecology.

A little to the east, the **Whitechapel Bell Foundry** (nos.32 & 34, 7247 2599, www. whitechapelbellfoundry.co.uk) continues to manufacture bells, just as it has since 1570,

Hands-on fun at the **V&A Museum of Childhood**. *See p166*.

most famously producing Big Ben. Displays in the foyer (open 9am-4.15pm Mon-Fri) include Big Ben's template, which surrounds the door; to join one of the fascinating tours you'll have to reserve a place (usually well in advance) on one of the scheduled Saturday tours.

But it's not bells needed at Whitechapel's current foremost place of worship. Instead, a muezzin summons the faithful each Friday: the **East London Mosque**, focal point for the largest Muslim community in Britain, can accommodate 10,000 worshippers. Behind is Fieldgate Street and the dark mass of **Tower House**, a former doss house whose 700 rooms are, inevitably, being redeveloped into flats. Joseph Stalin and George Orwell (researching *Down & Out in Paris and London*) were former tenants. The red-brick alleys around here give a good sense of Victorian Whitechapel, but also here is **New Tayyab** (nos.83-89, 7247 9543), which does cheap, impeccably lamby and aggressively spiced seekh kebabs.

East again is the Royal London Hospital and, in a small crypt on Newark Street, the small **Royal London Hospital Archives & Museum** (7377 7608, closed Sat, Sun). Inside are reproduction letters from Jack the Ripper (including the notorious missive 'From Hell', delivered with an enclosed portion of human kidney) and information on Joseph Merrick, the 'Elephant Man', so named for his fearsome congenital deformities. Rescued by surgeon Sir Frederick Treves, Merrick was given his own room in the Royal London Hospital. On nearby Turner Street, the brand new, high-tech **Centre of the Cell** (no.64, 7882 2562, www.centreof thecell.org) should open in spring 2008. It will give visitors a lively, interactive and occasionally grisly insight into cell biology in a purpose-built pod, suspended over labs that are engaged in investigating cancer and tuberculosis.

Back on Whitechapel Road, you can stock up on standard **street market** miscellanea (clothes, Bangladeshi fruit and veg, knock-off batteries, cigarettes from the roaming derelicts) or, at the corner of Whitechapel Road and Cambridge Heath Road, drop into the **Blind Beggar** (no.337, 7247 6195) where on 9 March 1966 East End gangster Ronnie Kray shot George Cornell dead.

Whitechapel Art Gallery

80-82 Whitechapel High Street, E1 7QX (7522 7888/www.whitechapel.org). Aldgate East tube. **Open** *Main gallery* closed for expansion until mid 2008. *Whitechapel Laboratory* 11am-6pm Wed-Sun. **Map** p405 S6.

Whitechapel's architecturally impressive art gallery has always been an unexpected cultural treat between the tatty clothing wholesalers, stripper pubs and the other flotsam of Whitechapel Road. Founded by a local vicar in the late 19th century to bring art to the working classes, it has presented contemporary, forward-thinking exhibitions for more than a century (Picasso's *Guernica*, for example, was shown here in 1939). The gallery is undergoing a complete overhaul as it expands into the former library next door – although the main entrance is boarded up, access via Angel Alley along the righthand side of the building gets you to the lively Whitechapel Laboratory. Keep an eye on the website: exhibitions of mainly lens-based work, readings and discussions, music nights (curated by out-there music mag *The Wire*) and the *Time Out*-sponsored First Thursday events are all still happening.

Shoreditch & Hoxton

Map p403

Old Street tube/rail.
This small area exerts a disproportionately large influence on London life thanks to its reputation as a hip arts and clubbing nexus.

The heart of all of this is a triangle formed by Old Street to the north, Shoreditch High Street (east) and Great Eastern Street (south-west). Anchoring the southernmost point of the triangle is the huge **Tea Building**, on the corner of Shoreditch High Street and Bethnal Green Road, a former tea warehouse that's now a hive of small creative studios, plus the fine **T Bar** (*see p321*) and **Hales Gallery** (*see p294*). **Les Trois Garçons** (*see p217*) and Brick Lane are just down the road, but the real landmark venues are places like **333**, **Cargo** and **Plastic People** (for all, *see p321*), plus a bunch of venues on and around Hoxton Square, including the **Hoxton Square Bar & Kitchen** (*see p321*).

It was artists who sparked the Hoxton resurgence; they took advantage of the area's large light industrial spaces and cheap rents to set up their studios here in the 1980s. The most high-profile legacy to result is the **White Cube Hoxton Square** (*see p294*). These days, City workers happy to pay serious money for some street cred have driven rents through the roof. The impecunious artists have moved east into Hackney and Bethnal Green, leaving the bars and clubs to fight a valiant rearguard action – that's right, 'No ties please'.

The area's sole bona fide tourist attraction is the exquisite **Geffrye Museum** (*see below*), which is a short walk north up Kingsland Road. The surrounding area is dense with Vietnamese restaurants, notably **Sông Quê** (*see p219*).

Geffrye Museum

Kingsland Road, E2 8EA (7739 9893/recorded information 7739 8543/www.geffrye-museum.org.uk). Liverpool Street tube/rail then 149, 242 bus/Old Street tube/rail then 243 bus. **Open** *Museum* 10am-5pm Tue-Sat; noon-5pm Sun. *Almshouse tours* 1st Sat of mth & 1st & 3rd Wed of mth – phone for times. **Admission** *Museum* free; donations appreciated. *Almshouse tours* £2; free under-16s. **Credit** (shop) MC, V. **Map** p403 R3.

The Geffrye Museum is a quite marvellous physical history of the English interior, housed in a set of converted almshouses. It recreates typical English living rooms from the 17th century to the present, and has a series of lovely gardens designed on similar chronological lines. There's an airy restaurant and special exhibitions are mounted throughout the year in a purpose-built downstairs space.

Rivington Place

6-8 Standard Place, Rivington Street, EC2A 3BE (7729 9616/www.rivingtonplace.org). Old Street tube/rail. **Open** 11am-6pm Tue, Wed, Fri; 11am-8.30pm Thur; noon-6pm Sat. **Admission** free. **Credit** (shop) MC, V. **Map** p403 R4.

Opening in October 2007, this fabulous structure is, astonishingly, the first new-build public gallery since the Hayward (*see p79*). Designed by David Adjaye, the ground-floor windows (with entrance to the side instead of at the front) serve almost as a shopfront for the exhibitions within. Dedicated to culturally diverse visual arts, two project spaces will show a range of British and international work, supported by the Stuart Hall members' library and the ground-floor café. Exhibitions in 2008 will include work from Cuba and photographs of the Bangladeshi independence struggle.

Bethnal Green

Bethnal Green tube/rail, Cambridge Heath rail or Mile End tube.

Once a suburb of spacious townhouses, by the mid 19th century Bethnal Green was one of London's poorest neighbourhoods. As in neighbouring Hoxton, a very recent upturn in fortunes has in part been occasioned by Bethnal Green's adoption as home by a new generation of artists. The new Bethnal Green is typified by the gallery **Between Bridges** (223 Cambridge Heath Road, 7729 8599), which occupies the entrance space to artist-photographer Wolfgang Tillmans's studio. The old Bethnal Green is best experienced through a trip to **E Pellicci** (*see p217*), the exemplary traditional London caff.

The area's other attraction is the famous **Columbia Road flower market** (*see p239*), a lovely way to fritter away a Sunday morning, whether you actually need any plants or not. A microcosmic retail community has grown up around the market: **Treacle** (nos.110-112, 7729 5657) is the place for groovy pieces of crockery and dinky cup cakes; **Angela Flanders** (no.96, 7739 7555; open Sun) is a lovely perfume shop; **Marcos & Trump** (no.146, 7739 9008) does vintage fashion.

V&A Museum of Childhood

Cambridge Heath Road, E2 9PA (8983 5200/ recorded information 8980 2415/www.museumof childhood.org.uk). Bethnal Green tube/rail/Cambridge Heath rail. **Open** 10am-5.45pm daily. **Admission** free; donations appreciated; *workshops* small charge. **Credit** MC, V.

Part of the Victoria & Albert Museum (*see p151*), the Museum of Childhood has had a recent refurb and emerged sparkling, with a brand new entrance and a variety of fresh exhibits and play areas spread over its two floors. The building is the original pre-fab used by the Kensington museum. The huge collection of children's toys, dolls' houses, games and costumes has been amassed since 1872, and continues to grow – our most recent visit uncovered *Incredibles* and new *Star Wars* figures to complement the bonkers 1970s puppets, Barbie Dolls, praxinoscopes and Victorian dolls' houses. The museum presents plenty of hands-on activities for kids, including dressing-up boxes and a zoëtrope, and runs free drop-in events and workshops. There's also a café to revive the grown-ups. *Photos p164.*

Ragged School Museum

46-50 Copperfield Road, E3 4RR (8980 6405/www. raggedschoolmuseum.org.uk). Mile End tube. **Open** 10am-5pm Wed, Thur; 2-5pm 1st Sun of mth. *Tours* by arrangement; phone for details. **Admission** free; donations appreciated.

Ragged schools were an early experiment in public education: they provided tuition along with food and clothing for destitute children. This one was the largest in London, and Dr Barnardo himself taught here. It's now a great little museum that contains a complete mock-up of a ragged classroom, where historical re-enactments are staged for schoolkids, as well as an Edwardian kitchen. There are displays on local history and industry in a downstairs room.

Docklands

London's docks were fundamental to the long prosperity of the British Empire. Between 1802 and 1921, ten separate docks were built between Tower Bridge in the west and Woolwich in the east employing tens of thousands of people.

Mudchute Park & Farm. *See p168.*

Yet by the 1960s the shipping industry was changing irrevocably. The new 'container' system of cargo demanded larger, deep-draught ships, as a result of which the work moved out to Tilbury. By 1980, the London docks had closed.

The London Docklands Development Corporation (LDDC), founded in 1981, spent £790 million of public money on redevelopment during the following decade, only for a country-wide property slump in the early 1990s to leave the shiny new high-rise offices and luxury flats unoccupied. Nowadays, though, that's just old history. As a financial hub, Docklands is a booming rival to the City of London, with an estimated 90,000 workers commuting to the area each day. For visitors, regular **Thames Clippers** (0870 781 5049, www.thames clippers.com) boat connections with central London and eastward extensions to the Docklands Light Railway (DLR) make the area easily accessible.

Wapping & Limehouse

Wapping tube or Limehouse DLR/rail.
In 1598, John Stowe described Wapping High Street as 'a filthy strait passage, with alleys of small tenements or cottages, inhabited by sailors' victuallers', which can still just about be imagined as you walk along it now, flanked by overbearingly tall Victorian warehouses. The historic **Town of Ramsgate** (no.62, 7481 8000), dating to 1545, also helps. Here 'hanging judge' George Jeffreys was captured in 1688, trying to escape to Europe in disguise as a woman. Privateer Captain William Kidd was executed in 1701 at Execution Dock, near **Wapping New Stairs**; the bodies of pirates were hanged from a gibbet until seven tides had washed over them. Further east, the **Prospect of Whitby** (57 Wapping Wall, 7481 1095) dates from 1520 and has counted Samuel Pepys and Charles Dickens among its regulars. It has good riverside terraces and a fine pewter bar counter. Opposite sits a more modern 'victualler': **Wapping Food** (*see p218*) occupies an ivy-clad Victorian hydraulic power station.

A riverpath connecting Wapping to easterly neighbour Limehouse offers a decent stroll during daylight hours (not at night, when one essential gate is locked). Dickens knew the way – and it is said that he based the Six Jolly Fellowship Porters tavern on the **Grapes** (*see p234*). Britain's first wave of Chinese immigrants, mostly seafarers, settled in Limehouse in the 19th century to create London's original Chinatown. Canton, Nankin and Pekin Streets are all nearby, and the city's first Chinese restaurant is thought to have been on Commercial Road just above **Limehouse**

Basin. This glossy marina is enlivened by some narrowboats, though luxury flats and a sense of self-satisfaction prevail.

Visible from the Basin is the white clock tower of magnificent **St Anne's Church**, another Hawksmoor construction. The gloomily pleasing churchyard has a narrow pyramid in its north-west corner that's taller than a man – more fodder for the masonic conspiracy theories.

Isle of Dogs

West India Quay, Mudchute or Island Gardens DLR/Canary Wharf tube/DLR.
The origin of the name 'Isle of Dogs' remains uncertain, but the first recorded use is on a map of 1588; one theory claims Henry VIII kept his hunting dogs here. One thing is clear: it isn't an island, but rather a peninsula, extending into the Thames to create the prominent loop that features in the title sequence of the BBC's indefatigable soap opera *EastEnders*. In the 19th century, a huge system of docks and locks completely transformed what had been no more than drained marshland; in fact, the West India Docks cut right across the peninsula, so the Isle did become some sort of island.

The natural isolation of the area and the formerly thriving docklands industry conspired to create a strong, compact community, one that took a heavy beating over the 20th century – during World War II, this was one of the hardest hit parts of London. At the height of the Blitz, the docks were bombarded on 57 consecutive nights. Yet as late as 1970 the community was cohesive enough to block the two entry roads to the Isle of Dogs and temporarily declare itself independent of the rest of Great Britain.

Almost all the interest for visitors is to be found in the vicinity of Cesar Pelli's dramatic **One Canada Square**, the country's tallest habitable building since 1991. The only slightly shorter HSBC and Citygroup towers joined it shortly after the millennium, and clones are springing up thick and fast (*see p32* **The only way is up...**). Shopping options are limited to the the mall beneath the towers (www.mycanary wharf.com), but there's a soothing if rather too crisp **Japanese garden** beside Canary Wharf tube station. Sit out front of **Carluccio's Caffè** (*see p218*) beneath Pelli's tower to sip an espresso among the clocks – a sculpture rather than functional timepieces – or splash out on a seriously luxury feed at the glass-walled, space-age French restaurant **Plateau** (4th floor, Canada Place, Canada Square, 7715 7100, www.danddlondon.com). Alternatively, head east on West India Avenue to the Thames bank for dim sum at a branch of the excellent

Royal China (30 Westferry Circus, 7719 0888, www.royalchinagroup.co.uk). In the opposite direction, within an 18th-century warehouse, is the **Museum in Docklands** (*see below*).

It's also well worth hopping on the DLR and heading to **Island Gardens** station at the southerly tip of the Isle of Dogs. Nearby, at **Mudchute Park & Farm** (Pier Street, Isle of Dogs, E14 3HP, 7515 5901, www.mudchute. org; *see also p275*) farmyard animals graze in front of the ultramodern skyscrapers. From the Island Gardens themselves, there are famous views across the river to Greenwich, which can be reached via a dank, Victorian pedestrian **tunnel** (lift service 7am-7pm Mon-Sat, 10am-5.30pm Sun).

Museum in Docklands

No.1 Warehouse, West India Quay, Hertsmere Road, E14 4AL (recorded information 0870 444 3856/box office 0870 444 3857/www.museumindocklands. org.uk). West India Quay DLR/Canary Wharf tube.
Open 10am-6pm daily. Last entry 5.30pm.
Admission (unlimited entrance for 1yr) £5; £3 reductions; free under-16s. **Credit** MC, V.
This huge museum explores the complex history of London's docklands over two millennia. Many exhibits are narrated by people who saw the changes for themselves; the Docklands at War section is particularly moving. There are also full-scale mock-ups of a quayside and a dingy riverfront alley. A new permanent gallery, due to open in November 2008, will explore links between the slave trade and sugar imports, with particular attention to the role of West India Dock. Expect partial closures and changes to exhibits while this is being finished.

Further east

Pontoon Dock or King George V DLR.
Pontoon Dock is the stop for the beautiful **Thames Barrier Park** (www.thamesbarrier park.org.uk). Opened in 2001, this was London's first new park in half a century. It has a lush sunken garden of waggly hedges and offers perhaps the best views of the fabulously sculptural Thames Barrier (*see p178*). Head to the terminus of this branch of the DLR at King George V for ready access to the jolly little **North Woolwich Old Station Museum** (Pier Road, 7474 7244, open 1-5pm Sat, Sun, 1-5pm Mon-Fri during school hols, closed Dec) and the free ferry (every 15mins daily, 8921 5786) that chugs pedestrians and cars across the river to Woolwich (*see p178*).

Hackney

London Fields or Hackney Central rail.
Few tourists ever make it out to this tube-less, north-eastern district of London – no wonder,

there's little to see. However, in anticipation of an East London Line extension and the arrival of Crossrail, which will finally connect Hackney with the rest of the city, the borough has begun to pull together its cultural assets. The core of these are the refurbished 1901 **Hackney Empire** (291 Mare Street, 8985 2424, www. hackneyempire.co.uk), together with the art deco **town hall** and the impressive little **Hackney Museum** (1 Reading Lane, 8356 3500, www.hackney.gov.uk/museum). Just to the east, **Sutton House** (*see below*) is the oldest house in east London.

A belwether for ongoing changes, **Broadway Market** has a suddenly thriving market, a wonderful deli, an inspiring independent bookshop and a fine pub – the **Dove** (nos.24-28, 7275 7617, www.belgianbars.com) has a great selection of Belgian beers and serves good booze fodder too. New and old east London are represented by two Broadway Market eateries: the nouveau Argentinian grill of **Santa Maria de Buen Ayre** (no.50, 7275 9900) and pie and mash at **F Cooke** (no.9, 7254 6458), here since the early 1900s.

Sutton House

2-4 Homerton High Street, E9 6JQ (8986 2264/ www.nationaltrust.org.uk). Bethnal Green tube then 254, 106, D6 bus/Hackney Central rail.
Open *Historic rooms* 12.30-4.30pm Thur-Sun. *Café, gallery & shop* noon-4.30pm Thur-Sun. *Tours* group tours phone for details; free tours on 1st Sun of mth. **Admission** £2.80; 70p 5-16s; £6.30 family; £2.40 group; free under-5s, National Trust members. **Credit** MC, V.
Built in 1535 for Henry VIII's first secretary of state, Sir Ralph Sadleir, this red-brick Tudor mansion is east London's oldest home. Miraculously, it has survived waves of development – as well as squatters in the 1980s. Now beautifully restored in authentic original decor, with a real Tudor kitchen to boot, it makes no secret of its history of neglect. Special events and activities are often held (check the website); there's also an art gallery exhibiting contemporary work by local artists. The house closes throughout January each year.

Lea Valley Park

Fight the boredom for long enough as you head east and Mile End Road becomes Bow Road. Where it crosses the River Lea, easily accessible by tube, is the delightful **Three Mills Island** (*see p170*). A short walk north-east up the canal-like tributary brings you to **Stratford**, nucleus of the transformation for the 2012 Olympics (*see p323*).

The River Lea wriggles north-west from Three Mills Island past the scrubby flats of Hackney Marsh and, either side of horrible

Sun, sound and sea

Where the River Lea flows into the Thames, almost opposite the great, white, deflated balloon of the O2 (*see p175*), **Trinity Buoy Wharf** (www.trinitybuoywharf.com) is pure incongruity. Built in the early 1800s – just as London's docks entered their period of global dominance – it was a depot and repair yard for shipping buoys, as well as a maintenance dock for lightships. And it was here, in the 1860s, that James Douglass – designer 20 years later of the amazing fourth Eddystone Light – built London's only lighthouse.

The Experimental Lighthouse was used for training lighthouse keepers and trialling new light technology (pioneering scientist of electricity Michael Faraday worked here), but now it's literally a work of art. The lighthouse is the magnificent setting for a 'sound art' composition by Jem Finer, a founder member of Irish punk-folksters the Pogues. **Longplayer** (http://longplayer.org), open 11am-4pm on the first weekend of each month, is a piece of music that started playing on 1 January 2000

as part of the Dome's millennium exhibition. Performed on gongs and Tibetan singing bowls (displayed on the first floor, beside the computer that now runs the performance), this meditative piece is designed not to repeat itself during a continuous performance lasting exactly 1,000 years. It is also a wonderfully soothing soundtrack as you look out over the vast river through the astragal bars of the lighthouse's lantern room.

The wharf is home to a gallery, a lightship, interesting historical information boards and the brightly coloured Container City, a series of offices and studios cunningly built from recycled ship containers. Take it all in over pastrami and rye in the genuine 1940s diner car **Fatboy's Diner** (7987 4334, www.fatboys diner.co.uk, open 10am-5pm Mon-Fri; 11am-3pm Sat), shipped here from the States.

The wharf is ten minutes' walk from East India DLR, round a small bird reserve where terns nest in summer; otherwise, get the 277 bus for Leamouth from near Mile End tube.

Lea Bridge Road, an ice rink, riding stables and the **WaterWorks Nature Reserve** (Lammas Road, 8988 7566, open 8am-9pm or dusk daily). A touchingly odd combination of golf course and nature reserve, these water-filter beds were built in 1849 to purify water during a cholera epidemic. The WaterWorks now house 322 species of plant and 25 species of breeding birds, observable from easily accessible hides. Further north are off-road cycle tracks, boating lakes and even an area where you can watch (or more likely hear) rare bitterns.

Olympic Park

Stratford, E15 (www.london2012.org). Stratford tube/rail/DLR/West Ham tube/rail/Pudding Mill DLR/Hackney Wick rail.
London is gearing up to host the 2012 Olympics, having pipped Paris with its bid in 2005. Different venues will be used across London, including the All England Tennis Club at Wimbledon (*see p327*) and Lord's Cricket Ground (*see p324*), but the main events will take place at the new Olympic site in Stratford. Currently under construction, the Olympic Park will include an 80,000-capacity stadium, an aquatic centre, a velopark, a hockey centre and the Olympic village. You'll find the site east of Victoria Park, around the western fringe of Stratford and north of Three Mills Island – but there really isn't all that much going on just yet.

Three Mills Island

Three Mill Lane, E3 3DU (8980 4626/www.house mill.org.uk). Bromley-by-Bow tube. **Tours** *May-Dec 1-4pm Sun.* **Admission** £3; £1.50 reductions; free under-16s. **No credit cards.**
This large island in the River Lea takes its name from the three mills that, until the 18th century, ground flour and gunpowder here. The House Mill, built in 1776, is the oldest and largest tidal mill in Britain and, though out of service, occasionally opens to the public. The island offers pleasant walks that can feel surprisingly rural once you're among the undergrowth. There's also a small café, a crafts market on the first Sunday of the month and, to puncture the idyll, part of the site is a TV studio.

Walthamstow to Epping Forest

Loughton/Theydon Bois tube/Walthamstow Central tube/rail.
Apart from the famous Walthamstow Stadium greyhound track (*see p325*), this area's best asset is quaint little **Walthamstow Village**, just a few minutes' walk east of the tube station. At the top of Orford Road is an ancient timber-framed cottage, relic of a settlement that stood here long before the Victorian terraces sprung up. Just opposite is **St Mary's Church**, parts of which date back to the 16th century although

there's been a church on the site since the 1100s. Across Vinegar Alley – so named because it was once a vinegar-filled ditch, intended as protection against plague – are the Monoux Almshouses. Further almshouses lead back along Church End to the modest **Vestry House Museum** (Vestry Road, 8509 1917, closed Sun & bank holidays), with its lovely garden and the reconstructed Bremer Car, London's first petrol-driven vehicle.

North of Walthamstow Central is the daily **street market**, which spans the length of Walthamstow High Street and is reputed to be the longest in Europe. Pie and mash shop **L Manze** (no.76, 8520 2855) retains its original decor from 1929. Further north, near the junction of Hoe Street and Forest Road, is peaceful **Lloyd Park**; the grand Georgian house at its entrance is home to the **William Morris Gallery** (*see below*) – the Arts and Crafts pioneer was a Walthamstow boy.

Forest Road is justly named. Follow it east past the extraordinary art deco **town hall** and it does indeed bring you to the southerly part of a long finger of ancient woodland. **Epping Forest** extends nearly eight miles north, its existence guaranteed by the Victorians: in 1878 Parliament granted the City of London the power to buy land within 25 miles of the city centre to be used for the recreation of city dwellers. Dedicated ramblers might stumble across the faint remains of two Iron Age forts, but Queen Elizabeth I's **hunting lodge**, now a free museum (8529 6681, May-Sept 1-5pm Wed-Fri, 11am-5pm Sat, Sun; Oct-Apr 1-4pm Sat, Sun), is easier to find. Drivers will want to stop at the High Beach visitors' centre (8508 0028) for information and maps. The self-propelled can get information from Guildhall Library before taking the Central Line to Loughton or Theydon Bois stations, either of which will bring you within striking distance of the forest's edge.

William Morris Gallery

Lloyd Park, Forest Road, E17 4PP (8527 3782/ www.lbwf.gov.uk/wmg). Walthamstow Central tube/rail/34, 97, 215, 275 bus. **Open** noon-4pm Thur, Fri; 10am-5pm Sat, Sun. *Tours* phone for details. **Admission** free; donations appreciated. **Credit** (shop) MC, V.
Artist, socialist and source of all that flowery wallpaper, William Morris lived here between 1848 and 1856. There are plenty of wonderful designs – in fabric, stained glass and ceramic – on show here, produced not only by Morris but also by his acolytes. There's even a medieval-style helmet and sword, props for Pre-Raphaelite paintings. Yet we prefer the humbler domestic objects: Morris's coffee cup and the satchel he used to carry his radical pamphlets around.

South-east London

Regenerating not gentrifying, the south-east is a work in progress.

Many consider the bottom right-hand corner of this city the 'deep south' – a little bit backward, slightly unsavoury and difficult to reach. In fact, the Elephant & Castle, a major transport hub, with tubes, trains and buses, is minutes from the South Bank and no further south than Sloane Square. Its main drawback has long been its ill-favoured looks, the result of careless reconstruction after bomb damage in World War II. True, areas around the Old Kent Road and Walworth Road are daunting after dark, but full-throttle regeneration of the 1960s estates can only have a positive effect, especially as far as visitors are concerned.

Further south, easily reached on the DLR or overland trains, other spots with an SE postcode cast a more kindly light: **Dulwich** is delightful, the **Horniman Museum** is a one-off, and **Greenwich** is glorious. You need only stand at the top of the hill in Greenwich Royal Park to see that you're still in the heart of the city: Canary Wharf looms surprisingly large just across the river. This humdinger of a view – where tourists gather with their cameras to capture both the panorama of London and each other straddling the Meridian Line (*see p177*) – is the pride of south-east London.

Kennington & the Elephant

Kennington tube/Elephant & Castle tube/rail.

As first impressions go, the Elephant & Castle, gateway to the south-east, is unlikely to augur well: a roundabout, where the thundering traffic spins off for the A2 into Kent and the A215 for the South Circular, is presided over by the famously awful 1960s shopping centre. As so often, there was many a slip 'twixt drawing board and reality when architects set about rebuilding what had once been, by all accounts, a rather handsome south London hub in the 1930s, reduced to rubble in World War II. They had envisaged a mixed-usage residential and shopping area; the reality was an alienated community cut off by increasing traffic and worn down by poorly designed housing connected by dank and frightening subways.

Not for too much longer. This area is on the receiving end of a £1.5 billion programme of home improvement. Already there are smart, pastel-coloured blocks of desirable apartments with aspirational balconies rising benignly over the Walworth Road, and residents can look forward to the shopping centre finally being replaced by green and pleasant pedestrianised

Sightseeing

There are all sorts of weird and wonderful things at the **Horniman Museum**. *See p174.*

areas, decent shops and new recreational facilities… by about 2014 (more details on www.elephantandcastle.org.uk). While you're waiting for that, walk north from the Elephant, up St George's Road, to the welcome respite of Geraldine Mary Harmsworth Park, where a Peace Garden is the best place to reflect after a visit to the **Imperial War Museum** (*see below*).

Behind the museum, tree-lined Kennington Road has smart, several-storey houses that are favoured by medics and lawyers requiring easy access to the city. Kennington Park is even greener, but the most lovingly tended greensward has to be that within the **Brit Oval**, the home of Surrey County cricket (*see p324*). Kennington has a colourful history. Once owned by the Duchy of Cornwall, Kennington Common (now Kennington Park) was the main place of execution for the county of Surrey. During the 17th and 18th centuries, preachers – notably John Wesley (*see p95*) – addressed audiences here.

Imperial War Museum

Lambeth Road, SE1 6HZ (7416 5320/www.iwm. org.uk). Lambeth North tube/Elephant & Castle tube/rail. **Open** 10am-6pm daily. **Admission** free. *Special exhibitions* prices vary. **Credit** MC, V. **Map** p404 N10.

Housed in what was originally the Bethlehem Royal Hospital (Bedlam), the collection covers the experience of armed conflicts, especially those involving Britain and the Commonwealth, from World War I to the present day. Tanks, aircraft and artillery are displayed in the main hall. A climb-in sub for kids comes complete with periscope. Descending to the lower floor devoted to the two World Wars, a sobering fact pulls you up sharp: a clock, set running at midnight on 1 January 2000, when the number of lives lost during the wars of the 20th century stood at 100 million, continues to count those dying in conflicts, calculated to be two per minute. There's some degree of levity allowed in the smelly Trench Experience on the World War I side, and the stouthearted Blitz Experience for World War II, but the mood gets darker as you ascend through the floors. On the third floor, the gut-wrenching Holocaust Exhibition traces the history of European anti-Semitism and its nadir in the concentration camps – it's not recommended for those under 14 years old. Upstairs, Crimes Against Humanity is a minimalist space in which a film exploring contemporary genocide and ethnic violence rolls relentlessly. This is unsuitable for under-16s. Special exhibitions for 2008 include 'Ian Fleming and James Bond' (from May); 'From War to Windrush' (from June) to coincide with the 60th anniversary of the arrival of the SS *Empire Windrush*, commemorating the West Indian contribution to World War II; and 'Remembering the Great War' (from September), in honour of the 90th anniversary of the Armistice.

Camberwell & Peckham

Denmark Hill, Nunhead or Peckham Rye rail.

Once rural enough to have a butterfly named after it (Camberwell Beauty), **Camberwell Green** is a little corner of parkland bracketed by multiple bus stops for Kennington, Elephant, Peckham and points south-east. Go east along Church Street, past **St Giles's Church**, designed by Sir George Gilbert Scott, designer of Bankside and Battersea power stations and St Pancras rail terminus. Further towards Peckham lies **Camberwell College of Arts** (Peckham Road, 7514 6300), London's oldest art college, and the **South London Gallery** (*see p296*). Studenty social life revolves around DJ bars and pubs such as Funky Munky (no.25, 7277 1806) and the Hermit's Cave (no.28, 7703 3188) on Camberwell Church Street.

In Peckham, Will Alsop's RIBA award-winning library is looking a bit dog-eared from the front, but is still a jaunty, multicoloured funbox from the back. Peckham High Street, diverse though it is, is characterised by a mix of bargain warehouses and open-fronted butchers. The best thing along here is the gratifying cheapness of seats at **Peckham Multiplex Cinema** (95A Rye Lane, 0870 042 9399). Beyond the Common, **Peckham Rye Park** – where Blake saw his angels – now looks heavenly after a makeover that reshaped its

gardens (Japanese, American, an arboretum). Keep walking south from Peckham Rye, or take a P4 or P12 bus, to enjoy views over London and Kent from Honor Oak and One Tree Hill, where Elizabeth I picnicked with Richard Bukeley of Beaumaris in 1602. Another reason to make this trip south is to discover the **Horniman Museum** (*see p174*) where the gardens also have fine views.

Less sculpted than Peckham Rye Park is the sublime **Nunhead Cemetery**, a mysterious maze of commemorative statuary half-buried by the undergrowth. North of Nunhead is **New Cross**, the only bit of south-east London with a tube station. That hatchery of Young British Artists, Goldsmith's College (part of the University of London) occupies various sites here. Its Ben Pimlott Building, a dramatic glass and steel edifice named after the late left-wing historian, is another Will Alsop creation.

Dulwich & Crystal Palace

Crystal Palace, East Dulwich, Herne Hill, North Dulwich or West Dulwich rail.
Inevitably described as 'leafy', **Dulwich Village** is a very posh enclave of south-east London. It has a mightily attractive park (once a favourite duelling spot), a historic boys' public school, founded by the actor Edward Alleyn in 1616, and, beside his school's original buildings, the **Dulwich Picture Gallery** (*see below*). East and west of the village, East Dulwich and Herne Hill represent the middle (class) way: smart, but not as expensive as Dulwich and less challenging than the relentless pace of Brixton (*see p179*). It's a pleasant, brisk half-hour's walk from Dulwich Picture Gallery across the park and up Lordship Lane to the **Horniman Museum** (*see p174*) in Forest Hill.

Crystal Palace is so-called because Joseph Paxton's famous structure, built for the Great Exhibition in Hyde Park in 1851, was moved to Sydenham, where it sat regally amid parkland until burning down in 1936. The original arches of its terraced platform and the sphinx from the exhibition's Egyptian-themed area can still be seen. Space was also given over to a **Dinosaur Park**, created by Benjamin Waterhouse-Hawkins, depicting a journey through prehistory via life-size dinosaur statues, which still pose around the lake. The **Crystal Palace Museum** (Anerley Hill, SE19 2BA, 8676 0700, www.crystalpalacemuseum.org.uk), opened by volunteers each weekend, has an 'exhibition of an exhibition' (the Great one).

Dulwich Picture Gallery

Gallery Road, SE21 7AD (8693 5254/www.dulwich picturegallery.org.uk). North Dulwich or West Dulwich rail. **Open** 10am-5pm Tue-Fri; 11am-5pm Sat, Sun. **Admission** £4; £3 reductions; free under-16s, students, unemployed, disabled. **Credit** MC, V.

Royal Observatory & Planetarium.
See p177.

Sightseeing

The first purpose-built art gallery in the country, this neoclassical building – designed by Sir John Soane in 1811 – remains one of the best. The gallery displays a small but outstanding collection of work by European Old Masters and offers a fine introduction to the baroque era through pieces by such as Rembrandt, Rubens, Poussin and Gainsborough. The big exhibitions of 2008 are 'The Agony and the Ecstasy: Guido Reni's paintings of Saint Sebastian' (5 Feb-11 May); 'Coming of Age: American Art, 1850s-1950s' (14 Mar-8 June) and a major exhibition focused on the De Bray family, who were at the heart of the Dutch Golden Age (2 July-2 Oct).

Horniman Museum

100 London Road, SE23 3PQ (8699 1872/www. horniman.ac.uk). Forest Hill rail/363, 122, 176, 185, 312, 356, P4, P13 bus. **Open** 10.30am-5.30pm daily. **Admission** free; donations appreciated. **Credit** MC, V.

Quieter during term-time than school holidays, this fascinating museum is one of the wonders of south-east London. Donated to the city by Frederick J Horniman, a tea trader and prodigious collector, it is housed in a jolly art nouveau building. The Natural History gallery has skeletons, pickled animals, stuffed birds and insect models in glass cases. The World Cultures exhibition is an atmospheric ethnographic display, while the Music Room has walls hung with instruments of every type, as well as touch tables that play their sound. The aquarium, following a £1.5m overhaul, is amazing. More than 200 species of aquatic animal and plant are housed in 14,000 litres of water across seven separate zones, the better to explain challenges now faced by the world's delicate ecosystems. The jellyfish are mesmerising. Outside, the delightful gardens have an animal enclosure, an elegant conservatory and a picnic spot with superb views. The café is terrific too. Of the temporary exhibitions for 2008, we're really looking forward to 'Every Third Mouthful…' (until 11 May) on the incredible impact of bees' pollinating activities on global food production. *Photo p171.*

Rotherhithe

Rotherhithe tube.

Once the centre for London's whaling trade, Rotherhithe was a shipbuilding village. Today the docks have been filled to make room for smart homes, but an atmospheric slice of old Rotherhithe remains in the conservation area where you'll find the **Brunel Engine House & Tunnel Exhibition** (*see below*) and the mariners' church of **St Mary's Rotherhithe** (St Marychurch Street, SE16 4JE, 7967 0518). This beloved community church is full of treasures, which have to be viewed through a glass door unless you attend a service or make an appointment. Completed in 1715, it was built by sailors and watermen, and contains many reminders of the area's links with the sea. The communion table in the Lady Chapel is made

from timber salvaged from the warship the *Fighting Temeraire*, immortalised by Turner's famous painting in the National Gallery (*see p135*). Captain Christopher Jones was buried here in 1622; his ship, the *Mayflower*, set sail from Rotherhithe in 1620 – a waterside pub of the same name marks the spot where the pilgrims embarked. The **Norwegian Church & Seaman's Mission** stands at the mouth of Rotherhithe's road tunnel, not completed until 1908, many years after Brunel's successful excavations. The number of Scandinavian churches, including a Finnish one with a sauna at 33 Albion Street (7237 1261), is a reminder of the area's links with Nordic sailors dating back to the Vikings. Across Jamaica Road, **Southwark Park**, London's oldest municipal park, has a community art gallery (7237 1230, www.cafegalleryprojects.com, open 11am-4pm Wed-Sun), an old bandstand, a landscaped lake and playgrounds.

Brunel Engine House & Tunnel Exhibition

Brunel Engine House, Railway Avenue, SE16 4LF (7231 3840/www.brunelenginehouse.org.uk). Rotherhithe tube. **Open** 10.30am-5pm daily. *Tours by appointment only.* **Admission** £2; £1 reductions; £5 family; free under-5s. **No credit cards.**

The Brunels, father and son – Sir Marc and Isambard Kingdom – worked together here to create the world's first tunnel beneath a navigable river, from 1825 until it was finally finished in 1843. The story of what the Victorians hailed as 'the Eighth Wonder of the World' is told in this museum in the original engine house. The tunnel is now used by the East London tube line. It was Isambard Kingdom Brunel's first project. The guided tours are well worth joining (check the website for details). Just a few hundred yards across the river in Millwall is the launch site of Brunel's last project, the monster SS *Great Eastern*.

Greenwich

Cutty Sark DLR for Maritime Greenwich.

Greenwich celebrated ten glorious years as a UNESCO World Heritage Site in 2007. Its wealth of attractions cluster round one of London's most inspirational Royal Parks. Henry VII rebuilt the Palace of Placentia, from around 1450 to 1650 one of the main English royal palaces, which was replaced by Sir Christopher Wren's **Old Royal Naval College** (*see p175*). The Greenwich Gateway Visitor Centre (0870 608 2000, www.greenwich.gov.uk) is a useful port of call. A short walk away, shoppers swarm round **Greenwich Market** and film buffs head for the plush **Greenwich Picturehouse Cinema** (180 Greenwich High Road, 0870 755 0065).

Keeping the river to your left, you reach the Thames-lapped **Trafalgar Tavern** (6 Park Row, 8858 2909), haunt of Thackeray, Dickens and Wilkie Collins, and the **Cutty Sark Tavern** (4-6 Ballast Quay, 8858 3146), which dates to 1695. Near the DLR stop, now with a Novotel hotel and cocktail bar on the forecourt, is **Greenwich Pier**. Every quarter of an hour at peak times the Thames Clipper commuter boat (0870 781 5049, www.thamesclippers.com) shuttles to and from central London.

The Pier is beside the charred old tea clipper, the **Cutty Sark** (www.cuttysark.org.uk). On 21 May 2007, fire devastated this historic vessel, which had been a quarter of the way through an ambitious conservation programme. Luckily, half the ship had been removed for conservation purposes. A temporary visitor centre explains what happened and what needs to happen for the ship to have a chance of reopening by 2010.

From the riverside it's a ten-minute walk (or you can take the park's shuttle bus) up the steep slopes of Greenwich Park to the **Royal Observatory**. This building looks even more stunning at night, when the bright green Meridian Line Laser illuminates the path of the Prime Meridian across the London sky.

From Greenwich the riverside Thames Path leads to the Greenwich Peninsula, which is dominated by the **O2**, a structure formerly known as the Millennium Dome. (For a guided stroll around the area's unsung attractions, *see p176* **Walk**.) Owned by the American billionaire Philip Anschutz, this is the world's largest single-roofed structure, around 1,200 feet in diameter. Mr Anschutz's lofty plans for the arena suffered a serious setback in February 2007 when it lost out to Manchester as a venue for a Supercasino, but he seems to have made a decent fist of it as a venue for sport (*see p323*) and concerts (*see p311*). The overfamiliar chain eateries are due to be joined by slightly plusher restaurants: Raan will serve grilled Indian food, while Britain and America do what it says on each tin.

Fan Museum

12 Crooms Hill, SE10 8ER (8305 1441/8293 1889/www.fan-museum.org). Cutty Sark DLR/ Greenwich DLR/rail. **Open** 11am-5pm Tue-Sat; noon-5pm Sun. **Admission** £4; £3 reductions; £10 family; free under-7s; OAPs, disabled free 2-5pm Tue. **Credit** MC, V.

The world's most important gathering of hand-held fans is housed in a pair of restored Georgian townhouses. There are more than 3,000 fans in the collection: only a proportion is on display at any one time, rotated every four months or so. If you come on a Tuesday or Sunday afternoon you can also take an elegant tea in the Orangery. Check the website for exhibition and workshop dates.

National Maritime Museum

Romney Road, SE10 9NF (8858 4422/information 8312 6565/tours 8312 6608/www.nmm.ac.uk). Cutty Sark DLR/Greenwich DLR/rail. **Open** *July, Aug* 10am-6pm daily. *Sept-June* 10am-5pm daily. *Tours* phone for details. **Admission** free; donations appreciated. **Credit** (shop) MC, V.

The nation's seafaring history is covered in some style by this bright and lively museum on three floors. Opened in 1937, its massive holdings include the world's largest collections of maritime art, cartography, ship's models, flags, instruments and costumes. More recent additions to the displays include, on Level 2, Your Ocean, which reveals our dependence on the health of the world's oceans. Also on this level, in Gallery 15, is Nelson's Navy, exhibiting more than 250 objects drawn from the museum's collection of naval memorabilia from this period, including the undress coat worn by Nelson at the Battle of Trafalgar, weaponry, artefacts and art. Elsewhere in the museum Explorers is devoted to pioneers of sea travel, and includes a small, chilling *Titanic* exhibition; Passengers is a paean to glamorous old ocean liners; and Maritime London tells the capital's nautical history through old prints and model ships. Seapower covers naval battles from Gallipoli to the Falklands, and the Art of the Sea is the world's largest maritime art collection. A colonnaded walkway takes you to the Queen's House (*see p177*). The Observatory and Planetarium (*see p177*), up the hill, are also part of the museum.

Old Royal Naval College

Greenwich, SE10 9LW (8269 4747/group tours 8269 4791/www.oldroyalnavalcollege.org.uk). Cutty Sark DLR/Greenwich DLR/rail. **Open** 10am-5pm daily. *Tours* by arrangement. **Admission** free. **Credit** (shop) MC, V.

Once known as the Greenwich Hospital, this architectural triumph was commissioned in 1694 for the relief and support of seamen and their dependants and for the improvement of navigation. Sir Christopher Wren planned the building, and his vision was completed by Hawksmoor and Vanbrugh, among others. Pensioners lived here from 1705 to 1869; they were given pocket money, which they supplemented by acting as caddies at Blackheath Golf Club and as tourist guides. The complex of buildings became the Royal Naval College in 1873, until the Navy left in 1998.

Now owned by the Greenwich Foundation, the neoclassical buildings of the Old Royal Naval College house part of the University of Greenwich and Trinity College of Music. The public are allowed into the rococo chapel, where there are free organ recitals, and the Painted Hall – a tribute to William and Mary that took Sir James Thornhill 19 years to complete. Nelson lay in state in the Painted Hall for three days in 1806, before being taken to St Paul's Cathedral for his funeral. The visitor centre contains an exhibition on Greenwich history and the story of the naval hospital. There's an ice rink outside in winter.

Walk Dome is where the art is

Start/finish North Greenwich tube.
Time 1hr 30mins.

A summer of high-profile rock concerts at the Dome in 2007 brought the public flooding to the **Greenwich Peninsula**. True, most came to see Prince, again and again – but the regular influx of 20,000 punters to the recently opened **02 Arena** (*see p175*) brings this much-maligned spit of land, a tongue poking out at Docklands, back into focus. Exactly ten years ago, national regeneration agency English Partnerships bought the 300-acre site. Here it planned the Greenwich Millennium Village, alongside the world's largest single-roofed structure. A year later, the Dome had proved a millennial flop, and the Thames Path around it had been opened, with specially commissioned artworks and colourful panels telling the site's history.

The result is still a work in progress. Emerge from North Greenwich tube and you will be drawn to the adjacent Dome, across **Peninsula Square**, its 147-foot steel spire and Meridian Line complemented by pavement plaques of poetic (Shakespeare, Larkin) reflections on time. Keep the Dome on your right and head west. Rebuilding works mean you'll soon have to take a narrow, temporary path to reach the Thames Path itself. This is the only tricky bit of the walk.

We now circumnavigate clockwise. Your eye will move from desolate pyramids of waste to the Manhattan-like cityscape of Docklands over the river. You soon pass a jetty-cum-nature reserve, the pier providing a home for

teasels and sea buckthorn... great googly moogly, what's that? Suddenly, you're struck by **A Slice of Reality**, Richard Wilson's dramatic, sheared-off boat, standing proud and bizarre as if awaiting embarkation. Old-style mileposts, guarding the now thriving mudflats below, remind you that historic London (Tower Bridge, in fact) is less than seven miles away. Take a lungful of the salty air and muse on the information panel's promise of teal, shore crabs and sea asters on the cunningly terraced banks below.

As you walk, planes zoom down close for London City Airport, and Thames Clippers whizz by, bound for the landing set by the four stout pillars supporting Antony Gormley's **Quantum Cloud**. From the correct angle, this apparent candy-floss of wires forms within it the figure of a man, as if shaping up for a free-kick. Perhaps it inspired David Beckham to place his Football Academy nearby.

Cut right on to the unpromising looking road heading inland, then left down East Parkside, a spacious, peaceful open road with elegantly manicured trees. This takes you to a little row of houses, one of which is the **Pilot Inn** (68 River Way, 8858 5910), a friendly Fuller's pub with fresh fish of the day, a garden and a plaque saying 'New East Greenwich' (dated 1801). Head south to where the horizon bristles with the rounded, red-topped housing blocks of alternating heights that make up the space-friendly **Millennium Village** – you can buy a four-bedroom 'überhaus' here for a mere £450,000. Turn left to rejoin the Thames Path, and south to enter **Greenwich Peninsula Ecology Park** (open 10am-5pm Wed-Sun, 8293 1904, www.urban ecology.org.uk). Through the gatehouse are bird hides and, depending on the season, house martins, damselflies, bumblebees, ducks and geese. No matter the season, you'll find educational drawings, colouring-in sets, crayons, quiz sheets and snacks.

When you've done with nature, head north up the Thames Path.

02 Arena.

An elongated 'History in Motion' panel –
cross-referring the depth of the Thames
at different periods with significant events,
from changes in shipping to sewerage –
seems all the more interesting given a
backdrop of gleaming modern buildings
and a waste dump, picked over by seagulls.
Back at the junction with Edmund Halley
Way, turn left, then first right to the tube.

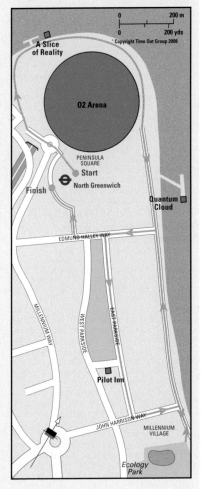

Queen's House

*Romney Road, SE10 9NF (8312 6565/www.
nmm.ac.uk). Cutty Sark DLR/Greenwich DLR/rail.*
Open 10am-5pm daily. *Tours* noon, 2.30pm.
Admission free; occasional charge for temporary
exhibitions. *Tours* free. **Credit** (over £5) MC, V.
Designed in 1616 by Inigo Jones for James I's wife,
Anne of Denmark, Queen's House was handed
unfinished to Charles I's queen, Henrietta Maria. It
was finally finished in 1640. The house is home to
the National Maritime Museum's art collection,
which includes portraits of famous maritime figures and works by Hogarth and Gainsborough. A
small exhibition charts the house's former life as a
boarding school for the sons of sailors. A colon-
nade, exceptionally striking in bright sunshine,
connects the building to the National Maritime
Museum (*see p175*).

Ranger's House

*Chesterfield Walk, SE10 8QX (8853 0035/www.
english-heritage.org.uk). Blackheath rail/Cutty Sark
DLR/53 bus.* **Open** *Mar-Sept* 10am-5pm Mon-Wed,
Sun. *Oct-Dec* group bookings only. **Admission**
£5.50; £2.80-£4.10 reductions; free under-5s.
Credit MC, V.
This Georgian villa, which dates back to 1723, was
from 1815 the residence of the Greenwich Park
Ranger, a post held by George III's niece, Princess
Sophia Matilda. It now contains the extraordinary
treasure amassed by millionaire Julius Wernher,
who was born in Germany and made his fortune in
the South African diamond trade. Wernher died in
1912. His collection of 19th-century art, including
jewellery, bronzes, tapestries, furniture, porcelain
and paintings, as well as quirky pieces such as
miniature coffins, is displayed in 12 lovely rooms.

Royal Observatory & Planetarium

*Greenwich Park, SE10 9NF (8312 6565/www.
rog.nmm.ac.uk). Cutty Sark DLR/Greenwich DLR/
rail.* **Open** 10am-5pm daily. *Tours* phone for details.
Admission free. *Tours* free. **Credit** MC, V.
The £15m Time and Space refurbishment has added
a new planetarium alongside the Observatory originally built for Charles II. As well as four galleries
charting the development of timekeeping since the
14th century, the observatory has a dome housing
the largest refracting telescope in the country – and
eighth largest in the world. In the courtyard is the
Prime Meridian Line – star of a billion snaps of
happy tourists with a foot in each hemisphere. The
new 120-seater planetarium in the South Building
opens up part of the site previously closed to visitors.
This new building's architecture cleverly reflects
its astrological position: the semi-submerged cone
tilts at 51.5 degrees, the latitude of Greenwich,
pointing to the north star, and its reflective disc is
aligned with the celestial equator. The Starlife show,
lasting half an hour, describes the birth and death of
stars – apparently, there are more of them in the
galaxy than the total number of heartbeats in human
existence. Several effects make stunning use of the

Sightseeing

planetarium's 3D capabilities and the projector is always operated by a trained astronomer, who will welcome any questions. *Photos pp172-173.*

Charlton & Woolwich

Charlton, Woolwich Arsenal or Woolwich Dockyard rail.

The once well-to-do area of Charlton still retains a certain villagey charm around the church and remnants of the green. **Charlton House** and park is the main attraction if you're not an Addicks fan (Charlton Athletic's football ground is just down the hill). The northernmost bit of the park leads to Woolwich Church Street and the river, spanned by the **Thames Barrier** (*see below*). This section of riverside London is at long last to be connected to the rest of civilisation courtesy of an extension of the DLR: it will run under the Thames from King George V station at North Woolwich to Woolwich Arsenal and should be completed in 2009. You can also use Thames Clippers for a high-speed commuter service to Canary Wharf.

Come to Woolwich for **Firepower** (*see below*), located in the buildings of the Woolwich Arsenal. Established in Tudor times as the country's main source of munitions, by World War I the Arsenal stretched 32 miles along the river, had its own internal railway system and employed 72,000 people. Much of the land was sold off during the 1960s, but the main section has been preserved. South of here, the Royal Artillery Barracks has the longest Georgian façade in the country. Another highlight – of greater eccentricity if less grandeur – is the the **Woolwich Ferry** (8921 5786). These diesel-driven boats take pedestrians and cars across the river every ten minutes daily. The ferry to the north shore lands you by North Woolwich Old Station Museum (*see p168*).

Charlton House

Charlton Road, SE7 8RE (8856 3951/www. greenwich.gov.uk). Charlton rail/53, 54, 380, 422 bus. **Open** *Library* 2-7pm Mon, Thur; 10am-12.30pm, 1.30-5.30pm Tue, Fri; 10am-12.30pm, 1.30-5pm Sat. *Toy library* 9.30am-12.30pm Mon, Tue, Thur, Fri. *Tearooms* 9am-3pm Mon-Fri. **Admission** free.

One of the finest examples of Jacobean domestic architecture in the country, this house was built between 1607 and 1612 by Sir Adam Newton. These days it's a community centre and library, but glimpses of its glorious past can be seen in the creaky oak staircase, marble fireplaces and ornate plaster ceilings. Outside, the venerable mulberry tree is still bearing fruit into its 400th year – if you're lucky, you can taste some of it in the cakes and chutneys sold in the Mulberry Café. There are two walled gardens, one of them a Peace Garden. Visit at 1pm on a Friday for a free concert by musicians from the Trinity College of Music, who also put on a soaring Christmas concert; check the website first for details.

Firepower

Royal Arsenal, SE18 6ST (8855 7755/www.fire power.org.uk). Woolwich Arsenal rail. **Open** *Nov-Mar* 10.30am-5pm Fri-Sun. *Apr-Oct* 10.30am-5pm Wed-Sun. **Admission** £5; £2.50-£4.50 reductions; free under-5s; £12 family. **Credit** MC, V.

The Gunners commemorated here are the soldiers of the Royal Artillery, not the north London premiership football team, whose Emirates Stadium has a couple of guns from this collection at its entrance. The footie team has its roots in Woolwich, though – in 1886 a group of workers in the armaments factory had a kickabout – and the rest is Arsenal FC history. This thrilling museum, which occupies a series of converted Woolwich Arsenal buildings close to the river, bristles with preserved artillery pieces, some of them many centuries old. The Queen became patron in 2007; on her birthday (21 April) a 25-pounder is fired in her honour. An introductory cinema presentation in the Breech Cinema tells the story of the Royal Artillery, leading on to 'Field of Fire', where four massive screens relay archive film and documentary footage of desert and jungle warfare. Smoke fills the air, searchlights pick out the ordinance that surrounds you and the sound of exploding bombs shakes the floor. Across the courtyard is a building containing a huge collection of trophy guns and the Cold War gallery, focused on the 'monster bits' (tanks and guns used from 1945 to the present). From June 2008, Out of the Dark celebrates the museum's 230th anniversary with a display of rarely seen pieces from the collection.

Thames Barrier Information & Learning Centre

1 Unity Way, SE18 5NJ (8305 4188/www. environment-agency.gov.uk/thamesbarrier). North Greenwich tube/Charlton rail/180 bus. **Open** *Apr-Sept* 10.30am-4.30pm daily. *Oct-Mar* 11am-3.30pm daily. **Admission** *Exhibition* £2; £1-£1.50 reductions; free under-5s. **Credit** MC, V.

Following the summer floods of 2007, there's been much discussion about whether the Thames Barrier, the world's largest adjustable dam, will be able to hold back the sort of deluge experts now fear for the Thames Estuary. The current barrier, spanning the 1,700ft of Woolwich Reach, was built in 1982 at a cost of £535m; since then it has saved London from flooding probably 70 times. The small Learning Centre explains how it all works and has a map that shows which parts of London would be submerged if it stopped working. Time your visit to see the barrier in action: every September there's a full-scale testing, with a partial test closure once a month (phone for dates and times). For a waterborne view of this immense feat of engineering Campion Cruises (8305 0300) runs trips to the barrier from Greenwich (Mar-Oct only); another fine vantage point is Thames Barrier Park (*see p168*), on the far bank.

South-west London

Flower gardens, black culture, the winding river and independent shops.

Even in a city well known for its cultural diversity, south-west London is astonishingly various. The semi-rural suburbs of Kingston, Richmond, Barnes, Putney and Wimbledon have some of the highest house prices outside central London, boosted by features that appeal as much to the casual visitor as one of the lucky residents: proximity to the river, leafy open spaces and first-rate attractions such as Kew Gardens and Hampton Court Palace. Closer to the centre of town, things get a bit more lived-in in such inner-city neighbourhoods as Stockwell and Brixton, vibrant places where it's easy to get under the skin of the capital.

Vauxhall, Stockwell & Brixton

Brixton or Vauxhall tube/rail/Stockwell tube.
The area now known as Vauxhall was, in the 13th century, home to a big house owned by one Falkes de Bréauté, a soldier rewarded for carrying out King John's dirtier military deeds. Over time Falkes' Hall became Fox Hall, Vaux Hall and finally Vauxhall.

Vauxhall's heyday was in the 18th century when the infamous Pleasure Gardens, built back in 1661, reached the height of their popularity. William Thackeray touched on the place's titillations in *Vanity Fair*, describing how the wealthy mingled briefly with the not-so-wealthy, getting into all kinds of trouble on so-dark-anything-could-happen 'lovers' walks'.

The Gardens closed in 1859 and the area became reasonably respectable – all that remains is Spring Garden, behind popular gay haunt the **Royal Vauxhall Tavern** (*see p300*). For a glimpse of old Vauxhall head to lovely, leafy **Bonnington Square**, a bohemian enclave thanks to its squatter heritage. Down on the river is the cream and emerald ziggurat designed by Terry Farrell for the Secret Intelligence Service (still almost universally referred to by its old title: MI6). On the other side of the south end of Vauxhall Bridge stands St George's Wharf, a glitzy apartment complex justifiably nicknamed the 'five ugly sisters'.

At the top end of the South Lambeth Road, **Little Portugal**, a cluster of Portuguese cafés, shops and tapas bars, is an enticing oasis of warmth and colour. At the other end, **Stockwell** is prime commuter territory, with

little to lure visitors except some charming Victorian backstreets: Albert Square, Durand Gardens and Stockwell Park Crescent. Van Gogh lived briefly at 87 Hackford Road.

South of Stockwell is **Brixton**, a lively hub of clubs and music, with its well-established black community. It's an interesting, often unpredictable area, with a vast street market, late-night clubs and live music venues. The main streets are modern and filled with chain stores, but attractive architecture is dotted here and there – check out the splendid 1911 **Ritzy Cinema** (*see p287*). Brixton's best-known street, **Electric Avenue**, was immortalised during the 1980s by Eddy Grant's eponymous song – it got its name when, in 1880, it became one of the first shopping streets to get electric lights. The Clash's 'Guns of Brixton' famously deals with the tensions felt here in the 1980s, but the rage and determination of the black community, still isolated and under suspicion 30 years after immigrants arrived from the West Indies at the government's invitation to find employment limited and their faces unwelcome, is far better expressed in the dub records by activist and poet Linton Kwesi Johnson – try 'Sonny's Lettah (Anti-Sus Poem)' for starters.

The riots of 1981 and 1985 around Railton Road and Coldharbour Lane left the district scarred for years. Start your Brixton wandering near the chaos of Brixton station, at the 21-year-old **Brixton Art Gallery** (35 Brixton Station Road, www.brixtonartgallery.co.uk), which has an excellent and constantly changing collection of contemporary art. Turn a corner from the station and you're in the extended, colourful and noisy mess of **Brixton Market**, which sells everything from kebabs to jewellery and bright African clothes.

Battersea

Battersea Park or Clapham Junction rail.
Battersea started life as an island in the Thames, before it was reclaimed by draining the marshes. Huguenots settled here from the 16th century and, prior to the Industrial Revolution, the area was mostly farmland. The riverside is dominated by Sir Giles Gilbert Scott's magnificent four-chimneyed **Battersea Power Station**, which can be seen close up from all trains leaving Victoria Station. Images

of this iconic building have graced album covers (notably Pink Floyd's *Animals*) and films (among them Ian McKellen's *Richard III*, Monty Python's *The Meaning of Life*, Michael Radford's *1984*), and its instantly recognisable silhouette pops up repeatedly as you move around the capital. Work started on what was to become the largest brick-built structure in Europe in 1929. The power station closed in 1983. Too impressive to be destroyed, the power station's future has been the subject of intense public debate (you can follow it on www.batterseapowerstation.org.uk), though the realisation of plans to turn the semi-derelict site into an entertainment complex seems remote.

Also overlooking the river, and rather less industrial, is nearby **Battersea Park**, with beautiful fountains, ponds and boating lakes. In 2004, it was relandscaped according to the original 19th-century plans, albeit with some modern additions left in place: a Peace Pagoda (built in 1985 to commemorate Hiroshima Day), a small zoo (7924 5826; *see p275*) and a tiny art gallery within a Grade II-listed building (the Pumphouse, 7350 0523, www.wandsworth. gov.uk/gallery). The park extends to the Thames; from the wide riverside walk you can see both the elaborate **Albert Bridge** and the simpler, but lovely, Battersea Bridge,

which was rebuilt between 1886 and 1890 to designs by the man who solved London's sewage problems, Joseph Bazalgette.

Further along the river, west of the bridges, and adjacent to a development of high-tech luxury flats by architect Richard Rogers is the beautiful church of **St Mary's Battersea** (Battersea Church Road); this was where Blake (*see p15* **City seer**) was married and from here JMW Turner painted the river.

Clapham & Wandsworth

Clapham Common tube/Wandsworth Common or Wandsworth Town rail.
In the 18th and 19th centuries, Clapham had recovered from effects of the plague and became home to the wealthy upper classes and social reformers. But the coming of the railways meant that the posh folk upped sticks, and from 1900 the area fell into decline.

Nowadays the area is once again one of the capital's desirable addresses. **Clapham Common** provides an oasis of peace amid busy traffic, with Holy Trinity Church, which dates from 1776, at its perimeter. During the summer, the common switches into music festival mode, attracting thousands to a series of high-profile events. From Clapham Common station, turn

WWT Wetland Centre.

north into the street called **The Pavement** – it leads to the pubs and shops of Clapham Old Town. Alternatively, head south to the smart shops and cafés of **Abbeville Road**, the centre of Abbeville Village. The area to the west of the common is known as 'Nappy Valley', because of the many young middle-class families who reside there. They're out in force at weekends, pushing prams. If you can fight your way between the baby carriages, head straight for **Northcote Road** (*see p185* **Street scene**).

It's a short stroll from Northcote Road to **Wandsworth Common**, arguably prettier than Clapham Common. The north-west side is dominated by a Grade II-listed Victorian heap, the Gothic **Royal Victoria Patriotic Building**. Originally an asylum for orphans of the Crimean War, it became a POW camp during World War II; now it contains flats, workshops and a drama school.

Putney & Barnes

East Putney or Putney Bridge tube/Barnes or Putney rail.
If you want proof of an area's well-to-do credentials, count the rowing clubs: Putney has a couple of dozen. Putney Bridge is partly to blame, as its buttresses made it difficult for large boats to continue upstream, creating a stretch of water conducive to rowing. The **Oxford & Cambridge Boat Race** (*see p265*) has started in Putney since 1845.

Putney was chic in Tudor times, when it was home to Thomas Cromwell. In 1647, another Cromwell – Oliver – chaired the Putney Debates in **St Mary's Church**, at which the establishment of an English constitution was discussed. The river has good paths in either direction; heading west along the Putney side of the river will take you past the **WWT Wetland Centre** (*see below*), which lies alongside **Barnes Common**. The main road across the expanse, Queen's Ride, humpbacks over the railway line below. It was here, on 16 September 1977, that singer Gloria Jones's Mini drove off the road, killing her passenger (and boyfriend) T-Rex singer Marc Bolan. The slim trunk of the sycamore tree hit by the car is covered with notes, poems and declarations of love; steps lead to a bronze bust.

WWT Wetland Centre

Queen Elizabeth's Walk, SW13 9WT (8409 4400/ www.wwt.org.uk). Hammersmith tube then 283 bus/ Barnes rail/33, 72 209 bus. **Open** *Mar-Oct* 9.30am-6pm daily. *Nov-Feb* 9.30am-5pm daily. **Admission** £8.75; £4.95-£6.60 reductions; £21.95 family; free under-4s. **Credit** MC, V.
The 43-acre Wildfowl & Wetlands Trust Wetland Centre may be a mere four miles from central London, but actually feels worlds away. Quiet ponds, rushes, rustling reeds and wildflower gardens all teem with bird life – some 150 species. Naturalists ponder its 27,000 trees and 300,000 aquatic plants, swoon over 300 varieties of butterfly, 20 types of dragonfly, four species of bat and the rare water vole. The site wasn't always this pretty. Until 1989, it consisted of four huge concrete reservoirs owned by the local water company. Then Sir Peter Scott transformed the marshy space into a unique wildlife habitat. There are weekly activities here virtually year-round, and the visitors' centre has a café with an outdoor terrace. If you forgot your binoculars, hire them on site.

Kew & Richmond

Kew Gardens or Richmond tube/rail/Kew Bridge rail.
Kew's big appeal is its vast and glorious **Royal Botanic Gardens** (*see p183*). The **National Archives** – formerly the Public Records Office – are housed here too, a repository for everything from the Domesday Book to recently released government documents. The place is always full of people researching their family trees. Overlooking the gardens is the newly refurbished **Watermans Arts Centre** (40 High Street, TW8 0DS, 8232 1010, www. watermans.org.uk), which contains a gallery,

London
at War

Experience life in wartime at the London
branches of the Imperial War Museum

Imperial War
Museum London
For Your Eyes Only
Ian Fleming and James Bond
17 April 2008 – 1 March 2009

Churchill Museum and
Cabinet War Rooms
Churchill and the Press
February 2008 – May 2008

The Last Post
October 2008 –
January 2009
Remembering the First World War

HMS Belfast
A Sailors Life for Me
Fun family events the last weekend
of every month

Visit www.iwm.org.uk for
details of our exhibitions,
events and activities

Visit www.iwm.org.uk/groups
for details of special group
rates and offers

cinema, 239-seater theatre, bar and restaurant. The centre focuses on British-Asian and South Asian arts in particular. Much of Kew has a rarified air, with leafy streets that lead you into a quaint world of teashops, tiny bookstores and gift shops, a sweet village green, ancient pubs and pleasant riverpaths.

Originally known as the Shene, the wealthy area of **Richmond**, about 15 minutes' walk west down Kew Road, has been linked with royalty for centuries: Edward III had a palace here in the 1300s and Henry VII loved the area so much that in 1501 he built another (naming it Richmond after his favourite earldom); this was where Elizabeth I spent her last summers. Ultimately, the whole neighbourhood took the palace's name, although the building itself is long gone – all that's left is a gateway on **Richmond Green**. Once the site of royal jousting tournaments, the green is less noble now, but it's still surrounded by gorgeous pre-Victorian architecture.

On the east side of the Green medieval alleys (such as Brewer's Lane) replete with ancient pubs lead to the traffic-choked high street. The **Church of St Mary Magdalene**, on Paradise Road, blends architectural styles from 1507 to 1904. A short walk away in Richmond's Old Town Hall, you'll find the small **Museum of Richmond** (Whittaker Avenue, 8332 1141, www.museumofrichmond.com, closed Mon & Sun). Nearby, the riverside promenade is eminently strollable and dotted with pubs; the **White Cross** (*see p235*), which has been here since 1835, has a special 'entrance at high tide' – the river floods regularly. The 13 arches of Richmond Bridge date from 1774 – this is the oldest surviving crossing over the Thames and offers fine sweeping views.

Royal heritage invariably means parkland, and the four square miles of **Richmond Park** make it London's largest park, a vestige of the region's once-dominant oak woodland. The meadows and remaining woods provide a natural habitat for free-roaming herds of red and fallow deer. Within the park's bounds are the Palladian splendour of White Lodge and Pembroke Lodge, childhood home to philosopher Bertrand Russell but now a café.

Royal Botanic Gardens (Kew Gardens)

Kew, Richmond, Surrey TW9 3AB (8332 5655/ information 8940 1171/www.kew.org). Kew Gardens tube/rail/Kew Bridge rail/riverboat to Kew Pier. Open Apr-Aug 9.30am-6.30pm Mon-Fri; 9.30am-7.30pm Sat, Sun. Sept-Oct 9.30am-6pm daily. Late Oct-early Feb 9.30am-4.15pm daily. Early Feb-late Mar 9.30am-5.30pm daily. **Admission** £12.25; £10.25 reductions; free under-17s. **Credit** AmEx, MC, V.

Kew's lush, landscaped beauty represents the pinnacle of our national gardening obsession. From the early 1700s until 1840, when the gardens were given to the nation, these were the grounds for two royal residences – the White House and Richmond Lodge. The 18th-century residents Henry II and Queen Caroline were enthusiastic gardeners; Caroline was particularly fond of exotic plants brought back by voyaging botanists. In the mid 1700s, Lancelot 'Capability' Brown began designing an organised layout for the property, using the plants Caroline had collected. Thus began the extraordinary collection that today attracts hundreds of thousands of visitors every year.

Covering around half a square mile, Kew feels surprisingly big – pick up a map at the ticket office and follow the handy signs. Any visit to Kew should take in the two huge 19th-century greenhouses, filled to the roof with plants – some of which have been here as long as the fanciful glass structures themselves. The sultry Palm House holds tropical plants: palms, bamboo, tamarind, mango and fig trees, not to mention fragrant hibiscus and frangipani. The

Kew view: the **Royal Botanic Gardens**.

Temperate House features *Pendiculata sanderina*, the Holy Grail for orchid hunters, with petals some 3ft long. Also of note here is the Princess of Wales Conservatory, which houses ten climate zones.

For an interesting perspective on 17th-century life, head to Kew Palace – the smallest royal palace in Britain. Little more than an addition to the now-gone White House, the lovely structure is, after years of renovation, open to the public. Also open 'for the first time in recent memory' is the 163ft pagoda, completed in 1762. Those who climb the 253 steps (it costs £3) are rewarded with views of Battersea Power Station and, to the far east and north respectively, Canary Wharf and Wembley Stadium.

Queen Charlotte's Cottage, with its dazzling springtime bluebell garden, repays return visits year after year. The Rose Garden and Woodland Garden are the stuff of fairytales, while Redwood Grove has a treetop walkway 33ft off the ground. Hungry? There are tearooms scattered throughout.

Wimbledon

Wimbledon tube/rail.

Beyond the world-famous tennis tournament, Wimbledon is little but a wealthy and genteel suburb. Turn left out of the station on to the uninspiring **Broadway**, and you'll wonder why you bothered. So turn right instead, climbing a steep hill lined with huge houses. At the top is **Wimbledon Village**, a trendy little enclave of posh shops, eateries and some decent pubs.

From here you can hardly miss Wimbledon Common, a huge, wild, partly wooded park, criss-crossed by paths and horse tracks. In an eccentric touch, the common has a **windmill** (Windmill Road, 8947 2825, www.wimbledon windmillmuseum.org.uk) where Baden-Powell wrote *Scouting for Boys* (1910). It now houses a tearoom and hands-on milling museum. If tea doesn't meet your needs, there are two decent pubs close to the common: the **Fox & Grapes** (9 Camp Road, 8946 5599) and **Hand in Hand** (6 Crooked Billet, 8946 5720). East of the common lies Wimbledon Park, with its boating lake, and the All England Lawn Tennis Club and **Wimbledon Lawn Tennis Museum** (*see below*). Two other attractions should be visited while you're here – pleasant Cannizaro Park and the gorgeous **Buddhapadipa Temple** (14 Calonne Road, Wimbledon Parkside, 8946 1357, www.buddhapadipa.org). When it was built in the early 1980s, this was the only Thai temple in Europe. The warm and sweet-smelling Shrine Room contains a golden statue of Buddha, a copy of the Buddhasihing in Bangkok's National Museum. Visitors are welcome, but shoes must be removed before entering the temple, you are not permitted to touch the monks and the soles of your feet must never face the Buddha.

Wimbledon Lawn Tennis Museum

Centre Court, All England Lawn Tennis Club, Church Road, SW19 5AE (8946 6131/www. wimbledon.org/museum). Southfields tube/39, 493 bus. **Open** 10.30am-5pm daily; ticket holders only during championships. **Admission** (incl tour) £15.50; £11-£13.25 reductions; free under-5s. **Credit** MC, V.

Highlights at this popular museum on the history of tennis include a 200° cinema screen that allows you to find out what it's like to play on Centre Court and a re-creation of a 1980s men's dressing room, complete with a 'ghost' of John McEnroe. Visitors get to grips with rackets, check changing tennis fashions and enjoy a behind-the-scenes tour.

Further south-west

If the water level allows, follow the river from Richmond south and west. You could stop at **Petersham**, home to Petersham Nurseries with its brilliant café (Church Lane, off Petersham Road, 8605 3627, www.petershamnurseries.com), or take in a grand country mansion, perhaps **Ham House** (*see below*) or **Marble Hill House** (*see p186*). Next to Marble Hill Park you'll find **Orleans House Gallery** (*see p186*).

Further along, the river meanders past Twickenham, home to rugby's **Twickenham Stadium** (*see p186*), to the evocatively named **Strawberry Hill** (0870 626 0402, www. friendsofstrawberryhill.org), home of Horace Walpole, who pretty much invented the Gothic novel with *The Castle of Otranto* (1764). Several miles further along the Thames, after a leisurely trip through suburban Kingston, the river passes the magnificent **Hampton Court Palace** (*see p186*). Few visitors will want to walk this far, of course – instead take a train from Waterloo or, for that extra fillip of adventure, a boat.

Ham House

Ham, Richmond, Surrey TW10 7RS (8940 1950/ www.nationaltrust.org.uk/hamhouse). Richmond tube/rail then 371 bus. **Open** *Gardens* 11am-6pm or dusk if earlier Mon-Wed, Sat, Sun. *House* Late Mar-Oct noon-4pm Mon-Wed, Sat, Sun. **Admission** *House & gardens* £9.90; £5.50 reductions; £25.30 family; free under-5s. *Gardens only* £3.30; £2.20 reductions; £8.80 family; free under-5s. **Credit** MC, V.

Built in 1610 for one of James I's courtiers, Thomas Vavasour, this lavish red-brick mansion is full of period furnishings, rococo mirrors and ornate tapestries. Detailing is exquisite, down to a table in the dairy with sculpted cows' legs. The restored formal grounds also attract attention: there's a lovely trellised Cherry Garden dominated by a statue of Bacchus. The tearoom in the old orangery turns out historic dishes (lavender syllabub, for instance) using ingredients from the Kitchen Gardens. A ferry crosses the river to Marble Hill House (*see p186*).

Street scene Northcote Road

A bustling English high street, full of eccentric shopkeepers, is something that many of us have only glimpsed in jovial Ealing comedies. Out-of-town shopping complexes, supposedly catering for our every need, sounded the death knell for many small businesses during the 1970s and '80s. But Clapham's Northcote Road stubbornly hung on, and today it's still providing a vibrant, healthy alternative to the weekly supermarket sweep.

Many Northcote Road emporiums are the results of 'downsizing': their proprietors gave up steady business careers to indulge their hobbies and feed the locals. Ruth and Liz left jobs in the arts to bake additive-free bread at the **Lighthouse Bakery** (no.64), while Mark, co-owner of cheese emporium **Hamish Johnston** (no.48), was once an IT director for an oil company before his regular visits to the shop prompted an abrupt lifestyle change. Both provide excellent picnic fodder.

To wet your whistle, drop in on Attila, proprietor of wine retailer **Vingt** (no.20), who left a lucrative post in management consultancy to turn his love of the finest French and Italian wines into not only a shop, but also boozy wine appreciation courses, with food and drink served up on a long, rickety table after the shop has shut for the day. Over the road is **Philglas & Swiggot** (no.21) – another highly rated wine outlet.

But Northcote Road isn't just about fresh produce and quality booze. There's an eye-opening range of outlets – from Mitch Tonks's highly rated **Fishworks** restaurant (no.54) to the 1970s-style launderette (no.102), from the hat hire company to the unpretentious corner shop; and the number of pushchairs is astounding – there are apparently more toddlers in this postcode than any comparable area in Europe. **QT Toys** (no.90) provide their fun and frolic, while children's clothes retailer **JoJo Maman Bébé** (no.68) waited for four or five years until the opportunity to open up here arose – and paid handsomely for the privilege.

Indeed, Northcote Road has become a veritable battleground for weightier high street outfits – note the ominous presence of Starbucks (no.33) – keen to muscle in on the action. But there are still such wonderful anomalies as the **Hive Honey Shop** (no.93), run by devoted beekeeper James. And it is on a Saturday that the road really starts buzzing, with gastronauts from all over London besieging the shops and vegetable stalls set up in the middle of the road. Some of the stalls have been a regular fixture here for over 40 years. After spending a couple of hours surrounded by some of the best food in town, it's all too easy to promise yourself that you'll never set foot in a supermarket again.

Sightseeing

Hampton Court Palace

East Molesey, Surrey KT8 9AU (0870 751 5175/
0870 752 7777/0870 753 7777/24hr information
0844 482 7777/www.hrp.org.uk). Hampton Court
rail/riverboat from Westminster or Richmond to
Hampton Court Pier (Apr-Oct). **Open** *Palace* Apr-
Oct 10am-6pm daily. Nov-Mar 10am-4.30pm daily.
Park dawn-dusk daily. **Admission** *Palace, courtyard,*
cloister & maze £13; £6.50-£10.50 reductions; £36
family; free under-5s. *Maze only* £3.50; £2 reductions.
Gardens only Apr-Oct £4; £2.50-£3 reductions.
Nov-Feb free. **Credit** AmEx, MC, V.
It may be a half-hour train ride from central
London, but this spectacular palace, once owned
by Henry VIII, is well worth the trek. It was built
in 1514 by Cardinal Wolsey, the high-flying Lord
Chancellor, but Henry liked it so much he seized it
for himself in 1528. For the next 200 years it was a
focal point of English history: Elizabeth I was
imprisoned in a tower by her jealous and fearful
elder sister Mary I; Shakespeare gave his first performance to James I in 1604; and, after the Civil
War, Oliver Cromwell was so besotted by the building he ditched his puritanical principles and moved
in to enjoy its luxuries.

Centuries later, the rosy walls of the palace still
dazzle. Its vast size can be daunting, so it's a good
idea to take advantage of the costumed guided
tours. If you do decide to go it alone, start with King
Henry VIII's State Apartments, which include the
Great Hall, noted for its splendid hammer-beam
roof, beautiful stained-glass windows and elaborate religious tapestries; in the Haunted Gallery, the
ghost of Catherine Howard – Henry's fifth wife,
executed for adultery in 1542 – can reputedly be
heard shrieking. The King's Apartments, added in
1689 by Sir Christopher Wren, are notable for a
splendid mural of Alexander the Great, painted by
Antonio Verrio. The Queen's Apartments and
Georgian Rooms feature similarly elaborate paintings, chandeliers and tapestries. The Tudor
Kitchens are great fun, with their giant cauldrons,
fake pies and blood-spattered walls (there were no
vegetarians in those days).

More spectacular sights await outside, where the
exquisitely landscaped gardens include perfectly
sculpted trees, peaceful Thames views and the
famous Hampton Court maze (in which, incidentally,
it's virtually impossible to get lost). In summer
there's a music festival and a flower show to rival
Chelsea's; in winter check out the ice-skating rink.

Marble Hill House

Richmond Road, Twickenham, Middx TW1 2NL
(8892 5115/www.english-heritage.org.uk). Richmond
tube/rail/St Margaret's rail/33, 90, 490, H22, R70
bus. **Open** *Apr-Oct* 10am-2pm Sat; 10am-5pm
Sun; group visits Mon-Fri by request. *Nov-Mar*
by request. **Admission** £4.20; £3.20 reductions;
free under-5s. **Credit** MC, V.
King George II spared no expense to win the favour
of his mistress, Henrietta Howard. Not only did he
build this perfect Palladian house (1724) for his
lover, he almost dragged Britain into a war while
doing so: by using Honduran mahogany to construct the grand staircase, he managed to spark a
diplomatic row with Spain. It was worth it. Over
the centuries, luminaries such as Alexander Pope,
Jonathan Swift and Horace Walpole have been
entertained in the Great Room; Pope and Swift are
said to have drunk the cellar dry. Picnic parties are
welcome, as are sporty types (there are tennis,
putting and cricket facilities). A programme of concerts and events keeps things busy in the summer,
and ferries regularly cross the Thames to neighbouring Ham House (*see p184*).

Museum of Rugby/
Twickenham Stadium

Twickenham Rugby Stadium, Rugby Road,
Twickenham, Middx TW1 1DZ (8892 8877/
www.rfu.com). Hounslow East tube then 281 bus/
Twickenham rail. **Open** *Museum* 10am-5pm Tue-
Sat; 11am-5pm Sun. *Tours* 10.30am, noon, 1.30pm,
3pm Tue-Sat; 1pm, 3pm Sun. **Admission** £10; £7
reductions; £34 family. **Credit** AmEx, MC, V.
The impressive Twickenham Stadium is the home
of English rugby union. Tickets for international
matches are extremely hard to come by, but the
Museum of Rugby offers some compensation. Tours
take in the England dressing room, the players' tunnel and the Royal Box. A permanent collection of
memorabilia, selected from 10,000 pieces that make
up the museum's collection, charts the game's development from the late 19th century. It includes the
oldest surviving international rugby jersey, the
Calcutta Cup (awarded annually to the winners of
the Scotland–England match) and the recently
acquired Melrose Winners Medal – awarded to one
of the winners of the first ever seven-a-side contest
at Melrose in 1883.

Orleans House Gallery

Riverside, Twickenham, Middx TW1 3DJ (8831
6000/www.richmond.gov.uk/orleans_house_gallery).
Richmond tube then 33, 490, H22, R68, R70 bus/
St Margaret's or Twickenham rail. **Open** *Apr-Sept*
1-5.30pm Tue-Sat; 2-5.30pm Sun. *Oct-Mar* 1-4.30pm
Tue-Sat; 2-4.30pm Sun. **Admission** free.
Secluded in pretty gardens, this Grade I-listed
riverside house was constructed in 1710. It was
built for James Johnson, Secretary of State for
Scotland, and named after the Duke of Orleans,
Louis-Philippe, who lived in exile here between
1800 and 1817, before returning to post-Napoleonic
France to claim the throne. Though the house was
partially demolished in 1926, the building retains
James Gibbs's neoclassical Octagon Room, which
houses the Richmond-upon-Thames collection, a
soothing pictorial record of the local countryside
since the early 1700s. A new display recreates the
Chinese wallpaper Henrietta Howard hung in the
dining room in 1751. Using historical references
and motifs, restorers designed a unique paper for
the room, each sheet different and, like the originals,
hand-painted by Chinese artists.

West London

Land of cash and history.

It was Edward the Confessor in the 11th century who began London's migration westwards, building the Palace of Westminster upriver and upwind of the City. After London had spread upriver, Kensington and Holland Park became the favoured locations for the rich and titled, a status that they largely retain. Fulham, erstwhile home of the Bishop of London, is home to many members of the new mediacracy, while Hammersmith offers access to the beautiful riverside walk to the many historic sites of Chiswick.

Kensington & Holland Park

Maps p394 & p396

High Street Kensington or Holland Park tube.
Kensington makes an appearance in the Domesday survey of 1086 as Chenesit and the earliest settlement was, most likely, around the still existing but often rebuilt St Mary Abbots Church. For the next 800 years the area

remained rural, and the rich and the noble began to build grand retreats that offered an escape to the country without the tiresome necessity of days spent travelling. Despite these aristocratic residences, the population at the start of the 19th century was less than 10,000; by 1901 there were 176,628 residents.

Today **Kensington High Street** is one of London's main shopping streets, although not one suited to those of limited means. Off the High Street, the streets and squares are lined with handsome 19th-century houses, most of which are still homes. Linking with Notting Hill to the north (*see p130*), **Kensington Church Street** has many antiques shops selling furniture so fine you could probably never use what you'd bought. **St Mary Abbots** (7937 6032, www.stmaryabbots church.org), at the junction of Church Street and High Street, is a wonderful Victorian neo-Gothic church, built by Sir George Gilbert Scott in 1869-72 on the site of the original

Kensington High Street, where sunglasses are obligatory.

12th-century church. Past worshippers include Sir Isaac Newton and William Wilberforce. As well as beautiful stained-glass windows, it has London's tallest spire (278 feet).

Across the road is a striking art deco building, once the department store Barkers, now taken over by Texan organic food giant **Whole Foods Market** (nos.63-97, 7368 4500, www.wholefoodsmarket.co.uk). South down Derry Street, past the entrance to the **Roof Gardens** (*see below*) six storeys above, is **Kensington Square**, which boasts one of London's highest concentrations of blue plaques. The writer William Thackeray lived at no.16, the painter Edward Burne-Jones at no.41 and at no.18 John Stuart Mill's maid made her bid for 'man from Porlock' status by using Carlyle's sole manuscript of *The French Revolution* to start the fire. Mrs Patrick Campbell, actress and famous beauty, resided at no.33. She was as well known for her exploits off stage as on, but settled here into 'the deep peace of the double bed as opposed to the hurly burly of the chaise longue'. The houses, though much altered, date from when the square was developed in 1685, and – hard to believe now – were until 1840 surrounded by fields.

Further to the west is one of London's finest green spaces: **Holland Park**. Holland Walk, which runs along the eastern edge of the park between Holland Park Avenue and Kensington High Street, is one of the most pleasant paths in central London, but the heart of the park is **Holland House**, originally built in 1606. Six years later, King James complained after a stay that he had been kept up by the wind blowing through the walls; the house was more seriously ventilated by World War II bombs. Left derelict, it was bought by the London County Council in 1952; the east wing now houses the city's best sited youth hostel (*see p72*), and the garden ballroom is the **Belvedere** restaurant (7602 1238, www.white starline.org.uk). In summer, open-air theatre and opera are staged on the front terrace.

There are three lovely formal gardens near the house and, a little further away, the Japanese-style **Kyoto Garden**. It has huge koi carp sucking noisily at the pool's surface and a bridge at the foot of a waterfall. It's a quiet and contemplative place. Elsewhere rabbits hop about (dogs must be kept on the lead) and peacocks stroll with the confidence of all beautiful creatures. Weary parents can let their under-fives roll around a safe playground, while older siblings get to enjoy an adventure playground with tree walks and rope swings.

Near Holland Park are two more fine historic houses: **Linley Sambourne House** and **Leighton House**.

Leighton House

12 Holland Park Road, W14 8LZ (7602 3316/ www.rbkc.gov.uk/leightonhousemuseum). High Street Kensington tube. **Open** 11am-5.30pm Mon, Wed-Sun. *Tours* 2.30pm Wed, Thur. **Admission** £3; £1 reductions. **Credit** MC, V. **Map** p396 A9.
From without, the house of the artist Frederic, Lord Leighton (1830-96) presents a sternly Victorian façade of red-brick respectability. But inside it's like a scene from *The Arabian Nights*, complete with tinkling fountain, oriental mosaics and a golden mosaic frieze. Instead of a kohl-eyed Scheherazade, visitors must make do with Lord Leighton's classical paintings, which are scattered through the house, along with those of contemporaries Edward Burne-Jones, John Everett Millais and Sir Lawrence Alma-Tadema. The garden offers a serene resting place – and an incongruous statue of an American Indian on horseback, spearing a rearing serpent.

Linley Sambourne House

18 Stafford Terrace, W8 7BH (Mon-Fri 7471 9160/Sat, Sun 7938 1295/www.rbkc.gov.uk/ linleysambournehouse). High Street Kensington tube. **Open** 18 Mar-10 Dec by appointment only. **Admission** £6; £4 reductions; £1 children. **Credit** MC, V. **Map** p396 A9.
The home of cartoonist Edward Linley Sambourne was built in the 1870s and has almost all of its original fittings and furniture. Tours must be booked in advance; they last 90mins, with weekend tours led by an actor in period costume.

Roof Gardens

99 Kensington High Street, W8 5SA (7937 7994/www.virgin.com/roofgardens). High Street Kensington tube. **Admission** free. **Map** p396 B9.
In 1936, the vice-president of Barkers, Trevor Bowen, established a garden six storeys above ground. Now more than 70 years old, the gardens remain largely unknown outside the world of corporate entertaining, but (as long as they are not booked for an event; phone ahead to check) they are open to all: simply take the lift up and emerge to find water gurgling into a brook. Follow the stream through a woodland garden, complete with trees rooted 100ft above the ground, past pools and over bridges. To complete the exotic scene a pair of Lesser Chilean flamingos sieve for crustaceans alongside various ducks. *Photos pp190-1.*

Earl's Court & Fulham

Map p396

Earl's Court, Fulham Broadway or West Brompton tube.
Earl's Court sells itself short, grammatically speaking. Once the site of the courthouse of both the Earl of Warwick and the Earl of Holland, it should be Earls' Court. The 1860s saw Earl's Court move from rural hamlet to investment opportunity as the Metropolitan Railway arrived. Some 20 years later it was much as we see it today, bar the fast food joints.

Odd curiosity stop
Kew Bridge Steam Museum

Kew Bridge Steam Museum (*see p191*) is one of London's most engaging museums, particularly at weekends when the great pumping engines are in steam. For those whose only association with steam is the railway, it may come as a surprise that steam engines were used to supply water to the city. This Victorian pumping station – a significant piece of industrial architecture in its own right – is now home to a simply extraordinary collection of different engines in addition to the two enormous Cornish beam engines around which it was originally built. The museum also illustrates how the rapidly expanding city brought water to its citizens and disposed of their effluvia.

There are lots of hands-on exhibits for children (and adults willing to get stuck in), a particularly appealing dressing-up box and even a small steam train for good measure. But the stars are the beam engines, four of them in all, gleaming behemoths whose pumping pistons and spinning wheels make an unearthly wooshing sound. Even those with only the slightest interest in engineering are likely to be impressed by the silky precision and visceral whomp of the Waddon engine's six-foot piston rod hammering home. There's a good café and a lovely garden that's ideal for picnics. Our only caveat? Try to visit on a cool weekend: all that steam certainly raises the temperature inside.

The terraces of grand old houses are mostly subdivided into bedsits and cheap hotels, once inhabited by so many Australians the area was nicknamed Kangaroo Valley. These days the transient population is more weighted towards Eastern Europe and South America.

In 1937, the **Earl's Court Exhibition Centre** was built, at the time the largest reinforced concrete building in Europe – a phrase that truly makes the heart sing. The centre hosts a year-round calendar of events, from trade shows and pop concerts (Pink Floyd built and tore down *The Wall* here) to the Ideal Home Show. Two minutes south down Warwick Road is an altogether different venue, with an equally impressive pedigree: the **Troubadour** (263-267 Old Brompton Road, 7370 1434, www.troubadour.co.uk) is a 1950s coffeehouse whose downstairs club hosted Jimi Hendrix, Joni Mitchell, Bob Dylan and Paul Simon in the 1960s. It still has a full programme of music, poetry and comedy, plus an excellent deli. There's a gallery on the first floor.

West along Warwick Road are the gates of **Brompton Cemetery**. It's full of magnificent monuments commemorating the famous and infamous, including suffragette Emmeline Pankhurst, shipping magnate Sir Samuel Cunard and, his grave marked by a lion, boxer 'Gentleman' John Jackson – 'Gentleman' John taught Lord Byron to box. Although Sioux chief Long Wolf was buried here in 1892 (he died while touring with Buffalo Bill's Wild West Show), his body was moved back to Pine Ridge, South Dakota, in 1997. The peace and quiet of the cemetery is regularly disturbed at its southern end by neighbouring **Stamford Bridge**, home of Chelsea FC. **Craven Cottage**, the home of west London's other Premiership football team, Fulham FC, and often a better bet for visitors looking to experience the football (*see p325*), is west of here, at the northern end of the park that surrounds **Fulham Palace**.

Fulham Palace & Museum

Bishop's Avenue, off Fulham Palace Road, SW6 6EA (7736 3233/www.fulhampalace.org). Putney Bridge tube/14, 74, 220, 414, 430 bus. **Open** *Museum & gallery* noon-4pm Mon, Tue; 11am-2pm Sat; 11.30am-3.30pm Sun. *Gardens* dawn-dusk daily. *Tours* 2pm 2nd & 4th Sun of mth. **Admission** free; under-16s must be accompanied by an adult. *Tours* £5; free under-16s. **No credit cards**.
The recent restoration of Fulham Palace revealed traces of human habitation going back to the Iron Age, but it was as the episcopal retreat of the Bishops of London that the site became known. The present building was built in Tudor times (try out the echo in the courtyard), with later significant Georgian and Victorian additions. It would be more accurate to call it a manor house than a palace, but it gives a fine glimpse into the changing lifestyles and architecture of nearly 500 years, from the Tudor hall to the Victorian chapel. The staff are among the most knowledgeable and enthusiastic we have met; the café (open 9am-5pm daily) serves excellent, although not cheap, food; and there's access to a glorious stretch of riverside walk – best of all, these delights still seem largely undiscovered by the majority of Londoners. The botanic gardens, in their current overgrown state already offering pleasant respite, are next in line for restoration. *Photo p192.*

Shepherd's Bush & Hammersmith

Goldhawk Road, Hammersmith or Shepherd's Bush tube.

Shepherd's Bush and its central green do not offer much in the way of sights to visitors – the green is now no more than a triangular patch of grass hemmed in by traffic. The **Bush** (*see p340*) and **Shepherd's Bush Empire** (*see p311*), a fine theatre and music venue respectively, are more likely to encourage a journey here. Just to the north, in **White City**, is BBC Television Centre (*see below*). Further up the road is the expansive green space of Wormwood Scrubs and the more restrictive confines of its prison.

Walk south down Shepherd's Bush Road and you'll see Hammersmith's dominating architectural feature: the grey concrete of the flyover. The A4 – the Great West Road – is one of the main trunk routes into London, with thousands of cars and lorries thundering along it each day. In the flyover's shadow, Hammersmith Broadway was once a bus garage, but has enjoyed the obligatory multi-million-pound redevelopment. Make it over the road and you'll find one of London's most notable rock venues, the **Hammersmith Apollo**. The Apollo started life in 1932 as the Gaumont Palace Hammersmith, entered rock legend as the Hammersmith Odeon (where Bowie killed off Ziggy) and was immortalised in the title of Motörhead's 1981 live album *No Sleep 'til Hammersmith*.

Hammersmith Bridge, the city's oldest suspension bridge, is a green and gold hymn to the strength of Victorian ironwork. Had a pedestrian not thrown the bomb in the river, the IRA might have succeeded in blowing the bridge up in 1939. They tried again in 2000, but all the explosion achieved was further snarling up of local traffic for the months it took to do the repairs. There's a lovely walk west along the Thames Path that takes in a clutch of historic pubs including the **Blue Anchor** (13 Lower Mall, 8748 5774) and the **Dove** (*see p236*); head in the opposite direction for **Riverside Studios** (Crisp Road, 8237 1111, www.riverside studios.co.uk), a cinema, theatre and arts venue, and to the still excellent **River Café** (*see p220*).

BBC Television Centre Tours

Wood Lane, W12 7RJ (0870 603 0304/www.bbc. co.uk/tours). White City tube. **Tours** by appointment only Mon-Sat. **Admission** £9.50; £8.50 reductions; £7 10-16s, students; £27 family. No under-9s. **Credit** MC, V.

Unusually, the British Broadcasting Corporation is publicly funded, costing the taxpayer more than £3bn a year in licence fees, plus £24m via Foreign Office grants. Tours of the BBC include visits to the news desk, the TV studios and the Weather Centre; you must book ahead, however, to secure a place. If you want to be part of a show (or, at least, part of the audience of a show), you can apply for free tickets at www.bbc.co.uk/whatson/tickets.

Kensington Roof Gardens. *See p188.*

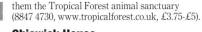

Chiswick

Turnham Green tube/Chiswick rail.
To walk the riverside path from Hammersmith
to Chiswick is to learn a lesson in transport
history. To your left the Thames would once
have resounded with the swearing of boatmen –
it is now quiet except for the rhythmic crump
and cursing of an occasional sweaty rowing
eight. To your right is the Great West Road
and its constant stream of traffic. Above there's
the main flight path into Heathrow Airport.
And, finally, there's you, on foot. Should
walking produce a thirst, never fear: just
off Chiswick Mall on Chiswick Lane South is
Fuller's Brewery. There's been a brewery
here since Elizabethan times – with so much
time to get it right, no wonder its London Pride
is a fine pint. The tours (£6; £4.50 children)
must be pre-booked on 8996 2063.

After refreshments, cross (under) the A4
to **Hogarth's House** and the rather grander
Chiswick House (for both, *see below*). A
bus might be necessary to reach **Kew Bridge
Steam Museum** (*see p189* **Odd curiosity
stop**), although it is possible to return to the
river path after visiting Chiswick House; the
wonderful **Kew Gardens** (*see p183*) are just
over the bridge. Further yet upstream is **Syon
House** (*see below*). If you do make the journey
out here, Syon Park has more than enough
attractions, in addition to the house and
grounds, to fill an expensive day – among

them the Tropical Forest animal sanctuary
(8847 4730, www.tropicalforest.co.uk, £3.75-£5).

Chiswick House

*Burlington Lane, W4 2RP (8995 0508/www.chgt.
org.uk). Turnham Green tube then E3 bus to Edensor
Road/Hammersmith tube/rail then 190 bus/Chiswick
rail.* **Open** 10am-5pm Wed-Fri, Sun; 10am-
2pm Sat. **Admission** £4.20; £3.20 reductions; £2.10
5-16s; free under-5s. **Credit** MC, V.
Richard Boyle, third Earl of Burlington, designed
this lovely Palladian villa in 1725 as a place to entertain the artistic and philosophical luminaries of his
day, including Alexander Pope, Jonathan Swift,
George Frideric Handel and Bishop Berkeley. The
Chiswick House and Gardens Trust recently took
over the site and aims to restore the gardens, which
were becoming rather tatty, to Burlington's original
design. The restoration will be helped by details
from the newly acquired painting *A View of
Chiswick House from the South-west* by Dutch landscape artist Pieter Andreas Rysbrack (c1685-1748).

Hogarth's House

*Hogarth Lane, Great West Road, W4 2QN
(8994 6757). Turnham Green tube/Chiswick
rail.* **Open** *Apr-Oct* 1-5pm Tue-Fri; 1-6pm Sat,
Sun. *Nov, Dec, Feb, Mar* 1-4pm Tue-Fri; 1-5pm
Sat, Sun. **Admission** free; donations appreciated.
No credit cards.
From the garden (a tranquil island next to the A4)
you can still appreciate this place as the country
retreat of the 18th-century painter, engraver and
social commentator William Hogarth. On display
are most of his engravings, including *Gin Lane,
Marriage à la Mode* and a copy of *Rake's Progress.*

Kew Bridge Steam Museum

*Green Dragon Lane, Brentford, Middx TW8 0EN
(8568 4757/www.kbsm.org). Gunnersbury tube/
Kew Bridge rail/65, 237, 267, 391 bus.* **Open**
11am-5pm Tue-Sun. **Admission** *Tue-Fri* £5; £4
reductions; free under-15s (must be accompanied by
an adult). *Sat, Sun* £7; £6 reductions; free under-15s
(must be accompanied by an adult). **Credit** MC, V.
See p189 **Odd curiosity stop.**

Syon House

*Syon Park, Brentford, Middx TW8 8JF (8560 0883/
www.syonpark.co.uk). Gunnersbury tube/rail then
237, 267 bus.* **Open** *House* (19 Mar-30 Oct only)
11am-5pm Wed, Thur, Sun. *Gardens* (year-round)
10.30am-dusk daily. *Tours* by arrangement.
Admission *House & gardens* £8; £4-£7 reductions;
£18 family. *Gardens only* £4; £2.50 reductions; £9
family. *Tours* free. **Credit** MC, V.
The Percys, Dukes of Northumberland, were once
known as 'the Kings of the North'. Syon House is
their southern pad, sufficiently imposing to have
starred in Robert Altman's *Gosford Park.* The house
stands on the site of a Bridgettine convent, sup-
pressed by Henry VIII in 1534. The building was
converted into a house in 1547 for the Duke of
Northumberland, its neoclassical interior created

by Robert Adam in 1761; there's an outstanding collection of Regency portraits by the likes of Gainsborough. The gardens, by Capability Brown, are enhanced by the splendid Great Conservatory and in Nov/Dec you can take an evening walk through illuminated woodland.

Southall

Southall rail.
Head west to go east. A stroll up Southall's South Road (which runs north from the railway station) and along the Broadway might have you wondering if some unsuspected wormhole has deposited you in Chennai: honking car horns, blaring Bollywood music, open shopfronts disgorging vibrant rolls of cloth and shimmering saris, and the air heavy with the pungent smell of spices.

This is London's Little India where, according to OriginsInfo, only 17.8 per cent of the area's 70,000 residents have English names – the lowest proportion in the country. Asians first started settling in the area in large numbers in the 1950s, although this first wave was composed mostly of men. Wives and families started arriving in the 1960s, mostly from the Punjab, and Sikhs still comprise the largest group in Southall, although there are also many Hindus and Muslims.

The secret joy of **Fulham Palace**. *See p189.*

If the **Broadway** isn't subcontinental enough for you, then try **Southall Market**, off the High Street and opposite North Road. What's on sale varies by the day, from squawking poultry on Tuesday, to horses (honestly) on Wednesday, general bric-a-brac on Friday and then, on Saturday, pretty well everything else. As unmissable is a show at the three-screen **Himalaya Palace** (*see p288*), a beautifully restored old movie house dedicated to Bollywood epics.

But it's the food that makes Southall special. **Madhu's** (39 South Road, 8574 1897) is one of the area's stars, with an Indo-Kenyan menu of food that's boldly spiced and expertly char-grilled. The best kebabs and superb yoghurt-based snacks can be had at the **New Asian Tandoori Centre** (114-118 The Green, 8574 2597), which is south of the station. Here the wholesome food is not only astonishingly cheap, but also as authentic as can be. There's even a Punjabi pub, the **Glassy Junction** (97 South Road, 8574 1626): all the trappings of a white working men's club – patterned carpet, pints of keg beer – plus the considerable boon of hot parathas. It's said to be the only pub in the UK that accepts payment in rupees.

A short walk south of Southall railway station, the **Gurdwara Sri Guru Singh Sabha Southall** (Havelock Road, 8574 4311, www.sgsss.org) is the largest Sikh place of worship outside India. Its golden dome is visible from the London Eye in the east and Windsor Castle to the west; it also provides vegetarian food from the langar, communal kitchen, free to all visitors. Non-Sikh visitors are welcome, but must take off their shoes before entering and women must wear a headscarf (provided, should you not have one to hand). Enthroned within is the Guru Granth Sahib, the Sikh scripture and supreme spiritual authority of Sikhism; most unusually, the Guru Granth Sahib contains, in addition to the writings of the ten Sikh Gurus, extracts from the scriptures of other religions.

The suburb of Neasden, six miles north-east of Southall, has its own claim to British Asian fame. It is the site of the **Shri Swaminarayan Mandir** (105-119 Brentfield Road, 8965 2651, www.mandir.org), which is the largest Hindu temple outside India to have been built using traditional methods. To this end, nearly 5,000 tons of stone and marble were shipped out to India, where craftsmen carved it into the intricate designs that make up the temple. Then the temple was shipped, piece by piece, to England, where the gigantic jigsaw was assembled on site. The shining marble temple stands incongruously close to one of IKEA's giant blue boxes.

Sightseeing

RAZ £16.00

'04 AUSTRALIA

E PIEROLA £35.00

VA '01 SPAIN

SOLARCE £14.50

PAIN   175ml/£3.80
         250ml/£5.00

BLANCO
         £13.50

Eat, Drink, Shop

Norfolk Arms. *See p226*.

Restaurants & Cafés

Bring an appetite – there's lots of great food to discover here.

Unbelievable, but true: 'British cuisine' is no longer a contradiction in terms. In this year's Eating & Drinking awards perhaps the mostly keenly contested category was Best British Restaurant: the **National Dinning Rooms** was the worthy winner, but **Geales**, **Great Queen Street** and **Magdalen** ran it close (*see also p219* **Best of British**). And it isn't all modern British, of course: whether you want old-school fish and chips (**Rock & Sole Plaice**, **Golden Hind**), a classic café (*see p206* **Cultured cafés**) or even stewed eels (**M Manze**) you have plenty of options.

Another area of excitement is the appearance of some top-quality, superbly authentic Chinese restaurants: **Bar Shu** and **Snazz Sichuan**, for example, specialise in 'hot and numbing' Sichuan food – and are both confident enough to confront timid Western palates with the likes of tripe and pigs' ears. Indeed, if you've a taste for the exotic, there can be few food cities better equipped than London. You'll find Bangladeshi, Burmese, Ethiopian, Indian, Iranian, Moroccan, Lebanese, Polish, Turkish and Vietnamese food represented in the following chapter, as well as fine exponents of the familiar French, Italian, Japanese, Spanish and Thai arts.

The truth is, avoid the tourist traps and it's hard to eat badly in London these days.

The best Restaurants

For British bites
For modern British, *see p219* **Best of British**. For something more old-fashioned, try **Golden Hind** (*see p206*), **M Manze** (*see right*) or **Sweetings** (*see p196*).

For pure cooking quality
Chez Bruce (*see p220*); **L'Atelier de Joël Robuchon** (*see p202*); **Nahm** (*see p213*).

For drop-dead style
Hakkasan (*see p200*); **Sketch** (*see p211*); **Wolseley** (*see p211*); **Yauatcha** (*see p205*).

For a nice price
Abeno Too (*see p202*); **Masala Zone** (*see p201*); the set lunch at **Wild Honey** (*see p211*); *see also p206* **Cultured cafés**.

DOS AND DON'TS
It's always best to book in advance. At many places it's absolutely essential and at a select few (notably Nobu and anything connected with Gordon Ramsay) you're going to have to book weeks in advance. Since the summer of 2007 smoking has been banned inside cafés and restaurants. Tipping is standard practice: ten to 15 per cent is usual. Many restaurants add this automatically to your bill, some of them doing so but still presenting the credit card slip 'open' – always check to avoid double-tipping.

We've listed a range of meal prices for each place. However, restaurants often change their menus, so these prices are only guidelines.

For the best places to eat with children, *see pp275-277*; for more on eating out in London, pick up the annual *Time Out London Eating & Drinking Guide* (£10.99) and *Time Out Cheap Eats in London* (£6.99).

The South Bank & Bankside

Borough Market (*see p255*), full of stalls selling all kinds of wonderful food, is a superb forage for gourmet snackers. **Tate Modern Café: Level 2** (*see p275*) is superb for those with children, and under the Royal Festival Hall the neighbouring outposts of **Wagamama** (*see p201*) and **Giraffe** (*see p273*) can be life-savers.

British

Magdalen
152 Tooley Street, Bankside, SE1 2TU (7403 1342/www.magdalenrestaurant.co.uk). London Bridge tube/rail. **Open** noon-2.30pm, 6.30-10.30pm Mon-Fri; 6.30-10.30pm Sat. **Main courses** £12-£21. **Credit** AmEx, MC, V. **Map** p405 Q8 ❶
Magdalen's very civilised interior – all dark wood, aubergine paintwork and florally accessorised elegance – leads you to suspect that its food will be as well mannered as its staff. A pleasant surprise, then, to be ambushed by spirited flavours on the daily changing menu. Try the likes of excellent rump of Hereford beef. *See also p219* **Best of British**.

> ❶ Purple numbers given in this chapter correspond to the location of each restaurant and café as marked on the street maps. *See pp394-407.*

M Manze

*87 Tower Bridge Road, Southwark, SE1 4TW
(7407 2985/www.manze.co.uk). Bus 1, 42, 188.*
Open 11am-2pm Mon; 10.30am-2pm Tue-Thur;
10am-2.15pm Fri; 10am-2.45pm Sat. **No credit
cards**. **Map** p405 Q10 ❷

Manze's is surely the finest remaining purveyor of
pie and mash – the dirt cheap traditional foodstuff
of London's working classes. It is not only the oldest pie shop, established in 1902, but also the most
beautiful, with tiled interior, marble-topped tables
and worn wooden benches. Expect mashed potatoes,
minced beef pies and liquor (a kind of parsley sauce);
braver souls should try the stewed eels.

Roast

*Floral Hall, Borough Market, Stoney Street,
Bankside, SE1 1TL (7940 1300/www.roast-
restaurant.com). London Bridge tube/rail.* **Open**
7-9.30am, noon-2.30pm, 5.30-10.30pm Mon-Fri;
8-10.30am, 11.30am-3.30pm, 6-10.30pm Sat; noon-
3.30pm Sun. **Main courses** £12-£20. **Credit**
AmEx, MC, V. **Map** p404 P8 ❸

Looking out over the market, Roast has a comfy bar
area that gives way to a handsome, high-ceilinged
restaurant with views of the cathedral and the railway line through huge windows. The place never
stops: it's open for breakfast (bacon and fried egg
butty) and tea (coronation chicken sandwiches), as
well as lunch and dinner (well-sourced meat and
fish). *See also p219* **Best of British**. *Photo p219.*

Cafés & brasseries

For authentic London café food, try the
stewed eels at **M Manze** (*see above*).

Shipp's Tea Rooms

*4 Park Street, Bankside, SE1 9AB (7407 2692).
London Bridge tube/rail.* **Open** 9.30am-5.30pm
Mon-Fri; 10am-7pm Sat; 11am-5pm Sun. **Main
courses** £2-£4. **Set tea** £17.50. **No credit cards**.
Map p404 P8 ❹

Shipp's caters perfectly for Borough Market shoppers with its nostalgic feel. Electrical contractor's
premises (right next to Neal's Yard Cheeses) have
become a shrine to last-century tea sets, scones and
victoria sponge cake, evoking an era when shoppers
were less caffeine-fuelled and had time to nibble
cakes over a cuppa in the afternoon.

Table

*83 Southwark Street, Bankside, SE1 0HX (7401
2760/www.thetablecafe.com). Southwark tube/
London Bridge tube/rail.* **Open** 7.30am-8.30pm
Mon-Thur; 7.30am-11pm Fri; 9am-4pm Sat. **Main
courses** £3-£8. **Credit** MC, V. **Map** p404 O8 ❺

Based in the ground floor of a Bankside architecture
company, the Table is a cut above your regular
office canteen. Mix and match a salad or choose from
hot meals that include flans, a daily risotto and sar-
dines, then hope to find a seat at the shared solid
wood tables. Multifunctional, cheap and stylish.

Eat, Drink, Shop

Skylon, for fine food and an excellent view. *See p196.*

East European

Baltic
74 Blackfriars Road, South Bank, SE1 8HA (7928 1111/www.balticrestaurant.co.uk). Southwark tube/ rail. **Open** noon-3pm daily; 6-11pm Mon-Sat; 6-10pm Sun. **Main courses** £10-£17. **Credit** AmEx, MC, V. **Map** p404 N8 ⑥
London's most glamorous east European restaurant, with high ceilings and a chandelier aglow with hundreds of amber shards. The place can be noisy, but the food is an excellent modern take on such dishes as nutty buckwheat blinis and kaszanka (Polish black pudding). The bar has over a dozen clear varieties of vodka, as well as home-infused specialities.

French

RSJ
33 Coin Street, South Bank, SE1 9NR (7928 4554/ www.rsj.uk.com). Waterloo tube/rail. **Open** noon-2pm, 5.30-11pm Mon-Fri; 5.30-11pm Sat. **Main courses** £12-£17. **Credit** AmEx, DC, MC, V. **Map** p404 N8 ⑦
Still fresh as just-dried paint after 25 years, RSJ's first-floor dining room is plain but smart. The concise menu of deftly cooked food is broadly French, given zest by English ingredients, but the place's reputation rests largely on its cellar of Loire wines.

Gastropubs

Anchor & Hope
36 The Cut, South Bank, SE1 8LP (7928 9898). Southwark or Waterloo tube/rail. **Open** 5-11pm Mon; 11am-11pm Tue-Sat; 12.30-5pm Sun. **Main courses** £11-£16. **Credit** MC, V. **Map** p404 N8 ⑧
With no bookings taken, customers happily wait for a table for up to 50 minutes, such is the reputation of the rustic, Med-slanted food here. The worn floorboards and high ceilings are appealing too. It even works as a boozer, with real ales and classic cocktails treated with proper respect. Come in the afternoon or after 9pm if you hope to avoid the crowds.

Japanese

Bincho
2nd floor, Oxo Tower Wharf, Barge House Street, South Bank, SE1 9PH (7803 0858/www.bincho.co. uk). Blackfriars or Waterloo tube/rail. **Open** noon-3pm, 5-11.30pm Mon-Fri; noon-11.30pm Sat; noon-10.30pm Sun. **Yakitori** £1-£11. **Credit** AmEx, DC, MC, V. **Map** p404 N7 ⑨
This new restaurant is a handsome interpretation of a yakitori-ya – a casual restaurant where office workers slug beer or saké while noshing hot snacks. The long dining room is done out in a mini-forest of wood and bamboo, the large windows giving great Thames views. Chefs at open charcoal grills prepare the meat and fish skewers.

Modern European

Skylon
Royal Festival Hall, Belvedere Road, South Bank, SE1 8XX (7654 7800/www.danddlondon.com). Waterloo tube/rail. **Open** Bar 11am-1am daily. *Brasserie* noon-11.45pm daily. *Restaurant* noon-2.30pm, 5.30-10.45pm daily. **Main courses** £9-£19. **Credit** MC, V. **Map** p401 M8 ⑩
Set at the front of the refurbished Royal Festival Hall, this lofty space – with fantastic river view – is divided into three: a central raised bar separates the formal restaurant from the brasserie. Winner of Best Design in our 2007 awards, the room is dominated by five enormous bronze chandeliers. Try the likes of Swedish classic jansson's temptation and Finnish-style hot-smoked fish dishes. Staff are friendly – and their Star Trek uniforms very swish. *Photos p195.*

Spanish

Tapas Brindisa
18-20 Southwark Street, Bankside, SE1 1TJ (7357 8880/www.brindisa.com). London Bridge tube/rail. **Open** noon-3pm, 5.30-11pm Mon-Thur; 9-11am, noon-4pm, 5.30-11pm Fri, Sat. **Tapas** £3.25-£9. **Credit** AmEx, MC, V. **Map** p404 P8 ⑪
The restaurant arm of the renowned Spanish deli turns out first-rate tapas, marrying fine imported ingredients with fresh, seasonal produce from closer to home. With its auspicious Borough Market location, the small space soon gets rammed – be prepared to wait, since no bookings are taken.

The City

Fish

Sweetings
39 Queen Victoria Street, EC4N 4SA (7248 3062). Mansion House tube. **Open** 11.30am-3pm Mon-Fri. **Main courses** £11-£28. **Credit** AmEx, MC, V. **Map** p404 P6 ⑫
Small and spartan (apart from a lovely mosaic-tiled floor), this century-old City institution remains determinedly old-fashioned – in the best way. Straightforward, simple fish dishes are served at linen-covered counters, followed by schoolyard fantasies such as spotted dick or fruit crumble.

French

1 Lombard Street
1 Lombard Street, EC3V 9AA (7929 6611/ www.1lombardstreet.com). Bank tube/DLR. **Open** Bar 11am-11pm Mon-Fri. Food served noon-3pm, 6-9.45pm Mon-Fri. **Main courses** Brasserie £16-£26. Restaurant £24-£35. **Credit** AmEx, DC, MC, V. **Map** p405 Q6 ⑬
If you're going to dine in the City, you may as well go the whole hog and dine in a bank. This temple of

Eat, Drink, Shop

Sure can pick 'em

Guy Dimond, Time Out Group's Food & Drink Editor, separates fiercely
spiced pig's ear from tired old frou-frou foam.

I'd like a millimetre off my waistline every time someone asks me 'What's the hot new trend in restaurants?'. Better make that a micrometre, or I might end up looking like a stick insect. Some restaurants are impervious to fashion: **St John** (*see p197*), the **Wolseley** (*see p211*), **Song Que** (*see p219*) and **Mandalay** (*see p207*) are diverse but outstanding examples. But for every culinary equivalent of this season's Louis Vuitton handbag there are several knock-offs, which threaten to bring any new culinary trend into disrepute before it's even started. Remember Pacific Rim cookery, savoury 'cappuccino' foams or oaked Aussie chardonnays? You start off with the Sugar Club's creative fusion, Gordon Ramsay's passion for seafood or Jilly Goolden sniffing vanilla-lined cigar boxes and end up with M&S ready meals, supermarket-branded cheap chocolates and jug wines with more oak than Robin Hood's forest.

The secret to eternal life, for chefs and restaurateurs at least, is to create something with enduring personality. A restaurant such as 2002's **Sketch** (*see p211*) almost defines 'fashionable' – the frequently updated interior design probably cost more than the new Eurostar terminal. Pundits said it wouldn't last, but it has become a modern classic because – I'd guess – diners love the look, the playfully creative food and, above all, the buzz.

The same cannot be said for the scores of me-too mid-range fast food chains popping up all over London, run by MBA graduates with more interest in their business plan and rolling out a 'concept' than customer satisfaction. Another flash-in-the-pan is the

recent fashion for badly executed pan-oriental restaurants. I think the pan-oriental bubble will burst soon, as diners become more sophisticated in their appreciation of Asian and oriental food. In contrast, the real jewels of the East are more resilient than a well-tempered wok: **Hakkasan** (*see p200*) for leading the way in modern Cantonese food since 2001; the Royal China chain for still making some of London's best dim sum; **Amaya** (*see p213*) and **Cinnamon Club** (*see p212*) for taking modern Indian food to new heights; and, despite their drawbacks, twins **Roka** (*see p200*) and **Zuma** (*see p214*) for helping make modern Japanese food cool, casual and (just about) affordable.

Londoners' obsession with the best new restaurants is not something it's wise for me to whinge about, as this fascination with the next week's hotspot keeps me in a job. But there is one 'concept' that consistently disappoints diners: celebrity restaurants, and especially celebrity-chef restaurants. **Nobu** (*see p211*), Jamie Oliver's **Fifteen** (*see p218*) and, above all, the Ivy polled badly in our summer 2007 reader survey, when we asked for London's most overrated restaurant. All three are perfectly good restaurants, but by no means London's best. Disappointment is bound to follow when the *Heat*-reading generation is duped into thinking London's longest queues for a table mean London's best restaurants. All a long queue indicates is that the other diners are suckers for joining in the mêlée. Bear that in mind if you find youself in an automated phone queue for the lottery of bagging a table months ahead.

Mammon is a Grade II-listed building, made bright and welcoming by big windows and neoclassical domed skylights. The food has won a Michelin star, merited both in the swish brasserie section and a restaurant area serving pricier haute cuisine.

Sauterelle

Royal Exchange, EC3V 3LR (7618 2483/www. danddlondon.com). Bank tube/DLR. **Open** noon-2.30pm, 6-10pm Mon-Fri. **Main courses** £16-£19. **Credit** AmEx, DC, MC, V. **Map** p405 Q6 **⑭**
With its stunning location around the gallery of the lovely Royal Exchange, Sauterelle doesn't have to worry about wow factor. Instead it focuses its energy

on food and service. The former is at the intersection between French and modern European: not so haute – nor expensive – as to discourage the middle management among its City clientele; the latter enjoyably mixes sycophancy and professionalism.

British

St John

26 St John Street, Clerkenwell, EC1M 4AY (7251 0848/4998/www.stjohnrestaurant.com). Barbican tube/Farringdon tube/rail. **Open** noon-3pm, 6-11pm

Eat, Drink, Shop

Mon-Fri; 6-11pm Sat. **Main courses** £13-£23.
Credit AmEx, DC, MC, V. **Map** p402 O5 ⑮
Fergus Henderson's St John has become a world-famous pioneer of British food, while managing to remain an extremely congenial restaurant where you can still get a table. *See p219* **Best of British.**
Other locations St John Bread & Wine,
94-96 Commercial Street, Spitalfields, E1 6LZ
(7251 0848/www.stjohnbreadandwine.com).

French

Club Gascon

*57 West Smithfield, Clerkenwell, EC1A 9DS
(7796 0600/www.clubgascon.com). Barbican tube/
Farringdon tube/rail.* **Open** noon-2pm, 7-10pm
Mon-Thur; noon-2pm, 7-10.30pm Fri; 7-10.30pm
Sat. **Main courses** £8-£28. **Credit** AmEx, MC,
V. **Map** p402 O5 ⑯
Bijou in the best possible way, Club Gascon was the original of a cluster of gems – Le Comptoir Gascon, Le Cercle, Cellar Gascon (*see p222*) – offering food and wine from south-west France. The menu is grouped by key ingredient (vegetables, seafood, lamb/beef and, famously, foie gras), from which you select three or four starter-size dishes. Expect dazzling flavours, and fabulous bread as the main carb.

Gastropubs

Eagle

*159 Farringdon Road, Clerkenwell, EC1R 3AL
(7837 1353). Farringdon tube/rail.* **Open** noon-11pm
Mon-Sat; noon-5pm Sun. **Main courses** £5-£15.
Credit MC, V. **Map** p402 N4 ⑰
The Eagle's renown as birthplace of London's gastropub movement means that, 15 years in, it's still near impossible to get a seat. To have a hope, come early: once people get settled, they shift for no one, tucking into steak sandwiches, tapas and heartier Med-influenced meat and fish dishes, all prepared behind the bar. Drinkers are well taken care of too.

Hat & Feathers

*2 Clerkenwell Road, Clerkenwell, EC1M 5PQ (7490
2244). Barbican tube/Farringdon tube/rail/55, 243
bus.* **Open** noon-midnight Mon-Sat. **Credit** AmEx,
MC, V. **Map** p402 O4 ⑱
Derelict for years, the Hat & Feathers reopened as a two-floor gastropub in 2006, the new management retaining its lovely acid-etched windows and wood panelling. Modern European cuisine is served on the first floor, where the interesting menu is more hit than miss. Massive new outdoor terrace as well.

Peasant

*240 St John Street, Clerkenwell, EC1V 4PH (7336
7726/www.thepeasant.co.uk). Angel tube/Farringdon
tube/rail.* **Open** noon-11pm Mon-Sat; noon-10.30pm
Sun. **Credit** AmEx, MC, V. **Map** p402 O4 ⑲
A model gastropub: classy but not condescending, adventurous without being ridiculous and, above all, blessed with a richness of personality. An array of

original fixtures – from mosaic tiled floor to grand horseshoe bar – hark back to its days as a Victorian gin palace, while the velvety red walls are replete with antique fairground art and framed rock posters.

Modern European

Ambassador

*55 Exmouth Market, Clerkenwell, EC1R 4QL (7837
0009/www.theambassadorcafe.co.uk). Farringdon
tube/rail/19, 38, 341 bus.* **Open** 8.30am-10.15pm
Mon-Sat. **Main courses** £9-£17. **Credit** AmEx,
MC, V. **Map** p402 N4 ⑳
A day-long café-style operation that aims to please all the people all the time and – due to skill, commitment and an eye for detail – succeeds. The various menus include breakfast waffles and pastries, a weekend brunch, dinner, and small sharing dishes for those primarily here to enjoy the beautifully crafted wine list. A fine restaurant.

Smiths of Smithfield

*67-77 Charterhouse Street, Clerkenwell, EC1M 6HJ
(7251 7950/www.smithsofsmithfield.co.uk). Barbican
tube/Farringdon tube/rail.* **Open** Bar 11am-11pm
Mon-Sat; noon-10.30pm Sun. *Café* 7am-4.30pm Mon-Fri; 9.30am-5.30pm Sat, Sun. *Dining Room* noon-2.45pm, 6-10.45pm Mon-Fri; 6-10.45pm Sat. **Main courses** *Café* £4-£8. *Dining Room* £10-£28. **Credit**
AmEx, DC, MC, V. **Map** p402 O5 ㉑
The popularity of John Torode's industrial chic, four-floor brick warehouse is testament to its reliability. No matter how bus it gets, standards remain constant. The ground-floor café-bar is packed with a democratic mix of City workers and night owls, but the hub of the operation is the second-floor Dining Room, its menu confidently focused on meat.

Spanish

Moro

*34-36 Exmouth Market, Clerkenwell, EC1R 4QE
(7833 8336/www.moro.co.uk). Farringdon tube/rail/
19, 38 bus.* **Open** 12.30-11.45pm Mon-Sat (last entry
10.30pm). **Tapas** £2-£12. **Main courses** £13-£18.
Credit AmEx, DC, MC, V. **Map** p402 N4 ㉒
The superb Moro has an unrivalled setting, coming into its own in summer when tables are placed outside. The softly lit open-plan dining room is no less pleasant – restrained, yet cosily romantic. But the food is the primary draw, a daily changing modern Mediterranean ensemble with heavy Spanish and North African accents. Book ahead.

Bloomsbury & Fitzrovia

British

Konstam at the Prince Albert

*2 Acton Street, Bloomsbury, WC1X 9NA (7833
5040/www.konstam.co.uk). King's Cross tube/rail.*
Open 12.30-3pm, 6.30-10.30pm Mon-Fri; 6.30-

10.30pm Sat. **Main courses** £10-£16. **Credit**
AmEx, MC, V. **Map** p399 M3 ㉓
The wild decor – dark green paint, even on the floor,
and talking-point lights made from plug chains – is
a welcome change after the identikit chains. Chef-
owner Oliver Rowe's menu doesn't play safe either:
about 90% of the ingredients come from within the
tube network; *see p212* **What a source**.

Cafés & brasseries

Acorn House
*69 Swinton Street, Bloomsbury, WC1X 9NT (7812
1842/www.acornhouserestaurant.com). King's Cross
tube/rail.* **Open** 8-11am, noon-3pm, 6-10.30pm Mon-
Fri; 10am-3pm, 6-10.30pm Sat. **Main courses** £12-
£18. **Credit** AmEx, MC, V. **Map** p399 M3 ㉔
'Eco-friendly training restaurant' doesn't convey the
charm of Acorn House. Yes, the place is committed
to seasonality and environmental responsibility (*see
p212* **What a source**), but visit for flavour-packed
food, a tempting wine list and warm staff. *Photo p212.*

Meals
*1st floor, Heal's, 196 Tottenham Court Road,
Bloomsbury, W1T 7LQ (7580 2522/www.heals.
co.uk). Goodge Street or Warren Street tube.*
Open 10am-6pm Mon-Wed, Fri; 10am-7.30pm
Thur; 9.30am-6.30pm Sat; noon-6pm Sun. **Main
courses** £9-£11. **Credit** AmEx, DC, MC, V.
Map p399 K5 ㉕
Cross an alpine lodge with a toddler's bedroom, add
cut-out cupboards that suggest a fairytale landscape, and marshmallow pink chairs on the ironic
side of twee – and you've got the runner-up for Best
Design in our 2007 awards. The food doesn't quite
taste as well as it reads, but it's enjoyable, cultured
and surprisingly generous. 'Squillionaire's short-
bread' isn't far short of sensational.

Italian

Ooze
*62 Goodge Street, Fitzrovia, W1T 4NE (7436 9444/
www.ooze.biz). Goodge Street tube.* **Open** noon-11pm
Mon-Sat. **Main courses** £5.25-£9.95. **Credit**
AmEx, MC, V. **Map** p398 J5 ㉖
It's a wonder Ooze is the first venture to concentrate
solely on different permutations of risotto. Contrary
to the dubious name, the dining room is clean, bright
and white, with the odd dash of colour. More colourful still are the risottos, over a dozen of which are
always available – comfort food, at comfy prices.

Oriental

Hakkasan
*8 Hanway Place, Fitzrovia, W1T 1HD (7907 1888).
Tottenham Court Road tube.* **Open** noon-12.30am
Mon-Wed; noon-1.30am Thur-Sat; noon-midnight
Sun. **Dim sum** £3-£20. **Main courses** £9-£58.
Credit AmEx, MC, V. **Map** p406 W1 ㉗

Upmarket Chinese restaurant Hakkasan whisks
customers off a horrible alley into a Narnia of other-
worldliness. Suddenly, you find yourself in a moody
1930s Shanghai-style basement dining room, a
three-dimensional Chinese woodcut of intimate,
interlocking booths, a super setting for sophisticated,
thought-provoking Chinese-inspired food. Cocktails
(£8.50) are the stuff of Asian-influenced fantasy and
DJs are on hand from 9pm daily.

Roka
*37 Charlotte Street, Fitzrovia, W1T 1RR (7580
6464/www.rokarestaurant.com). Goodge Street or
Tottenham Court Road tube.* **Open** noon-3.30pm,
5.30-11.30pm Mon-Fri; 12.30-3.30pm, 5.30-11.30pm
Sat; 5.30-10.30pm Sun. **Main courses** £3.60-£21.
Credit AmEx, DC, MC, V. **Map** p398 J5 ㉘
Everything about Roka, younger sibling of Zuma
(*see p214*), is enticing: from honey-coloured walls to
the aroma of wood burning at the centrepiece grill.
The food – a modern take on traditional Japanese
cuisine – might rock your budget, but it will rock
your taste buds too. The basement Shochu Lounge
is half 21st-century style bar, half feudal Japan.

Snazz Sichuan
*New China Club, 37 Chalton Street, Somers Town,
NW1 1JD (7388 0808). Euston tube/rail.* **Open**
12.30-10.30pm daily. **Main courses** £6-£27. **Credit**
MC, V. **Map** p399 K3 ㉙

Real Chinese at **Snazz Sichuan**.

The bizarre tone of the decor (flimsy magenta curtains, Cultural Revolution poster), the enthusiasm of the staff, the skill and exuberance of the chef and the wonderful aromas are testament to the authenticity of this Sichuanese food. This is ma-la (hot and numbing) fare, so don't expect familiar Cantonese dishes – instead sample the likes of spicy pigs' ears.

Wagamama
4A Streatham Street, Bloomsbury, WC1A 1JB (7323 9223/www.wagamama.com). Holborn or Tottenham Court Road tube. **Open** noon-11pm Mon-Sat; noon-10pm Sun. **Main courses** £5.95-£9.95. **Credit** AmEx, DC, MC, V. **Map** p407 X1 ③⓪
The mother of all London noodle bars. Since starting life in this basement in 1992, Wagamama has expanded to more than 80 restaurants with its clever concept of no bookings, communal tables, and a menu of Japan-easy noodle soups and 'side dishes'. **Other locations** throughout the city.

Spanish
Salt Yard
54 Goodge Street, Fitzrovia, W1T 4NA (7637 0657/ www.saltyard.co.uk). Goodge Street tube. **Open** noon-11pm Mon-Fri; 5-11pm Sat. **Tapas** £3-£9. **Credit** AmEx, DC, MC, V. **Map** p398 J5 ③①
The hybrid Spanish-Italian cooking at this classy restaurant is unique in London. The seasonal menu resembles traditional tapas in spirit, with unfussy recipes allowing the quality of the ingredients to tell; in its detail, the choice is fascinating. Signature dishes include fried courgette flowers stuffed with Spanish cheese, and confit of pork belly with cannellini beans. The only problem? Getting a table.

Covent Garden
Fancy a little people-watching? Celebs are still drawn to the elegant **Ivy** (1 West Street, 7836 4751, www.caprice-holdings.co.uk) – you might even (with some phone patience) nab same-day seats for lunch. **Joe Allen** (13 Exeter Street, 7836 0651, www.joeallen.co.uk) gathers a buzzy mix of audience members, cast and crew from across the West End's theatres each night… despite the food, rather than because of it.

British
Great Queen Street
32 Great Queen Street, WC2B 5AA (7242 0622). Covent Garden or Holborn tube. **Open** 6-10.30pm Mon; noon-2.30pm, 6-10.30pm Tue-Sat. **Main courses** £9-£18. **Credit** MC, V. **Map** p407 Z2 ③②
Sister to the revered Anchor & Hope (*see p196*), Great Queen Street shares the gastropub's buzzy lack of pretension, the pub-style room thrumming with bonhomie. Ranging from snacks to shared mains, the menu is designed to tempt and satisfy rather than educate or impress. *See p219* **Best of British**.

Cafés & brasseries
Bullet
3rd floor, Snow & Rock, 4 Mercer Street, WC2H 9QA (7836 4922/www.bullet-coffee.com). Covent Garden tube/Charing Cross tube/rail. **Open** 10am-6pm daily. **Main courses** £2.80-£6. **Credit** MC, V. **Map** p407 Y3 ③③
A jewel of a café, three flights of stairs up in a branch of Snow & Rock. It's worth the climb, even if you've forgotten your belays; *see p206* **Cultured cafés**.

Scoop
40 Shorts Gardens, WC2H 9AB (7240 7086/www. scoopgelato.com). Covent Garden tube. **Open** 9am-11.30pm daily. **Map** p407 Y2 ③④
We love the pinolo, made with pine kernels from Pisa. We adore the heady amaretto, with its ground biscuits and almond liqueur. Hell, we like everything in this ice-cream parlour. For those on special diets, there are appropriate sorbets and dairy-free ices.

Fish
J Sheekey
28-32 St Martin's Court, WC2N 4AL (7240 2565/ www.caprice-holdings.co.uk). Leicester Square tube. **Open** noon-3pm, 5.30pm-midnight Mon-Sat; noon-3.30pm, 6pm-midnight Sun. **Main courses** £13-£40. **Credit** AmEx, DC, MC, V. **Map** p407 X4 ③⑤
Behind mirrored windows that keep off prying eyes, this favoured haunt of the well-known is intimate and gentlemen's-club posh: a succession of little rooms (including a discreet bar) with black-and-whites of theatre stars and immaculately turned-out waiters. The menu offers stupendous fish and seafood platters, and a few meat and vegetarian dishes, all prepared with flair. Booking essential.

Fish & chips
Rock & Sole Plaice
47 Endell Street, WC2H 9AJ (7836 3785/www. rockandsoleplaice.com). Covent Garden tube. **Open** 11.30am-11pm Mon-Sat; noon-10pm Sun. **Main courses** £8-£14. **Credit** MC, V. **Map** p407 Y2 ③⑥
A sociable and busy little chippie in a handy location. The fish and chips are generally done well and in generous quantities. It's a great spot for alfresco dining in summer, under fairy lights and geraniums.

Indian
Masala Zone
48-51 Floral Street, WC2E 9DS (7379 0101/ www.masalazone.com). Covent Garden tube. **Open** noon-11pm Mon-Sat; noon-10.30pm Sun. **Main courses** £6-£9. **Credit** MC, V. **Map** p405 Y3 ③⑦
The latest in a rapidly expanding chain. Ceiling-hung Rajasthani puppets shout 'north Indian', but the menu's a round-up of adventurous fast food from

every region. The place is hugely popular, with (fast-moving) queues at busy times. Seating is comfortable, with secluded booths for private conversation. **Other locations** 9 Marshall Street, Soho, W1F 7ER (7287 9966); 80 Upper Street, Islington, N1 0NU (7359 3399); 147 Earl's Court Road, Earl's Court, SW5 9RQ (7373 0220).

Japanese

Abeno Too
17-18 Great Newport Street, WC2H 7JE (7379 1160/www.abeno.co.uk). Leicester Square tube. **Open** noon-11pm Mon-Sat; noon-10.30pm Sun. **Main courses** £7-£20. **Credit** AmEx, DC, MC, V. **Map** p407 X3 🟠
Okonomiyaki is fun, cheap comfort food – ingredients are added to a batter that is cooked and combined with noodles on a table-top hotplate in front of you. There are also noodle dishes and desserts. **Other locations** Abeno, 47 Museum Street, Bloomsbury, WC1A 1LY (7405 3211).

Modern European

L'Atelier de Joël Robuchon
13-15 West Street, WC2H 9NE (7010 8600/www. joel-robuchon.com). Leicester Square tube. **Open** *Bar* 2pm-2am Mon-Sat; 2-10.30pm Sun. *Restaurant* noon-2.30pm, 5.30-10.30pm daily. **Main courses** £15-£55. **Credit** AmEx, DC, MC, V. **Map** p407 X3 🟠
The London branch of French chef Joël Robuchon's international chain of high-concept brasseries is a three-floor extravaganza. Pools of darkness are illuminated by bright spots of colour in the otherwise all-black open kitchen, which is as well ordered as a monastery. You can't book after 7pm for the ground level, but you can for the lighter, brighter first floor. The food is terrific – fun and imaginative – but expect dinner for two to cost at least £150.

Spanish

Oops Restaurante & Vinateria
31 Catherine Street, WC2B 5JS (7836 3609). Covent Garden tube. **Open** noon- 11pm Mon-Sat. **Dishes** £2-£18. *Set menu* £12.95 (4 dishes & drink). **Credit** MC, V. **Map** p407 Z3 🟠
This is a demure little place, with dark wood and tasteful artwork. Most dishes are similarly restrained, creating good, old-fashioned tapas with fresh ingredients – but there's an occasional nod to modern Spanish techniques, as with the blue cheese ice-cream. Classics include marinated anchovies, Galician octopus, Jabugo ham and chorizo in cider.

Vegetarian & organic

Food for Thought
31 Neal Street, WC2H 9PR (7836 9072). Covent Garden tube. **Open** noon-8.30pm Mon-Sat; noon-5pm

Sun. **Main courses** £4.20-£6.90. **No credit cards. Map** p407 Y2 🟠
The customers patiently queuing down the street for a takeaway at peak hours attest to the popularity of this long-standing veggie hotspot; the space inside is scarcely less cramped. Rainbow hippie trousers will still be spotted here, but so will couples and shop workers grabbing lunch. Unpretentious and reliable.

Soho & Chinatown

British

Lindsay House
21 Romilly Street, Soho, W1D 5AF (7439 0450/ www.lindsayhouse.co.uk). Leicester Square tube. **Open** noon-2.30pm, 6-11pm Mon-Sat. **Set meals** £27-£57 3 courses. **Credit** AmEx, DC, MC, V. **Map** p406 W3 🟠
Justly famous, Lindsay House is an 18th-century Soho townhouse, with intimate dining rooms that really come into their own in the evening. Elegant restraint rules – impeccable service, quietly spoken diners – until the food arrives: one perfect, gutsily flavoured course after another. The wine list hasn't a single dull bottle. Booking advisable.

Mother Mash
26 Ganton Street, Soho, W1F 7QZ (7494 9644/ www.mothermash.co.uk). Oxford Circus tube. **Open** 8.30am-10pm Mon-Fri; noon-10pm Sat; noon-5pm Sun. **Main courses** £6.95-£7.95. **Credit** AmEx, MC, V. **Map** p406 U3 🟠
Sausages? Yes. Pies? Of course. Mashed spud? Now you're talking! A standard butter-and-milk mash is offered among a handful of variants, such as Irish champ. There's also a choice of gravies, including a traditional 'liquor' (parsley sauce). There are breakfast and salad options too, as well as wine and beer.

Cafés & brasseries

Yauatcha (*see p205*) has a chic ground-floor tea-house, but just three tables means huge waits. For a hefty snack, try **Mother Mash** (*see above*).

Fernandez & Wells
73 Beak Street, Soho, W1F 9RS (7287 8124). Oxford Circus or Piccadilly Circus tube. **Open** 8am-7pm Mon-Fri; 9am-7pm Sat. **Main courses** £3-£5. **Credit** (over £5) MC, V. **Map** p406 V3 🟠
Winner of our Best Coffee Bar gong in 2007, this bright room has ample seating and service that's all smiles (*see p206* **Cultured cafés**). They also run a takeaway/deli on Lexington Street, specialising in top-quality Spanish products. *Photo p206*.

Maison Bertaux
28 Greek Street, Soho, W1D 5DQ (7437 6007). Leicester Square, Piccadilly Circus or Tottenham Court Road tube. **Open** 8.30am-11pm Mon-Sat; 8.30am-7pm Sun. **Main courses** £1-£5. **No credit cards. Map** p407 X2 🟠

Even dining at the counter is suave at **L'Atelier de Joël Robuchon**.

Many consider the original Old Compton Street outpost of Pâtisserie Valerie (no.44, 7437 3466, www. patisserie-valerie.co.uk) to be essential Soho, but café nostalgics and connoisseurs of lost afternoon melancholy would do better heading to eccentric Maison Bertaux (*see p206* **Cultured cafés**).

Nordic Bakery

14 Golden Square, Soho, W1F 9JF (3230 1077/www. nordicbakery.com). Oxford Circus or Piccadilly Circus tube. **Open** 8am-8pm Mon-Fri; noon-7pm Sat. **Main courses** £2.80-£4. **Credit** MC, V. **Map** p406 V3 **45**
The simplicity of the Nordic Bakery formula takes a lot of beating: small range of food; high-ceilinged room decorated with impeccable Scandinavian good taste; good coffee. *See p206* **Cultured cafés**.

Indian

Red Fort

77 Dean Street, Soho, W1D 3SH (7437 2115/www. redfort.co.uk). Leicester Square or Tottenham Court Road tube. **Open** noon-2pm, 5.45-11pm Mon-Fri; 5.45-11pm Sat; 5.30-10pm Sun. **Main courses** £12-£20. **Credit** AmEx, MC, V. **Map** p406 W2 **47**
Seriously stylish, Red Fort's fine dining menu is a magnet for media moguls and moneyed tourists, offering north Indian classics and regal dishes from Lucknow. Sandstone walls, a sleek water feature and antique artefacts lend elegant restraint to the feng shui ordered interior. Booking advisable.

Modern European

Arbutus

63-64 Frith Street, Soho, W1D 3JW (7734 4545/ www.arbutusrestaurant.co.uk). Tottenham Court Road tube. **Open** noon-2.30pm, 5-11pm Mon-Sat; 12.30-3.30pm, 5.30-9.30pm Sun. **Main courses** £12-£16. **Credit** AmEx, MC, V. **Map** p406 W2 **49**
Always full (though counter-dining means casual diners are often accommodated), Arbutus has a alluring British and Mediterranean menu that is precise but unfussy. Braised pig's head with potato purée and caramelised onions is a trademark dish. The room is minimalist but pleasant, the diners a mixed bunch, and the staff friendly and prescient. Sister restaurant Wild Honey (*see p211*) is set to be just as big a hit.

Mediterranean

Hummus Bros

88 Wardour Street, Soho, W1F 0TJ (7734 1311/ www.hbros.co.uk). Oxford Circus or Tottenham Court Road tube. **Open** 11am-10pm Mon-Wed; 11am-11pm Thur, Fri; noon-11pm Sat; noon-10pm Sun. **Main courses** £2-£6. **Credit** AmEx, MC, V. **Map** p406 W2 **49**
Hummus Bros is a fine concept diner. The dip comes shaped around the inside of a bowl, which is filled with vibrant toppings (stewed beef, fava beans, guacamole). Those in the know order one of two daily changing specials. It isn't ideal for a quiet chat, but for a swift, nutritious lunch or early evening meal, the Bros are hard to beat. *Photo p208.*
Other locations Victoria House, 37-63 Southampton Row, Bloomsbury, WC1B 4DA (7404 7079).

Oriental

Chinatown stalwarts like **Mr Kong** (21 Lisle Street, 7437 7341) and **Wong Kei** (41-43 Wardour Street, 0871 332 8296) still ply their Anglo-Cantonese trade, but we're more excited by a new generation of Chinese restaurants

delicious noodles | rice dishes

freshly squeezed juices | salads

wine | sake | japanese beers

for locations visit wagamama.com

positive eating + positive living

wagamama.com

unafraid to combine authenticity with adventure. For atmosphere, drop in on one of Chinatown's bustling cafés – try a 'bubble tea' (sweet, icy and full of balls of jelly slurped up with a straw) at **Jen Café** (4-8 Newport Place, no phone) or late-night favourite **HK Diner** (22 Wardour Street, 7434 9544).

Bar Shu
28 Frith Street, Soho, W1D 5LF (7287 6688). Leicester Square or Tottenham Court Road tube. **Open** noon-11.30pm Mon-Sat; noon-11pm Sun. **Main courses** £7-£28. **Credit** AmEx, MC, V. **Map** p406 W2 ⓾
One of the few London restaurants dedicated to Sichuanese food, a cuisine characterised by fiery chilli and numbing Sichuan pepper. The menu provides clear descriptions and photographs of most dishes (thankfully it looks better in reality than it is portrayed). Not somewhere for the fainthearted, but perfect for those in search of authentic flavours.

Busaba Eathai
106-110 Wardour Street, Soho, W1F 0TR (7255 8686). Oxford Circus, Tottenham Court Road or Leicester Square tube. **Open** noon-11pm Mon-Thur; noon-11.30pm Fri, Sat; noon-10pm Sun. **Main courses** £5-£9. **Credit** AmEx, MC, V. **Map** p406 W2 ⓾
This is probably the handiest branch of Alan Yau's Thai fast food canteen. It combines shared tables and bench seating with a touch of oriental mystique (dark wood, incense, low lighting). The dishes are always intriguing, as you'd expect of a menu developed by David Thompson of Nahm (*see p213*). **Other locations** 8-13 Bird Street, Marylebone, W1U 1BU (7518 8080); 22 Store Street, Bloomsbury, WC1E 7DS (7299 7900).

Haozhan
8 Gerrard Street, Chinatown, W1D 5PJ (7434 3838). Leicester Square or Piccadilly Circus tube. **Open** noon-11.30pm Mon-Thur; noon-midnight Fri, Sat; noon-10.30pm Sun. **Main courses** £6-£26. **Credit** AmEx, MC, V. **Map** p407 X3 ⓾
This modern-looking venue's contemporary, globe-trotting menu is produced by a chef from Hakkasan (*see p200*), which means impeccable cooking. Many dishes are textural masterpieces, even something as simple as 'Sichuan vegetables'. Staff really know their dishes and are ultra-attentive. After which the low bill is a very pleasant surprise.

New Mayflower
68-70 Shaftesbury Avenue, Chinatown, W1D 6LY (7734 9207). Leicester Square or Piccadilly Circus tube. **Open** 5pm-4am daily. **Main courses** £7-£48. **Credit** MC, V. **Map** p406 W3 ⓾
A Chinatown stalwart. The lengthy Anglo-Cantonese menu has all the familiar dishes, plus some more esoteric concoctions. The decor is a bit rough around the edges, especially in the basement, and there is often a long wait for a table, but the very late hours are some compensation.

New World
1 Gerrard Place, Chinatown, W1D 5PA (7734 0396). Leicester Square or Piccadilly Circus tube. **Open** 11am-11.45pm Mon-Sat; 11am-11pm Sun. **Main courses** £5-£11. **Credit** AmEx, DC, MC, V. **Map** p406 W3 ⓾
One of Chinatown's most popular dim sum venues – not for the rather average food or the indifferent service, but for its trolley service, a disappearing custom that allows diners to glimpse dishes before they order. Reasonable prices too.

Yauatcha
15 Broadwick Street, Soho, W1F 0DL (7494 8888). Leicester Square, Oxford Circus, Piccadilly Circus or Tottenham Court Road tube. **Open** 11am-11.45pm Mon-Sat; 11am-10.45pm Sun. **Dim sum** £3-£27. **Credit** AmEx, MC, V. **Map** p406 V2 ⓾
Alan Yau's Michelin-starred Yauatcha is still shockingly popular. At dinnertime you have to fight through crowds waiting in the small space inside the entrance to reach the basement restaurant, which is a cacophony of music and media chat. Once there you can eat excellent dim sum (served until late into the evening), a small range of main courses or first-class pâtisserie. Decor blends cool minimalism with the ranked jars of a traditional Chinese teahouse.

Pizza

Spiga
84-86 Wardour Street, Soho, W1V 3LF (7734 3444/ www.vpmg.net). Leicester Square, Piccadilly Circus or Tottenham Court Road tube. **Open** noon-11pm Mon, Tue; noon-midnight Wed-Sat. **Main courses** £8-£18. **Credit** AmEx, MC, V. **Map** p406 W3 ⓾
Spiga's stablemates in the Vince Power Music Group include style bars and music venues. There are no musicians or DJs at this classy pizzeria, but a light jazz soundtrack accompanies casual daytime dining and picks up for the buzzier evening crowd. Modern decor, booth seating, a small bar and smart, black-clad Italian staff provide the good looks; food is well presented and competently put together.

Spanish

Barrafina
54 Frith Street, Soho, W1D 4SL (7813 8016/www. barrafina.co.uk). Tottenham Court Road tube. **Open** noon-3pm, 5-11pm Mon-Sat. **Tapas** £2-£17. **Credit** AmEx, MC, V. **Map** p406 W2 ⓾
There's an agreeable slickness and bustle about Sam and Eddie Hart's terrific tapas bar. Expect to queue unless you eat outside regular mealtimes, but staff work hard at keeping waiting diners happy, giving them updates on length of wait and plying them with drinks. Once you're seated at the L-shaped counter (which, apart from the open kitchen and grill, is pretty much the whole shebang), the fun really starts – watch the chefs cook squirming molluscs and perfect tortilla. Prices can be steep. *Photo p214.*

British

Rhodes W1

Cumberland, Great Cumberland Place, Marble Arch, W1A 4RF (7479 3737/www.garyrhodes.co.uk). Marble Arch tube. **Open** noon-2.30pm Tue-Fri; 7-10.30pm Tue-Sat. **Main courses** £22.50. *Set menus* £28-£45 3 courses. **Credit** AmEx, MC, V. **Map** p395 F6 ⑤⑧

The restaurant Gary Rhodes 'always dreamed of' – and boy, is it good. A forbidding black door opens on to a darkened cellar-cum-foyer, through which you enter a sparkly world of fun – every table has a Swarovski crystal chandelier. The food is equally stunning; not as flag-waving as you'd expect from the man who started the British food renaissance, but local ingredients are treated with light brilliance. **Other locations** Rhodes Twenty Four, Tower 42, Old Broad Street, the City, EC2N 1HQ (7877 7703/www.rhodes24.co.uk).

Cafés & brasseries

La Fromagerie

2-6 Moxon Street, Marylebone, W1U 4EW (7935 0341/www.lafromagerie.co.uk). Baker Street or Bond Street tube. **Open** 10.30am-7.30pm Mon; 8am-7.30pm Tue-Fri; 9am-7pm Sat; 10am-6pm Sun. **Main courses** £6-£12.40. **Credit** AmEx, MC, V. **Map** p398 G5 ⑤⑨

It's all about the ingredients in the 'tasting café' of this gourmet shop. The attractively skylit space is packed at weekends, when foodies and shoppers cram the central communal table. The cheese plate dominates a daily changing menu with selections from the walk-in cheese room (you can also take out), but don't ignore the house ploughman's: the pork and veal pie comes from the fine butcher next door. **Other locations** 30 Highbury Park, Highbury, N5 2AA (7359 7440).

Fish & chips

Golden Hind

73 Marylebone Lane, Marylebone, W1U 2PN (7486 3644). Bond Street tube. **Open** noon-3pm Mon-Fri; 6-10pm Mon-Sat. **Main courses** £5-£10.70. **Credit** AmEx, MC, V. **Map** p398 G5 ⑥⑩

Run by a group of Greek guys, this café-style chippie – established in 1914 – has the feel of a traditional English gaff, despite a couple of Greek touches on the menu. The small, no-frills dining room is blessed with a fabulous 1950s fish fryer (no longer in use); the place gets packed out by locals, drawn by reliable grub at cheap-for-the-area prices.

Cultured cafés

We were saddened in the winter of 2007 by the closure of classic 1950s café, the New Piccadilly. The food was nothing special, but those waiters' uniforms, the bright yellow Formica... Don't despair, though: London currently has a wealth of fine cafés.

Winner of our Best Coffee Bar award in 2007, bright, simply decorated **Fernandez & Wells** (see p202; pictured) is one of the newest. The staff here seem to enjoy what they're doing – you can tell from little touches of care, like bringing, unasked, a glass of water with your espresso. **Nordic Bakery** (see p203) is a more contemplative place, serving open sandwiches that feature a lot of cured salmon and classic Swedish Tosca cake.

Three floors up in a branch of sportswear chain wouldn't be our first place to look for a coffee bar, but that's where **Bullet** (see p201) serves its expert espressos, along with snacks and pies that are a cut above the average. It's perfect for a rest after Long Acre shopping.

There are also fantastic places for tea. The gourmet should head straight to **Tea Smith** (see p217) or **Postcard Teas** (see p254). For nostalgists, there's **Shipp's** (see p195), while **Maison Bertaux** (see p202) with its stern matriarch remains a Soho essential. And connoisseurs of the classic café are not entirely bereft – **E Pellicci** (see p217) and **Alpino's** (see p214) are both superb.

Global

Providores & Tapa Room

*109 Marylebone High Street, Marylebone, W1U 4RX
(7935 6175/www.theprovidores.co.uk). Baker Street
or Bond Street tube.* **Open** *Providores* noon-2.45pm,
6-10.30pm Mon-Sat; noon-2.45pm, 6-10pm Sun. *Tapa
Room* 9-10.30am, noon-10.30pm Mon-Fri; 10am-3pm,
4-10.30pm Sat; 4-10pm Sun. **Mains** £18-£25. *Tapas*
£2-£14. **Credit** AmEx, MC, V. **Map** p398 G5 **61**
Executive chef and co-owner Peter Gordon's fusion
cooking (South-east Asia meets New Zealand)
remains an inspiration. The up-tempo Tapa Room
is a buzzy drop-in for the pretty and privileged, who
enjoy refined, complex tapas, while the more grown-
up Providores upstairs serves even more fiendishly
complicated food. Yet each dish is precisely balanced.

Italian

Locanda Locatelli

*8 Seymour Street, W1H 7JZ (7935 9088/www.
locandalocatelli.com). Marble Arch tube.* **Open**
noon-3pm, 6.45-11pm Mon-Sat; noon-3.30pm, 6.45-
10pm Sun. **Main courses** £19-£30. **Credit** AmEx,
MC, V. **Map** p398 G6 **62**
Giorgio Locatelli has won numerous accolades for
the impossibly high quality of his regional Italian
food, and his kitchen team shows no sign of slacking. The 1970s lounge atmosphere of the dining room
feels louche and glamorous, although service can be
rushed (two sittings are squeezed into the evening).

Middle Eastern

Fairuz

*3 Blandford Street, Marylebone, W1U 3DA (7486
8108/8182/www.fairuz.uk.com). Baker Street or
Bond Street tube.* **Open** noon-11.30pm Mon-Sat;
noon-11pm Sun. **Main courses** £10.95-£18.95.
Credit AmEx, MC, V. **Map** p398 G5 **63**
Fairuz distinguishes itself from London's other top-
tier Lebanese restaurants with a very different vibe.
Instead of the usual smart-international look, it
resembles a generic Med-taverna, with rough white
walls and a fold-back frontage for fine weather. It's
a relaxed, pleasant spot, although tables are packed
quite tight. Food is excellent. Book for dinner.

Paddington & Notting Hill

Cafés & brasseries

Café García

*246 Portobello Road, Ladbroke Grove, W11 1LL
(7221 6119/www.cafegarcia.co.uk). Ladbroke Grove
tube.* **Open** 9am-5pm daily. **Tapas** £1-£5. **Credit**
AmEx, MC, V.
Shrewd Portobello Market shoppers nip into Garcia
for lunch. The café arm of the Spanish groceries
importer is hard to beat for hot or cold tapas, pastries

or a quick coffee. The bright, modern eaterie is often
peaceful and quiet, even when the market is bustling
– surprising, given the high standard of food.

Fish

Geales

*2 Farmer Street, Notting Hill, W8 7SN (7727 7528/
www.geales.com). Notting Hill Gate tube.* **Open** 6-
11pm Mon; noon-2.30pm, 6-11pm Tue-Fri; noon-11pm
Sat; noon-2.30pm, 6-10.30pm Sun. **Main courses**
£9-£14. **Credit** AmEx, MC, V. **Map** p395 A7 **64**
This long-time favourite local chippie (est 1939)
always had aspirations, and new owners have
turned it into a suave fish restaurant. Its roots
haven't been forgotten: the ketchup comes in jugs
rather than squeezy bottles, but the core of the
menu is fish in batter, with grilled or fried specials
from Devon and Cornwall, and they've retained the
original cover charge (15p!). *Photo p217.*

French

Ledbury

*127 Ledbury Road, Westbourne Grove, W11 2AQ
(7792 9090/www.theledbury.com). Westbourne Park
tube.* **Open** noon-2pm, 6.30-10.15pm Mon-Fri; noon-
3pm, 6.30-10.15pm Sat, Sun. **Set meals** £19-£50.
Credit AmEx, MC, V. **Map** p394 A6 **65**
The tone is set by plush parquet and swish leather
seats, with drapes for intimacy and mirrors to create a sense of space. Try to forget the £50 price tag
on the set dinner and feel the depth of the menu: fine
seasonal ingredients, ravishing presentation, a dash
of Ferran Adrià technology, and sublime flavours.

Gastropubs

Cow

*89 Westbourne Park Road, Westbourne Grove,
W2 5QH (7221 0021/www.thecowlondon.co.uk).
Royal Oak or Westbourne Park tube.* **Open** noon-
11pm Mon-Thur; noon-midnight Fri, Sat; noon-
10.30pm Sun. **Main courses** £9-£19. **Credit**
MC, V. **Map** p394 B5 **66**
The Cow is to Notting Hill as Aberdeen Angus is to
prime beef: one of the best breeds in its field. The
room above the pub is a pocket-sized, 1950s retro-
Irish restaurant. Although the menu specialises in
oysters, there's real finesse in starters ranging from
new-season garlic leaf soup to sublimely simple
scallops with herbs and tomatoes. It isn't cheap –
but, for the time being, there are no mains over £20.

Global

Mandalay

*444 Edgware Road, W2 1EG (7258 3696/www.
mandalayway.com). Edgware Road tube.* **Open** noon-
2.30pm, 6-10.30pm Mon-Sat. **Main courses** £3.90-
£6.90. **Credit** AmEx, DC, MC, V. **Map** p395 D4 **67**

Eat, Drink, Shop

Untarnished by a decade of success, with laudable lack of greed, the friendly Ali family (from Burma via Norway) refuse to hike prices or to dilute recipes. London's sole Burmese restaurant still operates from this 28-seater room, rudimentary but pepped up with etchings and travel posters. Expect an exciting mix of Thai, Indian and Chinese influences.

Italian

Assaggi

1st floor, 39 Chepstow Place, Bayswater, W2 4TS (7792 5501). Bayswater, Queensway or Notting Hill Gate tube. **Open** 12.30-2.30pm, 7.30-11pm Mon-Sat. **Main courses** £18-£24. **Credit** MC, V. **Map** p394 B6 ⑱
Renowned for celebrity custom and premium prices, you'll be surprised how informal Assaggi is. Upstairs from a pub, it is decorated in simple, bright colours and the brief menu is purist, but the cooking is superb. Saturday lunch is a good time to visit.

Middle Eastern

Maroush

21 Edgware Road, W2 2JE (7723 0773/www. maroush.com). Marble Arch tube. **Open** noon-2am daily. **Main courses** £14-£22. **Credit** AmEx, DC, MC, V. **Map** p395 F6 ⑲
Marouf Abouzaki launched this flagship Lebanese restaurant in 1981, and has since opened a further five. Here the menu runs to about 60 meze, plus mixed grills, and there's upmarket traditional entertainment (Arabic singers and belly dancers) nightly from 9.30pm. Service is male, besuited and formal, and there's a minimum £41 spend on Friday and Saturday. Café-style, cash-only Ranoush Juice (43 Edgware Road, 7723 5929) stays busy until 3am.

Patogh

8 Crawford Place, Edgware Road, W1H 5NE (7262 4015). Edgware Road tube. **Open** 12.30-11pm daily. **Main courses** £6-£12. **No credit cards**. **Map** p395 E5 ⑳
The Iranian equivalent of a chip shop, with grilled meat and rice in place of battered fish and potatoes. You get immaculately fresh salads, thick aubergine and yoghurt dips, and huge flatbread, hot from the oven. The meat, marinated for hours before cooking, is sensational. Just half a dozen cramped tables mean takeaway is a good option; bring your own alcohol.

Oriental

E&O

14 Blenheim Crescent, Ladbroke Grove, W11 1NN (7229 5454/www.rickerrestaurants.com). Ladbroke Grove or Notting Hill Gate tube. **Open** noon-midnight Mon-Sat; 12.30-11.30pm Sun. **Main courses** £9-£32. **Credit** AmEx, DC, MC, V.
Aussie restaurant whiz Will Ricker opened this Notting Hill celebrity magnet in 2001. Minimalist

and mirror-edged, it's a warm, dark and cosy space, full of lads with Hugh Grant hair and blondes with designer sunglasses pushed up. At night, Perrier Jouët ice buckets perch on tables covered with stylish bowls of edamame, tempura and futomaki rolls.

Piccadilly & Mayfair

Americas

Gaucho Piccadilly

25 Swallow Street, Piccadilly, W1B 4DJ (7734 4040/www.gauchorestaurants.co.uk). Piccadilly Circus tube. **Open** noon-midnight Mon-Sat; noon-11pm Sun. **Main courses** £8-£32. **Credit** AmEx, DC, MC, V. **Map** p406 V5 ⑦
Steakhouse chic is what the Gaucho flagship branch is all about – from its well-stocked Cavas wine shop to a pitch-dark cocktail bar and penchant for cowskin wallpaper and pouffes. The steaks? Good, with the *bife de lomo* (fillet) often outstanding. Service is a touch too slick, but that's the nature of smart chains. A new branch is to open in the O2 (*see p175*) in early 2008.
Other locations throughout the city.

British

Dorchester Grill Room

The Dorchester, 53 Park Lane, Mayfair, W1K 1QA (7629 8888/www.thedorchester.com). Hyde Park Corner tube. **Open** 7-10.30am, noon-2.30pm, 6.30-10.30pm Mon-Fri; 8-11am, noon-2.30pm, 6-11pm Sat;

Good, simple, **Hummus Bros**. *See p203.*

8-11am, 12.30-3pm, 7-10pm Sun. **Main courses** £19-£35. **Credit** AmEx, DC, MC, V. **Map** p400 G7 **72**
Brace yourself. Many-hued tartans cover every surface except the walls, which have strident murals of Scots. The cheerfully excessive decor was inspired by the grill room's signature ingredients – Aberdeen Angus beef, carved at the table from a domed trolley, and smoked salmon. Dress smart casual and be sure to book at weekends.

Cafés & brasseries

Parlour
1st floor, Fortnum & Mason, 181 Piccadilly, W1A 1ER (7734 8040/www.fortnumandmason.co.uk). Green Park or Piccadilly Circus tube. **Open** 10am-6pm Mon-Sat. **Credit** AmEx, MC, V. **Map** p406 V4 **73**
A celebration of sugar and spice and all things ice. The walls look like undulating layers of chocolate and vanilla, the counter is a pink and white mosaic. Floats, sundaes, cakes, shakes and ice-cream cocktails are the focus. You should expect to pay £25 for sundaes and coffee for two, but you get to enjoy them in an interior designed by David Collins.

Fish

Bentley's Oyster Bar & Grill
11-15 Swallow Street, Piccadilly, W1B 4DG (7734 4756/www.bentleysoysterbarandgrill.co.uk). Piccadilly Circus tube. **Open** *Oyster Bar* noon-midnight Mon-Sat; noon-10pm Sun. *Restaurant* noon-3pm, 6-11pm Mon-Sat; noon-3pm, 6-10pm Sun. **Main courses** £8-£38. **Credit** AmEx, MC, V. **Map** p406 V4 **74**
Irish chef Richard Corrigan (of the famous Lindsay House; *see p202*) relaunched this old-timer a couple of years ago, and it's been a great success. In the same lovely Victorian building for more than 90 years, the ground-floor oyster bar is more relaxed; there's also a smarter first-floor grill, with oak floor and crisp linen. Prices are Mayfair, but the food is first-rate.

French

La Petite Maison
54 Brooks Mews, Mayfair, W1K 4EG (7495 4774). Bond Street tube. **Open** noon-3pm, 7-11.30pm Mon-Sat. **Main courses** £9-£35. **Credit** AmEx, MC, V. **Map** p400 H6 **75**
Imported from a Nice original by the boss of Zuma (*see p214*) and Roka (*see p200*), La Petite Maison serves dishes to share, tapas-style – maybe courgette flowers or anchovies deep-fried with sage. There's not much space, but the linen curtains and frosted glass block out the ugly road and draw in daylight.

Indian

Tamarind
20-22 Queen Street, Mayfair, W1J 5PR (7629 3561/ www.tamarindrestaurant.com). Green Park tube.

Open noon-2.45pm, 6-11.30pm Mon-Fri; 6-11.30pm Sat; noon-2.45pm, 6-10.30pm Sun. **Main courses** £16-£28. **Credit** AmEx, DC, MC, V. **Map** p400 H7 **76**
The large basement interior is looking scuffed – despite a nouveau riche gilding and bronzing refurb a few years back – but a lily lies beneath. Chef Alfred Prasad produces consistently excellent north and south Indian dishes. Prices are high, but the food is great and the service friendly and attentive.

Japanese

Yoshino
3 Piccadilly Place, Piccadilly, W1J 0DB (7287 6622/ www.yoshino.net). Piccadilly Circus tube. **Open** noon-9pm Mon-Sat. **Set meals** £5.80-£19.80. **Credit** AmEx, MC, V. **Map** p406 V4 **77**
Maybe it's the waitresses' long, white aprons; maybe it's the clean, cool interior; maybe it's just the careful preparation that goes into the food – somehow Yoshino manages to feel posher than its prices suggest. The fully explained dinner list mainly comprises bentos and some à la carte sushi.

Modern European

Le Gavroche
43 Upper Brook Street, Mayfair, W1K 7QR (7408 0881/www.le-gavroche.co.uk). Marble Arch tube. **Open** noon-2pm, 6.30-11pm Mon-Fri; 6.30-11pm Sat. **Main courses** £27-£40. **Credit** AmEx, DC, MC, V. **Map** p400 G7 **78**
Le Gavroche is something special (and pricey – the minimum spend for dinner is £60 a head). We've yet to visit and not see wonder-chef Michel Roux Jr and manager Silvano hard at work, meaning the food is incredible: complex, fresh and cooked to split-second perfection. There's also a dizzying quantity of front-of-house staff – many restaurants achieve good service, but here it's amazing, with your every move not just catered for, but predicted.

Maze
13-15 Grosvenor Square, Mayfair, W1K 6JP (7107 0000/www.gordonramsay.com). Bond Street tube. **Open** noon-midnight daily. **Main courses** £16-£30. **Credit** AmEx, DC, MC, V. **Map** p400 G7 **79**
Sat lazily on a sunny afternoon, martini in hand, surrounded by buff leather, zebrano wood and lustrous glass panels, gazing out across the canopy of plane trees – you might conclude that Maze has one of London's loveliest locations. The name on the door is Gordon Ramsay, but the kitchen belongs to Jason Atherton: a man with a similar god complex and eye for perfection. You're free to order as much or as little as you like of the perfect tapas – a real treat.

St Alban
4-12 Regent Street, Piccadilly, SW1Y 4PE (7499 8558/www.stalban.net). Piccadilly Circus tube. **Open** noon-3pm, 5.30pm-midnight Mon-Sat; noon-3pm, 5.30-11pm Sun. **Main courses** £9.25-£26. **Credit** AmEx, DC, MC, V. **Map** p406 W4 **80**

Eat, Drink, Shop

At night this is a sleek, space-age restaurant, with big artworks and curvy white fittings. Owned by Chris Corbin and Jeremy King, of Wolseley fame (*see p211*), St Alban concentrates on mod Mediterranean food, with very reasonable prices for this level of cooking. It's the detail that counts: interesting breads and grissini with glorious olive oil; beautifully chewy mini-macaroons accompany the coffee; staff who are ultra-attentive without being bothersome.

Sketch
9 Conduit Street, Mayfair, W1S 2XZ (0870 777 4488/ www.sketch.uk.com). Oxford Circus tube. **Open** noon-2.30pm, 7-10.30pm Tue-Fri; 7-10.30pm Sat. **Main courses** £12-£59. **Credit** AmEx, DC, MC, V. **Map** p406 U3 **③①**
Of the three bits of Pierre Gagnaire's legendarily expensive Sketch – including extravagant destination dining at the Gallery and the Lecture Room's haute-beyond-haute cuisine – the Glade is the most egalitarian. The lunchtime brasserie (in which, horrors, the staff wear jeans) threatens to jar with Sketch's finely honed sensibilities, but the menus are appropriately artful and not unreasonably priced for the quality. But nothing can prepare you for the loos, each housed in a gleaming white egg.

Wild Honey
12 St George Street, Mayfair, W1S 2FB (7758 9160). Oxford Circus or Bond Street tube. **Open** noon-2.30pm, 5.30-10.30pm Mon-Sat; 12.30-3.30pm, 5.30-9.30pm Sun. **Set meals** £15-£18. **Credit** AmEx, MC, V. **Map** p398 H6 **③②**
Anthony Demetre and Will Smith, owners of Arbutus (*see p203*), have the magic touch. Winner of our 2007 award for Best New Restaurant, Wild Honey feels very different from the Soho original – this is a deeply convivial oak-panelled space that's subtly modern and just made for lingering. But the alluring combination of exceptionally good food at fair prices (especially for the set lunch) and a user-friendly wine list are the same. Booking essential.

Wolseley
160 Piccadilly, W1J 9EB (7499 6996/www. thewolseley.com). Green Park tube. **Open** 7am-midnight Mon-Fri; 8am-midnight Sat; noon-11pm Sun. **Main courses** £7-£30. **Credit** AmEx, DC, MC, V. **Map** p406 U5 **③③**
The Wolseley has the commodity money can't buy: glamour. It emanates from the gorgeous 1920s room, the battalions of waiters, and the sense that everyone in here (yourself included) could be in a 1950s film. The European grand-café schtick means a variety of eating and drinking options are offered here: crustacea and caviar, cocktails and coffee, breakfast and dinner and sundaes. Fabulous for afternoon tea.

North African

Momo
25 Heddon Street, Mayfair, W1B 4BH (7434 4040/ www.momoresto.com). Piccadilly Circus tube. **Open**
noon-2.30pm, 6.30-11pm Mon-Sat; 6.30-10.30pm Sun. **Main courses** £13-£23. **Credit** AmEx, DC, MC, V. **Map** p406 U3 **③④**
London's most high-profile Moroccan restaurant celebrated its tenth anniversary in 2007 with one hell of a party. But most nights here are a party, thanks to sexy decor, even sexier staff and excellent music. The food's not bad either. Moroccan isn't the most sophisticated of cuisines, but here it seems exotic: think wood pigeon pastilla dusted with a star-and-crescent design in icing sugar. Booking at weekends.

Oriental

Nobu
1st floor, the Metropolitan, 19 Old Park Lane, Mayfair, W1K 1LB (7447 4747/www.nobu restaurants.com). Hyde Park Corner tube. **Open** noon-2.15pm, 6-10.15pm Mon-Thur; noon-2.15pm, 6-11pm Fri, Sat; 12.30-2.30pm, 6-9.30pm Sun. **Main courses** £3-£30. **Credit** AmEx, DC, MC, V. **Map** p400 H8 **③⑤**
Nobu is no longer the celeb-magnet it used to be, but the modern Japanese dishes still dazzle. Service (charged at 15%) is charming and the restaurant is even quite child-friendly during the day. Panoramic views over Hyde Park give you something to gaze at even when the famous people fail to show up. **Other locations** 15 Berkeley Street, Mayfair, W1J 8DY (7290 9222); Ubon, 34 Westferry Circus, Canary Wharf, Docklands, E14 8RR (7719 7800).

Westminster & St James's

British

Inn The Park
St James's Park, St James's, SW1A 2BJ (7451 9999/ www.innthepark.com). St James's Park tube. **Open** 8am-9pm Mon-Fri; 9am-9pm Sat, Sun. **Main courses** £14-£23. **Credit** AmEx, MC, V. **Map** p401 K8 **③⑥**
Oliver Peyton's all-day lakeside 'café' has everything going for it: a stunning park location; a beautiful, flowing modern building; and a nicely varied British menu. There are famous poached egg and soldiers breakfasts and a summer barbecue (on the long terrace until 9pm); the à la carte isn't always so reliable.

National Dining Rooms
Sainsbury Wing, National Gallery, Trafalgar Square, WC2N 5DN (7747 2525/www.national gallery.co.uk). Charing Cross tube/rail. **Open** 10am-5.30pm Mon, Tue, Thur-Sun; 10am-8.30pm Wed. **Set meals** £17.50 1 course; £24.50 2 courses; £29.50 3 courses. **Credit** AmEx, MC, V. **Map** p407 X5 **③⑦**
Winner of our Best British Restaurant award in 2007, the National Dining Rooms has a slightly institutional feel, but don't be put off: the food is individual, delicate and inspiring. This is another Oliver Peyton restaurant, and in culinary terms his best. There's a prix fixe of great finesse, as well as afternoon tea, a bar menu and a counter of pies, tarts

Eat, Drink, Shop

What a source

There are certain questions restaurant-goers rarely ask, although they'd like to. Questions like 'did this meat live on antibiotics in a concrete bunker or graze a daisy-strewn pasture?' 'Was this fish farmed or caught wild?' 'Were these vegetables grown in Ghana or just down the road?' risk an unsympathetic response. Thank goodness, then, for the new breed of restaurants and foodsellers that believe in ethical sourcing and sustainable housekeeping. **Acorn House** restaurant (*see p200*; *pictured*) works tirelessly to an environmentally sound agenda, using green electricity, recycling packaging, composting waste and training young apprentices to be eco-restaurateurs. Admirable restraint is demonstrated in keeping to a seasonal menu with local ingredients, where possible. Nothing has been air-freighted to your plate. Cheeses, meats, fruits and vegetables come from independent suppliers; fish is bought according to Marine Conservation Society guidelines. So popular has the little Acorn grown that a new offshoot, the **Waterhouse**, is due to bloom in Hoxton (Canalside Works, Orsman Road, N1 5QJ) as we go to press.

The regeneration of the King's Cross area has encouraged a veritable green revolution. A short walk away from Acorn House is **Konstam at the Prince Albert** (*see p199*), which exploded on to restaurant critcs' collective consciousness in spring 2006 when its proprietor, Oliver Rowe declared that every foodstuff served here would be sourced within reach of the tube network. So Rowe uses beef from Harefield, honey from Tower Hill and pigeon from Amersham. Just up the road in Islington another public house works organic wonders. The **Duke of Cambridge** (*see p215*) was the first Soil Association certified organic pub. Its proprietor was recyling waste ten years ago, and it now proudly publicises its use of renewable energy suppliers and the dearth of air-freighted ingredients in its food.

It's not just a north London thing, this thirst for knowledge. **Borough Market** (*see p255*), the ancient market turned premier-league purveyor of fine foodstuffs, is darling of countless celebrity chefs because all the stallholders are happy to talk provenance. If you're passionate about sources, Borough has the ultimate in traceable comestibles.

and cakes. The National Café (7747 2525, www.thenationalcafe.com), a relaxed café-brasserie facing St Martin's church from the East Wing, stays open until 11pm, except on Sunday. *See also p219* **Best of British**.

Cafés & brasseries

Brilliantly located, **Inn The Park** and the **National Dining Rooms** do light bites and good afternoon teas. The **National Café** in the National Gallery's East Wing, another of Oliver Peyton's excellent establishments, stays open until 11pm on most days of the week. For all three, *see p211*.

Indian

Cinnamon Club
The Old Westminster Library, 30-32 Great Smith Street, Westminster, SW1P 3BU (7222 2555/www.cinnamonclub.com). St James's Park or Westminster tube. **Open** 7.30-9.30am, noon-12.30pm, 6-10.45pm Mon-Sat. **Main courses** £11-£29. **Credit** AmEx, DC, MC, V. **Map** p401 K9 ⬛
Destination of choice for power brokers and politicians, Cinnamon Club's spacious dining hall has the feel of a grand colonial club. The modern Indian food runs from dressed-up rustic staples to regal stalwarts, while the Indian-themed breakfasts are a great alternative to the hotel buffet.

Chelsea

Cafés & brasseries

Tom's Kitchen

27 Cale Street, SW3 3QP (7349 0202/www.toms kitchen.co.uk). South Kensington or Sloane Square tube. **Open** 7-10am, noon-3pm, 6pm-midnight Mon-Fri; 10am-3pm, 6pm-midnight Sat; 11am-3pm, 6pm-midnight Sun. **Main courses** £14-£25. **Credit** AmEx, MC, V. **Map** p397 E11 ⑱

Tom is acclaimed young British chef Tom Aikens, who runs his own haute cuisine restaurant not far from here (43 Elystan Street, 7584 2003, www.tom aikens.co.uk). This is his simpler, cheaper restaurant for the well-groomed Chelsea masses. With a big skylight and a marble counter (behind which you can see the chefs), it's an attractive space – though noisy. The menu is a crowd-pleasing mix of British and French, with plenty of meat alongside the likes of lemon sole 'à la française' and macaroni cheese.

Indian

Chutney Mary

535 King's Road, SW10 0SZ (7351 3113/www.real indianfood.com). Fulham Broadway tube/11, 22 bus. **Open** 6.30-11pm Mon-Fri; 12.30-2.30pm, 6.30-11pm Sat; 12.30-3pm, 6.30-10.30pm Sun. **Main courses** £14-£31. **Credit** AmEx, DC, MC, V. **Map** p396 C13 ⑳

One of the first restaurants to celebrate pairing wine with Indian cuisine, Chutney Mary – run by the Panjabi sisters, also behind Amaya (*see below*) and Masala Zone (*see p201*) – is innovative and classy. Smartly attired Americans, well-off Chelsea diners and youngish couples eat the likes of nihari shorba, a sublime cardamom-scented meaty broth, sealed under crisp golden puff pastry. There's a jazz lunch here on Sundays.

Modern European

Bluebird

350 King's Road, SW3 5UU (7559 1000/www. danddlondon.com). Sloane Square tube then 11, 19, 22, 49, 319 bus. **Open** *Bar* noon-midnight Mon-Thur; noon-1am Fri, Sat; noon-11.30pm Sun. *Restaurant* 12.30-2.30pm, 6-11pm Mon-Fri; noon-3.30pm, 6-11pm Sat; noon-3.30pm, 6-10pm Sun. **Main courses** £13-£25. **Credit** AmEx, DC, MC, V. **Map** p397 D12 ⑳

A cunning Conran conversion of a wonderful art deco garage into a food market, brasserie and fine-dining restaurant. Under new management, Bluebird unveiled a new look last year: the restaurant and bar now occupy a single, glorious upper room (not to be confused with the less formal ground-floor café, which has pleasant tables out-doors on the old forecourt). Service is bouncy and the user-friendly menu has been given a boost with an emphasis on local producers.

Knightsbridge & South Kensington

Fish

Olivomare

10 Lower Belgrave Street, Belgravia, SW1W 0LJ (7730 9022). Victoria tube/rail. **Open** noon-2.30pm, 7-11pm Mon-Sat. **Main courses** £14-£19. **Credit** AmEx, DC, MC, V. **Map** p400 H10 ⑫

A vision in white, gleaming even when the lights dim for dinner, this is one sleek restaurant. The food, a happy marriage of Sardinian recipes, fish and seafood, looks a treat; rustic in origin, it's served in a very suave fashion. Staff are charming, but if you're not a Euro-banker, you may feel the odd one out.

French

Racine

239 Brompton Road, Knightsbridge, SW3 2EP (7584 4477). Knightsbridge or South Kensington tube/14, 74 bus. **Open** noon-3pm, 6-10.30pm Mon-Sat; 6-10pm Sun. **Main courses** £12-£21. **Credit** AmEx, MC, V. **Map** p397 E10 ⑬

Push aside the heavy velvet curtains shielding the entrance door and you enter a lost world. Well-padded gents and their female consorts, Francophile and Francophone alike, revel in bourgeois French cooking and the timeless atmosphere. Try the likes of calves' brains with black butter and capers.

Indian

Amaya

19 Motcomb Street, Halkin Arcade, Knightsbridge, SW1X 8JT (7823 1166/www.realindianfood.com). Knightsbridge tube. **Open** 12.30-2.15pm, 6.30-11.15pm Mon-Sat; 12.45-2.30pm, 6.30-10.15pm Sun. **Main courses** £8-£25. **Credit** AmEx, DC, MC, V. **Map** p400 G9 ⑭

Darkly seductive decor with sparkly chandeliers and striking terracotta statues attracts a mix of expense-accounters and couples on that special date. An open counter means you can watch the chefs draw kebabs from clay ovens, glide sizzling patties across skillets, and spear meat on to skewers. A dressy Indian spin on the tapas formula.

Oriental

Nahm

The Halkin, Halkin Street, Belgravia, SW1X 7DJ (7333 1234/www.nahm.como.bz). Hyde Park Corner tube. **Open** noon-2.30pm, 7-10.45pm Mon-Fri; 7-10.45pm Sat; 7-9.45pm Sun. **Main courses** £11-£17. **Set meals** £26-£55. **Credit** AmEx, DC, MC, V. **Map** p400 G9 ⑮

David Thompson may not always be in the kitchen, but the influence of the master of Thai cooking at this quiet, understated hotel dining room is as strong as ever. Recently, he has revamped lunch to include more 'street food' – not that street food ever looked like this before. Appetisers of *ma hor* (minced prawns and chicken simmered in palm sugar) on fruit slices exemplify his distinctive style. Thai food is rarely this thrilling.

Zuma

5 Raphael Street, Knightsbridge, SW7 1DL (7584 1010/www.zumarestaurant.com). Knightsbridge tube. **Open** *Bar* noon-11pm Mon-Fri; 12.30-11pm Sat; noon-10pm Sun. *Restaurant* noon-2.15pm, 6-10.45pm Mon-Fri; 12.30-3.15pm, 6-10.45pm Sat; 12.30-2.45pm, 6-10.15pm Sun. **Main courses** £15-£70. **Credit** AmEx, DC, MC, V. **Map** p397 F9
Still one of the most exciting spots for dining and schmoozing, with a clientele of model types and their swains wearing designer gear they expect others to notice. From the robata grill, the barbecued tuna with umeboshi sauce and grilled veg is typically innovative – despite the 'modern izakaya' tag, this is high-end dining. Zuma also has one of the best saké lists in town, complete with saké sommelier. The two-hour sittings are strictly enforced.

Barrafina. *See p205.*

North London

African/Caribbean

Queen of Sheba

12 Fortess Road, Kentish Town, NW5 2EU (7284 3947/www.thequeenofsheba.co.uk). Kentish Town tube/rail. **Open** 6-11.30pm Mon-Sat; 1-10pm Sun. **Main courses** £5-£11. **Credit** MC, V.
Plain pale walls offset by assorted artefacts give little hint of the delights to come at this charming Ethiopian restaurant, where platters lined with injera (sourdough flatbread) come piled high with delicious meat or vegetarian selections, elegantly served under a tagine-shaped basket. Delicious food and loud funky music make for a cheerful night out.

Cafés & brasseries

Alpino's

97 Chapel Market, Islington, N1 9EY (7837 8330). Angel tube. **Open** 7am-4pm Mon-Fri; 7am-5pm Sat. **Main courses** around £5. **No credit cards. Map** p402 N2 ⑰
Founded in 1959, this popular local has held on to every ounce of its character. The plum-patterned cup and saucer sets alone are perfection, but fine booth seating, teak-veneer Formica and glorious lamp holders make the place a classic, especially in an area so heavily Starbucked. *See p206* **Cultured cafés.**

Haché

24 Inverness Street, Camden, NW1 7HJ (7485 9100/ www.hacheburgers.com). Camden Town tube. **Open** noon-10.30pm Mon-Sat; noon-10pm Sun. **Main courses** £5.95-£11.95. **Credit** AmEx, MC, V.

Haché is a cosy bistro-style restaurant specialising in superior burgers: good-quality Ayrshire steaks, chopped, grilled and served in ciabatta-like buns; the superiority of the meat compared to most rivals is undeniable. Sides too are a cut above – the fruit smoothies were delicious.

Ottolenghi

287 Upper Street, Islington, N1 2TZ (7288 1454/ www.ottolenghi.co.uk). Angel tube/Highbury & Islington tube/rail. **Open** 8am-10.30pm Mon-Sat; 9am-7pm Sun. **Main courses** £8-£14. **Credit** AmEx, MC, V. **Map** p402 O1 ⑱
Ottolenghi is a treat, with food to die for. Nothing here feels laboured, from the cool, minimalistic white furniture to the stylish but friendly staff. Seating is mainly at long, shared tables, but there are some small, solitary tables for those *à deux*. The place doubles as a bakery and deli, so after mains go and swoon over the cakes and tarts at the front counter.

S&M Café

4-6 Essex Road, Islington, N1 8LN (7359 5361/ www.sandmcafe.co.uk). Angel tube. **Open** 7.30am-11pm Mon-Fri; 8.30am-11pm Sat; 8.30am-10.30pm Sun. **Main courses** £6-£8. **Credit** MC, V. **Map** p402 O1 ⑲
A good balance between caff and trendy diner, S&M (that's sausage and mash) serves everyone from celebs to bricklayers. You can 'mix & mash' from ten sausages (including pork, chicken, vegetarian and gluten-free varieties), four types of mash and three of gravy. This branch has preserved features of the original Alfredo's café (which featured in *Quadrophenia*); the shopfront is an art deco classic.
Other locations 48 Brushfield Street, Spitalfields, E1 6AG (7247 2252); North Greenwich Centre, Peninsula Square, SE10 0DX (8305 1940); 268 Portobello Road, Ladbroke Grove, W10 5TY (8968 8898).

French

Morgan M

*489 Liverpool Road, Islington, N7 8NS (7609 3560/
www.morganm.com). Highbury & Islington tube/rail.*
Open 7-10pm Tue, Sat; noon-2.30pm, 7-10pm Wed-
Fri; noon-2.30pm Sun. **Set meals** £19-£43. **Credit**
DC, MC, V.
After so many overhyped but essentially ordinary
restaurants, it's a delight to find one that delivers.
Morgan Meunier's cooking is supremely skilful;
painstakingly intricate but without just-to-impress
gestures, producing multiple layers of subtle flavours.
Meunier is also known for his vegetarian creations:
there's an all-vegetarian menu. The wine list is on a
par with the food, the service utterly charming.

Gastropubs

Duke of Cambridge

*30 St Peter's Street, Islington, N1 8JT (7359 3066/
www.dukeorganic.co.uk). Angel tube.* **Open** noon-
11pm Mon-Sat; noon-10.30pm Sun. **Main courses**
£10-£18. **Credit** AmEx, MC, V. **Map** p402 O2 ⓿
In the decade since the Duke of Cambridge opened,
demand has soared for organic food (*see p212* **What
a source**). But aside from the conversion of the garden into a conservatory (a calm contrast to the loud
and busy front room), this all-organic gastropub
remains largely unchanged.

Marquess Tavern

*32 Canonbury Street, Islington, N1 2TB (7354 2975/
www.themarquesstavern.co.uk). Angel tube/Highbury
& Islington tube/rail.* **Open** 5-11pm Mon-Thur; 5pm-
midnight Fri; noon-midnight Sat; noon-11pm Sun.
Main courses £12-£17. **Credit** AmEx, MC, V.
The front half of the Marquess is a pub-like bar, with
great beer; the rear is a bright, glass-roofed dining
room. Simple British cooking is the aim, which is
admirably accomplished. This is one of the few
venues conscientious enough to note vintage changes
on the wine list, typical of its attention to detail.

Modern European

Odette's

*130 Regent's Park Road, Chalk Farm, NW1 8XL
(7586 8569/www.vpmg.net). Chalk Farm tube/31,
168, 274 bus.* **Open** 7-11pm Mon; 12.30-2.30pm,
7-11pm Tue-Sat; 12.30-2.30pm Sun. **Main courses**
£15-£23. **Credit** AmEx, MC, V.
Music venue impresario Vince Power has made
some striking improvements to this old-timer. The
interior, by Shaun Clarkson, is one example: egg-
yolk yellow leather chairs and banquettes against
white-painted walls in the back room, statement
wallpaper to the front and a dark, moody basement
bar. Bryn Williams cooks like a dream, from delicate
amuses-bouches to utterly delicious petits fours. The
prices (£3.50 for an espresso) are a bit at odds with
the local feel, but you do get haute food and service.

Oriental

Gilgamesh (*see p232*) serves consistent, assured
and sometimes inspired pan-Asian food.

Hi Sushi Salsa

*3A Camden Wharf Waterfront, 28 Jamestown Road,
Camden, NW1 7BY (7482 7088/www.hisushi.net).
Camden Town tube.* **Open** noon-10.30pm Mon-Wed;
noon-11.30pm Thur-Sun. **Main courses** £9-£17. *Set
meals* bento from £10.50. **Credit** AmEx, MC, V.
At this fun new Camden Lock spot – all dark wood
and disco beats – the aim is a fusion of Japanese and
Latin American themes, a concept popularised by
Nobu (*see p211*). The music, from a roster of DJs, is
great (if loud at times) and the outdoor waterfront
seating is an appealing destination on a sunny day.
Other locations throughout the city.

Spanish

Camino

*3 Varnishers Yard, Regents Quarter, King's Cross,
N1 9FD (7841 7331/www.barcamino.com). King's
Cross tube/rail.* **Open** *Bar* noon-midnight Mon-Wed;
noon-1am Thur-Sat. *Restaurant* 8am-3pm, 6.30-11pm
Mon-Fri; 8-11.30am Sat. **Main courses** £10-£20.
Credit AmEx, MC, V. **Map** p399 L3 ⓫
A new venture from the owners of Shoreditch's Cargo
(*see p321*). Rustic stripped wood and cork have been
used to create a clean, contemporary aesthetic that is
as much Spain as London. In the spacious bar and
outdoor courtyard, simple tapas are served; the
restaurant offers a longer menu including fish and
steaks from the charcoal grill. Top-notch.

Vegetarian & organic

The all-vegetarian menu at **Morgan M**
(*see above*) is an unforgettable treat.

Manna

*4 Erskine Road, Primrose Hill, NW3 3AJ (7722
8028/www.manna-veg.com). Chalk Farm tube/31,
168 bus.* **Open** 6.30-11pm Mon-Sat; 12.30-3pm, 6.30-
11pm Sun. **Main courses** £9-£13. **Credit** MC, V.
Taking its cue from the elegant location, Manna has
an easy composure that attracts a relaxed clientele.
Despite occasional blips in execution, details (a
deeply luscious red wine reduction, the intricate
presentation) prove there is real skill at work on the
far-reaching global menu. Safer dishes include the
tortillas and salads, which come piled high.

East London

The steaks at **Hawksmoor** (*see p234*) are
almost as notable as the imaginative cocktails.

Cafés & brasseries

On the Isle of Dogs and in need of a cream tea?
Check out the **Mudchute Kitchen** (*see p275*).

Eat, Drink, Shop

Brick Lane Beigel Bake

159 Brick Lane, E1 6SB (7729 0616). Liverpool Street tube/rail/8 bus. **Open** 24hrs daily. **No credit cards. Map** p403 S4
This charismatic little East End institution rolls out perfect bagels both plain and filled (egg, cream cheese, mountains of salt beef), superb bread and moreish cakes. Even at 3am, fresh baked goods are being pulled from the ovens at the back; no wonder the queue for bagels trails out the door when the innumerable local bars and clubs begin to close.

E Pellicci

332 Bethnal Green Road, Bethnal Green, E2 0AG (7739 4873). Bethnal Green tube/rail/8, 253 bus. **Open** 6.15am-5pm Mon-Sat. **Main courses** £5-£8. **No credit cards.**
This much-loved primrose caff, owned by the Pellicci family for over a century, has played an integral role in the social history of the East End, providing a home-from-home for gangsters (the Krays), artists (Gilbert & George), taxi drivers, local workers and families. The beautiful art deco interior is Grade II-listed: think marquetry panelling, laminate wood tables, framed family portraits and bottles of traditional condiments. Eat proper, good-value fry-ups, traditional English and Italian dishes, sarnies and classic puddings. *See p206* **Cultured cafés.**

Story Deli

3 Dray Walk, Old Truman Brewery, 91 Brick Lane, E1 6QL (7247 3137). Liverpool Street tube/rail. **Open** noon-4pm Mon-Fri; noon-6pm Sat, Sun. **Main courses** £6-£10. **Credit** AmEx, MC, V. **Map** p403 S5
On the corner of the bustling yard of the former brewery, this no-nonsense, 100% organic pizzeria and café makes a welcome break from the nu-rave neon with bags of flour and wooden slabs instead of plates. Lunches focus on pizza with innovative fresh toppings. Most people have a cool juice with their food, but the café also has a licence to serve wine.

Tea Smith

6 Lamb Street, Spitalfields, E1 6EA (7247 1333/ www.teasmith.co.uk). Liverpool Street tube/rail. **Open** 11am-6pm daily. **Teas** from £3.50. **Credit** MC, V. **Map** p403 R5
For tea-drinkers after something special, this little shop and tearoom on the edge of Old Spitalfields Market is a godsend. The interior has a recognisably Japanese aesthetic with simple, clean lines. The owner is a self-confessed tea geek who researched his teas in China and Japan and sources them direct from the Far East – their quality is matched by select accompanying nibbles. *Photo p220.*

French

Bistrotheque

23-27 Wadeson Street, Bethnal Green, E2 9DR (8983 7900/www.bistrotheque.com). Bethnal Green tube/rail/Cambridge Heath rail/55 bus. **Open** *Bar* 6pm-midnight Mon-Sat; 1pm-midnight Sun. *Restaurant* 6.30-10.30pm Mon-Thur; 6.30-11pm Fri; 11am-4pm, 6.30-11pm Sat; 11am-4pm, 6.30-10.30pm Sun. **Main courses** £10-£21. **Credit** AmEx, MC, V.
An all-white warehouse space, with louche cabaret and a classily funky bar, Bistrotheque hits the area's new demographic on the head with its blend of sophistication and streetwise cool. Service is friendly and committed, the relaxed clientele happy with a menu crafted to their whims: cocktails, brunch, grazing dishes, and a good prix fixe (even at weekends).

Les Trois Garçons

1 Club Row, Shoreditch, E1 6JX (7613 1924/www. lestroisgarcons.com). Liverpool Street tube/rail/8, 388 bus. **Open** 7-10pm Mon-Thur; 7-10.30pm Fri, Sat. **Main courses** £18-£32. **Credit** AmEx, DC, MC, V. **Map** p403 S4
Laughing in the face of simplicity with a room Dali might have co-conceived with Miss Havisham (taxidermy in tiaras among the *objets trouvés*), Les Trois Garçons does appropriately bold and complex food, offering technically demanding dishes in artistic (perhaps sometimes pretentious) presentations. Dishes are expensive, but there's a side of glamour with each one. The formal service can be a bit abstracted.

Gastropubs

Gun

27 Coldharbour, Docklands, E14 9NS (7515 5222/ www.thegundocklands.com). Canary Wharf tube/ DLR/South Quay DLR. **Open** 11am-midnight Mon-Fri; 11.30am-midnight Sat; 11.30am-11pm Sun. **Main courses** £11.95-£18. **Credit** AmEx, MC, V.

Geales. *See p207.*

Eat, Drink, Shop

Although this inordinately successful operation tucked down a skinny backstreet qualifies as a gastropub, it's effectively a smartish British restaurant (white tablecloths, subtle cooking, modest service) attached to a local boozer (heavy furniture, Thames-side terrace, roaring fire) with a more informal menu (roast beef sandwich £9.50, fat chips £2.75).

Indian

For years we've recommended visiting **Brick Lane** (*see p162* **Street scene**), just not for the curries – repeated visits have uncovered nothing better than the standard Anglo-Indian curries you find on any British high street. But there are signs of improvement. The formula curry houses are being joined by a few caffs offering proper Bangladeshi dishes, especially at the south end of Brick Lane. We've enjoyed the point-and-order dishes in **Sabuj Bangla** (102 Brick Lane, 7247 6222) and **Ruchi** (303 Whitechapel Road, 7247 6666).

Kolapata

222 Whitechapel Road, Whitechapel, E1 1BJ (7377 1200). Whitechapel tube. **Open** noon-11.30pm daily. **Main courses** £3.95-£8.95. **No credit cards**.
Whitechapel has long had little caffs serving a few home-style Bangladeshi dishes, but Kolapata seems intent on showcasing country's cuisine. True, there are simple things on the menu, but there are also the complex dishes you might find in Dhaka. Try the aloo chop, a perfectly cooked starter of potato cutlet filled with delicate shreds of beef. Booze isn't sold – Kolapata is pretty much a wipe-clean caff – so try the yoghurt-based wedding drink borhani.

Italian

Carluccio's Caffè

Reuters Plaza, Docklands, E14 5AJ (7719 1749/ www.carluccios.com). Canary Wharf tube/DLR. **Open** 7am-11pm Mon-Fri; 9am-11pm Sat; 10am-10.30pm Sun. **Main courses** £9-£13. **Credit** AmEx, DC, MC, V.
Antonio Carluccio's idea of providing traditional Italian food in unassuming café surroundings informs his successful chain. The utilitarian deli-cum-cafés are blessed with generously long opening hours, making them as perfect for breakfast as for lingering over a late dinner. They get busier and deafeningly noisy at lunchtime, but staff usually manage to stay charming and accommodating. **Other locations** throughout the city.

Fifteen

15 Westland Place, Shoreditch, N1 7LP (0871 330 1515/www.fifteenrestaurant.com). Old Street tube/ rail. **Open** *Trattoria* 7.30-11am, noon-3pm, 6-10pm Mon-Sat; 9-11am, noon-3.30pm Sun. *Restaurant* noon-2.30pm, 6.30-9.15pm daily. **Main courses** £11-£24. **Credit** AmEx, DC, MC, V. **Map** p403 Q3 **106**
Standards remain high at Jamie Oliver's Fifteen, set up to introduce disadvantaged youngsters to the restaurant trade. The modern Italian food is nigh-on flawless, while service is unpretentious yet professional. Opt for the informal ground-floor trattoria, now open for breakfast, or the funkily retro basement restaurant; in both you'll get a quirky, daily changing menu, using top-notch seasonal produce.

Mediterranean

Eyre Brothers

70 Leonard Street, Shoreditch, EC2A 4QX (7613 5346/www.eyrebrothers.co.uk). Old Street tube/rail. **Open** noon-3pm, 6.30-10.45pm Mon-Fri; 6.30-10.45pm Sat. **Main courses** £13-£22. **Credit** AmEx, DC, MC, V. **Map** p403 Q4 **107**
With its sleek, masculine decor, Eyre Brothers is a grown-up place, carefully thought out and very well executed. Tables are well spaced, allowing romantic tête-à-têtes and boozy family reunions to coexist, while service gives you the feeling you're in safe hands. The menu changes regularly, with some constants: such as huge Mozambican tiger prawns with pilau rice and cucumber, a long-term favourite.

Modern European

Wapping Food

Wapping Hydraulic Power Station, Wapping Wall, E1W 3ST (7680 2080/www.thewappingproject.com). Wapping tube/Shadwell DLR. **Open** noon-3.30pm, 6.30-11pm Mon-Fri; 10am-4pm, 7-11pm Sat; 1-4pm Sun. **Main courses** £11-£19. **Credit** AmEx, MC, V.
Both arts centre and restaurant, there are few more unusual spots to dine than this former hydraulic power station. Eat modern European food at stylish black tables with plastic chairs, set amid mint-coloured machinery in the old turbine hall.

Oriental

North-east London retains its monopoly on the most authentic and interesting Vietnamese restaurants in London – **Song Que** (*see right*) is still the best place to start.

Great Eastern Dining Room

54-56 Great Eastern Street, Shoreditch, EC2A 3QR (7613 4545/www.greateasterndining.co.uk). Old Street tube/rail/55 bus. **Open** *Ground-floor bar* noon-midnight Mon-Fri; 6pm-midnight Sat. *Restaurant* 12.30-3pm, 6.30-10.45pm Mon-Fri; 6.30-10.45pm Sat. **Main courses** £9-£18. **Credit** AmEx, DC, MC, V. **Map** p403 R4 **108**
You have to like the way Will Ricker (also behind E&O; *see p208*) puts a room together. Great Eastern is relaxed, good-looking and people-friendly, with squishy banquettes and paper-on-cloth tables conspiring to create a space you camp in as much as eat in. The menu tours South-east Asia (from dim sum and tempura to curries), with Thai a real strength.

Song Que

134 Kingsland Road, Shoreditch, E2 8DY (7613 3222). Old Street tube/rail/26, 48, 55, 67, 149, 242, 243 bus. **Open** noon-3pm, 5.30-11pm Mon-Sat; noon-11pm Sun. **Main courses** £4.70-£7.10. **Credit** MC, V. **Map** p403 R3

Song Que is still the culinary king of Little Vietnam. Despite spartan decor and brusque waiters, hungry Hoxtonites flock here for wonderful northern and southern Vietnamese specialities. Avoid the Chinese items and instead try bo tai chanh, a Vietnamese carpaccio; cua lot ('peeled crab'), with chillies spicing up the little shellfish; and tom sot me, massive king prawns, still in their crunchy shells, served in a bright orange sauce with a distinct tamarind taste.

Turkish

From Dalston Kingsland station up to Stoke Newington Church Street, you're in the Turkish and Kurdish heart of Hackney, which means superb grills: **19 Numara Bos Cirrik** (34 Stoke Newington Road, N16 7XJ, 7249 0400) and **Mangal Ocakbasi** (10 Arcola Street, E8 2DJ, 7275 8981, www.mangal1.com), by the **Arcola Theatre** *(see p333)* are favourites.

South-east London

Greenwich lacks stand-out eateries. Aside from some over-styled bistros and the high-street chains, **Inside** *(see p220)* is pretty much it.

Cafés & brasseries

Pavilion Tea House

Greenwich Park, Blackheath Gate, SE10 8QY (8858 9695/www.capergreen.co.uk). Blackheath rail/Greenwich rail/DLR. **Open** *Summer* 9am-6pm daily. *Winter* 9am-4pm daily. **Main courses** £2-£8. **Credit** MC, V.

Tip-top food in large portions, served by helpful staff in pleasant surroundings – what more could you ask from a park café? Well, breakfast served beyond 11am at weekends for a start. But the Welsh rarebit rarely disappoints.

Modern European

Inside

19 Greenwich South Street, SE10 8NW (8265 5060/ www.insiderestaurant.co.uk). Greenwich rail/DLR. **Open** noon-2.30pm, 6.30-11pm Tue-Fri; 6.30-11pm

Best of British

Fergus Henderson's enduringly excellent **St John** *(see p197)* is, for us, the real pioneer of British cuisine. His championing of 'nose-to-tail' eating a decade back effectively turned British foodies on to the forgotten wonders of offal. His approachable restaurant, a former smokehouse, has barely changed: it's still

a white, airy dining room with a semi-open kitchen, reached through a spacious bar. Although the menu changes daily, there are recurring treats – roast bone marrow and parsley salad being the most renowned.

In the early 2000s, the gradual reclaiming of **Borough Market** *(see p255)* by a bunch of fine-food enthusiasts helped turn Londoners on to local food. It also provided the perfect setting for an exciting new restaurant **Roast** *(see p195; pictured)*, whose arrival ushered in a new wave of British restaurants: among them the **National Dining Rooms** *(see p211)*, **Great Queen Street** *(see p201)* and **Magdalen** *(see p194)*. Nowadays even humble pie and mash (of which **M Manze**, *see p195*, is the finest original exponent) has been modernised at **Mother Mash** *(see p202)*, **Geales** *(see p207)* has done the same with good old fish and chips, and charmingly retro old tea shops like **Shipp's** *(see p195)* will soon be popping up like fairy mushrooms.

The future? The most spectacular new British restaurants are likely to be at **Fortnum & Mason** *(see p238)*, where the three venues (St James's, the Fountain and the Gallery) are being transformed by David Collins for the firm's 300th anniversary celebrations.

Sat; noon-3pm Sun. **Main courses** £11-£16. **Credit** AmEx, MC, V.

The decor here is deliberately understated in an art gallery sort of way, while the food is a rigorous representation of chef-patron Guy Awford's skills; the choice and flavour combinations arouse much deliberation among the diners, a lively mix of grateful gourmet locals and incomers after a good night out.

South-west London

French

Chez Bruce

2 Bellevue Road, Wandsworth, SW17 7EG (8672 0114/www.chezbruce.co.uk). Wandsworth Common rail. **Open** noon-2pm, 6.30-10.30pm Mon-Fri; 12.30-2.30pm, 6.30-10.30pm Sat; noon-3pm, 7-10pm Sun. **Set meals** £25.50-£37.50. **Credit** AmEx, DC, MC, V.

Chef-patron Bruce Poole's superb and enduringly popular restaurant continues to serve the best food at relatively reasonable prices. The menu doesn't change often and the decor rarely gets an update, but the place still feels vital. Sit downstairs if you can and seek immediate help from the smooth sommelier: the wine list shows care, flair and global reach.

Modern European

Glasshouse

14 Station Parade, Kew, Surrey TW9 3PZ (8940 6777/www.glasshouserestaurant.co.uk). Kew Gardens tube/rail. **Open** noon-2.30pm, 7-10.30pm Mon-Sat;

Tea Smith: finely wrought. *See p217.*

12.30-2.45pm, 7.30-10pm Sun. **Set meals** £17-£50. **Credit** AmEx, MC, V.

Kew's connection with lovely perennials bred from fine root-stock extends to this member of the small, well-rounded group that includes French restaurant Chez Bruce (*see above*). The glass-fronted room has a subtle, classy comfort (leather-upholstered chairs help) and the pace is perfectly calibrated. As good for a long, daylit lunch as an unrushed evening meal.

West London

Italian

River Café

Thames Wharf, Rainville Rd, Hammersmith, W6 9HA (7386 4200/www.rivercafe.co.uk). Hammersmith tube. **Open** 12.30-3pm, 7-9.30pm Mon-Sat; 12.30-3pm Sun. **Main courses** £23-£32. **Credit** AmEx, DC, MC, V.

Paper tablecloths, utilitarian glasses and a full view of the kitchen live up to the name, but that's where any similarity with a humble workers' caff ends. Prices at this famous establishment are steep, but match the freshness and seasonality of perfectly cooked food that never fails to impress, with gleamingly fresh ingredients allowed to speak for themselves. The outside tables are the ultimate weekend treat.

Modern European

Clarke's

124 Kensington Church Street, Kensington, W8 4BH (7221 9225/www.sallyclarke.com). Notting Hill Gate tube. **Open** 12.30-2pm Mon; 12.30-2pm, 7-10pm Tue-Fri; 11am-2pm, 7-10pm Sat. **Main courses** £14-£16. **Credit** AmEx, MC, V. **Map** p394 B7 ⑩

Sally Clarke was inspired by Alice Waters' Chez Panisse to bring Cal-Ital cooking to the UK. That was the mid 1980s, but her approach to food is still uncompromising. The crisp white tablecloths with bowls of roses, and the cut-glass-accented clientele are frightfully English, but sourcing is impeccable, preparation deceptively simple and everything tastes just-so: from terrific raisin and walnut bread to deep, dark chocolate truffles (available in the shop).

Vegetarian & organic

Gate

51 Queen Caroline Street, Hammersmith, W6 9QL (8748 6932/www.thegate.tv). Hammersmith tube. **Open** noon-2.45pm, 6-10.45pm Mon-Fri; 6-10.45pm Sat. **Main courses** £8-£14. **Credit** AmEx, MC, V.

London's grande dame of quality vegetarian cuisine occupies an elevated, airy attic above a pretty courtyard. A joy in daylight, it becomes deliciously cosy in the evening when staff come round with gem-coloured candles for each table. The food brims with interesting textures, tastes and touches. The smart-casual customers, from silver foxes to young sophisticates, usually fill the Gate to capacity – book ahead.

Pubs & Bars

The richer the pour, the happier the drinker.

Depending on who you listen to, London's pub scene is either in steep decline or in the best state it's been for years. We lean towards the latter. It's true, the really special pubs are few and far between – but they are worth seeking out. Take a trio of Lambs: there are the wonderfully well-preserved oldies such as Covent Garden's **Lamb & Flag**; pubs where staff take genuine pride in the beer they pour, as at Bloomsbury stalwart the **Lamb**; and recently opened crackers that tick all the right boxes, like Islington's near-perfect **Charles Lamb**. Four out of five pubs might be by-numbers, chain-affiliated and lacking in life, but with a careful eye and a *Time Out* guide to help, these can easily be avoided. One of the most encouraging developments in recent years has been the increased availability of real ale (*see p234* **Ale and hearty**), although some pubs still embrace ales more thoroughly than others – Borough's **Market Porter** (9 Stoney Street, Bankside, SE1 9AA, 7407 2495, www.markettaverns.co.uk), for example, has a fascinating selection – although these days there are comfier places to drink in the area.

Two genres in particular – gastropubs and wine bars – are thriving. Gordon Ramsay hogged the press attention in 2007 with the **Narrow**, his (excellent) first gastropub, but it's not all about the newbies: established faves like the **Pig's Ear** or the **Crown & Goose** continue to impress. (Further options are listed under 'Gastropubs' in the Restaurants & Cafés chapter; *see p194-220*.) The capital's wine bars have also improved dramatically over the last few years (*see p229* **Who's wine-ing now?**).

Overall? We're content, and you will be too. London's bar scene could do with some fresh invention, and maybe we'd like to see prices at the top gastropubs level out. But dip into the right spots of the city's fine pool – a chummy pub, legendary hotel bar, a gritty great or a classy corner – and you won't want to be drinking anywhere else in the world. For a full survey of London drinking options, pick up a copy of the annual *Time Out Bars, Pubs & Clubs* guide (£9.99).

> ❶ Pink numbers given in this chapter correspond to the location of each pub and bar as marked on the street maps. *See pp394-407.*

The South Bank & Bankside

The **Anchor & Hope** (*see p196*) is one of London's finest gastropubs, while sipping bellinis by the Thames in **Skylon** (*see p196*) is an essential – if expensive – London pleasure.

King's Arms
25 Roupell Street, South Bank, SE1 8TB (7207 0784). Waterloo tube/rail. **Open** 11am-11pm Mon-Fri; noon-11pm Sat, Sun. **Credit** AmEx, DC, MC, V. **Map** p404 N8 ❶
If you had to choose just one pub in the area, this is probably it. Hidden away amid the tiny yellow brick Victorian terraces on one of London's most atmospheric streets, it's a marvellous warren of a boozer with a fine selection of ales and a Thai menu.

Rake
Winchester Walk, Bankside, SE1 9AG (7407 0557). London Bridge tube/rail. **Open** noon-11pm Mon-Fri; 10am-11pm Sat. **Credit** AmEx, MC, V. **Map** p404 P8 ❷
The streets around Borough Market have never been short of places to drink, but this new pub has a few characteristics that help it stand out from the pack. For one thing, it's tiny, with a canopied, heated patio adjunct. And for another, it's run by the folks behind the Utobeer stall in the market; the list of brews is therefore varied and enticing.

The best Pubs & bars

For the latest thing
All Star Lanes (*see p225*); **Narrow** (*see p235*); **Rake** (*see p227*); **1707** (*see p230*).

For quirks and character
Golden Heart (*see p234*); **Gordon's** (*see p226*); **King's Arms** (*see above*); **Nag's Head** (*see p230*); **190 Queensgate** (*see p231*); **Seven Stars** (*see p223*).

For great beer
See p234 **Ale and hearty**.

For cocktails
Apartment 195 (*see p231*); **Duke's Hotel** (*see p230*); **Lonsdale** (*see p228*); **Lost Society** (*see p235*); **Player** (*see p227*).

Royal Oak
*44 Tabard Street, Bankside, SE1 4JU (7357 7173).
Borough tube.* **Open** 11am-11pm Mon-Fri; 6-11pm
Sat; noon-6pm Sun. **Credit** MC, V. **Map** p404 P9 **❸**
Tucked away around the back of Borough tube, this
Victorian corner pub is the only London outpost of
the long-serving Harveys brewery in Sussex. The
straightforward pub grub is very decent and priced
extremely keenly. And it's a very handsome place,
immaculately and unshowily maintained across its
two bars. But the atmosphere is really the thing.

Wine Wharf
*Stoney Street, Borough Market, SE1 9AD (7940
8335/www.winewharf.com). London Bridge tube/rail.*
Open 11.30am-11pm Mon-Sat. **Credit** AmEx, DC,
MC, V. **Map** p404 P8 **❹**
Set by Vinopolis (*see p81*), near Borough Market
under the railway arches, this industrial-chic wine bar
has a 100-glass selection and the buzz it creates is fun
and foxy. No aged noses sniffing into goblets here,
but busy post-work chatter and coupley entwine-
ment. Helping the wine along are Med delights from
the deli. Jazz plays from 7.30pm on a Monday and you
can buy takeout bottles for a picnic.
Other locations Brew Wharf, Stoney Street,
Bankside, SE1 9AD (7378 6601/www.brewwharf.com).

The City

Black Friar
*174 Queen Victoria Street, EC4V 4EG (7236 5474).
Blackfriars tube/rail.* **Open** 11am-11pm Mon-Wed,
Sat; 11am-11.30pm Thur, Fri; noon-10.30pm Sun.
Credit AmEx, MC, V. **Map** p404 O5 **❺**
Sir John Betjeman justifiably and successfully led
the campaign to save this remarkable venue. Built
in the 1880s on the site of a medieval Dominican fri-
ary, the Black Friar had its interior completely
remodelled by H Fuller Clark and Henry Poole of the
Arts and Crafts movement. Bright panes, intricate
friezes and carved slogans ('Industry is Ale', 'Haste
is Slow') make a work of art out of the main saloon.

Bonds Bar & Restaurant
*Threadneedle Hotel, 5 Threadneedle Street,
EC4R 8AY (7657 8088/www.theetongroup.com).
Monument tube/Bank tube/DLR.* **Open** 11am-11pm
Mon-Fri; 3-11pm Sat; 3-10.30pm Sun. **Credit** AmEx,
DC, MC, V. **Map** p405 Q6 **❻**
The best bar in the City? All is as it should be: the
attentive, black-shirted staff; the padded swivel bar-
chairs; the reading lights over the bar; and, above
all, the cocktails. Among the six dozen varieties
(most costing £8-£10) there's a truffle martini using
truffle liqueur, an Indian Touch with Stoli razberi
and cardamom, and a Bison Kick with Zubrówka
and kiwi syrup – divine.

Lamb Tavern
*10-12 Leadenhall Market, EC3V 1LR (7626
2454/www.thelambtavern.co.uk). Monument
tube/Bank tube/DLR.* **Open** 11am-midnight Mon-Fri.
Credit AmEx, DC, MC, V. **Map** p405 Q6 **❼**

In the 18th-century glory days of this photogenic
pub, it kept the market's meat, fish and fruit stallholders properly lubricated. These days most local
traders deal only in stocks and shares. The matey
main space is little more than a room with a bar in
it, but there are tables on the gallery above, and a
restaurant at the top.

Vertigo 42
*Tower 42, 25 Old Broad Street, EC2N 1HQ (7877
7842/www.vertigo42.co.uk). Bank tube/DLR/
Liverpool Street tube/rail.* **Open** noon-3pm, 5-11pm
Mon-Fri. **Credit** AmEx, DC, MC, V. **Map** p405 Q6 **❽**
Situated on the 42nd floor of the tallest edifice in the
City, Vertigo 42 enjoys a truly stunning London
panorama. Visitors have to earn their vista: the
check-in process, including X-ray machines and
guest passes, is reminiscent of arrival at an airport.
Champers is surely the only appropriate order, but
with a bowl of olives at £3.95, this view don't come
cheap – but it's a genuine London must-do.

Holborn & Clerkenwell

Clerkenwell also has a compelling claim to
being the birthplace of the now ubiquitous
gastropub: the still wonderful **Eagle** (*see p199*)
kicked things off, but the **Hat & Feathers**
and **Peasant** (for both, *see p199*) are also
worthy, more recent additions to the genre.
Another food pioneer that provides great
drinking is the fabulous **St John** (*see p197*).
Cittie of York (22 High Holborn, 7242 7670)
is perhaps the most visually arresting of the
many historic taverns, at least the market-sized
back room with its wooden snugs and endless
bar counter, while for contrast **Smiths of
Smithfield** (*see p199*) works the 1990s
bare-brick warehouse aesthetic.

Café Kick
*43 Exmouth Market, Clerkenwell, EC1R 4QL (7837
8077/www.cafekick.co.uk). Angel tube/Farringdon
tube/rail/19, 38 bus.* **Open** noon-11pm Mon-Thur;
noon-midnight Fri, Sat; 4-10.30pm Sun
(spring/summer only). **Credit** MC, V.
Map p402 N4 **❾**
This worn and weathered scout hut of a bar – long,
thin and dotted with footie memorabilia – is the setting for competitive high jinks of the highest order,
courtesy of three well-oiled René Pierre table football tables. A back area with Formica-topped café
tables offers sparse seating and menus listing a
Champions' League of Euro beers: 14 by the bottle.
Other locations Bar Kick, 127 Shoreditch High
Street, Shoreditch (7739 8700).

Cellar Gascon
*59 West Smithfield, Clerkenwell, EC1A 9DS (7600
7561/7796 0600/www.cellargascon.com). Barbican
tube/Farringdon tube/rail.* **Open** noon-midnight
Mon-Fri. **Credit** AmEx, MC, V. **Map** p402 O5 **❿**
See p229 **Who's wine-ing now?**

Pubs & Bars

Fluid
40 Charterhouse Street, Clerkenwell, EC1M 6JN (7253 3444/www.fluidbar.com). Barbican tube/ Farringdon tube/rail. **Open** noon-midnight Mon-Wed; noon-2am Thur; noon-4am Fri; 7pm-4am Sat. **Admission** £3 after 9pm; £5 after 10pm Fri, Sat. **Credit** AmEx, DC, MC, V. **Map** p402 O5 **⓫**
Epitomising Clerkenwell retro-chic, this bar draws a discerning flow of laid-back urbanites to its low-level leather seating. The Far East provides motifs galore, from giant koi carp strikingly engraved on the huge windows to 30 Asian nibbles (£3-£6).

Jerusalem Tavern
55 Britton Street, Clerkenwell, EC1M 5UQ (7490 4281/www.stpetersbrewery.co.uk). Farringdon tube/rail. **Open** 11am-11pm Mon-Fri. **Credit** AmEx, MC, V. **Map** p402 O4 **⓬**
With its wooden interior painted green and its clutter of tucked-away tables in countless nooks and crannies, the Jerusalem is like something straight out of Tolkien's Shire, and justly popular with punters of all ages and occupations. Run by St Peter's Brewery, it's certainly worth a trip.

Seven Stars
53 Carey Street, Holborn, WC2A 2JB (7242 8521). Chancery Lane or Holborn tube. **Open** 11am-11pm Mon-Fri; noon-11pm Sat; noon-10.30pm Sun. **Credit** AmEx, MC, V. **Map** p399 M6 **⓭**
By the Royal Courts of Justice, Roxy Beaujolais' magic little pub-cum-bar-cum-eaterie fulfils its (admittedly complex) brief to near perfection while keeping a healthy tongue in cheek. Posters for courtroom dramas overlook the legal fraternity tucking into well-chosen (and well-priced) merlots, malbecs and house Dulucs. Craftily conceived daily dishes chalked up by the bar (Napoli sausages and mash, dill-cured herring) are devoured in a side room.

Three Kings of Clerkenwell
7 Clerkenwell Close, Clerkenwell, EC1R 0DY (7253 0483). Farringdon tube/rail. **Open** noon-11pm Mon-Fri; 5.30-11pm Sat. *Food served* noon-3pm, 6.30-10pm Mon-Fri. **No credit cards. Map** p402 N4 **⓮**
In a town where characterful pubs succumb all too often to closure or, arguably worse, big chain buyouts, it's a relief to find a boozer with such brazen personality. From the frankly bonkers figurines standing guard over the entrance to the triumphant collection of tat cluttering every available surface inside (Egyptian cat statues, snowglobes, a fake rhino's head above the fireplace), the Three Kings is a true original. For all that, the pub takes one thing seriously: its music. Three real ales on tap and a range of board games complete the picture.

Vinoteca
7 St John Street, Clerkenwell, EC1M 4AA (7253 8786/www.vinoteca.co.uk). Farringdon tube/rail. **Open** 11am-11pm Mon-Sat. **Credit** MC, V. **Map** p402 O5 **⓯**
See p229 **Who's wine-ing now?**

English boozer meets continental charcuterie at the **Norfolk Arms**. *See p226.*

Sure can pick 'em

Tom Lamont, editor of *Bars, Pubs & Clubs*, gives the low-down on local boozers.

'Real ales' are a good place to start. The best pubs serve at least two regular and one guest cask ales (*see p234* **Ale and hearty**). A sure sign of the alehead landlord is the collection of brewery badges – look out for this display of previous ale incumbents around or behind the bar (a good example is Deptford's Dog & Bell). Staff in branded T-shirts generally points to a tourist pub or to chain affiliation – not always a bad thing (Wetherspoon's often have exemplary and extremely competitively priced ale; Sam Smith's pubs often have historic premises, always offer bracingly low prices and occasionally have decent ale), but staff at independents are generally proudly individualist and often better informed.

When it comes to gastropubs – devised as the perfect blend of pub and restaurant – central London suffers. For the best of the gastropubs, you'll need to edge outwards, to areas like Islington (home to estimable trio **Charles Lamb** (*see p232*), **Marquess Tavern** and **Duke of Cambridge** (for both, *see p213*) and Chelsea (where you'll find the wonderful **Pig's Ear** *see p231*). If you're after pub grub, avoid anywhere with a board outside that has chalked pictures of its food, particularly advertising 'traditional' fish and chips. Real ales are as important in a gastropub as any other boozer; if the bar hasn't bothered to source even one, it doesn't bode well for ingredients in the kitchen. The **Anchor & Hope** (*see p196*) and the pioneering **Eagle** (*see p199*) get both elements rights.

London is currently well furnished with cocktail bars. Take note of the menu: if it specifies the brand of spirit used in each creation, it's a good indicator that you're getting what you're paying for and that the head bartender knows a thing or two. I'm currently loving Dick Bradsell's menu at the reinvigorated **Lonsdale** (*see p228*) and the skills of the unpretentious bartenders at **Hawksmoor** (*see p234*). There are also first-rate hotel cocktail bars (the **Library**, *see p231*, or the **Donovan**, *see p230*, come to mind). All is not rosy at the bar stool, however. **Lost Society** (*see p235*) won our Best Bar award in 2006 and is still great, but Mocotó, nominated for its impressive Brazilian-themed decor and luscious cocktails, closed down before the awards took place. Eventual 2007 winner the **Rake** (*see p221; pictured*) is a worthy champion – but, specialising in bottled beer, it's as much of a pub as a bar.

One of my real bug-bears is the artificial creation of a queue by overzealous bouncers. Sure, it makes the joint look busy – but it ain't half a disappointment when you get inside and find it nearly empty. Better to find somewhere with a firmly open door: perhaps bar sports emporia **Café Kick** (*see p222*) or **All-Star Lanes** (*see p225*). The indoor smoking ban has meant an increase in crowds spilling on to the street, with the unexpected advantage that you can judge the mood of a venue before entering.

Second only to London's rise as a cocktail capital has been the improvement in its wine bars. The adoption of the *enoteca* (bar-shop) concept has been a revelation (*see p229* **Who's wine-ing now?**). As for wine lists themselves, I prefer simple, non-convoluted tasting notes to the effusions of a thesaurus-wielding sommelier. A better sign of true oenophilic knowledge is passionate advice about pairings, as at the excellent **Vinoteca** (*see p223*). And avoiding the chains is less decisive when it comes to wine bars: Balls Bros, Corney & Barrow and Davy's offer decent quality and price, especially given that their City stronghold has a surprising paucity of other good bars. But for pure atmosphere, I really love the gloriously old-fashioned **Gordon's** (*see p226*).

Vivat Bacchus

47 Farringdon Street, Holborn, EC4A 4LL (7353 2648/www.vivatbacchus.co.uk). Chancery Lane tube/ Farringdon tube/rail. **Open** noon-midnight Mon-Fri. **Credit** AmEx, DC, MC, V. **Map** p402 N5 ⑯
See p229 **Who's wine-ing now?**

Ye Old Mitre

1 Ely Court, Ely Place, at the side of 8 Hatton Gardens, Holborn, EC1N 6SJ (7405 4751/www. pub-explorer.com/yeoldmitre). Chancery Lane tube/ Farringdon tube/rail. **Open** 11am-11pm Mon-Fri. **Credit** AmEx, MC, V. **Map** p402 N5 ⑰
This oldie (established 1546) is only accessible through a narrow passage – incongruously described as 25m long. Still, the Mitre needs no yard conversion or 'ye olde' embellishment to prove its worth. Walk into its venerable, cramped three-room space, see what's on as the guest ale, then settle down amid the portraits of Henry VIII and sundry beruffed luminaries.

Bloomsbury & Fitzrovia

For sheer style, try the bar at **Hakkasan** or **Shochu Lounge** (for both, *see p200*); if the music is as important to you as the drinks, get happy at the **Big Chill House** (*see p318*).

All Star Lanes

Victoria House, Bloomsbury Place, WC1B 4DA (7025 2676/www.allstarlanes.co.uk). Holborn tube. **Open** 5-11.30pm Mon-Wed; 5pm-midnight Thur; noon-2am Fri, Sat; noon-11pm Sun. *Bowling* (per person per game) £7.50 before 5pm; £8.50 after 5pm. **Credit** AmEx, MC, V. **Map** p399 L5 ⑲
Doing for ten-pin bowling what the Elbow Room did for pool and Café Kick did for table football, All Star Lanes is a well-realised, high-end endeavour. It's the gold-card brigade's foil to grungier Bloomsbury Bowling nearby and sports four bowling lanes (plus two private ones) and a red leather bar serving up good cocktails. It's not a cheap night out – the kitchen serves lobster, for gawd's sake. A third location is due to open in Shoreditch in spring 2008. **Other locations** Whiteleys, Porchester Gardens, Bayswater, W2 4YQ (7313 8363).

Bloomsbury Bowling Lanes

Basement, Tavistock Hotel, Bedford Way, Bloomsbury, WC1H 9EU (7691 2610/www. bloomsburybowling.com). Russell Square tube. **Open** noon-2am Mon-Wed; noon-3am Thur-Sat; noon-midnight Sun. *Bowling* from £36/hr 1 lane. **Credit** AmEx, MC, V. **Map** p399 K4 ⑲
If you prefer a pint while you bowl, the freedom to spill it on worn carpeting, and a joystick-jiggle on retro arcade games such as Galactica, this is your venue. With low-key decor, booths in the restaurant (burgers for £6.75) and swivel stools dotted around, this is a more authentic representation of Americana. Two karaoke rooms have been added in the last year; and films are occasionally screened in the sloping entrance hall.

Bradley's Spanish Bar

42-44 Hanway Street, Fitzrovia, W1T 1UT (7636 0359). Tottenham Court Road tube. **Open** 11pm Mon-Sat; 3-10.30pm Sun. **Credit** MC, V. **Map** p406 W1 ⑳
This much-loved off-Oxford Street institution remains a fine place in which to spend a gloomy winter afternoon (tucked into a dark corner of the scruffy downstairs bar) or summery evening (when everyone spills out on to the street). It's a fabulously louche place to drink, as long as you don't mind a bit of grime: the men's toilets remain a bit of a challenge.

Crazy Bear

26-28 Whitfield Street, Fitzrovia, W1T 2RG (7631 0088/www.crazybeargroup.co.uk). Goodge Street tube. **Open** noon-10.45pm Mon-Fri; 6-10.45pm Sat. **Credit** AmEx, DC, MC, V. **Map** p399 K5 ㉑
Stylish, decadent yet supremely comfortable, the London outpost of the Oxfordshire-based hotel and pub chain comprises restaurant upstairs and opulent bar below. You may have trouble finding it – the building is almost entirely unmarked. You'll have no problem finding the swivel cowhide bar stools, red padded alcoves or low leather armchairs in the downstairs bar – a charming hostess will escort you down the ornate staircase. Fine dim sum keep hunger pangs at bay.

Lamb

94 Lamb's Conduit Street, Bloomsbury, WC1N 3LZ (7405 0713/www.youngs.co.uk). Holborn or Russell Square tube. **Open** 11am-midnight Mon-Sat; noon-10.30pm Sun. **Credit** AmEx, MC, V. **Map** p399 M4 ㉒
Founded in 1729, this beautifully restored etched glass and mahogany masterpiece is class itself. Today the snob screens have a decorative role above the horseshoe island bar, but, back in the days when music hall stars were regulars here, they were used to deflect unwanted attention. The Pit is a sunken back area that gives access to a summer patio with three tables outside. The beer is Young's and the menu seasonal, with most main plates costing under a tenner – try the own-made steak and mushroom pie (£8.75). Pub excellence.

Match Bar

37-38 Margaret Street, Fitzrovia, W1G 0JF (7499 3443/www.matchbar.com). Oxford Circus tube. **Open** 11am-midnight Mon-Fri; noon-midnight Sat; 4-10.30pm Sun. **Credit** AmEx, DC, MC, V. **Map** p406 U1 ㉓
As original as ever, even though they're now into a second decade, London's Match cocktail bars celebrate the craft of the bartender with a selection of authentic concoctions (£6.50-£7), such as a grapefruit julep (Wyborowa, grapefruit, lime, pomegranate, drizzled with honey) or Kamomilla Fizz, perhaps, made from Wyborowa and camomile syrup with fresh lemon and cucumber. DJs take to the decks from 7.30pm Thur-Sat.
Other locations 45-47 Clerkenwell Road, Clerkenwell, EC1M 5RS (7250 4002); 2 Tabernacle Street, Shoreditch, EC2A 4LU (7920 0701).

Bedford & Strand.

with impressive set lunch choices. The place buzzes at night and, in an area short of good beer options, the two real ales are very welcome. There are also tables outside. *Photo p223.*

Covent Garden & the Strand

Bedford & Strand

1A Bedford Street, The Strand, WC2E 9HH (7836 3033/www.bedford-strand.com). Charing Cross tube/ rail. **Open** noon-midnight Mon-Fri; 5pm-midnight Sat. **Credit** AmEx, MC, V. **Map** p407 Y4
See p229 **Who's wine-ing now?**

Coach & Horses

42 Wellington Street, Covent Garden, WC2E 7BD (7240 0553). Covent Garden tube. **Open** 11am-11pm Mon-Sat; noon-10.30pm Sun. **Credit** MC, V. **Map** p407 Z3
A stone's throw from the Piazza, this genuine expat Irish boozer packs a bundle of tradition and charm into a modest space. It pulls a good pint of Guinness, of course, with a couple of real ale alternatives. And tiny though the bar area is, it also boasts over 70 malts and whiskies. Hot roast beef, salt beef or Limerick ham sandwiches soak up the booze, and a lovely floral display hangs outside in summer.

Gordon's

47 Villiers Street, The Strand, WC2N 6NE (7930 1408/www.gordonswinebar.com). Embankment tube/Charing Cross tube/rail. **Open** 11am-11pm Mon-Sat; noon-10pm Sun. **Credit** AmEx, MC, V. **Map** p407 Y5
See p229 **Who's wine-ing now?**

Lamb & Flag

33 Rose Street, Covent Garden, WC2E 9EB (7497 9504). Covent Garden tube. **Open** 11am-11pm Mon-Sat; noon-10.30pm Sun. **Credit** MC, V. **Map** p407 Y3
A glance up Rose Street from Garrick Street after dark reveals a black street lantern throwing its light on to the frontage of the shamelessly traditional Lamb & Flag, Covent Garden's best pub. This pub wears its history on its sleeve, proudly displaying its classic boozer credentials of real ale and local memorabilia that adorn the walls. Jazz sessions liven up Sunday evenings.

Lobby Bar

One Aldwych, The Strand, WC2B 4RH (7300 1070/www.onealdwych.com). Covent Garden or Temple tube. **Open** 8am-11.30pm Mon-Sat; 8am-10.30pm Sun. **Credit** AmEx, DC, MC, V. **Map** p407 Z3
The lobby bar of the One Aldwych hotel innovates as much as it sparkles. It offers an improbable 30 kinds of martini (£9.40-£20). The six-strong house selection allows the use of crushed fresh chilli (with Agavero tequila liqueur) in a Chilli del Toro, and fresh tamarillo (with Wyborowa) in a tamarillo martini. Proceedings are overseen by impeccable staff and the setting is grand. Pure class.

Museum Tavern

49 Great Russell Street, Bloomsbury, WC1B 3BA (7242 8987). Holborn or Tottenham Court Road tube. **Open** 11am-11.30pm Mon-Thur; 11am-midnight Fri, Sat; noon-10.30pm Sun. **Credit** AmEx, DC, MC, V. **Map** p399 L5
A rare example of a pub as popular with locals as tourists, rejoicing in both a noble history (the current, splendid interior dates to a mid 19th-century refurb) and an ideal location (opposite the front gates of the British Museum). Ignore the logoed T-shirts for the six real ales that decorate an expansive bar backed by mirrors advertising liquor manufacturers. A row of flimsy tables cling to the pavement along Museum Street.

Norfolk Arms

28 Leigh Street, Bloomsbury, WC1H 9EP (7388 3937/www.norfolkarms.co.uk). Russell Square tube/King's Cross tube/rail. **Open** 11am-11pm Mon-Sat; noon-10.30pm Sun. **Credit** AmEx, MC, V. **Map** p399 L3
The Norfolk, now a gastropub, has much going for it. We love the design – English boozer meets European charcuterie – and the food is top-notch,

Lowlander

36 Drury Lane, Covent Garden, WC2B 5RR (7379 7446/www.lowlander.com). Covent Garden or Holborn tube. **Open** 9.30am-11pm Mon-Fri; 10am-11.30pm Sat; 10am-10.30pm Sun. **Credit** AmEx, MC, V. **Map** p407 Z2 ⓮

Choose from the finest Dutch and Belgian beers at Lowlander, a treat for hop-lovers. No fewer than 15 tall, gleaming chrome beer taps are lined up on the bar, offering pilsners, blondes, wheat beers, red and dark ales, fruit beers and miscellaneous speciality beers; there are also more than 40 bottled options.

Soho & Leicester Square

Cork & Bottle

44-46 Cranbourn Street, Leicester Square, WC2H 7AN (7734 7807/www.donhewitson.com). Leicester Square tube. **Open** 11am-11.30pm Mon-Sat; noon-10.30pm Sun. **Credit** AmEx, DC, MC, V. **Map** p407 X4 ⓭
See p229 Who's wine-ing now?

Courthouse Hotel

19-21 Great Marlborough Street, Soho, W1F 7HL (7297 5555/www.courthouse-hotel.com). Oxford Circus tube. **Open** 11am-midnight Mon-Sat; noon-11pm Sun. **Credit** AmEx, DC, MC, V. **Map** p406 V2 ⓮

Very smart, this place: both chic and clever. The court where Oscar Wilde, Christine Keeler and Mick Jagger were once tried has been transformed into the high-class cocktail bar of an upmarket off-Regent Street hotel. You can even hire a done-up cell, bucket urinal and all. Cocktails in the £10 range feature 20 martinis, nine classics, 20 short and long drinks, and four sparkling ones.

Dog & Duck

18 Bateman Street, Soho, W1D 3AJ (7494 0697). Tottenham Court Road tube. **Open** 11am-11pm Mon-Sat; noon-10.30pm Sun. **Credit** MC, V. **Map** p406 W2 ⓯

This historic Victorian gem, a two-floor landmark on the corner of Bateman and Frith Streets, has changed little since George Orwell drank here in the 1940s. The cosy bar upstairs is named after him. Downstairs, somehow squeezed into the narrow space, there's an old stamp machine and advertising mirrors for Virginia cigarettes and Brighton Seltzer mineral water – all authentic. Equally authentic are the ales, another attraction.

French House

49 Dean Street, Soho, W1D 5BG (bar 7437 2799/restaurant 7437 2477/www.frenchhousesoho.com). Leicester Square or Piccadilly Circus tube. **Open** noon-11pm Mon-Sat; noon-11pm Sun. *Restaurant* noon-3pm, 5.30-11pm Mon-Sat. **Credit** AmEx, DC, MC, V. **Map** p406 W3 ⓰

The famous French House pub is as popular now as when cabaret stars and a louche literary set were using it either side of the war. Most evenings you'll find yourself parked on the pavement outside, but if you make

Lobby Bar.

it to the bar (still sporting a photo of De Gaulle, whose Free French had their wartime offices upstairs), there's draught Kronenbourg and Breton cider.

Harp

47 Chandos Place, Leicester Square, WC2N 4HS (7836 0291/www.harpbarcoventgarden.com). Charing Cross tube/rail. **Open** 11am-11pm Mon-Sat; noon-10.30pm Sun. **Credit** MC, V. **Map** p407 Y4 ⓱

Fine ales and a genuine Irish atmosphere bring punters to this lovely little pub. Talk centres on the day's racing form; decor is provided by portraits lining the walls of the narrow saloon. O'Hagan's finest sausages, proudly announced on the board outside, sizzle in a pot on the hob atop the bar counter.

Player

8 Broadwick Street, Soho, W1F 8HN (7292 9945/www.thplyr.com). Oxford Circus or Tottenham Court Road tube. **Open** 5.30pm-midnight Mon-Wed; 5.30pm-1am Thur, Fri; 7pm-1am Sat. **Credit** AmEx, MC, V. **Map** p406 V2 ⓲

Few places hit the mark as meticulously as this subterranean cocktail lounge (open to non-members before 11pm), where the retroactively glamorous

1970s decor extends from Player-branded, turquoise carpet and sculpted wall panelling to the cluster of disco balls dangling behind the DJs, who can be relied on to crank it up from 8pm Thur-Sat (£5 entry after 9pm). Unpretentious and positively charged with cinematic elegance, the Player is the sort of place where even humble accountants can act like movie stars for the night.

Milk & Honey
61 Poland Street, Soho, W1F 7NU (7292 9949/ www.mlkhny.com). Oxford Circus tube. **Open** Non-members 6-11pm Mon-Fri; 7-11pm Sat. **Credit** AmEx, DC, MC, V. **Map** p406 V2 ⓣ

Tucked away behind unmarked Prohibition era-style black doors, this jazz-tinged speakeasy-style cocktail bar from the people behind the Player (*see p227*) is a charming mix of semi-exclusivity and unprecedented friendliness. Non-members will need to book in advance (and leave by 11pm), but will be treated like old friends by the staff.

Sun & Thirteen Cantons
21 Great Pulteney Street, Soho, W1F 9NG (7734 0934). Oxford Circus or Piccadilly Circus tube. **Open** noon-11pm Mon-Fri; 6-11pm Sat. **Credit** AmEx, DC, MC, V. **Map** p406 V3 ⓣ

Another pub veering from the traditional route to appeal to music fans and modern tastes in drinking. The rather smart Sun, diagonally opposite Alphabet, still bears the shiny wood and frosted glass of its pub heritage. Within, though, in the main bar adjoining an equally smart dining room (Thai food served throughout), you'll find pints of Kirin Ichiban and Peeterman and bottles of lager sunk to a contemporary aural backdrop. Thursday and Friday DJ sessions happen downstairs.

Two Floors
3 Kingly Street, Soho, W1R 5LF (7439 1007/ www.barworks.co.uk). Oxford Circus or Piccadilly Circus tube. **Open** noon-11.30pm Mon-Thur; noon-midnight Fri, Sat. **Credit** AmEx, DC, MC, V. **Map** p406 V3 ⓣ

A fine, fine bar this, reasonably priced, modest, understated. There's no sign – look out for an old no.3 along Kingly Street, now becoming bar central. Inside, furniture institutional and loungey fills an informal, long bar space, each table bearing a drinks menu with a black two of diamonds on the cover. Downstairs is Handy Joe's intimate Tiki Bar.

Oxford Street & Marylebone

Artesian
Langham Hotel, 1C Portland Place, Marylebone, W1B 1JA (7636 1000/www.artesian-bar.co.uk). Oxford Circus tube. **Open** 7.30am-2am Mon-Fri; 8am-2am Sat; 8am-midnight Sun. **Credit** AmEx, DC, MC, V. **Map** p398 H4 ⓣ

Some of the design features at the Langham Hotel's Artesian bar – reopened after a hugely expensive makeover by top designer David Collins – sail

nervously close to OTT, but a subdued colour scheme makes the total effect soothing rather than imposing, and it's a most suitable setting for an evening of grand cocktails, expertly made and served in remarkably beautiful glassware.

Moose
31 Duke Street, Marylebone, W1U 1LG (7224 3452/www.vpmg.net). Bond Street tube. **Open** 4pm-2am Mon-Thur; 4pm-3am Fri, Sat. **Credit** AmEx, MC, V. **Map** p398 G5 ⓣ

We can't imagine anyone not liking this place. The latest venture from the Vince Power Music Group is a rarity in the West End: cosy, reasonably priced and with decor that's simultaneously eccentric and inviting. There are two spaces: a small ground-floor bar and a much larger downstairs bar with DJs every night of the week except Sunday. An impressively long happy hour (5-9pm) offers ordinary cocktails at a delightfully cheap £3.75.

Windsor Castle
29 Crawford Place, Marylebone, W1H 4LJ (7723 4371). Edgware Road tube. **Open** 11am-11pm Mon-Sat; noon-10.30pm Sun. **Credit** MC, V. **Map** p395 E5 ⓣ

This delightful brewhouse is the pub version of the houses covered in St George's Cross flags that you see on England match days. Inside, every spare inch of wall space is plastered with patriotic memorabilia: a ceiling of Royal Family plates, souvenir mugs, royal tea tins, portraits of royals past and present, a photo of the Queen Mum pulling a pint. It should be awful, but it's actually rather charming.

Paddington & Notting Hill

Cow
89 Westbourne Park Road, Westbourne Grove, W2 5QH (7221 0021/www.thecowlondon.co.uk). Royal Oak or Westbourne Park tube. **Open** noon-11pm Mon-Thur; noon-midnight Fri, Sat; noon-10.30pm Sun. **Credit** MC, V. **Map** p394 A5 ⓣ

Gastrobar guru Tom Conran runs this two-storey operation: an Irish pub downstairs and renowned restaurant upstairs, with another dining area at the back of the pub. Plates of rock oysters sit atop the bar counter, invariably accompanied by a decent pint of Guinness, and equally invariably devoured by self-important regulars who swarm the modest interior and the two tables outside at the front.

Lonsdale
44-48 Lonsdale Road, Notting Hill, W11 2DE (7727 4080/www.thelonsdale.co.uk). Ladbroke Grove or Notting Hill Gate tube. **Open** 6pm-midnight Mon-Thur, Sun; 6pm-1am Fri, Sat. **Credit** AmEx, MC, V. **Map** p394 A6 ⓣ

Dick Bradsell's old establishment is back in contention with the launch of a fabulously original cocktail menu in spring 2007. Simple in concept, it traces the history of the London cocktail, from the mojito conceived in Cuba in 1586, the Sours of the

Who's wine-ing now?

The revival of London's wine bars continues apace – a sure sign being a trade show prediction in late 2007 of a trend for 'wine cocktails' (Sangria, Agua de Valencia, Tinto de Verano). There are still some wonderfully atmospheric old-timers: **Gordon's** (see p226) oozes charm, tucked under the low vaults on Villiers Street, where you can sit in semi-

darkness with a date and a dripping candle. Another is Don Hewitson's **Cork & Bottle** (see p227), where the decor surely hasn't changed since the place opened in 1971, but the enthusiasm of the winelist hasn't had to.

In the vanguard of the new school was **Vinoteca** (see p223), inspired by the Italian *enoteca* concept of attaching a wine shop to a bar, where the same bottles can be enjoyed with food. Perhaps bravely, takeaway wine prices are listed alongside the cost of drinking in; generally it works out at two-and-a-half times more if you stick around. **Vivat Bacchus** (see p225) is another classy operation, with tasting and teaching rooms on the premises. That these venues should both have appeared in Clerkenwell is perhaps down to a worthy predecessor – the excellent, stylish **Cellar Gascon** (see p222), with its clubby vibe and a fine list focused on the wines of south-west France.

Look out for more bars springing up in high-end wine merchants. East Dulwich's great deli, bar and shop, **Green & Blue** (see p235), has just doubled in size, while new arrivals in central London confirm the renaissance. **1707** (see p230; pictured), designed by David Collins, is at the heart of the new basement at Fortnum & Mason's famous food emporium. (The new Wonder Bar does the same job in Selfridges' wine department.) Our fave of the moment, though, is basement hideaway **Bedford & Strand** (see p226), a curiously compelling blend of Havana chic and 1970s wine lodge.

1700s, the Sangarees of the Antilles, the Flips of the 1860s, the Bucks of the 1920s and contemporary classics. It's a labour of love, a work of art, and it provides meticulously sourced concoctions (£6-£7.50) at fair prices. DJs play from 9pm on Fri, Sat.

Montgomery Place
31 Kensington Park Road, Notting Hill, W11 2EU (7792 3921/www.montgomeryplace.co.uk). Ladbroke Grove tube. **Open** 5pm-midnight Mon-Fri, Sun; 2pm-midnight Sat. **Credit** AmEx, MC, V.
This recently opened 'lounge bar kitchen' is above all else a cocktail bar – and a very good one. Alex Fitzsimmons and Matt Perovetz from sister bar Dusk have consulted on a cracking cocktail selection. Inspiration for the list comes from great bars of the 20th century. With live music on Sunday evenings, the Montgomery is an intimate space and it attracts a grown-up clientele. Recommended.

Portobello Gold
95-97 Portobello Road, Notting Hill, W11 2QB (7460 4900/www.portobellogold.com). Notting Hill Gate tube. **Open** 10am-midnight Mon-Thur; 10am-12.30am Fri; 9am-12.30am Sat; 10am-11.30pm Sun. **Credit** AmEx, DC, MC, V. **Map** p394 A6
Established enough to say 'Just Gold' outside, PG is the perfect Portobello hangout. With a firm grasp of pop culture – images of Sandie Shaw, the Stones on Thank Your Lucky Stars, and a California surfing scene that impressed Bill Clinton – Portobello Gold draws in discerning, music-savvy bohos. Happy hour is from 5.30-7pm daily, and there's also free internet access if that's your thang.

Trailer Happiness
177 Portobello Road, Notting Hill, W11 2DY (7727 2700/www.trailerhappiness.com). Ladbroke Grove or Notting Hill Gate tube. **Open** 5-11.30pm Tue-Fri; 6-11.30pm Sat; 6-10.30pm Sun. **Credit** AmEx, MC, V.

Ah, a proper bar, no messing. This basement might look trashy – part bordello, part South Pacific – but the drinking is serious. Bloody professional and bags of fun. Along with a homage to great contemporary mixologists, the bar does its own Grapefruit Julep and Hedgerow Sling. There are DJs on Wed-Sat evenings and five tables outdoors.

Piccadilly & Mayfair

Donovan Bar

Brown's Hotel, 33-34 Albemarle Street, Mayfair, W1S 4BP (7493 6020/www.roccofortecollection.com). Green Park tube. **Open** 11am-1am Mon-Sat; noon-11.30pm Sun. **Credit** AmEx, MC, V. **Map** p406 U4 ⓐ

The polarised black and whiteness of the diminutive Donovan Bar is a fitting testament to its muse, Stepney-born photographer Terence Donovan, whose monochrome prints of the international celebrities and semi-clad women that characterised swinging '60s London are liberally peppered over the walls. Live jazz plays every evening except Sundays. It's the epitome of nostalgia-chic, but the cocktail list is surprisingly forward-thinking.

Galvin at Windows

28th floor, London Hilton, 22 Park Lane, Mayfair, W1K 1BE (7208 4021/www.galvinatwindows.com). Hyde Park Corner tube. **Open** 10am-1am Mon-Wed; 10am-3am Thur, Fri; 5.30pm-3am Sat; 10am-10.30pm Sun. **Credit** AmEx, DC, MC, V. **Map** p400 G8 ⓐ

Windows is at the top of the Park Lane Hilton – the 28th floor, to be precise – and the views are, of course, sumptuous, but the cost of drinking here is pretty staggering too. The bar is stylish but not too trendy.

Red Lion

1 Waverton Street, Mayfair, W1J 5QN (7499 1307). Green Park tube. **Open** noon-11pm Mon-Fri; 6-11pm Sat. **Credit** AmEx, MC, V. **Map** p400 H7 ⓐ

A slice of the English countryside in the bowels of Mayfair, the Red Lion exudes rural bonhomie. Age-old pub ephemera hangs from hooks and sits on shelves, while an affable bunch of drinkers sup a well-kept range of ales and chow down on familiar pub grub. Only the foreign accents of the bar staff and the suits on a fair proportion of the clientele give away the pub's urban ethic.

1707

Fortnum & Mason, 181 Piccadilly, Piccadilly, W1A 1ER (7734 8040/www.fortnumandmason.com). Piccadilly Circus tube. **Open** 11am-8.30pm Mon-Sat; 11am-6pm Sun. **Credit** MC, V. **Map** p406 U5 ⓐ

See p229 **Who's wine-ing now?**

Westminster & St James's

The Parliament Street **Red Lion** (no.48, SW1A 2NH, 7930 5826) is a decent old boozer that is distinguished by the presence of a division bell (to call errant MPs in to vote) and by TVs that tirelessly screen BBC Parliament.

Dukes Hotel

35 St James's Place, St James's, SW1A 1NY (7491 4840/www.dukeshotel.co.uk). Green Park tube. **Open** noon-11pm Mon-Sat; noon-10.30pm Sun. **Credit** AmEx, DC, MC, V. **Map** p400 J8 ⓐ

Tucked away by the lobby of the Duke's Hotel, itself hidden away in a courtyard of St James's Place, this discreet cocktail bar comprises four seating areas of striped walls and stately portraits. Settle into your leather chair with your complimentary nuts and nibbles and peruse the famed martini (£14.50) menu – they'll even mix one at your table, if you wish.

Millbank Lounge

City Inn Hotel, 30 John Islip Street, Westminster, SW1P 4DD (7932 4700/www.millbanklounge.com). Pimlico or Westminster tube. **Open** 11am-11pm Mon-Sat; noon-10.30pm Sun. **Credit** AmEx, DC, MC, V. **Map** p401 K10 ⓐ

This quality hotel bar is criminally underused, hidden away down a backstreet on the first floor of a city hotel. You'll have no trouble finding a relaxing low chair in the expansive bar area – but you'll need to take your time over the long and impressive drinks menu.

Red Lion

2 Duke of York Street, St James's, SW1Y 6JP (7321 0782). Piccadilly Circus tube. **Open** noon-11.30pm Mon-Sat. **Credit** MC, V. **Map** p406 V5 ⓐ

Decimals – yet to disturb the **Nag's Head**.

Named in the early 1600s in honour of King James I (it was suddenly prudent to show the Red Lion as a sign of loyalty to the Scottish King who had just become King of England too) and given an ornate makeover by the Victorians, the Red Lion is a timeless English pub with classic dark wood decor. Two narrow bar areas are straddled by a beautifully carved, etched-glass island bar dispensing pints of real ale, as well as glasses of wine and generic Nicholson's food.

St Stephen's Tavern

10 Bridge Street, Westminster, SW1A 2JR (7925 2286). Westminster tube. **Open** 10am-11.30pm Mon-Thur, Sat; 10am-midnight Fri; 10.30am-10.30pm Sun. **Credit** MC, V. **Map** p401 L9 ⑤⑤

Most brewery bosses would give their drinking arm for a venue such as this one, diagonally opposite Big Ben. Somehow it seems apt that it should be traditional old Hall & Woodhouse running such a time-honoured establishment, and a thoroughly good job it's done of it too. The decor of this restored gem is all carved wood and etched glass, with towering displays of fresh flowers reaching up to the high, high ceilings.

Chelsea

Apartment 195

195 King's Road, SW3 5ED (7351 5195/www. apartment195.co.uk). Sloane Square tube then 11, 22 bus. **Open** 6-11pm Mon-Sat. **Credit** AmEx, MC, V. **Map** p397 E12 ⑤⑥

You need to press a buzzer to gain admittance to this discreet little number (a sure way to impress your mates). But despite the trappings of highfalutin' exclusivity, a warm welcome awaits at the top of the stairs. There's a Vivienne Westwood meets laid-back gentlemen's club feel to the decor. The drinking is all about the cocktails, with legendary mojitos, though the star turn is the aptly named Crown Jewels: a glass of honey-sweetened rare cognac topped with vintage champagne that'll set you back a staggering £350. Now that really would impress your friends.

Pig's Ear

35 Old Church Street, SW3 5BS (7352 2908/www. thepigsear.co.uk). Sloane Square tube then 11, 22 bus. **Open** noon-11pm Mon-Sun. **Credit** AmEx, MC, V. **Map** p397 E12 ⑤⑦

Brimming with bohemian London character, this Chelsea treat does indeed serve tasty, deep-fried porcine ears (as well as the excellent Pig's Ear ale from the Uley Brewery in Gloucestershire). Indeed, the food in both the bar and the smart dining room upstairs is decidedly adventurous. The crowd is refreshingly mixed: elderly Chelsea eccentrics, local builders and a group of girlfriends decadently getting drunk on red wine in the middle of the day, perhaps. Benches beneath the windows provide seating in front of the metal-topped bar. All in all, very English, very London and very good.

Knightsbridge & South Kensington

Anglesea Arms

15 Selwood Terrace, South Kensington, SW7 3QG (7373 7960/www.capitalpubcompany.com). South Kensington tube. **Open** 11am-11pm Mon-Sat; noon-10.30pm Sun. **Credit** AmEx, MC, V. **Map** p397 D11 ⑤⑧

Dickens and DH Lawrence both frequented this splendid free house, and both would probably still enjoy it today. There's a sympathetically dated feel to the sturdy wood interior but the drinks selection is bang up to date. Ales are the speciality, and there are 12 tables outside at which to sup them.

Library

Lanesborough Hotel, 1 Lanesborough Place, Hyde Park Corner, Belgravia, SW1X 7TA (7259 5599/ www.lanesborough.com). Hyde Park Corner tube. **Open** 11am-1am Mon-Sat; noon-10.30pm Sun. **Credit** AmEx, DC, MC, V. **Map** p400 G8 ⑤⑨

Walk through the lobby of the Lanesborough Hotel to the Library and you are handed a book by staff in Casablanca attire. Within it you'll find, as you survey the towering fresh flowers and roaring fire of the elegant surroundings, spell-binding cocktails. A pianist plays in the evenings. The magic may come at a price – £19 for spicy lobster nachos – but it's magic none the same.

Nag's Head

53 Kinnerton Street, Belgravia, SW1X 8ED (7235 1135). Hyde Park Corner or Knightsbridge tube. **Open** 11am-11pm Mon-Sat; noon-10.30pm Sun. **No credit cards. Map** p400 G9 ⑥⓪

No mobiles and no credit cards at this charming time warp of a pub – it's a wonder it accepts decimal coinage. The Nag's Head echoes a time when National Service was a given (note the cravats and regimental heraldry), James Mason was a sex bomb (note the line drawings) and glamorous destinations (Paris, New York) could only be glimpsed in crank-up machines, such as the one standing here beside a wireless-era Spangles sweets dispenser.

190 Queensgate

The Gore Hotel, 190 Queensgate, South Kensington, SW7 5EX (7584 6601/www.gorehotel.co.uk). Gloucester Road or South Kensington tube. **Open** noon-1am Mon-Wed, Sun; noon-2am Thur-Sat. **Credit** AmEx, DC, MC, V. **Map** p397 D9 ⑥①

The perfect pub, cocktail bar and destination lounge, this is the bar of the Gore Hotel, hiding between the Albert Hall and the Bulgarian Embassy. Upholstered seating and carved dark wood surround a sturdy bar. Underpinning it all is a 20-strong list of cocktails (£8.50), mules and martinis, while DJs liven up proceedings on Saturday nights from 10pm. At the back, tucked under the stairs, Cinderella's Carriage is a louche little nook done up in red velvet drapes and feather plumes that can be booked for intimate private parties.

North London

The **Lockside Lounge** (75-89 West Yard, Camden Lock Place, Camden, NW1 8AF, 7284 0007, www.locksidelounge.com) is an excellent Camden DJ bar, while the big terrace-cum-car park at Torquil's Bar at the **Roundhouse** (see p311) is typically north London urban. In Islington, the boisterous **King's Head** (see p340) is as good a pub as it is a theatre.

Charles Lamb

16 Elia Street, Islington, N1 8DE (7837 5040/www. thecharleslambpub.com). Angel tube. **Open** 4-11pm Mon, Tue; noon-11pm Wed-Sat; noon-10.30pm Sun. **Credit** MC, V. **Map** p402 O2 ⓒ

A gem of a pub consisting of two small rooms decorated in a down-home fashion, with fairy lights around the fireplace, framed maps and a notice saying 'Don't feed Mascha' (the cute, neckerchief wearing pub dog). As a gastropub, it's at the no-nonsense end of the spectrum, with hearty food (fish pie, pork rillettes on toast) and plenty of bar snacks.

Crown & Goose

100 Arlington Road, Camden, NW1 7HP (7485 8008). Camden Town tube. **Open** 11am-1am Mon-Thur, Sun; 11am-2am Fri, Sat. **Credit** MC, V. **Map** p398 J2 ⓒ

On a quiet side street off Camden High Street, this lovely little pub feels deliciously out of the way. With dark green-painted panelling, glimmering candlelight and an open fire on chilly nights, it's delightfully old-fashioned and romantic – especially when bar staff close the shutters towards the end of the evening. And it does simple but seriously good food.

Gilgamesh

Stables Market, Chalk Farm Road, NW1 8AH (7482 5757/www.gilgameshbar.com). **Open** 6pm-2.30am Mon-Thur; noon-2.30am Fri-Sun. **Credit** AmEx, DC, MC, V.

Inspired by the Babylonian epic of King Gilgamesh, this bar – centrepiece of the new Stables Market development – is an opulent, theatrical temple to excess. The scale is breathtaking, from the splendid lapis lazuli bar to the huge sphinxes that survey intricate hand-carved wall panels, pillars inset with polished stones, and an immense carved tree that stretches around the sweeping entrance staircase. Grab a table by the floor-to-ceiling windows to enjoy the cocktails – pricey, but blended with consummate skill – or the pricey, excellent pan-Asian food.

Holly Bush

22 Holly Mount, Hampstead, NW3 6SG (7435 2892/ www.hollybushpub.com). Hampstead tube/Hampstead Heath rail. **Open** noon-11pm Mon-Sat; noon-10.30pm Sun. **Credit** AmEx, MC, V.

Tucked away on a tiny lane amid some gorgeous NW3 piles, the Holly Bush is a gem of a place. It's a warren of little rooms, each offering their own distinctive historic patina alongside shared elements (burnished wood panels, low ceilings, sepia lighting). Only the rear dining room bucks the trend: it feels distinctly modern with its white painted walls and brighter lights, and a lot of people do check in for the food: quality nosh such as quails' eggs, smoked duck with fig and mint salad or a substantial organic rump steak.

Island Queen

87 Noel Road, Islington, N1 8HD (7704 7631). Angel tube. **Open** noon-11pm Mon, Sun; noon-11.30pm Tue, Wed; noon-midnight Thur-Sat. **Credit** MC, V. **Map** p402 O2 ⓒ

Buried in an anonymous row of terraced houses near the canal, the huge front windows showcase the welcoming, high-ceilinged Victorian saloon here, complete with delicately etched glass and heavy velvet drapes. Comfy sofas occupy the back room, and an upstairs section can accomodate larger parties. With its hum of indie rock and cheery buzz of conversation, the Island Queen is a supremely relaxing spot.

King Charles I

55-57 Northdown Street, King's Cross, N1 9BL (7837 7758). King's Cross tube/rail. **Open** noon-11pm Mon-Fri; 5-11pm Sat, Sun. **Credit** MC, V. **Map** p399 M2 ⓒ

This minute neighbourhood boozer has vintage, wood-heavy decor that radiates warmth whatever the season, and in winter the open fire is a perfect supplement. The drinks list is moderate but diligent, the perennial quality of the guest bitters deserving special mention. You can phone for food from the Royal Thai takeaway round the corner (7837 7755), and it'll be brought round to you, on proper plates. Even better, the bar billiards table is back out of storage.

Salmon & Compass

58 Penton Street, Islington, N1 9PZ (7837 3891/ www.salmonandcompass.com). Angel tube. **Open** 4pm-2am Mon-Thur, Sun; 4pm-4am Fri, Sat. **Admission** £3 after 9pm, £5 after 11pm Fri, Sat. **Credit** AmEx, MC, V. **Map** p402 N2 ⓒ

From the outside, you'd be forgiven for dismissing the Salmon & Compass as a old man's boozer. The interior, however, is a different story, with its sleek, black lacquered tables, moody lighting and expensive-looking art deco wallpaper. At the far end of the bar lies a mammoth DJ stack for the regular club nights Monday to Saturday. High-end lagers are on tap and the crowd is generally young, clubby and raring to dance.

East London

In Docklands, the **Gun** (see p217) is a decent pub as well as being a fine place to eat.

Big Chill Bar

Old Truman Brewery, off Brick Lane, E1 6QL (7392 9180/www.bigchill.net). Aldgate East tube/Liverpool Street tube/rail. **Open** noon-midnight Mon-Thur; noon-1am Fri, Sat; 11am-midnight Sun. **Credit** MC, V. **Map** p403 S4 ⓒ

The Big Chill franchise can do no wrong: its annual summer festival continues to increase in scale, while the Big Chill House (*see p318*) opened in King's Cross to great acclaim in 2006. This outlet – its original foray into the bar scene – is now firmly etched into the Brick Lane drinking landscape, drawing easy-going punters from London and beyond. Nightly changing DJs spin an enticing medley of laid-back tunes, and there's plenty of room to kick back on the brown leather sofas while sipping a freshly mixed mojito or raspberry caipirinha.

Camel

277 Globe Road, Bethnal Green, E2 0JD (8983 9888). Bethnal Green tube/rail. **Open** 4-11pm Mon-Wed; noon-11pm Thur-Sat; noon-10.30pm Sun. **Credit** MC, V.

Flock wallpaper, black and white photos, gourmet pies and an espresso machine might enrage those soapbox drinkers, forever complaining about the gentrification of London's old boozers. But wait – only the most cynically minded could fail to appreciate Matt Kenneston and Joe Hill's thoughtful, stylish refit of the Camel, purchased derelict two years ago after the building was saved from demolition by a local campaign. The same team is behind the excellent Florist (no.255, 8981 1100), the boozer cum bar almost next door.

Commercial Tavern

142 Commercial Street, Spitalfields, E1 6NU (7247 1888). Aldgate East tube/Liverpool Street tube/rail. **Open** 5-11pm Mon-Fri; noon-11pm Sat; noon-10.30pm Sun. **Credit** AmEx, MC, V. **Map** p403 R5 ⑱

Like the long-lost love child of Tiffany's and G.A.Y., the Commercial Tavern leaves no corner unadorned (walls are delicate duck-egg blue or plastered in old covers of *Interview*, sparkly umbrellas adorn the outside tables) and no punter unwelcomed. Fittingly, its motley crew of skinny rockers and Edie Sedgwick wannabes are more than willing to shove up, share tables and give you a shout when the pool table is free. It's grown out of its fresh-faced refurb into a Spitalfields stalwart well suited to the area's fussily cool crowd.

Dolphin

165 Mare Street, Hackney, E8 3RH (8985 3727). London Fields rail. **Open** 11am-2am Mon-Thur, Sun; 11am-4am Fri, Sat. **No credit cards**.

It might not look like much from the outside (or from the inside for that matter, apart from the cool tiled dolphin mural), but come Friday and Saturday everyone heads to the Dolphin for an East End knees-up – Hoxton-style. Expect punters with bad, mad haircuts, plenty of hats, gold lamé leggings and 1970s retro mixing it with the Turkish and Vietnamese locals. And the draw? The karaoke machine is cranked right up and it's not unusual to see 50 or more funsters crammed on the 'dancefloor' singing their hearts out. During the week, things are much more sedate.

dreambagsjaguarshoes

34-36 Kingsland Road, Shoreditch, E2 8DA (7729 5830/www.dreambagsjaguarshoes.com). Old Street tube/rail. **Open** 5pm-midnight Mon; 5pm-1am Tue-Sat; 5pm-12.30am Sun. **Credit** MC, V. **Map** p403 R3 ⑲

Mixology and meat are both done to a turn at **Hawksmoor**. *See p234.*

Ale and hearty

Chances are that you'll want to sample some British beer while you're in London. But it's not that simple. Broadly speaking the Shakespearean stuff you're after is called real ale. Not stout (like Guinness), nor heavy (that's Scottish) and definitely not lager (yellow, fizzy and usually foreign-made). Ale was first called 'real' in the 1970s by CAMRA, the campaign launched to save traditional beers from a rising tide of processed, keg stuff. Crucially, real ale matures and is managed in its barrel or cask (hence it is also known as 'cask ale' or 'cask-conditioned ale'). Stored in the cool cellar of the pub, it's served fresh on site, by hand pump (*pictured*), not electric tap. It's a living entity: the beer drinker's equivalent of farmhouse cheese.

Of many different styles, the most widely available ale is 'bitter', which can be Mild, Best, Special or Extra Special, in ascending order of potency. Bitter is a late Victorian derivative of Pale Ale, sometimes called India Pale Ale or IPA, first brewed for the colonies.

Where can you find this endangered beverage, brown as polished walnut and best enjoyed in pint glasses – in a 'jug', with a handle, or without, in a 'straight'? Fuller's (producer of London Pride, as well as ESB, and others) is now the last major London brewer of fine ale. Their many pubs include the **Dove** (*see p236*). Other brews we particularly like include Young's, Timothy Taylor's Landlord, and anything by Harvey's (at the **Royal Oak**, *see p222*). The **Museum Tavern** (*see p226*) and the **Anglesea Arms** (*see p231*) both keep a good range of ales. The **Jerusalem Tavern** (*see p223*) is the solitary London representative of Suffolk's truly outstanding St Peter's Brewery.

Dreambagsjaguarshoes has become the ultimate Shoreditch poster-bar. Thoughtfully shambolic, with massive floor-to-ceiling windows, a grungey cellar and an experimental music policy (DJs Wed-Sat from 8pm, Sun from 4pm), it's a fast-track education in Shoreditch cool. And remember, one man's terrifyingly trendy freak show is another man's bohemian love-in of like-minded souls.

Golden Heart
110 Commercial Street, Spitalfields, E1 6LZ (7247 2158). Liverpool Street tube/rail. **Open** 11am-11pm Mon-Sat; 11am-10.30pm Sun. **Credit** AmEx, MC, V. **Map** p403 S5 ⑩

'Stand still and rot' flashes a sign in this place, a motto for the East End arty types who see it as a home from home. Sandra Esqulant's famed corner boozer has stood still since the 1970s, which is precisely why they like it. And everyone knows the words to the Carpenters. This is retro at its most indulgent – and it's all marvellous fun.

Grapes
76 Narrow Street, Docklands, E14 8BP (7987 4396). Westferry DLR. **Open** noon-3pm, 5.30-11pm Mon-Thur; noon-11pm Fri, Sat; noon-10.30pm Sun. **Credit** AmEx, MC, V.

The Grapes isn't a large pub, but it is a lovely one. The roadside front is all greenery and etched glass, the interior has the requisite dark wood, beams and open fire, and there's a sweet, rickety balcony overhanging the Thames.

Hawksmoor
157 Commercial Street, Spitalfields, E1 6BJ (7247 7392/www.thehawksmoor.com). Liverpool Street tube/rail. **Open** noon-1am Mon-Sat. **Credit** AmEx, DC, MC, V. **Map** p403 R5 ⑪

This American-inspired restaurant and bar exists primarily for its meat and mixology. The former it does well, providing hefty cuts at around the £20 mark. The latter it does with excellence. As a standalone bar it's limited by space – much of the room is given over to dining tables. Also nearby is the same team's Green & Red (51 Bethnal Green Road, 7749 9670, www.greenred.co.uk), an excellent tequila bar serving great Mexican snacks. *Photo p233.*

Loungelover
1 Whitby Street, Shoreditch, E1 6JU (7012 1234/ www.loungelover.co.uk). Liverpool Street tube/rail. **Open** 6pm-midnight Mon-Thur, Sun; 6pm-1am Fri; 7pm-1am Sat. **Credit** AmEx, DC, MC, V. **Map** p403 S5 ⑫

Loungeloving is a popular pastime in these parts: Shoreditch loves this bar's OTT approach to glamorous, cocktail-swilling bonhomie. The luxe junkshop decor does much to impress: giant champagne glasses filled with flowers, palm-tree chandeliers, huge stage lights and glittery stag's horns cover every inch of available space. And the cocktails (£7.50-£11) are utterly fabulous. Tables need to be booked in advance.

Narrow

44 Narrow Street, Docklands, E14 8DP (7592 7950/www.gordonramsay.com). Limehouse DLR. **Open** noon-11pm Mon-Sat; noon-10.30pm Sun. **Credit** AmEx, MC, V.
The restaurant in Gordon Ramsay's first gastropub (due to be followed by nearly a dozen more over 2008) usually needs booking at least a month in advance, but the pub part is no slouch. Bar snacks include cockles and a soup, served in a striped mug, while the real food is served in the adjoining former boathouse: affordable dishes such as devilled kidneys on toast (£5.50), or pig's cheek and bashed neeps (£12.50). There are 36 tables outside on the riverside terrace.

Royal Oak

73 Columbia Road, Bethnal Green, E2 7RG (7729 2220/www.royaloaklondon.com). Bethnal Green tube/Old Street tube/rail/26, 48, 55 bus. **Open** 6-11pm Mon; noon-11pm Tue-Thur; noon-midnight Fri, Sat; noon-10.30pm Sun. **Credit** AmEx, MC, V. **Map** p403 S3 ⑦
This is a classic Bethnal boozer that's retained its original (inter-war) features, updated for contemporary tastes: original wood panelling throughout and a lovely low, central bar beneath a yellow glazed ceiling and original art deco wall lamps. It's busy on Sundays, of course, when shoppers at the flower market reward themselves for getting up early with a mighty roast (£13).

South-east London

Gipsy Moth

60 Greenwich Church Street, Greenwich, SE10 9BL (8858 0786). Cutty Sark DLR. **Open** noon-11pm Mon-Thur; noon-midnight Fri, Sat; noon-10.30pm Sun. **Credit** AmEx, DC, MC, V.
Overlooking the tarpaulined remains of the *Cutty Sark*, this formerly staid tourist pub has been transformed into a bright and busy bar, thanks to a bohemian refurb (loungey furniture, funky wallpaper, braided curtains, retro lamps, open kitchen at the back). Some conversation-level indie rattle and a colourful array of draught continental beers complete the makeover. There's also a huge garden.

Green & Blue

38 Lordship Lane, Dulwich, SE22 8HJ (8693 9250/ www.greenandbluewines.com). East Dulwich rail. **Open** 9am-11pm Mon-Sat; 11am-10.30pm Sun. **Credit** MC, V.
See p229 **Who's wine-ing now?**

Greenwich Union

56 Royal Hill, Greenwich, SE10 8RT (8692 6258/ www.greenwichunion.com). Greenwich rail/DLR. **Open** noon-11pm Mon-Fri; 11am-11pm Sat; 11.30am-10.30pm Sun. **Credit** MC, V.
Success itself, Alastair Hook's bright Meantime Brewery flagship offers traditional house brews to a loyal and lively thirtysomething clientele. They create a buzz in the functional front and arty back areas, around a narrow bar counter bearing the beer names, and at the tables outdoors in the garden.

South-west London

Dusk

339 Battersea Park Road, Battersea, SW11 4LF (7622 2112/www.duskbar.co.uk). Battersea Park rail. **Open** 6pm-12.30am Tue, Wed; 6pm-1.30am Thur; 6pm-2am Fri, Sat. **Credit** AmEx, MC, V.
A refurb at this long-established cocktail bar has been a resounding success. The absurdly friendly (without being pushy) waiting staff clearly love working here. And we love drinking here. The Mr Scruff soundtrack sums up the place perfectly: fun, clever and not prepared to take itself too seriously. The crowd of crepuscular hedonists knows, as do we, that Dusk is still way ahead of the pack in this part of town.

Lost Society

697 Wandsworth Road, Battersea, SW8 3JF (7652 6526/www.lostsociety.co.uk). Clapham Common tube/Wandsworth Road rail/77, 77A bus. **Open** 5-11pm Mon (winter only); 5pm-1am Tue-Thur; 4pm-2am Fri; 11am-2am Sat; 11am-1am Sun. **Admission** £5 after 9pm Fri, Sat. **Credit** AmEx, MC, V.
The winner of the Best Bar category in the 2006 Time Out Eating & Drinking Awards has sure become popular of late. Once you're past the queues and door staff, this is still the superbly crafted, fantasy country-house party that you wish you got invited to every night. Flat cap-clad barmen make knockout cocktails, classic and modern, while chaises longues and the hidden garden make for an intimate, classy and wonderfully original space. *Photo p236.*

White Cross

Water Lane, Richmond, Surrey TW9 1TH (8940 6844). Richmond tube/rail. **Open** 11am-11pm Mon-Sat; noon-10.30pm Sun. **Credit** AmEx, DC, MC, V.
This gorgeous waterfront pub is a local institution, and has been packing in the crowds like nobody's business for generations. The lovely interior boasts bay windows and an unusual, enclosed rectangular bar counter that resembles a front-facing wooden bus, ornately adorned with pumps, beer glasses and bottles.

White Horse

94 Brixton Hill, Brixton, SW2 1QN (8678 6666/ www.whitehorsebrixton.com). Brixton tube/rail/train 59, 118, 133, 159, 250 bus. **Open** 4pm-midnight Mon-Thur; 4pm-3am Fri; noon-3am Sat; noon-midnight Sun. **Credit** AmEx, MC, V.

In keeping with the media types that it attracts, the White Horse likes to be quirky. Jars of old-fashioned boiled sweets are available at 40p a tumbler, the drinks list announces the availability of cigarettes by declaring that they have 'no poxy 16s', and George, the landlord's black labrador, roams around nuzzling customers. It resembles a disused warehouse, with bare brick walls and painted steel girders. Funk and soul DJs take to the central booth from 9pm Thursday to Saturday and a crowd hits the floor.

West London

Dove
19 Upper Mall, Hammersmith, W6 9TA (8748 5405). Hammersmith or Ravenscourt Park tube. **Open** 11am-11pm Mon-Sat; noon-10.30pm Sun. **Credit** AmEx, MC, V.
British to its bones, the Dove is a 17th-century riverside inn with all the trimmings: low-beamed ceilings, dark panelled walls and historical gravitas. 'Rule Britannia' was penned in an upstairs room, and the manuscript hangs in a display case. Charles II and Nell Gwyn caroused here. The list of former regulars, posted above the roaring fire in the front bar, includes Tommy Cooper and Graham Greene.

Inn at Kew Gardens
292 Sandycombe Road, Kew, Surrey TW9 3NG (8940 2220/www.theinnatkewgardens.com). Kew Gardens tube. **Open** 11am-11pm Mon-Sat; 11am-10.30pm Sun. **Credit** AmEx, DC, MC, V.
Situated below the Kew Gardens Hotel, the Inn is an ambitious proposition. Downstairs is occupied by a tasteful clutter of big tables and easy chairs, with flock wallpaper adding a quaintly old-fashioned touch. A smart separate dining area lies at the back, serving up enticing, well-executed gastropub fare (lamb shank, pan-fried calf's liver and the like).

Ladbroke Arms
54 Ladbroke Road, Holland Park, W11 3NW (7727 6648/www.capitalpubcompany.com/ladbroke). Holland Park tube. **Open** 11am-11pm Mon-Sat; noon-10.30pm Sun. **Credit** AmEx, MC, V. **Map** p394 A7 🔞
Gorgeous within and without. The tree-shrouded front garden is packed in summer, with drinkers spilling out on to one of those majestic runs of lofty mini-mansions that west London does so well. A perch here, adjacent to the cobbled mews and the pub's trailing fronds of ivy, is about as soothing as London boozing gets. To the rear is a small dining room, where diners enjoy a Gallic-accented menu – all very snug, and very popular.

Prince Alfred & Formosa Dining Rooms
5A Formosa Street, Maida Vale, W9 1EE (7286 3287). Warwick Avenue tube. **Open** noon-11pm Mon-Sat; noon-10.30pm Sun. **Credit** MC, V.
Built in 1863, this magnificent old pub is visual testament to the divisions of Victorian society. Its five snugs are separated by ornately carved mahogany partitions, each with their own miniature door, designed to keep the classes and sexes apart. The beautiful, curved, etched plate-glass window at the front is another example of the fine 19th-century craftsmanship that went into creating this pub.

Fresh from a country-house party (the bar staff, at least): **Lost Society**. *See p235.*

Shops & Services

London bursts with relishable, reliable, redoubtable retail.

The magnificently refurbished **Fortnum & Mason**. *See p238.*

Packing in more than 40,000 shops and 80 markets, London is one of the world's most exciting and exhaustive retail centres. It's also one of the most eclectic, spanning multicultural street markets and deluxe department stores, mould-breaking fashion designers and traditional tailors, flashy modern furniture flagships and dusty antiquarian dens – not to mention a cornucopia of globe-spanning foodstuffs and some of the best places on the planet to buy books, records and second-hand clothes. We can only cover a fraction of it here, so we've concentrated on British brands and shops that are not only unique to the city, but also relatively central. For a breakdown of the key shopping areas, *see p243* **Where to shop**.

Most goods are subject to value added tax (VAT) of 17.5 per cent, usually included in the marked price. Books, children's clothes and food are exempt. Some shops operate a scheme allowing visitors from outside the EU to claim back VAT on goods – for details, *see p371*. Central London shops open late (7pm or 8pm) one night a week (Thursday in the West End; Wednesday in Chelsea and Knightsbridge).

For more listings and reviews covering the huge variety of shops in the city, pick up the annual *Time Out Shops & Services* (£9.99).

General

Shopping centres & arcades

The **Royal Arcades** in the vicinity of Piccadilly are a throwback to shopping past – the Burlington Arcade (*see below*) is the largest.

Burlington Arcade

Piccadilly, St James's, W1 (www.burlington-arcade. co.uk). Green Park tube. **Open** 9.30am-5.30am Mon-Fri; 10am-6pm Sat. **Credit** varies. **Map** p408 U4.
Opened in 1819, this genteel covered shopping promenade is patrolled by 'Beadles' (decked out in top hats and tailcoats). It was recently restored to its Regency glory and has attracted some stylish new tenants among the traditional purveyors of cashmere and jewellery. Highlights include Globe-Trotter and Mackintosh (iconic British luggage and rainwear), Parisian pâtisserie Ladurée and Jimmy Choo-trained shoe designer Beatrix Ong. *Photo p247.*

Kingly Court

Carnaby Street, opposite Broadwick Street, Soho, W1B 5PW (7333 8118/www.carnaby.co.uk). Oxford Circus tube. **Open** 11am-7pm Mon-Sat; noon-6pm Sun. **Credit** varies. **Map** p408 U3.

Not your average shopping centre, this compact, three-floor complex brings together a funky mix of established streetwear chains, boutiques and gift shops. The vintage selection is particularly good: check out Marshmallow Mountain for immaculate vintage shoes, clothes and bags, and Twinkled, which extends the retro look to the home. Also check out the recently relocated Microzine, which brings together an entire men's mag of fashion, furnishings and gadgets under one roof.

Department stores

High-street fave for undies and ready meals, **Marks & Spencer** (www.marksand spencer.co.uk) also offers several fashion ranges, including its designer Autograph collection for men and women, and the younger, trend-led Per Una line and Limited Collection.

Fortnum & Mason

181 Piccadilly, St James's, W1A 1ER (7734 8040/www.fortnumandmason.co.uk). Green Park or Piccadilly Circus tube. **Open** 10am-6.30pm Mon-Sat; noon-6pm Sun (food hall only). **Credit** AmEx, DC, MC, V. **Map** p406 V4.

London's oldest department store underwent a major nip and tuck for its 300th birthday in 2007, but it has been sensitively done, and courtly tail-coated staff still preside over the expanded food hall. The famed biscuits, confectionery, jams and preserves, coffee and tea are still on the ground floor. Downstairs you'll find fresh meat, game and fish, traiteur dishes and a wine bar designed by the man behind the decor of the Wolseley (*see p211*). The extended roster of restaurants now includes an ice-cream parlour serving knickerbocker glories and adults-only 'cocktail' sundaes. The upper floors are essentially a very large, classy gift shop – antique china teacups, bags by Lulu Guinness, leather backgammon sets and select perfumes (Miller Harris, Caron, Clive Christian). *Photo p237.*

Harrods

87-135 Brompton Road, Knightsbridge, SW1X 7XL (7730 1234/www.harrods.com). Knightsbridge tube. **Open** 10am-8pm Mon-Sat; noon-6pm Sun. **Credit** AmEx, DC, MC, V. **Map** p397 F9.

Harrods seems determined not to lose its reputation as the place where you can buy anything. By turns tasteful – the unrivalled food halls, the fifth-floor perfumerie curated by renowned 'nose' Roja Dove) and tacky – the life-size waxwork of owner Mohamed Al Fayed in menswear; the mawkish shrine to Dodi and Di in the basement), this cathedral to consumerism has long been one of London's top tourist attractions. The food halls are spectacular – chandeliers drip with ornamental grapes in fruit and veg, while the

meat and game room retains its original Edwardian tiling. The two Rooms of Luxury, plus the Egyptian Room with its friezes and a 10ft-high gold Ramses II pharaoh, cover luxury accessories by the likes of Louis Vuitton, Valextra and Chloé. There are more deluxe names in the fashion and beauty sections, but for a more keenly edited selection, we recommend Harvey Nichols up the road.

Harvey Nichols

109-125 Knightsbridge, SW1X 7RJ (7235 5000/www.harveynichols.com). Knightsbridge tube. **Open** *Store* 10am-8pm Mon-Sat; noon-6pm Sun. *Café* 8am-10.30pm Mon-Sat; 8am-6pm Sun. *Restaurant* noon-3pm, 6-11pm Mon-Fri; noon-4pm, 6-11pm Sat, noon-4pm Sun. **Credit** AmEx, DC, MC, V. **Map** p397 F9.

Harvey Nicks is a stylish receptacle of well-sourced labels with a restaurant (the Fifth Floor, 7235 5250) that knocks spots off every other department store eaterie. Fashion is the store's real forte, including less ubiquitous names such as Paris-based Canadian David Szeto and Californian sisters Kate and Laura Mulleavy's label Rodarte, which feature alongside catwalk supremos Chloé, Lanvin and Balenciaga. The women's shoe department features a glam new Christian Louboutin boutique. There's an outpost of Italian luxury brand Culti in the stylish home department and the food hall has been boosted by a concession and café from eco-chic leader Daylesford Organic (for their own premises, *see p255*).

Liberty

Regent Street, Soho, W1B 5AH (7734 1234/www.liberty.co.uk). Oxford Circus tube. **Open** 10am-8pm Mon-Wed, Fri; 10am-9pm Thur; 10am-7pm Sat; noon-6pm Sun. **Credit** AmEx, DC, MC, V. **Map** p406 U2.

Charmingly idiosyncratic, Liberty is housed in a 1920s mock Tudor structure. Walk in the main entrance on Great Marlborough Street, flanked by Paula Pryke's exuberant floral concession, and you'll find yourself in a room devoted to the store's own label, in the middle of a soaring, galleried atrium. As well as the famous scarves, Liberty's art nouveau prints now adorn a wide variety of goods from silk lingerie to chic stamped-leather handbags. The ground level is great for gifts: decorative notebooks, photo albums, unusual perfumes and toiletries and a wide range of jewellery. The basement menswear department is one of London's most stylish, and there's an emphasis on individualistic lines for both sexes rather than flashy superbrands. Don't miss the impressive display of Arts and Crafts furniture on the fourth floor. The in-store pitstops, including Tea at ground level and the champagne and oyster bar below, reflect the attention to interior design.

Selfridges

400 Oxford Street, Marylebone, W1A 1AB (0800 123 400/www.selfridges.com). Bond Street or Marble Arch tube. **Open** 9.30am-8pm Mon-Wed, Fri, Sat; 9.30am-9pm Thur; noon-6pm (browsing from 11.30am) Sun. **Credit** AmEx, DC, MC, V. **Map** p398 G6.

Spitalfields Market.

Selfridges' innovative displays, concession boutiques and themed events have brought a sense of theatre to shopping. And the store isn't resting on its laurels. The latest addition to the ground floor's glut of luxury accessories and beauty products is the Wonder Room – essentially a very flashy jewellery hall featuring an 'arcade' of perimeter boutiques, as well as rarefied gadgets and trinkets such as a miniature scale model of Lord Nelson's tomb. You can sample a cornucopia of international delicacies in the food hall and browse a branch of famed Foyles bookshop in the basement, while the exhaustive fashion collections cover every taste and budget, from the best of the high street to big international names and emerging British-based designers, such as Rodnik and Bï La Lï.

Markets

London's exuberant street markets are a great place to sample street life while picking up some bargains. Below is a selection of the best; for **Camden Market** (*see p155*).

Columbia Road Market

Columbia Road, Bethnal Green, E2. Liverpool Street tube/rail, then 26, 48, bus/Old Street tube/rail then 55, 243 bus. **Open** 8am-2pm Sun. **Map** p403 S3.
On Sunday mornings, this unassuming East End street is transformed into a green swathe of fabulous plant life and the air is fragrant with blooms. But it's not just about flora: alongside the flower market is a growing number of shops selling everything from pottery, groovy furniture and Mexican glassware to cupcakes and perfume. Refuel at Jones Dairy (23 Ezra Street, E2 7RH, 7739 5372, www.jonesdairy.co.uk). Get there early for the pick of the crop, or around 2pm for the best bargains.

Spitalfields Market

Commercial Street, between Lamb Street & Brushfield Street, E1 (7247 8556/www.visitspital fields.com). Liverpool Street tube/rail. **Open** *General* 10am-4pm Mon-Fri, 9am-5pm Sun. *Antiques* 9am-4pm Thur. *Food* 10am-5pm Wed, Fri, Sun. *Fashion* 10am-4pm Fri. *Records & books* 10am-4pm 1st & 3rd Wed of the mth. **Map** p405 R5.
In the final stages of its redevelopment as this guide is published, Spitalfields now consists of the refurbished 1887 covered market and an adjacent modern shopping precinct. Around the edge of Old Spitalfields Market, stands sell grub from around the world. The busiest day is Sunday, when the nearby Brick Lane Market and Sunday (Up)Market in the Old Truman Brewery (strong on edgy designer and vintage fashion; www.sundayupmarket.co.uk) create an *iD*-photo shoot-meets-Bangladeshi-bazaar vibe.

Shepherd's Bush Market

East side of railway viaduct between Uxbridge Road & Goldhawk Road, W12. Goldhawk Road or Shepherd's Bush tube. **Open** 8.30am-6pm Tue, Wed, Fri, Sat; 8.30am-1pm Thur.
There's a fantastic range of ethnic foodstuffs at this gritty, multicultural market, from Caribbean fruit to falafel. You'll also find vivid print fabrics, goatskin rugs and saris, and myriad cheap clothing, kitchenware and CDs.

Portobello Road Market

Portobello Road, Notting Hill, W10 & W11 (7229 8354/www.portobelloroad.co.uk). Ladbroke Grove or Notting Hill Gate tube. **Open** *General* 8am-6.30pm Mon-Wed, Fri, Sat; 8am-1pm Thur. *Antiques* 4am-4pm Sat. **Map** p394 A6.
Best known for antiques and collectibles, this is actually several markets rolled into one: antiques start at the Notting Hill end; further up are food stalls;

LET'S FILL THIS TOWN WITH ARTISTS

EASELS

£12.95
WINSOR & NEWTON
DART SKETCHING EASEL
RRP £39.99

75% OFF

70% OFF

£49.95
DALER-ROWNEY
SALISBURY EASEL
RRP £200

PAINTS

DALER-ROWNEY
SYSTEM 3 250ML ACRYLIC
ALL HALF PRICE

WINSOR & NEWTON
14ML ARTISTS WATERCOLOUR

UP TO 33% OFF

HALF PRICE

BRUSHES

£12.95
CASS ART
HOG BRUSH PACK SET OF 6

UP TO 40% OFF

WINSOR & NEWTON
ARTIST OIL 37ML

CANVAS

WINSOR & NEWTON
ARTIST QUALITY CANVAS
OVER 60 SIZES

HALF PRICE

SETS AND GIFTS

LESS THAN HALF PRICE

A4 - £3.50
A5 - £2.75
DALER-ROWNEY EBONY
HARDBACK SKETCH PAD
RRP (A4) £8.50, (A5) £6.25

HALF PRICE

£12.95
LETRASET MANGA PACK
RRP £31.86

LESS THAN HALF PRICE

£9.95
WINSOR & NEWTON 8X14ML
DRAWING INKS SET RRP £19.95

HALF PRICE

£4.75
FABER-CASTELL 9000 12 ART
PENCILS 8B-2H IN TIN RRP £9.50

CASS PROMISE – CREATIVITY AT THE LOWEST PRICES. WE'RE CONFIDENT OUR PRICES CAN'T BE BEATEN

ISLINGTON - FLAGSHIP STORE
66-67 COLEBROOKE ROW, N1
020 7354 2999 OPEN 7 DAYS

CHARING CROSS
13 CHARING CROSS RD, WC2
020 7930 9940 OPEN 7 DAYS

KENSINGTON
220 KENSINGTON HIGH ST, W8
020 7937 6506 OPEN 7 DAYS

SOHO
24 BERWICK STREET, W1
020 7287 8504 OPEN 7 DAYS

CASS ART
WWW.CASSART.CO.UK
INFO@CASSART.CO.UK

ALL OFFERS SUBJECT TO AVAILABILITY & PRICES SUBJECT TO CHANGE. ALL PRICES VALID TO 01/01/08. CASS PROMISE, ASK IN STORES.

under the Westway and along the walkway to Ladbroke Grove are emerging designer and vintage clothes on Fridays (usually marginally less busy) and Saturdays (invariably manic).

Specialist

Books & magazines

Central branches of the big chains include **Borders Books & Music** (203 Oxford Street, W1D 2LE, 7292 1600, www.borderssstores.co.uk) and the massive **Waterstone's** flagship (203-206 Piccadilly, SW1Y 6WW, 7851 2400, www.waterstones.co.uk), with a licensed bar-café and a branch of Trailfinders.

General

Daunt Books
83-84 Marylebone High Street, Marylebone, W1U 4QW (7224 2295/www.dauntbooks.co.uk). Baker Street tube. **Open** 9am-7.30pm Mon-Sat; 11am-6pm Sun. **Credit** MC, V. **Map** p398 G5.
A lovely Edwardian bookshop known for its travel section: books – related literature as well as guides –

are arranged by country in the expansive, three-floor back room complete with oak galleries and conservatory ceiling. The children's room is also excellent.
Other locations 193 Haverstock Hill, Belsize Park, NW3 4QL (7794 4006); 51 South End Road, Hampstead, NW3 2QB (7794 8206); 112-114 Holland Park Avenue, Holland Park, W11 4UA (7727 7022).

Foyles
113-119 Charing Cross Road, Soho, WC2H 0EB (7437 5660/www.foyles.co.uk). Tottenham Court Road tube. **Open** 9.30am-9pm Mon-Sat; noon-6pm Sun. **Credit** AmEx, MC, V. **Map** p407 X2.
Independently owned and open since 1906, Foyles is London's best-known bookshop, revered for the volume of its stock, which is spread over five floors. Ray's Jazz (*see p261*) and a café are on the first floor.
Other locations Riverside, Level 1, Royal Festival Hall, South Bank, SE1 8XX (7981 9739).

Hatchards
187 Piccadilly, St James's, W1J 9LE (7439 9921/ www.hatchards.co.uk). Piccadilly Circus tube. **Open** 9.30am-7pm Mon-Sat; noon-6pm Sun. **Credit** AmEx, DC, MC, V. **Map** p406 V5.
London's oldest bookshop (established 1797) is spread over five floors and has counted Disraeli, Byron and Wilde among its customers. It's particularly good for travel, biography and signed editions.

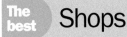

The best Shops

For unusual souvenirs
Bring home some London sauce from erotic emporium **Coco de Mer** (*see p255*), an exquisite hand-picked estate tea from **Postcard Teas** (*see p254*), or a limited-edition artwork from **Shelf** (*see p256*).

For cutting-edge fashion
Established avant-gardists and emerging talent rub shoulders at **b store** (*see p245*), **no-one** (*see p247*) is the ultimate Shoreditch style destination and über-boutique **Browns** (*see p245*) champions rising catwalk stars.

For unique accessories
Georgina Goodman's (*see p252*) shoes, **Bagman and Robin**'s bags (*see p250*), undies from **Miss Lala's Boudoir** (*see p251*) and jewellery from **Kabiri** (*see p251*).

For a taste of Britain
A Gold (*see p255*) provides an edible tour of the UK, **Neal's Yard Dairy** (*see p255*) is tops for regional cheeses, and **Daylesford Organic** (*see p255*) brings wholesome, organic country fare to town.

For budget style
Second-hand Savile Row suits go for a song at **Old Hat** (*see p249*) and there are acres of well-priced frocks at **Beyond Retro** (*see p249*). **Burberry** and **Paul Smith**'s discount outlets (*see p248*) offer bargain Brit style.

To revisit retail past
Old-fashioned specialists include **James Smith & Sons** (*see p256*) for brollies, **Bates the Hatter** (*see p250*), **Flittner** (*see p257*) barbers and **Benjamin Pollock's Toyshop** (*see p245*). A stroll through the **Burlington Arcade** (*see p237*) takes you back to a gentler age.

For green goods
Junky Styling (*see p248*) turns old clothes into hip gear, while **Terra Plana**'s (*see p252*) eco-conscious footwear is bang on trend.

For an atmospheric browse
Fashion imitates art at **Dover Street Market** (*see p246*), known for its theatrical displays. **Daunt Books**' (*see p241*) travel section is housed in a beautiful Edwardian conservatory, while **Weardowney Get-Up Boutique** (*see p247*) is within a charming converted pub.

Eat, Drink, Shop

John Sandoe

10 Blacklands Terrace, Chelsea, SW3 2SR (7589 9473/www.johnsandoe.com). Sloane Square tube. **Open** 9.30am-5.30pm Mon, Tue, Thur-Sat; 9.30am-7.30pm Wed; noon-6pm Sun. **Credit** AmEx, DC, MC, V. **Map** p397 F11.

Tucked away on a Chelsea side street, this 50-year-old independent looks just as a bookshop should. The stock is literally packed to the rafters, and of the 25,000 books here, 24,000 are a single copy – so there's serious breadth.

Specialist

Books for Cooks

4 Blenheim Crescent, Notting Hill, W11 1NN (7221 1992/www.booksforcooks.com). Ladbroke Grove tube. **Open** 10am-6pm Tue-Sat. **Credit** MC, V.

Books in this celebrated shop cover hundreds of cuisines, chefs and cookery techniques. Even better, the shop's kitchen-café tests different recipes every day, sold to eager customers from noon.

Magma

117-119 Clerkenwell Road, Holborn, EC1R 5BY (7242 9503/www.magmabooks.com). Chancery Lane tube/Farringdon tube/rail. **Open** 10am-7pm Mon-Sat. **Credit** AmEx, MC, V. **Map** p402 N4.

If you can visualise it, this art and design specialist has probably got a book on it. Magazines, DVDs, trendy toys, T-shirts and a series of commissioned limited-edition posters and cards arealso sold. **Other locations** 8 Earlham Street, WC2H 9RY (7240 8498); 16 Earlham Street, WC2H 9LN (7240 7571).

Stanfords

12-14 Long Acre, Covent Garden, WC2E 9LP (7836 1321/www.stanfords.co.uk). Covent Garden or Leicester Square tube. **Open** 9am-7.30pm Mon, Wed, Fri; 9.30am-7.30pm Tue; 9am-8pm Thur; 10am-7pm Sat; noon-6pm Sun. **Credit** MC, V. **Map** p407 Y3.

Three floors of travel guides, travel literature, maps, language guides, atlases and magazines. The basement houses the full range of British Ordnance Survey maps, and you can plan your next trip over Fairtrade coffee in the new Natural Café.

Used & antiquarian

Bookended by Charing Cross Road and St Martin's Lane, picturesque **Cecil Court** (www.cecilcourt.co.uk) is known for its line-up of antiquarian book, map and print dealers. Notable residents include children's illustrated book specialist **Marchpane** (no.16, 7836 8661) and 40-year veteran **David Drummond at Pleasures of Past Times** (no.11, 7836 1142), who specialises in theatre and magic. A more recent arrival is **Red Snapper** (no.22, 7240 2075) for small-press fiction, beat poetry and counter-culture classics.

Biblion

1-7 Davies Mews, Mayfair, W1K 5AB (7629 1374/www.biblion.com). Bond Street tube. **Open** 10am-6pm Mon-Fri. **Credit** MC, V. **Map** p398 H6.

Around 50 dealers display their various wares at these spacious premises in Grays Antique Market. The prices are as broad as the stock.

Simon Finch Rare Books

53 Maddox Street, Mayfair, W1S 2PN (7499 0974/www.simonfinch.com). Oxford Circus tube. **Open** 10am-6pm Mon-Fri. **Credit** AmEx, MC, V. **Map** p398 J6.

Housed in a narrow Mayfair townhouse, Simon Finch's era-spanning, idiosyncratic collection contains wonderful surprises, from one of the original copies of Hubert Selby Jr's *Last Exit to Brooklyn* to esoterica like *Mushrooms, Russia & History*. Prices start at around £20 or £30, so it's worth popping in even if you're not a serious collector.

Skoob

Unit 66, The Brunswick, Bloomsbury, WC1N 1AE (7278 8760/www.skoob.com). Russell Square tube. **Open** 10am-8pm Mon-Sat; 10am-6pm Sun. **Credit** MC, V. **Map** p399 L4.

A back-to-basics basement showcasing some 50,000 titles covering virtually every subject, from philosophy and biography to politics and the occult.

Children

Fashion

Baby superstore **Mamas & Papas** (256-258 Regent Street, W1B 3AF, 0870 850 2845, www.mamasandpapas.co.uk) sells everything from bibs to christening robes.

Caramel Baby & Child

291 Brompton Road, South Kensington, SW3 2DY (7589 7001/www.caramel-shop.co.uk). South Kensington tube. **Open** 10am-6pm Mon-Sat; 10am-5pm Sun. **Credit** AmEx, MC, V. **Map** p397 E10.

Tasteful togs for 0-12-year-olds. The look is relaxed, and well finished in modern, muted colour schemes; while clothes are clearly inspired by the sturdy styles of the past, they never submit to full-blown nostalgia. Prices are commensurate with quality: around £40 for a boy's polo shirt, £50-£60 for knitwear and £60 or £70 for a dress. **Other locations** 77 Ledbury Road, Notting Hill, W11 2AG (7727 0906/www.caramel-shop.co.uk).

Daisy & Tom

181-183 King's Road, Chelsea, SW3 5EB (7352 5000/www.daisyandtom.com). Sloane Square tube then 11, 19, 22 bus/49 bus. **Open** 9.30am-6pm Mon, Tue, Thur, Fri; 10am-7pm Wed; 9.30am-6.30pm Sat; 11am-5pm Sun. **Credit** AmEx, MC, V. **Map** p397 E12.

A boon for harassed parents, this all-rounder is the friendliest kids' shop in London. Four times a day there's a call to the children to gather at the ground-floor carousel for a gentle spin. There are half-hourly

Where to shop

Covent Garden & Soho

The famous former flower market-turned-shopping precinct is choked with chains and crowds, but **Neal Street** and the streets radiating off **Seven Dials** rule for trainers and streetwise gear. Another urbanwear hotspot is Soho's **Carnaby Street**, which has traded tacky tourist shops for hip chains and independents. **Berwick Street** is still hanging on to some record shops, while **Charing Cross Road** (especially Cecil Court) is prime browsing territory for bookish types.

Oxford Street & Marylebone

Oxford Street, London's commercial backbone, heaves with big chains and department stores, which spill over on to elegant, curving **Regent Street**. In contrast, **Marylebone** has a villagey atmosphere and a collection of small shops that sell everything from designer jewellery to farmhouse cheeses. Venture further north to **Church Street** for antiques.

Notting Hill

Best known for its antiques market on **Portobello Road**, Notting Hill also has an impressive cache of posh boutiques around the intersection of **Westbourne Grove** and **Ledbury Road** – a laid-back alternative to the West End and Chelsea. The area is also good for rare vinyl and vintage clothes.

Mayfair & St James's

The traditional home of tailors (**Savile Row**) and shirtmakers (**Jermyn Street**), this patch also retains venerable specialist hatters, cobblers and perfumers. **Bond Street** glitters with posh jewellers and designer flagships.

Chelsea & Knightsbridge

The legendary **King's Road** is pretty bland now, but punctuated with some interesting shops. Plush international designer salons line **Sloane Street** and mix with chains on **Knightsbridge**, which is anchored by deluxe department stores.

Kensington

Once a hub of hip fashion, **Kensington High Street** has given way to an influx of chains; it's still worth exploring the backstreets leading up to Notting Hill Gate, though. Rarefied antiques shops gather on **Kensington Church Street**. In South Ken, **Brompton Cross** has glossy contemporary furniture showrooms and designer boutiques.

East London

An unmissable destination for offbeat independent shops and some of the city's best markets. Head for **Brick Lane** and its offshoots for clothing, accessories and home goods by idiosyncratic young designers, and for heaps of vintage fashion. **Shoreditch** and **Hoxton** have further hip boutiques, furniture stores and bookshops.

North London

The sprawling, grungy markets of **Camden** are best left to the under-25s, but nearby leafy **Primrose Hill** has an exquisite selection of small shops selling, among other things, quirky lingerie and vintage clothes. Antiques dealers are thinning out on Islington's **Camden Passage**, but there is a growing number of other indies, including a gourmet chocolatier and an ethical boutique.

puppet shows in the clothing department too, which stocks its own Daisy & Tom label, Catimini, One Small Step One Giant Leap shoes and more. The vast toy selection covers everything from Lego kits to handmade rocking horses.

Their Nibs

214 Kensington Park Road, Notting Hill, W11 1NR (7221 4263/www.theirnibs.com). Ladbroke Grove or Notting Hill Gate tube. **Open** 9.30am-6pm Mon-Fri; 10am-6pm Sat; noon-5pm Sun. **Credit** AmEx, MC, V. **Map** p394 A6.
A visit to this shop is a treat. There's a play corner with a blackboard, books and toys to occupy tinies while older ones browse, and the vintage-inspired gear encompasses quirky little dungarees for crawling babes and demure summer frocks for preening

girls. Distinctive signature prints include cowboys, pirates, vintage cars and fairies. Toys and accessories are also sold here.

Toys

The many branches of the **Early Learning Centre** (www.elc.co.uk) are all dedicated to imaginative play. **Daisy & Tom** and **Their Nibs** (for both, *see above*) have great toy selections, while **Harrods** and **Selfridges** (for both, *see p238*) have dedicated toy departments.

Honeyjam

267 Portobello Road, Notting Hill, W11 1LR (7243 0449/www.honeyjam.co.uk). LadbrokeGrove

or Notting Hill Gate tube. **Open** 10am-6pm Mon-Sat; 11am-4pm Sun. **Credit** MC, V. **Map** p394 A6.
Despite the hype (the shop is co-owned by former model Jasmine Guinness), Honeyjam is full of fun, with a good selection of pocket money-priced trinkets.

Benjamin Pollock's Toyshop
44 The Market, Covent Garden, WC2E 8RF (7379 7866/www.pollocks-coventgarden.co.uk). Covent Garden tube. **Open** 10.30am-6pm Mon-Sat; 11am-4pm Sun. **Credit** AmEx, MC, V. **Map** p407 Z3.
Best-known for its toy theatres (from £2.95 for a tiny one in a matchbox to about £70 for elaborate models), Pollock's is also superb for traditional toys, such as knitted animals, china tea sets, masks, glove puppets, cards, spinning tops and fortune-telling fish.

Electronics & photography

General
Tottenham Court Road (map p399 K5) has the city's best electronics and computer shops.

Ask
248 Tottenham Court Road, Fitzrovia, W1T 7QZ (7637 0353/www.askdirect.co.uk). Tottenham Court Road tube. **Open** 10am-7pm Mon-Wed, Fri, Sat; 10am-8pm Thur; noon-6pm Sun. **Credit** AmEx, DC, MC, V. **Map** p399 K5.
Some shops on this thoroughfare feel gloomy and claustrophobic, but Ask has four capacious, well-organised floors that allow space to browse. Stock – spanning digital cameras, MP3 players, radios, laptops as well as hi-fis and TVs and all the requisite accessories – concentrates on the major consumer brands. Prices are competitive.

Specialist
The London **Apple Store**, complete with its trademark 'Genius Bar' offering technical support, is behind a grand façade in Regent Street (no.235, 7153 9000, www.apple.com). Several shops on Tottenham Court Road offer laptop repairs, but we recommend **Einstein Computer Services**, which operates on a call-out basis for £20 per hour (07957 557065, www.einsteinpcs.co.uk). **Adam Phones** (2-3 Dolphin Square, Edensor Road, W4 2ST, 0800 123 000, www.adamphones.com) rent out mobile phone handsets for £1 a day with reasonable call charges. For film processing, try citywide branches of **Boots** (*see p258*), **Jessops** (www.jessops.com) and **Jacobs Photo & Digital** (www.jacobsdigital.co.uk).

Calumet
93-103 Drummond Street, Somers Town, NW1 2HJ (7380 1144/www.calumetphoto.com). Euston tube/rail. **Open** 8.30am-5.30pm Mon-Fri; 9.30am-5.30pm Sat; 10am-4pm Sun. **Credit** AmEx, MC, V. **Map** p398 J3.

Caters mainly for professional snappers, students and darkroom workers. Lights, power packs, gels, tripods, printing and storage stock complement top-end digital gear. Also does repairs and rental.
Other locations 175 Wardour Street, Soho, W1F 8WU (7434 1848); 10 Heathmans Road, Parsons Green, SW6 4TJ (7384 3270).

Fashion

Designer
We've focused on boutiques that showcase a range of labels below, but key British designers with flagships in the capital include punk pioneer **Vivienne Westwood** (44 Conduit Street, W1S 2YL, 7439 1109, www.vivienne westwood.com), godfather of tailoring-with-a-twist **Paul Smith** (Westbourne House, 120 & 122 Kensington Park Road, W11 2EP, 7727 3553, www.paulsmith.co.uk), new guard **Stella McCartney** (30 Bruton Street, W1J 6LG, 7518 3100, www.stellamccartney.com) and **Alexander McQueen** (4-5 Old Bond Street, W1S 4PD, 7355 0088, www.alexander mcqueen.com), as well as rising stars **Preen** (5 Portobello Green, 281 Portobello Road, W10 5TZ, 8968 1542) and **PPQ** (47 Conduit Street, W1S 2YP, 7494 9789, www.ppqclothing.com).

b store
24A Savile Row, Mayfair, W1S 3PR (7734 6846/ www.bstorelondon.com). Oxford Circus tube. **Open** 10.30am-6.30pm Mon-Fri; 10am-6pm Sat. **Credit** AmEx, MC, V. **Map** p406 U3.
A platform for cutting-edge designers, b store is holding its own on trad tailors' enclave Savile Row. This is the place to preview the next big thing in fashion for both men and women, such as Belgrade-born Roksanda Ilincic and Dane Camilla Staerk, alongside more established iconoclasts such as Peter Jensen, Eley Kishimoto and Bi La Li. *Photos p253.*

Browns
23-27 South Molton Street, Mayfair, W1K 5RD (7514 0000/www.brownsfashion.com). Bond Street tube. **Open** 10am-6.30pm Mon-Wed, Fri, Sat; 10am-7pm Thur. **Credit** AmEx, MC, V. **Map** p398 H6.
Joan Burstein's venerable store has reigned supreme for 38 years. Among the 100-odd designers jostling for attention among its five interconnecting shops (menswear is at no.23) are Chloé, Dries Van Noten and Balenciaga. As well as the superbrands, the store champions rising stars, such as Central St Martins graduates Christopher Kane and Gareth Pugh. Across the road, Browns Focus is younger and more casual, while Browns Labels for Less is loaded with the leftovers from the previous season.
Other locations Browns Focus, 38-39 South Molton Street, Mayfair, W1K 5RN (7514 0063); Browns Labels for Less, 50 South Molton Street, W1K 5RD (7514 0052); 11-12 Hind Street, W1U 3BE (7514 0056); 6C Sloane Street, Chelsea, SW1X 9LE (7514 0040).

Dover Street Market

17-18 Dover Street, Mayfair, W1S 4LT (7518 0680/www.doverstreetmarket.com). Green Park tube. **Open** 11am-6pm Mon-Wed, Fri, Sat; 11am-7pm Thur. **Credit** AmEx, MC, V. **Map** p400 J7.
Comme des Garçons designer Rei Kawakubo's ground-breaking six-storey space combines the edgy energy of London's indoor markets – concrete floors, tills housed in corrugated-iron shacks, Portaloo dressing rooms – with rarefied labels. All 14 of the Comme collections are here, alongside exclusive lines such as Azzedine Alaïa and Veronique Branquinho and outposts of interesting shops such as Shoreditch's Labour and Wait and LA vintage-couture emporium Decades. The theatrical displays make it fun to browse, and there's an outpost of Parisian fave Rose Bakery on the top floor.

Koh Samui

65-67 Monmouth Street, Covent Garden, WC2H 9DG (7240 4280/www.kohsamui.co.uk). Covent Garden tube. **Open** 10.30am-6.30pm Mon-Wed, Fri, Sat; 10.30am-7pm Thur; noon-5.30pm Sun. **Credit** AmEx, DC, MC, V. **Map** p407 X3.

Vintage pieces sourced from around the world share rail space with a finely tuned selection of heavyweight designers at Koh Samui, resulting in a delightfully eclectic mix of stock. Marc by Marc Jacobs, Balenciaga and Dries Van Noten are always well represented, alongside small independent labels. Vast glass cabinets glint with beads and baubles by a global array of independent designers; prices start at around £50 for a pair of earrings.

Labour of Love

193 Upper Street, Islington, N1 1RQ (7354 9333/www.labour-of-love.co.uk). Highbury & Islington tube/rail. **Open** 11am-6.30pm Mon-Sat; noon-5pm Sun. **Credit** AmEx, MC, V. **Map** p402 O1.
Bored of seeing the same stock in every department store and gift shop in London, designer Francesca Forcolini decided to cram her own boutique with hand-picked clothes and accessories from London, Paris and beyond. Alongside her own idiosyncratic label are charming knitted accessories from Lowie and shirts remade from Savile Row offcuts by Yoko Brown (from £105). Antique-looking trinkets and coffee table books add up to a rewarding browse.

Sure can pick 'em

Come shopping! **Lisa Ritchie**, editor of Time Out's annual *Shops & Services* guide, knows what to avoid and what you'll enjoy.

Many of London's stores and markets are tourist attractions in their own right. Some really are unmissable, others unspeakable. Everyone has heard of **Harrods** (*see p238*), but the store has lost some of its English reserve since Mohamed Al Fayed bought the place. It's still worth a visit, if only to marvel at the spectacular Edwardian food halls and the extraordinary ego of the man who would plant a lifesize waxwork of himself among the designer menswear. But, unless you're after one of the store's exclusive lines (K by Karl Lagerfeld, for example, or the full range of hard-to-find French skincare brand Darphin), I don't advise spending your money here – I've seen the same goods cheaper elsewhere. And whatever you do, don't go on a Saturday.

Many of London's tourist-magnets are equally beloved by locals. **Liberty** (*see p238*) has retained its integrity through careful selection of unusual merchandise – from the latest niche labels to Arts and Crafts furniture in keeping with its heritage – and bringing its signature-print lines up to date instead of mass-manufacturing novelty teddy bears and mugs. I have a soft spot for **Fortnum & Mason** (*see p238*), which, although sensitively modernised for its 300th birthday,

maintains anachronistically attired staff and obscure relishes. It's expensive, but the quality is excellent – and hardly anyone ventures beyond the food halls, so the gift floors are delightfully quiet. Several shopping destinations once dismissed as 'for the tourists' are experiencing a renaissance. Take the **Burlington Arcade** (*see p237*). Once a staid shrine to dowdy cashmere twinsets and gent's velvet slippers, it is gradually being reinvented, with upstarts such as indie shoe designer Beatrix Ong, formerly of hip Primrose Hill, taking up residence. **Carnaby Street**, which had descended into tacky studded wristband/novelty hat territory, has been resurrected as a decent destination for streetwear, whereas 'alternative' **Camden** is giving in to full-scale tat. The most famous market of them all – **Covent Garden** – is best avoided unless you're after a toy theatre from the wonderful Benjamin Pollock's Toyshop. It's a chain- and crowd-clogged tourist trap. A better bet for a colourful scene and a mix of goods encompassing crafts, fashion and food is the **Spitalfields** and **Brick Lane** conglomeration on a Sunday (*see p239*). Other iconic markets, such as Petticoat Lane, are

no-one

*1 Kingsland Road, Shoreditch, E2 8AA (7613 5314/
www.no-one.co.uk). Old Street tube/rail.* **Open** 11am-
7pm Mon-Sat; noon-6pm Sun. **Credit** AmEx, DC,
MC, V. **Map** p403 01.

A favourite of Shoreditch locals and noncomformist
style icons such as Róisín Murphy and Björk, this
shop/café stocks a melange of cool merchandise: the
latest smock dresses from PPQ, limited-edition
men's cardies (from around £80), reasonably priced
feminine frocks by Mine (from £70) and Peter Jensen
plimsolls, plus quirky toys for grown-ups, vintage
sunglasses and cult magazines and books.

Shop at Bluebird

*350 King's Road, Chelsea, SW3 5UU (7351
3873/www.theshopatbluebird.com). Sloane Square
tube.* **Open** 9am-7pm Mon-Sat; noon-6pm Sun.
Credit AmEx, MC, V. **Map** p397 D12.

Sharing the landmark art deco garage with Terence
Conran's café/restaurant/deli complex, the Shop at
Bluebird is part lifestyle boutique, part design
gallery. The 10,000sq ft space is a shifting showcase
of clothing (for men, women and children) by a host
of non-ubiquitous designers from Britain and
abroad, lingerie, accessories, furniture, books and
gadgets. The constantly changing displays have a
sense of fun – the book section is illuminated by a
ceiling installation of over 1,000 lightbulbs, while
handbags sit on antique silver platters. The music
section is manned by guest DJs at weekends, and a
luxurious on-site spa should be open by the time this
guide is published.

Weardowney Get-Up Boutique

*9 Ashbridge Street, Marylebone, NW8 8DH
(7725 9694/www.weardowney.com). Edgware Road
tube/Marylebone tube/rail.* **Open** 10am-6pm Mon-
Wed, Fri, Sat; 10am-9pm Thur. **Credit** AmEx, MC,
V. **Map** p395 E4.

Former model and one-time knitwear designer for
John Galliano Gail Downey joined forces with fellow
model Amy Wear to create their own label in 2004.
Hand-knitted by an army of outworkers across the
UK, the clothes bear little resemblance to your gran's
cosy cardies, embracing such fashion-forward styles
as capes, minidresses reminiscent of Victorian
bathing costumes, legwarmer-style 'spats', even

known for cheap goods – but you get what
you pay for. And for bargains, you're in the
wrong city – unless you like **second-hand**
and **vintage gear** (*see p249*). The legendary
London street style can be found in an ever-
growing array of boutiques, but check the
provenance of the clothes you're buying.
American and Australian labels are currently
very much in vogue – with prices that are a
lot steeper than in their home countries.

A final tip: don't stay on the main drags,
where you'll largely find the ubiquitous
chains, but instead explore the backstreets.
Take a short detour from Sloane Square
to charming **Elizabeth Street** in Belgravia,
where you'll find everything from designer
dog collars to rare perfumes. Or slip behind
Carnaby for a hidden cache of indies on
cobbled **Newburgh Street**. There's blessed
respite from nerve-jangling Oxford Street in
the pedestrianised peace of **St Christopher's
Place**, and even in villagey Marylebone some
of the most interesting shops are off the High
Street on discreet, winding **Marylebone Lane**.

Eat, Drink, Shop

knitted knickers with rows of frills on the behind. The 'House of Weardowney', the tongue-in-cheek catch-all for their complex in a converted pub, contains the boutique, the 'School of Craftsmanship', where knitting and hand-sewing courses are held, and an on-site guesthouse (*see p53*). Vintagey cushions and smartly boxed Weardowney kits to create your own garments (£25-£78) are also for sale.

Discount

See also p245 **Browns Labels for Less**.

Burberry Factory Shop
29-53 Chatham Place, Hackney, E9 6LP (8328 4287). Hackney Central rail. **Open** 10am-6pm Mon-Sat; 11am-5pm Sun. **Credit** AmEx, DC, MC, V.
This warehouse space showcases seconds and excess stock reduced by 50% or more. Classic men's macs can be had for around £199 or less, while cashmere sweaters come in at £50.

Paul Smith Sale Shop
23 Avery Row, Mayfair, W1X 9HB (7493 1287/ www.paulsmith.co.uk). Bond Street tube. **Open** 10.30am-6.30pm Mon-Wed, Fri, Sat; 10.30am-7pm Thur; 1-5.30pm Sun. **Credit** AmEx, DC, MC, V. **Map** p400 H7.
Samples and previous season's stock at 30%-50% off – clothes for men, women and children, as well as accessories.

Primark
499-517 Oxford Street, Marble Arch, W1K 7DA (7495 0420/www.primark.co.uk). Marble Arch tube. **Open** 9am-9pm Mon-Fri; 9am-8pm Sat; noon-6pm Sun. **Credit** AmEx, MC, V. **Map** p398 G6.
There were scenes recalling the storming of the Bastille when the flagship of the trend-led, cheap as chips retailer opened in 2007.
Other locations throughout the city.

General

London's high-street chains have their finger on the fashion pulse. Among the best are young, streetwise **All Saints** (57-59 Long Acre, WC2E 9JL, 7836 0801, www.allsaints.co.uk) and chic, designer-look **Reiss** (Kent House, 14-17 Market Place, W1H 7AJ, 7637 9112, www.reiss.co.uk). **Topshop**'s massive, throbbing flagship (214 Oxford Street, W1W 8LG, 7636 7700, www.topshop.com) houses a boutique of high-fashion designer capsule ranges, concessions, and vintage clothes, and Hersheson's Blow Dry Bar (*see p257*). Also worth a look is H&M's new upmarket sibling **COS** (222 Regent Street, W1B 5BD, 7478 0400, www.cosstores.com), offering chic basics in luxurious fabrics.

A Butcher of Distinction
11 Dray Walk, Old Truman Brewery, off Brick Lane, Spitalfields, E1 6QL (7770 6111/www.butcherof distinction.com). Liverpool Street tube/rail. **Open** 10am-7pm daily. **Credit** AmEx, MC, V. **Map** p405 S5.
In contrast to the area's more experimental retail spaces, A Butcher embodies understated cool. The store is beautifully designed while looking artlessly thrown together, with garments laid out on chunky wooden tables and old-fashioned butchers' hooks dangling nicely aged leather accessories. The clothes have a similarly laid-back vibe: English heritage-based classics, such as check shirts and waxed jackets, by British label Steven Alan, and worn-in looking basics from New York's Nom de Guerre.

Junky Styling
12 Dray Walk, Old Truman Brewery, 91-95 Brick Lane, Spitalfields, E1 6RF (7247 1883/www.junky styling.co.uk). Liverpool Street tube/rail. **Open** 10.30am-6.30pm daily. **Credit** AmEx, MC, V. **Map** p403 S5.

Three Threads.

Junky offers an innovative take on second-hand clothes that fits in with our increased eco-awareness. Owners Kerry Seager and Anni Saunders take two or more formal garments (a pinstripe suit and a tweed jacket, say) and recycle them into an entirely new piece (skirts £50-£200, jackets £120-£350).

Three Threads
47-49 Charlotte Road, Shoreditch, EC2A 3QT (7749 0503/www.thethreethreads.com). Old Street tube/rail. **Open** 11am-7pm Mon-Sat; noon-5pm Sun. **Credit** MC, V. **Map** p403 R4.
Free beer, a jukebox well stocked with dad rock and conveniently placed bar stools around the till... the Three Threads tempts even the most shop-phobic male. While the threads themselves come in the form of exclusive, cult labels such as Japan's Tenderloin, Swedish outerwear by Fjall Raven, and New York's Built by Wendy, the vibe is more like a pal's house.

Tailors

Mr Eddie & Chris Kerr
52 Berwick Street, Soho, W1F 8SL (7437 3727/ www.eddiekerr.co.uk). Oxford Circus tube. **Open** 8am-5.30pm Mon-Fri; 8.30am-1pm Sat. **Credit** MC, V. **Map** p406 V2.
A Soho institution since the early 1960s, Eddie Kerr, and now his son Chris, turn out sharp bespoke gear in friendly, unostentatious surroundings. Suits cost from around £1,000.

Pokit
53 Lamb's Conduit Street, Holborn, WC1N 3NB (7430 9782/www.pokit.co.uk). Holborn tube. **Open** 11am-7pm Mon-Sat. **Credit** AmEx, MC, V. **Map** p399 L5.
Pokit's cool, contemporary custom-made suits for both men and women range from £500 to £800. Sturdy 'capsule' bags and sharp shoes are also sold.

Timothy Everest
35 Bruton Place, Mayfair, W1J 6NS (7629 6236/ www.timothyeverest.co.uk). Bond Street tube. **Open** 10am-6pm Mon-Fri; 11am-5pm alternate Sat. **Credit** AmEx, MC, V. **Map** p400 H7.
One-time apprentice to the legendary Tommy Nutter, Everest is a star of the latest generation of London tailors and known for his more relaxed 21st-century definition of style.

Vintage & second-hand

Luna & Curious (*see p256*) has a reasonably priced selection of reconditioned pieces, while **Dover Street Market** (*see p246*) houses an outpost of LA store Decades.

Beyond Retro
112 Cheshire Street, Spitalfields, E2 6EJ (7613 3636/ www.beyondretro.com). Liverpool Street tube/rail. **Open** 10am-6pm Mon-Wed, Fri-Sun; 10am-8pm Thur. **Credit** MC, V. **Map** p405 S4.

This enormous bastion of second-hand clothing and accessories is the starting point for many an expert stylist, thrifter or fashion designer on the hunt for mega-bargains and inspiration. The 10,000 items on the warehouse floor include 1950s dresses, cowboy boots and denim hot pants, many under £20.

Girl Can't Help It
Alfie's Antique Market, 13-25 Church Street, Marylebone, NW8 8DT (7724 8984/www.thegirl canthelpit.com). Edgware Road tube/Marylebone tube/rail. **Open** 10am-6pm Tue-Sat. **Credit** AmEx, MC, V. **Map** p395 E4.
Exuberant New Yorker Sparkle Moore and her Dutch partner Jasja Boelhouwer (AKA Cad Van Swankster) preside over this cache of vintage Hollywood kitsch at the front of Alfie's. For the ladies there are glamorous red-carpet gowns and 1950s circle skirts (£100-£350) decorated with everything from kitsch kittens to Mexican-style patterns, plus a great range of glam accessories from leopard-print shoes to seashell-encrusted straw bags. The suave menswear encompasses Hawaiian shirts (from £50), gabardine jackets, slick 1940s and '50s suits and camp accessories, such as tiki-themed bar glasses and pin-up ties.

Old Hat
66 Fulham High Street, Fulham, SW6 3LQ (7610 6558). Putney Bridge tube. **Open** 10.30am-6.30pm Mon-Sat. **Credit** MC, V.
A haunt of stylists and design teams from brands such as Burberry and Dunhill, David Saxby's menswear emporium is perfect for those with lord of the manor pretensions without the trust fund to match. Savile Row suits can be had for under £100.

Palette London
21 Canonbury Lane, Islington, N1 2AS (7288 7428/www.palette-london.com). Highbury & Islington tube/rail. **Open** 11.30am-6.30pm Mon-Wed, Fri; 11.30am-7pm Thur; noon-5.30pm Sun. **Credit** MC, V.
Palette sells a 50/50 mix of vintage and contemporary designers, selected to complement each other. Look out for Viennese designer Anna Aichinger, who trained with Viktor & Rolf and creates wonderful 1940s-inspired dresses and pencil skirts. Vintage glamour comes courtesy of legendary labels such as Pucci, Courrèges and homegrown talents Ossie Clark, Biba and Janice Wainwright. Prices are mid to high end, but the quality is superb. *Photo p250.*

Rellik
8 Golborne Road, Ladbroke Grove, W10 5NW (8962 0089/www.relliklondon.co.uk). Westbourne Park tube. **Open** 10am-6pm Tue-Sat. **Credit** AmEx, DC, MC, V.
Within spitting distance of the Trellick Tower, this celeb fave was set up in 2000 by three Portobello market stallholders: Fiona Stuart, Claire Stansfield and Steven Philip. The trio have different tastes, which means there's a mix of pieces by the likes of Halston, Vivienne Westwood, Bill Gibb, Christian Dior and the ever-popular Ossie Clark.

Palette London – a splash of vintage here, a splash of designer there. *See p249.*

Fashion accessories & services

Clothing hire

Lipman & Sons

22 Charing Cross Road, WC2H 0HR (7240 2310/ www.lipmanandsons.co.uk). Leicester Square tube. **Open** 9am-6pm Mon-Wed, Fri Sat; 9am-8pm Thur. **Credit** AmEx, DC, MC, V. **Map** p407 X4.
Reliable, long-standing formalwear specialist.

Cleaning & repairs

British Invisible Mending Service

32 Thayer Street, Marylebone, W1U 2QT (7935 2487/www.invisible-mending.co.uk). Bond Street tube. **Open** 8.30am-5.30pm Mon-Fri; 10am-1pm Sat. **No credit cards. Map** p398 G5.
Family-run for over 50 years, with a 24-hour service.

Celebrity Cleaners

9 Greens Court, Soho, W1F 0HJ (7437 5324). Piccadilly Circus tube. **Open** 8.30am-6.30pm Mon-Fri. **No credit cards. Map** p406 W3.
Dry-cleaner to West End theatres and the ENO. **Other location** Neville House, 27 Page Street, Pimlico, SW1P 4JJ (7821 1777).

Fifth Avenue Shoe Repairers

41 Goodge Street, Fitzrovia, W1T 2PY (7636 6705). Goodge Street tube. **Open** 8am-6.30pm Mon-Fri; 10am-6pm Sat. **Credit** (over £20) AmEx, MC, V. **Map** p398 J5.
High-calibre, speedy shoe repairs; reheeling can be done while you wait.

Hats

Bates the Hatter

21A Jermyn Street, St James's, SW1Y 6HP (7734 2722/www.bates-hats.co.uk). Piccadilly Circus tube. **Open** 9am-5.15pm Mon-Fri; 9.30am-4pm Sat. **Credit** AmEx, DC, MC, V. **Map** p400 J7.
With its wonderful topper-shaped sign and old fashioned interior, Bates is one of London's surviving specialist gems. The traditional headwear spans panamas to tweed deerstalkers by way of dapper flat caps and, of course, classy top hats.

Philip Treacy

69 Elizabeth Street, Belgravia, SW1W 9PJ (7730 3992/www.philiptreacy.co.uk). Sloane Square tube. **Open** 10am-6pm Mon-Fri; 11am-5pm Sat. **Credit** AmEx, MC, V. **Map** p400 G10.
The crowned king of couture headgear's hats are not for the faint-hearted – although the ready-to-wear collection, which tends to feature bold colours, graphic or animal prints and oversized details, is tamer than the OTT catwalk creations. Men are catered for with sleek styles, and Treacy has branched out into bags.

Bags & luggage

Harrods and **Selfridges** (for both, *see p238*) both have an excellent selection of high-quality luggage and bags.

Bagman & Robin

47 Exmouth Market, Clerkenwell, EC1R 4QL (7833 8780/www.bagmanandrobin.com). Farringdon tube then 19, 38 bus. **Open** 11am-6pm Mon-Sat. **Credit** AmEx, MC, V. **Map** p402 N4.

Marco Araldi and Keng Wai Lee's unique handmade bags – from roomy satchels to evening styles – are often characterised by a combination of vintage fabrics and skins and lined with printed fabric. Prices range from £33 to around £400.

Globe-Trotter
54-55 Burlington Arcade, Mayfair, W1J 0LB (7529 5950/www.globe-trotterltd.com). Green Park tube. **Open** 10am-6pm Mon-Sat. **Credit** AmEx, MC, V. **Map** p400 J7.
Globe-Trotter's indestructible steamer-trunk luggage, available in various sizes and colours, accompanied the Queen on honeymoon. Iconic Mackintosh macs share shop space.

Mimi
40 Cheshire Street, Spitalfields, E2 6EH (7729 6699/www.mimimika.com). Liverpool Street tube/rail. **Open** by appointment only Tue-Thur; 11am-6pm Fri-Sun. **Credit** MC, V. **Map** p405 S4.
Designer Mimi Berry's shop showcases a good range of roomy satchels, sleek clutches and supple purses in a generally desirable colour palette, including metallic finishes. Prices are reasonable (from £25 for a purse).

Lingerie & underwear

Agent Provocateur is now a glossy international chain but the original outpost of the shop that popularised high-class kink is still in seedy Soho (6 Broadwick Street, W1V 1FH, 7439 0229, www.agentprovocateur.com). **Marks & Spencer** (*see p238*) is a reliable bet for men's and women's smalls.

Alice & Astrid
30 Artesian Road, Notting Hill, W2 5DD (7985 0888/www.aliceandastrid.com). Notting Hill Gate tube. **Open** 10am-6pm Mon-Fri; 11am-6pm Sat, Sun. **Credit** AmEx, DC, MC, V. **Map** p394 A6.
The lingerie and loungewear displayed in this sweet little whitewashed shop is feminine and flirtatious rather than overtly sexy. Light cotton and silk dominate and seasonally changing prints include carrots, daisies and polka dots in tasteful pale shades, with items such as three-quarter-length bloomers, drawstring pyjama trousers and pretty camisoles.

Miss Lala's Boudoir
148 Gloucester Avenue, Primrose Hill, NW1 8JA (7483 1888/www.misslalasboudoir.co.uk). Chalk Farm tube. **Open** 10am-6pm Mon-Wed, Fri, Sat; 10am-7pm Thur; 11.30am-4.30pm Sun. **Credit** DC, MC, V.
This cute dressing-up box of a shop is brimming with prettily printed pants, frilly undies and retro-styled lingerie. There's also a fine selection of party dresses and glam accessories.

Rigby & Peller
22A Conduit Street, Mayfair, W1S 2XT (7491 2200/www.rigbyandpeller.com). Oxford Circus tube.
Open 9.30am-6pm Mon-Wed, Fri, Sat; 9.30am-7pm Thur. **Credit** AmEx, MC, V. **Map** p400 H7.
The royal corsetière is a service-oriented shop, rather than one that encourages casual browsing; customers are measured, fitted and shown suitable styles from a bank of drawers in the back. The stock is surprisingly contemporary. Pretty own-label bras start from £35, but the bulk of the stock consists of other upmarket brands, including La Perla, Aubade and Lejaby. A made-to-measure service is available. **Other locations** 2 Hans Road, Chelsea, SW3 1RX (0845 076 5545).

Jewellery

See also p256 **Contemporary Applied Arts**.

ec one
41 Exmouth Market, Clerkenwell, EC1R 4QL (7713 6185/www.econe.co.uk). Farringdon tube/rail. **Open** 10am-6pm Mon-Wed, Fri; 11am-7pm Thur; 10.30am-6pm Sat. **Credit** AmEx, MC, V. **Map** p402 N4.
Jos and Alison Skeates showcase jewellery from more than 50 designers. Jos Skeates's own designs are serious statement pieces, with prices to match. There's plenty of choice forthose on tighter budgets, however, including chic wooden bangles from Appartment A Louer and Alex Monroe's gorgeous fripperies for under £200.
Other locations 184 Westbourne Grove, Notting Hill, W11 2RH (7243 8811); 186 Chiswick High Road,Turnham Green, W4 1PP (8995 9515).

Kabiri
37 Marylebone High Street, Marylebone, W1U 4QE (7224 1808/www.kabiri.co.uk). Baker Street tube. **Open** 10am-6.30pm Mon-Sat; noon-5pm Sun. **Credit** AmEx, MC, V. **Map** p398 G5.
The work of more than 100 jewellery designers, from little-known talent to established names – is showcased in this small shop. Innovation and a sense of humour are linking themes. We love Central St Martins graduate Miss Bibi's (AKA Brigitte Giraudi) delightful Intrig collection, inspired by Cluedo, featuring telephone brooches, stiletto earrings and miniature chandeliers, pistols and meat cleavers dangling on delicate chains (from £115). Cairo-based jeweller Dima has collaborated with fashion designer Giles Deacon to create a collection that fuses the modern and ancient (from £585 for a garnet snake ring). There's now a concession in Selfridges.

Garrard
24 Albemarle Street, Mayfair, W1S 4HT (0870 871 8888/www.garrard.com). Bond Street or Green Park tube. **Open** 10am-6pm Mon-Fri; 10am-5pm Sun. **Credit** AmEx, DC, MC, V. **Map** p406 U5.
Whether Jade Jagger's contract as creative director will be renewed is a subject of much debate, but one thing's for certain: she has modernised the Crown Jeweller's diamond-studded designs to appeal to a new generation of bling-seekers.

Eat, Drink, Shop

Shoes

Among the best footwear chains are **Office** (57 Neal Street, WC2H 4NP, 7379 1896, www. office.co.uk), which offers fashion-forward, funky styles for guys and girls at palatable prices; **Kurt Geiger** (198 Regent Street, W1B 5TP, 3238 0044, www.kurtgeiger.com) and **Russell & Bromley** (24-25 New Bond Street, W1S 2PS, 7629 6903, www.russell andbromley.co.uk), which both turn out classy takes on key trends for both sexes; and **Clarks** (476 Oxford Street, W1C 1LD, 7629 9609, www.clarks.co.uk), inventor of the iconic Desert Boot and Wallabes.

Black Truffle

52 Warren Street, Fitzrovia, W1T 5NJ (7388 4547/ www.blacktruffle.com). Warren Street tube. **Open** 11am-6.30pm Mon-Sat. **Credit** AmEx, MC, V. **Map** p398 J4.

The second outpost of the Hackney favourite is stocked with shoes with plenty of personality from the likes of Audley, Chie Mihara, Eley Kishimoto, Rosa Mosa and Repetto, alongside bags and accessories. Owner Melissa Needham runs the Prescott & Mackay School of Fashion and Accessory Design in the basement, offering short courses in shoemaking, bag-making, millinery and other skills. *Photo p254.* **Other locations** 74 Broadway Market, E8 4QJ (7923 9450).

Foot Patrol

16A St Anne's Court, Soho, W1F 0BG (7734 6625/www.foot-patrol.com). Oxford Circus tube. **Open** 11am-7pm Mon-Fri; 11am-6.30pm Sat. **Credit** AmEx, MC, V. **Map** p406 W2.

Famous for its metal display cages (each housing a shoe), Foot Patrol has a special place in the little black books of trainer-heads everywhere. The rapidly changing stock mainly consists of Nike, Adidas and New Balance, with some vintage Californian Vans, fashion-led Chukkas and limited editions from newer brands like Billionaire Boys Club.

Georgina Goodman

12-14 Shepherd Street, Mayfair, W1J 7JF (7499 8599/www.georginagoodman.com). Green Park tube. **Open** 10am-6pm Mon-Sat. **Credit** AmEx, DC, MC, V. **Map** p400 H8.

Goodman started her business crafting sculptural, made-to-measure footwear from a single piece of untreated vegetan leather, and a couture service is still available at her airy, gallery-like shop (from £750 for women, or £1,200 for men). The ready-to-wear range (from £165 for her popular slippers) brings Goodman's individualistic approach to a wider customer base; signature flourishes include hand-painted materials (daubed in the workshop downstairs), unusual colour combinations and innovative heel shapes. Handmade crescent-shaped clutch bags, adorable baby bootees and patchwork leather cushions are further temptations.

Jeffery-West

16 Piccadilly Arcade, St James's, SW1Y 6NH (7499 3360/www.jeffery-west.co.uk). Green Park or Piccadilly Circus tube. **Open** 10am-6pm Mon-Wed, Fri, Sat; 10am-7pm Thur. **Credit** AmEx, MC, V. **Map** p406 V5.

With its playboy vampire's apartment feel – red walls, interesting objets d'art, an unexpected skeleton in the window – this shop is the perfect showcase for Marc Jeffery and Guy West's rakish men's shoes, much loved by modern day dandies. Made to exacting traditional standards in Northampton, the stand-out Punched Gibson in polished burgundy (£195) looks sharp and has a bewitching lustre. **Other locations** 16 Cullum Street, City, EC3M 7JJ (7626 4699).

Terra Plana

64 Neal Street, Covent Garden, WC2H 9PA (7379 5959/www.terraplana.com). Covent Garden tube. **Open** 10am-7pm Mon-Thur, Sat; 10am-7.30pm Fri; noon-6pm Sun. **Credit** AmEx, MC, V. **Map** p407 Y2.

Terra Plana is on a mission to revive artisan shoemaking, producing eco-friendly shoes that are stitched rather than glued and made from chrome-free, vegetable-tanned leather and, where possible, recycled materials. Better still, the utterly contemporary styles are cool, too, so you don't have to sacrifice fashion for your conscience.

Tracey Neuls

29 Marylebone Lane, Marylebone, W1U 2NQ (7935 0039/www.tn29.com). Bond Street tube. **Open** 11am-6.30pm Mon-Fri; noon-5pm Sat. **Credit** AmEx, MC, V. **Map** p398 G5.

Tracey Neuls challenges footwear conventions, right down to the way her shoes are displayed – here they dangle from the ceiling, suspended on ribbons. Her TN_29 label (from around £150) has gathered a cult following all the way from Seattle to Sydney, but the Cordwainers-trained Canadian designer is based in this small shop/studio. The idiosyncratic designs play on historical styles such as brogues and 1930s-style button shoes in worn-looking, muted leathers, complete with deliberate 'imperfections', such as an indented side that mimics stretched-out shoes. The new Tracey Neuls line is handmade in Italy using more luxurious materials.

Food & drink

Bakeries

Konditor & Cook

22 Cornwall Road, Waterloo, SE1 8TW (7261 0456/www.konditorandcook.com). Waterloo tube/rail. **Open** 7.30am-6.30pm Mon-Fri; 8.30am-2.30pm Sat. **Credit** AmEx, MC, V. **Map** p404 N10.

Gerhard Jenne caused a stir when he opened this bakery on a South Bank sidestreet in 1993, selling rudie gingerbread people for grown-ups and lavender-flavoured cakes. Success lay in fashion-forward ideas such as Magic Cakes that spell the recipient's

Independents' day? Clothes

The gradual demise of London's independent shops has been a hot topic in the London press and in Parliament over the past couple of years. Yet in the realm of fashion, business appears to be booming. Londoners are a trendy lot, while a mixture of increasing style-savvy and high-street fatigue has left consumers on the lookout for niche labels that will set them apart from the pack. If they get the formula right, boutiques can reap the benefits – even in areas with lighter foot traffic. Islington's **Labour of Love** (*see p246*), which opened four years ago on a stretch of Upper Street removed from busier Angel, is thriving, largely due to eclectic stock.

'The first couple of years were a little bit of a struggle,' says owner and designer Francesca Forcolini, 'but it's become a culty boutique that has spread through word of mouth. Once you reach a certain level you're OK because you have people who know about you and like you and come back – and they tell their friends.'

Rather than the kind of overwhelming selection you'd get in a department store, at an independent boutique the stock is edited for you. Another appeal is the insider element: 'We inform our customers about what they're buying and where it's made because we have a passion for the labels,' explains Forcolini. 'People are tired of the

whole high-street thing; they're becoming aware of one-off and small-production lines.'

It's not just about the goods. Now that shopping has become one of our favourite pastimes, customers come for the experience rather than just a pair of jeans. Avant-garde designer boutique **b store** (*see p245; pictured*) frequently doubles as a gallery, while the multi-faceted **Shop at Bluebird** (*see p247*) turns its displays into works of art (installation-style changing rooms, handbags displayed on silver platters) and lays on a DJ at weekends. Such shops become hip hangouts, where customers, united in taste, begin to feel they belong to an unspoken club. Shoreditch streetwear emporium the **Three Threads** (*see p249*) serves its own brand of beer, while nearby **no-one** (*see p247*) has an on-site café.

It stands to reason that the longer customers linger, the more money they'll spend. **Weardowney Get-Up Boutique** (*see p247*) takes the concept a step further, attracting customers with a shared hobby. The high-fashion knitwear label created by a pair of former models is showcased in a funky converted pub that also houses their craft school and guest house (*see p53*). So there are always people sitting among the vintagey cushions (also for sale) in the lounge, chatting over their clicking needles.

Black Truffle. See p252.

name in a series of individually decorated squares (Madonna ordered 100, spelling out her name seven times). The brand is now a mini-chain. Quality prepacked salads and sandwiches are also sold. **Other locations** 99 Shaftesbury Avenue, Covent Garden, W1D 5EY (7292 1684); 10 Stoney Street, Bankside, SE1 9AD (7407 5100); 46 Gray's Inn Road, Holborn, WC1X 8LR (7404 6300); 30 St Mary's Axe, City, EC3A 8DS (0845 262 3030).

Primrose Bakery
69 Gloucester Avenue, Primrose Hill, NW1 8LD (7483 4222/www.primrosebakery.org.uk). Camden Town or Chalk Farm tube. **Open** 8.30am-6.30pm Mon-Sat; 10am-5pm Sun. **Credit** MC, V.
Catch a serious sugar high with Martha Swift's pretty, generously sized cupcakes in vanilla, coffee and lemon flavours. The tiny, retro-styled shop also sells peanut butter cookies and layer cakes.

Drinks

Berry Bros & Rudd
3 St James's Street, St James's, SW1A 1EG (7396 9600/www.bbr.com). Green Park tube. **Open** 10am-6pm Mon-Fri; 10am-5pm Sat. **Credit** AmEx, DC, MC, V. **Map** p400 J8.
Britain's oldest wine merchant has been trading on the same premises since 1698 and its heritage is reflected in its panelled sales and tasting rooms. Burgundy- and claret-lovers will drool at the hundreds of wines, but there are also decent selections from elsewhere in Europe and the New World.

Cadenhead's Covent Garden Whisky Shop
3 Russell Street, Covent Garden, WC2B 5JD (7379 4640/www.coventgardenwhiskyshop.co.uk). Covent Garden tube. **Open** 11am-6.30pm Mon-Sat; noon-4.30pm Sun. **Credit** MC, V. **Map** p407 Z3.
Cadenhead's is a survivor of a rare breed: the independent whisky bottler. And its shop is one of a kind – at least in London. Cadenhead's selects barrels from distilleries all over Scotland and bottles them without filtration or any other intervention.

Gerry's
774 Old Compton Street, Soho, W1D 4UW (7734 4215/www.gerrys.uk.com). Leicester Square or Piccadilly Circus tube. **Open** 9am-6.30pm Mon-Thur; 9am-8pm Fri; 9am-9pm Sat. **Credit** MC, V. **Map** p406 W3.
Gerry's lays claim to the widest range of spirits in London. It offers 150 different vodkas – including exotic flavours – and no fewer than 60 tequilas and 100 rums, plus various absinthes, as well as novelties such as absinthe in an Eiffel Tower bottle (£37).

Postcard Teas
9 Dering Street, Mayfair, W1S 1AG (7629 3654/www.postcardteas.com). Bond Street or Oxford Circus tube. **Open** 10.30am-6.30pm Tue-Sat. **Credit** AmEx, MC, V. **Map** p398 H6.
The range in this exquisite little shop is not huge, but it is selected with care. At the time of writing, for instance, all its Darjeeling teas (£2.95-£4.75/50g) were sourced from the Goomtee estate, regarded as the best in the region. China, Ceylon and Assam are chosen just as carefully, and the range includes some real rarities. There's a table for those who want to try a pot; downstairs is a selection of vintage postcards from the collection of art dealer Antony d'Offay, father of the shop's owner Timothy.

General
You'll find outposts of supermarket chains **Sainsbury's** (www.sainsburys.co.uk) and **Tesco** (www.tesco.com) across the city. Superior-quality **Waitrose** has a central branch at 98-101 Marylebone High Street, W1U 4SD (7935 4787, www.waitrose.com).

Whole Foods Market
63-97 Kensington High Street, W8 5SE (7368 4500/www.wholefoodmarket.co.uk). High Street Kensington tube. **Open** 8am-10pm Mon-Sat; 10am-6pm Sun. **Credit** AmEx, DC, MC, V.
The London flagship of the American health-food supermarket chain occupies the former Barkers department store and also houses several eateries.

Markets
A resurgence of farmers' markets in the capital reflects Londoners' growing concern over provenance and environmental issues.

Two of the most central are in Marylebone (Cramer Street car park, corner of Moxton Street, off Marylebone High Street, 10am-2pm Sun) and Notting Hill (behind Waterstone's, access via Kensington Place, W8, 9am-1pm Sat). For more, contact **London Farmers' Markets** (7833 0338, www.lfm.org.uk).

Borough Market
Southwark Street, Borough, SE1 (7407 1002/www.boroughmarket.org.uk). London Bridge tube/rail. **Open** 11am-5pm Thur; noon-6pm Fri; 9am-4pm Sat. **Map** p404 P8.
The foodie's favourite market occupies a sprawling site near London Bridge, but campaigners are currently battling a threat in the form of a rail viaduct planned for above the space. Gourmet goodies run the gamut from Flour Power City Bakery's organic loaves to chorizo and rocket rolls from Spanish specialist Brindisa, plus rare-breed meats, fruit and veg, cakes and all manner of preserves, oils and teas – head out hungry to take advantage of the numerous free samples. The market is now open on Thursdays, when it tends to be quieter than at always-mobbed weekends.

Specialist

A Gold
42 Brushfield Street, Spitalfields, E1 6AG (7247 2487/www.agold.co.uk). Liverpool Street tube/rail. **Open** 11am-8pm Mon-Fri; 10am-6pm Sat; 11am-6pm Sun. **Credit** AmEx, MC, V. **Map** p405 R5.
A Gold was flying the flag for British foods long before it became fashionable to do so. Opposite Spitalfields Market, it resembles a village shop from a bygone era. The baked goods alone take customers on a whistlestop tour of Britain: Cornish saffron cakes, Dundee cakes, Welsh cakes, and (of course) Eccles cakes made in Lancashire. English mead, proper marmalade and teas, unusual chutneys and traditional sweets make great gifts.

Daylesford Organic
44B Pimlico Road, Belgravia, SW1W 8LP (7881 8060/www.daylesfordorganic.com). **Open** 8am-8pm Mon-Sat; 11am-5pm Sun. **Credit** MC, V. **Map** p400 G11.
Part of a new wave of chic purveyors of health food, this impressive offshoot of Lady Carole Bamford's Cotswold-based farm shop is set over three floors, and includes a café. Goods include ready-made dishes, store-cupboard staples such as pulses, pasta and sauces, cakes and breads, charcuterie and cheeses.

Neal's Yard Dairy
17 Shorts Gardens, Covent Garden, WC2H 9UP (7240 5700/www.nealsyarddairy.co.uk). Covent Garden tube. **Open** 11am-6.30pm Mon-Thur; 10am-6.30pm Fri, Sat. **Credit** MC, V. **Map** p407 Y2.
Neal's Yard buys from small farms and creameries and matures the cheeses in its own cellars until ready to sell in peak condition. Names such as

Stinking Bishop and Lincolnshire Poacher are as evocative as the aromas in the shop. It's best to walk in and ask what's good today – you'll be given various tasters by the well-trained staff. **Other locations** 6 Park Street, Borough Market, SE1 9AB (7645 3554).

Melrose & Morgan
42 Gloucester Avenue, Primrose Hill, NW1 8JD (7722 0011/www.melroseandmorgan.com). Chalk Farm tube. **Open** 8am-8pm Mon-Fri; 8am-6pm Sat; 9am-4pm Sun. **Credit** (over £7.50) AmEx, MC, V.
You may have to roll your tongue back up when you see the array of cakes, brownies, pasties and sausage rolls that cover the large table running down the centre of this excellent deli. At the far end a chef may be preparing joints of crumbed chicken to sell for dinner, while dishes of lentil salad and brightly coloured aubergine parmigiana vie for attention.

Paul A Young Fine Chocolates
33 Camden Passage, Islington, N1 8EA (7424 5750/ www.payoung.net). Angel tube. **Open** 11am-6pm Wed, Thur, Sat; 11am-7pm Fri; noon-5pm Sun. **Credit** AmEx, MC, V. **Map** p402 O2.
A gorgeous boutique with almost everything – chocolates, cakes, ice-cream – made in the downstairs kitchen and finished in front of customers. Young is a respected pâtissier as well as chocolatier and has an astute chef's palate for flavour combinations: the white chocolate with rose masala is addictive; so too are the salted caramels. *Photos p256.*

Prestat
14 Princes Arcade, St James's, SW1Y 6DS (7629 4838/www.prestat.co.uk). Green Park tube. **Open** 9.30am-6pm Mon-Fri; 10am-5pm Sat. **Credit** AmEx, MC, V. **Map** p406 V5.
England's oldest chocolatier offers unusual and traditional flavours in brightly coloured gift boxes.

Gifts

Coco de Mer
23 Monmouth Street, Covent Garden, WC2H 9DD (7836 8882/www.coco-de-mer.co.uk). Covent Garden tube. **Open** 11am-7pm Mon-Wed, Fri, Sat; 11am-8pm Thur; noon-6pm Sun. **Credit** AmEx, MC, V. **Map** p407 Y2.
Named after the curvaceous Seychelles nut that drove sailors to distraction, London's most glamorous erotic emporium sells a variety of tasteful books, toys and lingerie, from glass dildos that double as objets d'art to an exquisite Marie Antoinette costume of crotchless culottes and corset. Trying on items is a particular highlight as peepshow-style velvet changing rooms allow your lover to watch you undress from a 'confession box' next door.

Contemporary Applied Arts
2 Percy Street, Fitzrovia, W1T 1DD (7436 2344/ www.caa.org.uk). Goodge Street or Tottenham Court Road tube. **Open** 10am-5.30pm Mon-Sat. **Credit** AmEx, MC, V. **Map** p399 K5.

This airy gallery, run by the charitable arts organisation, represents more than 300 makers. Work embraces the functional – jewellery, tableware, textiles – as well as unique, purely decorative pieces. The ground floor hosts exhibitions by individual artists, or themed by craft, while in the basement shop are pieces for all pockets. Glass is always exceptional here.

James Smith & Sons

53 New Oxford Street, Bloomsbury, WC1A 1BL (7836 4731/www.james-smith.co.uk). Holborn or Tottenham Court Road tube. **Open** 9.30am-5.25pm Mon-Fri; 10am-5.25pm Sat. **Credit** AmEx, MC, V. **Map** p407 Y1.

More than 175 years after it was established, this charming shop, with Victorian fittings still intact, is holding its own in the niche market of umbrellas and walking sticks. The stock here isn't the throwaway type of brollie that breaks at the first sign of bad weather. Lovingly crafted brollies, such as a classic City umbrella with a hickory crook at £110, are built to last and a repair service is offered.

Luna & Curious

198 Brick Lane, Spitalfields, E1 6SA (7033 4411/www.lunaandcurious.com). Aldgate East tube/Liverpool Street tube/rail. **Open** noon-6pm Thur-Sun. **Credit** MC, V. **Map** p405 S4.

The stock here comes from a collective of young artisans, from the vintage cocktail dresses sourced, restored and accessorised by stylist Susie Coulthard, to the quintessentially English teacups and ceramics of Polly George. For a quirky gift idea, the shop's T-Shirt Patisserie (www.tshirt-patisserie.co.uk) takes some beating – choose a plain T-shirt, add the design of your choice and receive it hot off the press in particularly sweet packaging from £20.

Shelf

40 Cheshire Street, Spitalfields, E2 6EH (7739 9444/www.helpyourshelf.co.uk). Liverpool Street tube/rail. **Open** 1-6pm Fri, Sat; 11am-6pm Sun. **Credit** MC, V. **Map** p403 S4.

Artist Katy Hackney and costume designer Jane Petrie's gift shop-cum-gallery is a great place to pick up unique presents, such as Prague-based sculptor Pravoslav Rada's enigmatic ceramics, or one of the limited-edition collaborations with east London artist Rob Ryan, such as a recent series of 50 'polite notices' on vitreous enamel plaques (£250 each), produced by the supplier to London Underground.

Health & beauty

Complementary medicine

Hale Clinic

7 Park Crescent, Fitzrovia, W1B 1PF (7631 0156/www.haleclinic.com). Great Portland Street or Regent's Park tube. **Open** 9am-7pm Mon-Fri; 10am-5pm Sat. **Credit** (shop only) AmEx, MC, V. **Map** p398 H4.

Over 100 practitioners are affiliated to the Hale Clinic, which was founded with the aim of integrating complementary and conventional medicine and opened by the Prince of Wales in 1988. The treatment list is a veritable A-Z of alternative therapies, while the shop stocks supplements, skincare products and books.

Hairdressers & barbers

If the options we list below are out of your range, then you can get a great-value cut (£6 men; £10 women) at the nearest **Mr Topper's** (7631 3233).

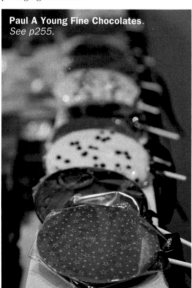

Paul A Young Fine Chocolates. *See p255.*

Daniel Hersheson
45 Conduit Street, Mayfair, W1S 2YN (7434 1747/www.danielhersheson.com). Oxford Circus tube.
Open 9am-6pm Mon-Wed, Sat; 9am-8pm Thur, Fri.
Credit AmEx, MC, V. **Map** p406 U3.
Despite its upmarket location, this modern two-storey salon isn't at all snooty, with a staff of very talented cutters and colourists. Prices start at £55 (£45 for men), though you'll pay £250 for a cut with Daniel. There's also a menu of therapies; the swish Harvey Nichols (*see p238*) branch has a dedicated spa. Hersheson's Blow Dry Bar at Topshop (*see p248*; call 7927 7888 to book) offers catwalk looks for £21.

Fish
30 D'Arblay Street, Soho, W1F 8ER (7494 2398/www.fishweb.co.uk). Leicester Square tube.
Open 10am-7pm Mon-Wed, Fri; 10am-8pm Thur; 10am-5pm Sat. **Credit** MC, V. **Map** p406 V2.
This relaxed and buzzing salon was a fishmonger's, hence the name. Staff are understatedly stylish and laid-back, offering a good mix of classic and fashion cuts for men and women, as well as own-brand hair products. Prices from £34 for men, £41 for women.

Flittner
86 Moorgate, City, EC2M 6SE (7606 4750/www. fflittner.com). Moorgate tube/rail. **Open** 8am-6pm Mon-Wed, Fri; 8am-6.30pm Thur. **Credit** AmEx, MC, V. **Map** p405 Q6.
In business since 1904, Flittner seems unaware the 21st century has begun. Hidden behind beautifully frosted doors (marked 'Saloon') is a simple, handsome room, done out with an array of classic barber's furniture that's older than you are. Within these hushed yet nonetheless welcoming confines, up to six black coat-clad barbers deliver straightforward haircuts (dry cuts £13.50-£15.50, wet cuts £18-£22) and shaves with skill and dignity.

Jo Hansford
19 Mount Street, Mayfair, W1K 2RN (7495 7774/www.johansford.com). Bond Street or Green Park tube. **Open** 8.30am-6pm Tue-Sat. **Credit** MC, V. **Map** p400 G7.
The undisputed queen of colour, Jo Hansford's clientele includes Yasmin Le Bon and Elizabeth Hurley. Prices start from £85 for a tint, or, for Jo's personal touch (she works three days a week), from £150.

Murdock
340 Old Street, Shoreditch, EC1V 9DS (7729 2288/www.murdocklondon.com). Old Street tube/rail. **Open** 11am-7pm Mon-Wed; 11am-8pm Thur, Fri; 10am-6pm Sat; noon-5pm Sun. **Credit** AmEx, MC, V. **Map** p403 R4.
Cool modern barber's Murdock opened in 2006 with the noble aim to revive the wet shave, while also offering moustache and beard trims, manicures and haircuts. The traditional wet shave (£32.50) is carried out using products from venerable chemist's DR Harris, while the Santa Maria Novella version (£38.50) employs the Florentine line. There's also an outpost in Liberty.

Opticians

Dollond & Aitchison (www.danda.co.uk) and **Specsavers** (www.specsavers.com) are chains with branches on most high streets.

Cutler & Gross
16 Knightsbridge Green, Knightsbridge, SW1X 7QL (7581 2250/www.cutlerandgross.com). Knightsbridge tube. **Open** 9.30am-7pm Mon-Sat; noon-4pm Sun. **Credit** AmEx, MC, V. **Map** p397 F9.
C&G's stock of handmade frames runs from Andy Warhol-inspired glasses to naturally light buffalo-horn frames. Vintage eyewear from the likes of Ray-Ban and Courrèges is at the sister shop down the road. **Other locations** 7 Knightsbridge Green, Knightsbridge, SW1X 7QL (7590 9995).

Michel Guillon Vision Clinic & Eye Boutique
35 Duke of York Square, Chelsea, SW3 4LY (7730 2142/www.michelguillon.com). Sloane Square tube. **Open** 10am-7pm Mon-Sat. **Credit** AmEx, MC, V. **Map** p397 F11.
Lined with striking blue cabinets, this ultra-modern shop was designed by Abe (son of architect Richard) Rogers. The changing range of designer frames is as edgy as the interior decor. Michel Guillon is also a leading contact lens specialist.

Pharmacies

National chain **Boots** (www.boots.com) has branches across the city, offering dispensing pharmacies and photo processing. The store on Piccadilly Circus (44-46 Regent Street, W1B 5RA, 7734 6126) is open until midnight (except Sunday when it closes at 6pm).

DR Harris
29 St James's Street, St James's, SW1A 1HB (7930 3915/www.drharris.co.uk). Green Park or Piccadilly Circus tube. **Open** 8.30am-6pm Mon-Fri; 9.30am-5pm Sat. **Credit** AmEx, MC, V. **Map** p400 J8.
Founded in 1790, this venerable chemist has a royal warrant. Wood-and-glass cabinets are filled with bottles, jars and old-fashioned shaving brushes and manicure kits. The smartly packaged own-brand products such as the bright blue Crystal Eye Gel have a cult following.

Shops

Eco pioneer **Neal's Yard Remedies** (15 Neal's Yard, WC2H 9DP (7379 7222, www.nealsyard remedies.com) now has several central London locations, offering excellent organic products, a herbal dispensary and complementary therapies. Ever-growing beauty chain **Space NK** (8-10 Broadwick Street, W1F 8HW, 7287 2667, www. spacenk.com) is a great source of niche skincare and make-up brands.

Eat, Drink, Shop

Liz Earle Naturally Active Skincare

53 Duke of York Square, King's Road, Chelsea, SW3 4LY (7730 9191/www.lizearle.com). Sloane Square tube. **Open** 10am-7pm Mon-Sat; 11am-5pm Sun. **Credit** AmEx, MC, V. **Map** p397 F11.

Former beauty writer Liz Earle's hugely successful botanical skincare range was previously only available from her HQ on the Isle of Wight. This new London flagship stocks the streamlined range of 23 products, based on a simple, no-fuss regime of cleansing, toning and moisturising. Superbalm is a calming treatment for dry skin (£13.50). The 'minis' are a great way to introduce yourself to the range (from £4).

Miller Harris

21 Bruton Street, Mayfair, W1J 6QD (7629 7750/www.millerharris.com). Bond Street or Green Park tube. **Open** 10am-6pm Mon-Sat. **Credit** AmEx, MC, V. **Map** p400 H7.

Grasse-trained British perfumer Lyn Harris's distinctive, long-lasting scents, in their lovely decorative packaging, are made with quality natural extracts and oils. Perennial favourites include Noix de Tubéreuse (£65/100ml), a lighter and more palatable tuberose scent than many on the market, and Citron Citron (£52/100ml), a summery citrus-based fragrance.

Other locations 14 Needham Road, Notting Hill, W11 2RP (7221 1545).

Spas & salons

Many luxury hotels, including the **Sanderson** (*see p46*) and the **Dorchester** (*see p59*), have spa facilities that are open to the public.

Cowshed

119 Portland Road, Notting Hill, W11 4LN (7078 1944/www.cowshedclarendoncross.com). Holland Park tube. **Open** 9am-8pm Mon-Fri; 9am-7pm Sat; 10am-5pm Sun. **Credit** AmEx, MC, V.

The (non-members') London outpost of Babington House's Cowshed does its country cousin proud. The chic, white ground floor is buzzy, with a tiny café area on one side, and a mani/pedi section on the other, complete with groovy retro mini-TVs. For facials, massages, waxing and more, head downstairs. The signature Cowgroom (£75/30mins, £105/hr), where two therapists work on you at once, comes in various packages (eg Maintenance, Teenage), or you can design your own combination.

Elemis Day Spa

2-3 Lancashire Court, Mayfair, W1S 1EX (7499 4995/www.elemis.com). Bond Street tube. **Open** 9am-9pm Mon-Sat; 10am-6pm Sun. **Credit** AmEx, MC, V. **Map** p398 H6.

This leading British spa brand's exotic, unisex retreat is tucked away down a cobbled lane off Bond

Eat, Drink, Shop

Independents' day? Words & music

Things haven't been easy for independent retailers of any kind in recent years, but booksellers are caught between price-slashing high-street chains and supermarkets on one side, and no-overheads internet sellers on the other. Record shops are facing an even more perilous future, with the growing popularity of music downloads. Now the game is all about getting people through the door and encouraging them to return.

'I see the bigger stores as book stockists rather than booksellers,' notes Phil Griffiths, proprietor of **Metropolitan Books** (49 Exmouth Market, Clerkenwell, EC1R 4QL, 7278 6900, www.metropolitanbooks.co.uk). 'I can order quickly and flexibly, I select all the stock myself, and I know many of my customers well.' As well as the usual readings, book launches, wine and nibbles, for example, classy indie **Crockatt & Powell** (119-120 Lower Marsh, Waterloo, SE1 7AE, 7928 0234, www.crockattandpowell.com) now hosts comedy evenings and runs its own blog. **Foyles** (*see p241*) made the interesting decision to host sub-specialists – such as a jazz shop evicted from its long-term premises

near Covent Garden. **Ray's Jazz** (*see p261*) now offers a varied programme of lunch and evening performances in the first-floor café it shares with the bookshop.

In summer 2007 – almost the same moment that low-cost chain retailer Fopp collapsed – long-standing indie stalwart **Rough Trade** (*see p261*; *pictured*) took the bold step of opening a 5,000sq ft shop in the Old Truman Brewery just off Brick Lane. Here beer is notable by its absence, but coffee and snacks are on offer at the front, there's a wireless community space and gallery of music-inspired art – and, most significantly, a state-of-the-art sound stage. 'Gigs will be up close and personal, and completely free,' says Rough Trade director Stephen Godfroy. 'Customers will get to see the greatest new talent while they're still hungry for success and unsullied by the pressures of fame. That said, it's just a small element of what we do, and it's nothing new: we've been hosting in-store gigs for more than 20 years now.'

Nor are they the only ones treating shopfloor shows as more than cynical marketing exercises. Pint-sized CD

Street. The elegantly ethnic treatment rooms are a lovely setting in which to relax and enjoy a spot of pampering, from wraps to results-driven facials.

Tattoos & piercings

Flamin' Eight

2 Castle Road, Kentish Town, NW1 8PP (7267 7888/www.flamineight.co.uk). Kentish Town tube. **Open** 10.30am-6pm Mon-Sat. **Credit** MC, V.
Friendly licensed studio with three artists offering a wide range of different styles as well as piercings.

Into You

144 St John Street, Clerkenwell, EC1V 4UA (7253 5085/www.into-you.co.uk). Farringdon tube/rail. **Open** noon-7pm Mon-Sat. **Credit** AmEx, MC, V. **Map** p402 O4.
The elaborate designs undertaken by Into You's eight artists are about as far from 'Mom' as you can get. Piercings also offered.

House & home

Antiques

Although it's not limited to antiques, **Portobello Road Market** (*see p239*) is London's biggest, best-known hunting ground.

Camden Passage in Islington (off Upper Street, N1, 7359 0190, www.camdenpassage antiques.com) was once lined with quirky dealers, but boutiques have encroached on its territory. A number still remain, however, especially in characterful Pierrepont Arcade, and Wednesday and Saturday are the best days to visit. Meanwhile, **Church Street**, NW8, in Marylebone has blossomed into antiques row, with a growing cluster of shops around Alfie's Antique Market (*see below*).

Alfie's Antique Market

13-25 Church Street, Marylebone, NW8 8DT (7723 6066/www.alfiesantiques.com). Edgware Road tube/Marylebone tube/rail. **Open** 10am-6pm Tue-Sat. **Credit** varies. **Map** p395 E4.
Alfie's boasts over 100 dealers in vintage furniture and fashion, art, accessories, books, maps and more. Dodo Posters (on the first floor) do 1920s and '30s ads.

Antiquarius

131-141 King's Road, Chelsea, SW3 5PH (7351 5353/www.antiquarius.co.uk). Sloane Square tube then 11, 19, 22, 211, 319 bus. **Open** 10am-6pm Mon-Sat. **Credit** varies. **Map** p397 E12.
Long-standing King's Road landmark houses around 60 dealers with specialisms from vintage trunks and jewellery to original film art. *Photo p260.*

retailer-cum-coffee lounge **Brill** (*see p260*) proves you don't need a large space and a fancy stage to host concerts. Owner Jeremy Brill fell for the idea after persuading US folkstress Alena Diane to give an impromptu show that packed the place to the rafters.

The success of the **Virgin Megastore** downstairs gig space on Oxford Street

suggests the chains are able to learn a trick or two from the independents. Ash promoted a recent single with a nationwide tour of Virgin outlets – clearly a sign that in-store appearances can do wonders for a band's record sales. Whether or not they have the power to save the humble record shop is another matter.

Collectibles at **Antiquarius**. *See p259.*

Core One

*The Gas Works, 2 Michael Road, Fulham, SW6 2AD.
Fulham Broadway tube.* **Open** 10am-6pm Mon-Fri;
11am-4pm Sat. **Credit** varies.
A group of antiques and 20th-century dealers has
colonised this industrial building in Fulham, including Dean Antiques (7610 6997, www.dean
antiques.co.uk) for dramatic pieces, Plinth (7371
7422) for quirky reconditioned vintage furniture and
De Parma (7736 3384, www.deparma.com) for
elegant mid-century design.

Grays Antique Market & Grays in the Mews

*58 Davies Street, Mayfair, W1K 5LP & 1-7 Davies
Mews, Mayfair, W1K 5AB (7629 7034/www.grays
antiques.com). Bond Street tube.* **Open** 10am-6pm
Mon-Fri. **Credit** varies. **Map** p398 H6.
Stalls in this smart covered market sell everything
from jewellery to rare books. More than 200 dealers.

General

Habitat (121-123 Regent Street, W1B 4TB,
0844 499 1134, www.habitat.co.uk) is a good
source of affordable modern design.

Conran Shop

*Michelin House, 81 Fulham Road, South Kensington,
SW3 6RD (7589 7401/www.conran.com). South
Kensington tube.* **Open** 10am-6pm Mon, Tue, Fri;
10am-7pm Wed, Thur; 10am-6.30pm Sat; noon-6pm
Sun. **Credit** AmEx, MC, V. **Map** p397 E10.
Terence Conran's flagship store in the Fulham
Road's beautiful 1909 Michelin Building showcases
furniture and design for every room in the house as
well as the garden; there are plenty of portable acces-
sories, gadgets, books, stationery and toiletries that
make great gifts or souvenirs.
Other locations 55 Marylebone High Street,
Marylebone, W1U 5HS (7723 2223).

Labour and Wait

*18 Cheshire Street, Spitalfields, E2 6EH (7729
6253/www.labourandwait.co.uk). Aldgate East
tube/Liverpool Street tube/rail.* **Open** 1-5pm Sat;
10am-5pm Sun. **Credit** MC, V. **Map** p403 S4.
This much-celebrated shop pays homage to
timeless, unfaddy domestic goods that combine
beauty with utility: think Victorian pantry crossed
with 1950s kitchen. The quintessentially British
homewares include traditional feather dusters (£8),
tins of twine (£6.50), simple enamelware and sturdy
canvas bags. Labour and Wait also has a space at
concept store Dover Street Market (*see p246*).

Mint

*70 Wigmore Street, Marylebone, W1U 2SF (7224
4406/www.mintshop.co.uk). Bond Street tube.* **Open**
10.30am-6.30pm Mon-Wed, Fri, Sat; 10.30am-7.30pm
Thur. **Credit** AmEx, DC, MC, V. **Map** p400 G6.
Surprising and inspirational, Mint is a compact
two-level space full of globally sourced pieces from
established designers and recent graduates alike. As
well as contemporary statement furniture, there
are plenty of smaller, more affordable items here,
such as Doris Banks' paper-thin ceramics glazed in
gorgeous greens and oranges (pot with cover, £65)
and Hella Jongerius's cushions (£150).

Music & entertainment

CDs & records

HMV (www.hmv.co.uk) and the **Virgin
Megastore** (www.virgin.com) are the most
prominent high-street chains. Serious browsers
should head for Soho, where indie record stores
cluster on Berwick and D'Arblay Streets.

Brill

*27 Exmouth Market, Clerkenwell, EC1R 4QL
(7833 9757). Angel tube/Farringdon tube/rail.*
Open 7.30am-6pm Mon-Fri; 9am-6pm Sat. **Credit**
AmEx, MC, V. **Map** p402 N4.
It may be small, but this CD shop-cum-café turns its
size to advantage with its selective approach: if it's
stocked here, it's going to be good. The knowledgeable owner Jeremy Brill dispenses fresh coffees,
Brick Lane Bagels and cakes at a smattering of outdoor and window seats.

Flashback

*50 Essex Road, Islington, N1 8LR (7354 9356/
www.flashback.co.uk). Angel tube.* **Open** 10am-7pm
Mon-Sat; noon-6pm Sun. **Credit** AmEx, MC, V.
Map p402 O1.
Stock is scrupulously organised at this second-hand
treasure trove. The ground floor is dedicated to CDs,
while the basement is vinyl-only: an ever-expanding

jazz collection jostles for space alongside soul, hip hop and a carpal tunnel-compressing selection of library sounds. A range of rarities is pinned in plastic sleeves to the walls.

Honest Jon's
278 Portobello Road, Notting Hill, W10 5TE (8969 9822/www.honestjons.com). Ladbroke Grove tube. **Open** 10am-6pm Mon-Sat; 11am-5pm Sun. **Credit** AmEx, MC, V.
Honest Jon's found its way here in 1979, where it was reportedly the first place in London to employ a Rastafarian. The owner helped James Lavelle set up Mo'Wax records. You'll find jazz, hip hop, soul, broken beat, reggae and Brazilian music on the shelves.

Ray's Jazz at Foyles
First Floor, Foyles Bookshop, 113-119 Charing Cross Road, Soho, WC2H 0EB (7440 3205/www.foyles.co.uk). Tottenham Court Road tube. **Open** 9.30am-9pm Mon-Sat; noon-6pm Sun. **Credit** AmEx, MC, V. **Map** p407 X2.
London's brightest and least beardy jazz shop shares a first floor café with Foyles and offers window seats for the consumption of coffees, cakes and quiches. The predominantly CD-based stock covers the entire spectrum (blues, avant-garde, gospel, folk, world), although modern jazz is the main draw.

Rough Trade
130 Talbot Road, Notting Hill, W11 1JA (7229 8541/www.roughtrade.com). Ladbroke Grove tube. **Open** 10am-6.30pm Mon-Sat; noon-5pm Sun. **Credit** AmEx, DC, MC, V.
A recent refit notwithstanding, Rough Trade remains instantly recognisable as a temple to all things alternative thanks to its wallpapering of posters featuring artists from Aphex Twin to the Butthole Surfers, and staff will happily blitz you with talk of releases so new they've barely been recorded. Despite the fading fortunes of many record shops, it recently opened a warehouse-style, 5,000sq ft store, café and gig space in a cluster of boutiques and bars off Brick Lane. *Photo p259.*
Other locations Dray Walk, off Brick Lane, E1 6QL (7392 7788).

Musical instruments

The site of legendary recording studio Regent Sounds in the 1960s, **Denmark Street**, WC2, off Charing Cross Road, remains a hub for music shops, and should be your first port of call if you're looking for a new, second-hand or rare vintage guitar.

Chappell of Bond Street
152-160 Wardour Street, Soho, W1F 8YA (7432 4400/www.chappellofbondstreet.co.uk). Tottenham Court Road tube. **Open** 9.30am-6pm Mon-Fri; 10am-5.30pm Sat. **Credit** AmEx, MC, V. **Map** p406 V2.
It's retained its old name, but Chappell recently moved from Bond Street (its home for nearly 200 years) to this amazing three-storey musical temple

in Soho. The shop is the leading Yamaha stockist in the UK, and the collection of sheet music (classical, pop, jazz) is reputedly the largest in Europe.

Sport & fitness

Selfridges (*see p238*) has a good fitness department, including specialist concessions such as Cycle Surgery. For trainers **JD Sports** (www.jdsports.co.uk) has branches all over town, and there's also **NikeTown** (236 Oxford Street, W1W 8LG, 7612 0800, www.nike.com).

King's Road Sporting Club
38-42 King's Road, Chelsea, SW3 4UD (7589 5418/www.krsc.co.uk). Sloane Square tube. **Open** 10am-6.30pm daily. **Credit** AmEx, MC, V.
Map p397 F11.
A reliable, family-run general sporting goods store, with a focus on women's active- and swimwear. You'll find everything here from yoga clothes to waterproof headphones.

Tickets

For London performances, it is well worth booking ahead – surprisingly obscure acts sell out, and high-profile gigs and sporting events can do so in seconds. It is almost always cheaper to bypass ticket agents and go direct to the box office – the former will charge booking fees that could top 20 per cent. Should you have to use them, booking agencies include **Ticketmaster** (0870 534 4444, www.ticketmaster.co.uk), **Stargreen** (7734 8932, www.stargreen.com), **Ticketweb** (0870 060 0100, www.ticketweb.co.uk), **See Tickets** (0871 220 0260, www.seetickets.com) and **Keith Prowse** (0870 840 1111, www.keithprowse.com). For specific tips on where to get tickets (and how to keep the cost down), *see p308, p333 and pp323-331.*

Travellers' needs

Independent travel specialist **Trailfinders** (European travel 0845 050 5945, worldwide flights 0845 058 5858, www.trailfinders.com) has several branches in the capital, including one in the flagship Piccadilly branch of Waterstone's (*see p241*).

The Excess Baggage Company
4 Hannah Close, Great Central Way, Wembley, NW10 0UX. (0800 783 1085, www.excess-baggage.com). **Credit** AmEx, MC, V.
This company ships goods to over 300 countries and territories worldwide, including the USA, Canada, Australia, New Zealand and South Africa, from a single suitcase to complete household removal. Prices are reasonable and include cartons and other packing materials.

'THIS SHOW IS A WONDER.
GO WITH AN OPEN HEART, WIDE-OPEN EYES, AND PREPARE FOR ENCHANTMENT'
The Times
THE LORD OF THE RINGS
The Times | London Lite | The Guardian
'ASTONISHING'
The Sunday Times
CALL +44 (0) 20 7087 7599
THEATRE ROYAL DRURY LANE LONDON
SZC lic. to KWL

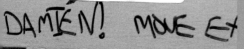
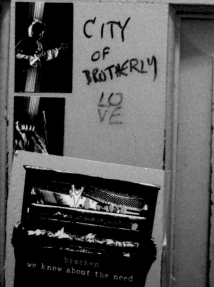

Arts &
Entertainment

Luminaire. *See p313.*

Festivals & Events

Wherever and whenever – the lowdown on what's going on.

Ceremony of the Keys.

Perhaps in part due to a succession of wonderful summers – which came to an end in the rains of 2007 – London has taken to outdoor events. Almost any weekend, there's a festival of some sort taking place somewhere in the city. We've included as many outdoor festivals, sponsored seasons and one-off events as we can here, but keep an eye on *Time Out* magazine for those arranged at short notice. If you're planning your trip around a particular event – or going out of your way to attend one – confirm the details beforehand: we've thoroughly checked the details published here, but dates change and events can be cancelled with little prior notice.

All year

For the **Changing of the Guard**, *see p143* Ceremonial city.

Ceremony of the Keys
Tower of London, Tower Hill, the City, EC3N 4AB (0870 751 5177/www.hrp.org.uk). Tower Hill tube/ Tower Gateway DLR. **Date** daily. *Apr-Oct* max party of 6. *Nov-Mar* max party of 15. **Map** p405 R7.
As part of this 700-year-old ceremony, the Yeoman Warders lock the entrances to the Tower at 9.53pm every evening. Assemble at the West Gate at 9pm, and it's all over by 10pm, when the last post sounds. Details of the ticket-application procedure are on the website – apply at least two months in advance.

Gun Salutes
Green Park, Mayfair & St James's, W1, & Tower of London, the City, EC3. **Date** 6 Feb (Accession Day); 21 Apr & 14 June (Queen's birthdays); 2 June (Coronation Day); 10 June (Duke of Edinburgh's birthday); 14 June (Trooping the Colour); State Opening of Parliament (*see p271*); 8 Nov (Lord Mayor's Show); 9 Nov (Remembrance Sunday); for state visits. **Map** p400 H8.
The King's Troop Royal Horse Artillery makes a mounted charge through Hyde Park, sets up the guns opposite the Dorchester Hotel and fires a 41-gun salute (at noon, except for the State Opening of Parliament). Not to be outdone, the Honourable Artillery Company fires a 62-gun salute at the Tower of London at 1pm.

January-March 2008

London International Mime Festival
Various venues across London (7637 5661/ www.mimefest.co.uk). **Date** 12-27 Jan.
Proving that mime isn't all black and white face paint and Marcel Marceau (RIP) impressions, the LIMF brings together companies from across the world to perform innovative shows. Free brochures are available from the website or by phone.

London Art Fair
Business Design Centre, 52 Upper Street, Islington, N1 0QH (7936 1290/www.londonartfair.co.uk). Angel tube. **Date** 16-20 Jan. **Map** p402 N2.

Arts & Entertainment

At this large-scale art sale millions of pounds are spent by collectors on modern British and contemporary works from such artists as Ben Nicholson, Barbara Hepworth, Keith Coventry and William Scott. More than 100 galleries participate.

Chinese New Year Festival

Around Gerrard Street, Chinatown, W1, Leicester Square, WC2, & Trafalgar Square, WC2 (7851 6686/www.chinatownchinese.co.uk). Leicester Square or Piccadilly Circus tube. **Date** 10 Feb. **Map** p406 W3.
In 2008, the Year of the Rat will take over from the Year of the Pig. Celebrations begin at 11am with a children's parade from Leicester Square south to Trafalgar Square, where the traditional lion and dragon dance teams perform. There are, of course, firework displays (both at lunchtime and at 5pm). Expect dense crowds – especially at the hub of the party on Gerrard Street.

Great Spitalfields Pancake Race

Dray Walk, Brick Lane, Spitalfields, E1 6QL (7375 0441/www.alternativearts.co.uk). Liverpool Street tube/ rail. **Date** 5 Feb (Shrove Tuesday). **Map** p403 S5.
Flippin' good fun in aid of charity. Relay teams race while simultaneously tossing pancakes. Festivities kick off at around 12.30pm. Call in advance to participate; just turn up if all you're after is seeing silly costumes and pancakes hitting the pavement.

National Science & Engineering Week

Various venues (www.the-ba.net). **Date** 7-16 Mar.
A week of scientific shenanigans in the capital, ranging from hands-on shows for youngsters to in-depth discussions for adults. Each event celebrates different aspects of science, engineering and technology. Not as dull as you might think, honest!

St Patrick's Day Parade & Festival

Various venues (7983 4100/www.london.gov.uk). **Date** 16 Mar.
This popular, thousands-strong parade through central London is followed by a free party. Expect plenty of Irish music and dance, and giant green hat and Guinness promotions everywhere in town.

London Lesbian & Gay Film Festival

BFI Southbank, Belvedere Road, South Bank, SE1 8XT (7928 3232/www.llgff.org.uk). Embankment tube/Waterloo tube/rail. **Date** 27 Mar-10 Apr.
The UK's third-largest film festival is 21 this year.

Oxford & Cambridge Boat Race

Thames, from Putney to Mortlake (01225 383483/ www.theboatrace.org). Putney Bridge tube/Putney, Barnes Bridge or Mortlake rail. **Date** 29 Mar.
Some 250,000 people are expected to line the Thames from Putney to Mortlake for the 154th edition of this historic annual grudge match (flag down at 4.30pm). Cambridge, kitted out in light blue, won the 2007 Boat Race in a time of 17 minutes and 15 seconds; Oxford wear dark blue. *Photo p266.*

April-June 2008

For the **City of London Festival** and **Hampton Court Palace Festival**, *see p305*; **Royal Ascot** and **Epsom Derby**, *see p326*; and **Wimbledon**, *see p327*.

La Linea

Various venues (8693 1042/www.comono.co.uk). **Date** 1-30 Apr.
Now in its eighth year, this festival celebrates Latin American music. In 2007, guest artists included Bebel Gilberto and Chango Spasiuk.

Spring Loaded

The Place, 17 Duke's Road, Bloomsbury, WC1H 9PY (7121 1100/www.theplace.org.uk). Euston tube/rail. **Date** 27 Mar-17 May.
Festival of new contemporary dance from British-based talent, with 16 companies performing over six weeks. *See also p284* **Dance festivals**.

Camden Crawl

Various venues (www.thecamdencrawl.com). Camden Town tube. **Date** 18-19 Apr.
A showcase of around 80 new musical acts, mostly of the indie guitar variety, in a dozen venues around Camden. *See also p309* **Festivals**.

East End Film Festival

Various venues (www.eastendfilmfestival.com). **Date** 17-24 Apr.
New films that explore the potential of cinema to cross cultural and political boundaries, and capture the atmosphere of London's East End.

Alternative Fashion Week

Spitalfields Traders Market, Crispin Place, Brushfield Street, Spitalfields, E1 6AA (7375 0441/www. alternativearts.co.uk). Liverpool Street tube/rail. **Date** 21-25 Apr.
Discover new designers at this fabulous fashion event; shows are at 1.15pm every day and feature over 70 original collections, from the sublime to the sensational. From noon to 3pm market stalls sell clothes, textiles and accessories.

London Marathon

Greenwich Park to the Mall via the Isle of Dogs, Victoria Embankment & St James's Park (7902 0200/ www.london-marathon.co.uk). Blackheath & Maze Hill rail or Charing Cross tube/rail. **Date** 13 Apr.
Hire a crazy costume and fill up on carbs for one of the world's biggest metropolitan marathons. It attracts some 35,000 starters, all of whom must have applied by the previous October. If you're joining the spectators lining most of the route, the front runners usually reach the halfway mark near the Tower of London at around 10am.

May Fayre & Puppet Festival

St Paul's Church Garden, Bedford Street, Covent Garden, WC2E 9ED (7375 0441/www.alternative arts.co.uk). Covent Garden tube. **Date** 11 May. **Map** p407 Y4.

Arts & Entertainment

Commemorating the first recorded sighting of Mr Punch in England (by diarist Samuel Pepys in 1662, here in Covent Garden), this free event offers puppetry galore from 10.30am to 5.30pm – and a church service with Mr Punch in the pulpit at 11.30am.

Playtex Moonwalk
Start & finish at Hyde Park, W1 (01483 741430/ www.walkthewalk.org). **Date** 17 May. **Map** p395 F7.
Power walk through the night in your best bra to raise money for breast cancer research. The 2007 event attracted over 15,000 participants, including a number of men. Choose either the marathon route (26.2 miles) or half-marathon (13.1 miles).

Chelsea Flower Show
Grounds of Royal Hospital, Royal Hospital Road, Chelsea, SW3 4SR (7649 1885/www.rhs.org.uk). Sloane Square tube. **Date** 20-24 May. **Map** p397 F12.
Elbow past the crowds of rich old ladies to admire perfect blooms, or get ideas for your own humble plot. The first two days are reserved for Royal Horticultural Society members and tickets for the open days are hard to come by. The show closes at 5.30pm on the final day; display plants are sold off from 4.30pm.

Kew Summer Festival
Royal Botanic Gardens, Kew, Richmond, Surrey TW9 3AB (8332 5655/www.kew.org). Kew Gardens tube/rail/Kew Bridge rail. **Date** 24 May-28 Sept.
Each season at Kew Gardens (*see p183*) brings its own programme of events: for summer 2008 there's a celebration of the special role of trees, featuring an 18m-high treetop walkway and rhizotron (an underground chamber revealing a tree's root structure).

Jazz Plus
Victoria Embankment Gardens, Villiers Street, Westminster, WC2R 2PY (7375 0441/www. alternativearts.co.uk). Embankment tube. **Date** 3 June-22 July. **Map** p407 Y5.
Free lunchtime concerts from contemporary jazz musicians, performed on Tuesdays and Thursdays.

Coin Street Festival
Bernie Spain Gardens (next to Oxo Tower Wharf), South Bank, SE1 9PH (7620 0544/www.coinstreet. org). Southwark tube/Waterloo tube/rail. **Date** June-Aug. **Map** p404 N8.
A series of themed – mostly weekend – events celebrating cultural diversity. Taking place beside the Thames, these events centre on live music, with some dance and theatre thrown in. There are food, drink and craft stalls in the gardens, and all of the entertainment is free; check the website for details.

Watch This Space Festival
Outside the National Theatre, South Bank, SE1 9PX (7452 3400/www.nationaltheatre.org.uk). Waterloo tube/rail. **Date** June-Aug. **Map** p401 M7.
Lively free festival of theatre, with some music and film performances too. Events take place on a large square of artificial grass right by the river.

Spitalfields Festival
Various locations across east London (7377 1362/ www.spitalfieldsfestival.org.uk). **Date** 2-20 June, 10-19 Dec.
An eclectic mix of concerts and events reflecting the local area and its many different communities; many events are held in historic local venues such as hospitals and churches.

Arts & Entertainment

Oxford & Cambridge Boat Race. *See p265.*

Beating Retreat

Horse Guards Parade, Whitehall, Westminster,
SW1A 2AX (information 7414 2271/tickets 7839
5323). Westminster tube/Charing Cross tube/rail.
Date 4-5 June. **Map** p401 K8.
This patriotic 'spectacle of sound and colour' begins
at 7pm, with the 'Retreat' beaten on drums by the
Mounted Bands of the Household Cavalry and the
Massed Bands of the Guards Division.

Open Garden Squares Weekend

Various venues (www.opensquares.org). **Date** 7-8 June.
Ever wondered what it's like in those enchanting
little private parks you see in the posher parts of
town? Every year the London Parks & Gardens
Trust opens to the public a selection of these squares
and roof gardens, ranging from secret 'children-only'
play areas to prison gardens.

Meltdown

South Bank Centre, Belvedere Road, South Bank,
SE1 8XX (0870 380 0400/www.rfh.org.uk).
Embankment tube/Waterloo tube/rail. **Date**
last 2wks in June. **Map** p401 M8.
This hugely successful and brilliantly unpredictable
festival of personally selected contemporary music
and culture was curated in 2007 by Jarvis Cocker;
Patti Smith and Scott Walker are among those
whose tastes have roamed free in previous years.

Trooping the Colour

Horse Guards Parade, Whitehall, Westminster,
SW1A 2AX (7414 2479/www.trooping-the-colour.
co.uk). Westminster tube/Charing Cross tube/rail.
Date 14 June. **Map** p401 K8.
Though the Queen was born on 21 April, this is her
official birthday celebration. At 10.45am she makes
the 15-minute journey from Buckingham Palace to
Horse Guards Parade, then scurries home to watch
a midday Royal Air Force flypast and receive a formal gun salute from Green Park.

Pride London

Parade from Oxford Street to Victoria Embankment
(7164 2182/www.pridelondon.org). Hyde Park
Corner or Marble Arch tube/Charing Cross tube/rail.
Date 28 June.
Always colourful, the Parade heads down Oxford
Street, Regent Street, Piccadilly and Whitehall, end-
ing up at Victoria Embankment, and is followed by
a Trafalgar Square rally. Around Soho and Leicester
Square, expect dance stages, market stalls, a food fes-
tival and cabaret. The two weeks leading up to the
Pride rally are Festival Fortnight, a mix of cultural
performances in various venues.

Greenwich & Docklands International Festival

Various venues in Greenwich & Docklands
(8305 1818/www.festival.org). **Date** 19-22 June.
An entertaining blend of free and family-friendly
theatrical, musical and site-specific outdoor events,
combining community arts with grander, often
visually stunning projects.

Watch This Space Festival.

London Biennale Festival of Architecture

Various venues (7436 8625/www.londonbiennale.
org.uk). **Date** 20 June-20 July.
A month of architecture-themed events, installations,
guided walks and cycle tours. The 2008 FRESH!
theme investigates innovative ideas, focusing on
new communities and green issues.

July-September 2008

For the **BBC Sir Henry Wood Promenade
Concerts**, *see p305* **Festivals**.

Henley Royal Regatta

Henley Reach, Henley-on-Thames, Oxon RG9 2LY
(01491 572153/www.hrr.co.uk). Henley-on-Thames
rail. **Date** 2-6 July.
First held in 1839 – and under royal patronage since
1851 – Henley is a five-day affair and as posh as can
be. Boat races range from open events for men and
women through student crews to junior boys.

Dance Al Fresco

Regent's Park, Marylebone, NW1 (www.dance
alfresco.org). Regent's Park tube. **Date** July-Aug.
Map p398 G3.
Held over three weekends, here's your chance to put
on your dancing shoes and ballroom dance (usually
on the Saturday) or tango (Sunday) outdoors to your
heart's content. The dancing runs from 2pm to 6pm;
novices can join the lessons at 1pm.

Chap & Hendrick's Olympics

Bedford Square, Bloomsbury, WC1 (8332 1188/
www.hendricksgin.com). Tottenham Court Road tube.
Date mid July.

Arts & Entertainment

It's terribly silly and terribly English: events start with the lighting of the Olympic Pipe; 'sports' include umbrella hockey, the three-trousered limbo and the pipe smokers' relay; and there's – hurrah! – free G&T.

Somerset House Summer Series

Somerset House, Strand, WC2 1LA (7845 4600/ www.somersethouse.org.uk/music). Temple tube/ Charing Cross tube/rail. **Date** July.

A spectacular outdoor setting for live music; last year's acts included Amy Winehouse and Lily Allen. *See also p309* **Festivals.**

Rushes Soho Shorts Festival

Various venues in Soho (7851 6207/www.soho shorts.com). **Date** 23 July-1 Aug.

Series of free screenings of short films and videos.

Great British Beer Festival

Earl's Court, Warwick Road, SW5 (01727 867201/ www.camra.org.uk). Earl's Court tube. **Date** 5-9 Aug.

Hiccups and hangovers are guaranteed at this unsurprisingly popular event – referred to by fans as 'the biggest pub in the world'. In 2007, some 67,000 visitors sampled more than 450 real ales, over 200 foreign beers and lager, cider and perry.

Innocent Village Fête

Regent's Park, Marylebone, NW1 (8600 3939/ www.innocentvillagefete.co.uk). Regent's Park tube. **Date** 2-3 Aug.

Free summer festival Fruitstock was remodelled in 2007 as a 'village fête'. Some fête it was too – 110,000 punters enjoyed live music, a farmers' market, posh food stalls and children's activities in Regent's Park.

Portobello Film Festival

Westbourne Studios *242 Acklam Road, Notting Hill, W10 5JJ. Ladbroke Grove tube.* **Inn on the Green** *2 Thorpe Close, Ladbroke Grove, W10 5XL. Westbourne Park tube.* **Both** *8960 0996/www.portobellofilmfestival.com.* **Date** 19 July-31 Aug.

Europe's largest indie film festival screens over 800 new films from around the world. There are also talks from top directors and art exhibitions. This year the theme will be 'Comedy & Comics'.

Time Out's 40th Birthday

www.timeout.com. **Date** 12 Aug.

A month of superb cultural activities, focused around the 40th birthday of London's best listings magazine.

Notting Hill Carnival

Notting Hill, W10, W11 (7727 0072/www. lnhc.org.uk). Ladbroke Grove, Notting Hill Gate & Westbourne Park tube. **Date** 24-25 Aug.

Calling itself Europe's biggest street party, Notting Hill Carnival welcomes approaching two million revellers. *See right* **Carnival of controversy.**

Kempton Park Fun Day

Kempton Park, Sunbury-on-Thames, Middx TW16 5AQ (01372 470047/www.kempton.co.uk). Kempton Park rail. **Date** 25 Aug.

Take the train from London Waterloo (it takes just 40 minutes) to enjoy a family-friendly day at the races; children's entertainment is free. For Christmas events, *see p331* **The sporting year.**

Crossing the Line Ceremony

HMS Belfast, Morgan's Lane, Tooley Street, SE1 2JH (7940 6300/www.hmsbelfast.org.uk). London Bridge tube/rail. **Date** 23-25 Aug.

Take part in Crossing the Line, one of the oldest rituals in the maritime world. Marking a sailor's first crossing of the equator, it involves getting wet and being gunged – which means the kids love it.

A Country Affair

Hampton Court Palace, Surrey KT8 9AU (8977 0705/www.hamptoncourtshow.com). Hampton Court rail/riverboat from Westminster or Richmond to Hampton Court Pier. **Date** 23-25 Aug.

Now in its fourth year, this family-friendly show has a host of hands-on activities for children, traditional fairground rides, morris dancers, maypole performers, falconry displays and animal shows, as well as live music and a farmers' market.

Regent Street Festival

Regent Street, Soho & Mayfair, W1B 4JN (7152 5853/www.regentstreetonline.com). Oxford Circus or Piccadilly Circus tube. **Date** 7 Sept. **Map** p406 U2.

An annual themed celebration that sees the horribly busy shopping street closed to traffic for the day to make room for fairground rides, theatre, street entertainers, storytelling and music. And, of course, lots of shopping.

London Gathering

Inner Temple Gardens, EC4 YBT (www.thelondon gathering.com). Temple tube or Blackfriars tube/rail. **Date** 8-9 Sept.

Scotland comes to London in this new two-day festival, celebrating contemporary culture north of the border. Literary, culinary, historical and musical events, plus a whisky marquee.

Great River Race

Thames, from Ham House, Richmond, Surrey, to Island Gardens, Isle of Dogs, E14 (8398 6900/ www.greatriverrace.co.uk). **Date** 13 Sept.

Watch over 260 vessels, from Chinese dragon boats to Viking longboats, vie for the UK 'traditional' boat championship over a 22-mile course. The race begins at 2pm; the best viewing points are Richmond, Hungerford, Millennium and Tower Bridges. You can also watch the action at close quarters from a passenger boat (phone for prices).

Spitalfields Show & Green Fair

Allen Gardens & Spitalfields City Farm, Buxton Street, E1 (7375 0441/www.alternativearts.co.uk). Whitechapel tube. **Date** 14 Sept.

Own-made produce and handicrafts, plus a wide range of stalls offering Fairtrade goods, healthy food and healing therapies, or promoting projects raising environmental awareness.

Carnival of controversy

For two days each summer a small, predominantly residential area of west London becomes heady with the colours, smells and, above all, the sounds of the Caribbean. Music is at the heart of the **Notting Hill Carnival** (*see left*), with traditional calypso and soca competing with massive sound systems belting out ragga, hip hop, dub and every other type of modern Afro-Caribbean music, but the parade, featuring spectacular floats and dancers, is the most traditional element. Hundreds of stalls sell anything from jerk chicken and rum punch to reggae albums and Jamaican flags. All in all, this is the second-largest street party in the world, after Rio, attracting around two million people every year.

Carnival began in 1959 as a response to the previous year's Notting Hill race riots. The event was conceived as a celebration of the large Caribbean presence in London, and as an inclusive festival to smooth race relations. Initially much smaller, it was held indoors until 1966. But several times in the 1970s, most notably in 1976, the parade gave way to riots, which left hundreds of policemen injured and several civilians dead. Carnival still attracts a certain amount of trouble, but over the past five years there's been a steady decline in the number of violent incidents, and these days it's easy to enjoy the event entirely oblivious of any sinister elements.

Nevertheless, worries remain about holding such a large party around narrow streets in such a limited area. Every year establishment figures and the conservative press renew calls for Carnival to be closed down or relocated. In 2004, Mayor Ken Livingstone created a Carnival Review Group with a remit to 'formulate guidelines to safeguard the future of Carnival'. The group recommended Hyde Park be used as a 'savannah' to accommodate some of Carnival's larger events, and in 2007 the first stage show took place there. This included the National Champions of Steel Competition, the steel-band battle that is traditionally one of the biggest attractions outside the main parade.

This move was heavily criticised by the majority of Carnival-goers, who saw it as an attempt to take the event out of the hands of the black community and to gain cheap, favourable publicity for the Mayor's Office. The event's organisers called the new stage show 'a local government showcase... [which] will never replace a community-based event that has grown to represent the essence of the Caribbean presence in the UK.' The Mayor responded that both events can happily co-exist. He may be right – but judging from the paltry attendance at its inception, the stage show has a long way to go before it becomes a serious alternative to its rowdier, messier neighbour.

Britain's largest independent film festival has been running for a decade and a half now; check the website for details on specific screenings and events.

For the **Frieze Art Fair**, *see p293* **Festivals**; the **Spitalfields Festival** (*see p266*) takes place in winter as well as summer.

Punch & Judy Festival

Covent Garden Piazza, Covent Garden, WC2E (0870 780 5001/www.coventgardenmarket.co.uk). Covent Garden tube. **Date** Oct. **Map** p407 Y3.

A festival of funny-voiced domestic incidents involving a bloke with a hooked nose, his wife, a crocodile and a policeman. For the May Fayre & Puppet Festival, *see p265*.

Pearly Kings & Queens Harvest Festival

St Martin-in-the-Fields, Trafalgar Square, Westminster, WC2N 4JJ (7766 1100/www.pearly society.co.uk). Leicester Square tube/Charing Cross tube/rail. **Date** 5 Oct. **Map** p407 X/Y4.

Pearly kings and queens – so-called because of the shiny white buttons sewn in elaborate designs on their dark suits – were early Victorian costermonger 'aristocracy', elected by their colleagues to safeguard their interests. Now charity representatives, the pearly monarchy gathers for this 3pm thanksgiving service in traditional 'flash boy' outfits.

London Film Festival

BFI Southbank, Belvedere Road, SE1 8XT (7928 3535/www.lff.org.uk). Embankment tube/Waterloo tube/rail. **Date** end Oct-early Nov. **Map** p401 M8.

Attracting big-name actors and directors from across the globe, the LFF screens around 180 new British and international features, mostly at BFI Southbank and the Odeon West End. *See also p289.*

London to Brighton Veteran Car Run

Serpentine Road, Hyde Park, W2 2UH (01327 856024/www.lbvcr.com). Hyde Park Corner tube. **Date** 2 Nov. **Map** p395 E8.

This parade of around 500 veteran (pre-1905) motors sets off at sunrise (7-8.30am) – though lazybones can watch the cars on Westminster Bridge a little later – on its stately way to Brighton, where the last arrivals are at 4.30pm. The cars are displayed along Regent Street the day before (11am-3pm).

Bonfire Night

Date 5 Nov.

This annual pyrotechnic frenzy sees Brits across the country gather – usually in inclement weather – to burn a 'guy' (an effigy of Guy Fawkes, who failed to blow up James I in the Gunpowder Plot of 1605) on a giant bonfire and set off loads of fireworks. Most public displays are held on the weekend nearest to 5 November; try Battersea Park, Alexandra Palace or Crystal Palace, or pre-book a late ride on the London Eye (*see p76*).

Visit the Gherkin at **Open House London**.

Mayor's Thames Festival

Between Westminster & Tower Bridges (7983 4100/www.thamesfestival.org). Blackfriars or Waterloo tube/rail. **Date** 13-14 Sept.

This popular celebration of the Thames gets more spectacular each year. Festivities kick off around noon on both days and culminate on the Sunday in an illuminated night carnival and lantern procession with firework finale. Food and crafts stalls are set up on the riverside, and there are dance and music performances and children's activities.

Open House London

Various venues (0900 160 0061/www.openhouse london.org). **Date** 20-21 Sept.

An annual event giving architecture-lovers and the merely curious free access to over 500 normally private or otherwise closed buildings, from palaces and private homes to office spaces. You can apply for a guide (print or downloaded) from the end of August; you'll need to book ahead for certain buildings.

Great Gorilla Run

Mincing Lane, the City, EC3 (www.gorillas.org/ greatgorillarun). Monument & Tower Hill tube/ Fenchurch Street rail. **Date** 27 Sept.

A 7km fun run – in furry gorilla suits – in aid of the Gorilla Organization.

Raindance

Various venues across the West End (7287 3833/ www.raindance.co.uk). **Date** 24 Sept-5 Oct.

Diwali

*Trafalgar Square, Westminster, WC2 (7983 4100/
www.london.gov.uk). Charing Cross tube/rail.* **Date**
19 or 26 Oct. **Map** p407 X5.
Join London's Hindu, Jain and Sikh communities to
celebrate the annual Festival of Light with fireworks, food, music and dance performances.

Lord Mayor's Show

*Various streets in the City (7332 3456/www.lord
mayorsshow.org).* **Date** 8 Nov.
This is the day when, under conditions laid down in
the Magna Carta, the newly elected Lord Mayor of
London is presented for approval to the monarch or
the monarch's justices. Amid 140 floats and 6,000
people, the Lord Mayor leaves Mansion House at
11am and processes to the Royal Courts of Justice
on the Strand, where he makes some vows before
returning to Mansion House by 2.30pm. The procession takes around an hour and a quarter to pass. At
5pm fireworks are set off from a barge.

Remembrance Sunday Ceremony

*Cenotaph, Whitehall, Westminster, SW1. Charing
Cross tube/rail.* **Date** 9 Nov. **Map** p401 L8.
In honour of those who lost their lives in World War
I, World War II and subsequent conflicts, the Queen,
the prime minister and other dignitaries lay wreaths
at the Cenotaph, Britain's war memorial. After a
two-minute silence at 11am, the Bishop of London
leads a service of remembrance.

State Opening of Parliament

*House of Lords, Palace of Westminster, Westminster,
SW1A 0PW (7219 4272/www.parliament.uk).
Westminster tube.* **Date** Nov. **Map** p401 L9.
In a ceremony that has changed little since the 16th
century, the Queen officially reopens Parliament
after its summer recess. Proceedings within are tele-
vised, but if you join the throngs on the streets you
can watch HRH arrive and depart in the state coach,
attended by the Household Cavalry.

London Jazz Festival

Various locations (www.londonjazzfestival.org.uk).
Date 14-23 Nov.
A ten-day jazz party, joining the dots between trad
jazz and the avant-garde, between America, the
West Indies and Africa. *See also p315* **Festivals**.

Christmas Tree & Lights

*Covent Garden (0870 780 5001/www.coventgarden
market.co.uk); Oxford Street (7462 0689/www.
oxfordstreet.co.uk); Regent Street (7152 5853/
www.regent-street.co.uk); Bond Street (www.bond
streetassociation.com); Trafalgar Square (7983 4234/
www.london.gov.uk).* **Date** Nov-Dec.
The main Christmas lights are an increasingly
commercialised affair, but the glittering lights of
St Christopher's Place, Bond Street, Marylebone
High Street and Kensington High Street still provide
a nostalgic thrill. Trafalgar Square's giant fir tree
is an annual gift from Norway, in gratitude for
Britain's role in liberating them from the Nazis.

Lord Mayor's Show: a festive City stroll.

VIP Day

*Oxford Street (7462 0689/www.oxfordstreet.co.uk);
Regent Street (7152 5853/www.regent-street.co.uk);
Bond Street (www.bondstreetassociation.com).*
Date early Dec.
London's major shopping areas are pedestrianised
for the day, with promotions and exhibits.

Bankside Frost Fair

*Tate Modern & Shakespeare's Globe, Bankside,
SE1 (7525 1139/www.visitsouthwark.com/frostfair).
London Bridge, Southwark & St Paul's tube.*
Date 12-14 Dec.
Held on the Riverwalk outside Tate Modern and
Shakespeare's Globe, Bankside Frost Fair is
London's largest free winter event, attracting over
100,000 people. Winter festivities include music,
food, shopping and fun workshops for families.

New Year's Eve Celebrations

Date 31 Dec.
Celebratory events in London tend to be quite
localised, although Trafalgar Square has traditionally been an unofficial (and alarmingly crowded)
gathering point; no booze is permitted, which may
not be a bad thing. For the cash-flash, almost all the
city's nightclubs hold ludicrously expensive New
Year parties. If you're feeling strong enough at noon
the next day, the New Year's Day Parade starts at
Parliament Square, finishes at Berkeley Square and
takes in Whitehall, Trafalgar Square and Piccadilly.

Arts & Entertainment

Children

London's a whole heap of fun for the sprogs.

The best city-break destination in the world can be as stimulating for children as it is for their parents. In fact, more so – your kids don't get the credit card bill. These pages can only scrape the surface of what's going on for children in London. Check the Around Town pages in the weekly *Time Out London* magazine for the latest shows and events, and log on to the Mayor's website for children at www.london. gov.uk/young-london. Useful information can also be found on www.kidslovelondon.com and www.whatson4kids.com. *Time Out London for Children* (£9.99) is a comprehensive, annually updated guide to getting the most out of the city with the children.

An economical way of touring London as a family is by bus: try the RV1 (Tower Hill to South Bank), the 12 (Westminster to Notting Hill) and the 52 (Kensington to Knightsbridge). Under-19s travel free on buses and under-11s travel free on all London transport; for further details, *see p357*.

Area guide

South Bank & Bankside pp76-87

Capital highlights when taking children on a dander down London's favourite tourist promenade are the **British Airways London Eye** (*see p76*), splendid on a clear day, and, across the way, the **London Aquarium** (*see p77*), a godsend on a rainy one. They're both expensive but rewarding. The National Theatre stages free entertainment in the summer – an open-air performance festival called **Watch This Space** runs from June to September. This, along with the **Coin Street Festival**, makes the South Bank an entertaining option in the summer holidays (for both, *see p266*). Further east, **Tate Modern** (*see p81*) looms large on the family agenda – weekend and school holiday art activities are free for all ages here and at **Tate Britain**, a boat ride downriver. A bit further east, the **Clink Prison Museum** offers ghoulish fun, while the **Golden Hinde** (for both, *see p80*) is justly famed for its educational sleepover programme. In nearby Tooley Street, the goriness of the **London Dungeon** (*see p83*) is appreciated by children over ten. All ages get a thrill from exploring warship museum **HMS Belfast** (*see p87*).

The City pp88-101

The best day out here is provided by the **Tower of London** (*see p99*), with regular Beefeater-guided tours. The best free attraction is the excellent **Museum of London** (*see p95*), notwithstanding the closure of the lower floor for an £18 million revamp.

Bloomsbury & Fitzrovia pp106-111

Check the **British Museum** (*see p107*) website for details of its next Eyeopener family tour; they run regularly through the school holidays, giving a fun introduction to specific galleries. Other tours, activity packs and sleepovers for Young Friends of the Museum (see the website for details) help to make this gargantuan collection more accessible to short attention spans. The best playground in central London, **Coram's Fields** (*see p278*), is nearby – with the **Foundling Museum** (*see p109*) next door. The **Cartoon Museum** (*see p107*) has regular children's workshops, as well as family fun days every second Saturday of the month. **Pollock's Toy Museum** (*see p111*) is a nostalgia trip for parents, but the shop is of far greater interest to their children.

Covent Garden pp112-115

Reopened in 2007 after an extensive refurb, **London's Transport Museum** (*see p113*) is better than ever for children. There's a bright and cheerful play area and loads of fantastic interactives, as well as a café overlooking the Piazza, a two-storey shop and a theatre. For more freestyle fun, the acts pulling in the crowds in front of **St Paul's Covent Garden** (*see p115*) are often worth a watch.

Trafalgar Square pp135-137

There are fewer pigeons but a lot more free weekend and summer holiday entertainment since London's central square was partially pedestrianised and turned into the city's 'best room'. Even if all is quiet in the Square, the **National Gallery** (*see p135*) has year-round paper trails and audio tours for children, as well as regular kids' workshops and storytelling

Great setting, great food and great fun at **Mudchute Kitchen**. *See p275.*

sessions for under-fives. For three- to 12-year-olds, the **National Portrait Gallery** (*see p137*) loans out free activity-filled rucksacks that correspond to the Tudor, Victorian and 20th-century galleries, and holds regular storytelling sessions. Nearby, the newly refurbished **St Martin-in-the-Fields** (*see p137*) has London's only brass-rubbing centre, as well as a fine café.

South Kensington pp149-152

Hands up who loves the **Natural History Museum**? Everyone, whether young or old. What's not to like? It's huge, it's free and it has dinosaurs. Explorer backpacks can be borrowed for the kids. You could try to see its equally splendid neighbour, the **Science Museum**, on the same day, but these giant places really deserve a day each. The Science Museum is divided into six play zones, and even toddlers are well catered for. Older children adore Launch Pad. You can even sleep over. These two big Beasts make it all too easy to forget about Beauty: the **Victoria & Albert Museum** (for all three, *see p151*). Its terrific Sunday and school holiday Activity Cart is a great way to focus on aspects of the collection. There are also tailor-made trails and a stylish shop, courtesy of an ongoing refurbishment programme.

Greenwich pp174-177

This World Heritage Site has a fantastic park, a huge **Maritime Museum** (*see p175*) full of seaworthy adventure, where there are frequent weekend and school holiday art and storytelling activities, an exciting weekend market and a spectacular new planetarium – the show is screened by an actual astronomer who will happily answer those complicated kiddie questions afterwards. The **Cutty Sark** (*see p175*) is under wraps for restoration and a little bit scorched after a mysterious fire – the information centre details current progress.

Eating & drinking

Of the places in the **Restaurants & Cafés** chapter, **Carluccio's Caffè** (*see p218*), **Geales** (*see p207*), **Inn The Park** (*see p211*), **Masala Zone** (*see p201*) and **Wagamama** (*see p201*) are notably child-friendly.

Giraffe

Units 1&2, Riverside Level 1, Royal Festival Hall, SE1 8XX (7928 2004/www.giraffe.net). Waterloo tube/rail. **Open** 8am-11pm Mon-Fri; 9am-11pm Sat; 9am-10.30pm Sun. **Main courses** £6.95-£13.95. *Set meals* (5-7pm) £6.95 2 courses. **Credit** AmEx, MC, V. **Map** p401 M8.

Teen sensation

When Victoria Park in Hackney hosted a huge Underage Festival for 5,000 teenagers in the summer of 2007, it prompted a puzzled news story on BBC Radio. 'Finally rock and roll is starting to embrace a brand new demographic,' announced a reporter. 'They're called teenagers.'

They were joking, of course, but perhaps not so very much. With the music business increasingly kept afloat by 'fifty quid man', that besuited forty-something bloke who stops off at the megastore on his way back from work to buy a handful of CDs and DVDs, and with those expensive summer festivals (Glastonbury, Reading, V) colonised by respectable, middle-aged punters, pop's initial target group has been steadily edged out of the picture over the past 50 years. A gap had opened up for someone to cater for a whole generation of pop-savvy teens, most of whom had learnt about music mostly or entirely through the internet.

The phenomenon started in 2005 when Keith Anderson set up the Way Out West nights in a bar at Brentford Football Club's ground, allowing in the under-18s. Soon an enterprising Camberwell 14-year-old by the name of Sam Killcoyne cottoned on to the idea, starting the Underage Club nights in south London, and before long you had the likes of All Age Concerts, Oops and Subverse springing up, advertising on web networks like MySpace and Bebo.

The format is similar to the covert afternoon bhangra gigs thrown by Asian kids in the 1980s and the posh 'public school parties' that were popular in the early 1990s. They usually start late afternoon on weekends in a variety of venues: the Barfly and the Underworld in Camden, the Islington Academy, the Coronet in Elephant and Castle, ULU in Bloomsbury, SeOne near London Bridge, or at the Pure Groove record shop in Holloway (679 Holloway Road, N19 5SE, 7281 4877, www.puregroove. co.uk). The bars sell only soft drinks, for obvious reasons. Invariably, the bands – usually up-and-coming indie acts in their late teens and early 20s (the Horrors, Patrick Wolf, the Klaxons, Cajun Dance Party, XX Teens, the Young Knives, Enter Shikari and Foals have all played over the past year) – are the oldest people at the venue.

The punters – aged between 14 and 18 – are sometimes dropped off by their parents and usually dress up for the events in skinny jeans, tight T-shirts and sparkly make-up (and that's just the boys). Concerned parents will be heartened to know that the gigs tend to attract kids from nice middle-class families, and you'll find no drugs, no fags, no drink and rarely a hint of any sexual or physical threat once you're inside.

For all the hormones buzzing around the clubs, girls in particular often find these nights less intimidating than sneaking into an adult gig. There are no leering students or older men trying to chat up teenage girls, there's none of the blokey machismo you get in the moshpit, no disapproving sneers from the oldies. Indeed, at the few youth-oriented gigs where over-18s aren't actually banned, anyone in their 20s or older will be assumed to be either a cab driver, a drug dealer or a predatory paedophile. Perhaps all three. It's probably the safest fun any teenager can enjoy – they can get involved on www.myspace.com, checking out the allageconcerts, underage_club or wayout west3 pages for upcoming events.

Like all outposts of the mini-chain, these spacious premises exude warmth, colour and good cheer – no wonder Giraffe is consistently near the top of the Most Child-Friendly Restaurant charts. Children can choose from their own menu. Brunch features combinations of fried or scrambled eggs, beans and sausage, and there's a choice of grills, such as burgers and chicken, plus veggie options and good ice-cream. The lunchtime deal (noon-3pm), including a drink and dessert is just £5.50.
Other locations throughout the city.

Mudchute Kitchen

Mudchute Park & Farm, Pier Street, Isle of Dogs, Docklands, E14 3HP (7515 5901/www.mudchute. org). Mudchute DLR. **Meals served** 9am-5pm Tue-Sun. **Main courses** £3-£8. **No credit cards**.
Mudchute Farm is a green and pleasant spot on the skyscraper-heavy Isle of Dogs; for family groups, the appeal is obvious. Across the yard from the squealing Gloucester Old Spot pigs and clucking Polish White Crest chickens sits the kitchen. Inside, you'll find farmhouse kitchen tables and settles, a big futon for babies, and a book and toy corner. Outside, picnic tables look out over riding stables. The bucolic has its disadvantages – flies, for one. But the tireless young chefs certainly know about wholesome seasonal grub and can make lashings of sparkling ginger beer. There are usually four or five hot options (also available in child portions), such as fried polenta topped with wild mushrooms, herbs and cream cheese. Plain eaters can have the farm's own eggs, own-made jam or beans on toast. The own-made cakes are ace and Mudchute does the best cream teas this side of Totnes. *Photos p273.*

Rainforest Café

20 Shaftesbury Avenue, Piccadilly, W1D 7EU (7434 3111/www.therainforestcafe.co.uk). Piccadilly Circus tube. **Meals served** noon-10pm Mon-Thur, Sun; noon-7.30pm Fri, Sat. **Main courses** £10.25-£16. **Credit** AmEx, DC, MC, V. **Map** p401 K7.
A ground-floor shop area leads to a basement restaurant, where animatronic apes, elephants and parrots continue to pump up the excitability levels. Children find the Rainforest Café delightful; grown-ups can take comfort from the number of organic items on the Rainforest Rascals kids' menu.

Smollensky's on the Strand

105 Strand, Charing Cross, WC2R 0AA (7497 2101/www.smollenskys.co.uk). Embankment tube/Charing Cross tube/rail. **Meals served** noon-11.30pm Mon-Sat; noon-10pm Sun. **Main courses** £8.95-£21.95. **Credit** AmEx, DC, MC, V. **Map** p401 L7.
The main reasons for lunching here at the weekend are the children's entertainment (clowns, face-painters and so on) and the fun packs. Children love the place, and we're fond of it too – the service is friendly and the food tasty, if rather on the fried side, especially on the children's menu (steaks, burgers, chicken, fish), but there is pasta and jambalaya. Puddings are great.

Tate Modern Café: Level 2

Second floor, Tate Modern, Sumner Street, SE1 9TG (7401 5014/www.tate.org.uk). St Paul's tube/Blackfriars tube/rail. **Meals served** 10am-5.30pm Mon-Thur, Sat, Sun; 10am-9.30pm Fri. **Main courses** £6.95-£9.95. **Credit** AmEx, MC, V. **Map** p404 O7.
Children are generally greeted with much enthusiasm here by the super-efficient waiters. As well as excellent views, the café provides distractions in the form of a junior menu of art and literacy activities, and a pot of wax crayons. The children's menu befits a top-of-the-range gallery restaurant, providing a choice of haddock goujons, spaghetti and meatballs or pasta and tomato bake, as well as a drink and ice-creamy or fruit pudding.

TGI Friday's

6 Bedford Street, Covent Garden, WC2E 9HZ (7379 0585/www.tgifridays.co.uk). Covent Garden or Embankment tube/Charing Cross tube/rail. **Open** noon-11.30pm Mon-Sat; noon-11pm Sun. **Main courses** £6.95-£17. **Credit** AmEx, MC, V. **Map** p401 L7.
The most child-centred of all the US chains, despite the entire restaurant being focused on a noisy bar. Perky staff, free activity packs, weekend face painting and entertainment… kids love it here and there's a devoted children's menu. Parents may be underwhelmed by the largely fried food (expect the usual chicken fingers and burger standards, plus ice-cream sundaes and a few veggie options), but it's fun for an occasional treat.
Other locations throughout the city.

Entertainment

City farms & zoos

London Zoo (*see p127*) houses some of the big hitters of the animal population, especially since Gorilla Kingdom opened, and there's loads to see and do. That's reflected in the admission charge, though. Young children will be just as enraptured by the very much cheaper **Battersea Park Children's Zoo** (www.batterseaparkzoo.co.uk) and there are city farms across the city that charge nothing to get in. Try **Freightliners City Farm** (www.freightlinersfarm.org.uk) and **Kentish Town City Farm** (www.aapi.co.uk/cityfarm) or, in the east, **Mudchute City Farm** (www.mudchute.org) with its fabulous new café (*see above*) and **Hackney City Farm** (www.hackneycityfarm.co.uk), with its more commercial venue Frizzante, which has a larger menu and quicker turnover than Mudchute's. Hackney Farm also runs all manner of health and craft workshops. Down by the river in south-east London **Surrey Docks Farm** (www.surreydocksfarm.org) has rampaging goats and a nice little café.

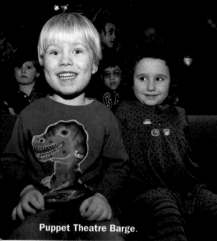

Puppet Theatre Barge.

Puppets

Little Angel Theatre

14 Dagmar Passage, off Cross Street, Islington, N1 2DN (7226 1787/www.littleangeltheatre.com). Angel tube/Highbury & Islington tube/rail. **Open** *Box office* 11am-6pm Mon-Fri; 10am-4.30pm Sat, Sun. **Tickets** £5-£15. **Credit** MC, V.

Established in 1961, London's only permanent puppet theatre stages diverse productions that cover all aspects of puppetry. There's a Saturday Puppet Club and Sunday Fundays for all the family. Phone for details of pay-what-you-can performances.

Puppet Theatre Barge

Opposite 35 Blomfield Road, Little Venice, W9 2PF (winter 7249 6876/summer 07836 202745 mobile/ www.puppetbarge.com). Warwick Avenue tube. **Open** *Box office* 10am-9pm daily. **Tickets** £8.50; £8 reductions. **Credit** MC, V.

Making the most of London's liquid assets, the barge is moored at Little Venice (*see p155*), a charming locale that will delight most children. The intimate little stage is the setting for quality puppet shows that put a modern twist on traditional tales and children's classics. The barge stays here between December and June; regular performances are held at 3pm on Saturday and Sunday, swelling to a daily programme during school holidays.

Science & nature

Camley Street Natural Park

12 Camley Street, King's Cross, NW1 0PW (7833 2311/www.wildlondon.org.uk). King's Cross tube/rail. **Open** 10am-5pm Thur-Sun. *School holidays* 10am-5pm daily. **Admission** free. **Map** p399 L2.

Right in the heart of noisy London, perched on the banks of the Regent's Canal, this is London Wildlife Trust's flagship reserve. It combines woods, ponds, marshes and flower meadows to lovely effect in an area that was once an industrial wasteland.

Greenwich Peninsula Ecology Park

Thames Path, John Harrison Way, Greenwich, SE10 0QZ (8293 1904/www.urbanecology.org.uk). North Greenwich tube/108, 161, 422, 472, 486 bus. **Open** 10am-5pm (or dusk) Wed-Sun. **Admission** free.

A pond-dipping, birdwatching wetland haven near the O2 (*see p311*). Family fun days, like Frog Day in March, and all-summer play activities are part of a busy calendar of events.

Theatre

Half Moon Young People's Theatre

43 White Horse Road, Stepney, E1 0ND (7709 8900/www.halfmoon.org.uk). Limehouse DLR/rail. **Open** *Box office* 10am-6pm Mon-Fri; 10am-5pm Sat. **Tickets** £4.50. **Credit** MC, V.

The Half Moon's inclusive policy places particular emphasis on engaging those often excluded by ethnicity and disabilities. Two studios provide a calendar of performances for children aged from six months, and they can join one of the seven youth theatre groups (for five- to 17-year-olds).

Polka Theatre

240 The Broadway, Wimbledon, SW19 1SB (8543 4888/www.polkatheatre.com). South Wimbledon tube/Wimbledon tube/rail then 57, 93, 219, 493 bus. **Open** *Phone bookings* 9.30am-4.30pm Mon; 9am-6pm Tue-Fri; 10am-4.30pm Sat. *Personal callers* 9.30am-4.30pm Tue-Fri; 10am-4.30pm Sat. **Tickets** £4-£14. **Credit** MC, V.

Arts & Entertainment

Sure can pick 'em

London's number one for family fun, says **Ronnie Haydon**, editor of
Time Out's *London for Children* guide.

In the seven years since the annual *Time Out London for Children* was first published, the capital has become markedly more family friendly. Museums are now free; parks and green spaces are flourishing; the Congestion Charge has unblocked the roads; buses are free for children, more accessible for pushchairs and plentiful... the list goes on.

Nowhere else in the world has so many museums and galleries specialising in so many subjects. They're full of surprises. Who would have thought, for example, that the stern features of the Old Lady of Threadneedle Street (**Bank of England Museum**; *see p96*) conceal a diverting exhibition that encourages a keen head for commerce among the very young? Children can pick up a solid gold bar, design their own banknotes or indulge in a spot of Foreign Exchange dealing. Another old eccentric, the **Horniman Museum** (*see p174*), has children making music, masks and marionettes in school holidays, but its disparate curiosities keep young children amused even when there are no special events. A firm favourite of ours, the Horniman – and it has superb gardens, but they cannot compare to **Kew** (*see p183*), an earthly paradise in south-west London, much loved by families for the dedicated indoor and outdoor play spaces, Climbers and Creepers. And although parent must pay, children get into Kew free. Yippee!

Which brings us to another reason why London is top for tots. The parks. You're usually within walking distance of one – if you aren't, you'll find one within a few stops on a bus. The **Royal Parks**, such as Hyde (*see p152*) and Regent's (*see p127*), make a big fuss of under-tens in the summer, but

the local ones are just as conscientious. Some of our favourites include **Highgate Woods** (sylvan setting, great playground, café; *see p159*), **Highbury Fields** (also with a terrific playground; *see p160*), **Thames Barrier Park** (playground, riverside ducks; *see p168*) and **Battersea Park** (riverside setting, great adventure playground and sports facilities, excellent little zoo; *see p180*). All these are perfect for picnics, but also have ultra-child-friendly places to eat.

If you're looking for a destination dining room, the majority of London restaurants are relaxed about catering for children, especially during the day. Every year we give an award to our favourite family eating place. It might be a well-known chain, such as **Giraffe** (*see p273*), but we also choose homely independents full of toys and good cheer, such as **Gracelands** up in Kensal Green (www.gracelandscafe.com) or farm-based **Frizzante** (www.frizzanteltd.co.uk). The winner for 2007/8 was the wonderful **Tate Modern Café** (*see p275*).

Of course, the reason so many visitors come to London – the shopping – is less likely to be cited by parents laden with buggies, prams and toddlers. There are, however, some outstanding children's shops. The self-appointed Best Toyshop in the World is **Hamleys**. It's certainly the biggest and it's full of fun, but for our money the cheeriest place to bring children on a spending spree is **Daisy & Tom** (*see p242*). It has everything under one roof, including a free carousel and puppet show. If your family party includes teens, especially those of an Emo disposition, point them to **Camden Market** (*see p155*) and stand well back.

This exceptional theatre has one of the best programmes of children's events in London. Touring companies stage daily shows (10.30am, 2pm) in the main auditoriums, with weekly (often puppet-based) performances for under-fours in the Adventure Theatre. There are free monthly World of Stories drop-in activities, and literature events.

Unicorn Theatre
Tooley Street, Bankside, SE1 2HZ (7645 0560/ www.unicorntheatre.com). London Bridge tube/rail/ Tower Hill tube. **Open** *Box office* 9.30am-6pm Mon-Fri; 10am-6pm Sat; noon-5pm Sun. **Credit** MC, V. **Map** p405 Q8.

This sleek-looking arts centre is the result of a three-year collaboration with local schoolchildren, whose thoughts are incorporated into the design. The 300-seat Weston Theatre is its large performance space, the Clore a more intimate studio for education and new work. Check the website for details of family workshops and the 2008 performance programme.

Spaces to play

London's parks are the envy of the rest of the world and provide great escapes for little visitors bored of pounding the pavement with their parents. **Hyde Park** (*see p152*) and **St James's Park** (*see p142*) are in the centre of town, but you don't have to travel far to reach **Regent's Park** (*see p127*) for boating and London Zoo (*see p127*); **Hampstead Heath** (*see p158*) for swimming and kite-flying; **Thames Barrier Park** (*see p168*) to watch the wildfowl; **Battersea Park** (*see p180*) for its adventure playground and zoo; **Greenwich Park** (*see p175*) for views and deer; and **Richmond Park** (*see p183*) for the Isabella Plantation, cycling and more deer.

Coram's Fields

93 Guilford Street, Bloomsbury, WC1N 1DN (7837 6138/www.coramsfields.org). Russell Square tube. **Open** *Apr-Sept* 8am-8pm Mon-Fri; 9am-8am Sat, Sun. *Oct-Mar* 8am-dusk Mon-Fri; 9am-dusk Sat, Sun. **Admission** free (adults only admitted if accompanied by child under 16). **Map** p399 L4.
This site dates back to 1747, when Thomas Coram established the Foundling Hospital (*see p109*). Coram's Fields opened as a park in 1936 and now has sandpits, a paddling pool, a football pitch, a basketball court, climbing towers, play areas and a zip wire. Other draws include a small café, animal enclosures and indoor facilities for the under-fives.

Diana, Princess of Wales Memorial Playground

Near Black Lion Gate, Broad Walk, Kensington Gardens, W8 2UH (7298 2117/recorded information 7298 2141/www.royalparks.gov.uk). Bayswater or Queensway tube. **Open** *Summer* 10am-6.45pm daily. *Winter* 10am-dusk daily. **Admission** free; adults only admitted if accompanied by under-12s. **Map** p395 E8.
This commemorative playground is a youngsters' wonderland. There's a huge wooden pirate ship, mermaids' fountain, rocky outcrops, wigwams and a tree-house encampment. The equipment and facilities have mostly been designed for use by children with special needs. Unaccompanied adults may view the gardens from 9.30am to 10am daily.

Discover

1 Bridge Terrace, Stratford, E15 4BG (8536 5555/www.discover.org.uk). Stratford tube/rail/ DLR. **Open** *Term-time* 10am-5pm Tue-Sun. *School holidays* 10am-5pm daily. **Admission Garden** free. *Story trail* £3.50; £2.50 reductions; free under-2s; half-price admission 3-5pm during term. **Credit** MC, V.
In a bleak area of London that was pretty much overlooked until the 2012 Olympics decided it would site itself nearby, Discover – an interactive 'story trail' – designed for under-eights – is a particular joy. The garden includes a wet-play area, a monster's-tongue slide, climbing frames and willow hide-and-seek tunnels. Indoors, children can hear and create stories using a wonderland of props, make characters at craft tables and be entertained by weekend puppet shows and art, dance and music workshops.

Theme parks

Always call or check the website for special events and for opening times, which vary throughout the year. Queues are unavoidable; arrive early in the morning to make the best of it. Also note that height and health restrictions apply on some rides.

Chessington World of Adventures

Leatherhead Road, Chessington, Surrey KT9 2NE (0870 444 7777/www.chessington.co.uk). **Getting there** *By rail* Chessington South rail then 71 bus or 10min walk. *By car* J9 off M25. **Open** times vary. Closed Nov-Feb. **Admission** £30; £20 under-12s; £12-£22 reductions; £61.50-£96 family; free under-4s. Check website for advance bookings for fast-track entry. **Credit** MC, V. **Map** p343.
Chessington is the softer option for young families after a theme park – witness the Animal Land zoo with its walk-through squirrel monkey enclosure, otters, sea lions, and monkey and bird gardens. All the rides in the Land of the Dragons, Pirate's Cove, Beanoland and Bubbleworks (indoor foamy fun) are fine for the under-12s.

Legoland

Winkfield Road, Windsor, Berks SL4 4AY (0870 504 0404/www.legoland.co.uk). **Getting there** *By rail* Windsor & Eton Riverside or Windsor Central rail then bus. *By car* J3 off M3 or J6 off M4. **Open** times vary. Closed late Nov-mid Mar. **Admission** *1-day ticket* £33; £23 reductions; free under-3s. *2-day ticket* £61; £47 reductions; free under-3s. **Credit** MC, V. **Map** p343.
Lovable Legoland is a top family day out (it won the 2007 Tommy's Parent Friendly award), so expect queues. All ages enjoy this beautifully laid-out park, where impressive cities around the world are recreated from nearly 40 million Lego pieces. Rides on the Dragon, Wave Surfer and Pirate Falls are a blast, and the impressive Vikings River Splash guarantees a soaking. Then there's the famous Driving School, bulldozers to manipulate, boats to row and live shows to see. The park is closed on selected Tuesdays and Wednesdays throughout the season.

Thorpe Park

Staines Road, Chertsey, Surrey KT16 8PN (0870 444 4466/www.thorpepark.com). **Getting there** *By rail* Staines rail then 950 bus. *By car* M25 J11 or J13. **Open** times vary. **Admission** £32; £14.50-£20 reductions; £88-£105 family; free for children under 1m. Check website or phone for advance bookings. **Credit** MC, V. **Map** p343.
This is the best option for older children, especially thrill seekers. It has Europe's fastest rollercoaster, Stealth, which launches you earthward from nought to 80mph in under two seconds. Other aptly named rides include Slammer, Rush, Colossus (the world's first ten-loop rollercoaster) and Vortex. There are plenty of tamer rides for younger visitors and a pleasant paddling area called Neptune's Beach, a godsend on hot days.

Comedy

Stand up for London's brilliant stand-ups.

Canal Café Theatre.
See p280.

To leave London without seeing some of the fun that goes on would be doing the capital a grave disservice. The stand-up scene – egged on by discerning audiences – is a world leader, though there is an element of seasonality to proceedings. August is a quiet month in town, as many acts head up to Scotland hoping to make a splash at the Edinburgh Festival. Conversely, April to July is preview time, which means you have a good chance to see big names try out material in small venues, often with reduced admission fees – try the **Etcetera Theatre** (265 Camden High Street, NW1 7BU, 7482 0378), **Lowdown at the Albany** or the **Hen & Chickens**. From September to December comics show off their Edinburgh successes to London audiences – often at the **Arts Theatre**, **Bloomsbury Theatre** (15 Gordon Street, WC1H 0AH, 7388 8822) or **Soho Theatre** (*see p340*), sometimes in a major West End playhouse. But the scene isn't just about Edinburgh. Bubbling away all through the year are plenty of terrific clubs with mixed bills – usually of three or four comics doing 20 minutes each. The venerable **Comedy Store** is the must-see: it was a key venue in the birth of 'alternative' comedy.

Names to watch out for this year include Cutting Edge-regular Andy Parsons and the outspoken Brendon Burns, who won

Edinburgh Festival's prestigious if.comedy award in 2007. We only list central venues below; for line-ups at neighbourhood venues, see *Time Out* magazine's weekly listings.

Amused Moose
Camden *The Washington, 50 England's Lane, NW3 4UE. Belsize Park or Chalk Farm tube.* **Shows** vary. **Admission** £5.
Soho *Moonlighting Nightclub, 17 Greek Street, W1D 4DR. Leicester Square or Tottenham Court Road tube.* **Shows** 8.30pm Sat. **Admission** £9-£12.50. **Map** p406 W2.
West End *Arts Theatre Comedy Cellar (see below).* **Shows** vary. **Admission** £5-£12.
All *7287 3727/www.amusedmoose.com.* **Credit** (bookings only) MC, V.
In its latest expansion, Amused Moose has taken over a space under the Arts Theatre. How long it'll last here we're not sure, given the awkward shape of the room, but for as long as it does, expect a good mix of big names and newcomers: Ricky Gervais, Bill Bailey and Graham Norton all raised a chuckle at the original venue. Heckling is discouraged – boo hiss.

Arts Theatre
6 Great Newport Street, Covent Garden, WC2H 7JB (information 7836 2132/www.artstheatrelondon. com). Leicester Square tube. **Shows/admission** phone for details. **Map** p407 X3.
In addition to plays, the Arts hosts a range of one-man comedy shows in its main auditorium. Expect the likes of Reginald D Hunter and Sean Hughes. Downstairs you'll find Amused Moose (*see above*).

Banana Cabaret
Bedford, 77 Bedford Hill, Balham, SW12 9HD (8682 8940/www.bananacabaret.co.uk). Balham tube/rail. **Shows** 9pm Fri, Sat. **Admission** £3 Tue; £13, £9 reductions Fri; £16, £13 reductions Sat. **Credit** (bookings only) MC, V.
Banana Cabaret has four or five stand-ups per show, usually of good quality – political agitator Mark Thomas warmed up for his TV shows here, and comedy Arab Omid Djalili has also appeared.

Boat Show/Monday Club
Tattershall Castle, Kings Reach, Victoria Embankment, SW1A 7HR (07932 658895 mobile). Embankment tube. **Shows** 8pm Fri, Sat; 8.30pm alternate Mon. **Admission** £8-£12. **Map** p401 L8.
Energetic promoter Christian Knowles regularly books top-notch stand-up for the Tattershall Castle boat. Big-name surprise guests are common, with the esteemed Dylan Moran, Harry Hill, Ross Noble and Daniel Kitson all having done turns here.

Making Hay?

Malcolm Hay, *Time Out*'s comedy editor for the last 20 years, reminisces.

Live comedy in Britain began a renaissance at the end of the 1970s. It has grown and expanded ever since. The London comedy circuit and *Time Out* have grown up alongside each other. No other city on the planet can rival it. What's most remarkable about this is that it's been achieved without any subsidy. There's always scope for innovation, but there's little room for self-indulgence. London audiences see to that. They're knowledgeable, comedy-literate, equipped with quite finely tuned crap detectors. Stag and hen parties remain the disgusting exception, although some promoters do actively discourage them. Comics sometimes talk about how audiences out of town, in places blessed with only occasional shows, can be so much more pleasant and appreciative. For this, read 'passive and undiscriminating'. The last thing live comedy needs right now is audiences who'll gratefully lap up anything they're given.

In 20 years as comedy editor, I've seen major comics start out and others fall by the wayside. The dividing line between success and failure looks frighteningly thin. Comedians who are stumbling today could be tomorrow's stars, so show every performer respect.

The memories? The memories would fill several virtual scrapbooks. Eddie Izzard in Crystal Palace early in his career, telling for the first time in my hearing how he was brought up by wolves. Lee Evans, long before he was famous, pumping himself up like a blow-up doll at the King's Head. Mark Thomas, at the Assembly Rooms in Edinburgh, hitting the button so accurately about female sexuality that members of the audience hugged each other in delighted recognition. And Stewart Lee's account of his encounter with Jesus in the aftermath of the Christian fundamentalist backlash against *Jerry Springer: The Opera*.

Canal Café Theatre

Bridge House, Delamere Terrace, Little Venice, W2 6ND (7289 6054/www.canalcafetheatre.com). Warwick Avenue tube. **Shows** *Newsrevue* 9.30pm Thur-Sat; 9pm Sun. Phone for details of other shows. **Admission** (incl membership) £10.50; £8.50 reductions. **No credit cards. Map** p394 C4.
Newsrevue, the Canal Café's topical comedy sketch show, was awarded a Guinness World Record in 2004 for the longest-running live comedy show (25 years); the show is updated each week. The venue also hosts comic plays and stand-up. *Photo p279.*

Chuckle Club

Three Tuns Bar, London School of Economics, Houghton Street, Holborn, WC2A 2AL (7476 1672/ www.chuckleclub.com). Holborn tube. **Shows** 8.30pm Sat. **Admission** £10; £8 reductions. **No credit cards. Map** p399 M6.
Bonkers resident compère Eugene Cheese introduces comics of the calibre of Simon Munnery and Scott Capurro, as well as open spots. Although everyone's welcome, the night is held in a student union – which means beer at student prices. Yay!

Comedy Café

66-68 Rivington Street, Shoreditch, EC2A 3AY (7739 5706/www.comedycafe.co.uk). Liverpool Street or Old Street tube/rail. **Shows** 9pm Wed, Thur, Sat; 8pm Fri. **Admission** free Wed; £8 Thur; £5 Fri; £15 Sat. **Credit** MC, V. **Map** p403 R4.
This purpose-built Shoreditch venue usually plays host to three to four stand-up comedians – most of them decent, and one of which is usually a big name (Mark Watson, for example). Wednesday is open mic night. It's almost directly opposite Cargo (*see p321*).

Comedy Camp

Barcode, 3-4 Archer Street, Soho, W1D 7AP (7483 2960/www.comedycamp.co.uk). Leicester Square or Piccadilly Circus tube. **Shows** 8.30pm Tue. **Admission** £10. **Credit** MC, V. **Map** p406 W3.
Jo Caulfield and Scott Capurro are the caustic regulars at this Soho haunt, which describes itself as a 'straight-friendly lesbian and gay club'. Fun weekly nights, hosted by Simon Happily, have welcomed Harry Hill, Al Murray and Graham Norton.

Comedy Store

1A Oxendon Street, Soho, SW1Y 4EE (Ticketmaster 0870 060 2340/www.thecomedystore.co.uk). Leicester Square or Piccadilly Circus tube. **Shows** 8pm Tue-Thur, Sun; 8pm & midnight Fri, Sat; Mon phone for details. **Admission** £15.25-£17.50; £8 reductions. **Credit** AmEx, MC, V. **Map** p406 W4.
The legendary Comedy Store made its name as the home of 'alternative comedy' in the 1980s. With those radical young comics now the mainstream of British comedy, the Store is the place every comic wants to play and has some of the best bills on the circuit. The venue is purpose-built for serious punters, with its gladiatorial semicircle of seats, and generally favours trad stand-up. Go on Tuesdays for the topical Cutting Edge shows, on Wednesdays for top improv outfit the Comedy Store Players.

Downstairs at the King's Head

2 Crouch End Hill, Crouch End, N8 8AA (8340 1028/office 01920 823265/www.downstairsatthe kingshead.com). Finsbury Park tube/rail then W7 bus. **Shows** 8pm Tue, Thur, Sat, Sun. **Admission** £4, £3 reductions Tue, Thur; £9, £7 reductions Sat; £7, £5 reductions Sun. **No credit cards**.

This Crouch Ender was there as the 'alternative comedy' scene started back in 1981. Now it's a favourite with many big-name comedians for trying out new material. It also showcases new talent: Thursday's 'try out night' – up to 16 new acts take the mic – kickstarted the careers of Mark Lamarr and Eddie Izzard.

Headliners Comedy

Ha Bloody Ha *Ealing Studios, Ealing Green, St Mary's Road, Ealing, W5 5EP. Ealing Broadway tube/rail.* **Shows** 8.45pm Fri, Sat.
Headliners *George IV, 185 Chiswick High Road, Chiswick, W4 2DR. Turnham Green tube.* **Shows** 9pm Fri, Sat.
Both *8566 4067/www.headlinerscomedy.com.* **Admission** £10; £7.50 reductions (Fri only). **No credit cards**.

In the studios where the Ealing Comedies were filmed, Ha Bloody Ha is a west London institution, with Headliners Chiswick its unfussy younger brother. The same guest acts shuttle between both clubs (only the MCs differ between them). Expect big names such as Bill Bailey and Ed Byrne.

Hen & Chickens

109 St Paul's Road, Highbury Corner, Islington, N1 2NA (7704 2001/www.henandchickens.com). Highbury & Islington tube/rail. **Shows** 7.30pm, 9.30pm. **Admission** £7-£10. **No credit cards**.

This well-established joint offers similar bills to its sister venue, Lowdown at the Albany (*see below*). A mix of big names (Jimmy Carr, Daniel Kitson) and newcomers are presented, with lots going on during the Edinburgh preview season.

Jongleurs

Battersea *The Rise, 49 Lavender Gardens, SW11 1DJ. Clapham Junction rail.* **Shows** 8.30pm Thur; 9pm Fri, Sat. **Admission** £9.50-£18.50.
Bow *221 Grove Road, E3 5SN. Mile End tube.* **Shows** 8.30pm Fri, Sat. **Admission** £14.50-£16.50.
Camden *Middle Yard, Camden Lock, Chalk Farm Road, NW1 8AB. Chalk Farm tube.* **Shows** 8.30pm Fri, Sat. **Admission** £18.50-£19.50.
All *0870 787 0707/www.jongleurs.com.* **Credit** AmEx, DC, MC, V.

Since it opened in 1983, Jongleurs has expanded nationwide – but the biggest doesn't necessarily mean best. You get the biggest names, but the Jongleurs are corporate-do and hen-night central, with boozed-up punters who eat, drink, dance – and laugh if they happen to notice the poor soul on stage.

Lee Hurst's Backyard Comedy Club

231 Cambridge Heath Road, Bethnal Green, E2 0EL (7739 3122/www.leehurst.com). Bethnal Green tube/rail. **Shows** 8pm Thur, Fri; 8.30pm Sat. **Admission** £10-£17; £2-£5 reductions. **Credit** MC, V.

Lee Hurst's purpose-built club offers four experienced comics each night, with the likeable Hurst usually compèring (he occasionally does solo shows too). Go on Thursday for £9.99 Night Out, where a show, food and three drinks cost… yep, £9.99.

Lowdown at the Albany

240 Great Portland Street, Marylebone, W1W 5QU (7387 5706/www.lowdownatthealbany.com). Great Portland Street tube. **Shows** 8pm. **Admission** £7-£10. **No credit cards**. **Map** p398 H4.

This rough-around-the-edges basement venue is a simple set-up that hosts stand-up, sketch shows and the odd play. Excellent for Edinburgh previews.

Red Rose

129 Seven Sisters Road, Finsbury Park, N7 7QG (7281 3051/07963 618333 mobile/www.redrose comedy.co.uk). Finsbury Park tube/rail. **Shows** 9pm Sat. **Admission** £10; £6 reductions. **Credit** (bookings only) MC, V.

A long-standing north London club established by outspoken comic Ivor Dembina, who dedicated it to cheap nights with big names but no frills. Food is available, though, and there is a late bar.

Up the Creek

302 Creek Road, Greenwich, SE10 9SW (8858 4581/ www.up-the-creek.com). Greenwich DLR/rail. **Shows** 9pm Fri; 8.30pm Sat. **Admission** £10, £6 reductions Fri; £15, £12 reductions Sat. **Credit** MC, V.

Malcolm Hardee ('To say that he has no shame is to drastically exaggerate the amount of shame that he has,' noted one journalist) established this bearpit in 1990. His legacy lives on: punters here are the rowdiest – some say, the most discerning – on the circuit.

Comedy Store.

Dance

London makes myriad moves.

The Royal Ballet at the **Royal Opera House**.

London dance is thriving, diverse and proudly multicultural. Though the capital is home to renowned traditional dance companies such as the **Royal Ballet** (www.roh.org.uk), the city is just as well known for producing performers who pride themselves on mixing it up: **Akram Khan** (www.akramkhancompany.net) has built a career out of incorporating modern moves with kathak traditions, and regularly collaborates with a wild array of artists, from musician Nitin Sawhney to actress Juliette Binoche; **DV8** (www.dv8.co.uk) continues to produce contemporary dance that dares to explore religion and sexuality; and Matthew Bourne's **New Adventures** (www.new-adventures.net) proudly popularises modern dance with narrative-based works. **Russell Maliphant** (www.rmcompany.co.uk), **Sylvie Guillem** (www.sylvieguillem.com), **George**

Piper Dances and **Michael Clark Company** (www.michaelclarkcompany.com) are all based in the capital, as are the all-female **Cholmondeleys** (pronounced 'Chumlees') and all-male **Featherstonehaughs** ('Fanshaws'). The most exciting new company is Christopher Wheeldon's **Morphoses/The Wheeldon Company**, which first performed in 2007 and promises to 'restore ballet as a force of innovation'. Interestingly, it has bases at both Sadler's Wells (www.sadlerswells.com) and New York's City Center (http://morphoses.org/).

Lovers of ballet can see the **Royal Ballet** at the Royal Opera House or, for those who like their lakes filled with lots of swans, catch one of the massive events hosted by the **English National Ballet** (www.ballet.org.uk) in the Royal Albert Hall (*see p306*). Visitors should also try and see a show by **Can*do*Co**, a company of disabled and non-disabled artists founded 16 years ago and still going strong (www.candoco.co.uk). The entrancing **Bawren Tavaziva** (www.tavazivadance.com) from Zimbabwe blends traditional African styles with contemporary dance.

Should you wish to strut your own stuff, London offers regular classes in just about everything, from capoiera to flamenco. *Time Out* magazine's regular dance listings publish a select list of current courses each week, alongside the best of what's on stage.

Major venues

Barbican Centre
For listings, *see p304* Barbican Centre.
The year-long Barbican International Theatre Event (BITE) is a boon for lovers of dance. The Barbican also nurtures resident artists including Michael Clark and commissions works in collaboration with continental and American companies. Visitors can also take the opportunity to note the love-it-or-hate-it architecture (*see also p94*), which has been dividing London opinion since it appeared in the City in the early 1970s.

Place
17 Duke's Road, Bloomsbury, WC1H 9PY (7121 1000/www.theplace.org.uk). Euston tube/ rail. **Box office** noon-6pm Mon-Sat; noon-8pm on performance days. **Tickets** £5-£15. **Credit** MC, V. **Map** p401 K3.
If you're looking for genuinely emerging or embryonic dance talent, the Place has plenty to offer, as both a site for professional training and a home for visiting acts. The 300-seat theatre makes for a more intimate experience than Sadler's Wells but doesn't have numbered seating, which can lead to a scrum when the doors are thrown open ten minutes before the show starts. It hosts an annual season of short, live dance works by emerging choreographers (in 2008 entitled 'Resolution!').

Royal Opera House
For listings, *see p307* Royal Opera House.
Being the home of the Royal Ballet, which features guest artists of the calibre of the marvellous Carlos Acosta, this is a must-see for visiting dance fans. The ROH's main lobby, the Vilar Floral Hall, is one of London's most handsome public spaces – it serves as the venue for afternoon tea dances. Also on the premises are the Linbury Studio Theatre and the Clore Studio Upstairs, which is used for edgier, more experimental fare.

Sadler's Wells
Rosebery Avenue, Islington, EC1R 4TN (box office 0870 737 7737/www.sadlerswells.com). Angel tube. **Box office** In person 9am-8.30pm Mon-Sat. *By phone* 24hrs daily. **Tickets** £10-£45. **Credit** AmEx, MC, V. **Map** p404 N3.

Rehearsal at the **Place**.

Sadler's Wells remains the epicentre of dance in London, with superb regular visitors including Momix and Alvin Ailey American Dance Theatre. The dazzling complex also provides a home for Matthew Bourne's New Adventures (his all-male Swan Lake premièred here back in 1995) and Wayne McGregor's Random Dance (www.randomdance. org). Among the venue's many associate artists are Jonzi D (www.jonzi-d.co.uk), Christopher Wheeldon, Jasmin Vardimon (www.jasminvardimon.com), Sylvie Guillem, Russell Maliphant, Akram Khan and George Piper Dances. Sadler's Wells also hosts a terrific roster of international visitors, ranging from Taiwan's Cloud Gate Dance Theatre to Spain's Paco Peña and New York's Savion Glover (the world's pre-eminent tap dancer). For added ease of egress, a specially chartered bus departs after each performance to Farringdon, Victoria and Waterloo stations. The adjacent Lilian Baylis Theatre (0844 412 4300) offers new work and theatre on a smaller scale, while the Peacock Theatre (Portugal Street, WC2A 2HT, 0844 412 4322) is a satellite venue for Sadler's Wells in Holborn.

Siobhan Davies Dance Studios
85 St George's Road, Southwark, SE1 6ER (box office 7091 9650/www.siobhandavies.com). Elephant & Castle tube/rail. **Box office** In person 9am-7pm Mon-Sat. **Tickets** £10-£45. **Credit** MC, V. **Map** p404 O10.

Arts & Entertainment

The Siobhan Davies Dance Company's beautiful new home was opened in 2006. It promptly won an architecture award, partly because it was designed in consultation with dancers to ensure the environment fulfilled their artistic needs. It now houses regular exhibitions in addition to dance performances. A veteran of the London Contemporary Dance School, Davies founded her own company in 1988. Check the website for details of shows, since the choreographer's interest in exploring different spaces means certain shows are staged elsewhere.

Southbank Centre

For listings, *see p307* Southbank Centre.
The refurbishment of the Royal Festival Hall has helped to fuel an ongoing revival in the Southbank Centre's dance programme, with companies such as CandoCo performing here and the Dance Umbrella festival being held in the complex's several spaces: the huge Festival Hall, the medium-sized Queen Elizabeth Hall and the more intimate Purcell Room.

Other venues

Blue Elephant Theatre

59A Bethwin Road, Camberwell, SE5 0XT (7701 0100/www.blueelephanttheatre.co.uk). Oval tube. **Tickets** £7-£10. **No credit cards.**
Not strictly a dance space, Blue Elephant Theatre nonetheless offers great value contemporary dance from emerging performers in an intimate setting.

Greenwich Dance Agency

Borough Hall, Royal Hill, Greenwich, SE10 8RE (8293 9741/www.greenwichdance.org.uk). Greenwich DLR/rail. **Box office** 9.30am-5.30pm Mon-Fri. **Classes** £6. **Tickets** £7-£15. **Credit** MC, V.
Greenwich Dance Agency provides a home to resident artist Temujin Gill of the Temujin Dance Company. It's a fun art deco space that runs a great programme of dance as well as hosting many classes and workshops. Of particular note are the unique gDA cabaret nights: samples of dance are performed among punters as they receive full table service.

Laban Centre

Creekside, Deptford, SE8 3DZ (information 8691 8600/tickets from Greenwich Theatre 8469 9500/ www.laban.org). Deptford DLR/Greenwich DLR/rail. **Open** 8.30am-8pm Mon-Sat. **Tickets** £1-£15. **Credit** MC, V.
The home of Transitions Dance Company, this beautiful independent conservatoire for dance training is renowned as the home of Rudolf Laban, founder and creator of a unique and enduring discipline for movement. Its stunning award-winning premises cost £22m. They were designed by Herzog & de Meuron (the architects who were responsible for the transformation of Bankside Power Station into Tate Modern) and completed back in 2003. You'll find an intimate 300-seat auditorium, as well as facilities for undergraduate and postgraduate research.

Dance festivals

London hosts a number of exciting dance festivals, giving you the chance not only to see the best in international performance, but to learn moves and participate (sometimes on the streets). **Dance Umbrella** (www.dance umbrella.co.uk) is the headline event, a key world dance festival that was founded back in 1978. Companies from Europe and as far afield as Australia perform at venues right across town.

Big Dance (www.london.gov.uk/bigdance) was launched in 2006 and returns for 2008 – a public celebration of flamenco, ballet, hip hop, folk, bhangra and disco. The first event witnessed a world record when 752 dancers in Trafalgar Square performed 44 different dance styles at the same time (everything from salsa to synchronised swimming). Big Dance features public lessons and ad hoc performances, such as tap dancing on the tube. Keep an eye out around July 2008.

Breakin' Convention (www.breakin convention.com) is an international hip hop dance festival that began in 2004 and is growing in popularity. In 2007, some 16,000 people enjoyed events spread over eight venues across the country, with global stars joining up with a range of local artists. Based primarily at Sadler's Wells and overseen by artistic director Jonzi D, the event is an exciting springboard for unknown London performers and has further established hip hop in the dance canon.

This year also sees the first of the **Spring Dance** festivals (www.sadlerswells.com), which are going to bring major dance companies from Stuttgart and New York (among other places) to the London Coliseum. It shouldn't be confused with **Spring Loaded** (www.theplace.org.uk), a showcase for emerging dance artists that thrived in the 1980s and '90s, but was retired in the noughties only to be revived in 2007. According to associate director of the Place Eddie Nixon, Spring Loaded represents 'where dance is going next'. Let's hope it remains a permanent fixture on London's dance calendar.

Film

Classic? Mainstream? Arthouse? Whatever your movie pleasure, we have it here.

London is a treat for film-goers. Keep a close eye on the listings and you'll be spoilt for choice every night of the week. The chain cinemas screen all the current mainstream releases: check the websites for **Cineworld Cinemas** (www.cineworld.co.uk), **Empire Cinemas** (www.empirecinemas.co.uk), **Odeon Cinemas** (www.odeon.co.uk), **Vue Cinemas** (www.my vue.com), consult *Time Out* magazine's weekly listings or visit www.timeout.com/film for full details of what's on. It's worth noting that the programmes change on a Friday in the UK.

For the best cinema experience, though, you often do well to avoid the obvious places. In the following chapter, we list the cinemas we think are the most fun. So there are a handful of impressive, film-première scale venues, several smaller first-run cinemas and the best of the rep houses. **Curzon Soho** impresses on all levels with first-rate refreshments and an excellent line-up of indie, foreign and arthouse fare. Archaeologists of cinema will head straight to the **BFI Southbank** (formerly the sensibly named National Film Theatre), with its reliably fascinating programme of cinematic and TV treasures; here the remarkable new Mediatheque (*see p289* **The film of history**) allows visitors to dig through the archives themselves. It's always worth checking what's on at the **Prince Charles**, with tickets costing as little as £3.50, and singalong sessions of *The Sound of Music* (*photo p287*) and *Rocky Horror*.

Films released in the UK are classified under the following categories: **U** – suitable for all ages; **PG** – open to all, parental guidance is advised; **12A** – under-12s only admitted with an over-18; **15** – no one under 15 is admitted; **18** – no one under 18 is admitted.

First-run cinemas

Most places charge less before 5pm Tuesday to Friday; some are cheap all day Monday.

Central London

Apollo West End

19 Lower Regent Street, Westminster, SW1Y 4LR (0871 2206 000/www.apollocinemas.co.uk). Piccadilly Circus tube. **Screens** 5. **Tickets** £12.50; £8.50 reductions. **Map** p398 J7. **Credit** MC, V.
A refurbished cinema with a stylish bar and modern interior, but pricey tickets.

The Compton organ at the **Odeon Leicester Square**. *See p287.*

Barbican

Silk Street, the City, EC2Y 8DS (7382 7000/www. barbican.org.uk). Barbican tube/Moorgate tube/rail. **Screens** 3. **Tickets** £8.50; £4.50-£6 reductions; £5.50 Mon. **Credit** AmEx, MC, V. **Map** p402 P5.
The three screens in the Barbican (*see p94*) show new releases of world and independent cinema.

Curzon

Chelsea *206 King's Road, Chelsea, SW3 5XP (7351 3742/www.curzoncinemas.com). Sloane Square tube then 11, 19, 22, 319 bus.* **Screens** 1. **Tickets** £9-£10.50; £6 reductions. **Map** p397 E12.
Mayfair *38 Curzon Street, Mayfair, W1J 7TY (7495 0500/www.curzoncinemas.com). Green Park or Hyde Park Corner tube.* **Screens** 2. **Tickets** £7; £3 reductions. **Map** p400 H8.
Renoir *Brunswick Square, Bloomsbury, WC1N 1AW (7837 8402). Russell Square tube.* **Screens** 2. **Tickets** £9-£10.50; £5-£6 reductions. **Map** p399 L4.
Soho *99 Shaftesbury Avenue, Soho, W1D 5DY (information 7292 1686/bookings 0870 756 4620/ www.curzoncinemas.com). Leicester Square tube.* **Screens** 3. **Tickets** £7; £5 reductions. **Map** p407 X3.
All *www.curzoncinemas.com.* **Credit** MC, V.
All the cinemas in the growing Curzon group are cosy locals with superb programming. You can expect a range of shorts, rarities, double bills and

The city is the star

With more films currently being shot in the capital per year than anywhere else bar Los Angeles and New York, there'll be no shortage of London locations gracing the silver screen. Which will, of course, mean thousands of lazy establishing shots of Big Ben, the London Eye and St Paul's Cathedral. It also means there's an established film-tourist trail you might wish to steer clear of: the owners of the Westbourne Park Road flat shared by Hugh Grant and Rhys Ifans in Roger Michell's *Notting Hill* (1999) entirely changed the look of their front in a failed bid to foil snap-happy tourists. And cash-in-fuelled confusion even saw a pub that was only ever called the Mother Black Cap in Bruce Robinson's superb *Withnail & I* (1986) briefly contrive to rename itself as, yes, the Mother Black Cap. If, one hungover morning, you feel the need for a large gin with iced cider chaser, you must now pay homage at an unrecognisable gastropub called Crescent House (41 Tavistock Crescent, W11 1AD).

Unsurprisingly, there are plenty of other film-related boozers at which to sup, although it's a stretch of the imagination to picture Tom Cruise ordering ale in a dimpled pint pot. *Mission: Impossible* (Brian De Palma, 1996) does, however, feature exactly such a scene. The oft-duped super-spy can be seen sharing a cheeky half with Ving Rhames in the Anchor (34 Park Street, SE1 9EF). Further unreality can be had in Clerkenwell's bar-restaurant Vic Naylor (40 St John Street), owned by Sting in Guy Ritchie's mockney classic *Lock, Stock & Two Smoking Barrels* (1998).

The river itself is never far away, and if you fancy a high-speed trip down it, why not book an RIB speedboat tour (*see p75*) in emulation of the powerboat set-piece in Michael Apted's James Bond blockbuster *The World is Not Enough* (1999)? Or perhaps public transport seems more sensible? Take the tube: Embankment station is the scene of Gwyneth Paltrow's lucky/unlucky tube train moment in *Sliding Doors* (Peter Howitt, 1998), while a considerably less lucky businessman is savaged by the beast at the foot of the escalators at Tottenham Court Road in horror classic *American Werewolf in London* (John Landis, 1981). If you're looking for the real Underground star, though, head to the Strand and disused Aldwych station (*pictured*), whose credits include films as various as *Death Line* (1972) and *Atonement* (2007).

Above ground things may not be much safer, particularly not if virally infected zombies have killed everyone, as in Danny Boyle's *28 Days Later* (2002), a film whose bravura opening sequence offers the spectacle of central London as a ghost town, complete with overturned Routemaster. In few of these films, though, is the city itself the star. Which is why our favourite London film is a kind of 'psychogeography' of the city, long before the term became fashionable: Patrick Keiller's *London* (1994) is a melancholy journey around the Big Smoke herself, in all her ancient shabby glory. Pass the popcorn.

mini-festivals, sat alongside new fare from around the world. The Renoir is a comfy little underground arthouse, surrounded by eating options in the newly refurbished Brunswick centre; the Curzon Soho has a great ground-floor café for cakes and pastries and, on a basement level, one of Shaftesbury Avenue's best bars – all in all, we reckon it's the best cinema in central London.

ICA Cinema
Nash House, the Mall, Westminster, SW1Y 5AH (information 7930 6393/bookings 7930 3647/www.ica.org.uk). Charing Cross tube/rail. **Screens** 2. **Tickets** £8; £7 reductions. **Credit** MC, V. **Map** p401 K8.
The cinema at the ICA is without doubt London's best place for harder-to-find world, experimental and

low-budget cinema (where else could you see both the silent monks of *Die Grosse Stille* and a wigged-out comics genius in *Mindscape of Alan Moore*?). The ICA's remit as testing ground for developments in the arts means you can expect the unusual.

Odeon Leicester Square
Leicester Square, Soho, WC2H 7LQ (0871 224 4007/www.odeon.co.uk). Leicester Square tube. **Screens** 1. **Tickets** £12.50-£17; £9-£14 reductions. **Credit** AmEx, MC, V. **Map** p407 X4.
London's archetypal red-carpet star-studded site for premières (despite pressure from the new giant screen at the O2 Vue, *see p288*), this cinema is an art deco masterpiece. If you can, catch one of the occasional silent movie screenings with live accompaniment on the 1937 organ (yes, it does come up through the floor; *photo p285*); if not, you'll get a comfy but expensive sight of most of the current blockbusters.
Other locations throughout the city.

Outer London

Electric Cinema
191 Portobello Road, Notting Hill, W11 2ED (7908 9696/www.the-electric.co.uk). Ladbroke Grove or Notting Hill Gate tube. **Screens** 1. **Tickets** £10-£12.50; £5-£7.50 Mon. **Credit** AmEx, MC, V.
One of London's oldest cinemas, the Electric is now also one of the city's most lavish. With leather armchairs and two-seater sofas, a bar inside the auditorium and superior snacks on offer, the Electric really does go to town on creature comforts – but expect to pay a high price for them. Just next door is the excellent Electric Brasserie.

Everyman Cinema
5 Hollybush Vale, Hampstead, NW3 6TX (0870 066 4777/www.everymancinema.com). Hampstead tube. **Screens** 2. **Tickets** £12-£15; £6-£10 reductions. **Credit** AmEx, MC, V.
Another cosy local, but recently enhanced with two-seater 'club suites'. These come complete with foot stools, wine cooler and plush upholstery, and ticket prices to match.

Notting Hill Coronet
103 Notting Hill Gate, W11 3LB (7727 6705/ www.coronet.org). Notting Hill Gate tube. **Screens** 2. **Tickets** £7; £4.50 reductions. **Credit** MC, V. **Map** p394 A7.
One of London's most charming local cinemas, the Coronet gives first runs a real sense of occasion.

Phoenix
52 High Road, East Finchley, N2 9PJ (8444 6789/ www.phoenixcinema.co.uk). East Finchley tube. **Screens** 1. **Tickets** £5-£7.50; £4.50-£6 reductions. **Credit** MC, V.
Another cinema with claims to be the capital's (and indeed the country's) oldest, this attractive one-screener has good programming with Sunday reps and parent and baby shows.

Picturehouse
Clapham *76 Venn Street, Clapham, SW4 0AT (0870 755 0061). Clapham Common tube.* **Screens** 4. **Tickets** £8.50; £7 reductions; £6.50 Mon.
Gate Cinema *87 Notting Hill Gate, Notting Hill, W11 3JZ (0870 755 0063). Notting Hill Gate tube.* **Screens** 1. **Tickets** £8-£11; £6-£9 reductions. **Map** p394 A7.
Greenwich *180 Greenwich High Road, Greenwich, SE10 8NN (0871 704 2059).* **Tickets** £7-£10; £5-£8 reductions; £5-£6 Mon.
Ritzy *Brixton Oval, Coldharbour Lane, Brixton, SW2 1JG (0871 704 2065). Brixton tube/rail.* **Screens** 5. **Tickets** £6.50-£8.50; £5.25-£7.25 reductions.
All *www.picturehouses.co.uk.* **Credit** AmEx, MC, V.
The Ritzy is London's biggest independent cinema, with 370,000 admissions a year. Like the other Picturehouses, it programmes a good mix of mainstream and indie, with lots of rep screenings and mini-festivals. They also run a range of kids' clubs and parent and baby screenings.

Rio Cinema
107 Kingsland High Street, Dalston, E8 2PB (7254 6677/www.riocinema.org.uk). Dalston Kingsland rail. **Screens** 1. **Tickets** £8; £6 reductions. **Credit** AmEx, MC, V.
East London's best independent cinema reflects the diversity of the Dalston area, with annual Turkish and Kurdish mini-festivals, on top of choice new releases year-round and a variety of arthouse screenings and special events.

Sound of Music singalong at the **Prince Charles**. *See p288.*

Screen on the Green
83 Upper Street, Islington, N1 0NP (7226 3520/
www.screencinemas.co.uk). Angel tube. **Screens** 1.
Tickets £8; £6-£6.50 reductions; £6 Mon. **Credit**
MC, V. **Map** p402 O2.
A jewel of a cinema with London's best old-style
neon billboard on its façade and super-comfy seats
in the auditorium. Programming is an appealing
blend of indie and mainstream.
Other locations Screen on Baker Street, 96-98
Baker Street, W1U 6TJ (7935 2772); Screen on the
Hill, 203 Haverstock Hill, NW3 4QG (7435 3366).

Tricycle Cinema
269 Kilburn High Road, Kilburn, NW6 7JR
(information 7328 1900/bookings 7328 1000/
www.tricycle.co.uk). Kilburn tube. **Screens** 1.
Tickets £8; £7 reductions; £5 Mon. **Credit** MC, V.
Part of an arts complex that includes the politically
conscious Tricycle Theatre (*see p340*), this cinema
supports small independent and world releases.

Vue O2 Multiplex
O2, Peninsula Square, North Greenwich, SE10 0AX
(08712 240 240/www.myvue.com). North Greenwich
tube. **Screens** 11. **Tickets** £6.80-£17.50; £5.50-£6
reductions. **Credit** MC, V.
The massive 11-screen Vue multiplex may not yet
make the Dome stately, but it certainly affords a bit
of grandeur: excluding the IMAX monsters (*see
below*), it has one of the largest screens in the
country, located in a 750-seat auditorium. Whether
it can pull in premières from the favoured West End
remains to be seen.
Other locations throughout the city.

Repertory cinemas
Several first-run cinemas also offer rep-style
fare – check *Time Out* magazine's weekly
listings for locations.

BFI Southbank
South Bank, SE1 8XT (information 7928 3535/
bookings 7928 3232/www.bfi.org.uk/nft).
Embankment tube/Waterloo tube/rail. **Screens** 3.
Tickets £8.60; £6.25 reductions; £4-£5 Tue. **Credit**
AmEx, MC, V. **Map** p401 M8.
A London institution, with an unrivalled programme of retrospective seasons and previews,
with regular director and actor Q&As. The
Thameside seating outside the rather underpow-
ered main café is hugely popular in good weather,
while museum-caterers Benugo run a handsome
new cocktail bar/restaurant on the other side of the
building alongside the terrific Mediatheque
(*see opposite* **The film of history**).

Ciné Lumière
Institut Français, 17 Queensberry Place, South
Kensington, SW7 2DT (7073 1350/www.institut-
francais.org.uk). South Kensington tube. **Screens** 1.
Tickets £7; £5 reductions. **Credit** MC, V.
Map p397 D10.

A plush cinema at the Institut Français that puts on
excellent seasons – and not all with a French focus.

Prince Charles
7 Leicester Place, Leicester Square, WC2H 7BY
(bookings 0870 811 2559/www.princecharles
cinema.com). Leicester Square tube. **Screens** 1.
Tickets £3.50-£4.50. **Credit** MC, V. **Map** p407 X3.
The best value in town for releases that have ended
their first run elsewhere. Singalong screenings too.
Photo p287.

Riverside Studios
Crisp Road, Hammersmith, W6 9RL (8237 1111/
www.riversidestudios.co.uk). Hammersmith tube.
Screens 1. **Tickets** £6.50; £5.50 reductions.
Credit MC, V.
Double-bills, special seasons and festivals.

Bollywood cinemas
Bollywood blockbusters regularly première at
the **Empire Leicester Square** (www.empire
cinemas.co.uk), but the Grade II-listed Himalaya
Palace is where to go for the real audience-
participation experience.

Himalaya Palace
14 South Road, Southall, Middx UB1 1RD (8813
8844/www.himalayapalacecinema.co.uk). Southall
rail. **Screens** 3. **Tickets** £5.95; £4.95 reductions.
Credit MC, V.

Uxbridge Odeon
Chimes Shopping Centre, Uxbridge, Middx UB8 1GD
(0871 224 4007/www.odeon.co.uk). **Screens** 9.
Tickets £6.60-£7.60; £5.20-£6.60 reductions.
Credit MC, V.

IMAX
BFI London IMAX Cinema
1 Charlie Chaplin Walk, South Bank, SE1 8XR
(0870 787 2525/www.bfi.org.uk/imax). Waterloo
tube/rail. **Screens** 1. **Tickets** *3D* £8.50; £5-£6.25
reductions. *2D* £12; £9.75 reductions. **Credit** AmEx,
MC, V. **Map** p401 M8.
The BFI's massive IMAX is the biggest screen in the
country. Made-for-IMAX children's fare and space/
submarine/mountain wow-factor documentaries are
usually what's on offer, but watch out for monster-
sized versions of mainstream films as well (*Alien,
300, Transformers*). The seating is set so that you
feel you're almost inside the screen.

Science Museum IMAX Theatre
Exhibition Road, South Kensington, SW7 2DD
(0870 870 4868/www.sciencemuseum.org.uk). South
Kensington tube. **Screens** 1. **Tickets** £7.50; £6
reductions. **Credit** MC, V. **Map** p397 D9.
Tends to screen documentaries and shorts in support of exhibitions of the parent museum (*see p151*),
rather than features. Experiencing these films is
usually impressive nonetheless.

Festivals

The city's largest international festival of cinema, the **London Film Festival** (*see p270*), takes place in late October and early November. Short films with a punk/DIY bent have their day at the ICA at the **Halloween Short Film Festival** (www.shortfilms.org.uk) in January (yes, January), while the **Rushes Soho Shorts Festival** (*see p268*) shows free short films and music videos by new directors at various Soho venues (23 July-1 Aug 2008). The **Human Rights Watch International**

Film Festival (7713 2773, www.hrw.org/iff), based at the Ritzy, runs from 12 to 21 March. The **London Lesbian & Gay Film Festival** (*see p265*), is at the BFI Southbank in late March. Indie festivals include the **Portobello Film Festival** (*see p268*) from 19 July to 31 August, and the **BFM International Film Festival** (8531 9199, www.bfmmedia.com, 8-14 Oct), a Black Filmmaker-programmed festival at the ICA, Prince Charles and Rio cinemas. Britain's largest indie film festival is **Raindance** (*see p270*) from 24 Sept-5 Oct at various venues across the West End.

The film of history

It began life during the 1953 Festival of Britain as the Telekinema before becoming the National Film Theatre. Now, the British Film Institute's flagship cinema has been transformed into **BFI Southbank** (*see opposite*). The deeply informed, deeply informative programming on which this London institution built its reputation remains in place within cunningly expanded premises: a chic new glass-and-steel main entrance (the 'light box'); an elegantly appointed, Wi-Fi equipped café-restaurant and bar; the return of the sorely missed film bookshop; a multimedia art gallery; and a new-media showpiece, the **BFI Mediatheque**. In a small, comfy room just off the impressive main foyer, 14 state-of-the-art viewing stations allow visitors free access to hundreds of hours of film and television recordings taken from the BFI archives. The footage is carefully

curated into themed categories, and though not everything in the BFI holdings will go up – it would take decades to upload it all – the plan is to have a large, select chunk of the archive accessible. You want to watch *The Elephant Man* from start to finish? You're interested in seeing a minute's worth of 1905 footage showing a Maharajah's procession on elephant-back? You can walk in off the street, for free, sit yourself in front of one of the computers, put on the headphones and – for up to two hours – watch whatever you like. (It can get busy, though, so it might be worth booking in advance, especially on a weekend). In a world where the promise of choice is usually just a fig-leaf worn on aggressive marketing, the Mediatheque is a fine innovation. Our sole criticism? It's open only from 11am until 8pm (with last admission at 7.15pm) and not on Mondays.

Galleries

London's art world enters the space race.

One space just isn't enough for London's top commercial galleries these days. The vogue for expansion that was kicked off in 2006 by **White Cube**, **Gagosian** and **Hauser & Wirth London** continued through autumn 2007 with **Sadie Coles** and **Timothy Taylor** each opening additional galleries in Mayfair. Just to the north of Oxford Street in Mortimer Street, a sister space to Bethnal Green's **Approach** opened, joining **Alison Jacques** and **Alexandre Pollazzon Ltd** and fuelling speculation that Fitzrovia might be the new place to be. In the East End, **Victoria Miro** expanded her empire with Victoria Miro 14, a vast top-floor space in an adjacent building to her Old Street headquarters.

Those mapping the shifting terrain of the art world have found much cause for excitement, but London's contemporary art scene, justifiably the most celebrated in Europe, resists easy categorisation. It's true that the majority of posh showrooms – like **Sprüth Magers London** and **Haunch of Venison** – have a W1 postcode, but the East End,

traditionally home to young and emerging spaces like **Hotel**, has its share of upmarket venues as well, headed by the redoubtable **Maureen Paley** gallery in Bethnal Green. In addition, a continuing, cross-capital trend has been the arrival of large-scale, non-profit venues. Joining philanthropic ventures like **Parasol Unit** and the **Louise T Blouin Institute** is **Project Space 176** in Chalk Farm, a flexible space where curators work with artists and the extensive Zabludowicz Collection of contemporary art to create experimental new work.

Before heading out we suggest you consult the weekly *Time Out* magazine (online listings at www.timeout.com) or the free pamphlet *New Exhibitions of Contemporary Art*, available from most galleries and also online at www. newexhibitions.com. Many galleries are closed in the early part of the week, and private views are often on Thursday evenings. For details of public galleries and exhibition spaces including Tate Britain, Tate Modern and the National Gallery, *see chapters* **Sightseeing**.

Louise T Blouin Institute.

Central

Alexandre Pollazzon Ltd

11 Howland Street, Fitzrovia, W1T 4BU (7436 9824/www.alex-pollazzon.com). Goodge Street tube. **Open** 10am-6pm Tue-Sat. **No credit cards.** **Map** p398 J5.

Formerly curator of the video programme at Sketch, Pollazzon opened this space in 2006 and quickly proved himself one of the smartest young operators, representing a mix of emerging and mid-career artists including Fabian Marti, Vidya Gastaldon and Jason Fox, all of whom will have solo shows in 2008.

Alison Jacques Gallery

16-18 Berners Street, Fitzrovia, W1T 3LN (7631 4720/www.alisonjacquesgallery.com). Goodge Street or Oxford Circus tube. **Open** 10am-6pm Tue-Sat. **No credit cards.** **Map** p398 J5.

Jacques relocated from Mayfair in 2007, inaugurating this swish, two-storey space with a show of paintings by British artist Tim Stoner. The gallery represents emerging and established international names including Liz Craft and Graham Little, as well as working with the estates of Hélio Oiticica, Robert Mapplethorpe and Hannah Wilke. In 2008, expect shows by Catherine Yass and Jon Pylypchuk.

Gagosian

6-24 Britannia Street, King's Cross, WC1X 9JD (7841 9960/www.gagosian.com). King's Cross tube/ rail. **Open** 10am-6pm Tue-Sat. **No credit cards.** **Map** p399 M3.

US super-dealer Larry Gagosian opened this vast gallery in 2004. While the location is a bit off the beaten track, visitors flock to see big names such as Cy Twombly, Jeff Koons and Francesco Clemente, plus a second tier of fashionable US and European artists including Carsten Höller and Cecily Brown. A second gallery, tiny by comparison, opened in 2006.

Other locations 17-19 Davies Street, Mayfair, W1K 3DE (7493 3020).

Haunch of Venison

6 Haunch of Venison Yard, off Brook Street, Mayfair, W1K 5ES (7495 5050/www.haunchof venison.com). Bond Street tube. **Open** 10am-6pm Mon-Wed, Fri; 10am-7pm Thur; 10am-5pm Sat. **Credit** AmEx, MC, V. **Map** p398 H6.

A few eyebrows were raised in 2007 when Haunch of Venison was bought from its founders by auction house Christie's International, but little appears to have changed in terms of the programme. In the eponymous yard, the splendid high-ceilinged converted Georgian townhouse hosts large-scale installations and exhibitions by major names (Turner Prize winners Keith Tyson and Richard Long) and also by emerging artists (Jamie Shovlin).

Hauser & Wirth London

196A Piccadilly, Mayfair, W1J 9DY (7287 2300/ www.hauserwirth.com). Piccadilly Circus tube. **Open** 10am-6pm Tue-Sat. **No credit cards.** **Map** p406 U5.

Founded in 1992 in Zurich, this Swiss-owned gallery opened in 2003 in a former bank, with intact basement vaults. Hauser & Wirth represents heavyweight artists including Louise Bourgeois, Dan Graham and Paul McCarthy, international names like Anri Sala and Pipilotti Rist, and home-grown talents such as Martin Creed.

Other locations Hauser & Wirth Colnaghi, 15 Old Bond Street, Mayfair, W1S 4AX (7399 9770).

Lisson

29 & 52-54 Bell Street, Marylebone, NW1 5DA (7724 2739/www.lisson.co.uk). Edgware Road tube. **Open** 10am-6pm Mon-Fri; 11am-5pm Sat. **No credit cards.** **Map** p395 E5.

One of London's longer established contemporary galleries, on its current site since 1991, the Lisson is a superb platform for major international names including the 'Lisson Sculptors': Anish Kapoor, Tony Cragg, Richard Wentworth and Richard Deacon. A second space nearby allows major exhibitions to be spread across both sites. Work by Tony Oursler, Lawrence Weiner, Shirazeh Houshiary and Julian Opie is due for display in 2008.

Other locations 29 Bell Street, Marylebone, NW1 5BY (7535 7350).

Louise T Blouin Institute

3 Olaf Street, Shepherd's Bush, W11 4BE (7985 9600/www.ltbfoundation.org). Latimer Road tube. **Open** 10am-8.30pm Tue; 10an-6pm Wed-Sun. **Admission** £9; £3 reductions. **Credit** MC, V.

Arts & Entertainment

CEO and president of the LTB Group of Companies, which publishes magazines *Art+Auction* and *Modern Painters*, Louise T Blouin MacBain opened this 35,000sq ft non-profit space in 2006. Housed over three storeys of a 1920s coachworks, the Institute has galleries, a conference centre, a cinema and a café. It hosts regular talks and events. *Photo p290.*

Project Space 176

176 Prince of Wales Road, Chalk Farm, NW5 3PT (7491 5720/www.projectspace176.com). Chalk Farm tube/Kentish Town West rail. **Open** 11am-3pm Thur, Fri; 11am-6pm Sat, Sun. **Admission** £5. **No credit cards.**
Launched in September 2007, this former Methodist chapel, a remarkable neoclassical building, holds three shows a year, enabling artists to create experimental new work and curators to build exhibitions around the Zabludowicz Collection of global emerging art in all media. The first show of 2008 is of work by British artist Gerald Fox, followed by the results of a curatorial residency.

Sadie Coles HQ

35 Heddon Street, Mayfair, W1B 4BP (7434 2227/ www.sadiecoles.com). Oxford Circus or Piccadilly Circus tube. **Open** 10am-6pm Tue-Sat. **No credit cards. Map** p406 U3.
Housed in a first-floor space just off Regent Street, Sadie Coles HQ represents some of the hippest artists from both sides of the Atlantic. The gallery opened a second space in 2007 in which to show the likes of John Currin, Sarah Lucas and Jim Lambie. **Other locations** 69 South Audley Street, Mayfair, W1K 2QZ (7434 2227).

Sprüth Magers London

7A Grafton Street, Mayfair, W1S 4EJ (7408 1613/ www.spruethmagers.com). Green Park tube. **Open** 10am-6pm Tue-Sat. **No credit cards. Map** p400 H7.
Karen Kilimnik, Cindy Sherman and Andreas Gursky are just three of the major-league international artists to have shown in this handsome gallery housed in an 18th-century building just off Old Bond Street.

Festivals Art and architecture

The London art scene offers plenty of visual stimulation at any time of the year, but if the focus of your trip to the capital is primarily contemporary art, it's worth considering the cultural calendar. Spring and autumn provide the richest pickings. Over Christmas and New Year and, more markedly, in late July and August, some galleries shut up shop or present uninspiring shows of gallery stock. Summer, however, is the perfect hunting season for fresh talent as London's colleges hold end-of-year exhibitions for graduating students, usually beginning in June with the **Royal College of Art** (www.rca.ac.uk) and ending in the second week of September with the **Chelsea College of Art & Design** (www.chelsea.arts.ac.uk). For the past six years Brick Lane's Truman Brewery has hosted **Free Range** (www.free-range.org.uk), a fast-changing display of work from final-year students, running from June to September.

By mid September, the art world is gearing up for the main event: the **Frieze Art Fair** (www.friezeartfair.com), which takes place 16-19 October 2008 and attracts all the major players from around the world. Frieze has been the catalyst for a string of fringe events, the best of which, **Zoo Art Fair** (www.zooartfair.com), outgrew its London Zoo venue and moved last year to the Royal Academy's Burlington Gardens site. A more relaxed and affordable version of Frieze, Zoo features the best of younger galleries.

You should also check out Year_art project, an annual fair organised by the **Keith Talent** gallery (*see p295*) that aims to provide a more experimental, installation-based antidote to the usual, and fairly soulless, arrangement of gallery booths. Also worth a look is **ScopeLondon** (www.scope-art.com), which showcases lesser-known galleries from around the world, and the **Affordable Art Fair** (www.affordableartfair.co.uk) in Battersea Park, notable for work by recent graduates. A more grass roots alternative is **Pilot** (www.pilotlondon.org), a rather chaotic platform for artists without commercial representation who have been selected by well-respected curators, collectors, critics and fellow artists.

Those who have a particular interest in photography should ensure that their visit coincides with **PhotoLondon** (www.photo-london.com), the annual, international photography fair held at Old Billingsgate Market in May. Architecture and design buffs, meanwhile, will find much to inspire during **Architecture Week** (www.architectureweek. org.uk) in June, the **London Architecture Biennial** (*see p267*) in June and July 2008, the **London Design Festival** (www.london designfestival.com) in September, and also **Open House** (*see p270*), the weekend in September when some of the capital's most famous and notorious buildings open their doors to the public.

Arts & Entertainment

Timothy Taylor Gallery

21 Dering Street, Mayfair, W1S 1TT (7409 3344/ www.timothytaylorgallery.com). Bond Street tube. **Open** 10am-6pm Mon-Fri; 10am-1pm Sat. **No credit cards. Map** p398 H6.

Emma Dexter, formerly chief curator at Tate Modern, joined Timothy Taylor Gallery in 2007 and immediately made her mark with a well-selected and beautifully installed show of works on paper by gallery artists – including Lucian Freud, Martin Maloney and Ewan Gibbs. The gallery also opened a second space with a retrospective of US painter Alex Katz, and now runs two distinct programmes. **Other locations** 15 Carlos Place, Mayfair, W1K 2EX (7409 3344).

White Cube

25-26 Mason's Yard, St James's, SW1 6BU (7930 5373/www.whitecube.com). Green Park tube. **Open** 10am-6pm Tue-Sat. **Credit** AmEx, MC, V. **Map** p406 V5.

Jay Jopling's gallery reasserted its West End presence in 2006 with the opening of this purpose-built 5,000sq ft space. White Cube Hoxton Square still runs a fine programme of exhibitions by the gallery's ever-expanding stable of international names but this larger space seems designated for A-list Young British Artists such as Damien Hirst, Tracey Emin and Gary Hume. **Other locations** 48 Hoxton Square, Shoreditch, N1 6PB (7930 5373).

East

Hoxton Square, Cambridge Heath Road and Vyner Street are all good places to start an exploration of east London's innumerable galleries, but it's worth planning the timing of your visit quite carefully. Bear in mind that many smaller galleries are closed at the start of the week and that when opening new shows they usually open their doors in the early evening later in the week.

Approach

Approach Tavern, 1st floor, 47 Approach Road, Bethnal Green, E2 9LY (8983 3878/www.the approach.co.uk). Bethnal Green tube. **Open** noon-6pm Wed-Sun; or by appointment. **No credit cards.**

Occupying a converted function room above a pub, the Approach, directed by Jake Miller, has a deserved reputation for showing both emerging artists and more established names. The location also makes it a great venue for combining an exhibition with Sunday lunch and a pint. As we go to press, a second space, Approach W1, is due to open in Fitzrovia (74 Mortimer Street, W1W 7RZ).

Carl Freedman Gallery

44A Charlotte Road, Shoreditch, EC2A 3PD (7684 8888/www.carlfreedmangallery.com). Old Street tube/rail. **Open** noon-6pm Thur-Sat. **Credit** MC, V. **Map** p405 R4.

Responsible for such seminal shows as 1990's 'Modern Medicine', Carl Freedman is an old hand at promoting Young British Art. From this smart Shoreditch gallery, he continues to focus his attention on mainly home-grown talent and represents a small stable of increasingly respected artists such as Michael Fullerton and Fergal Stapleton.

Chisenhale Gallery

64 Chisenhale Road, Bow, E3 5QZ (8981 4518/ www.chisenhale.org.uk). Bethnal Green or Mile End tube/8, 277, D6 bus. **Open** 1-6pm Wed-Sun. **No credit cards.**

With a reputation for recognising new talent, Chisenhale commissions up to five shows a year by emerging artists. Rachel Whiteread's *Ghost,* –concrete cast of a house, and Cornelia Parker's exploded shed *Cold Dark Matter* were both Chisenhale commissions. The 2008 programme will include shows by the painter Dan Perfect and also by the installation artists Anthea Hamilton and David Noonan.

Flowers East

82 Kingsland Road, Hoxton, E2 8DP (7920 7777/ www.flowerseast.com). Old Street tube/rail. **Open** 10am-6pm Tue-Sat. **Credit** AmEx, MC, V. **Map** p405 E3.

Flowers East might not garner the press attention of some of its neighbours, but it is an admired East End institution. It represents more than 40 artists, including Patrick Hughes, Derek Hirst and Nicola Hicks, some of them since the gallery's inception in Soho in 1970. The main gallery also houses Flowers Graphics, and there's a smaller West End space. **Other locations** Flowers Central, 21 Cork Street, Mayfair, W1S 3LZ (7439 7766).

Hales Gallery

Tea Building, 7 Bethnal Green Road, Shoreditch, E1 6LA (7033 1938/www.halesgallery.com). Liverpool Street or Old Street tube/rail. **Open** 11am-6pm Wed-Sat. **Credit** AmEx, DC, MC, V. **Map** p405 R4.

While the Tea Building never quite became the art world epicentre some suggested it might when it first opened, Hales operates successfully from a large ground-floor space, showing emerging and mid-career artists such as Turner Prize nominee Tomoko Takahashi. On the schedule for 2008 are shows by Jane Wilbraham, Hew Locke and Bob & Roberta Smith.

Hotel

53A Old Bethnal Green Road, Bethnal Green, E2 6QA (7729 3122/www.generalhotel.org). Bethnal Green tube/Cambridge Heath rail. **Open** noon-6pm Wed-Sun. **No credit cards.**

Thus named because the out-of-town artists who first showed in this home-cum-project-space treated the place like a hotel, this Bethnal Green gallery has grown in scale and gained an international reputation for representing painters such as Alan Michael and Michael Bauer, and the mixed media artist Duncan Campbell.

Keith Talent

*2-4 Tudor Road, Hackney, E9 7SN (8986 2181/
www.keithtalent.com). London Fields rail.* **Open**
noon-6pm Wed-Sat. **No credit cards.**
Named after a character in Martin Amis's novel
London Fields – itself named after the park located
just across Mare Street from here – Keith Talent is
one of the East End's most consistently inventive
galleries, running a diverse programme that has
recently included abstract sculpture by Young
British Artist Adam Gillam and the vintage homo-
erotica of Tom of Finland. Since 2004, the gallery
has published the magazine of contemporary culture
Miser & Now, and in 2006 founded the art fair
Year_art projects, which takes place each October.

Maureen Paley

*21 Herald Street, Bethnal Green, E2 6JT (7729
4112/www.maureenpaley.com). Bethnal Green tube/
rail.* **Open** 11am-6pm Wed-Sun; or by appointment.
No credit cards.
Paley opened her East End gallery long before the
area became the hip art mecca it is today. The

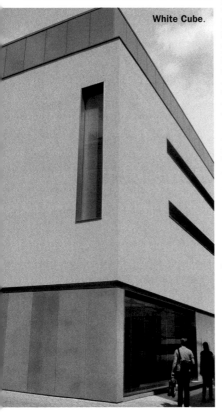

White Cube.

gallery represents high-profile artists such as
Turner Prize winners Wolfgang Tillmans and
Gillian Wearing, plus Paul Noble (best known for
drawings of the strange, fictitious town Nobson) and
sculptor Rebecca Warren. Highlights of 2008 include
new photographs by Tillmans, an installation by
Banks Violette and film work by Daria Martin.

Matt's Gallery

*42-44 Copperfield Road, Mile End, E3 4RR
(8983 1771/www.mattsgallery.org). Mile End tube.*
Open 10am-6pm Wed-Sun; or by appointment. **No
credit cards.**
Few galleries in town are as well respected as Matt's,
named after the dog of founder/director Robin
Klassnik. Since 1979, Klassnik has supported artists
in their often ambitious ideas for projects. Richard
Wilson's sump oil installation *20:50* and Mike
Nelson's *Coral Reef* were both Matt's commissions.
Willie Doherty, Paul Rooney and Roy Voss will
show during 2008.

Parasol Unit

*14 Wharf Road, Islington, N1 7RW (7490 7373/
www.parasol-unit.org). Angel tube/Old Street tube/
rail.* **Open** 10am-6pm Tue-Sat; noon-5pm Sun.
No credit cards. Map p402 P3.
This former warehouse (adjacent to Victoria Miro)
has been beautifully converted by architect Claudio
Silverstrin to create exhibition spaces on two floors
and a reading area. Opened by Ziba de Weck
Ardalan in 2004, the Unit shows work by emerging
and major-league figures; in 2008, expect Darren
Almond, Mona Hatoum and Charles Avery.

Victoria Miro

*16 Wharf Road, Islington, N1 7RW (7336 8109/
www.victoria-miro.com). Angel tube/Old Street tube/
rail.* **Open** 10am-6pm Tue-Sat; Mon by appointment.
Credit MC, V. **Map** p402 P3.
A visit to this ex-Victorian furniture factory rarely
disappoints – not just because it's a beautifully converted art space, but also due to the high calibre of
its artists, who include Chris Ofili, Peter Doig, Tal R
and Grayson Perry. In 2007, the gallery opened
Victoria Miro 14, a sleek, 9,000sq ft space adjacent
to the gallery that is used for exhibitions and special
projects. In 2008, look out for work by Chantal Joffe,
Inka Essenhigh, Elmgreen & Dragset and Jesper
Just. Parasol Unit is right next door.

Vilma Gold

*6 Minerva Street, Bethnal Green, E2 9EH (7729
9888/www.vilmagold.com). Bethnal Green tube/
Cambridge Heath rail.* **Open** 11am-6pm Wed-Sun.
No credit cards.
Steered by Rachel Williams and Steven Pippet,
Vilma Gold has rapidly gained a reputation as a
gallery to watch. The cognoscenti flock here for such
fashionable fare as the neo-expressionist paintings
of Sophie von Hellermann and the anti-heroic assem-
blages of Brian Griffiths. In 2008, Alexandre da
Cunha, Dubossarsky and Vinogradov, Jennifer West
and Charles Atlas will be on show.

Wilkinson Gallery

*50-58 Vyner Street, Bethnal Green, E2 9DQ
(8980 2662/www.wilkinsongallery.com). Bethnal
Green tube/Cambridge Heath rail.* **Open** 11am-
6pm Wed-Sat; noon-6pm Sun; or by appointment.
No credit cards.
Anthony and Amanda Wilkinson's gallery has
raised its profile over the past few years by showcasing trendy German painters including Tilo
Baumgartel, Matthias Weischer and Thoralf
Knobloch. In September 2007, they opened these
larger premises, the first purpose-built gallery in E2.

South

Albion

*8 Hester Road, Battersea, SW11 4AX (7801 2480/
www.albion-gallery.com). Sloane Square tube then
19 bus.* **Open** 9am-5.30pm Mon-Fri; Sat during
exhibitions. **No credit cards.**
Located since 2004 on the ground floor of this Foster
& Partners-designed riverside apartment block, the
Albion hosts a broad range of exhibitions, including
design by David Adjaye and the Campana Brothers,
photography by Wang Qingsong, and film and
installation by Mariko Mori. Xu Bing and Vito
Acconci will show in the first half of 2008.

Danielle Arnaud

*123 Kennington Road, Lambeth, SE11 6SF (7735
8292/www.daniellearnaud.com). Lambeth North tube.*
Open 2-6pm Fri-Sun. **Credit** AmEx, MC, V.
Established in 1995, Danielle Arnaud works with
artists like Janane Al-Ani, David Cotterell and Helen
Maurer. Exhibitions are installed in Grade II-listed
Georgian premises, or curated at off-site venues,
such as the Museum of Garden History (*see p77*).

Jerwood Space

*171 Union Street, Bankside, SE1 0LN (7654 0171/
www.jerwoodspace.co.uk). Borough or Southwark
tube.* **Open** 10am-5pm daily during exhibitions;
phone to check. **No credit cards. Map** p404 O8.
Part of a larger set-up of theatre and dance spaces –
and a great café – the Jerwood had an erratic visual
arts presence until recently. Now, under the banner
Jerwood Visual Arts, are grouped various prizes and
awards, including the Jerwood Applied Arts Prize
and the Jerwood Contemporary Painters.

South London Gallery

*65 Peckham Road, Peckham, SE5 8UH (7703 9799/
www.southlondongallery.org). Oval tube then 436
bus/Elephant & Castle tube/rail then 12, 171 bus.*
Open noon-6pm Tue-Sun. **No credit cards.**
On this site for over a century, the South London
Gallery became one of the main showcases for the
emerging Young British Artists in the 1990s, giving
solo shows to Tracey Emin, Marc Quinn and Gavin
Turk. Still one of the capital's foremost contemporary
art venues, the gallery completes its expansion into
an adjacent property in 2008, creating new exhibition
areas and a café.

Architecture & design

Architectural Association

*36 Bedford Square, Fitzrovia, WC1B 3ES
(7887 4000/www.aaschool.ac.uk). Tottenham
Court Road tube.* **Open** 10am-7pm Mon-Fri;
10am-3pm Sat. **Credit** MC, V. **Map** p399 K5.
Talks, events, exhibitions: three good reasons for
visiting these elegant premises. The café makes that
four. During the summer months, the gallery shows
work by students graduating from the AA School.

Crafts Council Gallery

*44A Pentonville Road, Islington, N1 9BY (7278
7700/www.craftscouncil.org.uk). Angel tube.* **Open**
11am-6pm Tue-Sat; 2-6pm Sun. **No credit cards.**
Map p402 N2.
Alongside its shop and resource centre, due to reopen
in 2008, the Crafts Council Gallery runs a programme
of innovative exhibitions showcasing contemporary
crafts, drawn from both its own collection and further
afield. It also organises 'Collect', the international craft
fair held at the V&A (*see p151*) in January, and
'Origin', the contemporary craft fair held at Somerset
House (*see p116*) in October.

Royal Institute of British Architects

*66 Portland Place, Marylebone, W1B 1AD (7580
5533/www.architecture.com). Great Portland Street
tube.* **Open** 10am-6pm Mon-Fri; 10am-5pm Sat.
Credit MC, V. **Map** p398 H5.
Temporary exhibitions are held in RIBA's Grade II-
listed headquarters, which houses a bookshop, café
and library, and hosts an excellent lecture series. In
2008/9, RIBA is bringing a major retrospective of
Le Corbusier to the Barbican Art Gallery (*see p94*).

Photography

Michael Hoppen Gallery

*3 Jubilee Place, Chelsea, SW3 3TD (7352 4499/
www.michaelhoppengallery.com). Sloane Square
tube.* **Open** noon-6pm Tue-Fri; 10.30am-4pm Sat;
or by appointment. **Credit** MC, V. **Map** p397 E11.
This three-storey space shows a mixture of vintage
and contemporary work, including Japanese photographer Nobuyoshi Araki. A 2007 highlight was Dr
Edgerton's famous motion-capture experiments.

Photographers' Gallery

*5 & 8 Great Newport Street, Covent Garden, WC2H
7HY (7831 1772/www.photonet.org.uk). Leicester
Square tube.* **Open** 11am-6pm Mon-Wed, Fri, Sat;
11am-8pm Thur; noon-6pm Sun. **Credit** AmEx,
DC, MC, V. **Map** p407 X3.
Home of the £30,000 Deutsche Börse Photography
Prize (8 Feb-6 Apr 2008), the Photographers' Gallery
also hosts a diverse range of exhibitions, as well as
running an excellent events programme. It occupies
two almost adjacent spaces at the moment, but
plans are under way to relocate to new premises
in nearby Ramillies Street, probably in 2010.

Gay & Lesbian

Dressed up, down or not at all: London's the place to be out.

London has the best gay scene in the world. A big call perhaps, but the evidence can be found across town every night of the week: London in 2008 has a wider and sexier variety of bars, clubs and venues than New York and Sydney combined. And, maybe thanks to London's rich theatrical tradition, dressing up (or down) for the occasion is of paramount importance. On any given night you might comfortably expect to don your business suit, superhero costume, drag outfit, leather gear, rubber suit, sports tackle, chav fatigues (young and poor), underwear, a towel only or, going full circle, nothing but your birthday suit.

There are now two main gay villages: an older-established scene in Soho and a newer, burgeoning scene in Vauxhall. That said, gay pubs and mini-scenes thrive in Islington, Earl's Court, the East End, Greenwich, King's Cross, Hampstead and Clapham. There's somewhere for every taste. For traditional noughties gayness (muscly handsome men and all-night clubbing) hit **Crash**, **Area** and **Fire** in Vauxhall. Legendary clubs **Heaven** and **G.A.Y.** still pack 'em in, even though they've not been flavour of the month for some years now.

If cocktails and drag are your thing, Trannyshack at the **Soho Revue Bar** (*see p318*) offers a cross-dressing bonanza, and the **Shadow Lounge** is still the swankiest place to meet someone with sharp collars, a chocolate martini and an attitude.

If your physique is more bloke than buff, then have a pint at **Comptons of Soho**, and another at **Bar Code** and one more at the **Yard**. If you're more bear than bloke, then don't miss a night at **XXL** in London Bridge – shangri-la for big hairy gents and those who admire them.

For indie and international music venues that are mixed, friendly and pumping head to **Ghetto**, **Trash Palace** and **Popstarz**, for ragga music visit **Club Caribana**, for bhangra and Bollywood visit **Club Kali** and for r'n'b go Bad at **Ghetto** every Sunday. The **Retro Bar** (2 George Court, off the Strand, Covent Garden, WC2N 6HH, 7321 2811) even holds a monthly evening of music from the annual Eurovision song contest.

Candy Bar is the biggest lesbian bar in town and, in keeping with London's reputation for licentiousnes, is replete with erotic dancers. More traditional women-only bars such as the **Glass Bar** are still around, but have struggled to stay open, with younger lesbians favouring mixed dance clubs.

The **Chariots** chain remains the sexiest bet for saunas, with outlets in Farringdon, Waterloo, Shoreditch, Vauxhall, Streatham and Limehouse. Of course you could also stay at home and cruise online at www.gaydar.com (the best hit for London), or check out the new gaydar-endorsed cyber bar **Profile**.

The annual **London Lesbian & Gay Film Festival** (*see p265*) highlights the best and edgiest lesbian and gay film and video, while the **Drill Hall** and the **Soho Theatre** (for both, *see p340*) regularly host top-drawer queer performance. Each June **Pride** (www.pridelondon.org; *see p267*) hosts a fortnight of cultural events.

The week out

In town with no time to do your research? Follow our simple daily guide to the best events each day of the week.

Monday
Cheap drinking debauchery at **G.A.Y. Bar**. *See p300.*

Tuesday
Comedy Camp at **Bar Code Soho**. *See p301.*

Wednesday
The amateur strip show at **BJ's White Swan**. *See p301.*

Thursday
Dresscode-night Boots Only at **Manbar**. *See p302.*

Friday
Indie stalwart **Popstarz** at the Scala. *See p300.*

Saturday
Ultra at Vauxhall's **Area**. *See p299.*

Sunday
Royal Vauxhall Tavern's drag show Dame Edna Experience. *See p300.*

Vauxhall vaudeville

Visitors to the capital might once have happily made do with the gay bars of Soho – but no more. The expanding gay village of Vauxhall is now officially a must. So much so that if you have only one night, you should spend it at the **Royal Vauxhall Tavern** (*see p300*). A quick walk under the railway bridge from Vauxhall tube (ten minutes from Oxford Circus down the Victoria line) and you're there. Both architecturally and culturally it is an anomaly: once a corner pub, its neighbours have long since fallen victim to history – now it stands solitary and proud like an enormous Trivial Pursuit pie piece.

There are events every night of the week – some of which have been running for years and attract devotees that make the Wicker Man's worshippers look half-hearted. Monday offers gay bingo with the insane Timberlina, while Tuesday nights provide the only gay jazz night in town, hosted by the fab Gill Manly, dragged kicking and shoo-wopping out of retirement. Comedy night Brou Ha Ha takes over on Wednesdays – the only regular rival to Barcode Soho's excellent Comedy Camp – while Vauxhallville on Thursdays stages 21st-century vaudeville. Fridays offer a shifting menu but do try to catch Kabarett with the incomparable Dusty Limits, an edgy chanteur with a good taste for the tasteless. Saturdays host Duckie, the notorious queer performance night. Hosted by Amy Lamé, an American lesbian who seems to have walked out of a Far Side cartoon, the night features three or four acts running for five minutes apiece. Quirky, edgy and rude are de rigueur: anything else – like singing Sondheim – can get viciously booed.

Then, every Sunday, there's the Dame Edna Experience. Held at 5pm and morphing into a club night, this rarely publicised drag show has moved beyond cult and can now surely be classified as an 'organised religion'. At the height of summer, queues begin outside the RVT as early as 2pm eager to avoid the almost inevitable sell-out.

So what's it all about? Jonathan Hellier is dressed as Oz icon Dame Edna and does a wicked Australian accent, but it's not long before you realise this initial impersonation is just the beginning. Hellier also does a mean stand-up routine – and his material always draws on the week's events. Then he sings, with a repertoire of vocal impressions that seems limitless: Karen Carpenter, Janis Joplin, Alanis Morissette, Michael Jackson and Diana Ross are just a sample – he even once sang the duet 'You Don't Bring Me Flowers' as both Neil Diamond and Barbara Streisand. Through it all the crowd chants and sings verses via prompts from the Dame – cues learnt from months spent attending the show. If you're seeking a very London gay experience, this is where to start.

London's finest gay bookshop remains **Gay's the Word** (66 Marchmont Street, Bloomsbury, 7278 7654), although it is still under threat of closure – do your bit while it lasts and drop in to pick up a souvenir Wilde *Collected*. For gay shopping of the hotpants and lube variety, visit **Clone Zone** (64 Old Compton Street, 7287 3530) and **Prowler** (3-7 Brewer Street, 7734 4031).

The listings here are just a sampler of the huge variety on offer. Time Out's *Gay & Lesbian London* guidebook (£9.99) gives a more thorough overview, while for weekly listings of clubs, meetings and groups, check the Gay & Lesbian section of *Time Out* magazine or the free press *Boyz* and *QX*. In shops, gay lifestyle is covered by *Attitude*, *Gay Times*, *Refresh* and dyke bible *Diva*.

Cafés & restaurants

Balans

60 Old Compton Street, Soho, W1D 4UG (7439 2183/www.balans.co.uk). Leicester Square or Piccadilly Circus tube. **Open** 8am-5am Mon-Thur; 8am-6am Fri, Sat; 8am-2am Sun. **Cover charge** £2.50 after midnight daily. **Credit** AmEx, MC, V. **Map** p406 W3.

Always busy and with a posse of gay waiters from around the globe, Balans' charm also lies in its location (smack in the middle of Soho, opposite Compton's bar) and reputation as the place to be seen. An added bonus: with the smoking ban the front windows are now open for non-smoking clientele – to give them prime viewing position after years of relegation to the rear. Oh, and the food's good too. The nearby Balans Café (no.34) serves up a shorter version of the menu. Both are open almost all night: good for a post-clubbing feast.

Other locations 239 Old Brompton Road, Earl's Court, SW5 9HP (7244 8838); 187 Kensington High Street, Kensington, W8 6SH (7376 0115); 214 Chiswick High Road, Chiswick, W4 1BD (8742 1435).

First Out

52 St Giles High Street, Covent Garden, WC2H 8LH (7240 8042/www.firstoutcafebar.com). Tottenham Court Road tube. **Open** 10am-11pm Mon-Sat; 11am-10.30pm Sun. **Credit** MC, V. **Map** p407 X1/2.

A touch of history here, as this lesbian and gay café was indeed London's first homosexual café (way back in 1986). Expect a decent vegetarian menu, a fun downstairs bar and a friendly atmosphere.

Steph's

39 Dean Street, Soho, W1D 4PU (7734 5976/www. stephs-restaurant.com). Tottenham Court Road tube. **Open** noon-3pm, 5.30-11.30pm Mon-Fri; 5.30-11.30pm Sat. **Credit** AmEx, DC, MC, V. **Map** p406 W3.

The decor may remain terribly 1980s (pink neon flamingos anyone?) but the vibe's warm and chatty – just the place for visitors expecting a bit of English cheer. There are board games to play and proper London food on the menu (try a Yorkshire pudding, but don't order ice-cream – it's savoury).

Clubs

Themed nights at London's many clubs change frequently – although stalwarts such as **G.A.Y.** and **Heaven** pull crowds in through the week.

Area

67-68 Albert Embankment, Vauxhall, SE1 7TP (7091 0080/www.areaclub.info). Vauxhall tube/rail. **Open** 9pm-4am Fri; 11pm-8am Sat. **Admission** free before 10pm, then £5 Fri; £13-£15 Sat. **No credit cards**.

One of the many clubs tucked under the railway arches at Vauxhall, this is just over a year old and proving hugely popular. Check out the mezzanine-level bar overlooking the dancefloor – perfect for a bit of pre-cruising reconnaisance.

Club Caribana

Factory, 65 Goding Street, Vauxhall, SE11 5AW (07939 393971 mobile/www.caribanaclub.com). Vauxhall tube/rail. **Open** 10.30pm-4am Sun. **Admission** £5 before midnight, then £6. **Credit** MC, V.

Held every Sunday, this mixed gay Caribbean night is hosted by DJs Biggy C, Kris/Celeste, and Alexxx, playing R&B, bashment ragga and soul.

Club Kali

The Dome, 1 Dartmouth Park Hill, Dartmouth Park, N19 5QQ (7272 8153/www.clubkali.com). Tufnell Park tube. **Open** 10pm-3am 3rd Fri of mth. **Admission** £8; £5 reductions. **No credit cards**.

Claiming to be the world's largest LGBT Asian music dance club spinning Bollywood, bhangra, Arabic, R&B and dance classics.

Crash

66 Albert Embankment, Vauxhall, SE1 7TP (7793 9262/www.crashlondon.co.uk). Vauxhall tube/rail. **Open** 10.30pm-5am Fri; 10.30pm-6am Sat; 10pm-5am Sun. **Admission** Fri, Sun £5, free-£4 reductions. Sat £15, £12 reductions. **Credit** (bar) MC, V.

Older, dirtier and more compact than its glitzy next-door neighbour Area, Crash remains the heartland of hard beats and nights with an edgy theme (such as Badladz, Fitladz and so on). Pick of the crop is still the eponymous Crash night.

Exilio Latino

LSE, 3 Houghton Street, off Aldwych, Covent Garden, WC2E 2AE (07931 374391 mobile/ www.exilio.co.uk). Holborn tube. **Open** 10pm-3am Sat. **Admission** £7 before 11pm; £8 after 11pm. **No credit cards**. **Map** p399 M6.

A gay club where you can actually salsa – a beacon of Latin music in a scene of gay pop with DJs Chaci and Tet playing merengue, salsa, cumbia and Latin for a lesbian and gay crowd.

Fiction

The Island, Hungerford Lane, Embankment, WC2N 5NG (0871 971 5861/www.myspace.com/ clubfiction). Embankment tube. **Open** 11pm-late Fri. **Admission** £12; £10 with flyer. **No credit cards**. **Map** p407 Y5.

The move from the Cross was big news for this very popular Friday night club, but it seems to have kept the beat at the new venue. The crowd is A-Gay, who love to dance.

Fire

South Lambeth Road, SW8 1UQ (7820 0550/www. fireclub.co.uk). Vauxhall tube/rail. **Open** 11pm-11am Fri; 11pm-11am Sat; 11am-8pm Sun. **Admission** £8-£12 Fri; £8-£15 Sat; £5 Sun. **No credit cards**.

The primary port of call for serious clubbers of any gender, with three rooms of DJs catering for most tastes (but big on tech house). Orange is followed by A:M very late on Friday; Later starts at noon (yes, that's noon) on Sunday.

Arts & Entertainment

G.A.Y.

Astoria, 157 Charing Cross Road, Soho, WC2H 0EN (7434 9592/www.g-a-y.co.uk). Tottenham Court Road tube. **Open** 11pm-4am Mon, Thur, Fri; 10.30pm-4.30am Sat. **Admission** £3-£10. **No credit cards. Map** p407 X2.

Divas with an album to flog (even as big as Madonna) will inevitably turn up at the Astoria on a Saturday night. It's the city's biggest gay venue.

Ghetto

5-6 Falconberg Court (behind the Astoria), Soho, W1D 3AB (7287 3726/www.ghetto-london.co.uk). Tottenham Court Road tube. **Open** 10.30pm-3am Mon-Wed; 10.30pm-4am Thur, Fri; 10.30pm-5am Sat; 9.30pm-2am Sun. **Admission** free-£8. **No credit cards. Map** p406 W1/2.

It's indie and gritty, certainly, and definitely the place for cool lesbians, skinny gays and bisexual, first-year ex-goths who share an aversion to 'commercial' gayness. Thursday's Miss-Shapes attracts a more lesbian crowd; Friday is the Cock for electro; Saturday is Wig Out for pop; Sunday is a new R&B night called Bad.

Heaven

The Arches, Villiers Street, Embankment, WC2N 6NG (7930 2020/www.heaven-london.com). Embankment tube/Charing Cross tube/rail. **Open** 10.30pm-late Mon, Wed, Fri, Sat. **Admission** £6-£18. **Credit** (bar) AmEx, DC, MC, V. **Map** p407 Y5.

London's most famous gay club is a bit like *Les Misérables* – it's camp, it's full of history and tourists seem to love it. Popcorn (Mon) and Fruit Machine (Wed) are good bets.

Popstarz

Scala, 275 Pentonville Road, King's Cross, N1 9NL (7833 2022/www.popstarz.org). King's Cross tube/rail. **Open** 10pm-4am Fri. **Admission** £8; £5 reductions, free before 11pm with flyer. **Credit** (bar) MC, V. **Map** p399 L3.

The original indie gay party. Three floors of different music in a stunning venue in the heart of King's Cross. Expect a mixed crowd with an eclectic taste in music – for anything but doof-doof dance music.

Royal Vauxhall Tavern (RVT)

372 Kennington Lane, Vauxhall, SE11 5HY (7737 4043/www.duckie.co.uk). Vauxhall tube/rail. **Open** 9pm-2am Sat. **Admission** £5. **No credit cards.**

Restored to its rightful place at the forefront of London's gay culture, the RVT operates a booking policy of pretty much anything goes and dress code that's principally 'no attitude' (*see p298* **Vauxhall vaudeville**).

South Central

349 Kennington Lane, Vauxhall, SE11 5QY (7793 0903/www.southcentrallondon.co.uk). Vauxhall tube/rail. **Open** 6pm-2am Sun. **Admission** £5. **No credit cards.**

The growth of the Vauxhall village has raised the popularity of this multi-purpose Kennington drinking hole, which on various nights attracts a leather and bear crowd and, once upon a time, a nude disco. The stalwart is Sunday night's Horse Meat Disco, where bears and fashionistas come together for a deliciously random music mix, from dance, disco and soul to new wave and punk.

XXL

51-53 Southwark Street, London Bridge, SE1 1TE (7403 4001/www.xxl-london.com). London Bridge tube/rail. **Open** 10pm-3am Wed; 10pm-6am Sat. **Admission** £8-£12. **No credit cards. Map** p404 P8.

The premier club for bears and their admirers, XXL is nirvana for the chubbier, hairier and blokier of London's gay men. True to its name the venue is bigger than average, with two dancefloors, two bars and an outdoor beer garden. Also home to musclebears and plenty of twinky admirers.

Candy Bar.

Pubs & bars

Unless otherwise indicated, all the pubs and bars listed here are open to both gay men and lesbians. Despite the fussy doorstaff, **Soho Revue Bar** (*see p318*) – with dance poles intact from its former incarnation as a strip club – is priceless entertainment and very Soho.

Admiral Duncan

54 Old Compton Street, Soho, W1U 5UD (7437 5300). Leicester Square tube. **Open** noon-11pm Mon-Sat; noon-10.30pm Sun.
Most famous as the site of a terrible homophobic bombing in 1999, the pub bounced back and is now home to an older crowd keen to enjoy a down to earth atmosphere.

Bar Code

3-4 Archer Street, Soho, W1D 7AP (7734 3342/ www.bar-code.co.uk). Leicester Square or Piccadilly Circus tube. **Open** 4pm-1am Mon-Sat; 4-10.30pm Sun. **Admission** £4 after 11pm Fri, Sat. **Credit** MC, V. **Map** p406 W3.
A lively and well-established men's bar just off Shaftesbury Avenue, Bar Code is home to a mostly gay comedy club (Comedy Camp, presented by Simon Happily on Tuesdays; *see p280*), the bearish Tonker Lite on Thursdays and a dancefloor for late-night Friday and Saturday sweaty moves.

Bar Code Vauxhall

Arch 69, Goding Street, Vauxhall, SE11 5AW (7582 4180/www.bar-code.co.uk). Vauxhall tube/rail. **Open** 4pm-1am Mon-Thur; 4pm-3am Fri, Sat; 4-10.30pm Sun. **Admission** £4 after 11pm Fri, Sat. **Credit** MC, V. **Map** p406 W3.
Brother club to Bar Code, this massive, lavish venue still draws a blokey-ish crowd despite its shiny surfaces. And BCV also attracts local boozers and pre-dancing punters.

BJ's White Swan

556 Commercial Road, Limehouse, E14 7JD (7780 9870/www.bjswhiteswan.com). Limehouse DLR. **Open** 9pm-2am Tue-Thur; 9pm-4am Fri, Sat; 5.30pm-midnight Sun. **Admission** £5 after 10pm Fri, Sat. **Credit** MC, V.
If you want to see what locals have to offer, don't miss Wednesday's amateur strip night. A big showcase for drag legends as well, with professional strippers and conventional clubbing on the weekends.

Black Cap

171 Camden High Street, Camden, NW1 7JY (7428 2721/www.theblackcap.com). Camden Town tube. **Open** noon-2am Mon-Thur; noon-3am Fri, Sat; noon-1am Sun. **Admission** £2-£5. **Credit** MC, V.
Drag central in the heart of north London – well worth a visit for a taste of England's talented, foul-mouthed, cross-dressing divas.

Candy Bar

4 Carlisle Street, Soho, W1D 3BJ (7494 4041/ www.thecandybar.co.uk). Tottenham Court Road tube. **Open** 5-11.30pm Mon-Thur; 3pm-2am Fri, Sat; 5-11pm Sun. **Admission** £5 after 9pm Fri; £6 after 9pm Sat; £3 after 10pm Thur. **Credit** (bar) MC, V. **Map** p406 W2.
The biggest and best lesbian bar in town also hosts erotic dancers and karoake nights. It's not women-only but the door policy is selective. It's also a little different from lesbian bars of yore: with more pole dancing than pool playing.

Coleherne

261 Old Brompton Road, Earl's Court, SW5 9JA (7244 5950). Earl's Court tube. **Open** noon-midnight daily. **Admission** free. **Credit** MC, V. **Map** p396 B11.
Once a notorious leather bar, this Earl's Court pub is now a regular gay bar, one of two in an area that were the birthplace of modern gay nightlife in London (the other being Bromptons, down the road).

Compton's of Soho

51-53 Old Compton Street, Soho, W1D 6HJ (7479 7961/www.comptons-of-soho.co.uk). Tottenham Court Road tube. **Open** noon-11pm Mon-Sat; noon-10.30pm Sun. **Credit** AmEx, MC, V. **Map** p406 W3.
Blokes are on tap at this popular venue, an unpretentious oasis in the heart of Soho. The upstairs lounge bar also offers regal portraits and velvet armchairs – so visitors can fulfil fantasies about visiting a 'real London pub' and still pick up.

Edge

11 Soho Square, Soho, W1D 3QE (7439 1313/ www.edge.uk.com). Tottenham Court Road tube. **Open** noon-1am Mon-Sat; noon-11.30pm Sun. **Credit** MC, V. **Map** p406 W2.
Just off the chaos of Oxford Street lies this monument to cocktails and a kind of glamour. Spread over four floors, it's still best patronised in summer, when takeaway Pimms and lemonades can be taken to Soho Square just opposite. Attracts a mixed crowd.

Friendly Society

The Basement, 79 Wardour Street, Soho, W1D 6QB (7434 3805). Piccadilly Circus tube. **Open** 4-11pm Mon-Fri; 2-11pm Sat; 2-10.30pm Sun. **Admission** free. **Credit** MC, V. **Map** p406 W3.
Down a flight of stairs lies a hidden gem – a mixed bar decorated with murals from lesbian pulp fiction novels, and cosy padded alcoves straight out of Austin Powers. Great for winter cocktails and as affable as the name suggests.

G.A.Y. Bar

30 Old Compton Street, Soho, W1D 4UR (7494 2756/www.g-a-y.co.uk). Leicester Square tube. **Open** noon-midnight daily. **Credit** MC, V. **Map** p406 W3.
Astoria has the celebrity cameos, but this popular bar is still a shrine to queer pop idols, with nightly cheap drink specials based on how quickly players pick up on pop anthems. There's also a women's bar in the basement, called (delightfully) Girls Go Down.

Glass Bar

West Lodge, 190 Euston Road, Euston, NW1 2EF (7387 6184/www.theglassbar.org.uk). Euston tube/ rail. **Open** 5-11pm Mon-Fri. **Admission** £1 day membership. **No credit cards. Map** p399 K3.
Reopened in late 2007 after threat of closure, this is London's only women-only bar, located down a spiral staircase in one of Euston Station's original stone-faced gatehouses.

Green Carnation

5 Greek Street, Soho, W1D 4DD (7434 3323/www. greencarnationsoho.co.uk). Tottenham Court Road tube. **Open** 4pm-2.30am Mon-Sat; 3pm-11.30pm Sun. **Admission** £5 after 10.30pm Fri, Sat. **Credit** AmEx, MC, V. **Map** p406 W2.
Formerly Element (itself formerly Sanctuary), the Green Carnation has had a major refit to spectacular effect. Head upstairs for cocktails in posh surroundings, with chandeliers and piano music to heighten the senses and raise the tone.

Hoist

Railway Arch, 47B&C South Lambeth Road, Vauxhall Cross, Vauxhall, SW8 1RH (7735 9972/ www.thehoist.co.uk). Vauxhall tube/rail. **Open** 8.30pm-midnight 3rd Thur of mth; 10pm-3am Fri; 10pm-4am Sat; 10pm-2am Sun. **Admission** £4 Thur; £5 Fri, Sun; £10 Sat. **No credit cards.**
One of two genuine leather bars in town – the other is in Bow (Backstreet, Wentworth Mews, off Burdett Road, E3 4UA, 8980 8557) – this club sits under the arches and makes the most of the underground and industrial setting. Wear leather, uniform, rubber, skinhead or boots only – trainers will see you shunned at the door. Men only.

King William IV

77 Hampstead High Street, Hampstead, NW3 1RE (7435 5747/www.kw4.co.uk). Hampstead tube/Hampstead Heath rail. **Open** 11am-11pm Mon-Thur; 11am-midnight Fri, Sat; noon-midnight Sun. **Credit** MC, V.
The perfect evening ending (or beginning!) to time spent on the Heath, this fab old local attracts a very Hampstead crowd (read: well-off and ready for fun). Summer cruisers can also enjoy the beer garden at King Willy (as it's known to all) if rambles on the Heath prove too much.

Manbar

82 Great Suffolk Street, Southwark, SE1 OBE (7928 3223/www.manbar.info). Southwark tube. **Open** 8pm-1am Mon-Sat; 2pm-midnight Sun. **Admission** £3-£7 depending on themed nights. **No credit cards. Map** p404 O8.
Manbar is – no surprises here – a men-only venue that offers you a particularly naughty night out. The themed nights include such offerings as Boots Only, a godsend for those who really can't decide what to wear midweek. The location in the backstreets of Southwark adds to the grimy appeal.

Profile

56 Frith Street, Soho, W1D 3JG (7734 8300/www. profilesoho.com). Tottenham Court Road tube. **Open** 4pm-1am Mon-Fri; noon-1am Sat; noon-12.30am Sun. **Admission** free. **Credit** AmEx, DC, MC, V. **Map** p406 W2.
A bar for fans of www.gaydar.com, this fab, brand-spanking new nightspot is spread over three floors and offers free internet access and an 'interactive text screen service'. Prepare yourself for some heavy laptop dancing.

Shadow Lounge

5 Brewer Street, Soho, W1F ORF (7287 7988/ www.theshadowlounge.com). Piccadilly Circus tube. **Open** 10pm-3am Mon, Wed; 9pm-3am Tue, Thur-Sat. **Admission** £5 after 11pm Mon-Thur; £10 Fri, Sat. **Credit** MC, V. **Map** p406 W3.
For professional cocktail waiters, celebrity sightings, suits, cutes and fancy boots this is your venue. Expect to have to pay a hefty cover charge and to queue on the weekend, but there's always a sublime atmosphere once inside.

Shadow Lounge.

Trash Palace

11 Wardour Street, Soho, W1D 6PG (7734 0522/
www.trashpalace.co.uk). Piccadilly Circus tube. **Open**
5.30pm-1am Mon-Thur; 5pm-3am Fri, Sat; 5.30-11pm
Sun. **Admission** £3 after 11pm Fri, Sat. **Credit** MC,
V. **Map** p406 W4.
Simon 'Popstarz' Hobart pioneered the indie gay
scene up to his death a couple of years back. This
was his final venture and it's well worth a visit – for
the zany DJs, cheap drinks and insane decor.

Two Brewers

114 Clapham High Street, Clapham, SW4 7UJ (7498
4971/www.the2brewers.com). Clapham Common tube.
Open 5pm-2am Mon-Thur, Sun; noon-4am Fri, Sat.
Admission free-£5. **Credit** AmEx, MC, V.
Clapham's high street is yet another gay village, and
visitors should make this their first stop. It's busy
on the weekends with locals happy to keep the fun
south of the river (and even south of Vauxhall).

Yard

57 Rupert Street, Soho, W1V 7BJ (7437 2652/www.
yardbar.co.uk). Piccadilly Circus tube. **Open** *Summer*
noon-11pm Mon-Sat; noon-10.30pm Sun. *Winter* 2-
11pm Mon-Sat; 2-10.30pm Sun. **Credit** AmEx, MC,
V. **Map** p406 W3.
Come for the courtyard in summer and stay for the
Loft Bar in winter. This unpretentious bar offers a
great open-air courtyard in a great location, which
attracts pretty boys, blokes and lesbians in just
about equal measure.

Saunas

Chariots

1 Fairchild Street, Shoreditch, EC2A 3NS (7247
5333/www.gaysauna.co.uk). Liverpool Street tube/
rail. **Open** noon-9am daily. **Admission** £15; £13
reductions. **Credit** AmEx, MC, V. **Map** p403 R4.
Chariots is a sauna chain with outlets all over town.
The original Shoreditch branch is the busiest, but
not necessarily the best. That accolade probably
goes to the newest one, in Vauxhall on the same
avenue as Area and Crash (for both, *see p299*). It
lacks the sleazy ambience of its brothers, but it is
certainly slick. The Waterloo branch has the UK's
biggest sauna (with enough steam for 50 guys) and
a baggage check for Eurostar customers. All aboard!
Other locations 57 Cowcross Street, Farringdon,
EC1M 6BX (7251 5553); 292 Streatham High Road,
Streatham, SW16 6HG (8696 0929); 574 Commercial
Road, Limehouse, E14 7JD (7791 2808); 101 Lower
Marsh, Waterloo, SE1 7AB (7247 5333); 63-64 Albert
Embankment, SE1 7TP (7735 6709).

Sauna Bar

29 Endell Street, Covent Garden, WC2H 9BA
(7836 2236). Covent Garden tube. **Open** noon-
midnight Mon-Thur; 24hrs from noon Fri-midnight
Sun. **Admission** £14; £10 reductions. **Credit** MC,
V. **Map** p407 Y2.
It's small, it's cosy but most of all it's the only sauna
in the heart of Soho.

Music

From Puccini to punk, it's all here.

Classical & opera

It's been all change in London's classical music world in recent years. The Royal Festival Hall on the South Bank reopened in summer 2007 after £90million worth of renovations. The year before, the Barbican Centre completed its own £30million refurbishment. In addition, a smaller recital room and arts complex is due to open in May 2008: Kings Place (York Way, King's Cross, N1, www.kingsplace.co.uk) is a 420-seat auditorium that will provide a home for both the London Sinfonietta and the Orchestra of the Age of Enlightenment. Add in the relatively recent opening of the Cadogan Hall and LSO St Luke's, the management changes at Wigmore Hall and various power struggles (and financial controversies) at the English National Opera, and it's clear that classical music in London is not letting the grass grow under its feet.

However, in other corners of the capital, the song remains the same. The **Proms** (see p305 **Festivals**) is still one of the highlights of the European cultural calendar. Ignore the riotously jingoistic Last Night and you'll find a spectacular two-month festival of superb variety and brilliance. The performances are broadcast on BBC television and Radio 3 (the latter can be listened to online for a limited period, following the original transmission). In the ever-traditional **Royal Opera House** and the always-excellent Barbican-based **London Symphony Orchestra** (LSO), the capital retains a pair of organisations of world renown.

On the opera front, as well as the big guns at the **Royal Opera House** and the **ENO**, venues such as **Sadler's Wells** (and the associated Peacock Theatre on Portugal Street in Covent Garden), the **Royal Albert Hall** and the **Hackney Empire** (291 Mare Street, Hackney, E8 1EJ, 8985 2424, www.hackney empire.co.uk) all stage some performances.

TICKETS AND INFORMATION

Tickets for most classical and opera events in London are available direct from the venues, online or by phone. Do book ahead, though, especially at small venues such as the Wigmore Hall. Several venues, such as the Barbican and Southbank, operate standby schemes, offering unsold tickets at cut-rate prices an hour before the show. Call or check online for details.

Classical venues

In addition to the venues detailed below, many places offer less frequent classical performances. The 18th-century **Grosvenor Chapel** (South Audley Street, Mayfair, W1K 2PA, 7499 1684, www.grosvenorchapel.org.uk) supplements its organ recital series with sporadic chamber concerts. The **Warehouse** (13 Theed Street, Waterloo, SE1 8ST, 7928 9250), home to the London Festival Orchestra (LFO), stages intimate and adventurous chamber concerts.

The capital's music schools all stage regular performances by pupils and visiting professionals. Check the websites of the **Royal Academy of Music** (7873 7373, www.ram. ac.uk), the **Royal College of Music** (7589 3643, www.rcm.ac.uk), the **Guildhall** (7628 2571, www.gsmd.ac.uk) and **Trinity College of Music** (8305 4444, www.tcm.ac.uk).

Barbican Centre

Silk Street, the City, EC2Y 8DS (7638 4141/box office 7638 8891/www.barbican.org.uk). Barbican or Moorgate tube/rail. **Box office** 9am-8pm daily. **Tickets** £6.50-£45. **Credit** AmEx, MC, V. **Map** p402 P5.

The Barbican recently spent millions on a refurbishment aimed at making its labyrinthine array of public spaces more welcoming. It hasn't really made this rabbit warren of a complex any easier to navigate, although the FreeStage area in front of the main hall has been tarted up a bit. The reworking of the acoustics in the arts centre's main concert hall (capacity 1,950) has proved more successful. At the core of the music roster, performing 90 concerts a year, is the London Symphony Orchestra (LSO), currently looking to consolidate its reputation as one of the world's best orchestras under the direction of principal conductor Valery Gergiev. For the centre's theatre, *see p333*; for its cinema, *see p285*.

Cadogan Hall

5 Sloane Terrace, Chelsea, SW1X 9DQ (7730 4500/ www.cadoganhall.com). Sloane Square tube. **Box office** *In person* 9am-7pm Mon-Fri; 10am-7pm Sat, Sun (performance days only). *By phone* 10am-7pm daily (Sun performance days only). **Tickets** £10-£65. **Credit** MC, V. **Map** p400 G10.

Built a century ago as a Christian Science church, this austere building was transformed into a light and airy auditorium in 2004. It's hard to imagine how the renovations could have been bettered: the 905-capacity hall is comfortable and the acoustics excellent. The

Festivals Classical

The daddy of all the classical festivals is the Proms – or, as they're officially known, the **BBC Sir Henry Wood Promenade Concerts** (www.bbc.co.uk/proms). They take place mainly at the Royal Albert Hall (see p306; pictured). Running annually from mid July until mid September, the event features around 70 concerts that take in a huge amount of the classical repertoire. You can buy reserved seats in advance, but many prefer to queue on the day for £5 tickets for the seatless promenade area in front of the stage (or for the gallery at the top of the auditorium, where the sound is far better).

Cadogan Hall (see left) hosts a few dozen 'overspill' Proms, and is also the focal point of the **Chelsea Festival** (www.chelseafestival. org.uk) every June, which hosts an ever-expanding range of international events. Other regular festivals in the calendar include

the **Hampton Court Palace Festival** (www. hamptoncourtfestival.com) throughout June, one of a series of pleasant 'picnic concerts' in the grounds of beautiful stately homes. Another excellent outdoor event is **Opera Holland Park** (0845 230 9769, www.opera hollandpark.com), where a canopied theatre hosts a season of opera each summer.

The **City of London Festival** (7796 4949, www.colf.org) takes place in and around the City from late June to mid July. The core of its adventurous and expanding programme remains chamber music concerts in churches and in the halls of ancient livery companies.

Nearby is the **Spitalfields Festival** (7377 1362, www.spitalfieldsfestival.org.uk), based around the lovely Christ Church Spitalfields (see p163). For three weeks in June and then a week before Christmas, it fields a strong line-up of early music and baroque works.

somewhat erratic Royal Philharmonic Orchestra is resident, though the hall also hosts smaller-scale ensembles, a smattering of jazz, world and pop acts, and a handful of lunchtime BBC Proms.

English National Opera

The Coliseum, St Martin's Lane, Covent Garden, WC2N 4ES (box office 0871 911 0200/www.eno. org). Leicester Square tube/Charing Cross tube/rail.

Box office *By phone* 10am-8pm Mon-Sat. *In person* from 10am on day of performance. **Tickets** £10-£85. **Credit** AmEx, DC, MC, V. **Map** p407 X4.
The Coliseum's 2,350-seat auditorium, built as a grand music hall in 1904 by the renowned architect Frank Matcham, was restored to its former glory in 2004 as part of a restoration that cost around £80m. Now all the ENO needs is a similarly impressive programme. Edward Gardner, a young conductor who

was artistic director at Glyndebourne, has taken over, promising to get the most out of the gifted orchestra. Unlike at the Royal Opera House (see p307), all works are performed in English.

LSO St Luke's

161 Old Street, the City, EC1V 9NG (information 7490 3939/Barbican box office 7638 8891/www.lso. co.uk/lsostlukes). Old Street tube/rail. **Box office** 9am-8pm daily. **Tickets** £6.50-£45. **Credit** AmEx, MC, V. **Map** p402 P4.

Although it was designed by the famous architect Nicholas Hawksmoor in the early 18th century, the Grade I-listed St Luke's church was left to decay during the 20th century. Its recent renovation and conversion by the London Symphony Orchestra into a rehearsal room, music education centre and a 370-seat concert hall cost around £20m, but it was worth

every penny. The programme takes in lunchtime recitals (some free), evening chamber concerts, and even some jazz and rock shows.

Royal Albert Hall

Kensington Gore, South Kensington, SW7 2AP (information 7589 3203/box office 7589 8212/www. royalalberthall.com). South Kensington tube/9, 10, 52, 452 bus. **Box office** 9am-9pm daily. **Tickets** £4-£150. **Credit** AmEx, MC, V. **Map** p397 D9.

Built as a memorial to Queen Victoria's husband, this rotunda can hold over 5,000 and is best known as the key BBC Proms venue, despite acoustics that do orchestras few favours. Occasional classical concerts are held throughout the year (look out for recitals on the overwhelming Willis pipe organ), alongside pop and rock gigs, sporadic boxing matches and the occasional opera. *Photos p305.*

Going for a song

Attempts to bring opera to the people usually end up an embarrassing farrago: think Glyndebourne's 2005 'punk operatic thriller' *Tangier Tattoo* or Asian Dub Foundation's ill-conceived 2006 disaster at the ENO, *Gaddafi: A Living Myth.* But this hasn't stopped opera companies from finding ever more novel ways of injecting new blood into the medium. The Gorillaz pairing of Damon Albarn and Jamie Hewlett premièred *Monkey: Journey to the West* at the Manchester International Festival,

just one of three big UK operas last year to have been guided by people from outside the opera tradition. Jazz pianist Julian Joseph wrote *Bridgetower: A Fable of 1807* (the story of black violinist George Bridgetower) for the City of London Festival, while the electronic composer Mira Calix co-wrote the unorthodox *Elephant & Castle* for the Aldeburgh Festival. Even more mainstream productions have started to inject some barbarian blood – the ENO's acclaimed take on Philip Glass's *Satyagraha* was directed and designed by the junkyard theatre company Improbable, and the ENO's other critical hit last season, a production of *Madame Butterfly,* was helmed by film director Anthony Minghella.

Now the acclaimed London opera company **Tête à Tête** (www.tete-a-tete.org.uk; *pictured*) has raised the stakes. Founder and director Bill Bankes-Jones describes them as working with 'opera's heightened world of fake reality', which means they take mundane events and elevate them into high art. To which end they've written mini-operas about walking to work and getting knocked over by a cycle courier, or about giving birth. They collaborate with weavers from the Shetland Islands, they've written work themed around speed-dating and line-dancing, they've even held writing 'jam sessions' with interested amateurs. They held their first festival in August 2007 at the Riverside Studios in Hammersmith, and look set to do something similar in 2008. And, amazingly, their work is rather impressive – without even a hint of 'punk opera' to put you off.

Royal Opera House

*Royal Opera House, Covent Garden, WC2E 9DD
(7304 4000/www.roh.org.uk). Covent Garden tube.*
Box office 10am-8pm Mon-Sat. **Tickets** £4-£190.
Credit AmEx, MC, V. **Map** p407 Z3.
While the ENO has spent the last few years being
bashed from pillar to post by critics, staff at the
ROH have been keeping their heads down, grateful
to be out of the spotlight for a change. The ROH
has quietly resumed its position as one of the
world's great opera houses. A massively expensive
renovation in 2000 gave the largely traditional productions the setting they deserve: the discreetly air-
conditioned auditorium and comfortable seating
(capacity 2,250) make a night here an appetising
prospect, whatever the performance. Book ahead to
enjoy one of the behind-the-scenes tours.

St James's Piccadilly

*197 Piccadilly, St James's, W1J 9LL (7381 0441/
www.sjpconcerts.org). Piccadilly Circus tube.* **Open**
8am-6.30pm daily. **Admission** free-£20; tickets
available at the door 30mins before performances.
No credit cards. **Map** p406 V4.
The only Wren church outside the City to hold free
lunchtime recitals (Mon, Wed, Fri at 1.10pm), pro-
grammed alongside less regular, mostly classical
evening concerts. The church also has a café.

St John's, Smith Square

*Smith Square, Westminster, SW1P 3HA (7222
1061/www.sjss.org.uk). Westminster tube.* **Box
office** 10am-5pm Mon-Fri, or up to 30mins after
start of performance; from 1hr before performance
Sat, Sun. **Tickets** £5-£45. **Credit** MC, V.
Map p401 K10.
This elegant 18th-century church hosts more or less
nightly orchestral and chamber concerts, with occasional vibrant recitals on its magnificent Klais
organ. There's a secluded restaurant in the crypt,
open regardless if there's a performance that night.

St Martin-in-the-Fields

*Trafalgar Square, Westminster, WC2N 4JJ
(concert information 7839 8362/www.stmartin-in-
the-fields.org). Charing Cross tube/rail.* **Box office**
10am-5pm Mon-Sat, or until start of performance.
Admission *Lunchtime concerts* free; donations
requested. *Evening concerts* £6-£18. **Credit** MC, V.
Map p407 X4.
As befits the church's location in the heart of tourist
London, the evening concert programme at the
atmospheric St Martin's is packed with crowd-
pleasers: expect lashings of Mozart and Vivaldi by
candlelight. The thrice-weekly lunchtime recitals
(Mon, Tue & Fri) offer less predictable fare.

Southbank Centre

*Belvedere Road, South Bank, SE1 8XX (switchboard
0871 663 2501/bookings 0871 663 2500/www.rfh.
org.uk). Embankment tube/Waterloo tube/rail.*
Box office *In person* 11am-8pm daily. *By phone*
9.30am-8pm daily. **Tickets** £5-£75. **Credit** AmEx,
MC, V. **Map** p401 M8.

The 3,000-capacity Royal Festival Hall reopened in
2007 after a £90m renovation. Access has been made
easier, but the real meat of the project is the acoustic
refurbishment of the main hall itself. The RFH's free
foyer gigs have also been expanded to include concerts in the ballroom. Showcase events include
Meltdown (where guest directors like Morrissey,
Scott Walker and David Bowie curate a two-week
programme), and the Shell Classic International
Season, which culminates in June 2008 with Ivan
Fischer's Budapest Festival Orchestra.
    Next door is the 900-seat Queen Elizabeth Hall, a
rather uninviting space that also houses pop and
jazz gigs, and the much smaller Purcell Room,
which hosts everything from chamber concerts to
poetry readings. The foyer of the QEH also hosts
free concerts before some gigs.

Wigmore Hall

*36 Wigmore Street, Marylebone, W1U 2BP (7935
2141/www.wigmore-hall.org.uk). Bond Street tube.*
Box office *In person* 10am-8.30pm daily. *By phone*
10am-7pm daily. **Tickets** £8-£60. **Credit** AmEx,
DC, MC, V. **Map** p398 G6.
Built in 1901 as the display and recital hall for
Bechstein Pianos, the Wiggy is a delight. Seating
up to 540 concertgoers – and with its perfect
acoustics, art nouveau decor and excellent basement restaurant – it is one of the world's top concert venues for chamber music and song. A £3m
refurbishment in 2004 added a new roof and ventilation system, better sight lines, new seats,
improved public spaces and sympathetic lighting.
Programming concentrates on the classical and
Romantic periods. Monday lunchtime recitals,
broadcast live on BBC Radio 3, are excellent value,
as are the Sunday morning coffee concerts.

Lunchtime concerts

Throughout the year the City of London
hosts low-key lunchtime recitals, given by
young musicians (many of them students)
in the many historic churches. Regular organ
recitals are held at **Grosvenor Chapel** (South
Audley Street, Mayfair, W1K 2PA, 7499 1684),
Temple Church (*see p90*) and **Southwark
Cathedral** (*see p83*).
St Anne & St Agnes *Gresham Street, the City,
EC2V 7BX (7606 4986). St Paul's tube.*
Performances 1.10pm Mon, Fri. **Map** p404 P6.
St Bride's *Fleet Street, the City, EC4Y 8AU
(7427 0133/www.stbrides.com). Blackfriars tube/
rail.* **Performances** 1.15pm Tue, Fri (except Aug,
Advent, Lent). **Map** p404 N6.
St John's *Waterloo Road, Waterloo, SE1 8TY
(7633 9819/www.stjohnswaterloo.co.uk). Waterloo
tube/rail.* **Performances** usually 1.10pm Fri.
Map p404 N8.
St Lawrence Jewry *Guildhall, the City, EC2V
5AA (7600 9478). Mansion House or St Paul's
tube/Bank tube/DLR.* **Performances** 1pm Mon,
Tue. **Map** p404 P6.

St Margaret Lothbury *Lothbury, the City, EC2R 7HH (7606 8330/www.stml.org.uk). Bank tube/DLR.* **Performances** 1.10pm Thur. **Map** p405 Q6.
St Martin within Ludgate *40 Ludgate Hill, the City, EC4M 7DE (7248 6054). St Paul's tube/ Blackfriars tube/rail/City Thameslink rail.* **Performances** 1.15pm Wed. **Map** p404 O6.
St Mary-le-Bow *Cheapside, the City, EC2V 6AU (7248 5139/www.stmarylebow.co.uk). Mansion House tube/Bank tube/DLR.* **Performances** usually 1.05pm Thur. **Map** p404 P6.

Rock, pop & roots

Whatever crisis the music industry is supposed to be facing, London's live scene remains one of the most exciting in the world. Meat and potatoes guitar bands are still the bedrock of a healthy grassroots scene, but any night of the week you'll also find Scandinavian death metallers, Appalachian banjo players, Celtic folk troubadours and Malian griots taking to the stage. The problem is that this buoyant scene can foster complacency, with many of the major venues getting away with wretched sound, surly staff, overpriced drinks and expensive tickets. Often smaller venues such as the **Luminaire**, **Bush Hall**, the **Union Chapel** and the **Scala** show 'em how it's done, with personable service, fair prices and eclectic booking policies.

TICKETS AND INFORMATION

Your first stop should be *Time Out* magazine, which lists literally hundreds of gigs each week. Most venues have websites detailing future shows. Always check ticket availability for shows before setting out: venues, large and small, can sell out weeks in advance. The main exceptions are small pub venues, which only sell tickets on the day. Prices vary wildly: on any given night, you could pay £150 to see Madonna at Earl's Court or catch a superb singer-songwriter for free.

There's often a huge disparity between door times and stage times; the Jazz Café opens at 7pm but the gigs often don't start until after 9pm. Some venues run club nights after the gigs, which generally means the show has to be wrapped up by 10.30pm; at other venues, the main act won't even come on until nearer 11pm.

Many venues offer tickets online via their websites, but beware: most online box offices are operated by ticket agencies, which add booking fees and service charges that can raise the ticket price by as much as 30 per cent. If you're going to a gig at any of the Mean Fiddler venues, cut out these ridiculous fees by paying in cash at the Jazz Café box office. Similarly, tickets for the Shepherd's Bush Empire, the

Carling Academy Brixton and the Carling Academy Islington can be bought at face value with cash from the Islington Academy's box office. If you absolutely must, there are four main ticket agencies; *see p261*.

Major venues

In addition to the venues below, the **Barbican** (*see p304*), **Southbank Centre** (*see p307*) and **Royal Albert Hall** (*see p306*) stage regular pop and rock gigs, with **Alexandra Palace** (*see p160*) occasionally getting in on the act. The **Coronet** club (26-28 New Kent Road, tickets 0870 060 0100, information 0871 971 3807, www.coronettheatre.co.uk) sometimes hosts rock shows, as does the **Troxy** (498 Commercial Road, Limehouse, E1 8HX, 7790 9000, 748 2728, www.troxy.co.uk), a gorgeous 2,600-capacity 1930s art deco former cinema.

Astoria & Astoria 2

157 Charing Cross Road, Soho, WC2H 0EL (information 8963 0940/box office 0871 231 0821/ www.festivalrepublic.com). Tottenham Court Road tube. **Box office** *In person* 10am-6pm Mon-Sat. *By phone* 24hrs daily. **Tickets** £10-£20. **Credit** MC, V. **Map** p406 W2.
That this old 2,000-capacity alt-rock sweatbox may have to close in 2008 to make way for Crossrail has outraged certain sections of the rock world, even though we've long found the Astoria to be a disappointing place to watch bands: we can't really recommend it for sound, decor or staff. Virtually an adjunct, Astoria 2 is a rather more agreeable place: sound and sight lines are better, although staff are just as apathetic. On Saturdays, the venue is home to student-indie night Frog, with a live band each week. If the music is terrible, there's always the glassed-off bar to the left of the balcony.

Bloomsbury Ballroom

Victoria House, Bloomsbury Square, WC1B 4DA (7287 3834/box office 0871 220 0260/www. bloomsburyballroom.co.uk). Russell Square tube. **Box office** *By phone* 24hrs daily. **Tickets** £10-£100. **Credit** MC, V.
A smart, well-appointed art deco concert hall that holds around 800, this has been putting on an excellent and varied bill (King Creosote, Lily Allen, Amy Winehouse) since its conversion in 2006 into a multi-purpose music venue and conference hall run by founder and former owner of the Mean Fiddler, Vince Power. Concerts can include dinner.

Carling Academy Brixton

211 Stockwell Road, Brixton, SW9 9SL (information 7771 3000/box office 0870 771 2000/www.brixton-academy.co.uk). Brixton tube/rail. **Box office** *By phone* 24hrs daily. **Tickets** £10-£40. **Credit** MC, V.
Built in the 1920s as a cinema and looking a little shabby after two decades as a rock venue, Brixton Academy remains London's most credible major

Festivals Rock, pop & roots

So you can't pitch tent and camp at any central London festivals – even on long weekenders, everyone gets the tube home each night – but every square inch of park and concrete seems to host some kind of festival between April and October. There's the **Camden Crawl** (www.thecamdencrawl.com), which takes place over two days in April – you buy a wristband in advance that entitles you to stagger around every music venue in Camden Town to see any of around 100 artists. It's hugely popular with teens and twentysomethings and usually sells out quickly. More grown-up is the **Tower Music Festival**, which takes place in late June and early July in the spectacular grounds of the Tower of London. Recent bookings include

Elvis Costello, Jamie Cullum and Bryan Ferry. And **Somerset House** hosts a series of big outdoor events in its Summer Series between June and August, featuring the likes of Lily Allen, the Roots and Beth Orton.

The **Wireless Festival** has become a regular fixture in mid June, with big acts like White Stripes, New Order and Kaiser Chiefs headlining over two nights in Hyde Park. The same stage is usually used again for another big event the following week. But – admitting a little bias – our favourite outdoor shindy of last year was **Time Out Lovebox Weekender** (*pictured*), a festival in Hackney's Victoria Park, which should be happening in the third week of July 2008. Blondie and Sly Stone headlined, you know.

rock venue. Despite being echo-ey when shows are half full, the 5,000-capacity space is popular because of its sloping surface, which allows pretty good sight lines from quite far back, and makes it a lot easier to move in and out of the moshpit. Pop acts like Mika and Groove Armada play here, but the programming leans more to metal, indie and alt-rock – bands like Hard Fi, the Klaxons and the Twang will use a run at Brixton to announce their arrival in the mainstream.

Carling Academy Islington
N1 Centre, 16 Parkfield Street, Islington, N1 0PS (information 7288 4400/box office 0870 771 2000/ www.islington-academy.co.uk). Angel tube. **Box office** *In person* noon-4pm Mon-Sat. *By phone* 24hrs daily. **Tickets** £3-£20. **Credit** MC, V. **Map** p402 N2. Located in a shopping mall and decorated like a multi-storey car park, this relatively new operation (800 capacity) is never going to be one of London's more atmospheric music venues. Still, the gigs are

East is Eden

Though the 'Shoreditch effect' has faced opposition from die-hard locals (witness the 'fuck off back to Portobello' graffiti), east London has become a kind of paradise for music fans. It started in Shoreditch itself, with clubby venues like the **333** (see p321), **Cargo** (see p321), **Catch Bar** (22 Kingsland Road, E2 8DA, 7729 6097) and **Old Blue Last** (38 Great Eastern Street, EC2A 3ES, 7739 7033). Soon the hype spread south to Brick Lane, with venues like **93 Feet East** (see p313; pictured) and the **Vibe Bar** (Old Truman Brewery, nos.91-95, E1 6QL, 7377 2899). Then venues started opening up in Hackney and Dalston, with the **Fleapit** (49 Columbia Road, Hackney, 7033 9986), **Barden's Boudoir** (see p312), **Chats Palace** (42-44 Brooksby's Walk, Hackney, E9 6DF, 8533 0227) and **Passing Clouds** (440 Kingsland Road, Dalston, E8, 7168 7146) all hosting weird and wonderful left-field acts. **Whitechapel Art Gallery** (see p165) began

regular music nights, not far from the **Rhythm Factory** (16-18 Whitechapel Road, E1 1EW, 7375 3774), which had been holding them for years. Bethnal Green got venues like **Pleasure Unit** (359 Bethnal Green Road, E2 6LG, 7729 0167), and the ultra-trendy **Bethnal Green Working Men's Club** (see p319). The effects have even been felt as far as Leytonstone, where the folk- and country-tinged What's Cookin' have Saturday gigs at the **Sheepwalk** (692 High Road, E11 3AA, 8556 1131) and Wednesday gigs upstairs at **Leytonstone Ex Servicemen's Club** (2 Harvey Road, E11, 8539 2954). With east London home to dozens of grime MCs (including Wiley, Dizzee Rascal, Lethal Bizzle and Roll Deep); countless indie bands (Babyshambles, the Rakes, Selfish Cunt, Ali Love, Infadels, Cazals) and 'nu-rave' bands, it's clear that this is set to remain the most heavenly place in the country to be a musician – or music fan – for some time to come.

decent – mostly fast-rising indie bands and cultured singer-songwriters, with the occasional tribute band – and the solid sound system ensures that the acts get their message across. The adjacent Bar Academy (250 capacity) hosts up-and-comers.

Cecil Sharp House
2 Regent's Park Road, NW1 7AY (7485 2206/www. efdss.org). Camden Town tube. **Open** phone or check website for details. **Tickets** free-£15. **Credit** MC, V.
This temple of English folk music is the home of the English Folk Dance & Song Society, with a huge research library and rehearsal spaces. It hosts barn dances, ceilidhs and folk dance classes in its 500-capacity hall, with Sharp's Folk Club on Tuesdays especially good fun.

Forum
9-17 Highgate Road, Kentish Town, NW5 1JY (information 7284 1001/box office 0871 230 1093/ www.meanfiddler.com). Kentish Town tube/rail. **Box office** *In person* noon-5pm Sat or from the Jazz Café (*see p313*). *By phone* 24hrs daily. **Tickets** £10-£30. **Credit** MC, V.
Dormant for a while, this grand old 2,000-capacity art deco hall (built as a cinema in 1934) is back hosting club nights (such as the Church and School Disco) and lots of alt-rock acts (the likes of Devendra Banhart, Turin Brakes and Deerhoof).

Hammersmith Apollo
Queen Caroline Street, Hammersmith, W6 9QH (information 8748 8660/box office 08448 444248/ www.getlive.co.uk). Hammersmith tube. **Box office** *In person* 4pm-event starts on performance days only. *By phone* 24hrs daily. **Tickets** £10-£40. **Credit** MC, V.
This 1930s cinema had a big refit in 2002 and now doubles as all-seater 3,600-capacity theatre (popular with comedy acts and children's shows) and 5,000-capacity standing-room-only gig space, hosting anyone from Gogol Bordello to the Proclaimers.

KOKO
1A Camden High Street, Camden, NW1 7JE (information 0870 432 5527/box office 0870 145 1115/www.koko.uk.com). Mornington Crescent tube. **Box office** *In person* 10.30am-5.30pm Mon-Fri. *By phone* 24hrs daily. **Tickets** £3-£18. **Credit** MC, V.
Opened in 1900 as a music hall, this venue scrubbed up very nicely during a 2004 refit and has since built up a roster of events to match. The 1,500-capacity auditorium stages a fair few club nights (including Club NME, Funkin You and Guilty Pleasures) alongside an indie-heavy gig programme.

O2 Arena & IndigO2
Formerly the Millennium Dome, Millennium Way, North Greenwich, SE10 0BB (8463 2000/box office 0871 984 0002/www.theo2.co.uk). North Greenwich tube. **Box office** *In person* noon-7pm daily. *By phone* 24hrs daily. **Tickets** £15-£85. **Credit** AmEx, MC, V.
The white elephant that was the Millennium Dome has finally been taken over and lavishly converted into a state-of-the-art 23,000-capacity enormodome,

with good acoustics and sight lines. Since opening in July 2007, it's hosted heavy-hitters including the Rolling Stones, Justin Timberlake and a mammoth two-month residency from Prince (it also hosts a variety of sports). Next door to the Arena but still inside the Dome is the smaller IndigO2 (0844 844 0002, www.theindigo2.co.uk), which holds a still impressive 3,000 to 4,000 people. Public transport links are excellent, especially the Thames Clipper (a 20-minute ride to London Bridge or Waterloo, leaving every 15mins after gigs) – the boats even have a little bar on board.

Roundhouse
Chalk Farm Road, Camden Town, NW1 8EH (information 7424 9991/box office 0870 389 1846/ www.roundhouse.org.uk). Chalk Farm tube. **Box office** *In person* 11am-6pm Mon-Sat. *By phone* 9am-7pm Mon-Sat; 9am-4pm Sun. **Tickets** £8-£25. **Credit** MC, V.
A one-time railway turntable shed and gin warehouse, the Roundhouse was used for experimental theatre and hippie happenings in the 1960s, becoming a legendary rock venue in the 1970s. Local businessman Torquil Norman reopened the venue with £30m of refurbishment, the USP being the huge, circular hall, which holds around 1,200 people. The programme mixes arty rock gigs with dance, theatre and multimedia events. The acoustics are good and the attendant bars, toilets and cafés excellent.

Scala
275 Pentonville Road, King's Cross, N1 9NL (7833 2022/www.scala-london.co.uk). King's Cross tube/rail. **Box office** 10am-6pm Mon-Fri. **Tickets** (cash only) £8-£15. **Map** p399 L3.
Built as a cinema shortly after World War I, this surprisingly capacious building in King's Cross (it holds 1,145) now features a laudably broad range of ultra-cool indie, electronica, avant hip hop and weird folk. Unlike many similar-sized venues, sound quality is decent and staff extremely personable.

Shepherd's Bush Empire
Shepherd's Bush Green, W12 8TT (8354 3300/box office 0870 771 2000/www.shepherds-bush-empire. co.uk). Shepherd's Bush tube. **Box office** *In person* 4-6pm, 6.30-9.30pm show nights only. *By phone* 24hrs daily. **Tickets** £8-£40. **Credit** MC, V.
This former variety hall and BBC theatre remains London's best mid-sized venue, holding 2,000 standing or 1,300 seated. The sound is decent (with the exception of the alcove behind the stalls bar) and the staff are among the friendliest in London. The booking policy takes in everything from Amy Winehouse to Athlete.

Wembley Arena
Arena Square, Engineers Way, Wembley, Middx HA9 0DH (8782 5566/box office 0870 060 0870/ www.livenation.co.uk/wembley). Wembley Park tube. **Box office** *In person* 10am-4pm Mon-Fri; noon-start of performance Sat, Sun. *By phone* 24hrs daily. **Tickets** £5-£100. **Credit**, MC, V.

A £30m refurbishment has improved this much-derided 12,500-capacity venue no end, with comfy seating, better acoustics and pretty good sight lines. The only thing the management needs to sort out is the food and drink – cheaper and better, please.

Club & pub venues

London's smaller venues (those that have a capacity of between 100 and 500) come in clusters. You'll find several in Soho, a fair few in Camden and a growing number out east in Shoreditch (*see p310* **East is Eden**), along with a smattering around Islington and Shepherd's Bush. In south London the venues are rather more scattered, but you'll find good sessions at **Jamm** (261 Brixton Road, Brixton, SW9 6LH, 7274 5537) and the **Amersham Arms** (388 New Cross Road, New Cross, SE14 6TY, 8469 1499).

In addition to the venues below, a handful of nightclubs stage regular gigs: try the **Notting Hill Arts Club** (*see p322*), venerable cabaret hangout **Madame Jo Jo's** (*see p318*) and the all-encompassing **ICA** (*see p144*). Fans of garage rock should check out the Dirty Water Club on Fridays at the **Boston Arms** (178 Junction Road, Tufnell Park, N19 5QQ, 7272 8153, www.dirtywaterclub.com), while fans of mellower fare might enjoy the **Enterprise** (2 Haverstock Hill, Camden, NW3 2BL, 7485 2659).

Bardens Boudoir
38-44 Stoke Newington Road, N16 7XJ (7249 9557/ www.bardensbar.co.uk). Dalston Kingsland rail/67, 76, 149, 243 bus. **Box office** phone for details. *Gigs* 8pm. **Tickets** £4-£6. **No credit cards.**
Having resolved a few licensing issues (it turned out that it didn't have one), this basement space of a Turkish social club on the Stokie/Dalston borders is open for business once more. The 300-capacity space is something of a shambles: the room is at least three times wider than it is deep, and the stage isn't really a stage at all. Which bothers neither the often out-there line-ups nor the hipsters that love them.

Barfly
49 Chalk Farm Road, Chalk Farm, NW1 8AN (7691 4244/box office 0870 907 0999/www.barfly club.com). Chalk Farm tube. **Open** 7.30pm-1am Mon-Thur; 7.30pm-3am Fri, Sat; noon-12am Sun. *Shows* from 8pm daily. **Admission** £6-£8. **No credit cards.**
This pokey, 200-capacity upstairs venue is a big part of the reason why indie guitar-meets-electro parties have done so well. Kill Em All Let God Sort It Out (held every couple of weeks on a Saturday) features bands guaranteed to get the crowd going, while Adventures Close to Home (once a month) also packs out the dancefloor.
Other locations Fly, 36-38 New Oxford Street, Bloomsbury, WC1A 1EP (7631 0862).

Luminaire.

Bull & Gate

389 Kentish Town Road, Kentish Town, NW5 2TJ
(8826 5000/www.bullandgate.co.uk). Kentish Town
tube/rail. **Open** *Shows* 8-11pm daily. **Tickets** £5-
£12. **No credit cards**.

This venerable old 150-capacity boozer (where
Nirvana played their first London gig) is perhaps the
best place to see unsigned bands, particularly at the
beginning of the week. Expect to find groups with
names such as Two Bear Mambo and Dancing With
Henry playing for the benefit of friends, family and
the occasional A&R scout.

Dublin Castle

94 Parkway, Camden, NW1 7AN (7700 0550/
7485 1773/www.bugbearbookings.com). Camden
Town tube. **Shows** 8.30pm-11.30pm Mon-Fri;
8pm-midnight Sat, Sun. **Admission** £5-£9.

An estimable old fleapit, which holds not many more
than 100 punters, this remains *the* place to catch
unsigned guitar bands, of variable quality. DJs play
after the live shows until 2am Thur-Sat.

Green Note

106 Parkway, Camden, NW1 7AN (7485 9899/
www.greennote.co.uk). Camden Town tube. **Open**
6pm-12.30am Wed-Fri; noon-midnight Sat, Sun.
Shows 9-11pm daily. **Tickets** £4-£8. **Credit** MC, V.

Roots music and vegetarian food make for a winning
combination here. Neither is particularly daring: the
music comes from a string of folkies, blues musicians
and singer-songwriters, while the menu contains a
variety of earthy dishes served tapas-style. But it all
hangs together nicely at what is clearly a charming
labour of love on the part of the young owners.
Regular open mic from 1pm to 6pm on Sundays.

Jazz Café

5 Parkway, Camden, NW1 7PG (information 7534
6955/box office 7485 6834/0870 060 3777/www.
jazzcafe.co.uk). Camden Town tube. **Box office** *In*
person 10am-2pm, 3-6pm Mon-Sat; noon-6pm Sun. *By*
phone 24hrs daily. **Tickets** £10-£30. **Credit** MC, V.

There is some jazz on the schedules here, but this
two-floor club (capacity 450) deals more in soul, R&B
and hip hop these days, and has become the first port
of call for soon-to-be-huge US acts (D'Angelo, Mary J
Blige, John Legend and the Roots all played their first
European dates here). Warning: tickets can cost a lot
more on the door than they do in advance.

Luminaire

307-311 Kilburn High Road, Kilburn, NW6 7JR
(7372 8668/www.theluminaire.co.uk). Kilburn
tube/Brondesbury rail. **Open** 7pm-midnight Mon-
Wed, Sun; 7pm-1am Thur; 7pm-2am Fri, Sat.
Tickets (cash only) £3-£20. **Credit** (bar) MC, V.

The booking policy here is fantastically broad, taking in everything from alt-rock legend Mark Eitzel
to hyper-hip electro-poppers Junior Boys; the sound
system is well up to scratch; the decor is stylish (with
seated areas away from the stage); the drinks are
fairly priced, and the staff are approachable, even
friendly. If only all venues were built this way.

93 Feet East

150 Brick Lane, Spitalfields, E1 6QL (7247 3293/
www.93feeteast.co.uk). Shoreditch or Aldgate East
tube or Liverpool Street tube/rail. **Open** 5-11pm Mon-
Thur; 5pm-1am Fri; noon-1am Sat; noon-10.30pm
Sun. *Shows* times and days vary. **Admission** free-
£5. **No credit cards. Map** p403 S5.

With three rooms, a balcony and a wrap-around
courtyard that's just made for summer barbecues,
93 Feet East (capacity 240) manages to overcome the
otherwise crippling lack of a late licence. There are
plenty of good nights: It's Bigger Than and Kiss
Kiss Bang Band are student house parties without
the puking on the carpet, while the winter season of
Rock 'n' Roll Cinema is a great mix of short films
and local ska and rockabilly bands. *Photos p310.*

100 Club

100 Oxford Street, Soho, W1D 1LL (7636 0933/
www.the100club.co.uk). Oxford Circus or Tottenham
Court Road tube. **Open** *Shows* 7.30pm-midnight
Mon; 7.30-11.30pm Tue-Thur; 7.30pm-12.30am Fri;
7.30pm-1am Sat; 7.30-11pm Sun. **Tickets** £6-£20.
Credit MC, V. **Map** p397 K6.

Perhaps the most adaptable venue in London, this
wide, 350-capacity basement room has provided a
home for trad jazz, pub blues, northern soul and
punk (the venue staged a historic show in 1976 that
featured the Sex Pistols, the Clash and the Damned).

Pigalle Club

215 Piccadilly, St James's, W1J 9HN (office 7734
8142/box office 0845 345 6053/www.vpmg.net/
pigalle). Piccadilly Circus tube. **Open** 7pm-2am
Mon-Wed; 7pm-3am Thur-Sat. **Tickets** free-£65.
Credit AmEx, DC, MC, V. **Map** p406 V4.

Vince Power sold his stake in the Mean Fiddler, the
company he founded in 1982, but he certainly isn't
about to retire. The Pigalle is his upmarket Jazz
Café, an old-fashioned, 400-capacity supper club
where prices imply a certain measure of sophistication. Acts are generally jazzy, with the occasional
big-name singer thrown in.

12 Bar Club

22-23 Denmark Place, Soho, WC2H 8NL (office
7240 2120/box office 7240 2622/www.12barclub.
com). Tottenham Court Road tube. **Open** *Café*
11am-9pm Mon-Sat. *Bar* 11am-1am Mon-Thur;
11am-3am Fri, Sat; 11-midnight Sun. *Shows* from
7.30pm; nights vary. **Admission** £5-£15. **Credit**
MC, V. **Map** p406 W4.

This minuscule and much-cherished hole-in-the-wall
books a real grab-bag of stuff. Its size (audiences of
around 100 people and a stage barely big enough for
three performers) dictates a predominance of singer-
songwriters, but that doesn't stop the occasional full
band from trying their luck.

ULU (University of London Union)

Malet Street, Bloomsbury, WC1E 7HY (7664 2000/
www.ulu.co.uk). Goodge Street tube. **Box office** *In*
person 8.30am-9.30pm Mon-Fri; 9.30am-7pm Sat, Sun.
Open *Shows* 7.30-11pm; nights vary. **Admission**
£8-£15. **No credit cards. Map** p399 K4.

ULU's 800-capacity hall was redecorated in 2005, when it also had a new sound system installed. Although these changes improved the venue, it's no more characterful than it was before. As a student venue, though, two things are guaranteed: the programme will rely heavily on dodgy major-label guitar bands and the drinks will be cheap.

Underworld

174 Camden High Street, Camden, NW1 0NE (7482 1932/box office 0870 060 0100/7734 8932/ www.theunderworldcamden.co.uk). Camden Town tube. **Box office** *In person* 11am-11pm daily. *By phone* 24hrs daily. **Open** *Shows* 7-10.30pm; nights vary. **Admission** £5-£20. **No credit cards.**
A dingy maze of pillars and bars in the bowels of Camden, this 500-capacity subterranean oddity is an essential for punk, metal and hardcore fans. The insalubrious interior is enlivened by youthful, friendly audiences and a real community feel. If you can tell friends you're going to see Pickled Dick supporting Necrophagist and keep a straight face, you'll fit in just fine.

Union Chapel

Compton Terrace, Islington, N1 2XD (7226 1686/ www.unionchapel.org.uk). Highbury & Islington tube/ rail. **Open** check website for details. **Tickets** free-£40. **No credit cards.**
This 500-capacity Victorian Gothic church (which still holds regular services each Sunday) has been one of London's best gig venues for the past decade. The acoustics are pretty dreadful for electric guitars, but great for unamplified world music acts and low-key acoustic performers like Bert Jansch, Davy Graham and José Gonzaléz.

Windmill

22 Blenheim Gardens, Brixton, SW2 5BZ (8671 0700/www.windmillbrixton.co.uk). Brixton tube/rail. **Open** *Shows* 8-11pm Mon-Thur; 8pm-1am Fri, Sat; 5-11pm Sun. **Admission** free-£6. **No credit cards.**
If you can live with the iffy sound system and amusingly taciturn barflies, you might think this pokey little L-shaped pub (a 20-minute walk from Brixton tube) is one of the city's best venues, thanks to adventurous bookings (country, techno, punk, folk, metal), cheap admission and friendly staff.

Jazz

In addition to the venues listed below, the **100 Club** (*see p313*) hosts trad jazz, the **Spice of Life** at Cambridge Circus (6 Moor Street, W1, 7739 3025) has excellent mainstream jazz singers and instrumentalists most nights of the week, while the **Pigalle Club** (*see p313*) specialises in the jazzier end of pop and cabaret. The **Jazz Café** (*see p313*) lives up to its name about half a dozen times a month, while both the **Barbican** (*see p304*) and **Southbank Centre** (*see p307*) host dozens of big jazz names every year, including the bulk of the **London**

Jazz Festival (*see right* **Festivals**). If you're after more left-field stuff, try the bonkers mix of improvised music, performance art, poetry and Super8 films at the **Klinker** (Tue at Stage B, Stoke Newington Church Street, N16; alternate Thur at Ivy House, 40 Stuart Road, Nunhead, SE15; alternate Fri at the Salisbury, Green Lanes, Harringay, N15, www.iotacism.com/ klinkerizer). Also check the London Musicians Collective website (www.l-m-c.org.uk) for details of experimental gigs at venues like the **Red Rose Club** (129 Seven Sisters Road, Finsbury, N7 7QG, 7263 7265). For full details, see jazzinlondon.net or *Time Out* magazine.

Bull's Head

373 Lonsdale Road, Barnes, SW13 9PY (8876 5241/www.thebullshead.com). Barnes Bridge rail. **Open** 11am-11pm Mon-Sat; noon-11pm Sun. *Shows* 8.30pm Mon-Sat; 1-3.30pm, 8.30-11pm Sun. **Admission** £5-£12. **Credit** AmEx, DC, MC, V.
A venerable riverside pub – specialising in mainstream British jazz and swing – has undergone a refurbishment of sound and lighting systems, leaving the Yamaha Jazz Room, as it's now known, in better shape than ever. Regular guests include pianist Stan Tracey, sax maestro Peter King and the almost legendary Humphrey Lyttelton.

Pizza Express Jazz Club

10 Dean Street, Soho, W1D 3RW (7439 8722/ www.pizzaexpress.co.uk). Tottenham Court Road tube. **Open** 7.30-11.15pm daily. *Shows* 9-11.15pm daily. **Admission** £15-£25. **Credit** AmEx, DC, MC, V. **Map** p406 W2.
The upstairs restaurant (7437 9595) is jazz-free, but the 120-capacity basement venue has become one of the most important modern jazz venues in Europe. It peaked a few years back under manager Peter Wallis, but you should still be able to find excellent residencies from the likes of Mose Allison, Scott Hamilton, Kenny Garrett, Lea DeLaria and Peter White, running the gamut through swing, mainstream, modern, contemporary and fusion.

Ronnie Scott's

47 Frith Street, Soho, W1D 4HT (7439 0747/ www.ronniescotts.co.uk). Leicester Square or Tottenham Court Road tube. **Open** 6pm-3am Mon-Sat; 6pm-midnight Sun. *Shows* 6.30pm daily. **Admission** (non-members) £25-£100. **Credit** AmEx, DC, MC, V. **Map** p406 W2.
This legendary institution, opened by the British saxophonist Ronnie Scott in 1959, was taken over in 2006 by theatre impresario Sally Greene, who closed it down for a mammoth refit under the auspices of Parisian designer Jacques Garcia. They tarted up the furniture, moved the main bar, expanded capacity to 250 and revamped the kitchen. It looks good – and the food is rather better – but it's come at a cost. Shows are expensive and the 'jazz' definition has got a little loose (Gabrielle? Alexander O'Neal? Craig David?), but you'll still find lots of excellent

bookings, including the Mingus Big Band, Wynton and Branford Marsalis, Georgie Fame, Stacey Kent, Ahmad Jamal and Monty Alexander.

606 Club
90 Lots Road, Chelsea, SW10 0QD (7352 5953/ www.606club.co.uk). Earl's Court or Fulham Broadway tube/11, 211 bus. **Open** *Shows* 9-11.45pm Mon; 7.30pm-12.30am Tue, Wed; 8pm-midnight Thur; 9.30pm-1.30am Fri, Sat; 8.30pm-1am Sun. **Admission** £8-£12. **Credit** AmEx, MC, V. **Map** p396 C13.
Only British-based jazz musicians play here, which would seem like commercial suicide, but it's testament to the talents of manager Steve Rubie that this charmingly furnished, 150-capacity club celebrated its 30th birthday in 2006. There's no entry fee:

instead, the bands are funded from a music charge that's added to your bill at the end of the night. Alcohol can only be served with food.

Vortex Jazz Club
Dalston Culture House, 11 Gillet Street, Dalston, N16 8JN (7254 4097/www.vortexjazz.co.uk). Dalston Kingsland rail. **Open** *Shows* 8.30-11.15pm daily. **Admission** free-£12. **Credit** MC, V.
A fixture on Stoke Newington Church Street for many years before a dispute with the landlord, the Vortex reopened in 2005 in a handsome new building (the estimable Il Bacio pizzeria is on the ground floor). The upstairs space (all blond wood and chrome) sometimes feels a little sterile, but the line-ups are as good as ever, packed with left-field talent from Britain, Europe and the US.

Festivals Jazz

The big event on London's jazz calendar each year is the **London Jazz Festival** (7324 1880, www.serious.org.uk). Held over ten days each November, the creatively curated event spans many genres and venues, from the Vortex to the Wigmore Hall, but usually centres on the Southbank Centre.

It isn't the only jazz festival in the city, though. July sees two annual events, both of them entirely free. **Jazz on the Streets** (www.jazzonthestreets.co.uk) is a week of low-key music in Soho cafés and bars,

while the westerly **Ealing Jazz Festival** (8825 6064, www.ealing.gov.uk) stages generally mainstream acts over five late July evenings in Walpole Park. And in late September, the **Riverfront Jazz Festival** in Greenwich (8921 4456, www.riverfrontjazz.co.uk) dishes up a spread of small-scale shows; the same organisers run a mini-festival in mid May.

The year-round **Barbican Jazz** session at the Barbican Centre (*see p304*) also brings a score of heroes (including the likes of Sonny Rollins) to the capital.

Nightlife

You can hide from time, but you can't avoid the night bus home.

Notting Hill Arts Club. *See p322.*

Those already familiar with London clubland will notice two changes: the closure of the King's Cross Goods Yard and, of course, the smoking ban. Three of London's best-loved clubs – the Cross, the Key and Canvas – were built out of warehouses and arches in a freight depot near King's Cross Station. The long-discussed redevelopment of the area is now happening and the clubs are due to close with a bang after their New Year's Eve 2007 celebrations – the owners hope to open at a new venue in spring 2008, but as we went to press no site had been finalised. The smoking ban that came into force in July 2007 hardly affected some clubs (**EGG** was already making use of its extensive outdoor space) but it has proved a headache for others, especially underground, windowless clubs like the **End** and **Fabric**. You can expect to queue for a cigarette break – and only have limited time in which to smoke.

Club fashion has become increasingly flamboyant of late and as yet there's no sign of a dressed-down, acid house-style backlash (*see p322* **Here come the freaks**). Fabulous and utterly OTT, alt-drag queens have been reviving the old NYC trend for vogueing. Madonna's 'Vogue' this ain't – it's a highly energetic and competitive danceform that's not for the fainthearted: stand well clear unless you want a stylised hand gesture in the eye. Club kids collect themselves into 'Houses' – perhaps Jonny Woo's House of Egypt or the House of FierceNest – and descend on dancefloors as one. Don't be surprised to see them at **Bar Music Hall** (*see p319*) or **Boombox** (*see p321*).

The cabaret juggernaut rolls on with burlesque and variety nights mushrooming at a phenomenal rate. Just two years into the burlesque revival and a girl stripping down to a sparkly pair of nipple pasties (trainspotting fact: they're the things to which the tassels are attached) seems positively middle of the road. While we love **Bearlesque** (the gay bear burlesque troupe), we're more excited by the strange variety acts that have been dragging cabaret into the modern clubbing era. To see the best of the latest, head to **VauxhallVille**, weekly Thursdays at the **Royal Vauxhall**

Tavern (*see p300*), and most things at **Bethnal Green Working Men's Club**. Whatever you do, go with an open mind.

Some things remain the same. Fabric and the End still pack 'em with quality line-ups, while the terrific sound system at **Plastic People** makes it a great choice for discerning fans of everything from psychedelic disco to electro. Still sounds too cool for school? Get a portion of retro-cheese, courtesy of Sean Rowley's indefatigable Guilty Pleasures, frequently hosted at **KOKO** (*see p311*).

For all that London rewards those who are willing to chance something new, not all risks are worth taking. If you can't walk home from the club, find out which night bus gets you home and (more importantly) where you get it from before you head out. Within even a minor proposal to extend tube closing times having foundered, you'll not regret working out the night-bus system: the tube doesn't start until around 7am on Sundays, black cabs are expensive and rare. If you must take a minicab, it's important to make sure that it's an official one (*see p361*).

Central

Bar Rumba
36 Shaftesbury Avenue, Soho, W1D 7EP (7287 6933/www.barrumba.co.uk). Piccadilly Circus tube. **Open** 9pm-3am Mon; 6pm-3am Tue; 7pm-3am Wed; 8pm-3.30am Thur; 6pm-3am Fri; 9pm-4am Sat; 9pm-2am Sun. **Admission** £3-£10; free before 10pm Mon, Sat; free before 9pm Tue-Fri. **Credit** AmEx, MC, V. **Map** p408 W4.
Smack bang in the middle of the West End, Bar Rumba is a small basement club offering deep, underground urban flavours for a surprisingly un-West End crowd. Most of the nights have been around forever: Movement is the weekly Thursday junglist session, salsa fans love Barrio Latino on Tuesday, while Fridays jump-jump to the hip hop of Get Down. Weekend door code is strictly over-21s.

Café de Paris
3-4 Coventry Street, Chinatown, W1D 6BL (7734 7700/www.cafedeparis.com). Piccadilly Circus tube. **Open** *Restaurant* 6-8pm Sat. *Club* 10pm-3am Fri, Sat; (special events) 7pm-2am Mon-Thur. **Admission** £10-£20. **Credit** AmEx, MC, V. **Map** p406 W4.
There aren't many London clubs that drip with as much glamour as the Café de Paris. Off the wretched tourist strip between Leicester Square and Piccadilly, head down the double staircase into this opulent club – admiring the people perched on chairs around the circular balcony – and the world becomes a classier place. Increasingly popular for one-off events and variety cabaret shows (the irregular Flash Monkey is always outstanding), so check the listings and dust off your most fabulous frock.

End & AKA
18 West Central Street, Holborn, WC1A 1JJ (7419 9199/www.endclub.com). Holborn or Tottenham Court Road tube. **Open** 10pm-3am Mon, Wed; 10pm-4am Thur; 10pm-5am Fri; 10pm-7am Sat; varies Tue, Sun. **Admission** £4-£16. **Credit** AmEx, MC, V. **Map** p409 Y1.
It's hard to think of a better club than the End, with its attached bare-brick bar AKA. Owned by Layo (of Layo & Bushwacka) and Mr C – yup, he of the Shamen all those years ago – it's not a bit like the mainstream West End parties happening further down Oxford Street. Here it's all about quality electronic music. On Saturdays the venue becomes 'As One', with promoters like the electro rockin' Bugged Out, Ibizan mayhem merchants Circo Loco or superstar DJs (Laurent Garnier, Timo Maas), all night long.

Fabric
77A Charterhouse Street, Clerkenwell, EC1M 3HN (7336 8898/advance tickets 0870 902 0001/www.fabriclondon.com). Farringdon tube/rail. **Open** 9.30pm Fri-5am Sat; 10pm Sat-7am Sun. **Admission** £12-£16. **Credit** AmEx, MC, V. **Map** p402 O5.

The best Clubs

Bar Music Hall
For freaks, uniques and plenty of cheek, the queues go down the block but the door whore doesn't care – dress up if you want to get in, club kids. *See p319*.

Bethnal Green Working Men's Club
Still a fave of the young burlesque, cabaret and vintage crowds, this is the coolest lil' working men's club around. *See p319*.

Soho Revue Bar
Made for those with a healthy dressing-up box – expect drag queens, lady DJs in kimonos and retro swing boys. *See p318*.

Fabric
Showing no signs of stepping back from the coalface, Fabric mines the very best electronic talent from around the world. *See p317*.

Notting Hill Arts Club
Keeping west London on the clubbing map, a great, shabby basement that punches leagues above its weight. *See p322*.

Turnmills
With so many rooms, it's a good thing this is London's friendliest rave space. *See p318*.

Arts & Entertainment

Fabric is the club that most party people come to see in London, with good reason. Fridays belong to the bass: guaranteed highlights include DJ Hype, who takes over all three rooms once a month for his drum 'n' bass night True Playaz, and Plump DJs' Eargasm party, which is a sure-fire sell-out every other month. Saturdays descend into techy, minimal, deep house territory, with plenty of live artists you just can't hear anywhere else. Too crowded, hot and sweaty for some; heaven on a stick for others.

Madame Jo Jo's
8 Brewer Street, Soho, W1F 0SE (7734 3040/ www.madamejojos.com). Leicester Square or Piccadilly Circus tube. **Open** 8pm-3am Tue; 9pm-3am Thur; 10pm-3am Fri, Sun; 7pm-3am Sat. **Admission** £4-£10. **Credit** AmEx, MC, V. **Map** p408 W3.
Calling itself 'the heart of Soho's darkness', Jo Jo's is a beacon for those seeking to escape the post-work chain pubs. The basement space is very red and slightly shabby, but that's how the DJs, dancers and performers like it. Treasured nights include variety (Finger in the Pie, first Sundays; Kitsch Cabaret, every Saturday), Keb Darge's long-running Deep Funk and Mark Moore's glitch-tastic Electrogogo.

Pacha London
Terminus Place, Victoria, SW1V 1JR (7833 3139/www.pachalondon.com). Victoria tube/rail. **Open** 10pm-6am Fri, Sat. **Admission** £15-£20. **Map** p400 H10.
One of the great unanswered questions in London's clubland remains why this outpost of the über-glamorous Ibizan superclub had to be located in… a bus depot. Attracting the suited, booted and mint-ed with a range of glamorous house parties, it's a swanky, stylish place for classy clubbers who have money to burn.

Social
5 Little Portland Street, Marylebone, W1W 7JD (7636 4992/www.thesocial.com). Oxford Circus tube. **Open** noon-midnight Mon-Wed; 1pm-midnight Thur-Sat; 5pm-midnight Sun. **Admission** free; £3 acoustic nights. **Credit** AmEx, MC, V. **Map** p408 U1.
The same (and as great) as it ever was, despite these days being surrounded by flashier venues – note the opulent Annex 3 bar-restaurant next door. A discreet, opaque front still hides this daytime diner and DJ bar of supreme quality, established by Heavenly Records in 1999. It remains popular with music industry workers, minor alt-rock celebs and other sassy trendies who, after drinks upstairs, descend to an intimate basement space rocked by DJs six nights a week. The monthly Hip Hop Karaoke night (www.hiphopkaraokelondon.com) is a giggle.

Soho Revue Bar
11-12 Walker's Court, off Brewer Street, Soho, W1F 0ED (7734 0377/www.sohorevuebar.com). Leicester Square or Piccadilly Circus tube. **Open** 5pm-4am Tue-Sat. *Performances* 7pm. **Admission** £10; £5 reductions. **Credit** AmEx, MC, V. **Map** p408 W3.

Soho's grooviest club. Formerly Too2Much and before that Raymond's Revuebar, it has two grand rooms that host the popular, monthly retro-rock grindfest Lady Luck and the ladies 'n' drag queens only Lotus Flower, plus cabaret most Sundays in a supper-club style. Jodie Harsh, London's drag queen du jour, hosts Friday's Circus nights.

Turnmills
63B Clerkenwell Road, Clerkenwell, EC1M 5NP (7250 3409/www.turnmills.com). Farringdon tube/rail. **Open** 9pm-1am Thur; 10.30pm-7.30am Fri; 10pm-6am Sat. **Admission** £8-£15. **Credit** MC, V. **Map** p402 N4.
A legend in its own lifetime, Turnmills is a true hedonists' playground. The Gallery draws the hard dance and trance kids every Friday, thanks to the likes of Paul Van Dyk and Sister Bliss, while Saturdays programme more credible fare, including the bi-monthly, festival-inspired Together and genre-crossing Party Proactive.

Volupté
7-9 Norwich Street, Holborn, EC4A 1EJ (7831 1622/www.volupte-lounge.com). Chancery Lane tube. **Open** noon-late Tue-Sat. **Admission** £8-£12. **Credit** MC, V. **Map** p406 N5.
Expect to suffer extreme wallpaper envy as you enter the ground-floor bar then descend to the club proper. Here tables are set beneath absinthe-inspired vines, surrounded by lush curtains and plenty of red, from where punters enjoy some of the best cabaret talent in town. Wednesday nights are Cabaret Salon and once a month the Black Cotton Club turns back the clock to the 1920s.

North London

Better known as live venues, **Barfly** (*see p312*), **KOKO** (*see p311*) and the **Scala** (*see p311*) all host feisty club nights.

Big Chill House
257-259 Pentonville Road, King's Cross, N1 9NL (7427 2540/www.bigchill.net). King's Cross tube/rail. **Open** noon-midnight Mon-Wed, Sun; noon-1am Thur; noon-4am Fri, Sat. **Admission** £5 after 10pm. **Credit** MC, V. **Map** p399 M3.
A festival, a record label, a bar and now also a house, the Big Chill empire rolls on. And a good thing too, if it keeps offering such interesting things as this three-floor space. It boasts an enormous sun-catcher of a terrace – perfect for the Sunday papers and brunch – while the likes of Sean Rowley and owner Pete Lawrence regularly handle deck duties.

EGG
200 York Way, King's Cross, N7 9AP (7609 8364/ www.egglondon.net). King's Cross tube/rail. **Open** 9pm Fri-6am Sat; 10pm Sat-2pm Sun; varies Mon-Thur. **Admission** £8-£15. **Credit** MC, V. **Map** p399 L2.
With its Mediterranean-styled three floors, garden and enormous terrace (complete with a small pool), EGG is big enough to lose yourself in but manages

Arts & Entertainment

Big Chill House.

to retain an intimate atmosphere. The upstairs bar in red ostrich leather is rather elegant, but the main dancefloor downstairs has a warehouse rave feel.

Lock Tavern
35 Chalk Farm Road, Chalk Farm, NW1 8AJ (7482 7163). Chalk Farm tube. **Open** noon-midnight Mon-Thur; noon-1am Fri, Sat; noon-11pm Sun. **Admission** free. **Credit** MC, V.
Excellent bar-pub with DJs most nights of the week, although Sundays are the musical staple, with off-duty DJs stumbling through the doors. Young indie bands on the up jostle for space with DJs from regular nights such as Kill Em All and Asbo. Plenty of outdoor areas for days when the sunshine shows.

East London

Aquarium
256 & 260 Old Street, Shoreditch, EC1V 9DD (7251 6136/www.clubaquarium.co.uk). Old Street tube/rail. **Open** 10pm Fri-11am Sat; 10pm Sat-11am Sun; 10pm Sun-4am Mon. **Admission** £7-£15. **Credit** MC, V. **Map** p403 Q4.
Don't let the Old Street location fool you, there's nothing edgy or cool about this ever-popular club. Queues of out-of-town girls on the raz for a hen night know to pack their bikinis – Club Aquarium is still the only venue in the UK to boast a swimming pool and jacuzzi. Carwash is the long-running Saturday night disco and funkfest, while the small roof terraces are popular in the summer months with electro afterparties that just go on and on. And on.

Bar Music Hall
134-146 Curtain Road, Shoreditch, EC2A 3AR (7729 7216/www.barmusichall.com). Old Street tube/rail. **Open** 11am-midnight Mon-Thur, Sun; 11am-2am Fri, Sat. **Admission** free. **Credit** AmEx, MC, V. **Map** p403 R4.
An enormous square room with an island bar. Not much to look at, it's true, but this club was home to the notorious polysexual debauchery that was AntiSocial. Nowadays, the queues run down Curtain Road on Saturday nights as Shoreditch's edgier club kids wait for the door to wave them into Scottee and Jodie Harsh's weekly electro party, Foreign. The dress code is extreme as you like and, despite lengthy queues (which surely aren't drawn by the poor-quality sound system), it's free to get in.

Bethnal Green Working Men's Club
42-44 Pollard Row, Bethnal Green, E2 6NB (7739 2727/www.workersplaytime.net). Bethnal Green tube. **Open** check website for details. **Admission** £5-£12 after 8pm Fri, Sat.
What was once a run-down East End working men's club threatened with closure is now one of London's coolest clubs, thanks to a canny local boy turned promoter. The sticky red carpet and broken lampshades perfectly suit its programme of quirky lounge, retro rock 'n' roll and fancy-dress burlesque parties, like Mexican wrestling cum darkside cabaret event Lucha Britannia or Grind a Go Go, for which burlesque starlets get a hip 1960s dancefloor. The mood is friendly, the playlist upbeat and the air full of playful mischief.

Arts & Entertainment

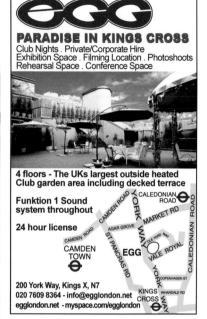

Cargo

Kingsland Viaduct, 83 Rivington Street, Shoreditch, EC2A 3AY (7739 3440/www.cargo-london.com). Old Street tube/rail. **Open** 11am-1am Mon-Thur; 11am-3am Fri; 6pm-3am Sat; 1pm-midnight Sun. **Admission** free-£12. **Credit** AmEx, MC, V. **Map** p403 R4.

Located down a side street and under a bridge, the bricks 'n' arches of Cargo keeps Shoreditch music fans in a blissful state of whatever-next-ness. It's increasingly about the live music here, but nights such as Ali B's seminal breaks party Air have also made this place home. Make sure you check out the great street-food café and take in the exceptional graffiti on the whitewashed walls of the spacious beer garden.

Catch

22 Kingsland Road, Shoreditch, E2 8DA (7729 6097/www.thecatchbar.com). Old Street tube/rail. **Open** 6pm-midnight Tue, Wed; 6pm-2am Thur-Sat; 6pm-1am Sun. **No credit cards. Map** p403 R3.

Another example of Shoreditch talent making the most of what they've got. Catch isn't anything special – expect sticky carpets, shabby brown decor and surly bar staff – but the small and dark upstairs room attracts a great mix of young, adventurous promoters. It's a bit hit and miss, of course, but we love Girlcore, a bouncy, buzzy collective of local girls who throw electro, indie and bashment parties on the first Thursday of the month.

Herbal

10-14 Kingsland Road, Hoxton, E2 8DA (7613 4462/www.herbaluk.com). Old Street tube/rail. **Open** 9pm-3am Fri, Sat; 9pm-2am Sun. **Admission** free-£10. **Credit** *Bar* MC, V. **Map** p403 R3.

A change in ownership of the Shoreditch stalwart meant that, for much of summer 2007, this much-loved but rather under-the-weather two-floor venue was closed except for Fridays and Saturdays. As the licensing process grinds along, Grooverider's outstanding weekly Sunday jungle-fest Grace is on hold, as is the killer beatbox and hip hop party Spitkingdom. Keith Reilly, who also owns Fabric, has bought into the club, and we're hearing talk of expansion in 2008. Fingers crossed.

Hoxton Square Bar & Kitchen

2-4 Hoxton Square, Hoxton, N1 6NU (7613 0709/www.hoxtonsquarebar.com). Old Street tube/rail. **Open** 11am-1am Mon-Thur, Sun; 11am-2am Fri, Sat. **Food served** noon-11pm daily. **Credit** MC, V. **Map** p403 R3.

A long, industrial bunker of a bar with a big square back room that's perfect for gigs and post-work drinkies. So far, so much whatever. Every Sunday, though, fashionistas, freaks and wannabes descend for Boombox: a riot of extreme outfits – dress merely as a Louis Vuitton bag or fetishist drag queen and you'll feel like a wallflower; dress like a civilian and you might not get in – and great mash-up DJs. It's one of the places that has recently seen a revival of New York's 'vogue' craze.

On the Rocks

25 Kingsland Road, Shoreditch, E2 8AA. Old Street tube/rail. **Open** 10.30pm-late Fri, 9pm-2am Sat. **Admission** £3 before 11pm, then £5 (£3 reductions). **Map** p403 R3.

There are run-down, after-the-after-party clubs… and then there's On the Rocks. Dark, small and full of UV lights, it's a haven for Shoreditch's dedicated party people. Hannah Holland is a cracking local DJ whose star is on the up and up; her twisted electro Trailer Trash party is here every fortnight.

Plastic People

147-149 Curtain Road, Shoreditch, EC2A 3QE (7739 6471/www.plasticpeople.co.uk). Old Street tube/rail. **Open** 10pm-2am Mon-Thur; 10pm-3.30am Fri, Sat; 7.30pm-midnight Sun. **Admission** £3-£8. **Map** p405 R4.

Plastic People subscribes to the old-school line that all you need for a kicking party is a dark basement and a sound system. What it lacks in size and decor it makes up for in sound quality (the rig embarrasses those in many larger clubs) and by staging some of London's most progressive club nights. Sounds range from Afro-jazz to Latin at Balance, and dubstep and grime at regular urban night FWD.

T Bar

Tea Building, 56 Shoreditch High Street, Shoreditch, E1 6JJ (7729 2973/www.tbarlondon.com). Liverpool Street tube/rail. **Open** varies. **Admission** free. **Credit** MC, V. **Map** p405 R4.

When T Bar opened in the over-saturated Shoreditch market, it changed the face of London's nightlife. A bunker-like place, it manages to book DJ stars such as Ivan Smagghe and Damian Lazarus – for no money whatsoever. Which means it's best to get down here early if you want to get in.

333

333 Old Street, Hoxton, EC1V 9LE (7739 5949/www.333mother.com/www.myspace.com/333mother). Old Street tube/rail. **Open** 10pm-4.30am Fri, Sat; 10pm-4am Sun. *Bar* 8pm-3am daily. **Admission** *Club* £5-£10. **Credit** MC, V. **Map** p405 Q4.

While no longer the be-all and end-all of East End clubbing, this three-floored clubbing institution still draws queues for indie-rave mash-ups at the weekends. The basement's dark and intense, which works well for the drum 'n' bass talent. Upstairs is just like a house party, complete with broken loos and random strangers falling over your shoes.

South London

Dogstar

389 Coldharbour Lane, Brixton, SW9 8LQ (7733 7515/www.thedogstar.co.uk). Brixton tube/rail. **Open** 4pm-2am Mon-Thur; noon-4am Fri, Sat; noon-2am Sun. **Admission** £3 after 10pm Fri, Sat; £5 after 11pm Fri, Sat. **Credit** MC, V.

A Brixton institution from back when Coldharbour Lane was somewhere people feared to go, Dogstar is a big street-corner pub exuding the urban

Arts & Entertainment

authenticity loved by clubbers. The atmosphere can be intense, but it's never less than vibrant. The music varies from night to night but quality stays high. It's a training ground for the DJ stars of tomorrow.

Jamm
261 Brixton Road, Brixton, SW9 6LH (7274 5537/ www.brixtonjamm.org). Brixton tube/rail. **Open** 5pm-2am Mon-Thur; 5pm-6am Fri; 2pm-6am Sat; 2pm-2am Sun. **Admission** £5-£10. **Credit** AmEx, MC, V.

This busy road isn't the classiest location for a club, but then this two-roomed place is more interested in slamming parties than swanky soirées. The music policy is as wide-ranging as the staff are welcoming: Hunk Papa's Pure Reggae turns Sundays into a proper friendly session, while the monthly Bosh showcases upcoming indie and funk talent.

Ministry of Sound
103 Gaunt Street, off Newington Causeway, Newington, SE1 6DP (0870 060 0010/www. ministryofsound.com). Elephant & Castle tube/rail. **Open** 10pm-3am Tue; 10.30pm-5am Fri; 11pm-7am Sat. **Admission** £12-£17. **Credit** AmEx, MC, V. **Map** p404 O10.

Cool it ain't (there's little more naff in all London than the VIP rooms here – avoid!) but home to a killer sound system the Ministry most certainly is. Nights chop and change, but whether it's electro house, trance or old-school garage, the line-up is sure to be superstar names. For those who missed legendary jungle night AWOL in its original early 1990s incarnation, it gets rolled out every other month throughout the year. Re-re-wind!

Plan B
418 Brixton Road, Brixton, SW9 7AY (7733 0926/www.plan-brixton.co.uk). Brixton tube/rail. **Open** 9pm-5am Fri, Sat; Mon-Thur, Sun varies. **Admission** varies. **Credit** MC, V.

It may be small, but Plan B punches well above its weight thanks to a constant flow of hip hop and funk stars at Fidgit on most Fridays and plenty of soulful house and international hip hop on Saturdays.

West London

Notting Hill Arts Club
21 Notting Hill Gate, Notting Hill, W11 3JQ (7460 4459/www.nottinghillartsclub.com). Notting Hill Gate tube. **Open** 6pm-2am Mon-Fri; 4pm-2am Sat; 4pm-1am Sun. **Admission** £5-£8; free before 8pm. **Credit** MC, V. **Map** p394 A7.

Cool west London folk are always grateful for this small, basement club. It may not be much to look at, but it almost single-handedly keeps this side of the capital on the clubbing radar thanks to influential nights like Thursday's YoYo – a haven for fans of eclectic cratedigging, from funk to 1980s boogie – and Nihal's globe trotting Asian underground Bombay Bronx (third Tuesday of every month). For grown-ups who still can. *Photo p316.*

Here come the freaks

It's hard to imagine that just ten years ago, London's clubbers were dressed head to toe in samey-same jeans, Converse trainers and T-shirt combos. Seems positively grandad in comparison to the current wave of full-on, DIY fashion that's swept across the clubbing spectrum. Sure, vintage and retro parties such as **Lady Luck** (monthly Thursdays at Soho Revue Bar, *see p318*) and almost anything at the **Bethnal Green Working Men's Club** (*see p319*) were always going to attract girls familiar with the workings of their grandmothers' wardrobes, but the fad for second-hand clothing (much more 'now', darling, to refer to one's frock as 'second-hand' instead of 'vintage') has seeped into the indie scene too. Gigs are full of girls in red lippy and heels and boys wearing cravats and, preserve us, trilbies. Nu-rave is still very much in evidence, championed by *Super Super* magazine, but this reappropriation of early 1990s music and day-glo 1980s clothes was a smoke screen for a wider, longer-lasting trend, that of the modern-day club kid. Just as early '90s New York had its fantastically dressed, hedonistic young things, Shoreditch is now full of kids barely out of puberty spending their last penny on a home-made outfit for Boombox or Foreign at **Bar Music Hall** (*see p319*).

Need inspiration? Check photographic blogs like www.dirtydirtydancing.com and see what London's clubbers are wearing the night they're wearing it. This post nu-rave generation is rapidly trying to distance itself from the nu-rave fad, and it will be interesting to see over the next year how the scene evolves. Drag queens are again having their moment in the sun, and they're *working* it. The alt-drag scene (think Leigh Bowery, not *Priscilla Queen of the Desert*) sends its great and good out into clubland every weekend. Catch Scottee who runs Foreign with Jodie Harsh, or the regular drag cabaret shows at **Bistrotheque** (*see p217*). Worried you didn't pack right for all this fabulousness? There's always time for some shopping – the city's best second-hand shops are on p249.

Sport & Fitness

Kicking, batting, rowing, running and jumping – roll on the Olympics.

Check the weekly Sport section of *Time Out* magazine for a comprehensive guide to the best of the week's action. For annual events, *see p329* **Silly season** *and p330* **The sporting year**.

Major stadiums

As well as providing London with a major new concert venue, the **O2 Arena** (*see p311*) is making a name for itself hosting American sporting events – including important ice-hockey and basketball fixtures.

Crystal Palace National Sports Centre

Ledrington Road, Crystal Palace, SE19 2BB (8778 0131/www.gll.org). Crystal Palace rail.
This Grade II-listed building has been in need of repair for some time now, and its very future was in doubt until it was given a reprieve in 2006 when the Mayor of London and the London Development Agency took over responsibility for running the site. So the popular summer Grand Prix athletics events continue here, although the new Olympic stadium being built in Stratford for the 2012 Games will, when completed, eclipse this one.

Wembley Arena & Conference Centre

Elvin House, Stadium Way, Wembley, Middx HA9 0DW (8782 5500/box office 0870 060 0870/www.whatsonwembley.com). Wembley Park tube/Wembley Stadium rail.
International boxing bouts, snooker and basketball tournaments and showjumping events take place infrequently at the refurbished Wembley Arena.

Wembley Stadium

Stadium Way, Wembley, Middx HA9 0WS (8795 9000/www.wembleystadium.com). Wembley Park tube/Wembley Stadium rail.
Britain's most famous sporting venue finally reopened in early 2007. The expansive redevelopment took more than six years to complete, three years longer than initially planned thanks to various wrangles with contractors and disputes among the sporting and political bodies overseeing it. Nonetheless, now it's complete, the new 90,000-seat Wembley, designed by architect Sir Norman Foster, is some sight, its futuristic steel arch an imposing feature of the skyline across large parts of the city. Inside, the sightlines and facilities are a huge improvement, for all the old venue's romantic associations with famous footballing moments such as England's 1966 World Cup Final victory. The eventual cost came in at

£798m, making it the most expensive stadium project ever launched, so some of these costs will be recouped by Wembley's staging of more events than ever before: all England football internationals and domestic cup finals are now played here, as are rugby league finals and other one-off sporting events, even gridiron and motorsport, as well as regular pop concerts. Tickets can still be difficult to come by, and there have been criticisms of the high percentage of spaces set aside for corporate guests. Nonetheless, a visit is thoroughly recommended. *Photo p324.*

Olympic Park

Lower Lea Valley (www.london2012.com).
London is gearing up to host the 2012 Olympics, having pipped Paris in 2005 to host the Games. Competitions will be held at venues across London, including the All England Tennis Club (*see p327*) and Lord's Cricket Ground (*see p324*), but the main events will take place at the new Olympic site currently under construction near Stratford, east London. The Olympic Park will include an 80,000-capacity Olympic stadium, an aquatic centre, velopark, hockey centre and Olympic village as part of a major regeneration of the area. Initial demolition and building work on the £600m stadium began in the summer of 2007, but the development is already dogged by political and financial disagreements. After the Games, the stadium will be remodelled into a 25,000-capacity venue, though exactly what role it will fulfil remains uncertain – various local professional football clubs have been linked with the venue, but none has made a firm commitment.

Spectator sports

Basketball

London Capital are currently the city's sole representatives in the professional, 13-strong British Basketball League. For information, including a list of indoor and outdoor courts, contact the **English Basketball Association** (0114 223 5693, www.englandbasketball.co.uk).

London Capital

Capital City Academy, Doyle Gardens, NW10 3ST (8838 8700/www.londoncapital.org).

Cricket

If you're pushed for time, catch a one-day international or a match in the C&G Trophy, Pro40 League or, shorter still, the hugely

Wembley Stadium. *See p323.*

popular evening Twenty20 matches (20 overs per side, taking perhaps an hour and a half). **Lord's** (home to Middlesex) and the **Brit Oval** (Surrey's home ground) also host Test matches and one-day internationals. Book well ahead; your best chance of seeing international cricket is on the last day of a Test, for which tickets are not normally sold in advance (play depends on the progress of the match, with Tests not infrequently being won in four of the allotted five days). Typically, the national team hosts Test and one-day series against two international sides each summer, and the domestic season runs from April to September.

Brit Oval

Kennington Oval, Kennington, SE11 5SS (7582 6660/7764/www.surreycricket.com). Oval tube. **Tickets** *International £40-£65. County £12-£15.*

Lord's

St John's Wood Road, St John's Wood, NW8 8QN (MCC 7289 1611/tickets 7432 1000/www.lords. org.uk). St John's Wood tube. **Tickets** *International £40-£65. County £12-£15.*

Cycling

The sport does not have the massive public profile it has in many other European countries, but cycling does have a dedicated following in the UK. The enthusiasm intensified with the stunning success of the capital's staging of the Grand Depart of the Tour de France in 2007. Each September the capital hosts a stage of the annual **Tour of Britain**, a road race that follows a different course round Britain every year. Since being granted world championship ranking status in 2004, the race has drawn crowds of up to 100,000 people. Those speed merchants who want a pedal themselves can try the **Herne Hill Velodrome** (Burbage Road, Herne Hill, SE24 9HE, 7737 4647, www.hernehillvelodrome.org.uk), the oldest cycle circuit in the world.

Football

Arsenal and Chelsea are the capital's major players in the lucrative and glamorous Barclays Premier League. **Chelsea** have been London's most successful club in recent years, winning consecutive league titles in 2005 and 2006, as well as both domestic cup competitions in 2007. Their success has been heavily dependent on the largesse of Russian oil tycoon Roman Abramovich, who lavished millions of pounds on players and brought in the astute and charismatic Portuguese manager Jose Mourinho. Mourinho's sudden resignation in September 2007, after a breakdown in relations with Abramovich, introduced unfamiliar anxiety to the club. **Arsenal** have won a string of trophies in the past 12 years under their cultured French coach Arsene Wenger, as well as reaching a Champions League final. They've also managed to boost their revenue to record-breaking levels by moving to a sparkling 60,000-capacity new ground at Ashburton Grove in the.

Big money continues to hold sway in English football's top flight, with Chelsea's Abramovich just one of a host of foreign businessmen investing in clubs in recent seasons. Arsenal have been the subject of much takeover speculation, while **West Ham United** were taken over by Icelandic magnate Eggert Magnusson in late 2006. The gap between big and small clubs seems more insurmountable by the year. Even well-supported and historically successful clubs such as **Tottenham Hotspur** (Arsenal's near neighbours and traditional rivals) have found it difficult to keep up. Yet London sustains ten professional clubs in the Premier League and the three divisions of the Football League, whose support bases have held up despite the lure of richer and often more successful neighbours.

Tickets for games in the Premier League can be difficult to get your hands on, especially for Chelsea and Arsenal; a visit to **Fulham**, however, is a treat: a superb setting by the river, a historic ground and seats in the 'neutral' section often available on the day. For London clubs in the lower leagues (in descending order the Coca-Cola Championship, Coca-Cola Football League 1, Coca-Cola Football League 2) tickets are cheaper and easier to obtain. Prices quoted are for adult non-members.

Arsenal
Emirates Stadium, Ashburton Grove, N7 7AF (7704 4040/www.arsenal.com). Arsenal tube. Tickets £13-£94. **Premier League**

Charlton Athletic
The Valley, Floyd Road, Charlton, SE7 8BL (0871 226 1905/www.cafc.co.uk). Charlton rail. **Tickets** £20; £10-£15 reductions. **Championship**

Chelsea
Stamford Bridge, Fulham Road, Chelsea, SW6 1HS (0870 300 1212/www.chelseafc.com). Fulham Broadway tube. Tickets £45-£60. **Premier League**

Crystal Palace
Selhurst Park, Whitehorse Lane, Selhurst, SE25 6PU (0871 200 0071/www.cpfc.co.uk). Selhurst rail/468 bus. Tickets £20-£40. **Championship**

Fulham
Craven Cottage, Stevenage Road, Fulham, SW6 6HH (0870 442 1234/www.fulhamfc.com). Putney Bridge tube. Tickets £25-£55. **Premier League**

Leyton Orient
Matchroom Stadium, Brisbane Road, Leyton, E10 5NF (8926 1111/tickets 0870 310 1883/www.leyton orient.com). Leyton tube/Leyton Midland Road rail. Tickets £20-£35. **League 1**

Millwall
The Den, Zampa Road, Bermondsey, SE16 3LN (7232 1222/tickets 7231 9999/www.millwallfc.co.uk). South Bermondsey rail. Tickets £20-£27. **League 1**

Queens Park Rangers
Loftus Road Stadium, South Africa Road, Shepherd's Bush, W12 7PA (0870 112 1967/ www.qpr.co.uk). White City tube. Tickets £20-£25. **Championship**

Tottenham Hotspur
White Hart Lane Stadium, 748 High Road, Tottenham, N17 0AP (0870 420 5000/www. tottenhamhotspur.com). White Hart Lane rail. Tickets £27-£71. **Premier League**

West Ham United
Upton Park, Green Street, West Ham, E13 9AZ (0870 112 2700/www.whufc.com). Upton Park tube. Tickets £39-£59. **Premier League**

Greyhound racing

For a cheap night out that could end up paying for itself, head to one of the four greyhound tracks around the capital. For an admission fee that's never more than £6, you can enjoy the art deco glories of **Walthamstow** (Chingford Road, 8531 4255, www.wsgreyhound.co.uk), the decent restaurants at **Wimbledon** (Plough Lane, 8946 8000, www.lovethedogs.co.uk), the chirpy charms of **Romford** (London Road,

01708 762345, www.trap6.com/romford) or the relaxed atmosphere at **Crayford** (Stadium Way, 01322 557836). Small stakes (we're talking coins rather than tenners) are accepted at most venues, but one judicious punt could keep you in drinks all evening. For more information, visit www.thedogs.co.uk.

Horse racing

The racing year is divided into the flat-racing season, from April to September, and the National Hunt season over jumps, from October to April. For more information about the 'sport of kings', visit www.discover-racing.com. The Home Counties around London are liberally sprinkled with a fine variety of courses, each of which offers an enjoyable day out from the city.

Epsom

Epsom Downs, Epsom, Surrey KT18 5LQ (01372 726311/www.epsomdowns.co.uk). Epsom Downs or Tattenham Corner rail. **Open** *Box office* 9am-5pm Mon-Fri. **Admission** £5-£35.
The Derby, held here each year in June, is one of the great events in Britain's social and sporting calendar. The impressive Queen's Stand and grandstand both offer fine viewing and restaurants.

Kempton Park

Staines Road East, Sunbury-on-Thames, Middx TW16 5AQ (01932 782292/www.kempton.co.uk). Kempton Park rail. **Open** *Box office* 9am-5pm Mon-Fri. **Admission** £11-£16.
Although it's far from glamorous, this course is the Londoner's local haunt. The year-round meetings are well attended, especially in summer.

Royal Ascot

Ascot Racecourse, Ascot, Berks SL5 7JX (0870 722 7227/www.ascot.co.uk). Ascot rail. **Open** 9am-5pm Mon-Fri. **Admission** phone for details.
The famous Royal Meeting takes place this year on 17-21 June. Get your top hats, posh frocks and credit cards ready for what is a society bash. Tickets to the public enclosure are usually available on the day, but it's best to ring before making a special journey. Other big races held at Ascot include the King George, which takes place in late July.

Sandown Park

Portsmouth Road, Esher, Surrey KT10 9AJ (01372 463072/www.sandown.co.uk). Esher rail. **Open** *Box office* 9am-5pm Mon-Fri. **Admission** £6-£35.
Most famous for hosting the Whitbread Gold Cup in April and the Coral Eclipse Stakes in July, Sandown pushes horses to the limit with a hill finish.

Windsor

Maidenhead Road, Windsor, Berks SL4 5JJ (01753 498400/tickets 0870 220 0024/www.windsor-racecourse.co.uk). Windsor & Eton Riverside rail. **Open** *Box office* 9.30am-5.30pm Mon-Fri. **Admission** £7-£22.

A pleasant Thameside location in the shadow of Windsor Castle helps to make the Royal Windsor Racecourse a lovely spot for first-timers and families, especially during the three-day festival in May or of a summer Monday evening.

Motorsport

Wimbledon Stadium (8946 8000, 01252 322920, www.speedworth.co.uk) is the place to come for pedal-to-the-metal action: every other Sunday bangers, hot rods and stock cars come together for family-oriented mayhem. **Rye House Stadium** (01992 440400) in Hoddesdon, on the northern edges of London near the M25 motorway, also hosts speedway, providing a home for the Rye House Rockets (www.ryehouse.com). Matches usually take place on Saturday.

Rugby league

North-of-England teams such as Leeds, Bradford, St Helens and Wigan rule the roost, but the capital's one Super League club, **Harlequins RL**, remain at the highest level of the domestic game despite leading a somewhat nomadic existence involving changes of home ground and name.

Harlequins Rugby League

Stoop Memorial Ground, Langhorn Drive, Twickenham, Middx TW2 7SX (0871 871 8877/www.quins.co.uk). Twickenham rail. **Admission** £12-£30.

Rugby union

Fans come out in force to watch the annual **Six Nations Championship** (Jan-Mar). The England team won the World Cup in 2003; then, to everyone's astonishment, a side that had struggled for much of the intervening four years dragged themselves to the final rounds again in France in 2007. Narrowly beating Australia in the quarter-finals, they defeated France in the semis, only to lose to South Africa in the final. Tickets for England's Six Nations games – which take place at **Twickenham** (Rugby Road, Twickenham, Middx, 8892 2000; *see also p186*), the home of English Rugby Union, are nigh impossible to get hold of, but other matches are more accessible. The Guinness Premiership, in which London and its immediate environs are well represented, and the three-division National League run from early September to May; most games are played on Saturday and Sunday afternoons. Matches in the Heineken Cup, the pan-European competition for the continent's elite domestic clubs, are also worth watching out for.

Arts & Entertainment

England take on France at **Twickenham**, the home of rugby union.

Arts & Entertainment

Listed below are the Premiership clubs that are based in the greater London area. For a more comprehensive list, contact the **Rugby Football Union** (8892 2000, www.rfu.com).

Harlequins
Stoop Memorial Ground, Langhorn Drive, Twickenham, Middx TW2 7SX (0871 871 8877/ www.quins.co.uk). Twickenham rail. **Tickets** £15-£40.

London Irish
Madejski Stadium, Shooters Way, Reading, Berks RG2 0SL (0870 999 1871/www.london-irish.com). Reading rail then £2 shuttle bus. **Tickets** £20-£30.

London Wasps
Adams Park, Hillbottom Road, High Wycombe, Bucks HP12 4HJ (8993 8298/tickets 0870 414 1515/www.wasps.co.uk). High Wycombe rail. **Tickets** £19-£43.

Saracens
Vicarage Road Stadium, Watford, Herts WD18 0EP (01923 475222/www.saracens.com). Watford High Street rail. **Open** *Box office* 9am-5.30pm Mon-Fri. **Tickets** £18-£50.

Tennis

Getting to see the action at the Wimbledon Championships at the **All England Lawn Tennis Club** (23 June-6 July 2008) requires forethought: seats on Centre and Number One courts are applied for by ballot the previous year, although enthusiasts who queue on the day may gain entry to the outer courts. You can also turn up later in the day and pay a reasonable rate for seats vacated by spectators who have left early. Wimbledon is preceded by the Stella Artois tournament at **Queen's Club**, where stars from the men's circuit can be seen warming up for the main event: the 2008 tournament will be held from 9 to 15 June.

All England Lawn Tennis Club
PO Box 98, Church Road, Wimbledon, SW19 5AE (8944 1066/tickets 8971 2700/information 8946 2244/www.wimbledon.org). Southfields tube.

Queen's Club
Palliser Road, West Kensington, W14 9EQ (7385 3421/www.queensclub.co.uk). Barons Court tube.

Participation & fitness

Circus skills

Circus Space
*Coronet Street, Hoxton, N1 6HD (7729 9522/www.
thecircusspace.co.uk). Old Street tube/rail.* **Open** 9am-
10pm Mon-Thur; 9am-9pm Fri; 10.30am-6pm Sat,
Sun. **Classes** phone for details. **Credit** MC, V.
Map p403 R3.
If you've ever wanted an honours degree in circus
arts, then here's the place to get one. It also offers
performances in its newly refurbished space.

Golf

You don't have to be a member to tee off at
either of the public courses below – but do book
in advance. For a list of clubs in the London
area, go to www.englishgolfunion.org.

Dulwich & Sydenham Hill
*Grange Lane, College Road, Dulwich, SE21 7LH
(8693 8491/www.dulwichgolf.co.uk). Sydenham Hill
rail.* **Open** 8am-dusk daily. **Admission** £40; £20
members' guests Mon-Fri.
A lovely course with fantastic views. Members only
at weekends, although they can bring in guests.

North Middlesex
*Manor House, Friern Barnet Lane, Arnos Grove,
N20 0NL (8445 3060/www.northmiddlesexgc.co.uk).
Arnos Grove or Totteridge & Whetstone tube.* **Open**
8am-dusk Mon-Fri; 1pm-dusk Sat, Sun. **Admission**
£15-£25 Mon-Fri; £25-£30 Sat, Sun.
An undulating course set in 74 acres and dating
back to 1905. Not one for beginners.

Health clubs & sports centres

Many clubs and centres admit non-members
and even allow them to join classes. Some of the
main contenders are listed below; for a list of all
venues in Westminster, call 7641 1846, or for
Camden, call 7974 4456. Note that last entry is
normally 45-60 minutes before the closing times
given. For more independent spirits, Hyde Park,
Kensington Gardens and Battersea Park have
particularly good jogging trails.

Central YMCA
*112 Great Russell Street, Bloomsbury, WC1B 3NQ
(7343 1700/www.centralymca.org.uk). Tottenham
Court Road tube.* **Open** 6.30am-10pm Mon-Fri; 10am-
8pm Sat; 10am-7pm Sun. **Map** p399 K5.
Conveniently located and user-friendly, the Y has a
good range of cardiovascular and weight-training
equipment, a pool and a squash court, as well as a
full timetable of excellently taught classes.

Jubilee Hall Leisure Centre
*30 The Piazza, Covent Garden, WC2E 8BE
(7836 4835/www.jubileehallclubs.co.uk). Covent*

Garden tube. **Open** 7am-10pm Mon-Fri; 9am-9pm
Sat; 10am-5pm Sun. **Map** p407 Z3.
A reliable and central venue that provides calm
surroundings for cardiovascular workouts.

Queen Mother Sports Centre
*223 Vauxhall Bridge Road, Victoria, SW1V 1EL
(7630 5522/www.courtneys.co.uk). Victoria tube/rail.*
Open 6.30am-10pm Mon-Fri; 8am-8pm Sat, Sun.
Map p400 J10.
The QM is a busy venue with a pool and decent
sweating and lifting facilities.

Soho Gym
*12 Macklin Street, Holborn, WC2B 5NF (7242 1290/
www.sohogyms.com). Holborn tube.* **Open** 7am-10pm
Mon-Fri; 8am-8pm Sat; noon-6pm Sun.
Busy and well-equipped, Soho Gym is notable for its
gay-friendly atmosphere.
Other locations 193 Camden High Street, NW1 7JY
(7482 4524); 95-97 Clapham High Street, SW4 7TB
(7720 0321); 254 Earl's Court Road, SW5 9AD (7370
1402); 11-15 Brad Street, SE1 8TG (0845 270 9270).

Westway Sports Centre
*1 Crowthorne Road, Ladbroke Grove, W10 6RP
(8969 0992/www.westway.org). Ladbroke Grove or
Latimer Road tube.* **Open** 8am-10pm Mon-Fri; 8am-
8pm Sat; 10am-10pm Sun.
A smart, diverse activity centre, with all-weather
pitches, tennis courts and the largest indoor climbing facility in the country.

Ice skating

Broadgate is London's only permanent outdoor
skating rink, but over recent years a variety of
temporary rinks have sprung up all over town –
Somerset House (*see p116*), **Hampton
Court Palace** (*see p186*) and **Kew Gardens**
(*see p183*) all provide spectacular backdrops.
Our favourite indoor year-round rink, **Queen's
Ice & Bowl** (17 Queensway, Bayswater, W2
4QP, 7229 0172, www.queensiceandbowl.co.uk),
is open 10am-11.30pm daily.

Riding

There are various riding stables in and around
the city; for a list of those approved by the
British Horse Society, see www.bhs.org.uk. The
following run classes for all ages and abilities.

Hyde Park & Kensington Stables
*63 Bathurst Mews, Lancaster Gate, W2 2SB
(7723 2813/www.hydeparkstables.com). Lancaster
Gate tube.* **Open** *Summer* 7.15am-5pm daily.
Winter 7.15am-3pm daily. **Fees** £49-£85/hr.
Map p395 D6.

Wimbledon Village Stables
*24 High Street, Wimbledon, SW19 5DX (8946
8579/www.wvstables.com). Wimbledon tube/rail.*
Open 9am-5pm Tue-Sun. **Fees** £45-£50/hr.

Silly season

Bored of paying through the nose to watch sporting prima donnas take themselves too seriously? Never fear, we have the answer.

February

February Fools Charity Cricket Match: Thespian XI v Broadcasters XI *Bank of England Sports Ground in Roehampton (Priory Lane, SW15 5JQ, 8876 8417).* Classic English foolhardiness as teams brave the weather to raise money for the Royal Marsden Hospital.

April

Motorsport Masters Historic Festival *Brands Hatch, Fawkham, Longfield, Kent DA3 8NG (01474 872331/www.motorsport vision.co.uk/brands-hatch).* Racing icons of yesteryear race Formula 1 cars from the 1970s and '80s.

July

Goodwood Festival of Speed *Goodwood, Chichester, West Sussex PO18 0PX (01243 755055/www.goodwood.co.uk/fos).* Historic vehicles compete in this hill climb.

Hendrick's Chap Olympics
Bedford Square Gardens, Bloomsbury, WC1 (www.thechap.net).
The estimable *Chap* periodical stages such decorum-upholding events as the martini knockout relay (where points can be deducted for the mere suggestion of vermouth).

Pimms Urban Regatta *Finsbury Square, EC2.* Dry-land 'racing' in bottomless boats, Fred Flintstone-style, in two- or four-person vessels. It's open to all, so visitors can turn up with their own customised boats.

Red Bull Air Race *O2 Arena (see p311; www.redbullairrace.com).*
Stunt-flying competition in which pilots race above the Thames through specially designed pylons known as 'air gates'.

Rollapaluza X *Waterloo Action Centre, 14 Baylis Road, SE1 7AA (www.rollapaluza.com).* Retro 1950s 'roller racing', in which two cyclists battle it out over a 500m sprint on a set of vintage rollers connected to a large clock, with different coloured hands for each rider.

September

Great River Race *Richmond to Island Gardens, Isle of Dogs (www.greatriverrace.co.uk).* For listings and review, *see p268.*

November

Unlimited Banger World Festival
Wimbledon Greyhound Stadium (see p325) Madcap, full-throttle action at the Wimbledon track, featuring all manner of eccentric motors.

Street sports

Baysixty6 Skate Park under the Westway in Acklam Road, W10, has a large street course and four halfpipes, all wooden and covered (8969 4669, www.baysixty6.com). Though **Stockwell Skate Park** (www.stockwellskatepark.com) is the city's most popular outdoor park, it's now rivalled by **Cantelowes Skatepark** (Cantelowes Gardens, Camden Road, NW1, www.cantelowesskatepark.co.uk), which opened in April 2007. Many prefer unofficial street spots such as the South Bank under the Royal Festival Hall. Skaters also collect at the **Sprite Urban Games** held on Clapham Common every July. Inliners should keep an eye on www.londonskaters.com for a diary of inline events across the city.

Swimming

To find your nearest pool check the Yellow Pages. For pools particularly well suited to children, check www.britishswimming.co.uk.

If alfresco swimming is more your thing, London still contains several **open-air lidos** at venues such as Parliament Hill Fields, the Serpentine, Tooting Bec and Brockwell Park, as well as the recently reopened London Fields Lido. The survival of such pools, and the reopening of some that had previously closed, is testament to the tireless work of the **London Pools Campaign**. See www.londonpools campaign.com for details, and a list of lidos.

Ironmonger Row Baths

Ironmonger Row, Finsbury, EC1V 3QF (7253 4011/ www.aquaterra.org). Old Street tube/rail. **Open** 6.30am-9pm Mon; 6.30am-8pm Tue-Thur; 6.30am-7pm Fri; 9am-5.30pm Sat; noon-5pm Sun. **Admission** £3.60; £1.60 reductions; free under-3s. A 31m pool with excellent lane swimming; the site also features good-value Turkish baths.

Oasis Sports Centre

32 Endell Street, Covent Garden, WC2H 9AG (7831 1804). Holborn tube. **Open** *Indoor* 6.30am-6.30pm Mon, Wed; 6.30am-5.30pm Tue; 6.30am-7pm Thur; 6.30am-4pm Fri; 9.30am-5pm Sat, Sun. *Outdoor* (lane swimming only) 7.30am-9pm Mon-Wed, Fri;

The sporting year

Athletics

Flora London Marathon
(see p265) Greenwich to the Mall. **Date** 13 Apr.

Norwich Union London Grand Prix
Crystal Palace National Sports Centre (see p323). **Date** 25 July (tbc). Big names turn out for this track and field event.

Australian rules football

AFL Challenge Trophy
Brit Oval (see p324). **Date** Oct. A yearly fixture for touring Australian sides.

Cricket

nPower Test Matches
Lord's (see p324). **Date** 15-19 May, 10-14 July.
Brit Oval (see p324). **Date** 7-11 Aug.

NatWest Series One-Day Internationals
Brit Oval. **Date** 25 June, 29 Aug.
Lord's. **Date** 28 June, 31 Aug.
This year England take on New Zealand (May-June), followed by South Africa (July-Aug).

Cycling

Tour of Britain
Date 7-14 Sept (tbc).

Join thousands on the streets of the capital for British cycling's biggest outdoor event.

Darts

Ladbrokes PDC World Darts Championship
Alexandra Palace (see p160). **Date** Dec-Jan. Widely regarded as of greater stature than the rival BDO World Darts Championship at Frimley Green (www.bdodarts.com) later in January.

Football

Carling Cup Final
Wembley Stadium (see p323). **Date** 24 Feb. The League Cup is now seen as the lesser of the country's domestic tournaments, though victory ensures a place in the UEFA Cup.

FA Cup Final
Wembley Stadium (see p323). **Date** 17 May. The climax of the historic knockout tournament with which Wembley is most famously associated.

Football League play-off finals
Wembley Stadium (see p323). **Date** 24-26 May. A promotion place is up for grabs for the winners of often enthralling end-of-season games between teams from the Championship and Leagues 1 and 2.

7.30am-8.30pm Thur; 9.30am-5.30pm Sat, Sun.
Admission £3.60; £1.40 reductions; free under-5s.
Renowned for its sun terrace and outdoor pool.

Tennis

Many parks around the city have council-run
courts that cost little or nothing to use. For
grass courts, phone the Lawn Tennis
Association's Information Department (8487
7000, www.lta.org.uk).

Islington Tennis Centre
*Market Road, Islington, N7 9PL (7700 1370/www.
aquaterra.org). Caledonian Road tube/Caledonian Road
& Barnsbury rail.* **Open** 7am-10pm Mon-Fri; 7am-9pm
Sat, Sun. **Court hire** *Indoor* £18.50; £12 reductions.
Outdoor £8.70; £6.80 reductions. **Credit** MC, V.
Non-members are welcome, but can only book a
maximum of five days in advance.

Ten-pin bowling

A useful first stop when looking for lanes is
the British Ten-pin Bowling Association (8478
1745, www.btba.org.uk). Less serious-minded
bowlers will do well to check out the more
nightlife-focused **All-Star Lanes** or its less
swanky counterpart **Bloomsbury Bowling
Lanes** (for both, *see p225*).

Rowans Bowl
*10 Stroud Green Road, Finsbury Park, N4 2DF
(8800 1950/www.rowans.co.uk). Finsbury Park
tube/rail or Crouch Hill rail.* **Open** 10.30am-12.30am
Mon-Thur, Sun; 10.30am-2.30am Fri, Sat.
Admission £1-£3/game. **Lanes** 24.

Yoga & Pilates

For something more substantial than just a
quick stretch in your hotel room, check out the
yoga activities and classes (and fully equipped
Pilates studio) at Triyoga. You may also want
to consult the **British Wheel of Yoga**
(www.bwy.org.uk).

Triyoga
*6 Erskine Road, Primrose Hill, NW3 3DJ (7483
3344/www.triyoga.co.uk). Chalk Farm tube.* **Open**
6am-10pm Mon-Fri; 8am-8.30pm Sat; 9am-9.30pm
Sun. **Cost** £11-£14/session.

Greyhound racing
Bigger events include the Arc in February and
the Victor Chandler Grand Prix in September
at Walthamstow; the William Hill Grand
National at Wimbledon in March; and the
Champion Stakes at Romford in July.

Horse racing
Epsom Derby Festival *Epsom Racecourse
(see p326).* **Date** 6-7 June.
One of Britain's key sporting events.

Royal Ascot *Ascot Racecourse (see p326).*
Date 17-21 June.
Major races include the Ascot Gold Cup, on
the Thursday, which is Ladies' Day. Expect
sartorial extravagance and fancy hats aplenty.

William Hill Tingle Creek Chase
Sandown (see p326). **Date** Nov.

Stan James Christmas Festival
Kempton Park (see p326). **Date** Dec.
The King George VI three-mile chase on
Boxing Day is the highlight of this festival.

Rowing
Boat Race *(see p265) Putney to Chiswick.*
Date 29 Mar.

Henley Royal Regatta *(see p267).*
Date 2-6 July.

Rugby league
Challenge Cup Final *Wembley Stadium
(see p323).* **Date** late Aug.
The north of England's big day out – clubs
from Lancashire and Yorkshire are dominant
– draws boisterous, convivial crowds.

Rugby union
Six Nations Championship *Twickenham
(see p326).* **Date** 2 Feb, 15 Mar.
England take on Wales, followed by Ireland.

EDF Energy Cup Final *Twickenham
(see p326).* **Date** 12 Apr.
The showpiece domestic knockout
competition reaches its climax.

Middlesex Sevens *Twickenham (see p326).*
Date Aug.
A curtain raiser to the season, featuring
short, fast seven-a-side matches.

Autumn international Test matches
Twickenham (see p326). **Date** Oct-Nov.

Tennis
Artois Tournament *Queen's Club (see p327).*
Date 9-15 June.

Wimbledon Championships
All-England Club, Wimbledon (see p327).
Date 23 June-6 July.

Theatre

All the world's on London's stages.

With pots of commercial and subsidised cash, cosmopolitan influences and increasing numbers of bums on seats, London is a true theatre capital. Its huge regional pull means most good UK productions end up here eventually. And it caters to all tastes – gay, straight, intellectual, in-yer-face or risibly sentimental, whatever wangs your twang.

Ever popular with punters are the musicals that illuminate – vibrantly or tackily, depending on your point of view – Piccadilly Circus and its surroundings. A recent craze for TV talent shows that audition hopefuls for roles in West End musicals seems to have run its course: however, reality-show winners are currently playing the lead in *The Sound of Music*, *Grease* and *Joseph & his Amazing Technicolor Dreamcoat*. The combination of songs, sets and choreography can be spectacular, but if you can get cut-price tickets at the last minute it can be a bad sign – better to book early, expecting to pay around £40.

Musicals have ruled the commercial sector for decades, but there are signs of a long-awaited return of serious theatre to non-subsidised West End theatre. At the Haymarket Theatre Royal, director Jonathan Kent is doing a whole 2007-08 season that includes Wycherley's Restoration comedy *The Country Wife*, Edward Bond's *The Sea* and a highbrow new musical based on *La Dame aux camélias* by Alexandre Dumas fils. For 2008-09 Donmar supremo Michael Grandage takes over Wyndham's Theatre for a season (*see p335* **Donmar marvels**).

Much excellent new European and American work finds its way to London. If your tastes are international, the Royal Court, the Barbican and the permanent programme of non-UK playwrights at Notting Hill's feisty little Gate Theatre are very good places to start.

London thesps are traditionally a left-wing lot and some of the best original recent drama has tackled the political issues of the day. Joe Penhall's *Landscape with Weapon*, which premièred at the National in 2007, investigated Western technological superiority and the concept of 'collateral damage' through the figure of an inventor of killer drones. The Tricycle has repeatedly called the government to account in transcript-based docu-dramas that double up as serious investigative journalism. And Caryl Churchill's new play *Drunk Enough*

to Say I Love You (which premièred at the Royal Court in 2006) played out the special relationship between the UK and America as a gay extra-marital affair on a flying sofa.

For the hippest theatregoers, site-specific, immersive and exploratory theatre is the leading edge of theatrical experience. Practitioners like Goat & Monkey or Punchdrunk – who take over 'found' spaces such as deserted warehouses and turn them into gloomy theatrical labyrinths, where masked theatregoers roam through sensational stage sets in search of the actors – are a cult phenomenon. Check the weekly theatre section of *Time Out* magazine to see what's current: it offers a brief but pertinent critique of every West End show running, as well as fuller reviews of the most intriguing Fringe and Off-West End shows.

WHERE TO GO AND WHAT TO SEE

In theatrical terms, the 'West End' is not strictly limited to the traditional theatre district, a bustling area bounded by Shaftesbury Avenue (home of the blockbuster) in the north, historic Drury Lane in the east, Haymarket in the west, and the Strand in the south. Most of London's musicals, big-money productions and transfers of successful smaller-scale shows end up here, though some of the city's best theatre takes place at innovative subsided venues like the South Bank's **National Theatre** and the **Royal Court** in Chelsea.

Off-West End denotes smaller budgets and smaller capacity. These theatres – many of which are sponsored or subsidised – push the creative envelope with new, experimental writing, often brought to life by the best acting and directing talent. The **Soho Theatre** and the **Bush** are good for up-and-coming playwrights, while the **Almeida** and **Donmar Warehouse** are safe bets for classy production values, sometimes with big international names. In north-west London the **Hampstead** and the **Tricycle** are very reliable.

Lurking under the Fringe moniker are dozens of smaller theatres, not always guaranteed to deliver quality, but supplied by a limitless number of hopefuls looking for their London stage debut. The area around and in the vaults underneath London Bridge Station is rapidly becoming home to some of the coolest fringe theatre. **Shunt Vaults** (7378 7776, www.shunt. co.uk), a members' club beneath the station, is a DJ-bar with live art and theatre installations (the 'day membership' scheme effectively means entry on the night for £5). The **Southwark Playhouse**, with experimental residents Goat & Monkey, has recently relocated to refurbished vaults nearby. Above ground, the **Menier Chocolate Factory** (51-53 Southwark Street, SE1 1TE, 7907 7060) is perhaps the classiest of them all, with accomplished production values and a restaurant attached – great for a glass of wine and food post-play. Out in Dalston, the **Arcola Theatre** (27 Arcola Street, E8 2DJ, 7503 1646) is worth the trek for new writing.

TICKETS AND INFORMATION
The first rule when buying tickets for London performances is to book ahead. The second rule is to bypass agents and, whenever possible, go direct to the theatre's box office. Booking agencies such as **Ticketmaster** (7344 4444, www.ticketmaster.co.uk) and **Keith Prowse** (0870 840 1111, www.keithprowse.com) sell tickets to many shows, but hit you with booking fees that could top 20 per cent. In a late bid to fill their venues, many West End theatres offer

Shunt Vaults.

reduced-price tickets for shows that have not sold out. These seats, available only on the night, are known as 'standby' tickets, and usually sell for about half the cost of a top-priced ticket. Always call to check the availability and conditions: some standby deals are limited to those with student ID, and when tickets go on sale varies. Reliable bargains are available at the National Theatre (Travelex sponsorship means that £10 tickets are available for many productions) and the Royal Court (on Cheap Mondays all tickets are available for a tenner; you can stand in the slips to watch any show in the Downstairs theatre for as little as 10p). **tkts**' cut-price booths are also worth a shot.

tkts
Clocktower Building, Leicester Square, Soho, WC2H 7NA (www.officiallondontheatre.co.uk). Leicester Square tube. **Open** *10am-7pm Mon-Sat; noon-3pm Sun.* **Credit** *AmEx, DC, MC, V.* **Map** *p407 X4.*
This non-profit organisation is run from Leicester Square by the Society of London Theatre, selling cut-price tickets for West End shows on a first come, first served basis on the day of performance. The Canary Wharf branch opens 11.30am-6pm Mon-Sat. **Other locations** Canary Wharf DLR, platforms 4/5.

West End

Barbican Centre
Silk Street, the City, EC2Y 8DS (0845 120 7550/ www.barbican.org.uk). Barbican tube/Moorgate tube/rail. **Box office** *9am-8pm daily.* **Tickets** *Barbican £7-£50. Pit £15.* **Credit** *AmEx, MC, V.* **Map** *p402 P5.*
The Barbican Centre hit the quarter-century mark in 2007, though thanks to a recent £14m facelift it isn't really showing its age. The annual BITE season (Barbican International Theatre Events) continues to cherry-pick exciting and eclectic theatre companies from around the globe: the Barbican's tiny Pit theatre hosts chic and atmospheric shorts, while the cross-cast Anglo-Russian Cheek By Jowl productions of *Three Sisters* and *Cymbeline* were a highlight of 2007 in the main house. Look out for more from Cheek By Jowl in May/June and Robert Lepage's *Lipsync*, a likely highlight of autumn 2008.

National Theatre
South Bank, SE1 9PX (information 7452 3400/ box office 7452 3000/www.nationaltheatre.org.uk). Embankment or Southwark tube/Waterloo tube/rail. **Box office** *9.30am-8pm Mon-Sat.* **Tickets** *Olivier & Lyttelton £10-£39.50. Cottesloe £10-£29.50.* **Credit** *AmEx, DC, MC, V.* **Map** *p401 M8.*
She's the concrete-clad, 1960s modernist grandmother of them all: no theatrical tour of London is complete without a visit to the National, whose three auditoriums and rolling repertory programme offer a choice of several productions in a single week. Nicholas Hytner's artistic directorship, with landmark successes such as Alan Bennett's *The*

Arts & Entertainment

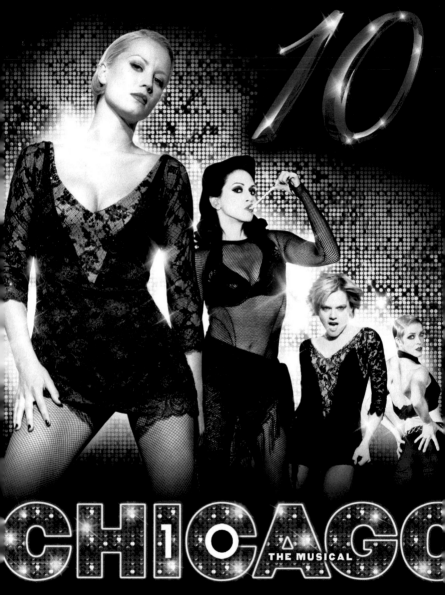

Celebrating a decade of decadence

10

CHICAGO
THE MUSICAL

Donmar marvels

Long-range theatrical predictions are about as reliable as long-range weather forecasts. But 2008 looks set to be the year of the **Donmar** (*see p340*). This classily converted 250-seater warehouse space in Covent Garden is dearly beloved – by virtue of its intimate stage, unfailingly intelligent productions and good-value tickets. In the last couple of years it's been responsible for sober, high-quality productions like *Frost/Nixon* (which transferred to the West End and Broadway). It's a favourite crossover spot for film actors to do serious stage-work. And it also has an edge of celebrity cool – Kate Moss got papped falling down the back steps after seeing Rhys Ifans star as *Don Juan of Soho* in Patrick Marber's cocaine-sprinkled rewrite of Molière's play.

In September 2008, the Donmar's redoubtable artistic director Michael Grandage will plant the Donmar's chic red and white flags in the West End, outside Wyndham's Theatre on Charing Cross Road, which the Donmar will take over for the year (while simultaneously staying open for business in Covent Garden). Wyndham's won't replicate the Donmar's intimacy, but Grandage is hoping to keep quality high and prices relatively low.

The 2008-09 season should fire a shot across the bows of commercial London theatre – not least because it's got some of the most bankable Britflick boys on board. The project was partly the brainchild of Kenneth Branagh, who will lead Chekhov's *Ivanov*, in a new translation by Tom Stoppard, directed by Grandage in September. At Christmas, Derek Jacobi will fulfil what's apparently a long-term ambition by squeezing himself into Malvolio's yellow stockings (cross-gartered) for *Twelfth Night*. The esoteric box is ticked by *Madame de Sade*, a play about the women behind the Marquis by Yukio Mishima – the Japanese writer as famous for his ritual suicide as his plays and poetry. Indeed, the only programming prospect likely to provoke disdainful critical sniffs could prove the most popular of all – in summer 2009 Jude Law will play the Dane in Kenneth Branagh's *Hamlet*.

History Boys, has shown that the state-subsidised home of British theatre can turn out quality drama at a profit. (*The History Boys* returns from Broadway in early 2008 to play across the river at Wyndham's.) The National looks set for a year of golden old boys, with *Oedipus the King* starring Ralph Fiennes and new plays by prestigious playwrights Michael Frayn and Sir David Hare. Hare also directs *The Year of Magical Thinking*, the acclaimed Broadway production of Joan Didion's one-woman play about mourning, starring Vanessa Redgrave. An upcoming collaboration between hip choreographer Akram Khan and Juliet Binoche offers extra youth appeal, as does the Travelex season, for which two-thirds of the seats are offered for £10. During summer the free outdoor performing arts stage called Watch This Space is a great way to see booty-shaking bhangra or fire-swallowing avant-gardists by the Thames.

Old Vic
Waterloo Road, Waterloo, SE1 8NB (0870 060 6628/www.oldvictheatre.com). Waterloo tube/rail. **Box office** 9am-9pm Mon-Sat. **Tickets** £12-£45. **Credit** AmEx, MC, V. **Map** p404 N9.
The combination of double-Oscar winner Kevin Spacey and top producer David Liddiment at this 200-year-old theatre continues to be a commercial success, if not a critical one. Spacey is a mesmerising stage (if not backstage) presence: look out for him in David Mamet's *Speed-the-Plow* (Feb-Apr).

Late spring 2008 heralds the first of Sam Mendes's *Bridge Projects*, an Anglo-American collaboration between Mendes, Spacey's Old Vic and Joseph V Melillo's Brooklyn Academy of Music. Expect Stephen Dillane as Hamlet and Prospero in Mendes's 2008 double bill, and Simon Russell Beale in *The Winter's Tale* and *The Cherry Orchard* in 2009.

Open Air Theatre
Regent's Park, NW1 4NR (7935 5756/box office 0870 060 1811/www.openairtheatre.org). Baker Street tube. **Tickets** £10-£35. **Credit** AmEx, MC, V. **Map** p398 G3.
The verdant setting of this alfresco theatre lends itself perfectly to summery Shakespeare romps in a season that runs from June to September. Standards are far above village green dramatics, with last year's delightful resurrection of old-school musical *The Boyfriend* showing that the diminutive stage need not cramp a production's style. Book well ahead and take an extra layer to fight chills during Act Three. If you don't want to bring a picnic, good-value, tasty grub can be bought on-site or you can eat at the funkily refurbed Garden Café.

Royal Court Theatre
Sloane Square, Chelsea, SW1W 8AS (7565 5000/ www.royalcourttheatre.com). Sloane Square tube. **Box office** 10am-6pm Mon-Sat. **Tickets** 10p-£25; all tickets £10 Mon. **Credit** AmEx, MC, V. **Map** p400 G11.

Arts & Entertainment

The Bard is back in town

When the RSC pulled out of its residency at the Barbican five years ago, it left a hole in the heart of London theatregoers. Summers are good for Shakespeare – groundlings at the **Globe** (*see right*) get an earthy experience in Elizabethan surroundings, and the London parks teem with fairies and ass-eared comedians. But after the Globe season's end in October, only the occasional RSC transfer to a commercial theatre – or the prospect of a long trip to Warwickshire with no return train home after the show – was left to cheer up the Shakespeare fan's winter of discontent. As if to rub it in, the dynamic RSC managed to perform Shakespeare's complete works in their 2006-07 season in Stratford-upon-Avon.

Thankfully, in 2008 the RSC is back with a bang, about a gallon of stage-gore and some spectacular rope-work, when the acknowledged highlight of the Complete Works season (artistic supremo Michael Boyd's own Histories Cycle) takes up residence at the **Roundhouse** (*see p311*) in April 2008. The eight History plays in the cycle include no Tom but pretty much every Dick and Harry, with *Henry VI* parts 1, 2 and 3, two *Henry IVs*, *Henry V*, *Richard II* and *Richard III*. What it all adds up to is a cycle of vicious family politicking, war and murder, in which our power-hungry royals outdo the Sopranos. And one ensemble plays all 264 parts – in practice, a lean and very meaningful way of embodying the bloody inheritances and ancestral ghosts that stain Shakespeare's portrait of a nation at war.

It is to be hoped that the RSC emerges victorious over the notorious Roundhouse reverb as well – it's so bad the company's actually rebuilding Stratford-upon-Avon's Courtyard Theatre inside the Roundhouse. Actors should be able to be heard as well as seen in the vaulting space, which has proved in the past to be brilliant for acrobatics but baffling for speeches.

The Courtyard in Stratford-upon-Avon, itself a temporary structure, will house a skeleton programme while the RSC's main theatres are closed for refurbishment; London audiences will have to wait and see if David Tennant's Hamlet (the *Doctor Who* star is directed by RSC associate Gregory Doran) transfers to the capital.

Meanwhile, Boyd has fulfilled his promise of commissioning new work from young dramatists who want to devise work with RSC actors and create epic pieces. The first fruits of these collaborations will be seen in London in 2008: at the **Tricycle** (*see p340*), Leo Butler's *I'll Be the Devil* and Roy Williams' *Days of Significance* will examine the corrupting influence of war on our lives, while the **Soho Theatre** (*see p340*) will be home for six weeks to a typically dark and wild new piece by Anthony Neilson (a richly maturing graduate of the 'in-yer-face' blood-and-jizz school of the 1990s), devised with 11 RSC actors. With all this on offer, it looks like this year it will be Stratford residents who are left cursing their train timetables.

A hard-hitting theatre in a well heeled location, the emphasis here has always been on new voices in British theatre – from John Osborne's *Look Back in Anger* in the inaugural year, 1956, to numerous discoveries over the past decade: Sarah Kane, Joe Penhall and Conor McPherson among them. New artistic director Dominic Cooke brought a political edge back in 2007, with a season that included Bruce Norris's swingeing satire on liberal complacency, *The Pain & the Itch*, and Ionesco's anti-conformist classic *Rhinoceros*. 2008 sees the return of the Court's works-in-progress season Rough Cuts, and more of the usual vividly produced British and international work by young writers. *Photo p339.*

Arts & Entertainment

Royal Shakespeare Company

Various venues including the New London Theatre, Roundhouse, Soho Theatre & Tricycle (01789 403444/box office 0844 800 1110/www.rsc.org.uk). **Box office** *By phone* 24hrs daily. **Tickets** £10-£45. **Credit** AmEx, MC, V.

The RSC has started massive reconstruction works on its main theatres in Stratford-upon-Avon. Bad news for them, but good news for London, as the capital will see the first fruits of Michael Boyd's RSC collaborations with living writers, as well as Boyd's Histories Cycle (*see left* **The Bard is back in town**).

Shakespeare's Globe

21 New Globe Walk, Bankside, SE1 9DT (7401 9919/ www.shakespeares-globe.org). Mansion House tube/ London Bridge tube/rail. **Box office** *Off season* 10am-5pm Mon-Fri. *Theatre* 10am-5pm daily. **Tickets** £5-£32. **Credit** AmEx, MC, V. **Map** p404 O7.

Sam Wanamaker's dream – to recreate the Bankside theatre where Shakespeare first staged many of his plays – has become a very successful reality, underpinned in part by the theatre's accomplished exhibition centre. Artistic director Dominic Dromgoole is an old hand of British theatre who is adamant that the Globe should showcase new writers alongside the Bard. The free-standing Pit tickets are excellent value, but the Heathrow flight path overhead can interrupt the peerless iambics.

Long-runners & musicals

Avenue Q

Noël Coward Theatre, St Martin's Lane, Covent Garden, WC2N 4BW (0870 850 9175/www. avenueqthemusical.co.uk). Leicester Square tube. **Box office** *In person* 10am-8pm Mon-Sat. *By phone* 24hrs daily. **Tickets** £10-£70. **Credit** AmEx, MC, V. **Map** p407 X3.

Sesame Street meets *South Park* in this Broadway smash, where the puppet and human residents of a down-at-heel New York share amusing songs and a cynical sense of humour. Highlights include 'If You Were Gay', 'The Internet is for Porn' – and one number in which a Japanese woman memorably informs us 'Everyone's a rittle bit lacist.'

Billy Elliot the Musical

Victoria Palace Theatre, Victoria Street, Victoria, SW1E 5EA (0870 895 5577/www.victoriapalace theatre.co.uk). Victoria tube/rail. **Box office** 10am-8.30pm Mon-Sat. **Tickets** £17.50-£55. **Credit** AmEx, MC, V. **Map** p400 H10.

Set during the miner's strike of 1984, this story of a working-class northern boy with balletic talent burning in his shoes transfers well from screen to stage, scored by Elton John and directed by Stephen Daldry.

Chicago

Cambridge Theatre, Earlham Street, Covent Garden, WC2H 9HU (0870 890 1102/www.cambridge theatre.co.uk). Covent Garden or Leicester Square tube. **Box office** *Seetickets* 24hrs daily. **Tickets** £17.50-£49. **Credit** MC, V. **Map** p407 Y2.

The jailbird roles are passed at regular intervals from one blonde TV star to the next, but this production still razzles and dazzles with high spirits.

Dirty Dancing

Aldwych Theatre, Aldwych, Covent Garden, WC2B 4DF (0870 400 0845/www.dirtydancinglondon.com). Covent Garden/Charing Cross tube/rail. **Box office** *In person* 10am-8pm daily. *By phone* 24hrs daily. **Tickets** £25-£60. **Credit** AmEx, MC, V. **Map** p399 M6.

With its raunchy choreography, archetypal ugly duckling story and powerful hit of nostalgia for '80s kids, it's no wonder *Dirty Dancing* took record advance bookings – so book well ahead.

Les Misérables

Queen's Theatre, Shaftesbury Avenue, Soho, W1D 6BA (7494 5040/www.lesmis.com/www.delfont mackintosh.co.uk). Leicester Square or Piccadilly Circus tube. **Box office** *In person* 10am-8pm Mon-Sat. *Seetickets* 24hrs daily. **Tickets** £15-£55. **Credit** AmEx, MC, V. **Map** p406 W3.

It's 21 years and counting since the RSC's version of Boublil and Schönberg's musical came to the London stage. When you've been singing these songs since your first audition, it's easy to take it that half-inch too far. Still, the voices are lush, the revolutionary sets are film-fabulous, and the lyrics and score (based on Victor Hugo's novel) will be considerably less chirpy than whatever's on next door.

Mamma Mia!

Prince of Wales Theatre, 31 Coventry Street, Soho, W1D 6AS (0870 850 0393/www.mamma-mia.com/ www.delfontmackintosh.co.uk). Leicester Square or Piccadilly Circus tube. **Box office** *In person* 10am-8pm Mon-Sat. *By phone* 24hrs daily. **Tickets** £27.50-£55. **Credit** AmEx, MC, V. **Map** p406 W4.

This feel-good musical links Abba's hits into a continuous but spurious story. Deathlessly popular.

Mousetrap

St Martin's Theatre, West Street, Cambridge Circus, Covent Garden, WC2H 9NH (0870 162 8787/www. vpsmvaudsav.co.uk). Leicester Square tube. **Box office** 10am-8pm Mon-Sat. **Tickets** £13.50-£37.50. **Credit** AmEx, MC, V. **Map** p407 X3.

This is the longest long-runner of them all: Agatha Christie's drawing-room whodunnit is a murder mystery Methuselah, and will probably still be booking when the last trump sounds.

Phantom of the Opera

Her Majesty's Theatre, corner of Haymarket & Charles II Street, St James's, SW1Y 4QR (0870 534 4444/www.reallyuseful.com). Piccadilly Circus tube. **Box office** *By phone* 24hrs daily. **Tickets** £25-£55. **Credit** AmEx, MC, V. **Map** p406 W5.

Once upon a time, if you threw a stone on Shaftesbury Avenue you'd hit an Andrew Lloyd Webber musical. The millionaire knight has fewer fluorescent lights in the West End now, but *Phantom* remains a beacon to those in search of madness, gothic tragedy, lavish sets and great love songs with loads of vibrato.

Arts & Entertainment

Spamalot

Palace Theatre, Cambridge Circus, Soho, W1D 5AY (0870 895 5579/www.montypythonsspamalot.com). Leicester Square tube. **Box office** *In person* 10am-8pm Mon-Sat. *By phone* 24hrs daily. **Tickets** £15-£60. **Credit** AmEx, MC, V. **Map** p407 X3.

The Tony Award-winning musical based on the lunacy that is *Monty Python & the Holy Grail*. All together now: 'We're knights of the Round Table/ We dance whene'er we're able/We do routines and chorus scenes/With footwork impec-cable…'.

Wicked

Apollo Victoria, Wilton Road, Victoria, SW1V 1LL (0870 400 0751/www.wickedthemusical.co.uk). Victoria tube/rail. **Box office** *In person* 10am-8pm Mon-Sat. *By phone* 24hrs daily. **Tickets** £15-£55. **Credit** AmEx, MC, V. **Map** p400 H10.

This hugely popular musical prequel to *The Wizard of Oz* reveals how the Wicked Witch of the West wasn't wicked at all, more a defender of those the Wizard sought to oppress. Focused on the on-off friendship between teenage prom queen Glinda ('the Good') and green-skinned radical Elphaba, it benefits from enjoyably sly wit, some serious lung-power and terrifying flying monkeys.

Off-West End

Almeida

Almeida Street, Islington, N1 1TA (7359 4404/www. almeida.co.uk). Angel tube. **Box office** *In person* 10am-6pm Mon-Sat. *By phone* 24hrs daily. **Tickets** £6-£29.50. **Credit** AmEx, MC, V. **Map** p402 O1.

Well groomed and with a funky bar, the Almeida turns out thoughtfully crafted theatre for grown-ups. Under artistic director Michael Attenborough it has drawn top directors like Howard Davies and Richard Eyre, and world premières.

BAC (Battersea Arts Centre)

Lavender Hill, Battersea, SW11 5TN (7223 2223/ www.bac.org.uk). Clapham Common tube/Clapham Junction rail/77, 77A, 345 bus. **Box office** *In person* 10am-6pm Mon-Fri; 2-6pm Sat. *By phone* 10am-6pm Mon-Fri; 2-6pm Sat. **Tickets** £5-£10; 'pay what you can' Tue (phone ahead). **Credit** MC, V.

The forward-thinking BAC, which inhabits the old Battersea Town Hall, plays alma mater to new writers and theatre companies – expect the very latest in quirky, fun and physical theatre. Artistic director David Jubb started up the famous Scratch programme, which shows a work in progress to larger and larger audiences until it's finished and polished. Over the next five years he aims to transform BAC into a radical promenade performance space. Autumn 2007 saw the first of the Playground Projects: cult theatre company Punchdrunk turned the Victorian municipal building into a Poe-inspired nightmare, with masked audience members searching out performers through a labyrinth of spooky sets.

Bush

Shepherd's Bush Green, Shepherd's Bush, W12 8QD (7610 4224/www.bushtheatre.co.uk). Goldhawk Road or Shepherd's Bush tube. **Box office** *In person* 5-8pm Mon-Sat (performance nights only). *By phone* 10am-7pm Mon-Sat. **Tickets** £10-£15. **Credit** AmEx, MC, V.

Arts & Entertainment

The **Royal Court Theatre** defies genteel surroundings with edgy new work. *See p335.*

A small, cash-poor champion of new writers and performers, the Bush has over 30 years' experience under its belt. Alumni include Stephen Poliakoff, Mike Leigh and Jim Broadbent, so watch that space.

Donmar Warehouse

41 Earlham Street, Covent Garden, WC2H 9LX (0870 060 6624/www.donmarwarehouse.com). Covent Garden or Leicester Square tube. **Box office** *In person* 10am-7.30pm Mon-Sat. *By phone* 9am-9pm Mon-Sat; 10am-6pm Sun. **Tickets** £12-£30. **Credit** AmEx, MC, V. **Map** p407 Y2.

The Donmar is less a warehouse than an intimate chamber. Artistic director Michael Grandage has kept the venue on a fresh, intelligent path, and will be running a dual season in the West End in 2008-09 (*see p335* **Donmar marvels**).

Drill Hall

16 Chenies Street, Bloomsbury, WC1E 7EX (7307 5060/www.drillhall.co.uk). Goodge Street tube. **Box office** 10am-9.30pm Mon-Sat; 10am-6pm Sun. **Tickets** £5-£17.50. **Credit** AmEx, MC, V. **Map** p399 K5.

Polyfunctional (it's a theatre, cabaret, gig venue and photo studio) and polysexual, Drill Hall is London's biggest gay and lesbian theatre.

Gate Theatre

Above the Prince Albert, 11 Pembridge Road, Notting Hill, W11 3HQ (7229 0706/www.gate theatre.co.uk). Notting Hill Gate tube. **Box office** *By phone* 10am-6pm Mon-Fri. **Tickets** £15; £10 reductions. **Credit** MC, V. **Map** p394 A7.

A doll's house of a theatre, with rickety wooden chairs as seats, the Gate devotes itself to foreign drama, often in specially commissioned translations.

Hampstead Theatre

Eton Avenue, Swiss Cottage, NW3 3EU (7722 9301/ www.hampsteadtheatre.com). Swiss Cottage tube. **Box office** 9am-7pm Mon-Sat. **Tickets** £10-£22. **Credit** MC, V.

This purpose-built space, opened in 2004, gave a home to one of the city's most reliable theatres. Its programme of fresh British and international playwrights is astute but accessible. For new artists, it organises Start Nights in which performers have 15 minutes to show off a slice of rehearsed material in the 80-seater Michael Frayn Space.

King's Head Theatre

115 Upper Street, Islington, N1 1QN (7226 1916/ www.kingsheadtheatre.org). Angel tube. **Box office** 10am-7.30pm daily. **Tickets** £10-£20. **Credit** MC, V. **Map** p402 N2.

Started in the 1970s on a spectacularly lean budget, London's first pub theatre is a tiny space tucked away at the back of a charming, if ramshackle, Victorian boozer. In the past it has launched a raft of stars, among them Hugh Grant; recently, Mick Jagger's son James made a promising stage debut in a double bill of Vietnam War comedies. It is also a favourite crossover spot for television actors to exercise their comedy muscles.

Lyric Hammersmith

Lyric Square, King Street, Hammersmith, W6 0QL (0870 050 0511/www.lyric.co.uk). Hammersmith tube. **Box office** 10am-6pm Mon-Sat; 10am-8pm performance nights. **Tickets** £7-£27. **Credit** MC, V.

The Lyric has a knack for vibrant, offbeat scheduling. It also offers good kids' theatre. Artistic director David Farr enjoys experimenting and in spring 2008 the Frank Matcham auditorium will be disguised as a run-down African theatre for a Mugabe-influenced production of Brecht's *The Resistible Rise of Arturo Ui*. Look out for site-specific shows on the terrace.

Soho Theatre

21 Dean Street, Soho, W1D 3NE (7478 0100/ box office 0870 429 6883/www.sohotheatre.com). Tottenham Court Road tube. **Box office** *In person* 10am-6pm Mon-Sat; 10am-7.30pm performance nights. **Tickets** £5-£20. **Credit** MC, V. **Map** p397 K6.

Its cool blue neon lights, front-of-house café and occasional late-night shows may blend it into the Soho landscape, but since taking up residence on Dean Street in 2000 this theatre has made quite a name for itself. It attracts a younger, hipper crowd than most theatres, and brings on aspiring writers with a free script-reading service and regular workshops.

Theatre Royal Stratford East

Gerry Raffles Square, Stratford, E15 1BN (8534 0310/www.stratfordeast.com). Stratford tube/rail/ DLR. **Box office** 10am-7pm Mon-Sat. **Tickets** £10-£20. **Credit** MC, V.

A community theatre with many shows written, directed and performed by black or Asian artists. Musicals are big here – whether about hip hop culture or the Windrush generation of immigrants.

Tricycle

269 Kilburn High Road, Kilburn, NW6 7JR (7328 1000/www.tricycle.co.uk). Kilburn tube. **Box office** 10am-9pm Mon-Sat; 2-9pm Sun. **Tickets** £8.50-£23. **Credit** MC, V.

Passionate and political, the Tricycle consistently finds original ways into difficult subjects. In the last few years it has pioneered 'tribunal' docu-dramas – transcript-based theatre that investigates highly political subjects, such as the murder of black teenager Stephen Lawrence, the Hutton Inquiry and Guantanamo Bay. The centre also has a buzzy bar.

Young Vic

66 The Cut, Waterloo, SE1 8LZ (7928 6363/www. youngvic.org). Waterloo tube/rail. **Box office** 10am-6pm Mon-Sat. **Tickets** £10-£24.50. **Credit** MC, V. **Map** p404 N8.

The Young Vic finally returned to its refurbished home in the Cut in 2007 with acclaimed community-based show *Tobias & the Angel*. As you would expect, it's got more verve and youthful nerve than its grown-up sibling across the road, and has fared better critically as well. Director David Lan's eclectic programming of rediscovered European classics (exemplified by 2007's bite-sized Big Brecht Fest) has proved especially popular with critics.

Arts & Entertainment

Trips Out of Town

Dungeness. *See p350.*

Trips Out of Town

Seaside, countryside and another side of life are all within reach.

Though London contains enough to occupy a lifetime, even the most enthusiastic visitor could be forgiven for occasionally wanting out. Fortunately, for those who make the break, there are many wonders to behold only an hour or so from the capital. We've picked five outstanding destinations each with their own particular appeal. Three of them are beside the seaside, though they could hardly be more different: Brighton is the easiest of the five to reach by train, with its breezy boho credentials and full-on nightlife; Dungeness, Romney and Rye amply reward the effort required to reach them – in fact, fairly simple by car – with their other-worldly atmosphere, cranky charm and weird maritime light; Chichester and Arundel are both accessible by train but best explored by car, offering Roman remains, a very fine cathedral, and a fairytale castle set amid the rolling splendours of the South Downs. Nestling in the lee of the North Downs, Canterbury is a medieval city embracing the mother church of Anglicanism. Woodstock, easily reached by bus from Oxford, is a charming town on the edge of the pretty Cotswolds hills, its main claim to fame being Blenheim, the only non-royal home in the country grand enough to call itself a palace. For the main attractions, we've included details of opening times, admission and transport, but be aware that these can change without notice: always phone to check. Major sights are open all through the year, but many of the minor ones close from November to March. Before setting out, drop in on the **Britain & London Visitor Centre** (*see p374*). More ideas for these areas and a score of others can be found in *Time Out Weekend Breaks in Great Britain & Ireland*.

Getting there

By train

For information on train times and ticket prices, call National Rail Enquiries on **0845 748 4950**. Ask about the cheapest ticket for the journey you are planning, and be aware that for long journeys the earlier you book, the cheaper the ticket. If you need extra help, there are rail travel centres in London's main-line stations, as well as Heathrow and Gatwick airports. These can give you guidance for things like timetables

and booking. We specify the departure station(s) in the 'Getting there' section for each destination; the journey times cited there are the fastest available. The website **www.virgin trains.co.uk** gives timetable information for any British train company. You can buy your tickets online for any train operator in the UK via **www.thetrainline.com**.

By coach

National Express (0870 580 8080, www.nationalexpress.com) coaches travel throughout the country and depart from Victoria Coach Station (*see below*), ten minutes' walk from Victoria rail and tube stations. **Green Line Travel** (0870 608 7261) also runs coaches.

Victoria Coach Station

164 Buckingham Palace Road, Victoria, SW1W 9TP (7730 3466/www.tfl.gov.uk). Victoria tube/rail. **Map** p400 G11.
Britain's most comprehensive coach company, National Express (*see above*), is based at Victoria Coach Station, as are many other companies that operate to Europe (some depart from Marble Arch).

By car

If you're in a group of three or four, it may be cheaper to hire a car (*see p362*), especially if you plan to take in several sights within an area. The road directions given in the listings below should be used in conjunction with a proper map.

By bicycle

Capital Sport (01296 631671, www.capital-sport.co.uk) offers gentle cycling tours along the Thames from London. Leisurely itineraries include plenty of time to explore royal palaces, parks and historic attractions. Or you could try **Country Lanes** (www.countrylanes.co.uk), who lead cycling tours of the New Forest in Hampshire (01590 622627/0845 370 0668).

Brighton

Britain's youngest city, England's most popular tourist destination after London, and every May host to the nation's biggest annual arts festival outside Edinburgh, Brighton is thriving. A welter of exciting new projects are reaching

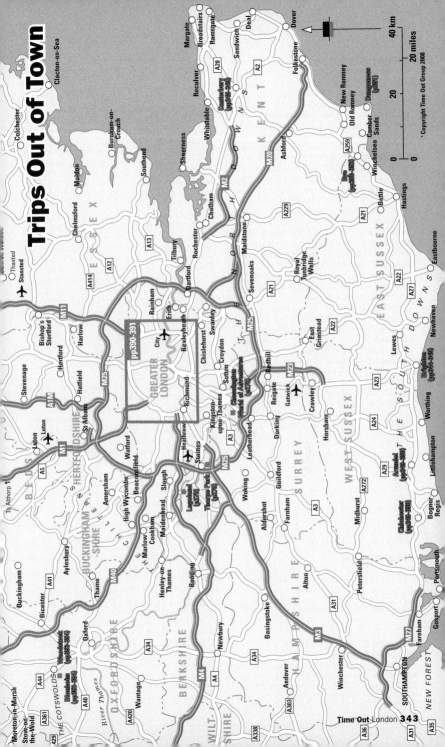

Trips Out of Town

* Copyright Time Out Group 2008

40 km
20 miles

ESSEX

Thaxted
Stansted
Bishop's Stortford
Harlow
Hertford
Stevenage
Hatfield
St Albans
Luton
ATM
BEDS
To Althorp

Colchester
Clacton-on-Sea
Maldon
Burnham-on-Crouch
Chelmsford
Southend
Tilbury
A13
A414
A12

GREATER LONDON
pp390-391

Rainham
Erith
City
Bexleyheath
Swanley
Chislehurst
Croydon
Sutton
Richmond
Kingston-upon-Thames
Leatherhead
Chessington World of Adventures (p276)
Heathrow
Staines
M25

Dartford
Rochester
Chatham
Sheerness
Whitstable
Reculver
Canterbury (pp345-349)
Margate
Broadstairs
Ramsgate
Sandwich
Deal
Dover
Folkestone
New Romney
Old Romney
Dungeness (p361)
Camber Sands
Winchelsea
Rye (pp358-359)
A28
A2
A259
A20
M20
M2
KENT
THE NORTH DOWNS
Maidstone
Sevenoaks
Royal Tunbridge Wells
A229
A21
A26
A22

Battle
Hastings
Eastbourne
Newhaven
Lewes
Brighton (pp354-357)
Worthing
Littlehampton
Bognor Regis
Arundel (pp350-351)
Chichester (pp352-353)
EAST SUSSEX
WEST SUSSEX
THE SOUTH DOWNS
A27
A22
A23
A24
A29
A272
A259
A21

East Grinstead
Crawley
Gatwick
Reigate
Redhill
M23
Dorking
Horsham
Midhurst
Petersfield
Guildford
Woking
Aldershot
Farnham
Alton
SURREY
HAMPSHIRE
A3
M25

Buckingham
Bicester
Aylesbury
Thame
Oxford
Woodstock (pp363-364)
Blenheim (pp365-366)
Moreton-in-Marsh
Stow-on-the-Wold
THE COTSWOLDS
A41
A44
A361
A429
A40
A420
A34
OXFORDSHIRE
BUCKINGHAMSHIRE
Amersham
High Wycombe
Beaconsfield
Marlow
Cookham
Henley-on-Thames
Maidenhead
Slough
Reading
Legoland (p276)
Thorpe Park (p276)
CHILTERNS
M40
M4

Watford
Luton
A5
M1
HERTFORDSHIRE
M11

Newbury
Basingstoke
Andover
Winchester
Southampton
Fareham
Gosport
Portsmouth
NEW FOREST
BERKSHIRE
WILTSHIRE
A34
A4
A303
A338
A36
A31
A35
A27
M3
M27
River Thames
Wantage

fruition (*see p348* **Boomtown Brighton**), but novelty is nothing new to Brighton. It began life as Brighthelmstone, a small fishing village, and so it remained until 1783, when the future George IV transformed it into a fashionable retreat. He kept the architect John Nash busy converting a modest abode into a faux-oriental pleasure palace. That building is now the **Royal Pavilion** (*see below*). Next door, the **Brighton Museum & Art Gallery** (Royal Pavilion Gardens, 01273 292882) has entertaining displays and a good permanent art collection. Only two of Brighton's three Victorian piers are still standing. Lacy, delicate **Brighton Pier** is a clutter of hot-dog stands, karaoke and fairground rides, filled with customers in the summertime. With seven miles of coastline, Brighton has all the traditional seaside resort trappings, hence the free **Brighton Fishing Museum** (201 King's Road Arches, on the lower prom between the piers, 01273 723064) and the **Sea-Life Centre** (*see below*), the world's oldest functioning aquarium.

Perhaps reflecting its singular character, the town has a huge number of independent shops, boutiques and art stores. The best shopping for clothes, records and gifts is found in and around **North Laine** and in the charming network of narrow cobbled streets known as the **Lanes**. A gay hub, a major international student town and child-friendly with it, Brighton still welcomes weekend gaggles of devil-horn-sporting hen parties, ravers, nudists, discerning vegetarians, surfers, sunseekers and all-round wastrels. Many are satisfied to tumble from station to seafront, calling in at a couple of bars down the hill before plunging on to the pier or the pebbles. But to get the best out of Brighton, seek out its unusual little pockets: the busy gay quarter of Kemp Town; the savage drinking culture of Hanover; and the airy terraces of Montpelier. Although hilly, all of the city is readily accessible by an award-winning bus network, with an all-night service on main lines.

Royal Pavilion

Brighton, BN1 1EE (01273 292820/www.royal pavilion.org.uk). **Open** *Apr-Sept* 9.30am-5.45pm daily. *Oct-Mar* 10am-5.15pm daily. *Tours* by appointment. Last entry 45mins before closing. **Admission** £7.70; £5.90 reductions; £5.10 under-16s; £6.70 groups 20+; free under-5s. **Credit** AmEx, MC, V.

Sea-Life Centre

Marine Parade, BN2 1TB (01273 604234/www. sealifeeurope.com). **Open** *Mar-Sept* 10am-6pm daily (last admission 5pm). *Oct-Feb* 10am-5pm (last admission 4pm). **Admission** £12.95; £8.95 reductions; free under-3s. **Credit** AmEx, MC, V.

Where to eat & drink

Brighton offers a ridiculous amount of dining possibilities for a town of its size. A handful, though, would hold their head up in any city in the UK. **One Paston Place** (1 Paston Place, 01273 606933, www.onepastonplace.co.uk) has a metropolitan buzz. The food is exquisite and presented by experienced, unstuffy staff eager to advise. **Gingerman** (21A Norfolk Square, 01273 326688, www.gingermanrestaurants.com) offers top-quality continental – mainly French – cuisine at accessible prices. **Seven Dials** (1-3 Buckingham Place, 01273 885555, www. sevendialsrestaurant.co.uk) – located in a former bank – does two- and three-course deals. **Terre à Terre** (71 East Street, 01273 729051, www.terreaterre.co.uk) is Brighton's reliably inventive flagship vegetarian restaurant. **La Capannina** (15 Madeira Place, 01273 680839) is hands down the best Italian in town, doing a set lunch at £8.95 for two courses. The most talked about fairly recent arrivals have been the ambitious and accomplished champagne and oyster bar **Riddle & Finns** (12B Meeting House Lane, 01273 323008, www.riddleand finns.co.uk, main courses £10-£30), and the stylish tapas bar **Pintxo People** (95 Western Road, 01273 732323, www.pintxopeople.co.uk, main courses £3-£14).

Of the city's countless drinking holes, **Brighton Rocks** (6 Rock Place, 01273 601139, www.brighton-rocks.com) is Kemp Town's most talked-up small bar, with a heated terrace, sparkling cocktails and superb organic cuisine. Of the pubs, the **Hand in Hand** (33 Upper St James Street, 01273 699595), is, in fact, neither a throbbing gay den of iniquity nor an indie student haunt, but a small, traditional boozer that attracts an older, discerning clientele thanks to its outstanding range of ales. The **Lion & Lobster** (24 Sillwood Street, 01273 327299) is a wonderful, wonderful little pub with a fine vibe, cool and communal. The **Sidewinder** (65 Upper St James Street, 01273 679927) is a pre-club bar with DJs. **Ali-Cats** (80 East Street, 01273 748103), the **Hampton** (57 Upper North Street 01273 731347) and **Riki-Tik** (18A Bond Street, 01273 683844) are also reliable bets for a good night out. Of the gay bars, the most fun is to be had at the **Amsterdam Hotel** (11-12 Marine Parade, 01273 688826, www.amsterdam.uk.com). **Doctor Brighton's** (16 King's Road, 01273 328765), on the seafront, is also worth a punt, with DJs playing house and techno. And lastly, but by no means least, one for the ladeeez... the **Candy Bar** (129 St James Street, 01273 622424, www.thecandybar.co.uk) is a strictly women-only lesbian hangout.

Where to stay

Given Brighton's popularity with tourists, it's perhaps not surprising that hotel prices can be on the high side. **Drakes** (43-44 Marine Parade, 01273 696934, www.drakesofbrighton.com, doubles £95-£300) is the latest of Brighton's high-end designer hotels. All 20 rooms have been individually created and the in-house restaurant is run by the best chef in town, Ben McKellar of Gingerman fame (*see above*). An interesting choice is the **Alias Hotel Seattle** (Brighton Marina, 01273 679799, www.aliashotels.com, doubles £125-£180), which is situated on the recently developed Brighton Marina and feels much like a state-of-the-art liner. **Blanch House** (17 Atlingworth Street, 01273 603504, www.blanchhouse.co.uk, doubles £130-£230) is a wonderfully conceived hotel, cocktail bar and restaurant. An unassuming Georgian terrace house with a dozen rooms themed after snowstorms, plus roses, rococo decor and a 1970s disco. **Nineteen** (19 Broad Street, 01273 675529, www.hotelnineteen.co.uk, doubles £80-£250) has just seven rooms in a stylish townhouse, and is one of the most pampering of Kemp Town's boutique hotels. Another good quality stop is **Hotel du Vin** (2-6 Ship Street, 01273 718588,www.hotelduvin.com, doubles £150-£410), which also has an estimable restaurant. The **Amherst** (2 Lower Rock Gardens, 01273 670131, www.amhersthotel.co.uk, doubles £90-£130) is one of the best bargains among new contemporary hotels, while the **George IV** (34 Regency Square, 01273 321196, www.georgeiv .hotel.co.uk, doubles £80-£150) is surely the best bargain with a sea view in the city.

Getting there

By train

Trains for Brighton leave from Victoria (50mins; map p400 H10) or King's Cross/London Bridge (1hr 10mins; map p399 L2/3).

By coach

National Express coaches for Brighton leave from Victoria Coach Station (1hr 50mins).

By car

Take A23, the M23, then the A23 again to Brighton (approx 1hr 20mins).

Tourist information

Tourist Information Centre

10 Bartholomew Square, Brighton, East Sussex, BN1 1JS (0906 711 2255/www.visitbrighton.com). **Open** *Summer* 10am-5pm Mon-Sat; 10am-4pm Sun. *Winter* 10am-5pm Mon-Sat.

Canterbury

The home of the Church of England since St Augustine was based here in 597, the ancient city of Canterbury is rich in atmosphere. Gaze up at its soaring spires, or around you at the enchanting medieval streets, and you'll soon feel blessed, even if you're not an Anglican. Its busy tourist trade and large university provide a colourful counterweight to the brooding mass of history present in its old buildings and, of course, the glorious **Canterbury Cathedral** (*see p347*), at its most inspirational just before dusk, especially if there is music going on within and the coach parties are long gone. Be prepared to shell out for entry, but it's well worth it. The cathedral has superb stained glass, stone vaulting and a vast Norman crypt. A plaque near the altar marks what is believed to be the exact spot where Archbishop Thomas à Becket was murdered. The Trinity Chapel contains the site of the original shrine, plus the tombs of Henry IV and the Black Prince. A pilgrimage to Becket's tomb was the focus of one of the earliest and finest long poems in all English literature, Geoffrey Chaucer's *Canterbury Tales* written in the 14th century. At the exhibition named after the book (*see p347*), visitors are given a device that they point at tableaux inspired by Chaucer's tales of a knight, a miller, a Wife of Bath, and others, enabling them to hear the stories.

Just down the road from Christ Church Gate, the **Royal Museum & Art Gallery** (High Street, 01227 452747) is a monument to high Victorian values. Permanent exhibitions include the national collection of the art of Thomas Sidney Cooper, the cattle painter, as well as work by Van Dyck, Gainsborough, Sickert and Epstein. Admission is free.

Eastbridge Hospital (25 High Street, 01227 471688), founded to provide shelter for pilgrims, retains the smell of ages past. Visitors can tour the hospital and admire the undercroft with its Gothic arches, the Chantry Chapel, the Pilgrims' Chapel and the refectory with an enchanting early 13th-century mural showing Christ in Majesty (there's only one other like this, in France). The **Roman Museum** (*see p347*) has the remains of a townhouse and mosaic floor among its treasures, augmented with reconstructions, computer reconstructions and time tunnels. From here you also get a super view of the cathedral tower. After the Romans comes **St Augustine**, or at least the ruins of the abbey he had built (Longport, 01227 767345, www.english-heritage.org.uk), now in the capable hands of English Heritage, which has attached a small museum and shop to the site. Everything you want to see, do or buy in

Canterbury is within walking distance, even the seaside – if you fancy a long (seven-mile) walk or cycle along the Crab and Winkle Way, a disused railway line to Whitstable, with its exceptional oysters.

Canterbury Cathedral

The Precincts, CT1 2EH (01227 762862/ www.canterbury-cathedral.org.uk). **Open** *Easter-Sept* 9am-5pm Mon-Sat; 12.30-2pm Sun. *Oct-Easter* 9am-4.30pm Mon-Sat; 12.30-2pm Sun. Admission restricted during services and special events. **Admission** £6.50; £5 reductions; free under-5s. **Credit** MC, V.

Canterbury Tales

St Margaret's Street, CT1 2TG (01227 454888/ 479227/www.canterburytales.org.uk). **Open** *Mid Feb-June, Sept, Oct* 10am-5pm daily. *July, Aug* 9.30am-5pm daily. *Nov-mid Feb* 10am-4.30pm daily. **Admission** £7.50; £5.50-£6.25 reductions; free under-4s. **Credit** MC, V.

Roman Museum

Butchery Lane, CT1 2JR (01227 785575/www. canterbury-museums.co.uk). **Open** *Nov-May* 10am-5pm Mon-Sat. *June-Oct* 10am-5pm Mon-Sat; 1.30-5pm Sun. Last entry 1hr before closing. **Admission** £3.10; £1.95 reductions; free under-5s. **Credit** MC, V.

Where to eat & drink

Michael Caines has brought a touch of Michelin glamour to the Canterbury eating scene. As well as his Fine Dining restaurant and champagne bar at his hotel **ABode** (*see below*), there's also his **Old Brewery Tavern** (High Street, 01227 826682, www.michaelcaines.com), where huge black and white prints of grizzled coopers rolling barrels hang on the walls. The MC OB doesn't look like a traditional boozer (far too trendy) but it also shies away from gastropub cliché. The food is solid and comforting – leek and potato soup, Romney Marsh lamb, fish and chips – but there are lighter numbers, such as fish pie and mixed meze. The **Goods Shed** (Station Road West, 01227 459153, main courses £10-£18) occupies a lofty Victorian building, formerly a railway freight store. On a raised wooden platform diners sit at scrubbed tables and choose from the specials chalked up on the board. Only ingredients on sale in the farmers' market below them are used in the restaurant. For people who care about their food and its provenance, this is heaven. **Café des Amis du Mexique** (93-95 St Dunstan's Street, 01227 464390, main courses £7.95-£24.95) is upbeat and also very popular. Pub wise, Canterbury is in thrall to its students, who take over the West Gate Inn Wetherspoons when they're tired of drinking on campus. Most of the better pubs are owned by Shepherd Neame (the local

brewery up the road in Faversham), and the best both happen to be in St Dunstan's Street. The **Unicorn** (no.61, 01227 463187) has a kitsch garden, real ales and also Deuchar's IPA from Edinburgh. The **Bishop's Finger** (no.13, 01227 768915) not surprisingly serves Bishops Finger, and attracts both students and more mature clientele. **Simple Simon**, near the West Gate (01227 762355), is recommended for its choice of ales and strong Biddenden cider.

Where to stay

ABode (30-33 High Street, 01227 766266, www.abodehotels.co.uk, doubles £125-£295) has brought a welcome breath of sleek and chic into Canterbury's somewhat chintzy accommodation options. It's the third in a small chain of smart hotels created by Andrew Brownsword. And the 72 rooms are a treat, ordered by price and size ranging from 'comfortable', through 'desirable' and 'enviable' to 'fabulous' (a penthouse with superior views and a tennis court-sized bed). Michael Caines Fine Dining Restaurant (01227 826684, www. michaelcaines.com, mains £17.50-£19.75) has a young, two Michelin-starred chef at the helm. Soothingly lit and a study in understated, chocolate brown decor, the restaurant's looks and the elaborate menu are all you would expect, though the most satisfying part of a meal here might prove to be the selection of British cheeses (£11.50). **Canterbury Cathedral Lodge** (The Precincts, 01227 865350, www.canterburycathedrallodge.org, doubles £89-£109) is right inside the cathedral precincts, and though not historic, being only five years old, the views certainly are, with bright and comfortable accommodation in a private courtyard. **Cathedral Gate Hotel** (36 Burgate, 01227 464381, www.cgate.co.uk, doubles £58-£130) is a splendid old hotel built in 1438 and pre-dates the Christ Church Gate it sits alongside. Its 25 rooms with sloping floors and ceilings are reached via dark narrow corridors and low doorways. 'Daybreak', 'Cathedral' and 'Joy' (oh joy! it's en suite) are the ones with cathedral views. **Greyfriars** (6 Stour Street, 01227 456255, www.greyfriars-house.co.uk, doubles £55-£100) is a city-centre hotel (and ancient but comfortable) with free parking to its guests, but like all the others it's booked up at graduation time and in high season. **Magnolia House** (36 St Dunstan's Terrace, 01227 765121, www.magnoliahouse canterbury.co.uk, doubles £65-£125) is quite compact, but highly recommended. And the breakfast is delicious and well worth lingering over. The walk to and from town takes you through peaceful Westgate Gardens. Further

Boomtown Brighton

Brighton hasn't exactly been letting visitors down since, ooh, about 1783 when 'Prinny', later King George IV, decided to hang up his funky wig at a local farmhouse. But this year, new developments could amount to something quite special.

First out of the traps comes **myhotel Brighton** (Jubilee Street, East Sussex BN1 1GE, www.myhotels.co.uk; *pictured*), the micro-chain's first new-build hotel – and its first venture outside London – due for completion in spring 2008. Sharing key features with myhotels Bloomsbury (*see p46*) and Chelsea (*see p63*), such as the foyer aquarium, superchill library area and Jinja treatment room, it should still be as different from its predecessors as they are from each other. We're told to expect 'Freddie Mercury meets the Maharishi' from designer Karim Rashid, which could mean wall-to-ceiling windows and curved rooms where beds can be rotated to make the most of every angle.

Long patronised by residents of the Big Smoke as 'London-by-Sea', Brighton has also this year decided to take the cheeky blighters at their word: the city is to have its very own Eye. **i360** will be 600 feet high, with a glass and steel pod transporting some 125 visitors 456 feet up to panoramic views spanning 25 miles on a clear day. Masterminding the project are David Marks and Julia Barfield, the husband-and-wife architectural team behind the London Eye. The observation mast is expected to attract half a million visitors a year, and will solve the thorny problem of what to do with Brighton's collapsed West Pier. Most of the wreckage will be cleared for the construction, with just the end section renovated for integration into the overall complex.

i360 is scheduled to open for summer 2008, by which time neighbouring Hove may also have discovered a thirst for the new: a controversial seafront leisure centre, designed by no less a figure than architect Frank Gehry, should have broken ground. At this rate, the good people of Brighton will soon be calling London 'Brighton-by-Thames'.

out, the **Ebury Hotel** (65-67 New Dover Road, 01227 768433, www.ebury-hotel.co.uk, doubles £75-£145) is really quite grand-looking, with a sweeping drive and a Gothic exterior. The best bedrooms have views of the garden, but most of them are large, light and comfortable.

Getting there

By train
From Victoria to Canterbury East (1hr 20mins; map p400 H10), or from Charing Cross (map p401 L7) to Canterbury West (1hr 30mins).

By coach
National Express from Victoria Coach Station (1hr 50mins).

By car
Take the A2, the M2, then the A2 again (approx 2hrs).

Tourist information

Tourist Information Centre
12-13 Sun Street, Buttermarket, Canterbury, Kent, CT1 2HX (01227 378100/www.canterbury.co.uk). **Open** *Mar-June; Sept, Oct* 9.30am-5pm Mon-Sat; 10am-4pm Sun. *July, August* 9.30am-6pm Mon-Sat; 10am-4pm Sun. *Nov-Feb* 10am-4pm Mon-Sat.

Chichester & Arundel

The south-west corner of West Sussex is green and pleasant England at its best. The rolling hills of the South Downs dominate the landscape, complemented by miles of sheltered coastline and characterful towns and villages. The area is also a walker's paradise, with over 2,500 miles of public footpaths traversing countryside dotted with wildflowers and butterflies. The historic city of Chichester exudes a peacefully quaint market-town charm. It was founded in AD 70 by the Romans, who laid out the main street plan and built the original city walls, which were subsequently rebuilt in flint in medieval times. The main streets of the city – called, with unimpeachable logic, North, South, East and West Streets – slice it neatly into four areas. The cathedral, best known for its spire and Marc Chagall stained-glass window, dominates the south-west sector, while the finest of the Georgian buildings are in the south-east, in the streets known as the Pallants where the **Pallant House Gallery** (*see below*) holds a truly outstanding collection of great 20th-century British art. Contemporary art shows here have also proved that the gallery has its finger firmly on the pulse. **Fishbourne Roman Palace** (*see below*) is a few miles east, the largest Roman residence excavated in Britain, and probably once the

finest accommodation north of the Alps, with about a hundred rooms. The foundations of around a quarter of them can still be seen, decorated with at least 20 different mosaics, including the famous Cupid on a Dolphin.

Seen from across the river, Arundel, with its castle and church at the top of the hill and the water at the bottom, looks more like a stage set than a real town. The imposing **Arundel Castle** (*see below*) was built in the 11th century by Roger de Montgomery but massively remodelled in the 18th and 19th centuries. Now the seat of the Dukes of Norfolk and Earls of Arundel, it's well worth exploring (though the cost of admission is high) for its fine collections of paintings, tapestries and furniture, and the gorgeous Fitzalan Chapel, otherwise only viewable through the wrought-iron gates in the parish church.

Pallant House Gallery
9 North Pallant, PO19 1TJ (01243 774557/ www.pallant.org.uk). **Open** 10am-5pm Mon-Wed; Fri, Sat. 10am-8pm Thur. 12.30-5pm Sun. **Admission** £6.50; £3.25 reductions; free under-5s & unemployed. **Credit** MC, V.

Fishbourne Roman Palace
Salthill Road, Fishbourne, PO19 3QR (01243 785859/www.sussexpast.co.uk/fishbourne). **Open** *Dec-Jan* phone for details. *Feb* 10am-4pm daily. *Mar-July; Sept, Oct* 10am-5pm daily. *Aug* 10am-6pm daily. *Nov-Dec* 10am-4pm daily. **Admission** £7; £3.70-£6 reductions; free under-5s. **Credit** MC, V.

Arundel Castle
Arundel, BN18 9AB (01903 882173/ www.arundelcastle.org). **Open** *Apr-Oct* 10am-5pm daily. **Admission** £12.50, £7.50 reductions. **Credit** MC, V.

Where to eat & drink

In Chichester, **St Martin's Organic Tearooms** (3 St Martin's Street, 01243 786715, www.organictearooms.co.uk, mains £5-£10) occupies an old terraced house, a charming labyrinth of nooks and crannies, offering carefully prepared organic, mostly vegetarian dishes and there's a lovely garden for alfresco summer eating. Both Arundel and Chichester have a decent spread of pubs and restaurants, but the best food is to be had out in the country, which makes a car even more useful for this trip. The **Duke of Cumberland** (Henley Village, 01428 652280, mains £8.50-£15.95) is a wonderfully isolated pub well known for its fresh fish and pints of prawns. The **Fox Goes Free** (Charlton, 01243 811461, www.thefoxgoesfree.com, mains £8.50-£17.95) is a 300-year-old country inn taking its name from William III's stopovers while on hunting trips. A definite cut above, the menu here features dishes such as roast partridge with cabbage and bacon, and grilled cod with garlic butter and prawns rather than scampi in a basket. The **George & Dragon** (Burpham, 01903 883131, mains £10.95-£19.95) is reached via a winding Downland road from Arundel. The pub itself is pretty ancient, with an 18th-century smugglers' spinning jenny set in the ceiling, a simple way to settle arguments over the spoils that came upriver. The place is now narrowly more restaurant than pub, though an excellent variety of thick-cut sandwiches is also available at the bar. A short walk up the way, the village cricket pitch occupies a remarkable Anglo-Saxon hillfort, built to oversee the Arun and still afffording wonderful views over the valley. The **White Horse Inn** (1 High Street, Chilgrove, 01243 535219, www.whitehorse chilgrove.co.uk, mains £14.95-£20) is a fine pub-restaurant-B&B where organic fare and fresh meat and fish are the specialities.

Where to stay

There's a huge range of accommodation in Chichester and, especially, in the towns and villages surrounding it: a few ineffably posh country retreats are supplemented by decent mid-range hotels and affordable B&Bs. No matter the grade, however, prices throughout the area soar in the summer during the Festival of Speed and Glorious Goodwood (www.good wood.co.uk); book months ahead or avoid them entirely. Pubs such as the Fox Goes Free and the White Horse Inn also do good rooms. The **Bailiffscourt Hotel & Health Spa** (Climping Street, Climping, nr Littlehampton, 01903 723511, www.hshotels.co.uk, doubles £245-£595) is one of the more extraordinary hotel properties in Sussex, a palimpsest of old English architectural styles in a delightfully secluded spot near the coast. A hotel since 1948, it is now run by Historic Sussex Hotels as a welcoming, efficient and laid-back high-end establishment with a decent restaurant (dining available in the candlelit courtyard in summer), a handsome new health spa (with indoor and outdoor pools, hot tub, steam room, sauna and well-equipped gym) and wide views over the marshes. And it's all just a five-minute walk from the pebbly beach. Futher inland, **West Stoke House** (Downs Road, West Stoke, Chichester, 01243 575226, www.weststoke house.co.uk, doubles £185-£215) is an elegant 'restaurant with rooms' in a really beautifully converted mansion house set in picture-perfect grounds. It combines period charm with contemporary comforts to great effect. And adventurous modern British cooking features at lunch and dinner.

Getting there

By train

From Victoria, Waterloo or London Bridge to Chichester (approx 1hr 40mins). From Victoria or London Bridge to Arundel (approx 1hr 20mins).

By coach

National Express from Victoria Coach Station (3hr 50mins).

By car

Take the A23, the M23, then the A29 (approx 2hrs).

Tourist information

Arundel Tourist Information

1-2 Crown Yard Mews, River Road, Arundel, West Sussex BN18 9JW (01903 882268/www.sussexby thesea.com). **Open** *Easter-Oct* 10am-5pm Mon-Sat; 10am-4pm Sun. *Jan-Easter* 10am-3pm daily.

Chichester Tourist Information

29A South Street, Chichester, West Sussex PO19 1AH (01243 775888/www.chichester.gov.uk). **Open** *Oct-Mar* 10.15am-5.15pm Mon; 9.15am-5.15pm Tue-Sat. *Apr-Oct* 10.15am-5.15pm Mon; 9.15am-5.15pm Tue-Sat; 11am-3.30pm Sun.

Dungeness, Romney & Rye

Perhaps because it's so difficult to reach from London (though there are rail links to Rye and Hastings), Romney Marsh is other-worldly in a way that conjures up science fiction scenarios in Tarkovsky movies; you half expect to see Steed and Mrs Peel in *The Avengers* supping ale in the eerily unchanged villages. It's a strange but hugely appealing mix of olde-worlde cobbled streets and ancient inns, miles of sandy beaches, a desolate promontory, the world's largest expanse of shingle and event-horizoned marshland, criss-crossed by canals and studded with tiny medieval churches and strange concrete defence constructions dating back to post-World War I. So long as the transport links remain as poor as they are, we suspect (and rather hope) that there won't be any real changes here for decades to come.

Hastings is the ideal starting point for a circular tour (by car) that takes in Winchelsea and Rye, Romney Marsh and Dungeness. Winchelsea was built on a newly-completed medieval grid pattern (first laid out by King Edward I) when the 'old' settlement was swept into the sea in the storms of 1287. The place is proud of its status as England's smallest town, but really it's a sleepy village of 400 residents. It's almost too quaint to be true, like Rye, which is a photogenic jumble of Norman, Tudor and Georgian architecture perched on one of the area's few hills. Apart from simply wandering the streets, it's worth taking a look at the medieval Landgate gateway and the **Castle Museum** and 13th-century **Ypres Tower** (*see below*). Rye Art Gallery (107 High Street, 01797 222433, www.ryeartgallery.co.uk) offers a changing series of excellent exhibitions, mostly by local artists.

East from Rye lies Romney Marsh, flat as a pancake and laced with cycle paths – bikes can be hired from Rye Hire (1 Cyprus Place, Rye, 01797 223033) – an ideal way to explore the lonely medieval churches that dot the level marsh. Heading out of Rye along the coast road takes you to the ever-popular Camber Sands, a vast and glittering sandy beach that's a haven for kite-flying, riding, sand-yachting and invigorating walks.

Beyond is Dungeness Point, a huge beach of flint shingle, stretching miles out into the sea. Clustered on this strange promontory are a lighthouse that offers wonderful views and a good café. The light on this remote, gloriously bleak patch of land is odd, reflected from the sea on both sides, and the oddness of the landscape is enhanced by the presence of the massive Dungeness nuclear power station that dominates the horizon; such man-made wonders are set against a truly magnificent natural backdrop. Then, when the miniature Romney, Hythe and Dymchurch Railway train barrels by, you know you're in an episode of *The Prisoner*. Proudly proclaiming to be the 'world's smallest public railway', it is fully functioning but one-third of the standard size. The diminutive train, built by the millionaire racing driver Captain Howey in 1927, even includes a buffet car. Sitting in one of the tiny carriages is a delightfully surreal experience, as you meander from the wide-open shingle of the Point behind back gardens and caravan parks, through woodland and fields to arrive at Hythe, 13.5 miles away.

Rye Castle Museum & Ypres Tower

3 East Street, TN31 7JY (01797 226728/www. ryemuseum.co.uk). **Open** *Museum* Easter-Oct 2-5pm Mon, Thur, Fri; 10.30am-5pm Sat, Sun. Closed Oct-Easter. *Tower* Easter-Oct 10.30am-5pm Mon, Thur-Sun. Oct-Easter 10.30am-3.30pm Sat, Sun. **Admission** *Museum* £2.50; £2 reductions. *Tower* £2.95; £2 reductions. *Both* £5; £4 reductions. **No credit cards.**

Where to eat & drink

You'll find some of the finest food on the south-east coast here. In Rye, the **Landgate Bistro** (5-6 Landgate, Rye, 01797 222829, www.landgatebistro.co.uk, mains £9.90-£15.90) once ruled the roost with its attractive,

inventive and pleasingly unfussy dishes, but now faces real competition from the **George in Rye** (98 High Street, 01797 222114, www.thegeorgeinrye.com, mains £12-£16.95) where the food is also scrumptious without being overpriced and the chef is Rod Grossmann, previously at London's Moro. It's also a hotel that is luxurious, stylish, welcoming and absolutely top of the range.

The light and informal **Fish Café** (17 Tower Street, 01797 222210, www.thefish cafe.com) serves some of the best seafood in town. If fancy isn't your thing, Rye has plenty of simpler eateries: authentic pasta at **Simply Italian** (The Strand, 01797 226024, www.simplyitalian.co.uk), great noodles at **Lemon Grass Thai Restaurant** (1-2 Tower Street, 01797 222327) or sound pub grub at any number of lovely boozers in town.

The finest option on the seaside is still the **Place** (New Lydd Road, Camber, 01797 225057, www.theplacecambersands.co.uk, mains £10.25-£17.95) at Camber Sands, which prides itself on its use of locally sourced and eco-friendly produce. Further east, the **Pilot** (Battery Road, Lydd, 01797 320314, www.the pilot.uk.com, mains £6.50-£11.95) has long been a Dungeness institution serving some of the best fish and chips in Kent. For a dinner with a difference, try the weekend Fly'n'Dine at **Lydd Airport** (Lydd, Romney Marsh, reservations 01797 322207, www.lyddair. com/flyanddine.html), which consists of drinks and canapés, a low-level 20-minute flight over the Kent coast and a five-course candlelit dinner in the 1960s-style Biggles Bar and Restaurant. At £59 it's quite a bargain, and there's also a lunch option at £39.

Of the many pubs, **Woolpack Inn** (Beacon Lane, nr Brookland, 01797 344321, mains £4.75-£23.95) is one of the best, with low ceilings and original 15th-century beams, sourced, rather enterprisingly, from local shipwrecks. The tiny, multi-award-winning **Red Lion** (Snargate, Romney Marsh, 01797 344648) is something of a Romney Marsh institution, famed for the fact that its interior hasn't been touched since World War II. It doesn't do food, but you are welcome to bring your own.

Where to stay

Even in the winter months, accommodation in Rye needs to be booked as far in advance as possible. If the tweeness of many of Rye's B&Bs is overly intimate for your tastes but you still want a place with character and also some individuality, the **Hope Anchor Hotel** (Watchbell Street, 01797 222216, www.thehope anchor.co.uk, doubles £85-£120) is a reliable bet.

It's set in a lovely location in the heart of town, at the end of a pretty, cobbled street. The **White Vine House** (24 High Street, 01797 224748, www.whitevinehouse.co.uk, doubles £125-£165) has seven individual and tastefully decorated bedrooms. Wonderfully located on Rye's quaintest cobbled street, the atmospheric 17th-century **Jeake's House** (Mermaid Street, 01797 222828, www.jeakeshouse.com) has 11 individually decorated rooms; the gold room features an impressive inglenook fireplace in which a lovely wood stove nestles. The 16th-century **Mermaid Inn** (Mermaid Street, 01797 223065, www.mermaidinn.com) offers olde-worlde tradition at its finest (including an accomplished restaurant), complete with wood panelling and stone fireplaces, four posters, wonky floors and secret passages, while the quirky **Simmons of the Mint** (68-69 The Mint, 07776 206203, www.simmonsofthe mint.co.uk) is an intriguing private house/B&B hybrid, with great breakfasts served by the proprietor, who runs the shop next door. Winchelsea's **Strand House** (Tanyard's Lane, 01797 226276, www.thestrandhouse. co.uk, doubles £70-£120) is a 15th-century house with ten rooms and a delightful garden.

The **Romney Bay House Hotel** (Coast Road, Littlestone-on-Sea, New Romney, 01797 364747, doubles £90-£160) is a ten-bedroom 1920s mansion designed for Hollywood gossip columnist Hedda Hopper by Sir Clough Williams-Ellis – of Portmeirion fame. It's perched on the seafront, right at the end of the bumpy coastal road, with welcoming, individually styled rooms (two with four-posters). And if you're looking for lovingly prepared food with an emphasis on locally sourced ingredients, you'd be hard pushed to find a better place to eat on the peninsula. In Hastings, the **Zanzibar International Hotel** (9 Eversfield Place, 01424 460109, www.zanzibarhotel.co.uk, doubles £89-£175) is a tall, thin seafront house that feels like a private house rather than a boutique hotel.

Getting there

By train

From London Bridge or Cannon Street to Rye via Ashford International (approx 1hr 45mins; map p404 P7). From Charing Cross, Waterloo East or London Bridge to Hastings (approx 1hr 30mins; map p401 L7).

Dungeness. *See p351*.

By car

Take the A20, the M20, then the A259 (approx 2hrs 30mins).

Tourist information

Hastings Tourist Information

Queen Square, Hastings, East Sussex TN34 1TL (0845 274 1001/www.visit1066country.com). **Open** 8.30am-6.15pm Mon, Tue, Thur, Fri; 10am-6.15pm Wed; 9am-5pm Sat; 10.30am-4.30pm Sun.

Folkestone Tourist office

103 Sandgate Road, Folkestone, East Sussex, CT20 2BQ (01303 258 594). **Open** 9am-5pm Mon-Fri.

Rye Tourist Information

Rye Heritage Centre, Strand Quay, Rye, East Sussex TN31 7AY (01797 226696/www.visitrye.co.uk). **Open** *Easter-Oct* 10am-5pm daily. *Oct-Easter* 10am-4pm daily.

Woodstock & Blenheim

The triangle of countryside between Oxford, Chipping Norton and Cirencester is one of the prettiest, most photogenic parts of England. The historic market town of Woodstock lies eight miles north of Oxford, perfectly placed

for those wishing to visit the twin monuments to extravagance, **Blenheim Palace** (*see p354*) and Bicester Village. The former is the country seat of the Duke of Marlborough and birthplace of Sir Winston Churchill; the luxury and splendour of Sir John Vanbrugh's design is breathtaking, and its sheer size will stop first-time visitors in their tracks. The same could be said of **Bicester Village** (50 Pingle Drive, 01869 323200, www.bicester-village.co.uk), a massive outdoor shopping mall that sells name brands at large discounts. The crowds at both are daunting; visit early in the day or later. The grounds of Blenheim Palace offer delightful walks to a variety of viewpoints.

Woodstock itself is best known for two trades – glove-making and decorative steel work. You can find out more about the area's heritage at the wide-ranging **Oxfordshire Museum** (*see p354*), but you won't see many signs of artisan life in the streets, which are filled with cars bringing custom to the classy pubs and restaurants. Garden-lovers should take a detour north to **Rousham House** (01869 347110, www.rousham.org), near Steeple Aston. The imposing – if rather gloomy – Jacobean mansion was remodelled

Trips Out of Town

in Tudor Gothic style by William Kent, an important predecessor of 'Capability' Brown, in the 18th century. But the real highlight here is his outstanding garden, inspired by Italian landscape painting. Rousham is determinedly and delightfully uncommercialised, with no shop or tearoom; you're encouraged to bring a picnic and wander the grounds.

Blenheim Palace

Woodstock, Oxon, OX20 1PX (01993 811091/ recorded information 08700 602080/www. blenheimpalace.com). **Open** *Feb-Oct* 10.30am-5.30pm daily. *Nov-Dec* 10.30am-5.30pm Wed-Sun. **Admission** £16; £9.75-£13.50 reductions; £43 family ticket. **Credit** MC, V.

Oxfordshire Museum

Park Street, Woodstock, Oxon, OX20 1SN (01993 811456/www.oxfordshire.gov.uk). **Open** 10am-5pm Tue-Sat; 2-5pm Sun. **Admission** free.

Where to eat & drink

Attractive country pubs and restaurants abound, but this is well moneyed land; while standards are high, so are prices, and tastes tend towards the conservative. Don't be surprised to see guests sporting black tie in your hotel dining room. The **Feathers Hotel** (*see below*) offers an intimate fine dining experience in its antique, oak-panelled dining room where a modern-leaning European menu is beautifully cooked and presented. The lunchtime 'market menu' is a gourmet steal at £19, offering hearty fare such as rump of lamb or roast mackerel. There's also a less formal bistro here. Elsewhere in town, there's the well-regarded Chinese restaurant **Chef Imperial** (22 High Street, 01993 813593, mains £4.50-£8.95), **Brothertons Brasserie** (1 High Street, 01993 811114, closed Tue), and **Hampers** deli and café (31-33 Oxford Street, 01993 811535) for light bites.

Further afield, but worth the trek, the **Red Lion** (South Side, Steeple Aston, 01869 340225, mains £7-£13) is a small, attractive country pub boasting a paved garden, low-ceilinged bar (complete with resident spaniel), separate lounge with squashy leather sofas, and wood-beamed conservatory dining room (children are permitted). Food is fairly traditional, but the ham is absolutely top-rate; game pie goes down a treat with a pint of Old Hookey.

Where to stay

Woodstock's finest accommodation remains the **Feathers Hotel** (16-20 Market Street, Woodstock, 01993 812291, www.feathers .co.uk, doubles £165-£275) made up of seven

interconnected 17th-century houses, and named by a stuffed bird-collecting former hotelier. It's a cosy maze of corridors and elegantly furnished bedrooms, the best of which is equipped with its own private steam room. The garden is pleasant on balmy afternoons; in winter, the wood-panelled lounge with huge fireplace is perfect for relaxed drinks. There's also a beauty salon, Preen (treatments must be pre-booked).

One step down is the **Bear Hotel** (Park Street, 0870 400 8202, www.bearhotel woodstock.co.uk, doubles £184-£230), Woodstock's largest hotel comprising an impressive 13th-century coaching inn and an adjoining glove factory, converted into guest rooms and conference facilities in the 1960s. Happily, the corporate aspects don't really detract from the main building's grandeur and appeal – there are still plenty of winding corridors, creaky wooden floors, oak beams and fireplaces for atmosphere, and a snug little bar for quiet drinks. Richard Burton and Elizabeth Taylor once famously holed up here. The **King's Arms Hotel** (19 Market Street, 01993 813636, www.kings-hotel-woodstock .co.uk, doubles £140-£150) is a comfortable, contemporary hotel, just across the road from the Feathers. The listed Georgian building has been painstakingly renovated to retain its character, but is carefully balanced with neutral tones and modern furnishings; the only dark furniture you'll find here are the leather chairs in the restaurant, a converted billiards room. The 15 bedrooms – all named after kings – are simply, stylishly and individually appointed, with Wi-Fi and good en suites. There's decent bistro fare (with appealing vegetarian options) in the restaurant, while the bar is popular with Woodstock's youth – so expect a bit of noise on your way up to bed.

Getting there

By train & coach

From Paddington to Oxford (1hr; map p395 D5), then bus no.20 to Woodstock (approx 40mins).

By car

Take the A40(M), the M40, then the A34.

Tourist information

Woodstock Tourist informaton

Oxfordshire Museum, Park Street, Woodstock, Oxon OX20 1SN (01993 813276/www.oxfordshire cotswolds.org). **Open** *Mar-Oct* 9.30am-5.30pm Mon-Sat; 2-5pm Sun. *Nov-Feb* 10am-5pm Mon-Sat; 2-5pm Sun.

Trips Out of Town

Directory

Features

Directory

Getting Around

Arriving & leaving

For London's domestic rail and coach stations, *see p342*.

By air

At the time of writing, heightened security measures remain in force at all UK airports. Each passenger may take only one item of hand baggage through security control. It must be no larger than 56cm (22in) tall, 45cm (17.7in) wide and 25cm (10in) deep. Only limited quantities of liquids may be carried through security control as hand baggage. Liquid items may only be carried in containers holding up to 100ml. They must be carried separately in a single transparent, re-sealable plastic bag (as provided by security control), no larger than 20cm x 20cm (8in x 8in), and all items must fit inside so that it closes properly. Liquid items larger than 100ml should be packed in your hold luggage – otherwise they will be confiscated. It is not yet known how long these restrictions will stand; visit www.baa.com for updates at the time of travel.

Gatwick Airport

0870 000 2468/www.baa.co.uk/ gatwick. About 30 miles south of central London, off the M23.
Of the three rail services that link Gatwick to London, the quickest is the **Gatwick Express** (0845 850 1530, www.gatwickexpress.co.uk) to Victoria Station, which takes about 30 minutes and runs from 3.30am to 12.30am daily. Tickets cost £15.90 single, £15.20 day return (after 9.30am) and £26.80 for an open return (valid for 30 days). Under-15s are £6.50 single, half-price open and cheap day returns; under-5s go free.

Southern (0845 748 4950, www.southernrailway.com) also runs a rail service between Gatwick and Victoria, with trains every 5-10 minutes (or every 25 minutes between 1am and 4am). It takes about 35 minutes, at £8.90 for a single, £9.20 for a day return (after 9.30am) and £17.80 for an open period return (valid for one month). Under-16s get half-price tickets; under-5s go free.

If you're staying in the King's Cross or Bloomsbury area, consider the **Thameslink** service (0845 748 4950, www.firstcapitalconnect.co.uk) via London Bridge, Blackfriars, Farringdon and King's Cross; journey times vary. Tickets cost £8.90 single, £9.50 day return (after 9.32am) and £17 for a 30-day open return.

Hotelink offers a shuttle service (01293 532244, www.hotelink.co.uk) at £20 each way (£24 online). A taxi costs about £100 and takes ages.

Heathrow Airport

0870 000 0123/www.baa.co.uk/ heathrow. About 15 miles west of central London, off the M4.
This year looks set to be a big one for Heathrow Airport. The new Terminal 5 is due to open in March 2008 – the £4.3 billion terminal complex will be the biggest free-standing building in the UK. BAA is already redeveloping Terminal 3 and, when Terminal 5 opens, will modernise Terminals 1 and 4. Planning permission has been granted to build a new, environmentally efficient terminal called Heathrow East (replacing Terminal 2 and the Queens Building). Terminal 5 has its own dedicated railway station with six platforms: two for the Heathrow Express; two for the Piccadilly Line tube; and two spare for future rail links to the west.

The **Heathrow Express** (0845 600 1515, www.heathrowexpress. co.uk) runs to Paddington every 15 minutes 5.10am-11.25pm daily, and takes 15-20 minutes. The train can be boarded at either of the airport's two tube stations. Tickets cost £15.50 single or £29 return (it's £1 cheaper if you book online and there is a £2 premium if you buy on board); under-16s go half-price. Many airlines have check-in desks at Paddington.

A longer but cheaper journey is by tube. Tickets for the 50- to 60-minute **Piccadilly Line** ride into central London cost £4 one way (£2 under-16s). Trains run every few minutes from about 5am to 11.57pm daily except Sunday, when they run from 6am to 11pm.

The **Heathrow Connect** (0845 678 6975, www.heathrowconnect. com) gives you direct access to Heathrow Airport from Hayes, Southall, Hanwell, West Ealing, Ealing Broadway and Paddington stations. The trains run every half-hour. It serves Terminals 1, 2 and 3 and, when Terminal 5 opens it will extend its route to Terminal 4, with a direct service from Paddington to the new Terminal 5. Ticket prices vary depending on where you board; a single from Paddington is £6.90 while an open return is £12.90.

National Express (0870 580 8080, www.nationalexpress.com) runs special coach services to London Victoria between 5am and 9.35pm daily, leaving Heathrow Central bus terminal around every 20-30 minutes. For a 90-minute journey to London, you can expect to pay £4 for a single (£2 under-16s) or £8 (£4 under-16s) for a return.

As at Gatwick, **Hotelink** (*see above*) offers an airport-to-hotel shuttle service for £19 per person each way. A taxi into town will cost roughly £100 and take an hour or more, depending on traffic.

London City Airport

7646 0000/www.londoncity airport.com. About 9 miles east of central London.
The Docklands Light Railway (DLR) now includes a stop for London City Airport. The journey to Bank in the City takes around 20 minutes, and trains run 5.30am-12.30am Mon-Sat or 7am-11.30pm Sun. A taxi costs around £20 to central London; less to the City or to Canary Wharf.

Luton Airport

01582 405100/www.london-luton. com. About 30 miles north of central London, J10 off the M1.
Luton Airport Parkway Station is close to the airport, but not in it; there's still a short shuttle-bus ride. The **Thameslink** service (*see above*)

calls at many stations (King's Cross and City, on Ludgate Hill, among them); it has a journey time of 35-45 minutes. Trains leave every 15 minutes or so and cost £11.90 single one-way and £21.50 return, or £11 for a cheap day return (after 9.30am Monday to Friday, weekends). Trains from Luton to King's Cross run at least hourly through the night.

The Luton to Victoria journey takes 60-90 minutes by coach. **Green Line** (0870 608 7261, www.greenline. co.uk) runs a 24-hour service every 30 minutes or so at peak times. A single is £11, while returns cost £16; under-16s go half-price. A taxi costs upwards of £50.

Stansted Airport

0870 000 0303/www.stansted airport.com/www.baa.co.uk/stansted. About 35 miles north-east of central London, J8 off the M11.
The quickest way to get to London from here is on the **Stansted Express** train (0845 748 4950) to Liverpool Street Station; the journey time is 40-45 minutes. Trains leave every 15-45 minutes depending on the time of day, and tickets cost £15 single, £25 return; under-16s travel half-price, under-5s free.

The **Airbus** (0870 580 8080, www. nationalexpress.com) coach service from Stansted to Victoria takes at least an hour and 20 minutes and runs 24 hours. Coaches run roughly every 30 minutes, more frequently at peak times. A single is £10 (£5 for under-16s), return is £17 (£8.50 for under-16s). A taxi is about £80.

By rail

Eurostar

St Pancras International Station, Pancras Road, NW1 (0870 518 6186/www.eurostar.com). Kings Cross tube/rail. **Map** p399 L3.
In November 2007, Eurostar relocated to the newly refurbished St Pancras International Station. The new station is served by a high speed rail line, cutting journey times by at least 20 minutes.

Public transport

Information

Details on public transport timetables and other travel information are provided by **Transport for London**

(7222 1234, www.tfl.gov.uk/ journeyplanner). Complaints or comments about almost any form of public transport can also be taken up with **London TravelWatch** (7505 9000).

Travel Information Centres

TfL's Travel Information Centres provide maps and information about the tube, buses and Docklands Light Railway (DLR; *see p363*). You can find them in the stations listed below. Call 7222 1234 for more information.
Heathrow Airport Terminals 1, 2 & 3 Underground station 6.30am-10pm daily.
Liverpool Street 7.15am-9pm Mon-Sat; 8.15am-8pm Sun.
Victoria 7.15am-9pm Mon-Sat; 8.15am-8pm Sun.

Fares & tickets

A flat cash fare of £4 per journey applies across zones 1-6 on the tube; customers save up to £2.50 per journey with a pre-pay Oyster card (*see below*). Tube and DLR fares are based on a system of six zones, stretching 12 miles out from the centre of London. Anyone caught without a valid ticket or Oyster card is subject to a £20 on-the-spot fine.

Oyster card

Oyster is the cheapest way of getting around on buses, tubes and the DLR. It's a pre-paid travel smart-card that you can charge up at tube stations, London Travel Information Centres (*see above*), some national rail stations and at newsagents. Oyster cards speed up passage through tube station ticket gates as they need only be touched on a special yellow card reader. There is a £3 refundable deposit payable for the card and you can put up to £90 on it.

Any tube journey within zone 1 using Oyster pay-as-you-go costs £1.50 (50p for under-16s). A single tube journey within zone 2, 3, 4, 5 or 6 costs £1 (50p for under-16s). Single tube journeys from zones 1-6 using Oyster to pay-as-you-go are £3.50 (7am-7pm Mon-Fri); £2 at other times and £1 for children.

If you make a number of journeys on the tube, DLR, buses or trams, Oyster pay-as-you-go fares will always be capped at 50p less than the price of an equivalent Day Travelcard, no matter how many

journeys are made. However, if you only make one journey using Oyster pay-as-you-go, you will only be charged a single Oyster fare.

You can also get up to three 7-Day, monthly or longer period (including annual) Travelcards and Bus Passes put on your Oyster card. For more details visit www.tfl.gov.uk/oyster.

Day Travelcards

If you are only using the tube, DLR, buses and trams, using Oyster to pay as you go will always be 50p cheaper than the equivalent Day Travelcard. If you are also using National Rail services, Oyster may not be accepted: opt for a Day Travelcard. Peak Day Travelcards can be used all day, Monday to Friday (except public holidays). They cost from £6.60 for zones 1-2 (£3.30 child), up to £13.20 for zones 1-6 (£6.20 child). All tickets are valid for journeys started before 4.30am the next day. The Off-Peak Day Travelcard meets most visitors' needs, allowing you to travel from 9.30am Monday to Friday and all day Saturday, Sunday and public holidays. It costs from £5.10 for zones 1-2, rising to £6.70 for zones 1-6.

1-Day Family Travelcards

Up to four under-11s can travel free on the tube (from 9.30am Monday to Friday, all day Saturday, Sunday and public holidays) as long as they are accompanied by a fare-paying adult. Another four can travel with an adult for £1 each (a Day Travelcard is issued) at the same times.

3-Day Travelcards

If you plan to spend a few days charging around town, you can buy a 3-Day Travelcard. The off-peak version can be used from 9.30am Monday to Friday and all day on Saturday and Sunday, and public holidays on the start date through to any journey that starts before 4.30am on the morning following the expiry date. It costs £20.10 for zones 1-6. The peak version can be used all day Monday to Friday on the start date and for any journey that starts before 4.30am on the day following the expiry date; it's available for £16.40 (zones 1-2) or £39.60 (zones 1-6).

Children

Under-14s travel free on buses and trams without the need to provide any proof of identity. 14- and 15-year-olds can also travel free, but

need to obtain an Under-16 Oyster photocard. For details of how to get this, visit www.tfl.gov.uk/fares or call 0845 330 9876. Under-11s travel free on the tube and DLR as well.

An 11-15 Oyster photocard is needed by 11- to 15-year-olds to pay as they go on the tube or DLR or to buy 7 -Day, monthly or longer period Travelcards and by 11- to 15-year-olds if using the tram to/from Wimbledon.

Photocards

Photocards are not required for adult rate 7-Day Travelcards, Bus Passes or for any adult rate Travelcard or Bus Pass charged on an Oyster card. For details of how to obtain under-14, 14-15 or 16-17 Oyster photocards visit www.tfl.gov.uk/fares or call 0845 330 9876.

London Underground

Delays are common. Escalators are often out of action. Some lines close at weekends for engineering. It's hot, smelly and crowded in rush hour (approximately 8am to 9.30am and 4.30pm to 7pm Mon-Fri). Nevertheless, the underground rail system – also known as 'the tube' – is still the quickest

way to get around London. Comments or complaints are dealt with by LU Customer Services on 0845 330 9880 (8am-8pm daily); for lost property, see p369.

Using the system

You can get Oyster cards from www.tfl.gov.uk/oyster, by calling 0870 849 9999, at tube stations, London Travel Information Centres, some National Rail stations and newsagents. Single or day tickets can be purchased from a ticket office or from self-service machines. You can buy most tickets and top up Oyster cards at self-service machines at most stations. Ticket offices in some stations close early (around 7.30pm); it's wise to carry a charged-up Oyster card to avoid being stranded.

To enter and exit the tube using an Oyster card, simply touch it to the yellow reader, which will open the gates. Make sure you also touch the card to the reader when you exit the tube, otherwise you will be charged a higher fare when you next use your Oyster card to enter a station.

To enter using a paper ticket, place it in the slot with the black magnetic strip facing down, then pull it out of the top to open the gates. Exiting at your destination is done in much the same way, though if you

have a single journey ticket, it will be retained by the gate as you leave.

There are 12 tube lines, colour-coded on the tube map (see p416).

Underground timetable

Tube trains run daily from around 5.30am (except Sunday, when they start an hour or two later, depending on the line). The only exception is Christmas Day, when there is no service. Generally, you should not have to wait more than ten minutes for a train, and during peak times services should run every two or three minutes. Times of last trains vary, though they're usually around 11.30pm-1am daily except Sunday, when they finish 30 minutes to an hour earlier. Other than on New Year's Eve, when the tubes run all night, the only all-night public transport is by night bus (see p360).

Fares

The single fare for adults across the network is £4. Using Oyster pay-as-you-go the fare varies by zone: zone 1 costs £1.50; zones 1-2 costs £1.50 or £2, depending on the time you travel; the zones 1-6 single fare is £2 or £3.50. The single fare for children aged 11-15 is £2 for any journey that includes travel in zone 1 and £1.50 for any journey not including zone 1. Under-11s travel free (see also p357).

Changing trains?

Though plans seem to have foundered for what in any other major city might be thought a minor extension to operating hours (just 30 minutes, folks), it's not all doom and gloom on the London Underground. The tube is getting a new station. Wood Lane is the first station to be built on an existing London Underground line for more than 70 years. It will appear on the Hammersmith & City Line between the existing Shepherd's Bush and Latimer Road stations, and the Hammersmith & City Line's Shepherd's Bush station will change its name to Shepherd's Bush Market, to avoid confusing it with the Shepherd's Bush station on the Central Line. Still with us? Good. Wood Lane station is to open in late 2008 to coincide with the completion of Westfield London, a £1.6 billion retail and leisure development being built on a 46-acre site just north of Shepherd's Bush. Spanning 1.5 million square feet, the development will

be supported by vital transport investment – with the expectation that 60 per cent of visitors will arrive and depart using public transport. Westfield says it has invested £170 million in transport improvements, with the money being spent on a new bus station and transport hub to the south-east of the site. Called the Southern Interchange, it will provide access to tubes, buses, trains, taxis and cycle routes, as well as supporting a proposed tram route.

So money talks while the rest of the city can walk? Perhaps not. As part of its grandly named £10 billion Five-Year Investment Programme, London Underground is looking at investing in the Central Line station at Shepherd's Bush, aiming to ease congestion and provide step-free access. And, as we went to press, White City station was due to join the rolling programme of refurbishments. So the network is changing, just not very fast.

Directory

Docklands Light Railway (DLR)

DLR trains (7363 9700, www.tfl.gov.uk/dlr) run from Bank (where they connect with the tube sytem's Central and Waterloo & City lines) or Tower Gateway, which is close to Tower Hill tube (Circle and District lines). At Westferry DLR the line splits east and south via Island Gardens to Greenwich and Lewisham; a change at Poplar can take you north to Stratford. The easterly branch forks after Canning Town to either Beckton or London City Airport. Trains run from 5.30am to 12.30am Monday to Saturday and 7am to 11.30pm Sunday. For lost property, *see p369*.

Fares

The adult single fares on DLR are the same as for the tube (*see p359*), except for a DLR-only zones 2-3 journey, which costs £1.50 (£1 using Oyster pay-as-you-go) or, for children 11-15, 70p (Oyster pay-as-you-go 50p).

The DLR also offers one-day 'Rail & River Rover' tickets, which combine one day's travel on DLR with hop-on, hop-off travel on City Cruises riverboats between Westminster, Waterloo, Tower and Greenwich piers (riverboats run 10am-6pm; call City Cruises on 7740 0400 for round-trip times). Starting at Tower Gateway, trains leave on the hour (from 10am), with a DLR guide giving a commentary as the train glides along. Tickets cost £11 for adults, £5.50 for kids and £27 for a family pass (two adults and up to three under-16s); under-5s free.

Family tickets can only be bought in person from the piers.

Buses

In the past couple of years hundreds of new buses have been introduced to the network as the old Routemasters have been phased out. All buses are now low-floor and accessible to wheelchair-users and buggies. The only exceptions are Heritage routes 9 and 15, which are served by the world-famous open-platform Routemaster buses. The introduction of 'bendy buses' with multiple-door entry and the fact that you *must* have a ticket or valid pass before getting on has at least contributed to speeding up boarding times at bus stops. Inspectors patrol and board buses at random; they can fine you £20 if you're on a bus and you haven't paid. You can buy a ticket (or 1-Day Bus Pass) from pavement machines, but, frustratingly, they're often out of order. Better to travel armed with an Oyster card or some other pass (*see p357*). For lost property, *see p369*.

Fares

Using Oyster pay-as-you-go costs £1 a trip and the most you will pay a day will be £3. Paying with cash at the time of travel costs £2 for a single trip. Under-16s travel for free (using an Under-14 or 14-15 Oyster photocard as appropriate; *see p357*). A 1-Day Bus Pass gives unlimited bus and tram travel for £3.50.

Bus Savers

A book of six Saver tickets costs £6, available from some newsagents and tube station ticket offices. They can't be used on the tram network.

Night buses

Many buses run 24 hours a day, seven days a week. There are also some special night buses with an 'N' prefix to the route number, which operate from about 11pm to 6am. Most night services run every 15 to 30 minutes, but many busier routes have a bus around every ten minutes. Fares for night buses are the same as for daytime buses. Travelcards and Bus Passes can be used on night buses at no additional charge – and until 4.30am of the morning after they expire. Oyster Pre Pay and bus Saver tickets are also valid on night buses.

Green Line buses

Green Line buses (0870 608 7261, www.greenline.co.uk) serve the suburbs and towns within a 40-mile radius of London. Its main office is opposite Victoria Coach Station (164 Buckingham Palace Road, Victoria, SW1W 9TP; Victoria tube/rail), and it runs 24-hour services.

Rail services

Independently run commuter services leave from the city's main rail stations. Travelcards are valid on these services within the right zones. One of the most useful is **Silverlink** (0845 601 4867, www.silverlink-trains.com; or National Rail Enquiries on 0845 748 4950), which runs from Richmond in the south-west through north London to Stratford in the east. Trains run about every 20 minutes daily except Sunday, when they run every half-hour. For lost property, *see p369*.

Tramlink

A tram service runs between Beckenham, Croydon, Addington and Wimbledon in south London. Travelcards that include zones 3, 4, 5 or 6 and all Bus Passes can be used on trams. Cash single fares are £2 (Oyster pay-as-you-go are £1 or 50p for 16-17 Oyster photocard holders who are ineligible for free bus travel). A 1-Day Bus Pass gives unlimited tram and bus travel at £3.50 for adults. For lost property, *see p369*.

Water transport

The times of London's various river services differ, but most operate every 20 minutes to one hour between 10.30am and 5pm. Services may be more frequent and run later in summer. Call the operators listed below for schedules and fares, or see www.tfl.gov.uk. **Thames Clippers** (www. thamesclippers.com) runs a reliable commuter-boat service, boarded at Embankment, Blackfriars, Bankside (for the Globe), London Bridge and Tower Pier. For lost property, *see p369*. The names in bold below are piers.

Royal Arsenal
Woolwich–Greenwich (15mins)–**Masthouse Terrace** (5mins)–**Greenland Dock**

(4mins)–**Canary Wharf**
(8mins)–**St Katharine's** (7mins)–
London Bridge City (4mins)–
Bankside (3mins)–**Blackfriars**
(3mins)–**Savoy** (4mins); Collins
River Enterprises 7252 3018/
www.thamesclippers.com.
Westminster–Festival (5mins)–
London Bridge City (20mins)–**St
Katharine's** (5mins); Crown River
7936 2033/www.crownriver.com.
Westminster–Greenwich (1hr);
Thames River Services 7930 4097/
www.westminsterpier.co.uk.
Westminster–Kew (1hr 30mins)–
Richmond (30mins)–**Hampton
Court** (1hr 30mins); Westminster
Passenger Service Association
7930 2062/www.wpsa.co.uk.
Westminster–Tower (40mins);
City Cruises 7740 0400/www.
citycruises.com.

Taxis

Black cabs

Licensed London taxis are
known as 'black cabs' – even
though they also come in other
colours – and are a much-loved
feature of London life. Drivers
must pass a test called 'the
Knowledge' to prove they know
every street in central London,
and the shortest route to it.

If a taxi's orange 'For Hire'
sign is switched on, it can be
hailed. If a taxi stops, the
cabbie must take you to your
destination, if it's within seven
miles. It can be hard to find a
free cab, especially just after
the pubs close. Expect to pay
slightly higher rates after 8pm
on weekdays and all weekend.

You can book black cabs in
advance. Both **Radio Taxis**
(7272 0272) and **Dial-a-Cab**
(7253 5000; credit cards only)
run 24-hour services (booking
fee £2). Any enquiries or
complaints about black cabs
should be made to the Public
Carriage Office. Note the cab's
badge number, which should
be displayed in the rear of the
cab and on its back bumper.
For lost property, see p369.

Public Carriage Office

*15 Penton Street, Islington, N1 9PU
(0845 602 7000/www.tfl.gov.uk/pco).*
Open *Phone enquiries* 9am-8pm
Mon-Fri. **Map** p402 N2.

Minicabs

Minicabs (saloon cars) are
generally cheaper than black
cabs, but only use licensed
firms (look for the yellow disc
in the front and rear windows)
and avoid those who tout for
business. These will be
unlicensed, uninsured and
possibly dangerous.

There are, happily, plenty of
trustworthy and licensed local
minicab firms. Londonwide
firms include **Lady Cabs** (7272
3300), which employs only
women drivers, and **Addison
Lee** (7387 8888). If you're on
the move and want to find a
licensed minicab firm, text
HOME to 60835 ('60tfl') and
Transport for London will send
you the phone numbers of the
two nearest licensed minicab
operators and the number for
Taxi One-Number, which
provides licensed black taxis in
London. The service costs 35p
plus your standard network
rate for a text message. Always
ask the price when you book
and confirm it with the driver.

Driving

London's roads are often slow
moving and clogged with
roadworks, and parking (*see
p362*) is a nightmare. So walk
or use public transport if you
can. If you do hire a car, you
can use any valid licence from
outside the EU for up to a year
after arrival. National speed
limits (70mph for motorways
and dual carriageways, 60mph
on single carriageways) rarely
apply in the capital's built-up
areas; here limits are set by the
local borough, and are often
around 20 or 30mph. Don't use
a mobile phone (unless it's
hands-free) while driving or
you risk a £1,000 fine.

Congestion charge

Drivers coming into central
London between 7am and 6pm
Monday to Friday have to pay

an £8 fee. The area is defined
as within King's Cross (N),
Old Street roundabout (NE),
Aldgate (E), Old Kent Road
(SE), Elephant & Castle (S),
Vauxhall, Chelsea, South
Kensington (SW), Kensington,
Holland Park, North
Kensington, Bayswater,
Paddington (W), Marylebone
and Euston (N). Expect a fine
of £50 if you fail to do so
(rising to £100 if you delay
payment). Passes can be
bought from newsagents,
garages and NCP car parks;
the scheme is enforced by
CCTV cameras. You can pay
any time during the day of
entry. Payments are also
accepted until midnight on the
next charging day after a
vehicle has entered the zone,
although it's £10 if you pay
then. You'll know when you're
about to drive into the
charging zone from the red 'C'
signs painted on the road.
Vauxhall Bridge Road,
Grosvenor Place and Park
Lane is the toll-free through-
route. There are no tollbooths;
instead you pay to register
your vehicle registration
number on a database. For
more information, phone
0845 900 1234 or go to www.
cclondon.com. The current
Congestion Charge zone is
marked on the Central London
by Area map on pp392-393.

Breakdown services

If you're a member of a
motoring organisation in
another country, check if it has
a reciprocal agreement with a
British one. The AA and the
RAC offer schemes that cover
Europe in addition to the UK.

AA (Automobile Association)
*Information 0870 550 0600/
breakdown 08457 887766/
membership 0800 444999/
www.theaa.com.* **Open** 24hrs daily.
Credit MC, V.
**ETA (Environmental Transport
Association)** *68 High Street,
Weybridge, Surrey KT13 8RS
(0845 389 1010/www.eta.co.uk).*
Open *Membership* 8am-6pm

Directory

Mon-Fri; 9am-4pm Sat. *Breakdown service* 24hrs daily. **Credit** MC, V.
RAC (Royal Automobile Club)
RAC House, 1 Forest Road, Feltham, Middx TW13 7RR (breakdown 0800 828282/office & membership 0870 572 2722/www.rac.co.uk). **Open** *Office* 8am-8pm Mon-Fri; 8.30am-5pm Sat. *Breakdown service* 24hrs daily. **Credit** AmEx, DC, MC, V.

Parking

Central London is scattered with parking meters, but free spots are rare. Meters cost up to £1 for 15 minutes, and are limited to two hours. Parking on a single or double yellow line, a red line or in residents' parking areas during the day is illegal, and you may end up being fined, clamped or towed.

However, in the evening (from 6pm or 7pm in much of central London) and at various times at weekends, parking on single yellow lines is legal and free. If you find a clear spot on a single yellow line during the evening, look for a sign giving the regulations for that area. Meters also become free at certain times during evenings and weekends. Parking on double yellow lines and red routes is illegal at all times.

NCP 24-hour car parks (0870 606 7050, www.ncp.co.uk) are numerous but pricey (£3-£12 for two hours). Central ones include Arlington House, Arlington Street, St James's, W1; Snowsfields, Southwark, SE1; and 4-5 Denman Street, Soho, W1.

Clamping

The immobilising of illegally parked vehicles with a clamp is commonplace in London. There will be a label on the car telling you which payment centre to phone or visit. You'll have to stump up an £80 release fee and show a valid licence.

The payment centre will de-clamp your car within four hours, but won't say exactly when. If you don't remove your car at once, it might get clamped again, so wait by your vehicle.

Vehicle removal

If your car has disappeared, the chances are (assuming it was legally

parked) it's been nicked; if not, it's probably been taken to a car pound. A release fee of £200 is levied for removal, plus £40 per day from the first midnight after removal. To add insult to injury, you'll also probably get a parking ticket of £60-£100 when you collect the car (which will be reduced by a 50% discount if paid within 14 days). To find out how to retrieve your car, call the Trace Service hotline (7747 4747).

Vehicle hire

To hire a car, you must have at least one year's driving experience with a full current driving licence; in addition, many car hire firms refuse to rent vehicles out to people under 23. If you're an overseas visitor, your driving licence is valid in Britain for a year.

Prices vary wildly; always ring several competitors for a quote. **Easycar**'s online-only service, at www.easycar.com, offers competitive rates, as long as you don't mind driving a branded car around town.
Alamo *0870 400 4508/www.alamo. com.* **Open** 7.30am-8pm Mon-Fri; 8am-4pm Sat; 10am-2pm Sun. **Credit** AmEx, MC, V.
Avis *0844 581 0147/www.avis. co.uk.* **Open** 7am-10pm daily. **Credit** AmEx, MC, V.
Budget *0844 581 9999/www. budget.co.uk.* **Open** 8am-8pm daily. **Credit** AmEx, DC, MC, V.
Enterprise *0870 607 7757/www. enterprise.com.* **Open** 7am-midnight Mon-Fri; 8am-midnight Sat, Sun. **Credit** AmEx, DC, MC, V.
Europcar *0870 607 5000/www. europcar.co.uk.* **Open** 24hrs daily. **Credit** AmEx, DC, MC, V.
Hertz *0870 599 6699/www.hertz. co.uk.* **Open** 24hrs daily. **Credit** AmEx, DC, MC, V.

Motorbike hire

HGB Motorcycles, 69-71 Park Way, Ruislip Manor, Middx HA4 8NS (01895 676451/www.hgbmotor cycles.co.uk). Ruislip Manor tube. **Open** 9am-6pm Mon-Sat. **Credit** AmEx, MC, V.
The rental prices here include 250 miles a day (with excess mileage at 10p a mile), AA cover, insurance and VAT. Bikes can only be hired with a valid credit card and you'll have to leave a deposit (between £350 and £1,600). You'll also need your own helmet.

Cycling

London isn't the friendliest of towns for cyclists, but the **London Cycle Network** (see www.londoncyclenetwork. org.uk) and **London Cycling Campaign** (7234 9310, www. lcc.org.uk) help make it better. Call **Transport for London** (7222 1234) for cycling maps.

Cycle hire

OY Bike (0845 226 5751, www.oybike.com) has 28 bike stations in west London from which you can rent a bike 24/7 (rates from 30p for 15 minutes) by calling in on a mobile phone (the lock is electronically released). You do have to pre-register with £10 credit.

Go Pedal!

07850 796320/www.gopedal.co.uk. Delivers and collects a bicycle and accessories. The website offers good advice about cycling in London.

London Bicycle Tour Company

1A Gabriel's Wharf, 56 Upper Ground, South Bank, SE1 9PP (7928 6838/www.londonbicycle.com). Southwark tube, Blackfriars or Waterloo tube/rail. **Open** 10am-6pm daily. **Hire** £3/hr; £18/1st day; £9/day thereafter. **Deposit** £180 cash or £1 by credit card. **Credit** AmEx, DC, MC, V. **Map** p404 N7. Bikes, tandems and rickshaw hire; bicycle tours Sat, Sun (£14.95 central London, £17.95 east and west).

Walking

The best way to see London is on foot, but the city is very complicated in its street layout – even many locals carry maps. We've included street maps of central London in the back of this book (starting on p394), with essential locations clearly marked, but the standard Geographers' *A–Z* and Collins' *London Street Atlas* are useful supplements. There's also route-planning advice at www.tfl.gov.uk/tfl/getting around/walkfinder.

Resources A-Z

Addresses

London postcodes are less helpful than they could be for locating addresses. The first element starts with a compass point – out of N, E, SE, SW, W and NW, plus the smaller EC (East Central) and WC (West Central) – which at least gives you a basic idea. However, the number that follows bears no relation to geography (unless it's a 1, which indicates that the address is central), though they apparently follow a rough alphabetical order. So N2, for example, is way out in the boondocks (East Finchley), whereas W2 includes the very central Bayswater.

Attitude & etiquette

Tolerance – of all manner of customs, costumes and weird antics – has long been one of the city's watchwords. But there are limits: nudity and sex in public are prohibited (as is smoking, see p373); churches, libraries, most theatres and cinemas expect a bit of shush; queues are there to be joined, not jumped. Don't mistake reserve for rudeness or indifference; strangers striking up a conversation are likely to be foreign, drunk, mad or in some kind of shared adversity. If you want to rile a Londoner in the underground, stand blocking the escalator during rush hour (the code is simple and works very well: stand on the right, walk on the left). While use of a map doesn't mark you out as a tourist in this sometimes bewildering city, trying to flag down a black cab with its orange light off surely does, as this means it's occupied (see p361). And, finally, those broad white stripes across the road,

sometimes with flashing orange beacons, indicate pedestrians have right of way and traffic is obliged to let you cross – but as some drivers flout the rules, you should still proceed with caution.

Age restrictions

You must be 17 or older to drive in the United Kingdom, and 18 to buy cigarettes or to buy or be served alcohol (if you look younger, carry photo ID). The age of heterosexual and homosexual consent is 16.

Business

As the financial centre of Europe, London is particularly well equipped to meet the needs of business travellers. The financial action is increasingly centred on Canary Wharf, although the City has maintained its dominance. Marketing, advertising and entertainment companies have a strong presence in the West End. As well as a plethora of dedicated conference facilities and meeting rooms, most hotels are thoroughly familiar with the exigencies of corporate clients.

Conventions & conferences

Visit London

7234 5800/www.visitlondon.com. Visit London runs a venue enquiry service for conventions and exhibitions. Call or email for an information pack that lists the facilities offered by various venues, or follow the links from the website.

Queen Elizabeth II Conference Centre

Broad Sanctuary, Westminster, SW1P 3EE (7222 5000/www.qeiicc. co.uk). Westminster tube. **Open** 8am-6pm Mon-Fri. *Conference facilities* 24hrs daily. **Map** p401 K9.
This purpose-built centre has some of the best conference facilities in the capital. Rooms have capacities ranging from 40 to 1,100, all with wireless LAN technology installed.

Couriers & shippers

DHL and FedEx (both with drop-off points all over London) offer local and international courier services; For the Excess Baggage Company, the UK's largest luggage shipper, see p261.
DHL *St Alphage House, 2 Fore Street, the City, EC2Y 5DA (7562 3000/www.dhl.co.uk). Moorgate tube/rail.* **Open** 9am-5.45pm Mon-Fri. **Credit** AmEx, DC, MC, V. **Map** p402 P5.

Travel advice

For current information on travel to a specific country – including the latest news on health issues, safety and security, local laws and customs – contact your home country's government department of foreign affairs. Most have websites with useful advice for would-be travellers.

Australia
www.smartraveller.gov.au

Canada
www.voyage.gc.ca

New Zealand
www.safetravel.govt.nz

Republic of Ireland
http://foreignaffairs.gov.ie

UK
www.fco.gov.uk/travel

USA
http://travel.state.gov

Directory

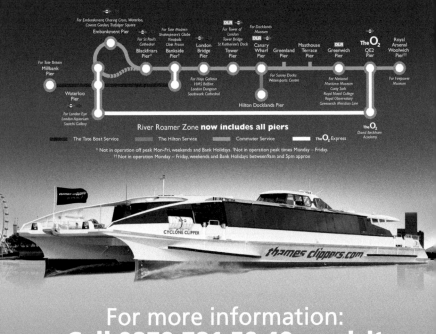

FedEx *0845 607 0809/www.fedex. com.* **Open** 7.30am-7.30pm Mon-Fri. **Credit** AmEx, DC, MC, V.

Office services

ABC rents office equipment, while British Monomarks offers communications services.

ABC Business Machines
17 Nottingham Street, Marylebone, W1U 5EW (7486 5634/www.abc business.co.uk). Baker Street tube. **Open** 9am-5pm Mon-Fri; Sat phone for details. **Credit** MC, V. **Map** p398 G5.

British Monomarks *Monomarks House, 27 Old Gloucester Street, Holborn, WC1N 3XX (7419 5000/ www.britishmonomarks.co.uk). Holborn tube.* **Open** *Mail forwarding* 9.30am-5.30pm Mon-Fri. *Telephone answering* 9am-6pm Mon-Fri. **Credit** AmEx, MC, V. **Map** p399 L5.

Consumer

Consumer Direct
0845 4040 506/ www.consumerdirect.gov.uk. Funded by the government's Office of Fair Trading, this is a good place to start for consumer advice on all goods and services.

Customs

See also www.hmrc.gov.uk; for details on how to claim VAT back on purchases, *see p371.*

From inside the EU

You may bring in the following quantities of tax-paid goods, as long as they are for your own consumption (there are some exceptions when coming from Eastern European countries).

● 3,200 cigarettes or 400 cigarillos or 200 cigars or 3kg (6.6lb) tobacco;
● 90 litres of wine and 110 litres of beer plus either 10 litres of spirits or liqueurs (more than 22% alcohol by volume) or 20 litres of fortified wine (under 22% ABV), sparkling wine or other liqueurs.

From outside the EU

These are total allowances, whether or not the goods were purchased duty-free.

● 200 cigarettes or 100 cigarillos or 50 cigars or 250g of tobacco;
● 2 litres of still table wine plus either 1 litre of spirits or strong liqueurs over 22% volume or 2 litres of fortified wine, sparkling wine or other liqueurs;
● £145 worth of all other goods including gifts and souvenirs.

Disabled

As a city that evolved long before the needs of disabled people were considered, London is a difficult place for disabled visitors, though legislation is slowly improving access and general facilities. In 2004, anyone who provides a service to the public was required to make 'reasonable adjustments' to their properties, and the capital's bus fleet is now much more wheelchair accessible. The tube, however, remains escalator-dependent and can therefore be of only limited use to wheelchair users. The *Tube Access Guide* booklet is free; call the Travel Information line (7222 1234) for more details.

Most major attractions and hotels offer good accessibility, though provisions for the hearing- and sight-disabled are patchier. Enquire about facilities in advance. *Access in London* is an invaluable reference book for disabled travellers, available for a £10 donation (sterling cheque, cash US dollars or online via PayPal to gordon.couch@virgin.net) from Access Project (www. accessproject-phsp.org), 39 Bradley Gardens, West Ealing, W13 8HE.

Artsline
54 Chalton Street, Somers Town, NW1 1HS (tel/textphone 7388 2227/www.artslineonline.com). Euston tube/rail. **Open** 9.30am-5.30pm Mon-Fri. **Map** p399 K3. Information on disabled access to arts and entertainment events.

Can Be Done
11 Woodcock Hill, Harrow, Middx HA3 0XP (8907 2400/www.can bedone.co.uk). Kenton tube/rail. **Open** 9.30am-5pm Mon-Fri.

This company runs disabled-adapted holidays and tours in London, around the UK and worldwide.

LDAF (London Disability Arts Forum)
20-22 Waterson Street, Hackney, E2 8HE (7739 1133/www.ldaf.org). Liverpool Street tube/rail then 149, 242 bus/Old Street tube/rail then 243 bus. **Enquiries** 11am-4pm Mon-Thur.
LDAF organises events for disabled people in London. It produces a bimonthly magazine called Arts Disability Culture (£15/yr waged, £9/yr unwaged).

Royal Association for Disability & Rehabilitation
12 City Forum, 250 City Road, Islington, EC1V 28AF (7250 3222/ textphone 7250 4119/www.radar. org.uk). Old Street tube/rail. **Open** 9am-5pm Mon-Fri. **Map** p402 P3. A national organisation for disabled voluntary groups that also publishes books and the bimonthly magazine *New Bulletin* (£35/yr).

Tourism for All
0845 124 9971/www.tourismforall. org.uk. **Open** *Helpline* 9am-5pm Mon-Fri.
Information for older people and people with disabilities in relation to accessible accommodation and other tourism services.

Wheelchair Travel & Access Mini Buses
1 Johnston Green, Guildford, Surrey GU2 9XS (01483 233640/www. wheelchair-travel.co.uk). **Open** 9am-5.30pm Mon-Fri; 9am-noon Sat. Hires out converted vehicles (driver optional), plus cars with hand controls and wheelchair-adapted vehicles.

Drugs

Illegal drug use remains higher in London than the UK as a whole, though is becoming less visible on the streets and in clubs, due to stricter police 'stop and search' policies. Despite fierce debate, cannabis remains a Class C drug, meaning that possession may only result in a warning or confiscation. More serious Class B and A drugs (ecstasy, LSD, heroin, cocaine and the like) carry stiffer penalties, with a maximum of seven years in prison for possession.

Directory

Electricity

The UK uses the standard European 220-240V, 50-cycle AC voltage. British plugs use three pins, so travellers with two-pin European appliances should bring an adaptor, as should anyone using US appliances, which run off 110-120V, 60-cycle.

Embassies & consulates

American Embassy *24 Grosvenor Square, Mayfair, W1A 1AE (7499 9000/www.london.usembassy.gov). Bond Street or Marble Arch tube.* **Open** 8.30am-5.30pm Mon-Fri. **Map** p400 G7.

Australian High Commission *Australia House, Strand, Holborn, WC2B 4LA (7379 4334/www.uk. embassy.gov.au). Holborn or Temple tube.* **Open** 9.30am-3.30pm Mon-Fri. **Map** p401 M6.

Canadian High Commission *38 Grosvenor Street, Mayfair, W1K 4AA (7258 6600/www.canada.org. uk). Bond Street or Oxford Circus tube.* **Open** 8-11am Mon-Fri. **Map** p400 H7.

Embassy of Ireland *17 Grosvenor Place, Belgravia, SW1X 7HR (7235 2171/passports & visas 7225 7700). Hyde Park Corner tube.* **Open** 9.30am-1pm, 2.30-5pm Mon-Fri. **Map** p400 G9.

New Zealand High Commission *New Zealand House, 80 Haymarket, St James's, SW1Y 4TQ (7930 8422/ www.nzembassy.com). Piccadilly Circus tube.* **Open** 9am-5pm Mon-Fri. **Map** p406 W4.

South African High Commission *South Africa House, Trafalgar Square, St James's, WC2N 5DP (7451 7299/www.southafricahouse. com). Charing Cross tube/rail.* **Open** 9.45am-12.45pm (by appoinment only), 3-4pm (collections) Mon-Fri. **Map** p407 X5.

Emergencies

In the event of a serious accident, fire or other incident, call **999** – free from any phone, including payphones – and ask for an ambulance, the fire service or police. For hospital Accident & Emergency departments, *see below*; for helplines, *see pp367-368*; for police stations, *see p372*.

Gay & lesbian

The *Time Out Gay & Lesbian London Guide* (£9.99) is the ultimate gay handbook to the capital. The phonelines below offer help and information; for information specific to HIV and AIDS, *see p367*.

London Friend *7837 3337/ www.londonfriend.org.uk.* **Open** 7.30-10pm daily.

London Lesbian & Gay Switchboard *7837 7324/ www.llgs.org.uk.* **Open** 24hrs daily.

Health

British citizens or those working in the UK can go to any general practitioner (GP). If you're not visiting your usual GP, you'll need to give their details so your records can be updated. People ordinarily resident in the UK, including overseas students, are also permitted to register with a National Health Service (NHS) doctor. If you fall outside these categories, you will have to pay to see a GP. Your hotel concierge should be able to recommend one.

A pharmacist will dispense medicines on receipt of a prescription from a GP. NHS prescriptions cost £6.85; under-16s and over-60s are exempt from charges. Contraception is free for all. If you're not eligible to see an NHS doctor, you'll be charged cost price for any medicines prescribed.

Free emergency medical treatment under the NHS is available to the following:

● European Union nationals, plus those of Iceland, Norway and Liechtenstein. They may also be entitled to treatment for a non-emergency condition on production of a European Health Insurance Card (EHIC). The EHIC is normally valid for three to five years and covers any medical treatment that becomes necessary during your trip, because of either illness or an accident. The card gives access to state-provided medical treatment only, and you'll be treated on the same basis as an 'insured' person living in the country you're visiting.

● Nationals of New Zealand, Russia, most former USSR states and the former Yugoslavia.
● Residents, irrespective of nationality, of Anguilla, Australia, Barbados, the British Virgin Islands, the Channel Islands, the Falkland Islands, Iceland, the Isle of Man, Montserrat, Poland, Romania, St Helena and the Turks & Caicos Islands.
● Anyone who has been in the UK for the previous 12 months.
● Anyone who has come to the UK to take up permanent residence.
● Students and trainees whose courses require more than 12 weeks in employment during the first year.
● Refugees and others who have sought refuge in the UK.
● People with HIV/AIDS at a special clinic for the treatment of STDs. The treatment covered is limited to a diagnostic test and counselling associated with that test.

There are no NHS charges for services including:

● Treatment in hospital Accident & Emergency departments.
● Emergency ambulance transport to a hospital.
● Diagnosis and treatment of certain communicable diseases, including STDs.
● Family planning services.
● Compulsory psychiatric treatment.

Accident & emergency

Below are listed most of the central London hospitals that have 24-hour Accident & Emergency departments.

Charing Cross Hospital *Fulham Palace Road, Hammersmith, W6 8RF (8846 1234). Barons Court or Hammersmith tube.*

Chelsea & Westminster Hospital *369 Fulham Road, Chelsea, SW10 9NH (8746 8000). South Kensington tube.* **Map** p396 C12.

Guy's Hospital *St Thomas Street (entrance Snowsfields), Borough, SE1 9RT (7188 7188). London Bridge tube/rail.* **Map** p404 P8.

Royal Free Hospital *Pond Street, Hampstead, NW3 2QG (7794 0500). Belsize Park tube/Hampstead Heath rail.*

Royal London Hospital *Whitechapel Road, Whitechapel, E1 1BB (7377 7000). Whitechapel tube.*

St Mary's Hospital *Praed Street, Paddington, W2 1NY (7886 6666). Paddington tube/rail.* **Map** p395 D5.

St Thomas's Hospital *Lambeth Palace Road, Lambeth, SE1 7EH (7188 7188). Westminster tube/ Waterloo tube/rail.* **Map** p401 L9.

University College Hospital
*235 Grafton Road, NW1 2BU
(0845 155 5000). Euston Square/
Warren Street tube.* **Map** p398 J4.

Complementary medicine

British Homeopathic Association
*0870 444 3950/www.trust
homeopathy.org.* **Open** *Phone
enquiries* 9am-5pm Mon-Fri.
The BHA will refer you to the nearest
homeopathic chemist/doctor.

Contraception & abortion

Family planning advice,
contraceptive supplies and
abortions are free to British
citizens on the NHS, and also
to EU residents and foreign
nationals living in Britain.
Phone the Contraception
Helpline on 0845 310 1334
or visit www.fpa.org.uk for
your local **Family Planning
Association**. The 'morning
after' pill (around £25),
effective up to 72 hours after
intercourse, is available over
the counter at pharmacies.

British Pregnancy Advisory Service
0845 730 4030/www.bpas.org.
Open *Helpline* 8am-9pm Mon-Fri;
8.30am-6pm Sat; 9.30am- 2.30pm Sun.
Callers are referred to their nearest
clinic for treatment. Contraceptives
are available, as is pregnancy testing.

Brook Advisory Centre
*7284 6040/helpline 0800 018 5023/
www.brook.org.uk.* **Open** *Helpline*
9am-5pm Mon-Fri.
Information on sexual health,
contraception and abortion, plus
free pregnancy tests for under-25s.
Call for your nearest clinic.

Marie Stopes House
*Family Planning Clinic/Well
Woman Centre, 108 Whitfield
Street, Fitzrovia, W1P 6BE (0845
300 8090/www.mariestopes.org.uk).
Warren Street tube.* **Open** *Clinic*
8.30am-4.30pm Mon-Fri.
Termination helpline 24hrs
daily. **Map** p398 J4.
For contraceptive advice, emergency
contraception, pregnancy testing, an
abortion service, cervical and health
screening or gynaecological services.
Fees may apply.

Dentists

Dental care is free for resident
students, under-18s and people
on benefits. All other patients
must pay. NHS-eligible
patients pay on a subsidised
scale. To find an NHS dentist,
contact the local Health
Authority or a Citizens'
Advice Bureau (*see p367*).

Dental Emergency Care Service
*Guy's Hospital, St Thomas Street,
Borough, SE1 9RT (7188 0511).
London Bridge tube/rail.* **Open** 9am-
5pm Mon-Fri. **Map** p404 Q8.
Queues start forming at 8am; arrive
by 10am if you're to be seen at all.

Hospitals

For a list of hospitals with
Accident & Emergency
departments, *see p366*; for
other hospitals, consult the
Yellow Pages directory.

Opticians

See p257.

Pharmacies

Also called 'chemists' in the
UK. Larger supermarkets and
all branches of Boots have a
pharmacy, and there are
independents on the high street
(*see p257*). Staff are qualified
to advise on over-the-counter
medicines. Most pharmacies
keep shop hours (9am-6pm
Mon-Sat).

STDs, HIV & AIDS

NHS Genito-Urinary Clinics
(such as the Centre for Sexual
Health, *see below*) are affiliated
to major hospitals. They
provide free, confidential
treatment of STDs and other
problems, such as thrush and
cystitis; offer counselling
about HIV and other STDs;
and can conduct blood tests.

The 24-hour **Sexual
Healthline** (0800 567 123,
www.playingsafely.co.uk) is

free and confidential. Visit the
website to find your nearest
clinic. For other helplines,
see below; for abortion and
contraception, *see above*.

Ambrose King Centre
*Royal London Hospital, Whitechapel
Road, Whitechapel, E1 1BB (7377
7306/www.bartsandthelondon.nhs.
uk). Whitechapel tube.* **Open** 9am-
4pm Mon, Thur; 9am-3pm Tue, Fri;
noon-4pm Wed.
Screening for and treatment of STDs,
HIV testing and counselling. Services
are provided on a walk-in basis. Doors
open 30 minutes before clinic hours.

Mortimer Market Centre for Sexual Health
*Mortimer Market, off Capper Street,
Bloomsbury, WC1E 6JB (7530 5050).
Goodge Street or Warren Street tube.*
Open *Bloomsbury clinic* 9am-5.30pm
Mon, Tue, Thur; 1-4pm Wed; 9am-
noon Fri. *GUM clinic (appointments
only)* 10.30am-6pm Mon; 9am-4.30pm
Tue; 1-4pm Wed; 9am-5pm Thur;
9am-12.30pm Fri. **Map** p398 J4.

Terrence Higgins Trust Lighthouse
*314-320 Gray's Inn Road, Holborn,
WC1X 8DP (office 7812 1600/
helpline 0845 122 1200/www.tht.
org.uk). King's Cross tube/rail.*
Open *Office* 9.30am-5.30pm Mon-
Fri. *Helpline* 10am-10pm Mon-Fri;
noon-6pm Sat, Sun. **Map** p399 M5.
This charity advises and counsels
those with HIV/AIDS, their relatives,
lovers and friends. It also offers free
leaflets about AIDS and safer sex.

Helplines

Sexual health helplines
are listed under **STDs,
HIV & AIDS** (*see above*).

Alcoholics Anonymous
*0845 769 7555/www.alcoholics-
anonymous.org.uk.* **Open** 10am-
10pm daily.

Citizens' Advice Bureaux
www.citizensadvice.org.uk.
The council-run CABs offer free
legal, financial and personal advice.
Check the phone book or see the
website for your nearest office.

NHS Direct
0845 4647/www.nhsdirect.nhs.uk.
Open 24hrs daily.
NHS Direct is a free, first-stop service
for medical advice on all subjects.

Directory

Missing People

*0500 700 700/www.missingpeople.
org.uk.* **Open** 24hrs daily.
This volunteer-run organisation
publicises information on anyone
reported missing, and helps to find
missing persons. Its 'Message Home'
freephone service (0800 700 740)
allows runaways to reassure friends
or family of their well-being without
revealing their whereabouts.

Rape & Sexual Abuse Support Centre

8683 3300/www.rapecrisis.org.uk.
Open *Helpline* noon-2.30pm, 7-
9.30pm Mon-Fri; 2.30-5pm Sat, Sun.
Provides support and information for
victims and families.

Samaritans

*0845 790 9090/www.samaritans.
org.uk.* **Open** 24hrs daily.
The Samaritans listen to anyone with
emotional problems. It's a busy
service, so persevere when phoning.

Victim Support

*Head office: Cranmer House, 39
Brixton Road, Brixton, SW9 6DZ
(0845 303 0900/www.victimsupport.
com).* **Open** *Support line* 9am-9pm
Mon-Fri; 9am-7pm Sat, Sun.
Volunteer provides emotional and
practical support to victims of crime,
including information and advice on
legal procedures. Interpreters can be
arranged where necessary.

ID

Unless you look young for
your age, you're unlikely to be
asked for ID in London when
buying alcohol or tobacco,
although many supermarkets
and some bars follow a policy
of checking anyone who looks
21 or under. Passports and
photographic driver's licences
are acceptable forms of ID.

Insurance

Insuring personal belongings
can be difficult to arrange once
you have arrived in London, so
do so before you leave home.
Medical insurance is usually
included in travel insurance
packages. Unless your country
has a reciprocal medical
treatment arrangement with
Britain (*see p366*), it's very
important to ensure you have
adequate health cover.

Internet

Most hotels have at least a
modem plug-in point (dataport)
in each room, if not broadband
or wireless access. Those that
don't have either usually offer
some other form of surfing.

There are lots of cybercafés
around town, including the
easyInternetCafé chain
(*see below*). You'll also find
terminals in public libraries
(*see below*). For more options,
check www.cybercafes.com.

Wireless access has taken off
slowly in Britain, but if your
machine is properly equipped
there are a number of options
– some free, some costly (*see
p368* **Wireless, with strings
attached**). For locations, check
with your provider or visit
www.wi-fihotspotlist.com.

easyInternetCafé

*456-459 Strand, Trafalgar Square,
WC2R 0RG (www.easyinternet
cafe.com). Charing Cross tube/rail.*
Open 8am-11pm daily. **Terminals**
393. **Map** p407 Y5.
Other locations throughout the city.

Left luggage

Airports

Gatwick Airport *South Terminal*
01293 502014/*North Terminal*
01293 502013.
Heathrow Airport *Terminal 1*
8745 5301/*Terminals 2-3* 8759
3344/*Terminal 4* 8897 6874.
London City Airport 7646 0162.
Stansted Airport 01279 663213.

Rail & bus stations

The threat of terrorism has
meant that London stations
tend to have left-luggage desks
rather than lockers; to find out
whether a train station offers
this facility, call 0845 748 4950.

Charing Cross *7930 5444.* **Open**
7am-11pm daily.
Euston *7387 8699.* **Open** 7am-
11pm daily.
King's Cross *7837 4334.* **Open**
7am-11pm daily.
Paddington *7313 1514.* **Open**
7am-11pm daily.
Victoria *7963 0957.* **Open** 7am-
midnight daily.

Legal help

Those in difficulties can visit a
Citizens' Advice Bureau (*see
p367*) or contact the groups
below. Try the Legal Services
Commission (7759 0000,
www.legalservices.gov.uk) for
information. If you are arrested,
your first call should be to your
embassy (*see p366*).

Community Legal Services Directory

0845 345 4345/www.clsdirect.org.uk.
Open 9am-6.30pm Mon-Fri.
Service providing free information
for those with legal problems.

Joint Council for the Welfare of Immigrants

*115 Old Street, Hoxton, EC1V 9RT
(7251 8708/www.jcwi.org.uk).*
Phone enquiries 2-5pm Tue, Thur.
JCWI's telephone-only legal advice
line offers guidance and referrals.

Law Centres Federation

*19 Whitcomb Street, Westminster,
WC2H 7HA (7839 2998/www.law
centres.org.uk). Piccadilly Circus
tube.* **Open** *Phone enquiries* 10am-
5.30pm Mon-Fri.
Local law centres offer free legal help
for people who can't afford a lawyer.
and are living or working in the
immediate area; this central office
connects you with the nearest.

Libraries

Unless you're a London
resident, you won't be able
to join a lending library.
Only the British Library's
exhibition areas are open to
non-members; other libraries
listed can be used for reference.

Barbican Library
*Barbican Centre, Silk Street, the
City, EC2Y 8DS (7638 0569/
www.cityoflondon.gov.uk/barbican
library). Barbican tube/Moorgate
tube/rail.* **Open** 9.30am-5.30pm
Mon, Wed; 9.30am-7.30pm Tue,
Thur; 9.30am-2pm Fri; 9.30am-4pm
Sat. **Map** p402 P5.
British Library *96 Euston Road,
Bloomsbury, NW1 2DB (7412 7000/
www.bl.uk). King's Cross tube/rail.*
Open *Reading room* 10am-8pm
Mon; 9.30am-8pm Tue-Thur; 9.30am-
5pm Fri, Sat. *Admissions office*
9.30am-6pm Mon, Wed, Thur;
9.30am-8pm Tue; 9.30am-4.30pm
Fri, Sat. **Map** p399 L3.

Wireless, with strings attached

London is fast becoming Europe's biggest Wi-Fi hotspot, with a number of different schemes covering Leicester Square, the Square Mile, Islington, bits of Westminster and a large part of the Thames, not to mention vast numbers of hotel lobbies, cafés, bars and clubs.

Several London councils have hopped on the bandwagon in the last few years. Back in 2005, the Borough of Islington was among the early adopters, introducing free Wi-Fi for all along its so-called 'Technology Mile', which runs from the Angel along Upper Street as far as the Odeon Cinema on Holloway Road. The free network remains solid, with approximately 8,000 users per month connecting to it, and no subscription or password is required.

In September 2007, Westminster City Council announced that central London will soon have the largest wireless network in Europe, with plans to extend it even further to a dramatic eight square miles by August 2008. The zone already covers Whitehall, Soho and several other areas within the borough. The City of London, meanwhile, is using new 'mesh' technology to transfer users automatically from base station to base station, allowing uninterrupted web use as they walk. All sounds pretty good, but of course these schemes cost. Westminster is using BT Openzone, with prices starting at £6 an hour. The City network, reputedly the most advanced of its kind in the EU, requires subscribers to register with the Cloud in order to gain a user name and password; they then pay either £4.50 for an hour, or take up an annual contract at £12 a month.

The group behind Free-hotspot.com, an online resource for those looking for Wi-Fi hotspots, and the Wi-Fi network infrastructure firm MeshHopper joined forces in 2007 to offer better news: free Wi-Fi access along a 22.3-mile stretch of the River Thames, from Millbank in central London to Greenwich in south-east London.

In hotels the picture is similarly confused. It seems mid-range properties (Hoxton Hotel, Vancouver Studios, the Sumner) are more likely to offer free Wi-Fi access in their rooms, whereas the swanky Great Eastern Hotel and Threadneedles charge £15-£20 a day for access. So if you're paying your own bills, it pays to do the research before you crack open your laptop for a surf.

Holborn Library *32-38 Theobald's Road, Bloomsbury, WC1X 8PA (7974 6345). Chancery Lane tube.* **Open** 10am-7pm Mon, Thur; 10am-6pm Tue, Wed, Fri; 10am-5pm Sat. **Map** p399 M5.

Kensington Central Library *12 Philimore Walk, Kensington, W8 7RX (7937 2542/www.rbkc.gov.uk/libraries). High Street Kensington tube.* **Open** 9.30am-8pm Mon, Tue, Thur; 9.30am-5pm Wed, Fri, Sat.

Marylebone Library *109-117 Marylebone Road, Marylebone, NW1 5PS (7641 1041/www.westminster.gov.uk/libraries). Baker Street tube/Marylebone tube/rail.* **Open** 9.30am-8pm Mon, Tue, Thur, Fri; 10am-8pm Wed; 9.30am-5pm Sat; 1.30-5pm Sun. **Map** p395 F4.

Victoria Library *160 Buckingham Palace Road, Belgravia, SW1W 9UD (7641 4287/www.westminster.gov.uk/libraries). Victoria tube/rail.* **Open** 9.30am-8pm Mon; 9.30am-7pm Tue, Thur, Fri; 9.30am-7pm Wed; 9.30am-5pm Sat. *Music library* 11am-7pm Mon-Fri; 10am-5pm Sat. **Map** p400 H10.

Westminster Reference Library *35 St Martin's Street, Westminster, WC2H 7HP (7641 4636/www.* *westminster.gov.uk/libraries). Leicester Square tube.* **Open** 10am-8pm Mon-Fri; 10am-5pm Sat. **Map** p407 X4.

Lost property

Always inform the police if you lose anything, if only to validate insurance claims. *See p372* or the Yellow Pages for your nearest police station. Only dial 999 if violence has occurred. Report lost passports both to the police and to your embassy (*see p366*).

Airports

For items left on the plane, contact the relevant airline; Otherwise, phone the following:

Gatwick Airport *01293 503162.*
Heathrow Airport *8745 7727.*
London City Airport *7646 0000.*
Luton Airport *01582 395219.*
Stansted Airport *01279 663293.*

Public transport

If you've lost property in an overground station or on a train, call 0870 000 5151, and give the operator the details.

Transport for London
Lost Property Office, 200 Baker Street, Marylebone, NW1 5RZ (7918 2000/www.tfl.gov.uk). Baker Street tube. **Open** 8.30am-4pm Mon-Fri. **Map** p398 G4.
Allow three working days from the time of loss. If you lose something on a bus, call 7222 1234 and ask for the phone numbers of the depots at either end of the route. If you lose something on a tube, pick up a lost property form from any station.

Taxis

The **Transport for London** office (*see above*) deals with property found in registered black cabs. You are advised to allow seven days from the time of loss. For items lost in a minicab, you must contact the office of the relevant company.

Media

Magazines

Time Out remains London's only quality listings magazine. Widely available in central London every Tuesday, it gives listings for the week from Wednesday. If you want to know what's going on and whether it's going to be any good, this is where to look.

Nationally, *Loaded*, *FHM* and *Maxim* are big men's titles, while women read handbag-sized *Glamour* and glossy weekly *Grazia*, alongside *Vogue*, *Marie Claire* and *Elle*. The appetite for celebrity magazines like *Heat*, *Closer* and *OK* doesn't seem to have abated, while style mags like *i-D* and *Dazed & Confused* have found a profitable niche.

The *Spectator*, *Prospect*, the *Economist* and the *New Statesman* are at the serious, political end of the market, with the satirical *Private Eye* bringing a little levity to the subject. The *London Review of Books* ponders life and letters in considerable depth. The laudable *Big Issue* is sold across the capital by registered homeless vendors.

Newspapers

London's main daily paper is the dull, right-wing *Evening Standard*, published Monday to Friday. *Metro*, an *Evening Standard* spin-off, led what in 2006 became a deluge of free dailies: *London Lite* (the *Standard* again) and the *London Paper* are overpriced at gratis – pick up one of the copies discarded on the tube or a bus to see what we mean.

Quality national dailies include, from right to left, the *Daily Telegraph* and The *Times* (which is best for sport),

the *Independent* and the *Guardian* (best for arts). All go into overdrive on Saturdays and have bulging Sunday equivalents bar the *Guardian*, which has a sister Sunday paper, the *Observer*. The pink *Financial Times* (daily except Sunday) is the best for business. In the middle market, the leader is the right-wing *Daily Mail* (and *Mail on Sunday*); the *Daily Express* (and *Sunday Express*) tries to compete. Tabloid leader is the right-wing *Sun* (and Sunday's *News of the World*). The left-wing *Daily Star* and *Mirror* are the main lowbrow contenders.

Radio

The stations listed below are broadcast on standard wavebands as well as digital, where they are joined by some interesting new channels, particularly from the BBC. The format is not yet widespread, but you might be lucky enough to have digital in your hotel room or hire car.

BBC Radio 1 *97-99 FM.* Standard mix of youth-oriented pop, indie, metal and dance.
BBC Radio 2 *88-91 FM.* Bland during the day, but good after dark.
BBC Radio 3 *90-93 FM.* Classical music dominates, but there's also discussion, world music and arts.
BBC Radio 4 *92-95 FM, 198 LW.* The BBC's main speech station. News agenda-setter *Today* (6-9am Mon-Fri, 7-9am Sat) exudes self-importance.
BBC Radio 5 Live *693, 909 AM.* Rolling news and sport. Avoid the morning phone-ins, but *Up All Night* (1-5am nightly) is terrific.
BBC London *94.9 FM.* Robert Elms (noon-3pm Mon-Fri) is good.
BBC World Service *648 AM.* A distillation of the best of all the other BBC stations; transmitted worldwide.
Capital FM London's best-known station: chat and music.
Classic FM *100-102 FM.* Easy-listening classical.
Heart FM *106.2 FM.* Capital for grown-ups.
Jazz FM *102.2 FM.* Smooth jazz (aka elevator music) now dominates.
LBC *97.3 FM.* Phone-ins and features. The cabbies' favourite.
Resonance *104.4 FM.* Arts radio – an inventively oddball mix.
Xfm *104.9 FM.* Alternative rock.

Television

With a multiplicity of formats, there are plenty of pay-TV options. However, the relative quality of free TV (most notably the BBC's new digital channels) keeps subscriptions from attaining US levels.

Network channels

BBC1 The Corporation's mass-market station. Relies too much on soaps, game shows and lifestyle TV, but has quality offerings too, notably in nature and drama. As with all BBC stations, there are no commercials.
BBC2 A reasonably intelligent cultural cross-section and plenty of documentaries, but upstaged by the BBC's digital arts channel, BBC4 (*see below*).
ITV1 ITV London provides monotonous weekday mass-appeal shows. ITV2 does much the same on digital.
Channel 4 C4's output includes a variety of extremely successful US imports (the likes of *Ugly Betty*, *ER*, *The Sopranos*), many of which get previewed on digital counterpart E4), but it still comes up with gems of its own, particularly documentaries.
Five Sex-oriented programmes, TV movies, rubbish comedy and the occasional good documentary.

Selected satellite, digital & cable

BBC3 *EastEnders* reruns and other light fare, plus quality comedy.
BBC4 Highbrow stuff, including earnest documentaries and dramas.
BBC News 24 Rolling 24hr news.
BBC Parliament Live debates and highlights from Parliament.
Discovery Channel Science and nature documentaries.
E4/Film4 C4's entertainment and movie channels.
Five US US sport, drama and documentaries.
ITV4 'Challenging' drama, comedy and film.
Sky News Rolling news.
Sky One Sky's version of ITV.
Sky Sports Screens most Premiership football and cricket live. There are also Sky Sports 2 and 3.

Money

Britain's currency is the pound sterling (£). One pound equals 100 pence (p). Coins are copper (1p, 2p), silver (round: 5p, 10p; seven-sided: 20p, 50p), yellow-gold (£1) or silver in the centre with a yellowy-gold edge (£2).

Directory

Paper notes are blue (£5), orange (£10), purple (£20) or red (£50). You can exchange foreign currency at banks, bureaux de change and post offices; there's no commission charge at the last of these (for addresses of the most central, *see below*). Many large stores also accept euros (€).

Western Union
0800 833833/www.westernunion.co.uk. The old standby for bailing out cash-challenged travellers. Chequepoint (*see below*) also offers this service.

Banks & ATMs

As well as inside and outside banks, cash machines can be found in some supermarkets and in larger tube and rail stations. Some commercial premises have 'pay-ATMs', which charge for withdrawals (usually £1.50 per transaction). If you are visiting from outside the UK, your cash card should work via one of the debit networks, but check charges in advance. ATMs also allow you to make withdrawals on your credit card if you know your PIN number; you will be charged interest plus, usually, a currency exchange fee. Generally, getting cash with a card is the cheapest form of currency exchange but increasingly there are hidden charges, so do your research. Bank of America customers can use Barclays ATMs free.

Credit cards, especially MasterCard and Visa, are accepted in pretty much every shop (except small corner shops) and restaurant (except caffs) in the capital. However, American Express and Diners Club tend to be accepted at more expensive outlets.

Britain has moved over to the Chip and PIN system, whereby you are required to enter your PIN number rather than sign a credit or debit card slip. You will usually not be allowed to make a purchase with your card without your

PIN. For more information, see www.chipandpin.co.uk.

No commission is charged for cashing sterling travellers' cheques if you go to one of the banks affiliated with the issuing company. You do have to pay to cash travellers' cheques in foreign currencies, and to change cash. You will always need to produce ID to cash travellers' cheques.

Bureaux de change

You'll be charged for cashing travellers' cheques or buying and selling foreign currency at bureaux de change. The commission varies. Major rail and tube stations have bureaux, and there are many in tourist areas and on major shopping streets. Most open 8am-10pm.

Chequepoint *550 Oxford Street, Marylebone, W1C 1LY (7724 6127/www.chequepoint.com). Marble Arch tube.* **Open** 8am-11pm daily. **Map** p398 G6.
Other locations throughout the city.
Garden Bureau *30A Jubilee Market Hall, Covent Garden, WC2E 8BE (7240 9921). Covent Garden tube.* **Open** 9.30am-6pm daily. **Map** p407 Z3.
Thomas Exchange *13 Maddox Street, Mayfair, W1S 2QG (7493 1300/www.thomasexchange.co.uk). Oxford Circus tube.* **Open** 8.45am-5.30pm Mon-Fri. **Map** p406 U3.

Lost/stolen credit cards

Report lost/stolen credit cards immediately to both the police and the services below.

American Express *01273 696933.*
Diners Club *01252 513500.*
MasterCard/Eurocard *0800 964767.*
Switch *0870 600 0459.*
Visa/Connect *0800 895082.*

Tax

With the exception of food, books, newspapers, children's clothing and a few other items, UK purchases are subject to VAT – Value Added Tax, aka

sales tax – of 17.5%. Unlike in the US, this is included in prices quoted in shops. In hotels, always check that the room rate quoted includes tax.

You may be able to take advantage of a scheme allowing you to claim back the VAT you have been charged on most of the goods you take out of the EC (European Community). The scheme is typically advertised in UK shops as 'Tax Free Shopping'. To be able to claim a refund you must be an eligible traveller who is a non-EC visitor to the UK, or a UK resident emigrating from the European Community. When you buy the goods the retailer will ask to see your passport. They will then ask you to fill in a simple refund form. You need to have one of these forms to make your claim; till receipts alone will not do.

If you are leaving the UK direct for a destination outside the EC, you must show your goods and refund form to UK Customs at the airport/port you are leaving from. If you are leaving the EC via another EC country, you must show your goods and refund form to Customs staff of that country.

After Customs have certified your form you can get your refund by posting the form to the retailer from whom you bought the goods, posting the form to a commercial refund company or handing your form in at a refund booth to get immediate payment. Customs are not responsible for making the refund, so when you buy the goods it's worth asking the retailer how the refund is paid.

Opening hours

The following are general guidelines. Government offices all close on every bank (public) holiday (*see pp375-376*); shops are increasingly remaining open, with only Christmas Day seeming sacrosanct. Most

Directory

attractions remain open on the other public holidays, but always call first.

Banks 9am-4.30pm (some close at 3.30pm, some 5.30pm) Mon-Fri; sometimes also Saturday mornings.
Businesses 9am-5pm Mon-Fri.
Post offices 9am-5.30pm Mon-Fri; 9am-noon Sat.
Pubs & bars 11am-11pm Mon-Sat; noon-10.30pm Sun.
Shops 10am-6pm Mon-Sat; some to 8pm. Many are also open on Sunday, usually 11am-5pm or noon-6pm.

Police stations

The police are a good source of information about the area and are used to helping visitors. If you've been robbed, assaulted or involved in an infringement of the law, go to your nearest police station. (We've listed a handful in central London; look under 'Police' in Directory Enquiries or call 118 118, 118 500 or 118 888 for more). If you have a complaint, ensure that you take the offending officer's identifying number (it should be displayed on his or her epaulette). You can then register a complaint with the **Independent Police Complaints Commission** (90 High Holborn, WC1V 6BH, 0845 300 2002). For emergencies, *see p366*.

Belgravia Police Station *202-206 Buckingham Palace Road, Pimlico, SW1W 9SX (7730 1212). Victoria tube/rail.* **Map** p400 H10.
Camden Police Station *60 Albany Street, Fitzrovia, NW1 4EE (7404 1212). Great Portland Street tube.* **Map** p398 H4.
Charing Cross Police Station *Agar Street, Covent Garden, WC2N 4JP (7240 1212). Charing Cross tube/rail.* **Map** p407 Y4.
Chelsea Police Station *2 Lucan Place, Chelsea, SW3 3PB (7589 1212). South Kensington tube.* **Map** p397 E10.
Islington Police Station *2 Tolpuddle Street, Islington, N1 0YY (7704 1212). Angel tube.* **Map** p402 N2.
Kensington Police Station *72-74 Earl's Court Road, Kensington, W8 6EQ (7376 1212). Earl's Court tube.* **Map** p396 B11.
Marylebone Police Station *1-9 Seymour Street, Marylebone, W1H 7BA (7486 1212). Marble Arch tube.* **Map** p395 F6.

West End Central Police Station *27 Savile Row, Mayfair, W1X 2DU (7437 1212). Piccadilly Circus tube.* **Map** p406 U3.

Postal services

You can buy stamps at all post offices and many newsagents and supermarkets. Current prices are 34p for first-class and 24p for second-class letters and small items weighing less than 100g, or 48p for letters to the EU and 78p to the United States. Rates for other letters and parcels vary with weight, size and destination. *See also p363* **Business: Couriers & shippers**.

Post offices

Post offices are usually open 9am-6pm Mon-Fri and 9am-noon Sat, with the exception of **Trafalgar Square Post Office** (24-28 William IV Street, WC2N 4DL, 0845 722 3344), which opens 8.30am-6.30pm Mon-Fri and 9am-5.30pm Sat. Listed below are the other main central London offices. For general enquiries, call 0845 722 3344 or consult www.postoffice.co.uk.

43-44 Albemarle Street *Mayfair, W1S 4DS (0845 722 3344). Green Park tube.* **Map** p406 U5.
111 Baker Street *Marylebone, W1U 6SG (0845 722 3344). Baker Street tube.* **Map** p398 G5.
54-56 Great Portland Street *Fitzrovia, W1W 7NE (0845 722 3344). Oxford Circus tube.* **Map** p398 H4.
1-5 Poland Street *Soho, W1F 8AA (0845 722 3344). Oxford Circus tube.* **Map** p406 V2.
181 High Holborn *Holborn, WC1V 7RL (0845 722 3344). Holborn tube.* **Map** p407 Y1.

Poste restante

If you want to receive mail while you're away, you can have it sent to Trafalgar Square Post Office (*see above*), where it will be kept for a month. Your name and 'Poste Restante' must be clearly marked on the letter. You'll need ID to collect it.

Religion

Times may vary; always phone to check.

Anglican
St Paul's Cathedral *For listings details, see 93.* **Services** 7.30am, 8am, 12.30pm, 5pm Mon-Fri; 8am, 8.30am, 12.30pm, 5pm Sat; 8am, 10.15am, 11.30am, 3.15pm, 6pm Sun. **Map** p404 O6.
Westminster Abbey *For listings details, see p138.* **Services** 7.30am, 8am, 12.30pm, 5pm Mon-Fri; 8am, 9am, 12.30pm, 3pm Sat; 8am, 10am, 11.15am, 3pm, 5.45pm Sun. **Map** p401 K9.

Baptist
Bloomsbury Central Baptist Church *235 Shaftesbury Avenue, Covent Garden, WC2H 8EP (7240 0544/www.bloomsbury.org.uk). Tottenham Court Road tube.* **Open** 10am-4pm Mon-Fri. *Friendship Centre* Oct-June noon-2.30pm Tue. **Services & meetings** 11am, 6.30pm Sun. **Classical concerts** phone for details. **Map** p399 Y1.

Buddhist
Buddhapadipa Thai Temple *14 Calonne Road, Wimbledon, SW19 5HJ (8946 1357/www.buddhapadipa.org). Wimbledon tube/rail then 93 bus.* **Open** *Temple* 9-6pm Sat, Sun. *Meditation retreat* 7-9pm Tue, Thur; 4-6pm Sat, Sun. *See also p184.*

Catholic
Oratory Catholic Church *For listings, see p148.* **Services** 7am, 8am (Latin mass), 10am, 12.30am, 6pm Mon-Fri; 7am, 8.30am, 10am (tridentine), 11am (sung Latin), 12.30pm, 3.30pm, 4.30pm, 7pm Sun. **Map** p397 E10.
Westminster Cathedral *For listings, see p141.* **Services** 7am, 8am, 9am, 10.30am, 12.30pm, 5pm Mon-Fri; 8am, 9am, 12.30pm, 6pm Sat; 7am, 8am, 9am, 10.30am, noon, 5.30pm, 7pm Sun. **Map** p400 J10.

Islamic
Islamic Cultural Centre & London Central Mosque *146 Park Road, Marylebone, NW8 7RG (7724 3363/www.iccuk.org). Baker Street tube/74 bus.* **Open** dawn-dusk daily. **Services** phone 7725 2213 for details.
East London Mosque *82-92 Whitechapel Road, Whitechapel, E1 1JQ (7650 3000). Aldgate East or Whitechapel tube.* **Open** 10am-10pm daily. **Services** *Friday prayer* 1.30pm (1.15pm in winter). **Map** p405 S6.

Directory

Jewish

Liberal Jewish Synagogue
28 St John's Wood Road, St John's Wood, NW8 7HA (7286 5181/ www.ljs.org). St John's Wood tube. **Open** 9am-5pm Mon-Thur; 9am-1pm Fri. **Services** 6.45pm Fri; 11am Sat.
West Central Liberal Synagogue *21 Maple Street, Fitzrovia, W1T 4BE (7636 7627/ www.wcls.org.uk). Warren Street tube.* Services 3pm Sat. **Map** p398 J4.

Methodist

Methodist Central Hall *Central Hall, Storey's Gate, Westminster, SW1H 9NH (7222 8010/www. c-h-w.co.uk). St James's Park tube.* **Open** *Chapel* 8am-6pm daily. **Services** 12.45pm Wed; 11am, 6.30pm Sun. **Map** p401 K9.

Quaker

Religious Society of Friends (Quakers) *173-177 Euston Road, Bloomsbury, NW1 2BJ (7663 1000/ www.quaker.org.uk). Euston tube/ rail.* **Open** 8.30am-9.30pm Mon-Fri; 8.30am-4.30pm Sat. **Meetings** 6.30pm Mon; 11am Sun. **Map** p399 K3.

Safety & security

There are no 'no-go' areas in London as such, but thieves haunt busy shopping areas and transport nodes as they do in all cities. Use common sense and follow these basic rules.

● **Keep** wallets and purses out of sight, and handbags securely closed.
● **Don't** leave briefcases, bags or coats unattended; even if they aren't stolen, they are currently likely to trigger a bomb alert.
● **Don't** leave bags or coats beside, under or on the back of a chair.
● **Don't** put bags on the floor near the door of a public toilet.
● **Don't** take short cuts through dark alleys and car parks.
● **Don't** keep your passport, money, credit cards etc together.
● **Don't** carry a wallet in your back pocket.
● **Be aware** of your surroundings.

Smoking

July 2007 saw the introduction of a ban on smoking in all enclosed public spaces, including pubs, bars, clubs, restaurants, hotel foyers and shops, as well as on public transport. Smokers now face a penalty fee of £50 or a maximum fee of £200 if they

are prosecuted for smoking in a smoke-free area. Many bars and clubs offer smoking gardens or terraces.

As of October 2007 it is also illegal to sell tobacco products to anyone under the age of 18 (prior to that the age was 16).

Study

Being a student in London is as expensive as it is exciting, but certain places do offer discounted student admission. In our listings, these are designated as 'reductions'. You'll need to show ID (an NUS or ISIC card) to qualify.

Universities

Brunel University *Cleveland Road, Uxbridge, Middx UB8 3PH (01895 274000/students' union 01895 269269/www.brunel.ac.uk). Uxbridge tube.*
City University *Northampton Square, Clerkenwell, EC1V 0HB (7040 5060/students' union 7040 5600/www.city.ac.uk). Angel tube.* **Map** p402 O3.
Imperial College *Exhibition Road, Kensington, SW7 2AZ (7589 5111/ students' union 7594 8060/www. imperial.ac.uk). South Kensington tube.* **Map** p397 D9.
London Metropolitan University *166-220 Holloway Road, Holloway, N7 8DB (7607 2789/students' union 7133 2769/www.londonmet.ac.uk). Holloway Road tube.*
South Bank University *Borough Road, Borough, SE1 0AA (7815 7815/students' union 7815 6060/www.lsbu.ac.uk). Elephant & Castle tube/rail.* **Map** p404 O10.
University of Greenwich *Old Royal Naval College, Park Row, Greenwich, SE10 9LS (8331 8000/students' union 8331 7629/www.gre.ac.uk). Greenwich DLR/rail.*
University of Middlesex *Trent Park, Bramley Road, Cockfosters, N14 4YZ (8411 5968/ students' union 8411 6450/www. mdx.ac.uk). Cockfosters tube.*
University of Westminster *309 Regent Street, Mayfair, W1B 2UW (7911 5000/students' union 7915 5454/www.wmin.ac.uk). Oxford Circus tube.* **Map** p398 J5.

University of London

The university consists of 19 separate colleges, spread across the city, of which the

largest are listed below. All are affiliated to the National Union of Students (NUS; 0871 221 8221, www.nusonline.co.uk).
Goldsmiths' College *Lewisham Way, New Cross, SE14 6NW (7919 7171/students' union 8692 1406/www.goldsmiths.ac.uk). New Cross tube/rail.*
King's College *The Aldwych, Strand, Covent Garden, WC2R 2LS (7836 5454/students' union 8481 5588/www.kcl.ac.uk). Temple tube.* **Map** p401 M7.
Kingston University *Penrhyn Road, Kingston, Surrey KT1 2EE (8547 2000/students' union 8547 8868/www.kingston.ac.uk). Kingston rail.*
London School of Economics (LSE) *Houghton Street, Holborn, WC2A 2AE (7405 7686/students' union 7955 7158/www.lse.ac.uk). Holborn tube.* **Map** p399 M6.
Queen Mary, University of London *327 Mile End Road, Stepney, E1 4NS (7882 5555/ students' union 7882 5390/www. qmul.ac.uk). Mile End or Stepney Green tube.*
University College London (UCL) *Gower Street, Bloomsbury, WC1E 6BT (7679 2000/students' union 7387 3611/www.ucl.ac.uk). Euston Square, Goodge Street or Warren Street tube.* **Map** p399 K4.

Useful organisations

More useful organisations for students, including BUNAC and the Council on International Educational Exchange, are on p378.
National Bureau for Students with Disabilities *Chapter House, 18-20 Crucifix Lane, Bermondsey, SE1 3JW (7450 0620/www.skill. org.uk).* **Open** 9am-5pm Mon-Fri.

Telephones

Dialling & codes

London's dialling code is 020; standard landlines have eight digits after that. You don't need to dial the 020 from within the area, so we have not given it in this book. If you're calling from outside the UK, dial your international access code, then the UK code, 44, then the full London number, omitting the first 0 from the code. For example, to make a call to 020 7813 3000 from the

US, dial 011 44 20 7813 3000. To dial abroad from the UK, first dial 00, then the relevant country code from the list below. For more international dialling codes, check the phone book or www.kropla.com/dialcode.htm.

Australia 61; **Canada** 1; **New Zealand** 64; **Republic of Ireland** 353; **South Africa** 27; **USA** 1.

Mobile phones

Mobile phones in the UK work on either the 900 or 1800 GSM system. If you're a US traveller, your home service provider will use the GSM system, and your phone probably runs on the 800 or 1900 MHz band, so you'll need to acquire a tri- or quad-band handset.

The simplest option may be to buy a 'pay-as-you-go' phone (about £50-£200); there's no monthly fee, you top up talk time using a card. Check before buying whether it can make and receive international calls. Phones4u (www.phones4u.co.uk) or Carphone Warehouse (www.carphonewarehouse.com), which both have stores throughout the city, offer a wide range of options. For phone rental, *see also p245*.

Operator services

Operator

Call **100** for the operator if you have difficulty in dialling; for an alarm call; to make a credit card call; for information about the cost of a call; and for help with international person-to-person calls. Dial **155** for the international operator if you need to reverse the charges (call collect) or if you can't dial direct, but be warned that this service is very expensive.

Directory enquiries

This service is now provided by various six-digit 118 numbers. They're pretty pricey to call: dial (free) 0800 953 0720 for a rundown of options and prices. The best known is **118 118**, which charges 49p per call, then 14p per minute thereafter. **118 888** charges 49p per call, then 9p per minute. **118 180** charges 25p per call, then 30p per minute. Online, use the free www.ukphonebook.com.

Yellow Pages

This 24-hour service lists the phone numbers of thousands of businesses in the UK. Dial **118 247** (49p/min) and identify the type of business you require, and in which area of London.

Public phones

Public payphones take coins or credit cards (sometimes both). The minimum cost was to increase in November 2007 to 40p, which buys a 110-second local call. Some payphones, such as the counter-top ones found in many pubs, require more. International calling cards, offering bargain minutes via a freephone number, are widely available.

Telephone directories

There are several telephone directories for London, divided by area, which contain private and commercial numbers. Available at post offices and libraries, these hefty tomes are also issued free to all residents, as is the invaluable Yellow Pages directory (also online at www.yell.com), which lists businesses and services.

Time

London operates on Greenwich Mean Time (GMT), which is five hours ahead of the US's Eastern Standard time. In spring (30 March 2008) the UK puts its clocks forward by one hour to British Summer Time. In autumn (26 October 2008) the clocks go back to GMT.

Tipping

In Britain it's accepted that you tip in taxis, minicabs, restaurants (some waiting staff rely heavily on tips), hotels, hairdressers and some bars (not pubs). Ten per cent is normal, with some restaurants adding as much as 15%. Always check whether service has been included in your bill: some restaurants include an automatic service charge, but also leave space for a gratuity on your credit card slip.

Toilets

Public toilets are scandalously few in London, yet all pubs and restaurants reserve the use of their toilets for customers only. However, all mainline rail stations and a few tube stations – Piccadilly Circus, for one – have public toilets (you will often be charged a small fee). Department stores usually have loos that you can use free of charge, and museums (most of which no longer charge an entry fee) generally have good facilities. At night, options are worse. For a few years Westminster has provided pop-up urinals (they rise up out of the street in time for the post-pub exodus), but there is no such provision for women. The scattering of coin-operated toilet booths around the city may be your only option.

Tourist information

Visit London (7234 5800, www.visitlondon.com) is the city's official tourist information company. There are tourist offices in Leicester Square and by St Paul's (*see p93*), and the new St Pancras International station (*see p357* **Eurostar**) will also have a visitor centre.

Britain & London Visitor Centre *1 Lower Regent Street, Piccadilly Circus, SW1Y 4XT (7808 3800/ www.visitbritain.com). Piccadilly Circus tube.* **Open** 9.30am-6.30pm Mon; 9am-6.30pm Tue-Fri; 10am-4pm Sat, Sun. **Map** p406 W4.
London Information Centre *Leicester Square, WC2H 7BP (7292 2333/www.londontown. com). Leicester Square tube.* **Open** 8am-6pm Mon-Fri; 10am-6pm Sat, Sun. *Helpline* 8am-midnight Mon-Fri; 9am-10pm Sat, Sun.
Greenwich Tourist Information Centre *Pepys House, 2 Cutty Sark Gardens, SE10 9LW (0870 608 2000). Cutty Sark DLR.* **Open** 10am-5pm daily.
Richmond Tourist Information Centre *Old Town Hall, Whittaker*

Avenue, Surrey TW9 1TP (8940 9125/www.visitrichmond.co.uk). Richmond tube/rail. **Open** 10am-5pm Mon-Sat.
Southwark Tourist Information Centre *Tate Modern: Level 2, Bankside, SE1 9TG (7401 5266/ www.visitsouthwark.com). Southwark tube or Blackfriars tube/rail.* **Open** 10am-6pm daily.

Visas & immigration

EU citizens do not require a visa to visit the UK; citizens of the USA, Canada, Australia, South Africa and New Zealand can also enter with only a passport for tourist visits of up to six months as long as they can show they are able to support themselves during their visit and plan to return home afterwards. Use www.ukvisas.gov.uk to check your visa status well before you travel, or contact the British embassy, consulate or high commission in your own country. You can arrange visas online at www.fco.gov.uk. For work permits, *see p376*.
Home Office *Border & Immigration Agency, Lunar House, 40 Wellesley Road, Croydon, Surrey CR9 2BY (immigration information 0870 606 7766/nationality information 0845 010 5200/www.ind.homeoffice. gov.uk).* **Open** *Phone enquiries* 9am-4.45pm Mon-Thur; 9am-4.30pm Fri.

Weights & measures

It has taken some time but the UK is slowly moving towards full metrication. Distances are still measured in miles but all goods are officially sold in metric quantities, with no legal requirement for the imperial equivalent to be given. In May 2007, it was announced that retailers are still permitted to show imperial measurements. A reversal of the European Union's previous position on the matter, this was viewed as a victory over the Eurocrats by some, and a matter of supreme indifference to others. We've

used the still more common imperial measurements throughout this guide.
Some useful conversions:

1 inch (in) = 2.54 centimetres (cm)
1 yard (yd) = 0.91 metres (m)
1 mile = 1.6 kilometres (km)
1 ounce (oz) = 28.35 grammes (g)
1 pound (lb) = 0.45 kilogrammes (kg)
1 UK pint = 0.57 litres (l)
1 US pint = 0.8 UK pints or 0.46 litres

1 centimetre (cm) = 0.39 inches (in)
1 metre (m) = 1.094 yards (yd)
1 kilometre (km) = 0.62 miles
1 gramme (g) = 0.035 ounces (oz)
1 kilogramme (kg) = 2.2 pounds (lb)
1 litre (l) = 1.76 UK or 2.2 US pints

When to go

Climate

The British climate is famously unpredictable, but Weathercall on 0906 850 0401 (60p/min) can offer some guidance. *See also below* **Weather report**. The best websites for weather news and features include www.met office.com, www.weather.com and www.bbc.co.uk/london/ weather, which all offer good detailed long-term forecasts and are easily searchable.
Spring extends from March to May, though frosts can last into April. March winds and April showers may be a month early or a month late, but May is often very pleasant.
Summer (June, July and August) can be unpredictable, with searing heat

one day followed by sultry greyness and violent thunderstorms the next. There are usually pleasant sunny days, though they vary greatly in number from year to year. High temperatures, humidity and pollution can create problems for those with hay fever or breathing difficulties, and temperatures down in the tube can be uncomfortably hot in rush hour. Do as the locals do and carry a bottle of water.
Autumn starts in September, although the weather can still have a mild, summery feel. Real autumn comes with October, when the leaves start to fall – on sunny days the red and gold leaves can be breathtaking. When the November cold, grey and wet sets in, though, you'll be reminded that London is situated on a northerly latitude.
Winter can have some delightful crisp, cold days, but don't bank on them. The usual scenario is for a disappointingly grey, wet Christmas, followed by a cold snap in January and February, when London may even see a sprinkling of snow – and immediate public transport chaos.

Public holidays

On public holidays (bank holidays), many shops remain open, but public transport services generally run to a Sunday timetable. On Christmas Day almost everything, including public transport, closes down.

Good Friday Fri 21 Mar 2008.
Easter Monday Mon 24 Mar 2008.
May Day Holiday Mon 5 May 2008.

Weather report

Average daytime temperatures, rainfall and hours of sunshine in London

	Temp (°C/°F)	Rainfall (mm/in)	Sunshine (hrs/dy)
Jan	6/43	54/2.1	1.5
Feb	7/44	40/1.6	2.3
Mar	10/50	37/1.5	3.6
Apr	13/55	37/1.5	5.3
May	17/63	46/1.8	6.4
June	20/68	45/1.8	7.1
July	22/72	57/2.2	6.4
Aug	21/70	59/2.3	6.1
Sept	19/66	49/1.9	4.7
Oct	14/57	57/2.2	3.2
Nov	10/50	64/2.5	1.8
Dec	7/44	48/1.9	1.3

Directory

Spring Bank Holiday Mon 26 May 2008.
Summer Bank Holiday Mon 25 Aug 2008.
Christmas Day Thur 25 Dec 2008.
Boxing Day Fri 26 Dec 2008.
New Year's Day Thur 1 Jan 2009.

Women

London is home to dozens of women's groups and networks, from day centres to rights campaigners; www.gn.apc.org and www.wrc.org.uk provide information and many links.

Women visiting London are unlikely to be harassed. Bar the very occasional sexually motivated attack, London's streets are no more dangerous for women than for men if you follow the usual precautions (*see p373*). For helplines, *see pp367-368*; for health issues, *see pp366-367*.

The Women's Library
25 Old Castle Street, Whitechapel, E1 7NT (7320 2222/www.the womenslibrary.ac.uk). Aldgate or Aldgate East tube. **Open** *Reading room* 9.30am-5pm Tue, Wed, Fri; 9.30am-8pm Thur; 10am-4pm Sat. **Map** p405 S6.
Europe's largest women's studies archive, with changing exhibitions.

Working in London

Finding temporary work in London can be a full-time job. Those with a reasonable level of English, who are EU citizens or have work permits, should be able to find work in catering, labouring, bars/pubs, coffee bars or shops. Graduates with an English or foreign-language degree could try teaching. Ideas can be found in *Summer Jobs in Britain*, published by Vacation Work, 9 Park End Street, Oxford OX1 1HJ (£10.99 plus £1.75 p&p); its website is www.vacationwork.co.uk.

The *Evening Standard*, local/national newspapers and newsagents' windows are all good sources of job information. Vacancies for temporary and unskilled work are often

displayed on Jobcentre noticeboards; your nearest Jobcentre can be found under 'Employment Agencies' in the Yellow Pages. If you have good typing (over 40 wpm) or word processing skills, you could sign on with some temp agencies. Many have specialist areas beyond the obvious administrative or secretarial roles, such as translation.

Work permits

With few exceptions, citizens of non-European Economic Area (EEA) countries have to have a work permit before they can legally work in the United Kingdom. Employers who are unable to fill particular vacancies with a resident or EEA national must apply for a permit to the Home Office Border & Immigration Agency (*see below*). Permits are issued only for high-level jobs.

Au Pair Scheme
Citizens aged 17 to 27 from the following non-EEA countries (along, of course, with EEA nationals) are permitted to make an application to become au pairs: Andorra, Bosnia-Herzegovina, Bulgaria, Croatia, the Faroe Islands, Greenland, Macedonia, Monaco, Romania, San Marino, Turkey. A visa is sometimes required, so make sure you check. See the appropriate page of www.workingintheuk.gov.uk for details, or contact the **Border & Immigration Agency** (*see below* **Home Office**).

Sandwich students
Approval for course-compulsory sandwich placements at recognised UK colleges must be obtained for potential students by their home country college from the **Border & Immigration Agency** (*see below* **Home Office**).

Students
Visiting students from the US, Canada, Australia or Jamaica can sign up for the BUNAC programme, which allows them to work in the UK for up to six months. Contact the Work in Britain Department of the **Council on International Educational Exchange** (from the US, call 1-800 407 8839 or visit www.ciee.org) or call **BUNAC** direct (*see below*). Students should get an

application form OSS1 (BUNAC) from BUNAC, and submit it to a UK Jobcentre to obtain permission to work. Students may not exceed 20 hours' work during term-time.

Working holidaymakers

Citizens of Commonwealth countries aged from 17 to 27 are allowed to apply to come to the UK as a working holidaymaker. Start by contacting your nearest British diplomatic post in advance. You are then allowed to take part-time work without a DfEE permit. Contact the **Border & Immigration Agency** (*see below* **Home Office**) for more information.

Useful addresses

BUNAC
16 Bowling Green Lane, Clerkenwell, EC1R 0QH (7251 3472/www. bunac.org.uk). Farringdon tube/rail. **Open** 9.30am-5.30pm Mon-Thur; 9.30am-5pm Fri. **Map** p402 N4.

Council on International Educational Exchange
300 Fore Street, Portland, ME 04101, USA (7553 4000/www.ciee. org). **Open** 9am-5pm Mon-Fri.
The CIEE helps young people to study, work and travel abroad.

Home Office
Border & Immigration Agency, Lunar House, 40 Wellesley Road, Croydon, Surrey CR9 2BY (0870 606 7766/www.ind.homeoffice. gov.uk). **Open** *Phone enquiries* 9am-4.45pm Mon-Fri; 9am-4.30pm Fri.
The Home Office is able to provide advice on whether or not a work permit is required; application forms can be downloaded from the website.

Overseas Visitors Records Office
180 Borough High Street, Borough, SE1 1LH (7230 1208). Borough tube. **Open** 9am-4pm Mon-Fri. **Map** p404 P9.
The Overseas Visitors Records Office charges £34 to register a person if they already have a work permit.

Working in the UK
0114 207 4074/www.working intheuk.gov.uk. **Open** *Phone enquiries* 9am-5pm Mon-Fri.
The website has information provided by the Border & Immigration Agency for foreign nationals and UK-based employers about the various routes open to those who want to come and work in the UK, plus the relevant application forms.

Directory

Further Reference

Fiction

Peter Ackroyd *Hawksmoor; The House of Doctor Dee; Great Fire of London; The Lambs of London* Intricate studies of arcane London.
Monica Ali *Brick Lane* Arranged marriage in Tower Hamlets.
Martin Amis *London Fields* Darts and drinking way out east.
Jonathan Coe *The Dwarves of Death* Mystery, music, mirth, male violence and the like.
Norman Collins *London Belongs to Me* Witty saga of 1930s Kennington.
Sir Arthur Conan Doyle *The Complete Sherlock Holmes* Reassuring sleuthing shenanigans.
Joseph Conrad *The Secret Agent* Anarchism in seedy Soho.
Charles Dickens *Oliver Twist; David Copperfield; Bleak House; Our Mutual Friend* Four of the master's most London-centric novels.
Maureen Duffy *Capital* The bones beneath us and the stories they tell.
Christopher Fowler *Soho Black* Walking dead in Soho.
Anthony Frewin *London Blues* One-time Kubrick assistant explores 1960s Soho porn movie industry.
Graham Greene *The End of the Affair* Adultery and Catholicism during the Blitz.
Patrick Hamilton *Twenty Thousand Streets Under the Sky* Dashed dreams at the bar of the Midnight Bell in 1950s Fitzrovia.
Alan Hollinghurst *The Swimming Pool Library; The Line of Beauty* Gay life around Russell Square; beautiful, ruthless look at metropolitan debauchery – won the 2004 Booker.
Hanif Kureishi *The Buddha of Suburbia* Sexual confusion and identity crisis in the 1970s.
Colin MacInnes *City of Spades; Absolute Beginners* Coffee 'n' jazz, Soho 'n' Notting Hill. Tour of rock history's blue plaque sites.
Derek Marlowe *A Dandy in Aspic* A capital-set Cold War classic.
Michael Moorcock *Mother London* A love letter to London.
Alan Moore *From Hell* Amazing, dark graphic novel on the Ripper.
George Orwell *Keep the Aspidistra Flying; Nineteen Eighty-Four* Saga of a struggling writer; bleak vision of totalitarian takeover.
Derek Raymond *I Was Dora Suarez* The blackest London noir.
Nicholas Royle *The Matter of the Heart; The Director's Cut* Abandoned buildings and secrets.
Edward Rutherfurd *London* A city's history given a novel voice.

Iain Sinclair *Downriver; Radon Daughters; White Chappell/Scarlet Tracings* The Thames's *Heart of Darkness*; William Hope Hodgson; Ripper murders/book dealers.
Sarah Waters *Nightwatch* The Home Front during World War II.
HG Wells *War of the Worlds* Early SF classic with a suburban London setting and Primrose Hill finale.
Virginia Woolf *Mrs Dalloway* A kind of London *Ulysses*.

Non-fiction

Peter Ackroyd *London: The Biography; Thames: Sacred River* Loving but wilfully obscurantist histories of the city and its river.
Nicholas Barton *The Lost Rivers of London* Fascinating studies of old watercourses and their legacy.
James Boswell *Boswell's London Journal 1762-1763* Rich account of a ribald literary life.
Geoffrey Fletcher *The London Nobody Knows* Long out of print discourse on the capital by a great forgotten London writer.
Ed Glinert *A Literary Guide to London; The London Compendium* Essential London minutiae.
Sarah Guy (ed) *Time Out Book of London Walks volumes 1 & 2* Writers, cartoonists, comedians and historians walk the capital.
Neil Hanson *The Dreadful Judgement* The embers of the Great Fire raked over.
Sarah Hartley *Mrs P's Journey* Biography of Phyllis Pearsall, the woman who created the *A-Z*.
Edward Jones & Christopher Woodward *A Guide to the Architecture of London* What it says on the cover. A brilliant work.
Jack London *The People of the Abyss* Poverty in the East End.
Tim Moore *Do Not Pass Go* Hilarious Monopoly addict's London.
George Orwell *Down and Out in Paris and London* Waitering, begging and starving.
Samuel Pepys *Diaries* Fires, chat, plagues and bordellos. (Blog www.pepysdiary.com has been posting an entry of the diary a day since 2003.)
Liza Picard *Dr Johnson's London; Restoration London* London past, engagingly revisited.
Patricia Pierce *Old London Bridge* The story of the world's longest inhabited bridge.
Roy Porter *London: A Social History* An all-encompassing history.
Iain Sinclair *Lights Out for the Territory; London Orbital* Time-warp visionary crosses London; time-warp visionary circles it on the M25.

Iain Sinclair (ed) *London: City of Disappearances* Scraps, clippings and faded post-it notes from a host of contemporary city mythologisers.
Stephen Smith *Underground London: Travels Beneath the City Streets* Absorbing writing on the subterranean city.
Richard Tames *Feeding London; East End Past* Eating history from coffee houses onwards; a close look at the East End.
Adrian Tinniswood *His Invention So Fertile* Illuminating biography of Sir Christopher Wren.
Richard Trench & Ellis Hillman *London Under London: A Subterranean Guide* Tunnels, lost rivers, disused tube stations, military bunkers – simply fascinating.
Ben Weinreb & Christopher Hibbert (eds) *The London Encyclopaedia* Brilliant, thorough, indispensable reference guide.
Jerry White *London in the 20th Century: A City and Its People.* How London became a truly global city.

Films

Alfie (Lewis Gilbert, 1966) What's it all about, Michael?
Blow-Up (Michelangelo Antonioni, 1966) Swinging London captured in an unintentionally hysterical fashion.
Breaking and Entering (Anthony Minghella, 2006) Star-studded thievery in Kings Cross.
A Clockwork Orange (Stanley Kubrick, 1971) Kubrick's vision still shocks – but so does Thamesmead, location for many Orange scenes.
Closer (Mike Nichols, 2004) Infidelity and emotional uncertainty in and around Clerkenwell.
Da Vinci Code (Ron Howard, 2006) Film version of Dan Brown's blockbuster novel, partly filmed in London (Inner Temple gets a look-in).
Death Line (Gary Sherman, 1972) The last of a Victorian cannibal race is found in a lost tube station. Yikes.
Dirty Pretty Things (Stephen Frears, 2002) Drama centred on immigrant hotel workers.
The Krays (Peter Medak, 1990) The life and times of the most notorious of East End gangsters.
Life is Sweet; Naked; Secrets & Lies; Career Girls; All or Nothing; Vera Drake (Mike Leigh, 1990-2004) Metroland; study of misanthropy; familial tensions; old friends meet; family falls apart; problems of post-war austerity.
Lock, Stock & Two Smoking Barrels; Snatch (Guy Ritchie, 1998-2000) Mr Madonna's pair of East End faux-gangster flicks.

London; Robinson in Space (Patrick Keiller, 1994-1997) Quality arthouse fiction meets documentary.

The Long Good Friday (John MacKenzie, 1989) Bob Hoskins stars in the classic London gangster flick.

Mona Lisa; The Crying Game (Neil Jordan, 1986-1992) Prostitution, terrorism, transvestism.

Notting Hill (Roger Michell, 1999) Hugh Grant and Julia Roberts get it on in west London.

Peeping Tom (Michael Powell, 1960) Powell's creepy murder flick: a young man films his dying victims.

Performance (Nicolas Roeg & Donald Cammell, 1970) This cult movie to end all cult movies made west London cool for life.

28 Days (Danny Boyle, 2002) Post-apocalyptic London.

Wonderland (Michael Winterbottom, 1999) Love, loss and deprivation in Soho and south London.

Music

Lily Allen *Alright, Still* Feisty, urban reggae-pop, perfect for summer.

Babyshambles *Down in Albion* Pete Doherty's vision of an idealised England oddly takes in unglamorous Deptford and Catford.

Blur *Modern Life is Rubbish; Parklife* Modern classics by the Essex exiles.

Billy Bragg *Must I Paint You a Picture? The Essential Billy Bragg* The bard of Barking's greatest hits.

Chas & Dave *Don't Give a Monkey's* Cockney singalong revivalists.

The Clash *London Calling* Epoch-making punk classic.

Dizzee Rascal *Maths + English* Rough-cut sounds and street-smart lyrics from grime's crossover king.

Ian Dury *New Boots & Panties* Cheekily essential listening from the Essex pub maestro.

The Good, the Bad & the Queen *The Good, the Bad & the Queen* Damon Albarn, Paul Simenon, Simon Tong and Tony Allen form London-centric supergroup.

The Jam *This is the Modern World* Weller at his splenetic finest.

The Kinks *Something Else* Classic album, 'Waterloo Sunset' and all.

Madness *Rise & Fall* The nutty boys at their lyrical best.

The Rolling Stones *December's Children (& Everybody's)* Moodily cool evocation of the city.

Saint Etienne *Tales from Turnpike House* Kitchen-sink opera by London-loving indie dance band.

Small Faces *Ogdens' Nut Gone Flake* Concept album by band fronted by East End-born Steve Marriott.

Squeeze *Greatest Hits* Lovable south London geezer pop.

The Streets *Original Pirate Material* Geezer pop for a new millennium: garage meets Madness.

Websites

www.allinlondon.co.uk Links site.

www.bbc.co.uk/london London-focused news, travel, weather, sport.

www.classiccafes.co.uk London's finest 1950s and '60s caffs.

www.filmlondon.org.uk London's film and movie agency.

www.gumtree.com Very useful online community noticeboard.

www.hiddenlondon.com The city's undiscovered gems.

www.london-footprints.co.uk Free walks to print out.

www.london.gov.uk The Greater London Assembly's official website.

www.pubs.com London's traditional boozers.

www.riverthames.co.uk Places along the riverbank.

www.streetmap.co.uk Grid references and postcodes.

www.timeout.com A vital source giving access to our eating and drinking reviews, as well as features and listings from the magazine.

www.tfl.gov.uk/tfl Transport for London journey planners and maps.

www.uktravel.com Click on a tube station and find nearby attractions.

Reading corners

Read curled up in the safety of your hotel room if you like, but why not grab that book and step out into the streets that inspired it. There's hardly a district that doesn't have its fictional double, hardly a pub without it's one-time writer-in-residence.

Poet's Corner in **Westminster Abbey** (*see p138*) is the permanent and final residence of luminaries such as Chaucer and Tennyson, as well as Charles Dickens, surely the archetypal London writer. Too obvious a homage for us, though: instead, take your *Bleak House* to **Lincoln's Inn Fields** (*see p102*), near the Chancery Law Courts where the interminable Jarndyce v Jarndyce case unfolds. Not far away to the north-west is Fitzroy Square; park yourself on a bench and you can open Ian McEwan's *Saturday* in the company of protagonist Henry Perowne, who we are told lives nearby.

If the weather's poor, stroll to the **British Museum** (*see p107*). The new Great Court centres on the former British Library Reading Room, where many eminent writers famously laboured. Do check with your other half before setting out, though: Karl Marx spent so much time here his wife hid his trousers in an attempt to keep him at home. Rudyard Kipling and George Orwell are among the many who put pen to paper here. Having struggled through the first few pages of *Das Kapital*, perhaps it's time for a pint. Head to the Covent Garden's **Lamb & Flag** (*see p226*), said to be the inspiration for Orwell's fictional pub the Moon under Water, which crops up in an essay describing the ideal boozer and, troublingly, in *1984*.

Drink is seldom far from the agenda in London novels, and few capture the seamier side of the city better than Patrick Hamilton's superb *Hangover Square*. You can sample the hospitality at the **Courtfield** (187 Earl's Court Road, 7370 2626), renamed the Rockingham in the book. Worried about the perdition of your soul? The sinister spire of **Christ Church Spitalfields** (*see p163*) will give you scant solace, especially if you're accompanied by *Hawksmoor*, Peter Ackroyd's fictionalised life of its architect. Perhaps the hotel room wasn't such a bad idea.

Directory

Index

Advertisers' Index

Please refer to the relevant pages for contact details

Major sight or landmark	▇
Railway or coach station	▇
Underground station	⊖
Park	▇
Hospital or place of learning	▇
Casualty unit	✚
Church	✚
Synagogue	✡
Congestion Zone	Ⓒ
District	MAYFAIR
Theatre	●

Maps

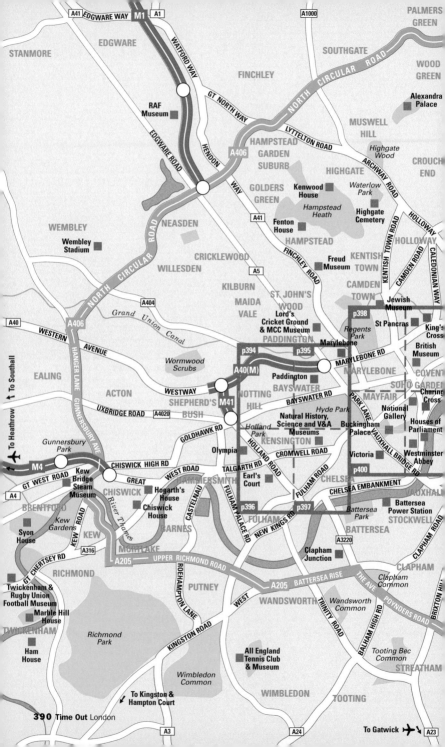

London Overview

© Copyright Time Out Group 2008

Central London
by Area

© Copyright Time Out Group 2008

0   1 km

0   0.5 mile

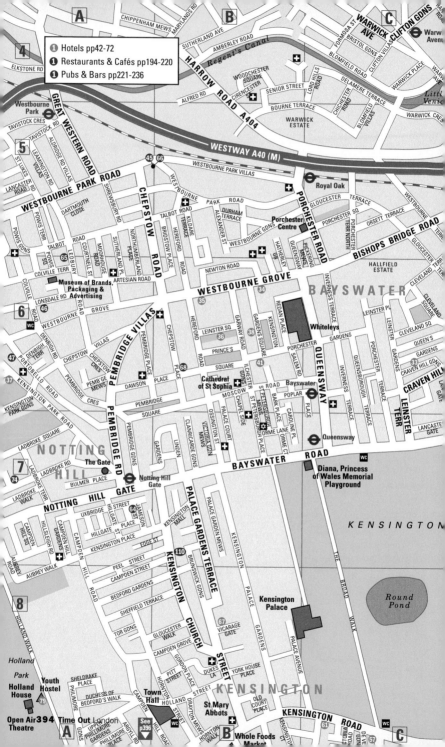

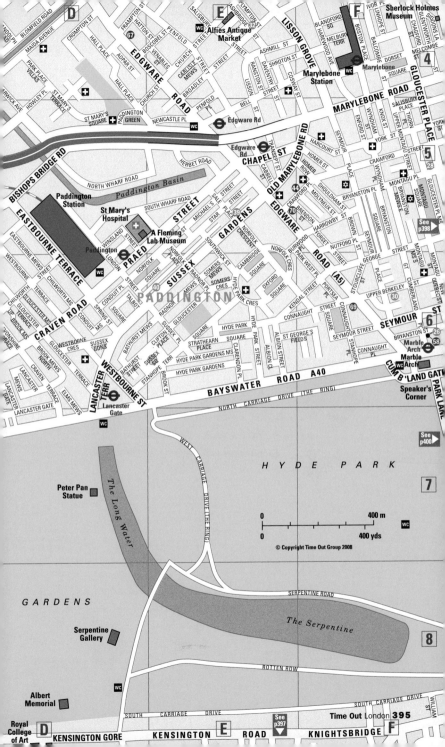

D
E
F

Sherlock Holmes Museum

4

Alfies Antique Market

Marylebone Station

Marylebone

MARYLEBONE ROAD

5

Edgware Rd

CHAPEL ST

OLD MARYLEBONE RD

Paddington Station

St Mary's Hospital

A Fleming Lab Museum

PRAED STREET

EDGWARE ROAD (A5)

SUSSEX GARDENS

PADDINGTON

6

Marble Arch

Marble Arch

SEYMOUR ST

Speaker's Corner

CUMBERLAND GATE

PARK LANE

EASTBOURNE TERRACE

CRAVEN ROAD

WESTBOURNE ST

LANCASTER TERR

Lancaster Gate

BAYSWATER ROAD A40

NORTH CARRIAGE DRIVE (THE RING)

See p400

Peter Pan Statue

The Long Water

WEST CARRIAGE DRIVE (THE RING)

H Y D E   P A R K

7

0   400 m
0   400 yds
© Copyright Time Out Group 2008

G A R D E N S

SERPENTINE ROAD

Serpentine Gallery

The Serpentine

8

ROTTEN ROW

Albert Memorial

SOUTH CARRIAGE DRIVE

WILLIAM

Time Out London **395**

Royal College of Art

D KENSINGTON GORE

E KENSINGTON ROAD

See p397

F KNIGHTSBRIDGE

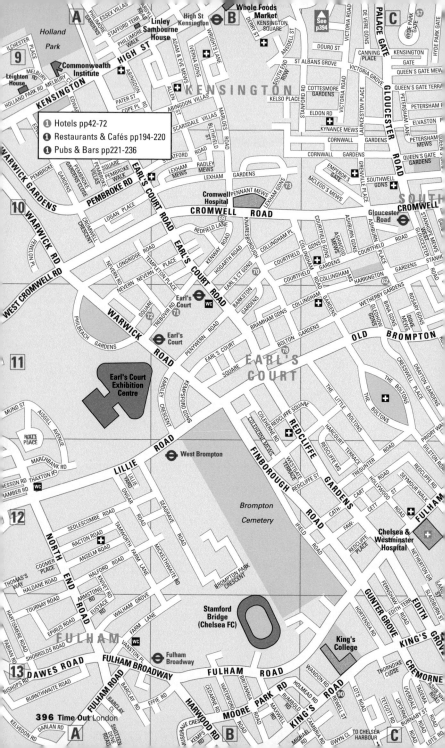

❶ Hotels pp42-72
❶ Restaurants & Cafés pp194-220
❶ Pubs & Bars pp221-236

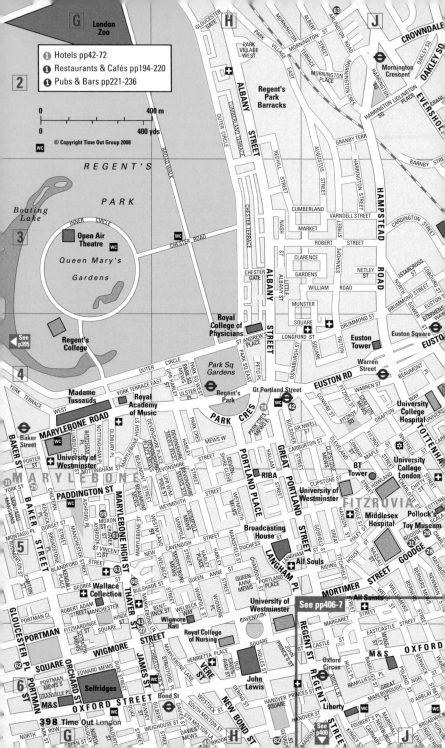

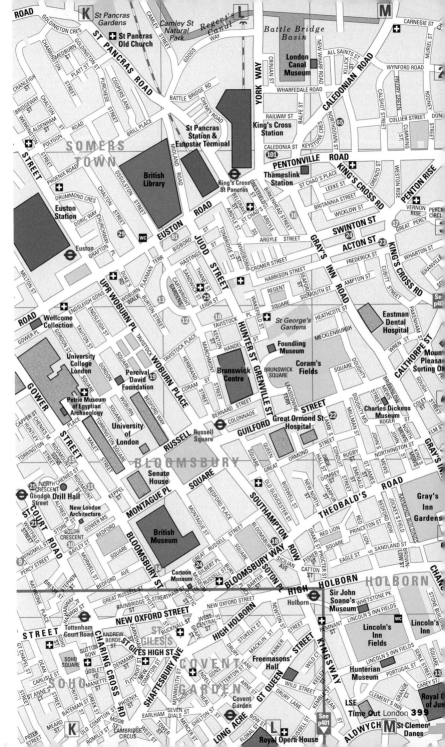

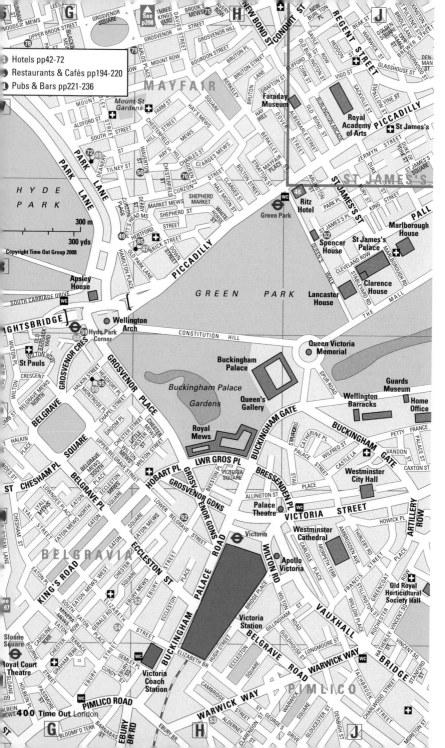

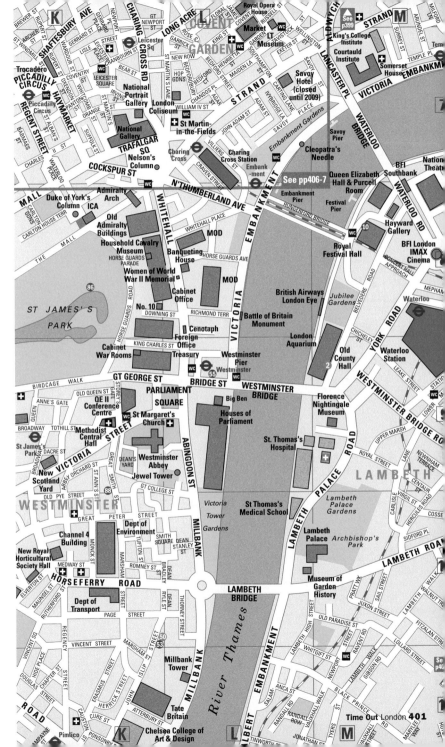

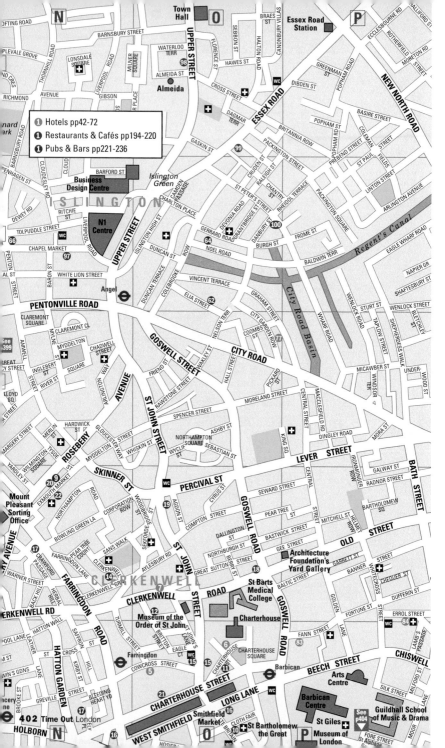

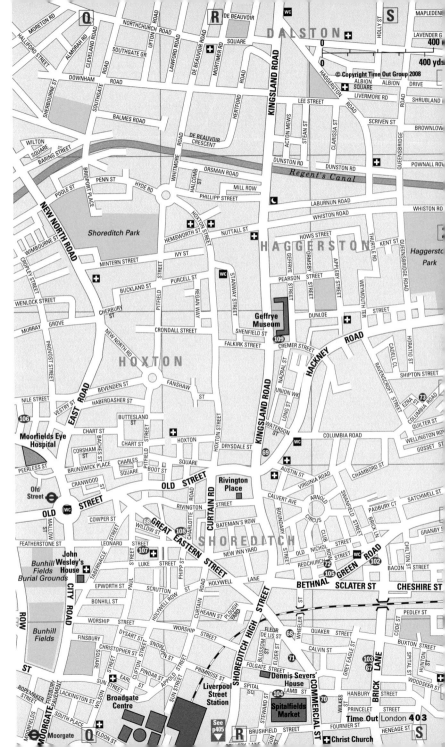

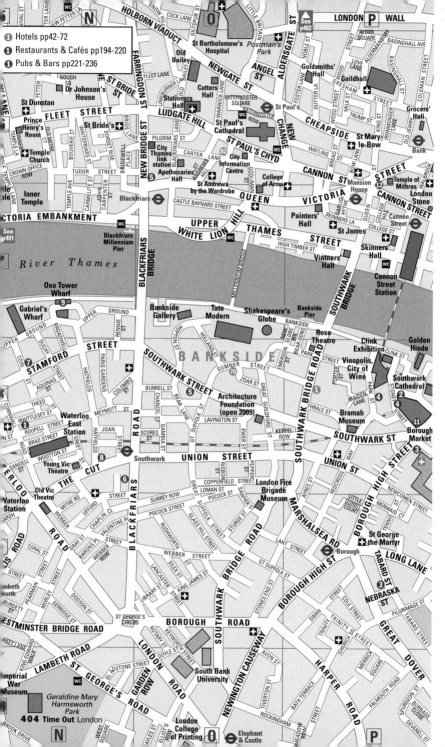

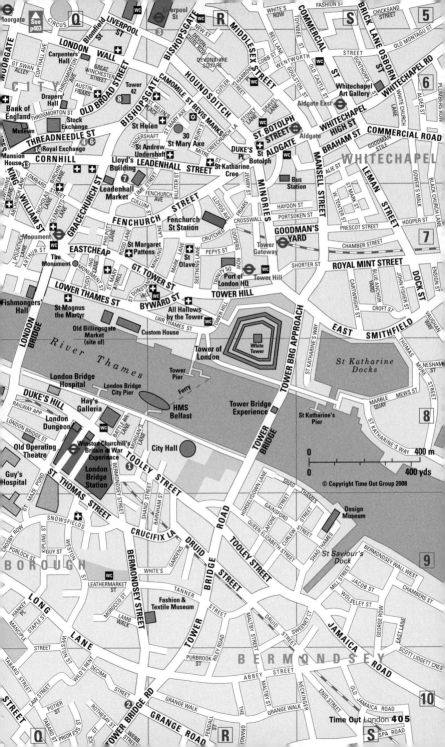

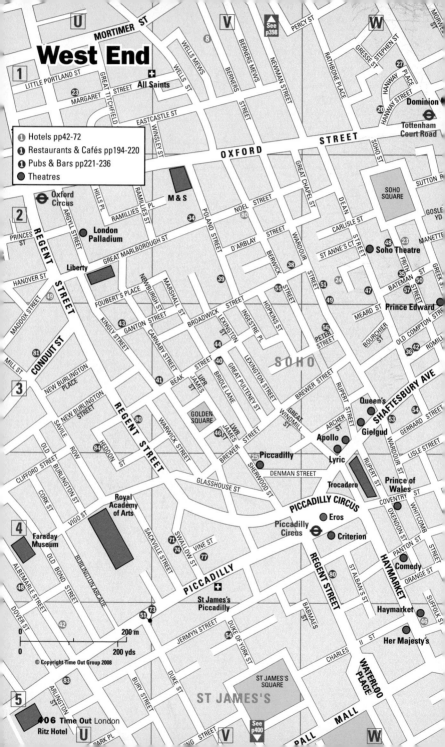

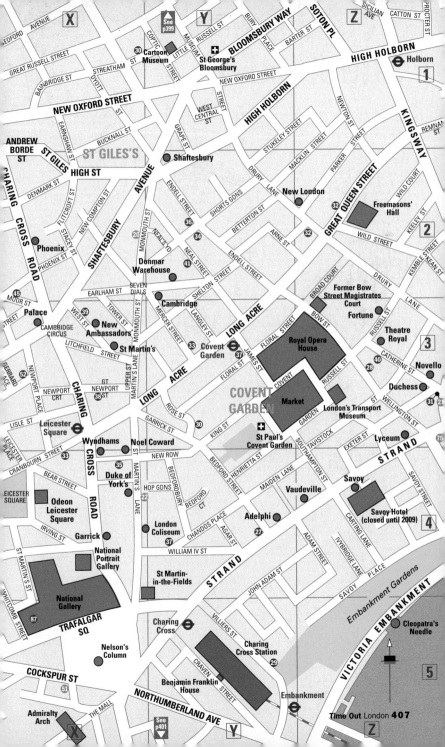

Street Index

Cutler Street - 405 R6
Cynthia Street - 399 M2
Cyrus Street - 402 O4

Dacre Street - 401 K9
Dagmar Terrace - 402 O1
Dallington Street - 402 O4
Danbury Street - 402 O2
Danube Street - 397 E11
Danvers Street - 397 D12/E12
D'Arblay Street - 398 J6,
406 V2
Darlan Road - 396 A13
Dartmouth Close - 394 A5
Daventry Street - 395 E4/5
Davies Mews - 398 H6
Davies Street - 398 H6,
400 H6/7
Dawes Road - 396 A13
Dawson Place - 394 B6
De Beauvoir Crescent - 403 Q1
De Beauvoir Road - 403 R1
De Beauvoir Square - 403 R1
De Vere Gardens - 394 C9,
396 C9
Deal Street - 403 S5
Dean Bradley Street -
401 K10/L10
Dean Ryle Street -
401 K10/L10
Dean Stanley Street - 401 L10
Dean Street - 399 K6,
406 W2/3
Deanery Street - 400 G7
Dean's Yard - 401 K9
Decima Street - 405 Q10
Delamere Terrace - 394 C4
Denbigh Road - 394 A6
Denbigh Street - 400 J11
Denbigh Terrace - 394 A6
Denman Street - 400 J7,
406 V4/W4
Denmark Street - 399 K6,
407 X2
Denyer Street - 397 F10
Derby Street - 400 H8
Dering Street - 398 H6
Derry Street - 396 B9
Deverell Street - 404 P10
Devonia Road - 402 O2
Devonshire Close - 398 H4/5
Devonshire Mews South -
398 H5
Devonshire Mews West -
398 H4
Devonshire Place - 398 G4/H4
Devonshire Place Mews -
398 G4
Devonshire Row - 405 R6
Devonshire Square - 405 R6
Devonshire Street - 398 H4
Devonshire Terrace - 395 D6
Dewey Road - 402 N2
Dibden Street - 402 P1
Dilke Street - 397 F12
Dingley Road - 402 P3
Dock Street - 405 S7
Dodson Street - 404 N9
Dombey Street - 399 M5
Donegal Street - 399 M2,
402 N2
Doric Way - 399 K3
Dorset Rise - 404 N6
Dorset Square - 395 F4
Dorset Street - 398 G5
Doughty Mews - 399 M4
Doughty Street - 399 M4
Douglas Street - 401 K11
Douro Street - 396 C9
Dove Mews - 396 C11
Dovehouse Street - 397 E11/12
Dover Street - 400 H7/J7,
406 U5
Down Street - 400 G8/H8
Downham Road - 403 Q1
Downing Street - 401 K8/L8
Doyle Street - 404 O10
Drake Street - 399 M5
Draycott Avenue - 397 E10/F12

Draycott Place - 397 F11
Draycott Terrace - 397 F10
Drayton Gardens - 396 C11,
397 D11/12
Drayton Mews - 394 B8
Druid Street - 405 R9/S10
Drummond Crescent - 399 K3
Drummond Street - 398 J3/4
Drury Lane - 399 L6/M6,
407 Y2/Z2/3
Drysdale Street - 403 R3
Duchess of Bedford's Walk
394 A8
Duchess Street - 398 H5
Duchy Street - 404 N8
Dufferin Street - 402 P4
Duke of York Street - 400 J7,
406 V5
Duke Street - 398 G6
Duke Street, St James's -
400 J7/8, 406 V5
Duke's Hill - 405 Q8
Dukes Lane - 394 B8
Duke's Place - 405 R6
Duke's Road - 399 K3
Duncan Street - 402 O2
Duncan Terrace - 402 O2
Dunloe Street - 403 S3
Dunraven Street - 400 G6
Dunston Road - 403 R2/S2
Durham Terrace - 394 B5
Dyott Street - 399 L6, 407 X1
Dysart Street - 403 Q5

Eagle Court - 402 O4/5
Eagle Street - 399 M5
Eagle Wharf Road - 402 P2,
403 Q2
Eardley Crescent - 396 B11
Earl Street - 403 Q5
Earlham Street - 399 K6/L6,
407 X2
Earl's Court Square - 396 B11
Earl's Court Gardens - 396 B10
Earl's Court Road - 396
A9/10/B10/11
Earls Walk - 396 E10
Earnshaw Street - 399 K6,
407 X1/2
East Lane - 405 S9
East Road - 403 Q3
East Smithfield - 405 S7
Eastbourne Mews - 395 D5/6
Eastbourne Terrace - 395 D5/6
Eastcastle Street - 398 J5/6,
406 U1/V1
Eastcheap - 405 Q7
Eaton Mews - 400 H10
Eaton Place - 400 G9/10
Eaton Square - 400 G10/H10
Eaton Terrace - 400 G10/12
Ebury Bridge - 400 H11
Ebury Bridge Road - 400 G11
Ebury Mews - 400 H10
Ebury Square - 400 G11
Ebury Street - 400 G10/11/H10
Ecclesbourne Road - 402 P1
Eccleston Mews - 400 G9
Eccleston Place - 400 H10
Eccleston Square - 400 H11
Eccleston Street - 400 G10/H10
Edge Street - 394 A7
Edgware Road - 395 D4/E4/5
Edith Grove - 396 C12/13
Edith Terrace - 396 C13
Edward Mews - 398 G6
Edwardes Square - 396 A9/10
Effie Road - 396 A13/B13
Egerton Crescent - 397 E10
Egerton Gardens - 397 E10
Egerton Terrace - 397 E10
Elcho Street - 397 E13
Elder Street - 403 R5
Eldon Road - 396 C9
Eldon Street - 403 Q5
Elia Street - 402 O2
Elizabeth Avenue - 402 P1,
403 Q1
Elizabeth Bridge - 400 H11

Elizabeth Street - 400 G10/H10
Elkstone Road - 394 A4
Elliot's Row - 404 O10
Elm Park Gardens - 397 D11/12
Elm Park Lane - 397 D12
Elm Park Road - 397 D12
Elm Place - 397 D11
Elm Street - 399 M4
Elms Mews - 395 D6
Elvaston Place - 396 C9,
397 D9
Elverton Street - 401 K10
Ely Place - 402 N5
Elystan Place - 397 F11
Elystan Street - 397 E11
Emerald Street - 399 M5
Emerson Street - 404 O8
Emperor's Gate - 396 C10
Endell Street - 399 L6, 407 Y2
Endsleigh Gardens - 399 K3/4
Endsleigh Street - 399 K4
Enford Street - 395 F5
Enid Street - 405 S10
Ennismore Gardens - 397 E9
Ennismore Mews - 397 E9
Ensign Street - 405 S7
Epirus Road - 396 A13
Epworth Street - 403 Q4
Erasmus Street - 401 K11
Errol Street - 402 P4
Essex Road - 402 O1/P1
Essex Street - 401 M6
Essex Villas - 396 A9
Eustace Road - 396 A13
Euston Road - 398 J4,
399 K3/4/L3/4
Euston Street - 398 J3
Evelyn Gardens - 397 D11
Evershott Street - 398 J2,
399 K3
Ewer Street - 404 O8
Exeter Street - 401 L7, 407 Z3
Exhibition Road - 397 D9/10
Exmouth Market - 402 N4
Exton Street - 404 N8

Fabian Road - 396 A13
Falkirk Street - 403 R3
Falmouth Road - 404 P10
Fann Street - 402 P5
Fanshaw Street - 403 R3
Farm Lane - 396 A13/B13
Farm Street - 400 H7
Farringdon Lane - 402 N4
Farringdon Road - 402 N4/5
Farringdon Street - 404 N6/O6
Fashion Street - 405 S5
Fawcett Street - 396 C12
Featherstone Street - 403 Q4
Fenchurch Avenue - 405 R7
Fenchurch Street - 405 Q7/R7
Fendall Street - 405 R10
Fenelon Place - 396 A10
Fernshaw Road - 396 C12/13
Fetter Lane - 404 N6
Finborough Road - 396 B12/C12
Finsbury Circus - 403 Q5,
405 Q5
Finsbury Pavement - 403 Q5
Finsbury Square - 403 Q5
First Street - 397 E10
Fisher Street - 399 L5
Fitzalan Street - 401 M10
Fitzhardinge Street - 398 G6
Fitzroy Square - 398 J4
Fitzroy Street - 398 J4
Flaxman Terrace - 399 K3
Fleet Lane - 404 O6
Fleet Street - 404 N6
Fleur de Lis Street - 403 R5
Flitcroft Street - 399 K6,
407 X2
Flood Street - 397 E12/F12
Flood Walk - 397 E12
Floral Street - 399 L6, 401 L6,
407 Y3
Florence Street - 402 O1
Foley Street - 398 J5
Folgate Street - 403 R5

Fore Street - 402 P5
Formosa Street - 394 C4
Forset Street - 395 F5/6
Fortune Street - 402 P4
Foster Lane - 404 P6
Foubert's Place - 398 J6,
406 U2
Foulis Terrace - 397 D11
Fournier Street - 403 S5
Frampton Street - 395 D4
Francis Street - 400 J10
Franklin's Row - 397 F11
Frazier Street - 404 N9
Frederick Street - 399 M3
Friend Street - 402 O3
Frith Street - 399 K6,
406 W2/3
Frome Street - 402 P2
Fulham Broadway -
396 A13/B13
Fulham Road - 396 A13/
B13/C12/13/D12,
397 D11/12/E11
Furnival Street - 404 N5

Gainsford Street - 405 R9/S9
Galway Street - 402 P3/4
Gambia Street - 404 O8
Garden Row - 404 O10
Garlichythe - 404 P7
Garrick Street - 401 L7
Garway Road - 394 B6
Gaskin Street - 402 O1
Gate Place - 397 D10
Gaunt Street - 404 O10
Gee Street - 402 O4/4
Geffrye Street - 403 R2
George Row - 405 S9
George Street - 395 F5/6,
398 G5
Gerald Road - 400 G10
Gerrard Road - 402 O2
Gerrard Street - 401 K6/7,
406 W3
Gerridge Street - 404 N9
Gertrude Street - 397 D12
Gibson Road - 401 M11
Gibson Square - 402 N1
Gilbert Place - 399 L5
Gilbert Street - 398 H6
Gillingham Street - 400 H10/J10
Gilston Road - 396 C12
Giltspur Street - 404 O5
Gladstone Street - 404 N10/O10
Glasshill Street - 404 O9
Glasshouse Street - 400 J7,
406 V4
Glebe Place - 397 E12
Gledhow Gardens - 396 C11
Glendower Place - 397 D10
Glentworth Street - 395 F4
Gloucester Gate - 398 H2
Gloucester Mews - 395 D6
Gloucester Place - 395 F5,
398 G5/6
Gloucester Place Mews -
395 F5
Gloucester Road - 396 C9/10
Gloucester Square - 395 E6
Gloucester Street - 400 J11
Gloucester Terrace - 394 C5,
395 D6
Gloucester Walk - 394 B8
Gloucester Way - 402 N3
Godfrey Street - 397 E11
Godliman Street - 404 O6
Golden Lane - 402 P4/5
Golden Square - 400 J7,
406 V3
Goldington Crescent - 399 K2
Goldington Street - 399 K2
Goodge Place - 398 J5
Goodge Street - 398 J5,
399 K5
Goodman's Yard - 405 R7/S7
Goods Way - 399 L2
Gordon Place - 394 B8
Gordon Square - 399 K4
Gordon Street - 399 K4

King Street SW1 - 400 J8
King Street WC2 - 401 L7, 406 V5, 407 Y3
King William Street - 405 Q6/7
Kingly Street - 398 J6, 406 U3
King's Cross Road - 399 M3
King's Mews - 399 M4
King's Road - 396 C13, 397 D12/13/E11/12/F11
King's Road - 400 G10
Kingsland Road - 403 R1/2/3
Kingsway - 399 M6, 407 Z1/2
Kinnerton Street - 400 G9
Kipling Street - 405 Q9
Kirby Street - 402 N5
Knightsbridge - 400 G8
Knivet Road - 396 A12
Knox Street - 395 F5
Kynance Mews - 396 C9

Laburnun Road - 403 R2/S2
Lackington Street - 403 Q5
Ladbroke Road - 394 A7
Ladbroke Square - 394 A7
Ladbroke Terrace - 394 A7
Ladbroke Walk - 394 A7
Lafone Street - 405 R9
Lamb Street - 403 R5
Lamb Walk - 405 Q9
Lambeth Bridge - 401 L10
Lambeth High Street - 401 L10
Lambeth Palace Road - 401 L10/M9
Lambeth Road - 401 M10, 404 N10
Lambeth Walk - 401 M10/11
Lamb's Conduit Street - 399 M4/5
Lamb's Pass - 402 P5
Lamont Road - 397 D12
Lancaster Gate - 394 C6/7, 395 D6/7
Lancaster Mews - 395 D6
Lancaster Place - 401 M7
Lancaster Street - 404 O9
Lancaster Terrace - 395 D6
Langham Place - 398 H5
Langham Street - 398 H5/J5
Langley Street - 399 L6, 407 Y3
Langton Street - 396 C12/13
Lansdowne Terrace - 399 L4
Lant Street - 404 O9/P9
Launceston Place - 396 C9/10
Laurence Pountney Lane - 405 Q7
Lavender Grove - 403 S1
Lavington Street - 404 O8
Law Street - 405 Q10
Lawford Road - 403 R1
Lawrence Street - 397 E12
Leadenhall Street - 405 Q6/R6
Leake Street - 401 M9
Leamington Road Villas - 394 A5
Leather Lane - 402 N5/11 N5
Leathermarket Street - 405 Q9
Ledbury Road - 394 A6
Lee Street - 403 R1/S1
Leeke Street - 399 M3
Lees Place - 400 G6
Leicester Place - 401 K7, 407 X3/4
Leicester Square - 401 K7, 407 X4
Leigh Street - 399 L3
Leinster Gardens - 394 C6
Leinster Square - 394 B6
Leinster Terrace - 394 C6/7
Leman Street - 405 S6/7
Lennox Gardens - 397 F10
Lennox Gardens Mews - 397 F10
Leonard Street - 403 Q4
Lever Street - 402 P3
Lexham Gardens - 396 B10
Lexham Mews - 396 B10
Lexington Street - 398 J6, 400 J6, 406 V3

Lidlington Place - 398 J2
Lillie Road - 396 A12/B11
Lillie Yard - 396 A12
Lime Street - 405 Q7/R6
Limerston Street - 397 D12
Lincoln Street - 397 F11
Lincoln's Inn Fields - 399 M5/6
Linden Gardens - 394 B7
Linhope Street - 395 F4
Linton Street - 402 P2
Lisle Street - 401 K7, 406 W3/4, 407 X3
Lisson Grove - 395 E4/F4
Lisson Street - 395 E4/5
Litchfield Street - 401 K6, 407 X3
Little Albany Street - 398 H3
Little Britain - 402 O5, 404 O5
Little Chester Street - 400 H9
Little Dorrit Court - 404 P9
Little Portland Street - 398 J5, 406 U1
Little Russell Street - 399 L5, 407 Y1
Livermore Road - 403 S1
Liverpool Road - 402 N1/2
Liverpool Street - 405 Q5/6
Lloyd Baker Street - 402 N3
Lloyd Square - 402 N3
Lloyds Avenue - 405 R7
Lofting Road - 402 N1
Logan Place - 396 A10
Lollard Street - 401 M10/11
Loman Street - 404 O8
Lombard Street - 405 Q6/7
London Bridge - 405 Q7/8
London Bridge Street - 405 Q8
London Road - 404 O10
London Street - 395 D5/6
London Wall - 404 P5/Q6
Long Acre - 399 L6, 401 L6/7, 407 Y3
Long Lane EC1 - 402 O5
Long Lane SE1 - 404 P9/Q9
Long Street - 403 R3
Longford Street - 398 H4/J4
Longmoore Street - 400 J10/11
Longridge Road - 396 A10
Lonsdale Road - 394 A6
Lonsdale Square - 402 N1
Lord Hills Road - 394 C4
Lorenzo Street - 399 M3
Lots Road - 396 C13, 397 D13
Love Lane - 404 P6
Lower Belgrave Street - 400 H10
Lower Grosvenor Place - 400 H9
Lower James Street - 400 J7, 406 V3
Lower Marsh - 401 M9
Lower Sloane Street - 400 G11
Lower Thames Street - 405 Q7/R7
Lowndes Square - 397 F9
Lowndes Street - 400 G9
Lucan Place - 397 E10/11
Ludgate Hill - 404 O6
Luke Street - 403 Q4/R4
Lumley Street - 398 G6
Luxbough Street - 398 G4/5
Lyall Mews - 400 G10
Lyall Street - 400 G10

Macclesfield Road - 402 P3
Macklin Street - 399 L6, 407 Z1/2
Maddox Street - 398 J6, 406 U2/3
Maguire Street - 405 S9
Maida Avenue - 395 D4
Maiden Lane WC2 - 401 L7, 407 Y4
Maiden Lane SE1 - 404 P8
Malet Street - 399 K4/5
Mallow Street - 403 Q4
Maltby Street - 405 R9/10

Malvern Road - 403 S1
Manchester Square - 398 G5/6
Manchester Street - 398 G5
Manciple Street - 405 Q9
Manette Street - 399 K6, 406 W2
Manresa Road - 397 E11/12
Mansell Street - 405 S6/7
Mansfield Street - 398 H5
Manson Mews - 397 D10
Manson Place - 397 D10
Maple Street - 398 J4
Mapledene Road - 403 S1
Marble Quay - 405 S8
Marchbank Road - 396 A12
Marchmont Street - 399 L4
Margaret Street - 398 J5/6
Margaretta Terrace - 397 E12
Margery Street - 402 N3
Mark Lane - 405 R7
Market Mews - 400 H8
Markham Square - 397 F11
Markham Street - 397 F11
Marlborough Road - 400 J8
Marloes Road - 396 B9/10
Marshall Street - 398 J6, 406 V2/3
Marshalsea Road - 404 P9
Marsham Street - 401 K10/11
Marylands Road - 394 B4
Marylebone High Street - 398 G4/5
Marylebone Lane - 398 G5/H6
Marylebone Mews - 398 H5
Marylebone Road - 395 F4/5, 398 G4
Marylebone Street - 398 G5
Marylee Way - 401 M11
Maunsel Street - 401 K10
Maxwell Road - 396 B13
Mayfair Place - 400 H7
Mcleod's Mews - 396 C10
Meadow Row - 404 P10
Meard Street - 399 K6, 406 W3
Mecklenburgh Square - 399 M4
Medburn Street - 399 K2
Medway Street - 401 K10
Melbury Court - 396 A9
Melbury Road - 396 A9
Melbury Terrace - 395 F4
Melcombe Street - 395 F4
Melton Court - 397 D10
Melton Street - 399 K3
Mepham Street - 401 M8
Mercer Street - 399 L6, 407 Y3
Merlin Street - 402 N3
Mermaid Court - 404 P9
Merrick Square - 404 P10
Mews Street - 405 S8
Meymott Street - 404 N8
Micawber Street - 402 P3
Michael Road - 396 B13/C13
Micklethwaite Road - 396 B12
Middle Temple Lane - 404 N6/7
Middlesex Street - 405 R5/6
Middleton Road - 403 S1
Midland Road - 399 L2/3
Milford Lane - 401 M6/7
Milford Street - 402 P5
Milk Street - 404 P6
Mill Street W1 - 400 H6/J6, 406 U3
Mill Street SE1 - 405 S9
Millbank - 401 L10/11
Millman Street - 399 M4
Milman's Street - 397 D12/13
Milner Place - 402 N1/O1
Milner Square - 402 N1/O1
Milner Street - 397 F10
Mincing Lane - 405 R7
Minera Mews - 400 G10
Minories - 405 R6/7
Mintern Street - 403 Q2
Mitchell Street - 402 P4
Mitre Road - 404 N9
Molyneux Street - 395 F5
Monck Street - 401 K10

Monmouth Street - 399 L6, 407 X2/3
Montagu Mansions - 398 G5
Montagu Mews South - 395 F6
Montagu Place - 395 F5
Montagu Square - 395 F5
Montagu Street - 395 F6
Montague Place - 399 K5
Montague Street - 399 L5
Montpelier Place - 397 E9
Montpelier Street - 397 E9
Montpelier Terrace - 397 E9
Montpelier Walk - 397 E9
Montrose Place - 400 G9
Monument Street - 405 Q7
Moor Lane - 402 P5
Moor Street - 399 K6, 407 X2/3
Moore Park Road - 396 B13
Moore Street - 397 F10
Moorfields - 403 Q5
Moorgate - 403 Q5, 405 Q5/6
Moorhouse Road - 394 A5/6
Mora Street - 402 P3
Moreland Street - 402 O3/3
Moreton Road - 402 P1
Moreton Street - 400 J11
Morgan's Lane - 405 Q8
Morley Street - 404 N9
Mornington Crescent - 398 J2
Mornington Place - 398 J2
Mornington Street - 398 H2/J2
Mornington Terrace - 398 H2/J2
Morocco Street - 405 Q9
Morpeth Terrace - 400 J10
Mortimer Road - 403 R1
Mortimer Street - 398 J5, 406 U1
Morwell Street - 399 K5, 406 W1
Moscow Road - 394 B6
Mossop Street - 397 E10
Motcomb Street - 400 G9
Mount Pleasant - 399 M4
Mount Row - 400 H7
Mount Street - 400 G7
Moxon Street - 398 G5
Mund Street - 396 A11
Munster Square - 398 H3/4/J3/4
Muriel Street - 399 M2
Murray Grove - 402 P3, 403 Q3
Museum Street - 399 L5/6, 407 Y1
Musgrave Crescent - 396 B13
Myddelton Square - 402 N3
Myddelton Street - 402 N3/O3
Mylne Street - 402 N3

Napier Grove - 402 P2
Nash Street - 398 H3
Nassau Street - 398 J5
Nazral Street - 403 R3
Neal Street - 399 L6, 407 Y2
Neal's Yard - 407 Y2
Nebraska Street - 404 P9
Neckinger - 405 S10
Nelson Terrace - 402 O3
Nesham Street - 405 S8
Netherton Grove - 396 C12
Netley Street - 398 J3
Nevern Place - 396 A10/B10
Nevern Square - 396 A11
Neville Street - 397 D11
New Bond Street - 398 H6, 400 H6/7
New Bridge Street - 404 O6
New Burlington Place - 400 J6, 406 U3
New Cavendish Street - 398 G5/H5/J5
New Change - 404 O6
New Compton Street - 399 K6, 407 X2
New Fetter Lane - 404 N5
New Globe Walk - 404 O8/P7
New Inn Yard - 403 R4

Ravenscroft Street - 403 S3
Ravent Road - 401 M10/11
Rawlings Street - 397 F10
Rawstone Street - 402 O3
Raymond Buildings - 399 M5
Red Lion Square - 399 M5
Red Lion Street - 399 M5
Redan Place - 394 B6
Redburn Street - 397 F12
Redchurch Street - 403 R4/S4
Redcliffe Gardens -
 396 B11/C12
Redcliffe Mews - 396 C12
Redcliffe Place - 396 C12
Redcliffe Road - 396 C12
Redcliffe Square -
 396 B11/C11
Redcliffe Street - 396 C12
Redcross Way - 404 P8/9
Redesdale Street - 397 F12
Redfield Lane - 396 B10
Redhill Street - 398 H2/3
Reece Mews - 397 D10
Reeves Mews - 400 G7
Regan Way - 403 R2/3
Regency Street - 401 K10/11
Regent Square - 399 L3
Regent Street - 398 J6, 400
 J6/7, 401 K7, 406 U1/2/3/
 V4/W4/5
Remnant Street - 399 M6,
 407 Z1
Rennie Street - 404 N7
Rewell Street - 396 C13
Rheidol Terrace - 402 P2
Richmond Avenue - 402 N1
Richmond Crescent - 402 N1
Richmond Terrace - 401 L8
Ridgmount Gardens -
 399 K4/5
Ridgmount Street - 399 K5
Riding House Street -
 398 J5
Riley Road - 405 R9/10
Riley Street - 397 D13
Ripplevale Grove - 402 N1
Risbor Street - 404 O8
Ritchie Street - 402 N2
River Street - 402 N3
Rivington Street - 403 R4
Robert Adam Street -
 398 G5
Robert Street - 398 H3/J3
Rochester Row - 400 J10
Rockingham Street - 404
 O10/P10
Rodmarton Street - 398 G5
Rodney Street - 399 M2
Roger Street - 399 M4
Roland Gardens - 396 C11,
 397 D11
Romilly Street - 399 K6,
 406 W3, 407 X3
Romney Street - 401 K10
Rood Lane - 405 Q7
Ropemaker Street - 403 Q5
Ropley Street - 403 S3
Rosary Gardens - 396 C11
Rose Street - 401 L7, 407 Y3
Rosebery Avenue - 402 N3/4
Rosemoor Street - 397 F10
Rotary Street - 404 O9
Rotherfield Street - 402 P1,
 403 Q1
Rothesay Street - 405 Q10
Rotten Row - 395 E8/F8
Roupell Street - 404 N8
Royal Avenue - 397 F11
Royal Hospital Road -
 397 F11/12
Royal Mint Street -
 405 S7
Royal Street - 401 M9
Rugby Street - 399 M4
Rumbold Road - 396 B13
Rupert Street - 401 K6/7,
 406 W3/4
Rushworth Street - 404 O9
Russell Square - 399 L4/5

Russell Street - 399 L6,
 401 L6, 407 Z3
Russia Row - 404 P6
Rutherford Street - 401 K10
Rutland Gate - 397 E9
Rutland Street - 397 E9

Sackville Street - 400 J7,
 406 U4/V4
Saffron Hill - 402 N5
Sail Street - 401 M10
St Alban's Street - 401 K7,
 406 W4
St Alphage Gardens - 402 P9
St Andrews Hill - 404 O6
St Andrew's Place - 398 H4
St Anne's Court - 399 K6,
 406 W2
St Anne's Street - 401 K9/10
St Botolph Street - 405 R6
St Bride Street - 404 N6
St Chad's Place - 399 L3/M3
St Chad's Street - 399 L3
St Christopher's Place -
 398 H6
St Clement's Lane - 399 M6
St Cross Street - 402 N5
St Dunstens Hill - 405 Q7
St George Street - 398 H6,
 400 H6
St George's Circus -
 404 N9
St George's Drive -
 400 H11/J11
St George's Fields -
 395 E6/F6
St George's Road -
 404 N10/O10
St Giles High Street - 399 K6,
 407 X2
St Helen's Place - 405 R6
St James's Place - 400 J8
St James's Square - 400 J7/8,
 406 V5
St James's Street - 400 J8
St John Street - 402 O3/4/5
St John's Lane - 402 O4/5
St Katherine's Way - 405 S8
St Leonard's Terrace - 397 F11
St Loo Avenue - 397 F12
St Luke's Road - 394 A5
St Luke's Street - 397 E11
St Mark Street - 405 S7
St Martin's Lane - 401 L7,
 407 X4
St Mary At Hill - 405 Q7
St Mary Axe - 405 R6
St Mary's Square - 395 D5
St Mary's Terrace - 395 D4
St Matthews Row - 403 S4
St Michael's Street - 395 E5
St Pancras Road - 399 K2
St Paul Street - 402 P1/2
St Paul's Churchyard - 404 O6
St Peters Street - 402 O2
St Petersburgh Mews -
 394 B6/7
St Petersburgh Place -
 394 B6/7
St Swithins Lane - 405 Q6/7
St Thomas Street - 405 Q8/9
St Vincent Street - 398 G5
Salamanca Street - 401 L11
Sale Place - 395 E5
Salem Road - 394 B6
Sandell Street - 404 N8
Sandland Street - 399 M5
Sandwich Street - 399 L3
Sans Walk - 402 N4
Savile Row - 400 J7,
 406 U3/4
Savoy Place - 401 L7/M7,
 407 Z4
Savoy Street - 401 M7, 407 Z4
Sawyer Street - 404 O8/9
Scala Street - 398 J5
Scarsdale Villas - 396 A10/B9
Sclater Street - 403 S4
Scores Street - 404 O8

Scott Lidgett Crescent -
 405 S10
Scriven Street - 403 S1
Scrutton Street - 403 Q4/R4
Seacoal Lane - 404 O6
Seaford Street - 399 L3
Seagrave Road - 396 B12
Searles Close - 397 E13
Sebastian Street - 402 O3
Sebbon Street - 402 O1
Sedlescombe Road - 396 A12
Seething Lane - 405 R7
Sekforde Street - 402 O4
Selwood Terrace - 397 D11
Semley Place - 400 G11/H11
Senior Street - 394 B4
Serle Street - 399 M6
Serpentine Road - 395 E8/F8
Seven Dials - 399 L6, 407 X2
Seward Street - 402 O4/4
Seymour Place - 395 F5/6
Seymour Street - 395 F6
Seymour Walk - 396 C12
Shad Thames - 405 R8/S9
Shaftesbury Avenue -
 401 K6/7/L6, 406 W3,
 407 X2/Y1/2
Shaftesbury Street - 402 P2
Shalcomb Street - 397 D12
Shand Street - 405 Q9/R8
Shawfield Street - 397 E11/F12
Sheffield Terrace - 394 A8/B8
Sheldrake Place - 394 A8
Shelton Street - 399 L6,
 407 Y2/3
Shenfield Street - 403 R3
Shepherd Street - 400 H8
Shepherdess Walk - 402 P2/3
Shepherds Market - 400 H8
Shepperton Road - 402 P1,
 403 Q1
Sherbourne Street - 403 Q1
Sherwood Street - 400 J7,
 406 V4
Shipton Street - 403 S3
Shoe Lane - 404 N5/6
Shoreditch High Street -
 403 R4/5
Shorter Street - 405 R7/S7
Shorts Gardens - 399 L6,
 407 Y2
Shottendene Road - 396 A13
Shouldham Street - 395 F5
Shrewsbury Road - 394 A5
Shroton Street - 395 E4
Shrubland Road - 403 S1
Sicilian Avenue - 399 L5,
 407 Z1
Siddons Lane - 395 F4
Sidford Place - 401 M10
Sidmouth Street - 399 L3/M3
Silex Street - 404 O9
Silk Street - 402 P5
Skinner Street - 402 N4/O4
Skinners Lane - 404 P7
Slaidburn Street - 396 C12/13
Sloane Avenue - 397 E10/F11
Sloane Gardens - 400 G11
Sloane Street - 397 F9/10
Smith Square - 401 K10/L10
Smith Street - 397 F11/12
Smith Terrace - 397 F11
Snowden Street - 403 R5
Snowsfields - 405 Q9
Soho Square - 399 K6,
 406 W2
Soho Street - 399 K6,
 406 W1/2
Somers Crescent - 395 E6
Soton Place - 399 L5
South Audley Street - 400 G7
South Carriage Drive -
 395 E8/F8/G8
South Crescent - 399 K5
South Eaton Place - 400 G10
South End Row - 396 B9
South Molton Lane - 398 H6
South Molton Street - 398 H6
South Parade - 397 D11

South Place - 403 Q5
South Street - 400 G7
South Terrace - 397 E10
South Wharf Road - 395 D5/E5
Southampton Row - 399 L5
Southampton Street - 401 L7,
 407 Z3/4
Southgate Grove - 403 Q1
Southgate Road - 403 Q1
Southwark Bridge - 404 P7
Southwark Bridge Road -
 404 O9/10/P7/8
Southwark Street - 404 O8/P8
Southwick Street - 395 E5/6
Spa Road - 405 S10
Spencer Street - 402 O3
Spital Square - 403 R5
Spital Street - 403 S5
Sprimont Place - 397 F11
Spring Street - 395 D6
Spur Road - 400 J9
Spurgeon Street - 404 P10
Stableyard Road - 400 J8
Stacey Street - 399 K6, 407 X2
Stafford Place - 400 J9
Stafford Terrace - 396 A9
Stag Place - 400 J9
Stamford Street - 404 N8
Stanford Road - 396 B9
Stanford Street - 400 J11
Stanhope Gardens - 396 C10,
 397 D10
Stanhope Mews East -
 397 D10
Stanhope Mews West -
 396 C10
Stanhope Place - 395 F6
Stanhope Street - 398 J3
Stanhope Terrace - 395 E6
Stanway Street - 403 R2/3
Staple Street - 405 Q9
Star Street - 395 E5
Station Road - 401 M9
Stean Street - 403 R1
Stephen Street - 399 K5,
 406 W1
Stephenson Way - 398 J3/4
Steward Street - 403 R5
Stillington Street - 400 J10
Stone Buildings - 399 M6
Stone Street - 404 N6
Stones End Street - 404 O9
Stoney Lane - 405 R6
Stoney Street - 404 P8
Store Street - 399 K5
Storey's Gate - 401 K9
Stourcliffe Street - 395 F6
Strand - 401 L7/M6/7,
 407 Y4/5
Stratford Place - 398 H6
Stratford Road - 396 B10
Strathearn Place - 395 E6
Stratton Street - 400 H7/8
Streatham Street - 399 K5/L5,
 407 X1/Y1
Stukeley Street - 399 L6,
 407 Y1/2/Z1
Sturge Street - 404 O9
Sturt Street - 402 P2
Suffolk Street - 401 K7,
 406 W4/5
Sumner Place - 397 D10/11
Sumner Street - 404 O8/P8
Sun Street - 403 Q5
Surrey Row - 404 O8/9
Surrey Street - 401 M6/7
Sussex Gardens - 395 E5/6
Sussex Place - 395 E6
Sussex Square - 395 D6/E6
Sutherland Avenue - 394 B4
Sutherland Place - 394 A5/6
Sutton Row - 399 K6, 406 W2
Swallow Street - 400 J7,
 406 V4
Swan Street - 404 P9
Swan Walk - 397 F12
Swanfield Street - 403 S4
Sweeney Court - 405 S10
Swinton Street - 399 M3

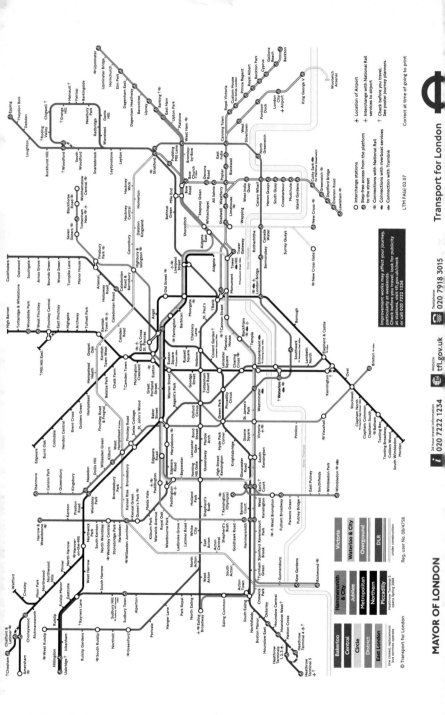

MAYOR OF LONDON

Transport for London

i 24 hour travel information
020 7222 1234

Textphone
020 7918 3015

Website
tfl.gov.uk

Correct at time of going to print

© Transport for London

Reg. user no. 08/4758

LTM FA(a) 02.07